"The world and our communities are changing at a rapid pace. Public and nonprofit leaders need skills, knowledge, and tools to respond effectively and swiftly to translate planning into action. This book combines both practical and useful insights with realistic examples, intellectual rigor, and clarity to help your organization successfully navigate the complexity of an ever-changing environment. This book is a 'must-read' for government and nonprofit leaders who wish to be successful in thinking, planning, and improving systems and organizational outcomes. John Bryson has done it again!"
—Gary L. Cunningham, vice president of programs and chief program officer, Northwest Area Foundation

"As organizational ties get more complicated and resources get ever tighter, Bryson's approach to strategic governance has more resonance than ever. In this new edition that builds on what's already a classic, Bryson helps us understand not only how to do strategic management, but also how to get strategic results."
—Donald F. Kettl, dean, School of Public Policy, University of Maryland, and author, *The Next Government of the United States: Why Our Institutions Fail Us and How to Fix Them*

"Time and again I attend conferences on strategic management and John Bryson's books and articles are either required reading, cited in the materials, or highlighted by the presenter. John Bryson's work on strategic management is clearly the gold standard."
—Jocelyn Hale, executive director, The Loft Literary Center

"John Bryson's book on strategic management has long been the touchstone in the field for practitioners and academics alike. This new edition promises to continue its preeminence and will be required reading for all with an interest in this topic."
—Stephen P. Osborne, professor of international public management, University of Edinburgh, Scotland, and editor, *Public Management Review*

"John Bryson is one of those rare academics who is so respected, skillful, and reflective that he is invited in to help large and important public and nonprofit organizations deal with their most sensitive and significant strategic issues. This book shows why."
—Colin Eden, professor of strategic management and management science, University of Strathclyde, Scotland, and coauthor, *Making Strategy: Mapping Out Strategic Success*

An Instructor's Guide for the fourth edition of *Strategic Planning for Public and Nonprofit Organizations* is available free online. If you would like to download and print a copy of this guide, please visit:

www.wiley.com/college/bryson

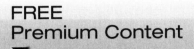

FREE
Premium Content

JOSSEY-BASS™
An Imprint of
WILEY

This book includes premium content that can be accessed from our Web site when you register at
www.josseybass.com/go/johnbryson
using the password *professional*.

Strategic Planning for Public and Nonprofit Organizations

A Guide to Strengthening and Sustaining Organizational Achievement

Fourth Edition

John M. Bryson

JOSSEY-BASS
A Wiley Imprint
www.josseybass.com

Published by Jossey-Bass
A Wiley Imprint
989 Market Street, San Francisco, CA 94103-1741—www.josseybass.com

Additional credit lines are listed on page 548.

Readers should be aware that Internet Web sites offered as citations and/or sources for further information may have changed or disappeared between the time this was written and when it is read.

Limit of Liability/Disclaimer of Warranty: While the publisher and author have used their best efforts in preparing this book, they make no representations or warranties with respect to the accuracy or completeness of the contents of this book and specifically disclaim any implied warranties of merchantability or fitness for a particular purpose. No warranty may be created or extended by sales representatives or written sales materials. The advice and strategies contained herein may not be suitable for your situation. You should consult with a professional where appropriate. Neither the publisher nor author shall be liable for any loss of profit or any other commercial damages, including but not limited to special, incidental, consequential, or other damages.

Jossey-Bass books and products are available through most bookstores. To contact Jossey-Bass directly call our Customer Care Department within the U.S. at 800-956-7739, outside the U.S. at 317-572-3986, or fax 317-572-4002.

Jossey-Bass also publishes its books in a variety of electronic formats. Some content that appears in print may not be available in electronic books.

Library of Congress Cataloging-in-Publication Data

Bryson, John M.

Strategic planning for public and nonprofit organizations: a guide to strengthening and sustaining organizational achievement / John M. Bryson. —4th ed.

p. cm. —(Bryson on strategic planning)

Includes bibliographical references and index.

ISBN 978-0-470-39251-5 (hardback); ISBN 978-1-118-04993-8 (ebk); ISBN 978-1-118-05051-4 (ebk); ISBN 978-1-118-05053-8 (ebk)

1. Strategic planning. 2. Nonprofit organizations—Management. 3. Public administration. I. Title.

HD30.28.B79 2011

658.4'012—dc23

2011017844

Printed in the United States of America
FOURTH EDITION
HB Printing   10 9 8 7 6 5 4 3 2

CONTENTS

FIGURES AND EXHIBITS

Figures

Exhibits

*This book is dedicated to all of my students over
the last thirty-five years, the people who have been kind enough
to read and comment on this book in its several editions, and
all the organizations with whom I have been privileged to work.
I owe you all a sincere debt of gratitude—not least for all that
I have learned from you.*

PREFACE

How can the leaders and managers of public and nonprofit organizations cope with the challenges that confront their organizations, now and in the years ahead? How should they respond to the increasingly uncertain and interconnected environments in which their organizations operate? How should they respond to dwindling or unpredictable resources; new public expectations or formal mandates; demographic changes; deregulation or reregulation; upheavals in international, national, state, and local economies and polities; and new roles for public, nonprofit, and business organizations, including calls for them to collaborate more often? What should their organizations' missions be? How can they create greater and more enduring public value? How can they build on organizational strengths and take advantage of opportunities while minimizing organizational weaknesses and overcoming challenges to their organizations? How can they formulate desirable strategies and implement them effectively? These are the questions this book addresses.

SCOPE

Strategic Planning for Public and Nonprofit Organizations is based on two premises. The first is that *leaders and managers of public and nonprofit organizations must be effective strategists* if their organizations are to fulfill their missions, meet their mandates, satisfy their constituents, and create public value in the years ahead. These leaders and managers will need to exercise as much discretion as possible in the areas under their control. They need to develop effective strategies to cope with changed and changing circumstances, and they need to develop a coherent and defensible basis for their decisions. They also need to build the capacity of their organizations to respond to significant challenges in the future.

The second premise is that leaders and managers are most likely to discern the way forward via a reasonably disciplined process of deliberation with others when the situations faced require more than technical fixes. They will need to design and construct, remodel, or repair existing processes or pathways for deliberation among speakers and audiences that include analysis, synthesis, and judgment; intellect and emotion; reasonable objectivity, but also partiality and passion; at times transparency and publicity, at other times secrecy; and at all times listening to and respecting what others say, at least until final choices are made (Garsten, 2006, 127–129, 131, 191–194). This honorable tradition of deliberation goes back at least to Aristotle and Cicero, both of whom wrote eloquently of its virtues. But to succeed, deliberative practices and processes also need institutional and organizational processes and structures in place to support them. The deliberative tradition of Aristotle and Cicero nowhere implies that there is "one best answer" to major challenges, only that there is the possibility of gaining understanding, finding common ground, and making wise choices via the deliberative process.

Strategic planning at its best makes extensive use of analysis and synthesis in deliberative settings to help leaders and managers successfully address the major challenges that their organization (or other entity) faces. This book begins by *defining* strategic planning as a deliberative, disciplined approach to producing fundamental decisions and actions that shape and guide what an organization (or other entity) is, what it does, and why it does it. Strategic planning has an important role to play as part—but only a part—of complex social problem solving. Specifically, it can be helpful for: (1) gathering, analyzing, and synthesizing information to consider its strategic significance and frame possible choices; (2) producing considered judgments among key decision makers about desirable, feasible, defensible, and acceptable missions, goals, strategies, and actions, along with complementary initiatives, such as new, changed, or terminated policies, programs, and projects, or even overall organizational designs; (3) addressing key organizational challenges now and in the foreseeable future; (4) enhancing continuous organizational learning; and (5) creating significant and enduring public value.

As experience with this kind of deliberative approach has grown, a substantial and expanding inventory of knowledge, concepts, guidance, procedures, tools, and techniques has also developed to assist leaders and managers. In the past forty-five years, strategic planning of this kind has become a standard part of management thinking and practice in the business world. In the past twenty-five years strategic planning has also become the standard practice of large numbers of public and nonprofit organizations. Of course, strategic planning isn't always called for, doesn't always work, or can work quite badly. This book is intended to help practitioners make suitable, wise, and effective use of strategic planning.

The first three editions of this book played an important role in promoting the use of strategic planning by public and nonprofit organizations. The practice of strategic planning has progressed substantially, and new areas of concern have emerged. Thus, although this fourth edition covers the same topics as the first three editions, it also focuses on additional areas requiring special attention. All of the chapters have been updated and new cases have been added. New material has been included on:

- The importance and logical structure of deliberative arguments and the requirements for effective deliberation intended ultimately to create public value
- Competencies and distinctive competencies
- Collaboration
- New approaches to strategic issue identification
- The difference between strategic and operational issues and what that implies for subsequent action
- The importance of strategy mapping for developing strategies, identifying and making use of competencies and distinctive competencies, and managing performance
- Performance management and balanced scorecards
- Organizational learning and formative and summative evaluations
- The applicability of Web 2.0 (and beyond) technologies throughout the process

The third edition's resource on strategic planning in collaborative settings has been dropped and—because of its importance—has been incorporated in the main text. A new resource section is devoted to developing a *livelihood scheme*, which links competencies and distinctive competencies directly to organizational aspirations. A livelihood scheme essentially articulates the core logic of a strategic plan (Bryson, Ackermann, & Eden, 2007; Eden & Ackermann, 2010). A second new resource section summarizes information on using the Web as part of a strategic planning process.

The fourth edition reflects a continuing major trend in the field by explicitly blending leadership, strategic planning, and ongoing management. People realize that strategic planning is no substitute for leadership and ongoing effective management. Instead, strategic planning comprises a deliberative approach and set of concepts, procedures, and tools that can help leaders, managers, and those with whom they engage to enhance the achievements of their organization (collaboration or community). People also realize that strategic thinking, acting, and learning must go together for strategic planning to serve its function as a deliberative process focused on important organizational issues. Of course, these points were all emphasized in the previous editions, but they are emphasized even more in the fourth edition. The book is therefore as much about *strategic management*—and indeed *strategic governance*—as it is about *strategic planning.* I have kept the original title, however, because of the recognition and following that the first three editions have achieved worldwide.

The new edition also reflects another continuing trend in the field by highlighting the importance of inclusion, analysis and synthesis, and speed as means to increasing organizational and community effectiveness (Bryson, 2003). The idea is to get more people of various kinds and skills involved, increase the sophistication and quality of analysis and synthesis used to inform action, and do it all more quickly than in the past. The challenge, of course, is that doing any two of the three is not so hard, but doing all three together is very hard. For example, there are methods that enable large numbers of stakeholders to be in the same room at the same time working on strategic planning, but informing their efforts with sophisticated analysis and synthesis is time-consuming. Alternatively, sophisticated analyses and syntheses often can be done quickly, but not when they involve a large group of people. One of the challenges the book presents, but does not really solve, is how to be inclusive, analytic, synthetic, and quick all at once. Figuring out how to address that challenge effectively is one of the continuing tasks for the field.

In sum, this edition places a renewed emphasis on the fact that strategic planning is *not* the same as strategic thinking, acting, learning, or deliberation. What matters most is strategic thinking, acting, and learning in a deliberative context. Strategic planning is useful only if it improves strategic thought, action, and learning; it is not a substitute for them. Strategic planning also does not produce deliberation unless it is designed into the process. The reader also should keep clearly in mind that the formation, or realization, of strategies in practice has a variety of sources (the vision of new leaders, intuition, group learning, innovation, what already works, chance) and strategic planning is only one of them. Wise strategic thought, action, and learning take all of them into account. As Mintzberg (1994, p. 367) notes, "Strategy formation cannot be helped by people blind to the richness of its reality."

Specifically, this book:

- Reviews the reasons public and nonprofit organizations (collaborations and communities) should embrace strategic planning and management as ways of improving their performance.

- Describes the elements of effective deliberation and deliberative practices.

- Presents an effective strategic planning and management process for public and nonprofit organizations that has been successfully used by many thousands of public and nonprofit organizations around the world; this approach, called the Strategy Change Cycle, enhances the process presented in the third edition by more attention to the design of pathways for deliberation, including the use of Web-based tools; competencies, distinctive competencies, and livelihood schemes; strategic and operational issues and the different approaches needed to address each; new approaches to strategic issue identification; additional strategy mapping methods; performance measurement and management; and organizational learning and formative and summative evaluations.

- Offers detailed guidance on applying the process, including information on specific tools and techniques that might prove useful in various circumstances within organizations, across organizations, and in communities.

- Discusses the major roles that must be played by various individuals and groups for strategic planning to work and gives guidance on how to play the roles.

- Clarifies the various ways in which strategic planning may be institutionalized so that strategic thinking, acting, and learning may be encouraged, embraced, and embedded across an entire organization.

- Includes many new examples of successful (and unsuccessful) strategic planning practice.

- Relates the entire discussion to relevant research and literature.

AUDIENCE

This book is written for two main groups. The first consists of elected and appointed policymakers, managers, and planners in governments, public agencies, and nonprofit organizations who are responsible for and who want to learn more about strategic planning and management. The book will help them understand what strategic planning and management are and how to make use of them in their own organizations and, to a lesser extent, their communities. Thus, the book speaks to city council members, mayors, city managers, administrators, and planners; sheriffs, police chiefs, fire chiefs, and their staffs; school board members, administrators, and staff; county commissioners, administrators, and planners; governors, state cabinet secretaries, administrators, and planners; legislators; chief executive officers, chief administrative officers, chief financial officers, and chief information officers; executive directors, deputy directors, and unit directors; presidents and vice presidents; elected and appointed officials of governments and public agencies; and boards of directors of nonprofit organizations.

The second major audience consists of academics and students of strategic planning and management. For-credit and professional development courses on strategic planning and management are now typically offered in schools of public affairs, public administration, planning, and public policy. This book offers participants in these courses a useful blend of theory and practice.

Others who will find the book interesting are businesspeople and citizens interested in increasing their understanding of how to improve the operations of governments, public agencies, and nonprofit organizations. To a lesser extent, the book is also intended to help these individuals understand and improve their communities.

OVERVIEW OF THE CONTENTS

Part One introduces the reader to the dynamics of strategic planning. Chapter One introduces the concept of strategic planning and why such planning is important for governments, public agencies, nonprofit organizations, and communities. Attention is focused on strategic planning for: (1) public agencies, departments, or major organizational divisions; (2) general purpose governments; (3) nonprofit organizations; (4) a function, such as transportation, health care, or education that bridges organizational and governmental boundaries; (5) interorganizational networks and collaborations; and (6) entire communities, urban or metropolitan areas, regions, or states seen as economic, social, and political entities.

Benefits of strategic planning are emphasized as are the conditions under which strategic planning should *not* be undertaken. In this chapter I also argue that the practice of public and nonprofit strategic planning will become further institutionalized and improved over time. The reason is that—at its best—strategic planning can accommodate substantive rationality; technical and administrative feasibility; legal, ethical, and moral justifiability; and, of crucial importance, political acceptability. Finally, readers will be introduced to three organizations whose experience with strategic planning will be used through-out the book to illustrate key points. All three are based in Minnesota and are nationally and internationally recognized for their good work. The first is the Minneapolis Park and Recreation Board, which is responsible for managing, preserving, and enhancing one of the nation's great municipal park systems. The second is a nonprofit organization—The Loft Literary Center—famed for supporting the artistic development of writers, fostering a writing community, and building a broader audience for literature. The third is an award-winning public, private, and nonprofit collaboration responsible for developing and maintaining a geographic information system in the Twin Cities metropolitan area: MetroGIS.

In Chapter Two, I present my preferred approach to strategic planning and management, which I call the Strategy Change Cycle. This approach has been used effectively by a very large number of governments, public agencies, and nonprofit organizations in the United States, Canada, United Kingdom, and Australia, and indeed on every continent—except perhaps Antarctica! Since Peking University Press published a Chinese-language version of the third edition of the book, use of the approach is also on the rise in China. (Readers of the third edition will note that the Strategy Change Cycle in the fourth edition differs slightly from the process outlined previously; the changes reflect changes in my own thinking based on the advice of colleagues as well as general developments in the field.) Chapters Three through Ten, which make up Part Two, describe in detail how to apply the approach.

Chapter Three covers the initial agreement, or readiness assessment and "plan for planning," phase of the strategic planning process. Chapter Four focuses on identification of mandates and the clarification of mission and values. Chapter Five addresses the assessment of an organization's external and internal environments. Chapter Six discusses strategic issues—what they are, how they can be identified, and how to critique them. Chapter Seven is devoted to the development of effective strategies and plans, along with their review and adoption. Chapter Eight covers the development of the organiza-tion's "vision of success," that is, what the organization should look like as it fulfills its mission and achieves its full potential. Chapter Nine attends to development of an effective implementation process. Chapter Ten covers reas-sessment of strategies and the strategic planning process as a prelude to a new round of strategic planning. Chapters Three through Seven thus emphasize the *planning* aspect of the Strategy Change Cycle, and Chapters Eight through Ten highlight the *management* aspects. Jointly, the eight chapters together encom-pass the *strategic management* process.

Part Three includes two chapters designed to help leaders know what they will need to do to get started with strategic planning and to make it work. Chapter Eleven covers the many leadership roles and responsibilities necessary for the exercise of effective strategic leadership for public and nonprofit organizations. These roles include sponsoring, championing, and facilitating a reasonably deliberative process in such a way that an organization's situation is clearly understood, wise decisions are made and implemented, residual conflicts are handled well, and the organization is prepared for the next round of strategy change. Chapter Twelve assesses the strategic planning experiences of the three organizations used as examples throughout the text. This chapter also provides guidance on how to begin strategic planning.

Four resource sections are included at the end of the text. Resource A presents an array of stakeholder identification and analysis methods designed to help organize participation, create strategic ideas worth implementing, organize a coalition of support in favor of the ideas, protect the ideas during implementation, and build capacity for ongoing implementation, learning, and change. Resource B presents information on how Web-based tools may be used to support a strategy change cycle. Resource C provides guidance on how to develop a livelihood scheme for an organization that links competencies and distinctive competencies to aspirations; such a scheme can serve as the core logic of a strategic plan. Finally, Resource D provides guidance on how to use *action-oriented strategy mapping* to identify strategic issues and formulate effective strategies. Other uses for the mapping process are covered as well.

Strategic Planning for Public and Nonprofit Organizations will provide most of the guidance leaders, managers, and planners need to engage in a deliberative strategic planning and management process aimed at making their organizations (collaborations and communities) more effective and responsive to their environments. This book presents a simple yet effective strategic planning and management process designed specifically for public and nonprofit organizations, detailed advice on how to apply the process, and examples of its application. The entire exposition is grounded in the relevant research and literature, so readers will know where the process fits in with prior research and practice and can gain added insight on how to apply the process.

COMPANION STRATEGIC PLANNING WORKBOOKS

The third edition benefited from having a companion strategic planning workbook to help groups and organizations work through both the conception and nuts and bolts of the strategic planning and management process, with a particular focus on the strategic planning aspects. I have again teamed with Farnum Alston, a highly skilled and experienced consultant, to coauthor a new edition of *Creating Your Strategic Plan, Third Edition* (2011).

The workbook is designed primarily to help those who are relatively new to strategic planning—along with those who are experienced old hands—to guide themselves through the Strategy Change Cycle. The workbook, however, is clearly not a substitute for the book. Effective strategic planning is an art that involves thoughtful tailoring to specific contexts. *Strategic Planning for Public and Nonprofit Organizations* provides considerable guidance on how to think about the tailoring process, including many process guidelines, caveats, and case examples. Thus, the book should be read first before the workbook is used, and should be consulted on a regular basis throughout the course of a Strategy Change Cycle.

The fourth edition is accompanied by a second workbook designed to provide more detailed attention to the implementation and management of strategies. I am pleased to team with longtime consultant, colleague, and friend Sharon Roe Anderson, along with Farnum, to coauthor *Implementing and Sustaining Your Strategic Plan.* Again, the book should be read before the workbook is used.

Minneapolis, Minnesota   John M. Bryson
April 2011

ACKNOWLEDGMENTS
FOR THE FOURTH EDITION

Space limitations prevent me from thanking again by name all those who contributed to the previous three editions of this book; I remain deeply grateful to them. Without their insights, thoughtfulness, advice, and other forms of help, neither those editions nor this one would have been written. I carry their wisdom with me every day.

There is space, however, for me to thank the people who contributed their insights, advice, and support to the fourth edition. Deep thanks and appreciation must go to Colin Eden and Fran Ackermann, two colleagues at the University of Strathclyde in Glasgow, Scotland; and David Andersen and George Richardson, colleagues at the Rockefeller College of Public Affairs of the University at Albany of the State University of New York. The five of us have been carrying on a dialogue about public and nonprofit strategic management for twenty years, and this continuing seminar has been one of the most significant sources of my own learning.

A number of academic colleagues (many of whom are also skilled consultants and practitioners) at various institutions in the United States, the United Kingdom, and elsewhere have contributed to the fourth edition through their writing and conversations with me. I would like to give special thanks to Michael Barzelay at the London School of Economics and Political Science, where I was a visiting fellow for the 2009–10 academic year. His intelligence, thoughtfulness, graciousness, and desire to help me improve this book are deeply appreciated. His probing questions, suggestions for reading, instructive classroom lectures, and willingness to engage in extended in-person and e-mail dialogues all helped me gain a far richer understanding of what I was up to and how best to do it than I ever would have achieved otherwise. Others who helped directly or indirectly (and may be surprised to know they have) include: Stu Albert, Rhys Andrews, Fran Berry, Kim Boal, Tony Bovaird, George Boyne, Barry Bozeman, Jim Bryant, David Chrislip, Steve Cropper, Barbara Crosby (who is also my spouse), Andre Delbecq, Bob Denhardt, Ann Doucette, Jane Dutton, Dean Eitel, Martha Feldman, Marlena Fiol, Norman Flynn, John Forester, George Frederickson, Arie Halachmi, Patsy Healey, Alfred Ho, Marc Holzer, Christopher Hood, Chris Huxham, Judy Innes, Gerry Johnson, Robert Kaplan, Don Kettl, Anne Khademian, Martin Krieger, Bruno Latour, Paul Light, Russell Linden, Larry Lynn, Alfie Marcus, Ken Meier, Brint Milward, Henry Mintzberg, Mark Moore, Don Moynihan, Sam Myers, Kathy Newcomer, Paul Niven, Paul Nutt, Rosemary O'Leary, Wanda Orlikowski, Stephen Osborne, Larry O'Toole, Michael Patton, Guy Peters, Ted Poister, Keith Provan, Beryl Radin, Joe Raelin, Hal Rainey, Sue Richards, Peter Ring, Nancy Roberts, Olaf Rughase, Jodi Sandfort, Otto Scharmer, Donna Rae Scheffert, Melissa Stone, Colin Talbot, John Clayton Thomas, Fred Thompson, Andy Van de Ven, David Van Slyke, Siv Vangen, Karl Weick, Chris Wheeland, Kaifeng Yang, Dennis Young, Jerry Zhou, and many others.

A number of practitioners also provided immense help. I am reminded of the old adage: A practitioner is a theorist who pays a price for being wrong. These thoughtful, public-spirited, good-hearted friends and colleagues have shared with me their hard-won insights and have provided invaluable knowledge and encouragement necessary to produce the fourth edition. Their number includes Farnum Alston, a friend for thirty-five years and coauthor of *Creating Your Strategic Plan, Third Edition*, a companion workbook focused primarily on developing a strategic plan; and of *Implementing and Sustaining Your Strategic Plan*, a second companion workbook focused on plan implementation. Farnum has an amazing store of experience, insights, techniques, and wisdom gained as a political appointee serving former Governor Pat Lucey in Wisconsin (where we first met); a high-ranking federal civil servant; head of KPMG Peat-Marwick's national consulting practice for strategic planning in the public sector; and deputy mayor and budget director for San Francisco. I am indeed fortunate that Farnum has been willing to share his prodigious talents with me. Farnum now heads The Crescent Company, a strategic planning and management consulting firm located in Bozeman, Montana.

Another outstanding practitioner who has been an immense source of wisdom and insight is Sharon Roe Anderson, my coauthor (along with Farnum) on a new companion workbook called *Implementing and Sustaining Your Strategic Plan*. Sharon also has an incredible store of practical experience gained through long service as a program director of several different programs at the Humphrey School (where I am on the faculty), co-owning a successful strategic planning consulting firm, and through dedicated service on a number of nonprofit boards of directors and to many government and nonprofit organizations. She is also a champion bridge player, so thinking about strategy and tactics comes easily to her. She now describes herself as a *time philanthropist*, a label I love.

All who finish reading this book will know how grateful I am to three practitioners in particular: Jennifer Ringold of the Minneapolis Park and Recreation Board; Jocelyn Hale of The Loft Literary Center; and Randall Johnson, an employee of the Twin Cities' Metropolitan Council and staff coordinator of MetroGIS, the regional geographic information system and network. All three organizations feature prominently in the book as case studies in the successful use of strategic planning and management practices. This book could not have been written without these three and their willingness to spend hours discussing their experiences and the lessons they have gleaned from them—and hours going over what I had written about their organizations to make sure I got it right! Many of their colleagues also helped contribute information and insights.

Four other truly outstanding and generous practitioner-academics deserve special mention: my sometime coauthor Gary Cunningham, vice president of the Northwest Area Foundation in St. Paul, Minnesota; my Humphrey School colleagues Senior Fellows Jay Kiedrowski and Lee Munnich; and Tom Walkington, a faculty member at Hamline University, adjunct faculty member at the Humphrey School, and successful strategic management consultant. All four have deepened my knowledge of the subject and I also greatly value their friendship.

Other practitioners (several of whom have also been academics) who have advanced my knowledge of strategic planning and deserve special thanks include Bill Barberg, Bryan Barry, Ronnie Brooks, Anne Carroll, Steve Cramer, Lonnie Helgeson, Joyce Hoelting, Richard Johnson, Tom Kingston, Milne Kintner, Sean Lusk, Leah Goldstein Moses, David O'Fallon, Jon Pratt, David Riemer, Randy Schenkat, Dick Senese, Bev Stein, Becky Stewart, and Lyle Wray. I would like to offer special thanks as well to President Bob Bruininks, Executive Vice President and Provost Tom Sullivan, Vice President Kathy Brown, Vice President Kathleen O'Brien, former Dean of the Graduate School Gail Dubrow and Graduate School staff members Vicki Field and Char Voight of the University of Minnesota, all of whom drew on my expertise to help the university we all treasure. I would also like to thank President J. B. Milliken of the University of Nebraska and his able assistant Dara Troutman for engaging me to help their admirable university with strategic planning. Marie-Andrée Lachapelle and her colleagues at the City of Edmonton, Alberta, Canada, were wonderful hosts who helped me understand more about their great city and its strategic planning efforts. I would also like to thank the Senior Minister of Plymouth Congregational Church in Minneapolis, James Gertmenian, and the church's strategic planning champions Sonia Cairns and Claire Kolmoden for asking me to serve on an advisory committee to the church's strategic planning process. I didn't help much, but I certainly learned a lot about this marvelous religious organization. I must thank Sławomir Stefaniak and his colleagues in Poland for helping me understand a great deal about the challenges facing businesses in Poland as the country shakes off the last vestiges of communism and enters the European Union. And finally, I also must express deep gratitude to the many readers who gave me valuable feedback on the previous editions of this book.

Since 1987 I have served as a strategic planning consultant to various health and social service organizations in Northern Ireland, and I would like to thank several people there who have been especially helpful. These include David Bingham, Seamus Carey, Dympna Curley, Irene Hewitt, William McKee, Denis McMahon, and Brian White, among many others. The results of that engagement with Northern Ireland show up in several places in this book. The opportunity to work over a long period of time on strategic planning projects in a different country, in a sector undergoing often radical change, and in especially difficult political circumstances has immeasurably improved my understanding of both the limits and possibilities of strategic planning.

I would also like to thank The Evaluators' Institute of George Washington University for providing numerous opportunities for me to teach evaluators how to make use of many of the ideas and skills presented in this book—and to learn from these savvy evaluators how to improve strategic planning. Midge Smith was the first director of TEI and has been ably followed by Ann Doucette. Kathy Newcomer helped manage TEI's move from independent nonprofit organization to part of GWU. Michelle Baron and Alexandra Fernandez Jefferson make sure everything works exceedingly well. My sincerest thanks to all of you.

At the Humphrey School, I would like to thank in addition to those already mentioned, former Dean Brian Atwood; Interim Dean Greg Lindsey; Assistant Dean Margaret Chutich; all of the staff in the Dean's Office; all of our marvelous staff in the Public and Nonprofit Leadership Center—Kim Borton, Emily Saunoi-Sandgren, Mary Maronde, Karen McCauley, and a host of terrific research assistants and teaching assistants; Harry Boyte; Gary DeCramer; Kathy Fennelly; Ed Goetz; Steve Kelly; Bob Kudrle; Kathy Quick; Carissa Schively Slotterback; Joe Soss; and research assistants Jackie Aman and Justin Elston. Brian Atwood was an outstanding dean and also is the best boss I've ever had. Brian tapped me to be an associate dean from 2004 to 2008 to help implement a strategic agenda at the school, and I will be forever grateful for his confidence in me, his willingness to provide whatever support was needed, and his literally world-class diplomatic skills (he was administrator of the

United States Agency for International Development and has now taken a leave of absence to chair the Development Advisory Committee of the Organization for Economic Cooperation and Development in Paris). As I finish writing this book I am not sure that writing about strategic planning is easier than doing it, but while I was associate dean I certainly felt that way! Regardless, the Humphrey School is in the best shape it has ever been and Brian is a big part of the reason why.

Much of the third edition was written while Barbara Crosby and I were on sabbatical leave in London, England, for 2009–10—a year that has to count as one of the best years of our lives. As already noted, I was a visiting fellow at the London School of Economics and Political Science. In addition to Michael Barzelay, I would particularly like to thank faculty members Gwyn Bevan and Alec Morton, and of course the extremely helpful group manager Brenda Mowlam. No mention of our year in London would be complete without mentioning our stay at Bankside House, an LSE-owned dormitory. We rented a flat on the top floor with a view out of our living room and bedroom windows of the Thames, Globe Theater, Tate Modern, and St. Paul's Cathedral. What a location! We would like to thank the manager Richard Anderson and all of his extremely friendly, helpful, and solicitous staff. They all helped make our experience a delightfully memorable one. We would also like to thank our many old and new British friends who helped make the year so good. In particular, in addition to the many already mentioned, we would like to thank Malcolm Foley, Gayle McPherson, and their son (our godson) Michael Foley McPherson; Katherine Bowden Bradley; Richard Bradley; Amy Colori; Roger Colori; Christine Eden; Lone Hummelshoj; Brian Leonard; and Maggie Meade-King. We treasure the times we had with these wonderful human beings.

Some of the material in the book appeared elsewhere, and I would like to thank the editors and publishers of these earlier publications for allowing revised versions to be printed here. Some ideas in Chapters One and Two appeared in Bryson and Einsweiler (1987); Bryson and Roering (1987); and in a book coedited with Bob Einsweiler (1988). Parts of Chapter Seven appeared in Bryson (1988). Parts of Chapter Four and Resource A appeared in Bryson (2004b). Earlier versions of some material in Chapters Nine, Ten, and Eleven appeared in Bryson and Crosby (1992) and Crosby and Bryson (2005). Resource C is a major revision of Bryson, Ackermann, and Eden (2007).

Finally, I must thank my spouse, Barbara Crosby, herself a skilled academic, and our two wonderful children, Jessica and John ("Kee"), for their love, support, understanding, intelligence, and good humor. Barbara is my best friend, closest adviser, and the person who more than any other has helped me understand and appreciate what love could be. She has also taught me a great deal about leadership and strategic planning. Our children are marvels, and I love them very deeply and am very proud of them. I am also delighted that we now have a daughter-in-law, Megan, who brings all the more intelligence, charm, good humor, and love to the family. She and Kee are the parents of the newest member of the family, grandson Benjamin, who more than anyone helps put work in perspective. My hope for this book is that it will help make the world a better place for our children and grandchildren—and everyone's children. If it does, I could not be more thankful.

J.M.B.

THE AUTHOR

John M. Bryson is the McKnight Presidential Professor of Planning and Public Affairs in the Hubert H. Humphrey School of Public Affairs, University of Minnesota, Twin Cities. He works in the areas of leadership, strategic management, and the design of organizational and community change processes. He wrote the best-selling and award-winning book, *Strategic Planning for Public and Nonprofit Organizations* (1988, 1995, 2004, 2011), and cowrote (with Barbara C. Crosby) the award-winning book *Leadership for the Common Good* (1992, 2005).

Dr. Bryson is a Fellow of the National Academy of Public Administration. He has received many awards for his work, including four best book awards, three best article awards, the General Electric Award for Outstanding Research in Strategic Planning from the Academy of Management, and the Distinguished Research Award and the Charles H. Levine Memorial Award for Excellence in Public Administration given jointly by the American Society for Public Administration and the National Association of Schools of Public Affairs and Administration. In 2011, he received the Dwight Waldo Award from the American Society for Public Administration. The award honors persons who have made "outstanding contributions to the professional literature of public administration over an extended scholarly career of at least 25 years." He serves on the editorial boards of the *American Review of Public Administration, Public Management Review, International Public Management Journal*, and *Journal of Public Affairs Education*.

From 2004 to 2008 he served as associate dean of the Humphrey School. From 1998 to 2000 he was director of the Institute's Master of Public Affairs degree; from 1997 to 2000 he was collegiate program leader for the University of Minnesota Extension Service; from 1997 to 1999, he was director of the Institute's Reflective Leadership Center; and from 1983 to 1989, he was associate director of the University's Strategic Management Research Center. He has consulted with a wide variety of governing bodies, government agencies, nonprofit organizations, and for-profit corporations in North America and Europe. Bryson is a regular presenter in many practitioner-oriented training programs, including the programs of The Evaluator's Institute of George Washington University. He holds a doctorate and master of science degree in urban and regional planning and a master of arts degree in public policy and administration, all from the University of Wisconsin. He has a bachelor of arts degree in economics from Cornell University.

PART ONE

UNDERSTANDING THE DYNAMICS OF STRATEGIC PLANNING

The environments of public and nonprofit organizations have become not only increasingly uncertain in recent years but also more tightly interconnected; thus changes anywhere in the system reverberate unpredictably— and often chaotically and dangerously—throughout the society. This increased uncertainty and interconnectedness requires a fivefold response from public and nonprofit organizations (collaborations and communities). First, these organizations must think and learn strategically as never before. Second, they must translate their insights into effective strategies to cope with their changed circumstances. Third, they must develop the rationales necessary to lay the groundwork for the adoption and implementation of their strategies. Fourth, they must build coalitions that are large enough and strong enough to adopt desirable strategies and protect them during implementation. And fifth, they must build capacity for ongoing implementation, learning, and strategic change.

Strategic planning can help leaders and managers of public and nonprofit organizations think, learn, and act strategically. Chapter One introduces strategic planning, its potential benefits, and some of its limitations. The chapter discusses what strategic planning is not and in which circumstances it is probably not appropriate, and presents my views about why strategic planning is an *intelligent practice* that is here to stay—because of its capacity, at its best, to incorporate both substantive and political rationality. The chapter concludes by introducing three organizations that have used a strategic planning process to produce significant changes. Their experiences will be used throughout the book to illustrate the dynamics of strategic planning.

Part One concludes with an overview of my preferred strategic planning process (Chapter Two). The process was designed specifically to help public and nonprofit organizations (collaborations and communities) think, act, and learn strategically. The process, called the Strategy Change Cycle, is typically very fluid, iterative, and dynamic in practice, but nonetheless allows for a reasonably orderly, participative, and effective approach to determining how best to achieve what is best for an organization and create real public value. Chapter Two also highlights several process design issues that will be addressed throughout the book.

A key point to be emphasized again and again: the important activities are *strategic thinking, acting, and learning*, not strategic planning per se. Indeed, if any particular approach to strategic planning gets in the way of strategic thought, action, and learning, that planning approach should be scrapped!

CHAPTER ONE

Why Strategic Planning Is More Important Than Ever

Usually, the main problem with life conundrums
is that we don't bring to them enough imagination.
—Thomas Moore, *Care of the Soul*

Leaders and managers of governments, public agencies of all sorts, non-profit organizations, and communities face numerous and difficult challenges. Consider, for example, the dizzying number of trends and events affecting the United States in the past two decades: we have experienced an aging and diversifying population; extensive immigration and geographic shifts in population; the changing nature of families; huge bubbles in housing and stock markets followed by long bear markets and recessions; an apparent conservative political shift in electoral politics, coupled with major support among the populace for education and health care reform; tax cuts, levy limits, and indexing at the same time the federal government and most states are facing unprecedented debt; dramatic shifts in federal and state responsibilities and funding priorities; first a closing of the gap between the rich and poor, and then a reopening of the gap; the emergence of children as the largest group of poor Americans; dramatic growth in the use of information technology, e-commerce, and e-government; the changing nature of work and a redefinition of careers; fears about international terrorism; and even the emergence of obesity as an important public health concern, as the United States is by far the most obese country in the world. Perhaps most ominous, we have experienced a dramatic decline in social capital in recent decades, especially among the less educated and less well off. Social capital, defined as goodwill, fellowship, sympathy, and social intercourse, is a crucial factor in building and maintaining personal and family physical and mental health and strong communities. The 2008 presidential campaign notwithstanding, the younger generation in general is not very interested in politics, not very trustful of politicians or others, cynical about public affairs, and less inclined to participate in enduring social organizations, such as unions, political parties, or churches (Putnam, 2000; Putnam, Feldstein, and Cohen, 2004). Beyond that, in spite of economic growth, citizens in the United States and other developed countries appear to be no more happy now than they were thirty years ago (Eaton & Eswaran, 2009; Veenhoven, 2009).

Not surprisingly, we have seen sustained attention paid to questions of government and nonprofit organizational design, management, performance, and accountability as part of the process of addressing these and other concerns. Indeed, in the public sector *change*—though not necessarily dramatic or rapid change—*is the rule, rather than the exception* (Light, 1997, 2000; Kettl, 2002).

Globally, the spread of democracy and a beneficent capitalism seemed almost inevitable after the collapse of the Soviet Union some twenty years ago (Schwartz, Leyden, & Hyatt, 1999; Giddens, 2002). Although democracy has spread, progress seems far more uneven (Huntingdon, 1998). Thomas Friedman has argued that the world is becoming "flatter" as a result of globalization (Friedman, 2000, 2007); Richard Florida (2007), in contrast, argues that the world continues to be very "spiky," with many peaks and valleys. Can both be right? In some ways, yes—but across the board, probably not. In 2009, twenty years after the adoption of the U.N. Convention on the Rights of the Child, somewhat under *nine million* children under the age of five died worldwide of causes mostly preventable by inexpensive means, such as clean water, immunization, or access to generic drugs. The number of deaths is a big improvement over the 12.5 million under-fives who died in 1990, but there are still almost 25,000 mostly needless child deaths *every day* (UNICEF, 2007, p. 15.). The World Bank (2011) estimates that in 2005 something like 2.6 billion people subsisted on less than two dollars a day (although the fraction of people living at that level had declined from 1981 from 70 percent to 48 percent). Using that criterion of two dollars per day, most readers of this book are astronomically wealthy. Feiock, Moon, and Park (2008) conclude that the landscape is indeed spiky, and that active governments, businesses, and nonprofit organizations working together, especially on a regional scale, are needed to help communities stay out of the valleys.

Beyond that, most Western nations and many others face a scenario of low growth for perhaps a decade, as the excesses of the "noughties" (as the British call the first decade of the twenty-first century) and costs of the 2007–2009 global recession work themselves out. (In a somewhat parallel way, the third edition of this book was written in the wake of the 2000 stock market collapse, subsequent recession, and long bear market following the bursting of the 1990s "dot-com" frenzy; history may not repeat itself, but as Mark Twain noted, it rhymes a lot.) It is clearly possible that Japan might once again be the low growth, deflationary "model" for the future, as it was in a very different way in the 1980s when its economic and business prowess were the envy of all. Dictators—even tyrants—still abound; concerns about huge labor migrations, dislocations, and exploitation persist in the United States, European Union, China, and elsewhere; unemployment rates are high in many, perhaps most, developed and developing countries; awful catastrophes involving earthquakes, tsunamis, and epidemics occur all too frequently; many of the world's forest and fish stocks are depleted; and so on. As noted, poverty and ill health are far too widespread, even when some of the worst effects of ill health might be removed for literally pennies per person per day. Global environmental change shows up in hotter average temperatures, changed rainfall patterns, prolonged droughts, an increasing number of catastrophic storms, and increased skin cancer rates. The Worldwatch Institute claims in *State of the World 2010* that worldwide consumerism has put us on a collision course with environmental disaster. Terrorism in several parts of the globe is real and deeply threatening, and must be countered, if democracy, sane and sustainable economic growth, and peaceful conflict management are to occur. The United States has been involved in extraordinarily expensive wars of unclear benefit in Iraq and Afghanistan. The first was undertaken under demonstrably false pretenses and, though it has brought democracy of a sort to Iraq, has also cost upwards of 500,000 civilian deaths as a consequence of criminally negligent planning for the occupation (Rieff, 2003; Allawi, 2008). And Sir Martin Rees, a renowned astrophysicist and the British royal astronomer, guesses that the world has only a 50–50 chance of escaping a devastating global catastrophe of some kind sometime in this century (Rees, 2003).

So do I have your attention? Organizations that want to survive, prosper, and do good and important work must respond to the challenges the world presents. Their response may be to do what they have always done, only better; but they may also need to shift their focus and strategies. Although organizations typically experience long periods of relative stability when change is incremental, they also typically encounter periods of dramatic and rapid change (Gersick, 1991; Baumgartner & Jones, 2009; Mintzberg, Ahlstrand, & Lampel, 2009). These periods of organizational change may be exciting, but they also can be anxiety producing—or even terrifying. As geologist Derek V. Ager notes, "The history of any one part of the earth . . . consists of long periods of boredom punctuated by short periods of terror" (Gould, 1980, p. 185). He might as well have been talking about organizational life!

These economic, social, political, technological, environmental, and organizational changes are aggravated by the interconnectedness of the world. Changes anywhere typically result in changes elsewhere, making efficacious self-directed behavior problematic at best. As Booker Prize–winning novelist Salmon Rushdie says, "Most of what matters in your life happens in your absence" (1981, p. 19). More recently, Pulitzer Prize–winning novelist Junot Díaz asserts: "It's never the changes we want that change everything" (2008, p. 51). Only if you are lucky are the changes for the better and often "the best things in life happen when you don't get what you think you want" (Bakewell, 2010, p. 333).

This increasing interconnectedness is perhaps most apparent in the blurring of three traditionally important distinctions—between domestic and international spheres; between policy areas; and between public, private, and nonprofit sectors (Cleveland, 2002; Kettl, 2002, 2008). These changes have become dramatically apparent since the mid-1970s. The U.S. economy is now intimately integrated with the economies of the rest of the world, and events abroad have domestic repercussions. My wife and I own an American-made car—a Toyota Camry. The Chinese government is both keeping the United States afloat by buying our debt, and causing trouble with its undervalued currency for U.S. manufacturing and other industries, and to our balance of payments. It is hard to see how long this bilateral system can be sustained— because it simply is unsustainable in the long run. When I was growing up, the Soviet Union was the enemy; now the Evil Empire, as President Ronald Reagan called it, does not exist, and my young Eastern European students don't have much knowledge of it. The current Russian Federation is an ally on many fronts, but clearly problematic, just as Russia was in World War II. Threats to U.S. oil and natural gas supplies from abroad prompt meetings in, and actions by, the White House, intelligence agencies, and Departments of State, Defense, and Homeland Security. And the Middle East remains a powder keg affecting interests across the globe.

Distinctions between policy areas are also hard to maintain. For example, both educational policy and arts or cultural policy are seen as a type of economic development and industrial policy to help communities and firms compete more effectively. Strengthening the economy will not eliminate government human service and Social Security costs, but letting it falter will certainly increase them. Physical education programs, educational programs promoting healthy lifestyles, and parks and recreation budgets are viewed as a way of controlling health care costs.

Finally, the boundaries between public, private, and nonprofit sectors have eroded. National sovereignty has "leaked up" to multinational corporations, international organizations, and international alliances. Sovereignty has "leaked out" to businesses and nonprofit organizations. Taxes are not collected by government tax collectors but are withheld by private and nonprofit organizations from their employees and turned over to the government. The nation's health, education, and welfare are rightly seen as public—and not just government—responsibilities, and we increasingly rely on private and non-profit organizations and associations for the production and coproduction of services in these areas. Weapons systems are not produced in government arsenals but by private industry. When such fundamental public functions as tax collection; health, education, and welfare; and weapons production are handled by private and nonprofit organizations, then surely the boundaries between public, private, and nonprofit organizations are irretrievably blurred. But beyond that, sovereignty has also "leaked down," as state and local governments have been the big gainers in power in the last fifteen years, and the federal government the big loser. As the second decade of the twenty-first century begins, the federal government is quite frequently the *last* resort when it comes to dealing with the most complex social and economic problems. (The Treasury and the Federal Reserve Bank really were the last resort in avoiding a depression as a result of the 2007–2009 financial crisis, but now the resulting massive federal debt makes federal responses to important challenges perhaps no less needed, but even harder to sell.) State and local governments now are typically more important as the problem solvers, even though they often lack the knowledge, resources, legitimacy, and political will to do so effectively. The result of this "leakage" of sovereignty up, out, and down, and the irretrievable blurring of boundaries between public, private, and nonprofit sectors, is the creation of what Brinton Milward and his colleagues call "the hollow state," in which government is simply an actor—and not necessarily the most important actor—in the networks we rely on to do the public's work (Milward & Provan, 2000; Frederickson & Frederickson, 2006).

The blurring of these boundaries means that we have moved to a world in which no one organization or institution is fully in charge, and yet many are involved, affected, or have a partial responsibility to act (Cleveland, 2002; Kettl, 2002, 2008; Crosby & Bryson, 2005). This increased jurisdictional ambiguity—coupled with the events and trends noted previously—requires public and nonprofit organizations (and collaborations and communities) to think, act, and learn strategically as never before. Strategic planning is designed to help them do so. The extensive experience of public, nonprofit, and private organizations with strategic planning in recent decades offers a fund of research and advice on which we will draw throughout this book.

DEFINITION, PURPOSE, AND BENEFITS
OF STRATEGIC PLANNING

What is strategic planning? Drawing in part on the work of Olsen and Eadie (1982, p. 4), I define strategic planning as a *deliberative, disciplined approach to producing fundamental decisions and actions that shape and guide what an organization (or other entity) is, what it does, and why.* Strategic planning may be thought of as a "way of knowing" intended to help leaders and managers discern what to do, how, and why (Bryson, Crosby, & Bryson, 2009). Strategic planning of this kind can help leaders and managers successfully address major issues or challenges facing an organization (or some other entity), by which I mean issues or challenges not amenable to simple technical fixes. As noted in the Preface, deliberative strategic planning can be helpful for purposes of: (1) gathering, analyzing, and synthesizing information to consider its strategic significance and frame possible choices; (2) producing considered judgments among key decision makers about desirable, feasible, defensible, and acceptable missions, goals, strategies, and actions, along with complementary initiatives, such as new, changed, or terminated policies, programs, and projects, or even overall organizational designs; (3) addressing in effective ways key organizational issues or challenges now and in the foreseeable future; (4) enhancing continuous organizational learning; and (5) creating significant and enduring public value. As experience with this kind of deliberative approach has grown, a substantial and expanding inventory of knowledge, concepts, procedures, tools, and techniques has also developed to assist leaders and managers in their deliberations. Much of that inventory is highlighted in this book.

As a deliberative approach, strategic planning must attend to the design and use of the settings within which constructive deliberation is most likely to occur (Crosby & Bryson, 2005, pp. 401–426). First and foremost, these settings include formal and informal forums linking speakers and audiences in order to create and communicate meaning and foster learning (Moynihan & Landuyt, 2009). In addition, formal and informal arenas—in which legislative, executive, and administrative decisions are made—and formal and informal courts— where underlying laws and norms are reinforced or modified, and residual conflicts left over from policymaking or executive decisions are managed— must be designed and used. The most important court is probably the court of public opinion. Of the three types of characteristic settings, forums are the most amenable to design, in contrast to formal arenas and courts, which often are quite rigidly structured. Fortunately, however, in my experience forums are the most important kinds of settings, because they are where meaning is created and communicated—meaning that is extraordinarily consequential for shaping what follows, including what gets considered in arenas and courts.

In each of these settings for deliberation, participants must take into account the "deliberative pathways" that are possible and available for use as part of mutual efforts at persuasion. The term was coined by Bryan Garsten (2006, p. 131) to describe Aristotle's sense of "the landscape of thoughts and patterns" that might exist in an audience, and thus "the pathways" that might exist from one belief to another. These pathways are the starting point for understanding how mutual understanding, learning, and judgment might proceed. The pathways will influence a listener's beliefs via the structure and logic of an argument (*logos*), trust in the judgment and goodwill of the speaker (*ethos*), or because he or she felt moved by an emotion (*pathos*) (Garsten, 2006).

Strategic planning approached as the design and use of settings for deliberation must include an awareness of the features of effective deliberation, including the deliberative pathways that might be available for use. In other words, the overall process of designing a pathway (or process) for deliberation must take into account the deliberative pathways already existing within audiences' heads. Other features of effective deliberation include: speakers and audiences; information gathering, analysis, and synthesis; the development and framing of choices; the development of persuasive arguments; judgment; intellect and emotion; reasonable objectivity, but also partiality and passion; at times transparency and publicity, and at other times secrecy, so that people can develop and consider the full range of options, including the "unthinkable" or "unspeakable"; and at all times listening and respecting what others say, at least until final choices are made (Garsten, 2006, pp. 127–129, 131, 191–194). The basic form of a reasonable statement is to make a claim because of reasons based on evidence. Deliberation occurs in situations requiring choice; the basic form of a deliberative statement is *choice* based on *reasons* in order to *achieve ends* (Barzelay, 2009; see also Simons, 2001, pp. 155–178; Dunn, 2004, pp. 89–134). This honorable tradition of reasonable deliberation goes back at least to Aristotle and Cicero, both of whom analyzed and promoted its virtues.

But to succeed, deliberative processes and practices also need institutional and organizational arrangements in place to support them. Cicero in particular emphasized this point, as one would expect. He may have been Rome's greatest orator—whose oratory once saved the Republic from a coup, thereby earning himself the Senate's accolade of *pater patriae*, "father of his country"—but he also faced more than one angry mob and the likes of Julius Caesar, Mark Antony, and their armies. He endured exile and in the end had his throat slit by one of Mark Antony's henchmen (Everitt, 2003; Freeman, 2008). Deliberation certainly should be a part of politics, but its constructive role must be supported and protected or the politics can get very nasty indeed!

The deliberative tradition requires a willingness on the part of would-be deliberators to: resist rushing to judgment; tolerate uncertainty, ambiguity, and equivocality; consider different views and new information; and be persuaded— but also a willingness to end deliberations at some point and go with the group's considered judgment. The deliberative tradition doesn't presume that there is a "correct" solution or "one best answer" to addressing major challenges, only that there is wisdom to be found via the process (Stone, 2002). Many find the lack of definitiveness in deliberation frustrating. It takes time to build and maintain an appreciative audience for deliberation—as with poetry, classical music, and jazz.

In short, at its best, strategic planning requires deliberation informed by broadscale yet effective information gathering, analysis, and synthesis; clarification of the mission and goals to be pursued and issues to be addressed along the way; development and exploration of, and choice among, strategic alternatives; and an emphasis on the future implications of present decisions. Strategic planning can help facilitate communication, participation, and judgment; accommodate divergent interests and values, foster wise decision making informed by reasonable analysis; promote successful implementation and accountability; and enhance ongoing learning. In short, at its best strategic planning can prompt in organizations the kind of imagination—and commitment—that psychotherapist and theologian Thomas Moore thinks are necessary to deal with individuals' life conundrums.

One useful way to think about strategic planning is presented in Figure 1.1. The figure presents a capsule summary of what strategic planning is all about. Necessary richness and detail can be added as needed to this basic understanding. "A" is figuring out, via a deliberative process, where you are, "B" is where you want to go, and "C" is how to get there. Leaders and other process participants come to understand A, B, and C as they formulate, clarify, and resolve strategic issues—the fundamental policy choices or challenges the organization has to face. The content of A and B are the organization's existing or new mission, structure, communications systems, programs and services, people and skills, relationships, budgets, and other supports. The content of C is the strategic plan; plans for various functions; ways to restructure, reengineer, reframe, or repurpose (Scharmer, 2009); budget allocations; and other strategies and vehicles for change. Getting from A to B involves clarifying vision, mission, and goals. Getting from A to C is the process of strategy formulation; getting from B to C is strategy implementation. To do strategic planning well, you need to figure out A, B, and C and how they should be connected as you go along. You accomplish this principally by understanding the issues that A, B, C and their interconnections must address effectively. Think of the arrows as pathways for deliberation that result in the final choices of what is in A, B, and C. The summary also makes it clear that strategic planning is an approach, not a detailed, rigidly sequential, step-by-step, technocratic process. As an approach, it requires effective deliberation—and leadership—and a variety of concepts, activities, procedures, tools, and techniques can contribute to its success.

So that is how strategic planning is defined and briefly what it is. But why engage in strategic planning? At its best, the purpose of strategic planning in the United States and elsewhere is to help public and nonprofit organizations "create public value," in Mark Moore's compelling and evocative phrase

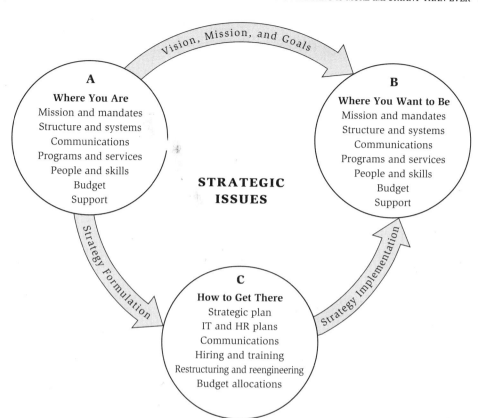

Figure 1.1. The ABCs of Strategic Planning.

Source: Bryson & Alston, 2004.

(Moore, 1995, 2000). Moore discusses creating public value primarily as the responsibility of individual managers, whereas I see creating public value more broadly as an individual, group, organizational, and community responsibility. Creating public value means producing enterprises, policies, programs, projects, services, or physical, technological, social, political, and cultural infrastructure that advance the public interest and the common good at a reasonable cost. At a very general level, in the United States creating public value means enhancing life, liberty, and the pursuit of happiness for all, while also fostering a more perfect union. It means ensuring that the beneficial effects of our institutions and efforts carry on into the indefinite future, and that we change what we must, so that the world is always left better off than we found it. Strategic planning is about listening to "the better angels of our nature," as Abraham Lincoln called them in his First Inaugural—it is about organizing our best and most noble hopes and dreams, making them reasonable and actionable, and bringing them to life. In this sense, strategic planning is about "the manufacture of transcendence" (Krieger, 2000) and finds its inspiration in the deepest sources of "the real American Dream" (Delbanco, 1999). Beyond that—in the United States and elsewhere—strategic planning is meant to help its practitioners and beneficiaries "pursue significance" (Denhardt, 1993)—in short, to create significant and enduring public value.

Most of the work on strategic planning has focused on for-profit organizations. Until the early 1980s, strategic planning in the public sector was applied primarily to military strategy and the practice of statecraft on a grand scale (Bracker, 1980). That situation changed, however, with the publication in 1982 of J. B. Olsen and D. C. Eadie's book, *The Game Plan: Governance with Foresight*, which marks the beginning of sustained applications of strategic planning to the broad range of public organizations, and of scholarship on how best to do so. Strategic planning for nonprofit organizations has proceeded in parallel, with the most important early publication being Barry (1986). I am pleased to say that the first three editions of this book, published in 1988, 1995, and 2004, also played an important role in expanding the use of strategic planning by public and nonprofit organizations.

Experience has clearly demonstrated that strategic planning can be used successfully to help:

- Public agencies, departments, or major organizational divisions (for example, Barzelay & Campbell, 2003)
- General-purpose governments, such as city, county, state, or tribal governments (for example, Kissler, Fore, Jacobson, Kittredge, & Stewart, 1998; Hendrick, 2003)
- Nonprofit organizations providing what are basically public services (for example, Stone, Bigelow, & Crittenden, 1999; Vila & Carnales, 2008)
- Purpose-driven interorganizational networks (such as partnerships, collaborations, and alliances) in the public and nonprofit sectors designed to fulfill specific functions, such as transportation, health, education, or emergency services—that bridge organizational and governmental boundaries (for example, Nelson & French, 2002; Burby, 2003; Innes & Booher, 2010)
- Entire communities, urban or metropolitan areas, regions or states (for example, Chrislip, 2002; Wheeland, 2004)

This book concentrates primarily on strategic planning for public and nonprofit organizations, including the collaborations of which they may be a part. It considers applications for communities in lesser detail. (The term *community* is used throughout the book to refer to communities, urban or metropolitan areas, and regions or states.) Though the process detailed in this book is applicable to all the entities listed above, the specifics of its implementation may differ for each case. When strategic planning is focused on an organization, it is likely that most of the key decision makers will be "insiders"— although considerable relevant information may be gathered from "outsiders." Certainly this would be true of public agencies, local governments, and non-profit organizations that deliver "public" services. When most of the key decision makers are insiders, it will likely be easier to get people together to decide important matters, reconcile differences, and coordinate implementation activities. (Of course, whether or not the organization's board of directors or governing body consists of insiders or outsiders may be an open question, particularly if they are publicly elected. For instance, are elected city council members insiders, outsiders, or both? Regardless of the answer, it remains true that typically a major proportion of the key decision makers will be insiders.)

In contrast, when strategic planning is focused on a function—often crossing organizational or governmental boundaries—or on a community, almost all of the key decision makers will be outsiders. In these situations, the focus of attention will be on how to organize collective thinking, action, and learning more or less collaboratively within an interorganizational network or networks where no one person, group, organization, or institution is fully in charge, but in which many are involved, or affected, or have a partial responsibility to act. One should expect that it might be more difficult to organize an effective strategic planning process in such a "shared-power" context. More time probably will need to be spent on organizing forums for discussion, involving various diverse constituencies, negotiating agreements in existing or new arenas, and coordinating the activities and actions of numerous relatively independent people, groups, organizations, and institutions (Bardach, 1998; Burby, 2003; Huxham & Vangen, 2005; Innes & Booher, 2010).

Organizations engage in strategic planning for many reasons. Proponents of strategic planning typically try to persuade their colleagues with one or more of the following kinds of statements:

- "We face so many conflicting demands we need to figure out what our focus and priorities should be."

- "The rules are changing on us. We are being told to emphasize measurable outcomes, the competition is stiffer, funding is getting tighter, collaboration is being pushed, and we need to figure out what we do or can do well that fits with the changing picture."

- "We have gone through total quality management, reinvention and reengineering, downsizing and rightsizing, along with the revolution in information technology. Now people are asking us to take on performance management, balanced scorecards, knowledge management, and who knows what else? How can we make sure all of this effort is headed in the right direction?"

- "We can expect a severe budget deficit next year and the public will suffer unless we drastically rethink the way we do business. Somehow we need to figure out how to do more with less through better integration of our activities, finances, human resources, and information technology."
- "Our city is changing and in spite of our best efforts, things do not seem to be getting better."
- "Issue X is staring us in the face and we need some way to help us think about its resolution, or else we will be badly hurt."
- "We need to integrate or coordinate better the services we provide with those of other organizations. Right now things are just too fragmented and poorly resourced and our clients needing more than one service are suffering."
- "Our funders (or board of directors, or new chief executive) have asked us to prepare a strategic plan."
- "We know a leadership change is coming and want to prepare for it."
- "We want to use strategic planning to educate, involve, and revitalize our board and staff."
- "Our organization has an embarrassment of riches, but we still need to figure out how we can have the biggest impact; we owe it to our stakeholders."
- "Everyone is doing strategic planning these days; we'd better do it, too."

Regardless of why public and nonprofit organizations engage in strategic planning, however, similar *benefits* are likely to result. Many authors argue that strategic planning can produce a number of benefits for organizations (for example, Nutt & Backoff, 1992; Barry, 1997; Nutt, 2002). The first and perhaps most obvious potential benefit is the *promotion of strategic thinking, acting, and learning,* especially through "strategic conversation" and deliberation among key actors (Van der Heijden, 2005). Let me define these terms. The *Oxford Reference Dictionary* (Hawkins, 1986, p. 855, defines *thinking* as meaning "(1) to exercise the mind in an active way, to form connected ideas, (2) to have as an idea or opinion, (3) to form as an intention or plan, (4) to take into consideration, or (5) to call to mind, to remember." In keeping with the spirit of this definition, I define *strategic thinking* as thinking in context about how to pursue purposes or achieve goals. This also includes thinking about what the context is and how it might or should be changed; what the purposes are or should be; and what capabilities or competencies will or might be needed, and how they might be used, to achieve the purposes. *Strategic acting* is acting in context in light of future consequences to achieve purposes and/or to facilitate learning. And drawing in part on Simon (1996, p. 100), I define *strategic learning* as any change in a system that by better adapting it to its environment produces a more or less permanent change in its capacity to pursue its purposes. The learning thus is focused pragmatically on what works, which likely includes knowing something about what doesn't. Learning of this sort doesn't have to be by design; much of it will be tacit and epiphenomenal (Bryson, 2010a; Vila & Carnales, 2008). In short, strategic planning is an approach to facilitate these kinds of thinking, acting, and learning.

Strategic thinking, acting, and learning are promoted by more systematic information gathering about the organization's external and internal environment and various actors' interests, thoughtful examination of the organization's successes and failures, clarification of future direction, establishment of organizational priorities for action, and in general attention to the acquisition and use of productive knowledge and skills. For many organizations, "strategic planning has become a natural part of doing business"—the regular deliberations about key concerns are a central feature of "moving the organization forward and increasing its effectiveness" (Barry, 1997, p. 10). In short, strategic planning can be used to help organize and manage effective organizational change processes in which the best is kept, while the organization figures out what to change.

The second benefit is *improved decision making.* Improved decision making is really crucial, since recent studies have indicated that at least half of all strategic decisions fail as a result of poor decision-making processes (Nutt, 2002)! Strategic planning helps because it focuses attention on the crucial issues and challenges the organization faces, and it helps key decision makers figure out what they should do about them. It can help them make today's decisions in light of their future consequences. It can help them develop a coherent and defensible basis for decision making and then coordinate implementing the resulting decisions across levels and functions. It can help them exercise maximum discretion in the areas under their organization's control, and influence actions and outcomes in those areas that are not. Strategic planning thus can help organizations formulate and clearly communicate their strategic directions and intentions to relevant audiences, and also act on those intentions.

The third benefit is *enhanced organizational effectiveness, responsiveness, and resilience*, which flow from the first two. Organizations engaging in strategic planning are encouraged to clarify and address major organizational issues, respond wisely to internal and external demands and pressures (including those for accountability), and deal effectively with rapidly changing circumstances. They are encouraged, in other words, to be well managed. And while it almost sounds tautological to say so, it clearly is not: The evidence is fairly clear that organizations that are managed well and are relatively stable perform better, are appropriately responsive to external demands, are innovative in effective ways, have greater influence, are more accountable, and are more resilient than organizations that are not managed well (Light, 1998, 2000; O'Toole & Meier, 2003; Coggburn & Schneider, 2003; Boyne & Gould-Williams, 2003; Meier & O'Toole, 2009). Good management helps create good organizational systems and response repertoires; in other words, good management is a process that draws on resources of many kinds to produce the outputs and outcomes that indicate organizational effectiveness, and that trigger the resource flows the organization needs to sustain itself and continue to create public value into the future (Bryson, Gibbons, & Shaye, 2001). Porter (1985, pp. 33–61) refers to this linkage of inputs, processes, and outputs in firms as a "value chain," and if the chain does not produce value in the marketplace at reasonable cost, the firm is in danger of going out of business. In the case of public and nonprofit organizations, we can say that the value chain must create public value at reasonable cost, or else serious consequences are likely to ensue. Increasingly, integrated use of human resources, information technology, and financial management are crucial elements of organizing, strengthening, protecting, and sustaining organizational capabilities for creating public value (Bryson, 2003; Heintzman & Marson, 2005).

The fourth benefit is *enhanced organizational legitimacy.* Organizations that satisfy their key stakeholders according to the stakeholders' criteria and that create real public value at reasonable cost have earned the right to exist (Eden & Ackermann, 1998). Said differently, public and nonprofit organizations are externally justified in that they exist to provide real service; those that do, and continue to find ways to do so as circumstances change, typically continue to exist (Holzer, Lee, & Newman, 2003; Hill & Lynn, 2009). These survivors therefore can concentrate on doing better without having to worry quite so much as they otherwise might about having to justify their claims on others' resources (Suchman, 1995).

Fifth, beyond organizational effectiveness, strategic planning can help produce *enhanced effectiveness of broader societal systems.* Most of the public problems we face these days stretch beyond any one organization's boundaries. As Don Schön (1971) pointed out long ago, our big challenges in education, health, employment, poverty, the environment—you name it—typically need to be conceptualized at the supra-organizational or *system* level, not the *organizational* level. Those systems are what really need to work better if our lives and the world are to be made better and broadly based public value is to be created. Organizations can contribute to better functioning of these systems, but typically must do so in partnership with others or by somehow taking those others into account (Kettl, 2002, 2008; Crosby & Bryson, 2005; Mulgan, 2009). Strategic planning can help organizations take the broader environment into account and can help them figure out how best to partner with other organizations so that they jointly can create better environments (Agranoff, 2007; Crosby & Bryson, 2010). The result probably should be some sort of concerted institutional redesign effort at the system level (for example, Brandl, 1998; Lake, Reis, & Spann, 2000; Bryson & Crosby, 2008) that enhances intellectual, human, and social capital at both the societal and organizational levels (Nahapiet & Ghoshal, 1998).

Finally, strategic planning can directly *benefit the people involved.* Policymakers and key decision makers can be helped to fulfill their roles and responsibilities, and teamwork and expertise are likely to be built among participants in the process (Kim, 2002). Human, social, political, and intellectual capital can increase. Morale can improve based on task accomplishment. Further, employees or organizations that can create real, demonstrable public value are more likely to have a job in the future. Reduced anxiety may result from a job well done, increased competency, strengthened relationships, and enhanced job prospects.

In short, strategic planning at its best surely must count as a "smart practice," which Bardach defines as a "method of interacting with a situation that is intended to produce some result; . . . [and] also involves taking advantage of some latent opportunity for creating value on the cheap" (1998, p. 36). Strategic planning is smart, because it is relatively easy to do; is not all that time- and resource-intensive, particularly when matched against the costs of potential failure; seeks out relevant information; makes use of deliberative argumentation, which is an important route to producing wise judgments; and would seem to go hand in hand with the craft of creating public value (Lynn, 1996; Bardach, 1998; Hill & Lynn, 2009). Strategic planning can be a highly cost-effective tool for finding or creating useful ideas for strategic interventions and for figuring out how to organize the participation and coalition needed to adopt the ideas and protect them during implementation (Mulgan, 2009). When not overly formalized, bereft of participation, and obsessed with numbers, strategic planning can make effective use of deliberation to produce enhanced organizational responsiveness, performance, and accountability.

Although strategic planning *can* provide all these benefits, there is *no* guarantee that it will. Indeed, it is highly unlikely that any organization would experience all or even most of the benefits of strategic planning the first time through—or perhaps even after several cycles of strategic planning. For one thing, the process depends on its participants' willingness to engage in deliberation. In addition, strategic planning must be adapted to its context, even as its purpose may be to change aspects of that context. Leaders, managers, and planners therefore need to be very careful—and strategic—about how they engage in strategic planning because their success will depend at least in part on how they tailor the process to their situations. This book will present a generic approach to strategic planning for governments, public agencies, and nonprofit organizations that is based in considerable research and experience. Advice will be offered on how to apply the process in different circumstances. But the process will work only if enough key decision makers and planners support it and use it with common sense and sensitivity to the particulars of their situation. And even then, success is never guaranteed, particularly when very difficult and fraught strategic issues are addressed.

Furthermore, strategic planning is not always advisable (Mintzberg, 1994; Barry, 1997; Mintzberg, Ahlstrand, & Lampel, 2009). There are two compelling reasons for holding off on a formal strategic planning effort. First, strategic planning may not be the best first step for an organization whose roof has fallen—keeping in mind, of course, that every crisis should be managed strategically (Mitroff & Anagnos, 2005; Weick & Sutcliffe, 2007). For example, the organization may need to remedy a cash-flow crunch before undertaking strategic planning. Or the organization may need to postpone strategic planning until it fills a key leadership position. Or it could be that showing compassion for people who have faced some sort of disaster is the first order of business (Dutton, Frost, Worline, Lilius, & Kanov, 2002). Second, if the organization lacks the skills, resources, or commitment of key decision makers to engage in deliberative strategic planning, or implementation of the results is extremely unlikely, strategic planning will be a waste of time. Such a situation embodies what Bill Roering and I have called "the paradox of strategic planning": it is most needed where it is least likely to work, and least needed where it is most likely to work (Bryson & Roering, 1988, 1989). If strategic planning is undertaken in such a situation, it probably should be a focused and limited effort aimed at developing the necessary skills, resources, and commitment.

A number of other reasons also can be offered for not engaging in strategic planning. Too often, however, these "reasons" are actually excuses used to avoid what should be done. For example, one might argue that strategic planning will be of little use if the costs of the process are likely to outweigh any benefits, or the process takes time and money that might be better used elsewhere. These concerns may be justified, but recall that the purpose of strategic planning is to produce fundamental decisions and actions that define what an organization (or other entity) is, what it does, and why it does it. In Chapter Three I will argue that strategic planning probably shouldn't take more than 10 percent of the ordinary work time available to any key decision maker during a year. When is the cost of that time likely to outweigh the benefit of focusing on the production of fundamental decisions and actions by their organization? In my experience, hardly ever.

Many organizations—particularly small nonprofit organizations—may prefer to rely on the intuition and vision of extremely gifted leaders instead of on formal strategic planning processes. If these leaders are strategically minded and experienced, there may be no need for strategic planning for purposes of developing strategies. It is rare, however, for any leader to have all the information necessary to develop an effective strategy, and rarer still for any strategy developed by a single person to engender the kind of commitment necessary for effective implementation. A reasonably structured and formalized deliberative strategic planning process helps organizations gather and assess the information necessary for effective strategy formulation. It also provides the discipline and commitment necessary to effectively implement strategies.

In addition, many organizations—particularly those that have enormous difficulty reaching decisions that cut across levels, functions, or programs— find that incremental decision making and mutual adjustments of various sorts among interested partisans is the only process that will work. "Muddling through" of this sort, as Charles Lindblom (1959) described it, legitimizes the existing distribution of power and resources in the organization and allows the separate parts of the organization to pursue opportunities as they arise. Interesting and useful innovations may develop that enhance learning and promote useful adaptations to changing circumstances. In fact, if the muddling occurs within a general agreement on overall direction, everyone may be better off (Behn, 1988; Barzelay & Campbell, 2003; Mintzberg, Ahlstrand, & Lampel, 2009). Unfortunately, muddling typically results in a chronic suboptimization of organizational performance, and key external and internal constituencies therefore may be badly served (Barzelay, 1992; Osborne & Plastrik, 1997; Andrews, Boyne, Law, & Walker, 2009).

Strategic planning also probably should not be undertaken if implementation is extremely unlikely. To engage in strategic planning when effective implementation will not follow is the organizational equivalent of the average New Year's resolution. On the other hand, when armed with the knowledge that implementation will be difficult, key decision makers and planners can focus extra attention on ensuring implementation success.

Finally, organizations simply may not know how and where to start and stop the process. The good news is that strategic planning actually can begin almost anywhere—the process is so interconnected that you end up covering most phases via conversation and dialogue, no matter where you start.

What Strategic Planning Is Not

Strategic planning clearly is no panacea. As noted, strategic planning is simply a deliberative, disciplined *approach* to helping key decision makers in organizations figure out what they think they should be doing, how, and why. It may not be possible to design or use the needed formal and informal forums, arenas, and courts; the key decision makers may not participate. Even if they do take part, needed deliberations may not necessarily occur. And if these deliberations do occur, needed actions may not necessarily be taken as a result. There is an available set of concepts, procedures, tools, and practical guidance designed to help leaders, managers, and planners think, act, and learn strategically, but those needed in any particular situation may not be used or used effectively. Indeed, in my experience—in life generally and in strategic planning specifically—there are more ways to fail than to succeed, and so possible failure is always lurking in the footsteps of incipient success.

When used in wise and skillful ways by a coalition of interested parties, strategic planning can help organizations focus on producing effective decisions and actions that create public value, further the organization's mission, meet its mandates, and satisfy key stakeholders. But one must always remember that strategic planning is not a substitute for strategic thinking, acting, and learning. Only caring and committed people can do that—and almost always via deliberative processes. Unfortunately, when used thoughtlessly, obsessively, or with excessive formality or rigidity, strategic planning can drive out precisely the kind of strategic thinking, acting, and learning it was supposed to promote. That kind of approach may be worse than no approach at all.

Furthermore, strategic planning is not a substitute for leadership broadly conceived. In my experience there is simply *no* substitute for leadership when it comes to engaging in strategic planning effectively. At least some key decision makers and process champions must be committed to it; otherwise, any attempts to use strategic planning are bound to fail. An effective strategic planning team also is typically needed. And skilled facilitators are often necessary.

A standard distinction is to argue that leadership is "doing the right things" whereas management is "doing things right." My own view is that leadership and management *both* involve doing the right things *and* doing them well, but if one sticks with this rather simplistic distinction, clearly strategic planning is first and foremost about articulating mission, mandates, vision, goals, and the nature of the common good and public value to be created—doing the right things—and management is about making sure those things are done well through strategies and operations at reasonable cost. But no matter what your view of the similarities and differences between leadership and management, both matter, and both are needed if strategic planning is to succeed—since it won't succeed by itself!

In addition, strategic planning is not synonymous with creation of an organization's strategies. Organizational strategies have numerous sources, both planned and unplanned. Strategic planning is likely to result in a statement of organizational *intentions*, but what is *realized* in practice will be some combination of what is intended with what *emerges* along the way (Mintzberg,

Ahlstrand, & Lampel, 2009). Strategic planning can help organizations develop and implement effective strategies, but organizations also should remain open to unforeseen opportunities as well. Too much attention to strategic planning and reverence for strategic plans can blind organizations to other unplanned and unexpected—yet incredibly useful—sources of information, insight, and action.

It should be clear now that the *deliberation* among key actors in strategic planning—and especially among key decision makers—is of a very special kind: it is thoughtful, reflective, informed, appreciative, situation- and stakeholder-sensitive, mission-oriented, careful, and *political*—in the best sense. Deliberation of that sort involves a special kind of *discipline* harkening back to the Latin roots of the word emphasizing instruction, training, education, and learning. Of course, there is a second meaning of discipline embodied in later interpretations emphasizing order, control, and punishment. I personally prefer the emphasis on education and learning, although there clearly are occasions when imposing order, taking control, and imposing appropriate sanctions are appropriate. Key leaders, managers, and planners can best use strategic planning as a deliberative educational and learning tool to help them figure out what is really important and what should be done about it. Sometimes this means following a particular sequence of steps and preparing formal strategic plans, but not necessarily. The ultimate end of strategic planning should not be rigid adherence to a particular process or the production of plans. Instead, strategic planning should promote wise strategic thought, action, and learning on behalf of an organization and its key stakeholders. It should be used to create noteworthy public value. If it does not, then it has been a waste of time other than to fulfill some symbolic or procedural requirement.

Why Strategic Planning Is Becoming a Standard Intelligent Practice

The vast majority of public and nonprofit organizations now claim to engage in strategic planning (Poister & Streib, 1994; Berry & Wechsler, 1995; Berman & West, 1998; Joyce, 1999; Poister & Van Slyke, 2002; Poister, 2003). Exactly what they mean when they say that is unclear. All that is really clear is that strategic planning in general is an idea whose time appears to have come. Specifically, the idea that strategic planning is something that skilled leaders and managers do is well past the "tipping point" (Gladwell, 2002) and is now an idea "in good currency" (Schön, 1971). Doing strategic planning has become accepted practice—and indeed, when done well, it is an intelligent practice.

Having said that, many leaders and managers no doubt groan at the prospect of having to go through another round of strategic planning. They may have "been there, done that," and, depending on their experience, may not want to do it again! They also have seen cost-benefit analysis, planning-programming-budgeting systems, zero-based budgeting, management by objectives, continuous improvement, downsizing, contracting out, reinvention, reengineering, and a host of other techniques trumpeted by a cadre of authors and management consultants. They have also, all too often, seen the techniques fall by the wayside after a burst of initial enthusiasm. Managers in particular are frequently, and justifiably, tired of "buzzword bingo" and feel as if they are the victims of some sort of perverse management hazing or status degradation ritual (Schein, 1987, pp. 84–86).

But strategic planning is far from a passing fad, at least not the sort of deliberative strategic planning proposed in this book. The reason is that the strategic planning process presented here builds on the nature of *political* intelligence and decision making. So many other management techniques have failed because they ignore, try to circumvent, or even try to counter the political nature of life in private, public, and nonprofit sector organizations. Too many planners and managers, at least in my experience, just do not understand that such a quest is almost guaranteed to be quixotic. Politics is the method that we humans use to answer the analytically unresolvable questions of what should be done for collective purposes, how, and why (Moore, 1995, p. 54; Christensen, 1999; Stone, 2002; Mulgan, 2009).

Most of these new management innovations have tried to improve government decision making and operations by trying to impose a formal rationality on systems that are not rational, at least in the conventional meaning of that word. Public and nonprofit organizations (and communities) embody a *political* intelligence and rationality, and any technique that is likely to work well in such organizations must accept and build on the nature of political rationality (Wildavsky, 1979; March & Olsen, 1995; Stone, 2002).

Let us pursue this point further by contrasting two different kinds of decision making: the "rational" planning model and political decision making. The rational planning model, a rational-deductive approach to decision making, is presented in Figure 1.2. This model begins with goals; policies, programs, and actions are then deduced to achieve those goals. If there is a traditional plan-

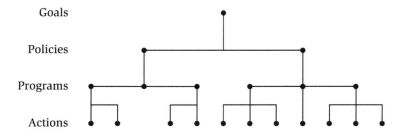

Figure 1.2. Rational Planning Model.

ning theology, this model is one of its icons. Indeed, if there were a Moses of planning, Figure 1.2 would have been etched on his tablets when he came down from the Mount.

Let us now examine a fundamental assumption of the rational planning model—that in the fragmented, shared power settings that characterize many public and nonprofit organizations, networks, and communities there will either be a *consensus* on goals, policies, programs, and actions necessary to achieve organizational aims, or there will be someone with enough *power and authority* that consensus does not matter. The assumption just does not hold in most circumstances. Only in fairly centralized, authoritarian, and quasi-military bureaucracies will the assumption hold—maybe (Roberts & Wargo, 1994).

Let us now examine a model that contrasts sharply with the rational planning model, the political decision-making model presented in Figure 1.3. This model is inductive, not rational-deductive. It begins with issues, which almost by definition involve conflict, not consensus. The conflicts may be over ends, means, timing, location, political advantage, reasons for change, or philosophy and values—and the conflicts may be severe. As efforts proceed to resolve the issues and learn how to move ahead, policies and programs emerge that address the issues and are politically rational—that is, they are politically acceptable to involved or affected parties. Over time, more general policies may be formulated to capture, frame, shape, guide, or interpret the policies, programs, and learning developed to deal with the issues. The various policies and programs are in effect treaties among the various stakeholder groups and, though they may not exactly record a consensus, at least they represent a reasonable level of agreement among stakeholders (Lindblom, 1965, 1990; March & Olsen, 1989, 1995; Weick, 2009).

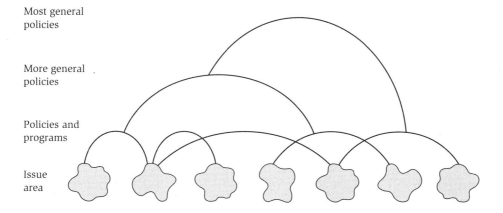

Most general
policies

More general
policies

Policies and
programs

Issue
area

Figure 1.3. Political Decision-Making Model.

Now, the heart of the strategic planning process discussed in Chapter Two is the identification and resolution of strategic—that is, very important and consequential—issues. The process, in other words, accepts political decision making's emphasis on issues and seeks to inform the formulation and resolution of those issues. Effective strategic planning therefore should make political decision makers more effective, and, if practiced consistently, may even make their professional lives easier (Janis, 1989; Nutt, 2002). Since every key decision maker in a large public or nonprofit organization is, in effect, a political decision maker (Bolman & Deal, 2008), strategic planning can help these decision makers and their organizations. Strategic planning—at least as described in this book—therefore will last in government and nonprofit organizations because it accepts and builds on the nature of political decision making. If done well, it actually improves political decisions, as well as programs, policies, and learning how to do better, by joining political acceptability to administrative feasibility and substantive rationality.

Having drawn a sharp distinction between the rational planning and political decision-making models, I must now emphasize that the two models are not inherently antithetical. Indeed, research by Judith Innes (1996; Innes & Booher, 2010) and her colleagues demonstrates that multiparty efforts to reach consensus on important issues fraught with conflict often can look extremely messy in practice, but then meet very high standards of rationality after all of the political, technical, administrative, procedural, and legal issues have been sorted out. The challenge in this case is simply to sequence the approaches appropriately. The political decision-making model is necessary to work out consensual agreements on what programs (services, projects, and so on) and policies will best resolve key issues. Then the rational planning model can be used to recast that consensus in the form of goals, policies, programs, and actions. While the planning and decision making that go into the formulation of a strategic plan may look fairly sloppy to an outsider, once a consensus is reached on what to do, the resulting strategic plan can be rewritten—rationalized—in a form that is in fact quite rational by ordinary definitions of the term. Furthermore, the rational planning model may be used to sort out and address any minor (and perhaps major) inconsistencies embedded in the political consensus. Clear goals, when backed by political agreement and authority, can help foster and guide organizational innovation and effectiveness (Nutt, 2002; Moynihan & Pandey, 2010; Mulgan, 2009).

To use another example, in many organizations and communities there exists a broad-based consensus on basic purposes and values—and often on many policies, programs, and actions as well. There may even be a consensus on the organization's or community's vision. This consensus can be recast using the rational planning model. The political model can then be used to address remaining issues on which there is no agreement. In particular, the remaining issues are likely to revolve around what would have to be done in order to achieve the agreed-upon goals or vision.

To summarize: A great advantage of the strategic planning process outlined in this book is that the process does not presume consensus where it does not exist, but can accommodate consensus where it does exist. Because there is no presumption of consensus, the process is more suitable for politicized circumstances than purely "rational" approaches. An intense attention to, and deliberation about, stakeholders and their interests, external and internal environments, and strategic issues means that the actions that are ultimately agreed-upon are more likely to be *politically* wise, and that organizational survival and prosperity are, therefore, more likely to be assured. Furthermore, by gathering relevant information, asking probing questions, and focusing on how best to raise the issues, the process can be used to inform political decision making in such a way that virtuous public and nonprofit purposes are better served than they would be if only the rawest forms of political decision making prevailed (Flyvbjerg, 1998). The process, in other words, provides a way of blending substantive rationality (that is, the content of the final answer makes sense), procedural rationality (that is, the steps followed make reasonable sense to the parties involved or affected), *and* political rationality (that is, acceptability to the interested parties)—content *and* process *and* politics—in wise ways to the betterment of the organizations and communities that use it (March & Olsen, 1989, 1995; Nutt, 2002; Stone, 2002; Innes & Booher, 2010; Eden & Ackermann, 2010).

DEFINITION, PURPOSE, AND BENEFITS OF STRATEGIC MANAGEMENT

What is strategic management and how does strategic planning relate to it? Strategic management is a more inclusive concept than strategic planning, because strategic management is the reasonable integration of strategic planning and implementation across an organization (or other entity) in an ongoing way to enhance the fulfillment of mission, meeting of mandates, continuous learning, and sustained creation of public value (see Exhibit 1.1). Strategic management should thus be considered a part of organizational *governance*, which as Owen Hughes (2010, pp. 87–88) points out, "is about running organizations, about setting up structures to enable the organization to be run. . . . In English, the verb *govern* derives from the Latin *gubernare*, meaning steer, direct, rule."

Functionally, strategic planning involves the kind of deliberative, disciplined work intended to help clarify organizational purposes, mandates, goals, and

Exhibit 1.1. Strategic Planning and Strategic Management: Definitions, Functions, and Approaches.

	Strategic Management The integration of strategic planning and implementation across an organization (or other entity) in an ongoing way to enhance the fulfillment of mission, meeting of mandates, and sustained creation of public value	
	Strategic planning A deliberative, disciplined effort to produce fundamental decisions and actions that shape and guide what an organization (or other entity) is, what it does, and why it does it.	**Implementation** The effort to realize in practice an organization's (or other entity's) mission, goals and strategies, the meeting of its mandates, continued organizational learning, and the ongoing creation of public value.
Functions	Designing and integrating kinds of *work* that have to be done in a reasonably *formalized way*, for the sake of clarifying organizational purposes, mandates, goals, issues, strategies, and requirements for success; the work includes use of deliberative settings to foster collective strategic thinking, acting, and learning around key issues. Addressing the kinds of *work* that should be done in a reasonably *formalized way*, for the sake of building the enterprise's *capacity for, and delivery of success over time*; the work includes linking purposes, people, structures, processes, resources, political support, and learning in productive ways. Clarifying the purpose and placement of the strategic planning function within a governmental or nonprofit organizational design.	Designing an appropriate formal *strategic management system* and the placement and role of strategic and operational planning within it. Linking budgeting, performance measurement, and performance management to: meet mandates; achieve agreed mission, goals, strategies, and requirements for success; allow for desirable changes in ends and means to emerge over time; and achieve significant public value. Making use of forums and formative evaluations to tailor and adjust strategies during implementation to increase chances of success. Making use of forums and summative evaluations to help judge the degree to which success has been achieved, and whether new ends and means should be pursued.

Approaches to Fulfilling the Functions	A strategic planning approach is a kind of *response* to circumstances recognized as *challenges* that people judge to require a considered, collective, and often novel *response*.
	
	Such responses are part of complex social problem solving, inseparable—and in many ways indistinguishable from—other parts of the same thing. Still, for purposes of discussing enterprises in which planning plays a role, it is advantageous to use *strategic planning* to characterize this "part" of response scenarios to challenges.
	
	A widely used approach is the Strategy Change Cycle (Bryson, 2004), which includes attending to context and developing and linking purposes, strategies, participation, and the coalitions of support needed to adopt desirable changes and protect them during implementation, as well as building capacity for ongoing implementation, learning, and change.
		Approaches to, or kinds of, *strategic management systems*:
		
		Integrated units of management (or layered or stacked units of management), including use of cascaded Balanced Scorecards
		
		Strategic issues management, including PerformanceStat systems
		
		Contract models
		
		Portfolio approaches
		
		Collaboration models:
		
		  Lead organization
		
		  Shared governance
		
		  Partnership administrative organization
		
		Goals or benchmark approaches
		
		Hybrid models, that is, combinations of two or more of the above

Source: Adapted in part from M. Barzelay and J. M. Bryson, "Two Views of Strategic Planning," unpublished manuscript, January 2010; and Bryson, 2010a, p. S256.

strategies. It also includes designing an effective and responsive strategic management system that will build the enterprise's capacity for, and delivery of, success over time. Implementation, however, involves the effort to realize in practice an organization's mission, goals, and strategies, the meeting of its mandates, continued organizational learning, and the ongoing creation of public value. Doing so requires actually developing a useful strategic management system, including linking budgeting, performance measurement, and performance management, and allowing desirable changes in ends and means to emerge over time. Conceptually, it is useful to view strategic planning as the "front end" of strategic management, even though most strategic planning efforts begin amid the implementation of previously designed, or currently emerging, strategies.

There are many different ways to approach strategic planning in practice. This book focuses on one, the Strategy Change Cycle, which is presented in some detail in the next chapter. The approach is generic and must be tailored in an ongoing way to fit specific purposes and circumstances. It is also important to keep in mind that strategic planning is just one of the ways in which important strategy change is brought about; those using the process must be attentive to other sources and avenues of positive change and figure out ways for the strategic planning effort to make use of or complement them.

Similarly, there are many different approaches to designing a strategic management system in practice, where the approach again must be tailored in an ongoing way to fit specific purposes and circumstances. Seven different major approaches are listed in Exhibit 1.1, of which the most important is perhaps the last: hybrid models. Because purposes and circumstances are often so situation-specific, most effective strategic management systems are hybrids of two or more of the other approaches. All seven approaches are discussed in Chapter Ten. To summarize, this book is mainly but not exclusively about *strategic planning*, but I will always emphasize the need to do the planning with the requirements for, and function of, implementation and strategic management kept clearly in mind.

Three Examples of Strategic Planning

Throughout this book the experiences of three organizations (one public, one nonprofit, and the third a cross-sector collaboration) are used to illustrate key points about strategic planning—including its capacity for accommodating procedural, substantive, and political rationality. Each of these organizations used a variant of the strategic planning process outlined here, explicitly or implicitly adapting it for their own purposes. I was a strategic planning consultant for two of the organizations, although the extent of my involvement varied. Each of these projects represented an action research project in which the aims included developing theory and guidance for practice (Eden & Huxham, 1996). I had no involvement in the third organization's planning effort other than the fact that the chief planner was a former student and a student team in my strategic planning class prepared a case study of the process (Enke, Nguy, Sullivan, & Zenk, 2009).

The first of the three organizations described here is the Minneapolis Park and Recreation Board (the Park Board), which oversees one of the nation's premier municipal park systems. The Park Board is a semi-autonomous part of the government of the City of Minneapolis, Minnesota. The Park Board has its own separately elected board and its own taxing powers, subject to some oversight by other parts of Minneapolis government. The nonprofit is

The Loft Literary Center, a nationally famous writers' support organization founded in 1974 and headquartered in Minneapolis. The Loft serves thousands of people each year through classes, mentoring, readings, in-school and in-community programs of many kinds, and efforts to build an audience for literature.

The third organization is MetroGIS, a cross-sector, completely voluntary collaboration of three hundred units of government, businesses, and nonprofit organizations serving the seven-county Minneapolis–St. Paul, Minnesota, metropolitan area, whose purpose is to help its members address their shared geographic information needs and help them get the most out of their existing resources. This purpose is accomplished through the collaboration's voluntary efforts to: (1) implement regional solutions to geospatial information needs shared by its stakeholder organizations, and (2) address policy and procedural barriers that inhibit widespread sharing of geospatial data or geographic information. MetroGIS's sole purpose is to foster collaborative solutions and it does so by providing a forum (or fora) for defining collaborative solutions to shared geospatial needs; it does not own any geospatial data or operate any geographic information system (GIS). The forum is coordinated by a small group of public servants housed within—but not reporting to—the region's metropolitan government, the Metropolitan Council (MC). The MC is the primary sponsor of MetroGIS. One full-time MetroGIS staff coordinator, along with 3–4 members of the Council's GIS Unit—who together average approximately 1.5 full-time equivalent (FTE) for this purpose—comprise the dedicated support team. These individuals, in turn, leverage support resources on a project-by-project basis from the stakeholder community to define and implement the subject regional solutions. Although the support team is employed by the MC, MetroGIS does not report to the Council. The MC has representation on the MetroGIS Policy Board. Decisions of the board, which are made by consensus by all affected and relevant parties, authorize the regional solutions to shared geospatial needs. MetroGIS has won numerous national and international awards for its work. A number of other less detailed examples are used as well to clarify the discussion.

The Minneapolis Park and Recreation Board (Park Board). The Park Board was created in 1883 through an act of the Minnesota Legislature and is a semi-autonomous body of nine independently elected commissioners overseeing one of the country's largest and best municipal park systems. The Park Board has dual roles of natural resource steward and program provider and has received numerous awards and accolades for its work—including having *USA Today* say it is the "closest to park nirvana" among U.S. park systems (http://www.minneapolisparks.org).

The Park Board is responsible for governing, maintaining, and developing the Minneapolis park system, which serves millions of visitors each year

(Minneapolis Park and Recreation Board, 2007). The Park Board manages 182 park properties comprising 6,732 acres of land and water. The properties include local and regional parks, playgrounds, golf courses, gardens, picnic areas, biking and walking paths, nature sanctuaries, and a 55-mile parkway system, as well as cultural and historical sites such as the Minneapolis Sculpture Garden and the nineteenth-century Stone Arch Bridge (that my wife and I see from our living room window) across the Mississippi River.

Minneapolis voters elect Park Board commissioners during general elections every four years; three are elected at-large and six represent geographical park districts. Commissioners, among other responsibilities, develop park policies, enact ordinances governing the use of park facilities, and hire the superintendent of parks. At the end of 2009 the superintendent oversaw approximately 450 permanent year-round, 225 part-time, and many seasonal employees. At the end of fiscal year 2009 the Park Board had revenues of approximately $71.7 million and expenditures of approximately $68.9 million.

As noted, the Park Board is semi-autonomous. This has led to occasionally complicated relationships with other governmental bodies, particularly the City of Minneapolis, depending on who the mayor and city council members are. The commissioners' powers include the ability to levy property taxes and own land within and outside the City of Minneapolis. However, the city can determine a cap for the property tax levy. Resulting power struggles have sometimes created a difficult political environment for the Park Board. For example, in 2002 a majority of Park Board commissioners voted to spend almost $5.8 million to purchase and rehabilitate a riverfront building (Brandt, 2002). Some vocal citizens and elected officials felt that the tax dollars could be better spent on park services or infrastructure improvements at park centers. Minneapolis mayor R. T. Rybak vetoed the decision, but the Park Board overrode the veto, which heightened strains between the city and its Park Board (Brandt, 2002). The action led to temporary budgetary difficulties.

By the early part of the new millennium, the Park Board was in an uncomfortable position. The commissioners' internal bickering made it very difficult to hire a new superintendent (Grow, 2003). The agency faced financial difficulties, city demographics were changing, other agencies' planning efforts required a response, and a series of public missteps strained the Park Board's relationships with some government bodies and parts of the community at large. As a 2003 *Minneapolis Star Tribune* article lamented: "The Park Board has been a sorely divided body for several years, at war internally over matters of staff, budget and procedure" (Grow, 2003, p. 2B).

In 2001, the Park Board contracted with a planning consultant to begin a strategic planning process. Although the consultant conducted initial interviews with commissioners, the planning process was delayed by budgetary and administrative changes. At the beginning of 2004, new Interim

Superintendent Jon Gurban began reorganizing the staff and procurement processes. He began by restructuring the organization into cross-functional teams across three newly delineated districts and assigned a district administrator to each one. These changes provided needed vertical and horizontal integrative capacity and accountability that had not existed before. He also promoted Jennifer Ringold in July 2005 to Citywide Planner to lead an upcoming strategic planning effort. She began working on the project in earnest in August 2005 and made her first presentation to the board in October 2005. In January 2006, four new commissioners, who had run on a platform of change and been elected, joined the Park Board. Under Gurban's leadership, Ringold's day-to-day direction, and the new board, the strategic planning process was fully under way.

The Loft Literary Center (The Loft). The Loft began in the early 1970s when a group of then-unknown writers who wanted to learn from and support each other gathered in a loft above a Minneapolis bookstore. The Loft was officially founded in 1974 and incorporated as a nonprofit organization in 1975. Many of the Loft's founders went on to national and international fame, including Garrison Keillor, Robert Bly, Patricia Hampl, Jim Moore, Phebe Hanson, and others. The organization has grown to include 2,800 members and the list of established writers of regional, national, and international renown has grown as well. The Loft has become the nation's largest and most comprehensive literary center. It is now located in the award-winning Open Book literary arts building in Minneapolis, Minnesota. The Loft both grew out of, and helped build, one of the most literate and book-friendly regions in the country (http://www.loft.org). (And it pleases me greatly to live across the street from the Loft and the Open Book and its coffee shop.) At the end of 2007, when the strategic planning process began, the Loft had 19 full-time employees. At the end of 2009, that number had been trimmed to 15 full-time and one part-time employees and a pool of about two hundred regular contract creative writing teachers. Total revenues at the end of fiscal year 2009 in the midst of the recession were around $1.8 million, whereas expenses were around $2.0 million, prompting the reduction in staff and a new, quicker round of strategic planning.

The Loft offers services for readers and writers at every level. Children's literature, poetry, playwriting, novels, memoirs, the spoken word, and other literary forms and media are all featured. There are readings by well-known local, national, and international authors; classes; weekend genre festivals; competitions and grants; open groups; writer's studios; mentoring programs; and so on. The list of the Loft's alumni and guests reads much like a *Who's Who* of American letters.

The Loft also has a tradition of strategic planning, having prepared plans for 1996–2001, 2002–2007, and now 2007–2012. This last planning effort is the focus in this book (although some attention will be devoted to a shorter effort begun in 2010 to update the plan and address the consequences of pressing financial challenges). The effort took about 18 months from start to finish. It began early in 2006 and was initiated by the then–executive director Linda Myers, the executive committee, and the board of directors. They knew the current plan would expire in June 2007 and wanted to take enough time to have a widely participative process. Writers are a notably independent group and lots of participation would be needed to build the kind of consensus the Loft's leadership wanted in support of the final plan. Besides, all the major goals in the 2002–2007 Strategic Plan had been achieved so it was time to begin articulating the next major goals.

Although there were no crises to attend to, there were some concerns involving ongoing financing, changes in the demography of the region, the potentials and threats posed by new media, and leadership succession, as Myers was reaching an age when retirement might be a consideration. She had been in the post for 13 years and was widely admired for her work on behalf of the organization. But her very effectiveness and centrality to the organization's success meant it was wise to at least consider some succession planning. Two members of the board served as the strategic planning secretariat, including Jocelyn Hale, an accomplished businesswoman, nonprofit manager, community activist, writer, and mid-career student at the Humphrey School. Hale took a course from me in strategic planning and used the Loft as a real-life case study (Hale, 2007). We met regularly throughout the process to talk about how things were going and what might be done next. Then in March 2007 Myers announced that she would retire in October of that year. Some board members thought the strategic planning process should be held in abeyance until a new executive director was hired, but the board as a whole concluded it was best to proceed and to use the plan to help attract the right kind of director. The plan was finalized and formally adopted by the board in May 2007. Later in the summer Hale was hired as executive director (after a national search) and worked with Myers to effect a seamless transition (Hale, 2007).

MetroGIS. Before introducing MetroGIS, we first need to say something about geographic information systems and the Twin Cities regional government, the Metropolitan Council.

Geographic Information Systems (GIS). Technological innovations in recent decades have produced powerful Web-based geospatial mapping tools that can help a variety of groups solve problems and achieve ambitious goals. Users of the tools might be, for example, nonprofits or governments seeking to combat public health problems or a business entrepreneur wanting to corner new markets. Yet putting together a mapping system that draws on expertise and databases of multiple organizations (at multiple levels of government and across sectors) is a challenging endeavor for leaders like those who were central to the creation and continuation of MetroGIS under the sponsorship of the Twin Cities Metropolitan Council.

Maps, of course, have been used throughout human history to visually represent geographic space, the elements making it up, and the relationships among the elements. The creation of an analogical space representing a larger geography is one of the great accomplishments of human history, on par with the development of language and numeracy (Robinson, 1982). Maps are crucial to knowing where anything is and to navigating between points; to assertions of sovereignty and the rights and duties of those under the sovereign power; to understanding amounts, capacities, or flows of various things (land, water, weather, traffic); to establishing ownership and the legitimacy of real property exchanges; and to a host of other purposes. Maps typically are two-dimensional, but represent three-dimensional spaces. They also can be three-dimensional, as in globes, or four-dimensional via time-lapsed presentations.

Since the 1960s, it has become possible to produce digitized geospatial information in order to create computerized maps (models) and to format, reformat, and analyze them using various analytic tools. Geographic information systems (GIS) are computerized models containing digitized, manipulable, geospatially referenced data. In a GIS, the maps are made up of layers (think of the zoom feature on Google Earth). Each layer consists of features (cities, jurisdictions, tracts of land) or surfaces (lakes, land uses, snow cover). The features have shapes and sizes; the surfaces have values (elevation, slope, temperature, depth). Features have specific locations identified by coordinate systems and can also be displayed at different sizes (scales) (Ormsby, Napoleon, Burke, Groessl, & Feaster, 2004, pp. 2–10). Google Maps (http://www.maps.google.com) is the best-known GIS, but doesn't come close to the functionality of cutting-edge GISs. Each version of Google Maps includes more and increasingly accurate data, including geospatially referenced video feeds. Automobiles increasingly come with onboard GIS systems as standard equipment to assist with navigation; most include voice directions.

The Metropolitan Council (MC). The Metropolitan Council (MC) was created in 1967 to be the regional planning and coordinating agency for the Minneapolis–St. Paul region of Minnesota. It formally sponsors MetroGIS and has assumed primary responsibility for its support.

Since the 1960s the Minneapolis–St. Paul region has experienced many of the same problems as other metropolitan centers in the United States and other developed nations. Leaders in the region responded over many years by creating regional government structures—especially the MC—that increased the capacity of local, state, and federal governments to tackle regional public problems (Bryson & Crosby, 1992; Metropolitan Council, 2010). The council works with local communities to provide the following services:

- Operating the region's largest bus system
- Collecting and treating wastewater
- Engaging communities and the public in planning for future growth
- Providing forecasts of the region's population and household growth
- Providing affordable housing opportunities for low- and moderate-income individuals and families
- Providing planning, acquisitions, and funding for a regional system of parks and trails
- Providing a framework for decisions and implementation for regional systems including aviation, transportation, parks and open space, water quality, and water management

The MC's governing board consists of 17 members, 16 of whom represent a geographic district and one chair who serves at large. They are all appointed by and serve at the pleasure of the governor. At present, the MC has staff of 3,700 and an annual operating budget of about $700 million, 90 percent of which is funded by state appropriations and user fees such as wastewater treatment charges and transit fares. Ten percent comes from local property taxes. The bulk of the MC's employees operate the region's transit and regional wastewater treatment systems.

Although the MC had accomplished many things since its establishment, by the early 1990s regional officials and planners were still struggling to have timely, accurate, reliable, and comparable geospatial information about local conditions so they could understand the contours of transportation, housing, open space, and waste treatment challenges; generate solutions that were more finely tuned to local and regional realities; and build the coalitions needed for necessary policy changes and resource allocation choices. Said differently, in any democratic society based on the rule of law, accurate, timely, geospatially referenced information is absolutely necessary for effective governance, planning, and coordination. The MC had for years produced information, but it was often based on estimates and projections that did not take into account the carrying capacity of the land.

MetroGIS grew out of the efforts of a group of public officials and managers, along with partners in other sectors, to remedy this shortcoming. They sought to create a shared GIS for the region that linked and made easily accessible business, government, and nonprofit databases of accurate, timely, standardized, and needed geospatially referenced information; and acquired or developed the software applications to make use of the data to solve public problems.

These leaders strove to improve multiple governments' capacities for public problem solving around a host of issues affecting the Twin Cities metropolitan region, including urban traffic congestion, economic development, affordable housing, threats to water availability and quality, provision of parks and other recreational opportunities, waste management, and crime. Government structures and tools often are simply inadequate to allow government agencies to carry out responsibilities and partner effectively with other organizations (Kettl, 2008; Osborne, 2010). Developing these structures and tools can be a major leadership challenge—and certainly was in the MetroGIS case.

MetroGIS. In this book we will trace the efforts of MC administrators and appointed officials, along with several county commissioners and others, to develop a sustainable cross-governmental, cross-sector system for sharing detailed geographic information (for example, exact location of land parcels, streets, sewer, and utility lines) across numerous jurisdictional boundaries (MetroGIS, 2009; Bryson, Crosby, & Bryson, 2009; Crosby & Bryson, 2010).

MetroGIS is now fourteen years old and involves three hundred governmental units, businesses, and nonprofit organizations. The organization's small coordinating staff is housed in the MC. Its policy board consists exclusively of government representatives, but its management-level coordinating committee and technical advisory team consist of members representing a variety of units of government, businesses, and nonprofits.

MetroGIS is now nationally and internationally recognized as one of the best collaborative GIS organizations in the world. Its accomplishments include, among other things (MetroGIS, 2009):

- Implementing, or making substantial progress on implementing, regional solutions for eight of the MetroGIS community's thirteen priority information needs: jurisdictional boundaries; street addresses/ where people live; parcels/parcel identifiers; highway and road networks; census boundaries; lakes, wetlands, water courses; land cover; and planned land use.

- Implementing MetroGIS DataFinder as a registered node of the Federal National Spatial Data Infrastructure, fully integrated into the State of Minnesota's Geographic Data Clearinghouse, supporting not only traditional downloading of geospatial data but also accessing geospatial data via emerging Web service technology. Over two hundred datasets are currently accessible via DataFinder. Over eight hundred data downloads per month occur and the trend is a steady increase in the form of data and Web services.

- Executing agreements that provide access by all government interests serving the seven-county metropolitan area, without fee and subject to identical access requirements, to parcel and other geospatial data produced by all seven metro area counties and the MC.

- Maintaining active involvement of key stakeholder representatives at the policy, management, and technical levels since MetroGIS's inception in 1995.

The road to these achievements has been a long and not necessarily easy one. In this book we will discuss the two major strategic planning efforts undertaken by MetroGIS. The first took place in the mid-1990s and resulted in the creation of the organization. The second occurred in 2007–2008 and resulted in a new and expanded mission for the organization.

Comparisons and Contrasts. These three organizations offer a number of comparisons and contrasts. All are Minnesota-based, but they differ in size, staff, budgets, and legal status. The Park Board is a unit of local government. The Loft is an independent nonprofit organization. And MetroGIS is a cross-sector collaboration whose coordinating staff consists of public servants well down the organizational hierarchy of the regional government that serves as its primary sponsor.

The strategic planning effort for these organizations differed in the extent to which it focused directly on the organization and what it should do or on what should happen in the community of which the organization is a part. The Park Board focused on both organizational and community planning. MetroGIS focused on itself—where "itself" is a virtual enterprise linking three hundred organizations from across the broad regional community. MetroGIS also was intent on building the capabilities of its stakeholders to leverage the power of GIS technology and collaborative solutions to shared geospatial needs to improve their organizational effectiveness. Most of the stakeholders were governments having both organizational and community responsibilities. Finally, the Loft was focused mostly on the organization and its members, but also saw its role and mission as building the audience for literature. In short, for these organizations the boundary between what is "inside" and what is "outside" the organization is somewhat blurred.

In addition, the three organizations engaged in strategic planning for different reasons. The Park Board had never really had a strategic plan and also faced some serious issues, including financial challenges, changing city demographics, the need to respond to planning efforts by the City of Minneapolis and the Metropolitan Council, and at times difficult relationships on its board and with some leaders of Minneapolis's city government and the community at large. The process could provide a way for everyone to come together around the preservation and enhancement of the park system. The Loft had a habit of regular strategic planning and the time had come to produce the next plan. The Loft didn't face an emerging crisis, but its funding environment had become tougher and the match with the organization's capabilities had to be explored in relation to changing community demographics and emerging technologies and media. In addition, the need for leadership succession planning had to be considered. MetroGIS engaged in two strategic planning efforts, one in the mid-1990s and the other in 2007–08. The first effort was to determine exactly what the purpose, goals, strategies, and structure of a new regional GIS should be. The establishment of a functioning, effective regional GIS altogether took a decade and was hardly easy to do. The second effort took place after the organization had achieved its initial goals and survived a major challenge to its existence. The new mission that emerged from this process was to help participating organizations build their *own* capacities to address "shared geographic information technology needs and maximize investments in existing resources through widespread collaboration of organizations serving the area" (MetroGIS, 2010). The new mission takes MetroGIS into a whole new territory.

There are a number of similarities in the three cases as well. First, each organization succeeded because it had leaders willing to act as *process sponsors* to endorse and legitimate the effort. The sponsors were not always particularly active participants, and they were not always at the top of the organizational hierarchy, but they did let it be known that they wanted important decision makers and managers to give the effort a good try. Second, each organization had *process champions* committed to making the process work. The champions did not have preconceived ideas about what specific issues and answers would emerge from the process, although they may have had some good hunches. They simply believed that the process would result in good answers and pushed until those answers emerged (Bryson & Roering, 1988, 1989).

Third, each organization ultimately developed a fairly clear understanding and agreement among key decision makers about what strategic planning was and what they expected from the process. Fourth, each followed a reasonably structured strategic thinking, acting, and learning process. Fifth, each had a decision-making or advisory body to oversee the process. Sixth, each had a strategic planning team to manage the process, collect information and prepare for meetings, engage in serious strategic dialogue, and draft a strategic plan. Seventh, each identified critical issues that required effective action if the organization were to capitalize on important opportunities, avoid being victimized by serious threats, or both. Eighth, each worked hard to develop strategies that created public value and were politically acceptable, technically workable, administratively feasible, and ethically responsible. Ninth, each relied on outside assistance, including consultants, to help with the process—though particularly in the Park Board's case consultants were typically used to train staff to do the work consultants might otherwise do. Tenth, each made a point of not getting so bogged down in the process that they lost sight of what was truly important: strategic thinking, acting, and learning. And finally, each gained many of the potential benefits of strategic planning outlined above.

SUMMARY

This chapter has discussed what strategic planning is and why it is important. Its importance stems from its ability to help organizations and communities anticipate and respond to change in wise and effective ways. Not only have the environments of public and nonprofit organizations and communities changed dramatically in the recent past, more upheaval is likely in the future. The post-industrial, post-modern, post-structural, post-9/11, post-2007–2009 financial meltdown era is one in which continuous progress can hardly be taken for granted. In fact, we should *expect* periods of stability and small changes—interrupted by instability and significant change; uncertainty, ambiguity, and equivocality; happy surprises but also unhappy jolts—and occasional terror. In the last century we experienced world wars, big booms, big busts, modernism, post-modernism, post-structuralism, and major new roles for government and nonprofit organizations. In the last half century or so, the United States experienced the effects of the Korean War, the civil rights movement, the women's movement, major student disruptions, the disastrous war in Vietnam, the antiwar movement, the environmental movement, the collapse of the Soviet Union, dramatic shifts in the dominant political ideology in the United States, HIV/AIDS, lengthy wars in the Middle East, growing public cynicism, staggering new technologies, unprecedented economic growth but a continuation of sometimes brutal business cycle downturns, the emergence of the European Union, China, and India as serious economic competitors, a dramatic spread of democracy, and globalization—plus all the other changes noted in the opening paragraphs of this chapter. The current century opened with all the hope of a new millennium—and was quickly followed in the United States by the appalling 2000 presidential election process; the terrorist attack on the World Trade Center; the collapse of Enron, Worldcom, Adelphi, and a host of other once-famed, yet ultimately corrupt corporations; wars in Afghanistan and Iraq; the worst economic recession since the Great Depression; and now the biggest federal debt in our history, with really deep government budget cuts at all levels to follow. It all reminds me of a quotation attributed to Lord Salisbury (Robert Gascoyne-Cecil), three-time British Prime Minister in the nineteenth century: "Change, change, who needs change? Aren't things bad enough already?" Or a handwritten sign on a tip jar filled with coins at a cash register in a coffee shop in Portland, Oregon: "If you don't like change, leave it here." If only it were that simple!

Strategic planning is one way to help organizations and communities deal with their changed circumstances. Strategic planning is intended to enhance an organization's ability to think, act, and learn strategically. It can help organizations clarify and resolve the most important issues they face. It can help them build on strengths and take advantage of major opportunities, while they overcome or minimize weaknesses and serious challenges. It can help them be much more effective in what seems to be a more hostile world. If it does not do that, it probably was not worth the effort, even though it may have satisfied certain legal mandates or symbolic needs.

Figure 1.1 showed how strategic planning can help an organization (or other entity) deliberate about how it might get from where it is to where it wants to be. Figure 1.4 shows another way to think about strategic planning that more forcefully demonstrates its importance in terms of purposes and functions—namely, that strategic planning is meant to help public and non-profit organizations and communities create public value through meeting their mandates and fulfilling their missions. In order to do so, it must help produce fundamental decisions and actions that shape and guide what the organization is, what it does, and why it does it. Producing those decisions and actions requires an interconnected set of activities that organizes effective participation;

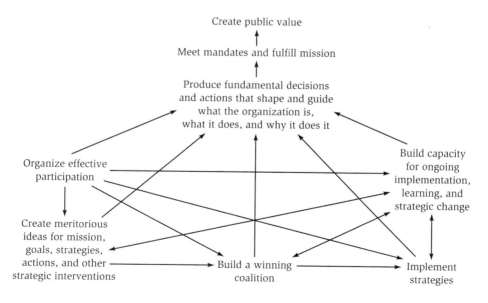

Figure 1.4. Purposes and Functions of Strategic Planning and Management.
Source: Adapted from Bryson, 2004a, p. 28.

creates meritorious ideas for mission, goals, strategies, actions, and other strategic interventions; builds a winning coalition; implements strategies; and builds capacity for ongoing implementation, learning, and strategic change.

Strategic planning clearly is a leadership and management innovation that is likely to persist because, unlike many other recent innovations, it accepts and builds on the nature of *political* decision making. Raising and resolving important issues is the heart of political decision making, and the heart of strategic planning. Strategic planning seeks to improve on raw political decision making, however, by helping to ensure that issues are raised and resolved in ways that benefit the organization, its key stakeholders, and society.

Chapter Two presents my preferred approach to strategic planning for governments, public agencies, nonprofit organizations, boundary-crossing collaborations, and communities. Subsequent chapters will discuss how to apply the process to help public and nonprofit organizations, collaborative networks, and communities create public value, fulfill their missions, meet their mandates, and serve their stakeholders effectively, efficiently, and responsibly. The good news in this book is of two sorts: There is lots of good work to do, and strategic planning can help you do it. The bad news is also of two sorts: strategic planning is not necessarily easy, and there is no guarantee of success. That's when it helps to remember the words of former senator and vice president Hubert H. Humphrey (1959): "Sometimes we get so overwhelmed by the problems of today that we forget the promise of tomorrow." Indeed, it may be even more helpful to consider the words of Samuel Beckett, winner of the Nobel Prize for Literature, in *Worstward Ho* (1984): "Ever tried. Ever failed. No matter. Try Again. Fail again. Fail better." Beckett's words are helpful because often failure of various sorts prompts the strategic thinking, acting, and learning necessary for success (Weick, Sutcliffe, & Obstfeld, 2005; Bryson & Crosby, 2008). The key is to use a deliberative, disciplined process that allows strategic thinking, acting, and learning to be joined for the ultimate benefit of those involved or affected. The next chapter presents such a process.

CHAPTER TWO

The Strategy Change Cycle: An Effective Strategic Planning Approach for Public and Nonprofit Organizations

*No, I can't say as I ever was lost, but once
I was bewildered pretty bad for three days.*
—Daniel Boone

*Make-believe is at the heart of play, and
also at the heart of so much that passes for work.
Let's make-believe we can shoot a rocket to the moon.*
—Diane Ackerman, poet and essayist

This chapter presents my preferred approach to strategic planning for public and nonprofit organizations, collaborations of various sorts, and communities. This generic approach, called the Strategy Change Cycle, does what Poister and Streib (1999, pp. 309–310) assert public and nonprofit strategic planning should do. Specifically, they believe strategic planning should:

- Be concerned with identifying and responding to the most fundamental issues facing an organization
- Address the subjective question of purpose and the often competing values that influence mission and strategies
- Emphasize the importance of external trends and forces as they are likely to affect the organization and its mission
- Attempt to be politically realistic by taking into account the concerns and preferences of internal, and especially external, stakeholders

41

- Rely heavily on the active involvement of senior level managers, and sometimes elected officials, assisted by staff support where needed
- Require the candid confrontation of critical issues by key participants in order to build commitment to plans
- Be action oriented and stresses the importance of developing plans for implementing strategies, and
- Focus on implementing decisions now in order to position the organization favorably for the future

The Strategy Change Cycle becomes a *strategic management* process—and not just a *strategic planning* process—to the extent that it is used to link planning and implementation and to manage an organization in a strategic way on an ongoing basis (see Exhibit 1.1). As Poister and Streib (1999, pp. 311–312) argue, "The overall purpose of strategic management is to develop a continuing commitment to the mission and vision of the organization (both internally and in the authorizing environment), nurture a culture that identifies and supports the mission and vision, and maintains a clear focus on the organization's strategic agenda throughout all its decision processes and activities." The Strategy Change Cycle draws on a considerable body of research and practical experience, applying it specifically to public and nonprofit organizations. Subsequent chapters will provide detailed guidance on moving through the cycle to make use of its logic in specific situations.

The epigraphs at the beginning of this chapter help make the point that strategic thinking, acting, and learning are more important than any particular approach to strategic planning. Consider the humorous statement of Daniel Boone, the famous eighteenth- and nineteenth-century American frontiersman (Faragher, 1992, p. 65). When you are lost in the wilderness—*bewildered*—no fixed plan will do. You must think, act, and learn your way to safety. Boone had a destination of at least a general sort in mind, but not a route. He had to wander around reconnoitering, gathering information, assessing directions, trying out options, and in general thinking, acting, and learning his way into where he wanted to be. As Weick, Sutcliffe, and Obstfeld (2005, pp. 412–413) put it, he had to "act thinkingly . . . [knowing] there are truths of the moment that change, develop, and take shape through time" and that "may signal a progression from worse to better." Or as Behn (1988) says more prosaically, he had to "manage by groping along." Ultimately—but not initially, or even much before he got to where he was going—Boone was able to establish a clear destination and a route that worked to get him there. Boone thus had a strategy of purposeful wandering, and it is true that he was not exactly lost; rather, he was working at finding himself where he wanted to be. So wandering with a purpose is an important aspect of strategic planning, in which thinking, acting, and learning clearly matter most.

Diane Ackerman's statement makes the point that almost anything is possible with enough imagination, ambition, direction, intelligence, competence, education and training, organization, resources, will, and staying power. A long list, to be sure, but sometimes they can be assembled and the triumph attained: humans have been to the moon, Mars, Venus, and a host of other places. We as citizens of the world have won world wars and cold wars, ended depressions and avoided others, virtually eliminated smallpox, unraveled the human genome, watched a reasonably united and integrated Europe emerge, and seen democracy spread where it was thought unimaginable. Now let's think about shared efforts to create good jobs for everyone, adequate food and housing for everyone, fully universal health care coverage at reasonable cost, drastically reduced crime, effective educational systems, secure pensions and retirements, a dramatic reduction in greenhouse emissions, the elimination of weapons of mass destruction, the elimination of HIV/AIDS, the realization in practice of the Universal Declaration on Human Rights and the Convention on the Rights of the Child, and so on. There is plenty of necessary, good, and exalting work to do. Committed leaders and followers can create institutions, policies, programs, projects, products, and services of lasting public value by drawing on diverse talents—and have done so again and again throughout history (Boyte & Kari, 1996; Light, 2002; Boyte, 2004). And they can use strategic planning to help think, act, and learn strategically—to figure out what is desirable and why, and how to get it. Think of strategic planning as the organization of hope, as what makes hope reasonable (Baum, 1997).

A TEN-STEP STRATEGIC PLANNING PROCESS

Now, with the caution that strategic thinking, acting, and learning matter most, let us proceed to a more detailed exploration of the ten-step Strategy Change Cycle. The process (presented graphically in Figure 2.1) is more orderly, deliberative, and participative than the process followed by an essayist such as Ackerman, or a wanderer like Boone. The process is designed to organize effective participation; create meritorious ideas for mission, goals, strategies, actions, and other strategic interventions; build the winning coalition needed to adopt and protect strategies during implementation; provide needed guidance and resources for implementation; and build competence and knowledge to sustain implementation and engage in the next round of strategic planning (see Figure 1.4). The Strategy Change Cycle may be thought of as a *process strategy* (Mintzberg, Ahlstrand, & Lampel, 2009, pp. 201, 208), *processual model of decision making* (Barzelay, 2001, p. 56), *activity-based view of strategy* (Johnson, Langley, Melin, & Whittington, 2007, pp. 35–36), or just an *approach* to identify and respond to challenges in which a leadership group manages

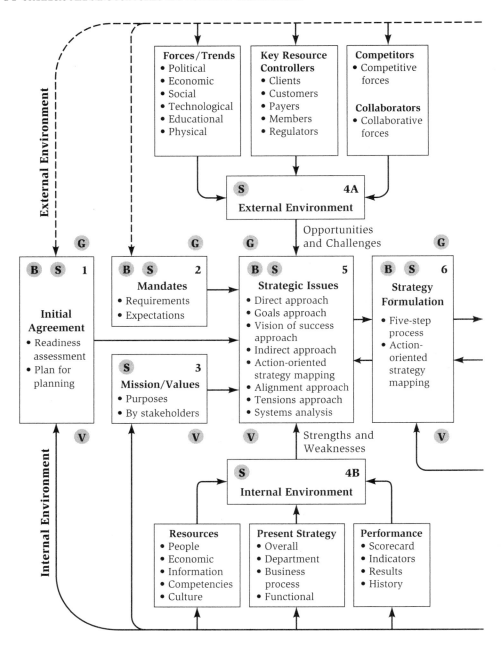

Figure 2.1. The Strategy Change Cycle.

Copyright © John M. Bryson, 1995, 2003, 2011.

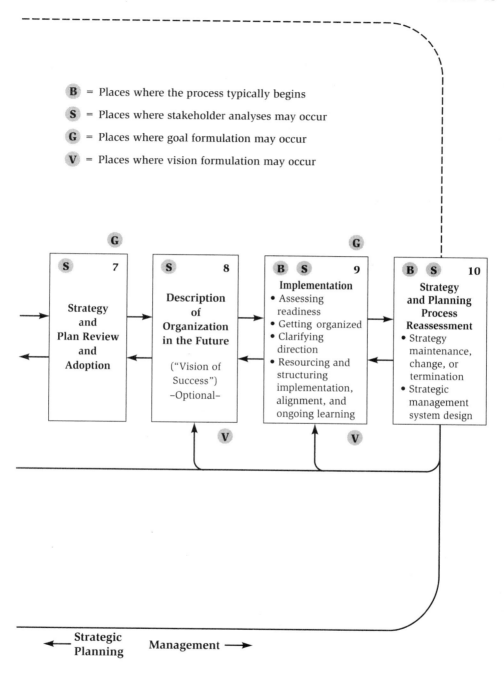

the main activities in the process and often leaves much of the content of the responses and implementation methods to others. The ten steps (or occasions for deliberation and decision) are as follows:

1. Initiate and agree on a strategic planning process
2. Identify organizational mandates
3. Clarify organizational mission and values
4. Assess the external and internal environments to identify strengths, weaknesses, opportunities, and threats
5. Identify the strategic issues facing the organization
6. Formulate strategies to manage the issues
7. Review and adopt the strategic plan or plans
8. Establish an effective organizational vision
9. Develop an effective implementation process
10. Reassess strategies and the strategic planning process

These ten steps should lead deliberatively to actions, results, evaluation, and learning. It must be emphasized that these outcomes should emerge at each step in the process. In other words, implementation and evaluation should not wait until the end of the process, but should be an integral and ongoing part of it.

The process is applicable to public and nonprofit organizations, collaborations of various sorts, and communities. The only general requirements are a "dominant coalition" (Thompson, 1967), or at least a "coalition of the willing" (Cleveland, 2002) able to sponsor and follow the process, and a process champion or champions willing to push it. For small organizations, well-informed strategic planning teams that are familiar with, believe in, and are committed to the process should be able to complete most of the steps in a two- or three-day retreat, with an additional one-day meeting scheduled three to four weeks later to review the resulting strategic plan. Responsibility for preparing the plan can be delegated to a planner assigned to work with the team, or the organization's chief executive may choose to draft the plan personally. More time may be needed for additional reviews and sign-offs by key decision makers, or to secure information or advice for specific parts of the plan, especially its recommended strategies. For large organizations, however, more time and effort are likely to be needed for the process. And when applied to a collaboration or community, the effort is likely to be considerably more time-consuming in order to promote the involvement of substantial numbers of leaders, organizations, and in a community, citizens, and to develop necessary agreements to proceed.

As you learn more about the steps of the Strategy Change Cycle, note that in practice it bears little resemblance to the caricature of strategic planning occasionally found in the literature as a rigid, formal, overly analytic, and detached process (for example, Mintzberg, Ahlstrand, & Lampel, 2009, pp. 49–84). (The criticisms seem to be based primarily on an exegesis and critique of historic texts and outdated private sector practice.) Instead, the Strategy Change Cycle is intended to enhance strategic thinking, acting, and learning; to engage key actors with what is as well as with what can be; to engage with the most important details while abstracting the strategic message within them; and to link strategy formulation with implementation in ways that are wise, technically and administratively workable, politically intelligent, and legal, moral, and ethical—and, not least, that create enduring public value.

Step 1: Initiating and Agreeing on a Strategic Planning Process

The purpose of the first step is to negotiate agreement among key internal (and perhaps external) decision makers or opinion leaders about the overall strategic planning effort and the key planning steps. The support and commitment of key decision makers are vital if strategic planning in an organization is to succeed. Further, the involvement of key decision makers outside the organization usually is crucial to the success of public and nonprofit programs if implementation will involve multiple parties and organizations (Nutt & Backoff, 1996; Light, 1998; Fernandez & Rainey, 2006; Innes & Booher, 2010).

Obviously, some person or group must initiate the process. One of the initiators' first tasks is to identify exactly who the key decision makers are. The next task is to identify which persons, groups, units, or organizations should be involved in the effort. These two steps will require some preliminary stakeholder analysis, which is discussed in more detail below. The initial agreement will be negotiated with at least some of these decision makers, key opinion leaders, groups, units, or organizations. In practice, a *series* of agreements typically must be struck among various parties as support for the process builds and key stakeholders and decision makers sign on. Strategic planning for a public or nonprofit organization, collaboration, or community is especially likely to work well if an effective policy- and decision-making body is in place to oversee the effort.

The agreement turns a general approach into a specific process design. The agreement should cover:

- The purpose of the effort
- A statement of desired outcomes (however sketchy) to be achieved

- Preferred steps in the process and the way ongoing feedback and learning will be accomplished
- The form and timing of reports
- The role, functions, and membership of any group or committee empowered to oversee the effort, such as a strategic planning coordinating committee (SPCC)
- The role, functions, and membership of the strategic planning team
- A general sense of how stakeholders will be engaged over the course of the process (see Resource A)
- A general sense of how the World Wide Web (the Web) will be used to help the process along (see Resource B)
- The likely requirements for success
- Any important limitations or boundaries on the effort
- Commitment of resources necessary to proceed with the effort

As noted, at least some stakeholder analysis work will be needed in order to figure out whom to include in the series of initial agreements. A *stakeholder* is defined as any person, group, or organization that can place a claim on an organization's (or other entity's) attention, resources, or output, or is affected by that output. Examples of a government's stakeholders are citizens, taxpayers, service recipients, the governing body, employees, unions, interest groups, political parties, the financial community, other businesses, and other governments. Examples of a nonprofit organization's stakeholders include members, clients or customers, third-party payers or funders, employees, the board of directors, volunteers, other nonprofit organizations providing complementary services or involved as co-venturers in projects, banks holding mortgages or notes, and suppliers.

Attention to stakeholder concerns is crucial: *the key to success in public and nonprofit organizations (and communities) is the satisfaction of key stakeholders according to their criteria, or at least ones they can accept* (Light, 1998; Fernandez and Rainey, 2006; Rainey, 2009). A stakeholder analysis is a way for the organization's decision makers and planning team to immerse themselves in the networks and politics surrounding the organization. An understanding of the relationships—actual or potential—that help define the organization's context can provide invaluable clues to identifying strategic issues and developing effective strategies (Moore, 1995; Bryson, 2004b). In this regard, note that the stakeholder definition is deliberately quite broad for both practical and ethical reasons. Thinking broadly, at least initially, about who the stakeholders are is a way of opening people's eyes to the various webs of relationships within which the organization exists (Feldman & Khademian,

2002; Rainey, 2009), and of assuring the organization is alerted to its ethical and democratic accountability responsibilities, since they always involve clarifying *who* and *what* counts (Mitchell, Agle, & Wood, 1997; Behn, 2001; Lewis & Gilman, 2005).

For many public and nonprofit organizations, the label *customer* will be given to their key stakeholder, particularly if the organization is trying to *reinvent* itself (Osborne & Plastrik, 1997, 2000; Osborne & Hutchinson, 2004), *reengineer* its operations, or employ *continuous improvement processes* (Cohen, Eimicke, & Heikkila, 2008). The customer label can be useful, particularly for organizations that need to improve their customer service. In other situations, the customer language actually can be problematic. One danger is that focusing on a single customer may lead these organizations inadvertently to ignore other important stakeholder groups. Another danger is that the customer label can undermine the values and virtues of active citizenship (deLeon & Denhardt, 2000; Denhardt & Denhardt, 2000; Hill & Hupe, 2009). The public sector is not as simple as the private sector; there typically are many "bottom lines" (Rainey, 2009). Many community-based nonprofit organizations and those relying on government funding also face very complex stakeholder environments.

Resource A at the end of the book provides an overview of a range of stakeholder identification and analysis techniques, and Chapter Three provides more detail on how to get started. The organizers of the planning effort should count on using several different techniques, including what I call the Basic Stakeholder Analysis Technique. This technique requires the strategic planning team to brainstorm a list of the organization's stakeholders, identify their criteria for judging the performance of the organization (that is, their *stake* in the organization or its output), and assess how well the organization performs against those criteria *from the stakeholders' points of view.* If there is time, additional steps (perhaps involving additional analysis techniques) should be considered, including understanding how the stakeholders influence the organization, identifying what the organization needs from its various stakeholders (money, staff, political support), and determining in general how important the various stakeholders are. Looking ahead, a stakeholder analysis will help clarify whether the organization needs to have different missions and perhaps different strategies for different stakeholders, whether it should seek to have its mandates changed, and in general what its strategic issues are.

Step 2: Identifying Organizational Mandates

The formal and informal mandates placed on the organization consist of the various "musts" it confronts—that is, the various requirements, restrictions, expectations, pressures, and constraints it faces (Simons, 1995). Actually, it is surprising how few organizations know precisely what they are (and are not) formally mandated to do. Typically, few members of any organization have ever read, for example, the relevant legislation, policies, ordinances, charters, articles, and contracts that outline the organization's formal mandates. Even if they have read these materials, too many strategic plans do not include explicit reference to many of the applicable formal mandates, so that they may be overlooked (Piotrowski & Rosenbloom, 2002). In addition, many organizational members also do not understand the informal mandates—typically political in the broadest sense—that the organization faces. It may not be surprising, then, that most organizations make one or more of three fundamental mistakes. First, by not articulating or knowing what they must do, they are unlikely to do it. Second, they may believe they are more tightly constrained in their actions than they actually are. And third, they may assume that if they are not explicitly told to do something, they are not allowed to do it.

Step 3: Clarifying Organizational Mission and Values

An organization's mission, in tandem with its mandates, provides the organization's most obvious *raison d'être* and social justification for its existence. An organization's mission and mandates also point the way toward the ultimate organizational end of creating public value at reasonable cost. This ultimate end corresponds to Aristotle's *final* cause, where "final" comes from the Latin word *finis* or end, corresponding to the Greek word *telos* or goal. A final cause thus provides the explanation for change by pointing to the goal (*telos*) on account of which, or for the sake of which, the changes are undertaken (Vella, 2008, p. 77). The Strategy Change Cycle thus represents a primarily teleological—meaning goal- or purpose-oriented—theory of change (Van de Ven & Poole, 1995) in which actions are undertaken and justified in terms of their efficacy for achieving goals or purposes (which will often be more intermediate than final, since ultimate ends may not be clearly understood at the beginning of the process). Causation in the Aristotelian sense is thus broader than our modern conception: "For Aristotle, a cause is an explanation or a reason why something is the case" (Vella, 2008, p. 48). Deliberations informed by the Strategy Change Cycle are thus guided by the need for *choices* based on *reasons* in order to *achieve ends.* The goal-oriented nature of strategic planning places a premium on ongoing feedback and learning, since they provide information necessary to stay on track (or perhaps to revise the goals) (Simon, 1996).

For a government, government agency, or nonprofit organization, this means there must be identifiable social or political demands or needs that the organization seeks to fill. Viewed in this light, organizations must always be seen as a means to an end (*finis*), not as an end in and of themselves (Frederickson, 1997). For a collaborative, it means identifying the *collaborative advantage* to be gained by working together, that is, what can be gained together that creates public value that cannot be achieved alone (Huxham & Vangen, 2005). Communities, too, must justify their existence based on how well they meet their stakeholders' social, political, economic, and environmental needs—including the stakeholders' need for a sense of community. Communities, however, are less likely to think they have a mission; they are more likely to talk about their purposes, values, and identity.

Identifying the mission or purpose of the organization, however, does more than justify the organization's existence. Clarifying purpose can eliminate a great deal of unnecessary conflict in an organization and can help channel discussion and activity productively (Nutt, 2002; Thompson, 2008). Agreement on purpose also defines the arenas within which the organization will collaborate or compete and, at least in broad outline, charts the future course of the organization. Agreement on purpose thus serves as a kind of *primary framework* (Goffman, 1986; Bryant, 2003, pp.96–99) or *boundary system* (Simons, 1995) that circumscribes the plausibility and acceptability of arguments. Agreement on purpose can go even further and provide a kind of *premise control* that constrains thinking, learning, and acting (Perrow, 1986; Weick, 1995), and even legitimacy (Suchman, 1995). Moreover, an important and socially justifiable mission is a source of inspiration and guidance to key stakeholders, particularly employees (Weiss & Piderit, 1999; Kouzes & Posner, 2008). Indeed, it is doubtful whether any organization ever achieved greatness or excellence without a basic consensus among its key stakeholders on an inspiring mission (Collins & Porras, 1997; Rainey & Steinbauer, 1999; Rughase, 2007).

I think that some careful stakeholder analysis work should precede development or modification of an existing mission statement, so that attention to purpose can be informed by thinking about purpose *for whom*. If the purposes of key stakeholders are not served, then the organization may be engaging in what historian Barbara Tuchman (1984) aptly calls folly. The mission statement itself might be very short, perhaps not more than a paragraph or a slogan, but development of the mission statement should grow out of lengthy dialogue about the organization's identity, its abiding purpose, desired responses to key stakeholders, its philosophy and core values, and its ethical standards. These discussions may also provide a basic outline for a description of the organization in the future, or its vision of success, described in Step 8. Considerable intermediate work is necessary, however, before a complete vision of success can be articulated.

Step 4: Assessing the Organization's External and Internal Environments

The planning team should explore the environment outside the organization to identify the opportunities and challenges (or threats) the organization faces (Step 4a). It should explore the environment inside the organization to identify strengths and weaknesses (Step 4b). Basically, "outside" factors are those the organization can't control, whereas "inside" factors are those it can (Pfeffer &

Salancik, 1978). Opportunities and challenges usually (though not necessarily) are more about the future than the present; strengths and weakness are more about the present than the future (Nutt & Backoff, 1992). Note that communities are more likely to think in terms of assets rather than strengths (Kretzmann & McKnight, 1997). The analysis of strengths, weaknesses, opportunities, and challenges (or threats) will be referred to in this book as a SWOC/T analysis.

Monitoring a variety of forces and trends—including political, economic, social, educational, technological, and physical environmental ones—can help planners and decision makers discern opportunities and challenges. Unfortunately, organizations all too often focus only on the negative or threatening aspects of serious challenges, and not on the genuine opportunities they may present, so care must be taken to assure a balanced view (Nutt, 2001; Eden & Ackermann, 2010). In other words, attending to challenges and weaknesses should be seen as an opportunity to build strengths and improve performance (Weick & Sutcliffe, 2007).

Besides monitoring trends and events, the strategic planning team also should monitor particularly important external stakeholder groups, especially those that affect resource flows (directly or indirectly). These groups would include customers, clients, payers or funders, dues-paying members, regulators, and relevant policy bodies. The team also should attend to competitors, competitive forces, and possible sources of competitive advantage; as well as to collaborators, collaborative forces, and potential sources of collaborative advantage.

The organization might construct various scenarios to explore alternative futures in the external environment, a practice typical of much strategic planning in large business organizations (Van der Heijden, 2005; Marcus, 2009). Scenarios are particularly good at demonstrating how various forces and trends are likely to interact, which are amenable to organizational influence, and which are not. Scenarios also offer an effective way of challenging the organization's "official future" when necessary. The "official future" is the presumed or taken-for-granted future that makes current strategies sensible. Organizations unwilling to challenge this future are the ones most likely to be blindsided by changes (Schwartz, 1996; Barzelay & Campbell, 2003). Communities also may wish to develop scenarios (Neuman, 1998; Myers & Kitsuse, 2000).

Members of an organization's governing body (particularly if they are elected) are often better at identifying and assessing external opportunities and challenges (particularly present ones) than are the organization's employees. This is partly due to a governing board's responsibility for relating an organization to its external environment and vice versa (Carver, 2006). Unfortunately, neither governing boards nor employees usually do a systematic or effective job of external scanning. As a result, most organizations are often like ships trying to navigate troubled or treacherous waters without benefit of human lookouts, global positioning systems, radar, or sonar. All too often the result is a very unwelcome surprise (Schwartz, 2004; Weick & Sutcliffe, 2007).

Because of this, both employees and governing board members should consider relying on a somewhat formal external assessment process to supplement their informal efforts. The technology of external assessment is fairly simple, and allows organizations to cheaply, pragmatically, and effectively keep tabs on what is happening in the larger world that is likely to have an effect on the organization and the pursuit of its mission. Basically there are three steps: scanning the environment to identify key trends, analyzing trends to interpret their importance and identify issues, and providing reports that are useful for planning and decision making (Pflaum & Delmont, 1987). Clip services, Web aggregators such as Google Reader, listserv queries, monthly discussion groups, and periodic retreats, for example, might be used to explore forces and trends and their potential impact. The key, however, is to avoid being captured by existing categories of classification and search, since they tend to formalize and routinize the past, rather than open one to the surprises of the future (Weick & Sutcliffe, 2007; Mintzberg, Ahlstrand, & Lampel, 2009).

Attention to opportunities and challenges, along with a stakeholder analysis, can be used to identify the organization's "critical success factors" (CSF). These may overlap with mandates, in the sense that they are the things the organization must do, or criteria it must meet, in order for it to be successful in the eyes of its key stakeholders, especially those in the external environment. Ideally, the organization will excel in these areas, and must do so in order to outperform or stave off competitors. In the private sector CSFs are often discussed in relation to specific products and services (Johnson, Scholes, & Whittington, 2008, pp. 79–81); here we are using the term more broadly as a category of requirements for success in addition to those that emanate from mission and mandates.

To identify internal strengths and weaknesses, the organization might monitor resources (inputs), present strategy (process), and performance (outputs). Most public and nonprofit organizations, in my experience, have volumes of information on many of their inputs, such as salaries, supplies, physical plant, and full-time equivalent (FTE) personnel. Unfortunately, fewer organizations have a very clear idea of their philosophy, core values, distinctive competencies, and culture, a crucial set of inputs both for ensuring stability and managing change.

Organizations also tend to have an unclear idea of their present strategy, either overall, by subunit, or by function. And typically they cannot say enough about their outputs, let alone the effects, or outcomes, those outputs create for clients, customers, or payers, although this, too, is changing. For example, traditionally schools have been able to say how many students they graduate—an output—but most cannot say how educated those students are. National and state requirements for standardized testing at different grade levels are an attempt to measure outcomes in order to remedy this shortcoming. We know tests of this sort are almost always imperfect, but the need to demonstrate accountability for performance to politicians and the citizenry virtually requires that believable testing of some sort be used. As Moynihan (2008) argues, much of the value of performance information is the dialogue that it prompts with stakeholders about performance.

A lack of performance information presents problems both for the organization and for its stakeholders. Stakeholders judge an organization according to the criteria *they* choose, which are not necessarily the same criteria the organization would choose. For external stakeholders in particular, these criteria typically relate to performance. If an organization cannot effectively meet its stakeholders' performance criteria, then regardless of its "inherent" worth, the stakeholders are likely to withdraw their support (Epstein, Coates, Wray, & Swain, 2005). The need to address this potential threat—particularly from key stakeholders, or so-called customers—is one of the reasons organizations initiate reinvention, restructuring, reengineering, or continuous improvement efforts (Light, 1997; Kettl, 2002, 2008).

An absence of performance information may also create—or harden—major organizational conflicts. Without performance criteria and information, there is no way to evaluate with reasonable objectivity the relative effectiveness of alternative strategies, resource allocations, organizational designs, and distributions of power. As a result, organizational conflicts are likely to occur more often than they should, serve narrow partisan interests, and be resolved in ways that don't further the organization's mission (Flyvbjerg, 1998; Thompson, 2008).

The difficulties of measuring performance are well known (Osborne & Plastrik, 2000; Berman, 2006; Moynihan, 2008). But regardless of the difficulties, organizations are continually challenged to demonstrate effective performance to their stakeholders. Employees of government agencies and nonprofit organizations receiving government funds might see the public's desire to limit or decrease taxation and funding as selfishness, which it may be for some. Alternatively, one might interpret these limitations on public expenditure as an unwillingness to support organizations that cannot demonstrate unequivocally effective performance. The desire for demonstrable performance was clearly behind the Government Performance and Results Act (GPRA) of 1993 (Public Law 103–62), which requires all federal agencies to complete a strategic plan based on outcomes rather than inputs or throughputs. The assessment of GPRA is mixed (Radin, 2006; Frederickson & Frederickson, 2006), but the impulse behind the act will remain. Several states initiated performance-oriented systems prior to GPRA (Broom, 1995), and large numbers of local governments embrace performance management as well (Berman, 2006).

A consideration of the organization's strengths and weaknesses can also lead to an identification of its *distinctive competencies* (Selznick, 1957), or *core competencies* (Prahalad & Hamel, 1990; Johnson, Scholes, & Whittington, 2008). The precise meanings of these terms differ, but in general they indicate the organization's strongest *abilities* that draw on resources (broadly conceived) and underpin effective strategies and actions that allow the organization to routinely perform well. What makes these abilities distinctive is the inability of others to replicate them easily, if at all, because of the way they are interlinked with one another (Bryson, Ackermann, & Eden, 2007; Eden & Ackermann, 2010). Resource C provides a method for identifying distinctive competencies and linking them directly to organizational aspirations.

Finally, a consideration of how inputs, process, and outputs are linked can help the organization more clearly understand what its strategies are and precisely what the *value proposition* is that the organization offers its stakeholders (Moore, 2000). In other words, what story does it or can it tell about the *logic model* (McLaughlin and Jordan, 2010) or *value chain* (Porter, 1985; Heintzman & Marson, 2005; Williams & Lewis, 2008) that the organization pursues to convert inputs into outputs that meet its mandates, fulfill its mission, satisfy its stakeholders, and create public value? Being clear about what *is* can be an extraordinarily helpful prelude to discerning what *ought* to be (Weick, 1995; Weick, Sutcliffe, & Obstfeld, 2005). For one thing, standing back and understanding what the strategy is in practice can help open people's eyes to what is going on in the environment more generally. As Mintzberg, Ahlstrand, and Lampel (2009, p. 19) note in reference to strategies' ability to put blinders on people, "the very encouragement of strategy to get on with it—its very role in protecting people in the organization from distraction—impedes their capacity to respond to changes in the environment." Understanding the current strategy also can sensitize people to the ways in which integrating human resources management, information technology, and financial management might be used to sustain, strengthen, and protect desirable strategies.

Step 5: Identifying the Strategic Issues Facing an Organization

Together the first four elements of the process lead to the fifth, the identification of strategic issues. *Strategic issues* are fundamental policy questions or critical challenges affecting the organization's mandates, mission and values, product or service level and mix, clients, users or payers, costs, financing, organization, or management. Finding the best way to frame these issues typically requires considerable wisdom, dialogue, and deep understanding of organizational operations, stakeholder interests, and external demands and possibilities. The first four steps of the process are designed deliberately to slow things down so that there is enough information and interaction to inform deliberations so that needed wisdom might emerge. More colloquially, the process is designed to increase deliberators' knowledge so as to avoid too much *bullshit*. As Frankfurt (2005, p. 63) notes, "Bullshit is unavoidable whenever circumstances require someone to talk without knowing what he [or she] is talking about." The process is designed, in other words, to *unfreeze* people's thinking (Lewin, 1951; Dalton, 1970; Fiol, 2001) so that knowledge exploration, development, and learning might occur (March, 1991; Nonaka & Takeuchi, 1995; Crossan, Lane, & White, 1999). This knowledge will be exploited in this and later phases.

Strategic planning focuses on achieving the best *fit* between an organization and its environment. Attention to mandates and the external environment, therefore, can be thought of as planning from the *outside in*. Attention to mission and organizational values and the internal environment can be considered planning from the *inside out*. Usually, it is vital that pressing strategic issues be dealt with expeditiously and effectively if the organization is to survive and prosper. An organization that does not respond to a strategic issue can expect undesirable results from a threat, a missed opportunity, or both.

The iterative nature of the strategic planning process often becomes apparent in this step when participants find that information created or discussed in earlier steps presents itself again as part of a strategic issue. For example, many strategic planning teams begin with the belief that they know what their organization's mission is. They often find out in this step, however, that one of the key issues the organization faces is exactly what its mission ought to be. In other words, the organization's present mission is found to be inappropriate, given the team members' new understanding of the situation the organization faces, and a new mission must be created. The organization must be repurposed.

Strategic issues, virtually by definition, involve conflicts of one sort or another. The conflicts may involve ends (what); means (how or how much); philosophy (why); location (where); timing (when); and who might be advantaged or disadvantaged by different ways of resolving the issue (who). In order for issues to be raised and resolved effectively, the organization must be prepared to deal with the almost inevitable conflicts that will occur. Conflict, shifts in understanding, and shifts in preferences will all evoke participants' emotions (Weick, 1995; Bryant, 2003). It is therefore in this stage that the importance of emotion will become dramatically apparent, along with the concomitant need for emotional and social intelligence on the part of participants if emotions are to be dealt with effectively (Goleman, 1995, 2007; Heifetz, 1994; Heifetz, Linsky, & Grashow, 2009).

A statement of a strategic issue should contain three elements. First, the issue should be described succinctly, preferably in a single paragraph. The issue should be framed as a question that the organization can do something about. If the organization cannot do anything about it, it is best not to think of it as an issue for the organization; it is simply a condition (Wildavsky, 1979). An organization's attention is limited enough without wasting it on issues it cannot address effectively. The question also should have more than one answer, as a way of broadening the search for viable strategies. Too often organizations "jump to solutions" without fully understanding what else might be possible, and without learning more about the issue by understanding more about the range of possible answers (Eden & Ackermann, 1998, 2010; Nutt, 2002).

Second, the factors that make the issue a fundamental challenge should be listed. In particular, what is it about the organization's mandates, mission, values, or internal strengths and weaknesses, and external opportunities and challenges that make this a strategic issue for the organization? Listing these factors will become useful in the next step, strategy development. Every effective strategy builds on strengths and takes advantage of opportunities while minimizing or overcoming weaknesses and challenges. The framing of strategic issues is therefore very important because it will provide much of the basis for the issues' resolution (Eden & Ackermann, 1998; Nutt, 2002; Bolman & Deal, 2008).

Finally, the planning team should prepare a statement of the consequences of failure to address the issue. This will help organizational leaders decide just how strategic, or important, various issues are. If no consequences will ensue from failure to address a particular issue, then it is not a strategic issue. At the other extreme, if the organization will be destroyed or will miss a valuable opportunity by failing to address a particular issue, then the issue is clearly *very* strategic and is worth attending to immediately. Thus, the step of identifying strategic issues is aimed at focusing organizational attention on what is truly important for the survival, prosperity, and effectiveness of the organization.

Once statements of the issues are prepared, the organization will know what kinds of issues it faces, just how strategic they are, and what some of the important requirements are for their successful resolution. There are several kinds of strategic issues:

- Issues that alter the organization and especially its core business and those which do not. Heifetz (1994) refers to the former as *adaptive* challenges and the latter as *technical* problems, while Nutt (2001) calls the former *developmental* issues and the latter *nondevelopmental* issues. Adaptive challenges involve a fundamental change in products or services, customers or clients, service or distribution channels, sources of revenue, identity or image, or some other aspect of the organization. They also are issues for which there is no real organizational precedent. In other words, the resolution of these issues may well hinge on clarifying a new vision, set of goals, and accompanying strategies. Deep dialogue almost certainly will be needed to sort these issues out (Scharmer, 2009). Technical or nondevelopmental issues, however, involve less ambiguity because most of the aspects of the organization's mission, goals, and overall strategy will not change. Resolving these issues is more likely to require reprogramming strategies, rather than vision, goals, and whole new strategies.

- Issues that require no organizational action at present, but which must be continuously monitored.

- Issues that are on the horizon and are likely to require some action in the future, and perhaps some action now. For the most part, these issues can be handled as part of the organization's regular strategic planning cycle.

- Those that require an immediate response and therefore cannot be handled in a more routine way.

In Chapter Six, eight basic approaches to the identification of strategic issues will be discussed. The *direct* approach goes straight from a discussion of mandates, mission, and SWOC/Ts (strengths, weaknesses, opportunities, and challenges or threats) to the identification of strategic issues. The *indirect* approach begins with brainstorming about several different kinds of options before identifying issues. Each option is put on a separate card or self-adhesive label. The options include actions the organization could take to meet its mandates, fulfill its mission, and create public value; to meet stakeholders' performance expectations; to build on strengths, take advantage of opportunities, and minimize or overcome weaknesses and challenges; and to incorporate any other important aspect of background studies. These options are then merged into a single set of potential actions and clustered into potential issue categories. The *goals* approach starts with goals (or CSFs or performance indicators) and then identifies issues that must be addressed before the goals (CSFs or indicators) can be achieved. And the *vision of success* approach starts with at least a sketch of a vision of success in order to identify issues that must be dealt with before the vision can be realized. This approach is most likely to be necessary in situations involving adaptive challenges—where fundamental change is needed but the organization lacks a precedent (Nutt, 2001). For example, development of a vision is often recommended for organizations about to engage in a serious way in e-government or e-commerce (Abramson & Means, 2001). In addition, many community strategic planning efforts use a visioning approach to identify issues (Chrislip, 2002).

The *action-oriented strategy mapping* approach involves creation of word-and-arrow diagrams in which ideas about actions the organization might take, how it might take them, and why, are linked by arrows indicating the cause-effect or influence relationships between them. In other words, the arrows indicate that action A may cause or influence B, which in turn may cause or influence C, and so on; if the organization does A, it can expect to produce outcome B, which in turn may be expected to produce outcome C. These maps can consist of hundreds of interconnected relationships, showing differing areas of interest and their relationships to one another. Important clusters of potential actions may comprise strategic issues. A strategy in response to the issue would consist of the specific choices of actions to undertake in the issue area, how to undertake them, and why (Eden & Ackermann, 1998; Bryson, Ackermann, Eden, & Finn, 2004). The approach is particularly useful when participants are having trouble making sense of complex issue areas, time is short, the emphasis must be on action, and commitment on the part of those involved is particularly important.

The *tensions* approach was developed by Nutt and Backoff (1992) and elaborated in Nutt, Backoff, and Hogan (2000). These authors argue that there are always four basic tensions around any strategic issue. These tensions involve human resources, especially *equity* concerns; *innovation and change*; maintenance of *tradition*; *productivity improvement*; and their various combinations. The authors suggest critiquing the way issues are framed using these tensions separately and in combination in order to find the best way to frame the issue. The critiques may need to run through several cycles before the wisest way to frame the issue is found. *Systems analysis* can be used to help discern the best way to frame issues when the system contains complex feed-back effects and must be formally modeled in order to understand it (Sterman, 2000; Mulgan, 2009). Finally, the *alignment* approach addresses problems of misalignment of the organization's mission, mandates, goals, strategies, actions, and systems—or misalignment of other features or requirements for proper functioning—that are inhibiting success.

By stating that there are eight different approaches to the identification of strategic issues, I may raise the hackles of some planning theorists and practitioners who believe you should *always* start with either issues, or goals, or vision, or analysis. I argue that what will work best depends on the situation, and that the wise planner should choose an approach accordingly. What matters most is simply that those involved have as clear a picture as possible of the challenges facing the organization.

Step 6: Formulating Strategies and Plans to Manage the Issues

A *strategy* is defined as a pattern of purposes, policies, programs, projects, actions, decisions, or resource allocations that define what an organization is, what it does, and why it does it. Strategies can vary by level, function, and time frame, and obviously vary in terms of how well they perform against expectations or requirements. Strategies are developed to deal with the issues identified in the previous step.

This definition is purposely broad, in order to focus attention on the creation of consistency across *rhetoric* (what people say), *choices* (what people decide and are willing to pay for), *actions* (what people do), and the *consequences* of those actions. Effective strategy formulation and implementation processes link rhetoric, choices, actions, and consequences into reasonably coherent and consistent patterns across levels, functions, and time (Eden & Ackermann, 1998). They also will be tailored to fit an organization's culture, even if the purpose of the strategy or strategies is to reconfigure that culture in some way (Johnson, Scholes, & Whittington, 2008).

The definition makes clear that every organization has strategies, in the sense that there is always some sort of pattern across purposes, actions, resource allocations, and so on. But the pattern may not be a very good one. Indeed, most public and nonprofit organizations seem to have issues with misalignment, which is why one of the approaches to strategic issue identification is to discern misalignments, which often become painfully apparent during times of resource shortages.

Draft strategies, and perhaps drafts of formal strategic plans, will be formulated in this step to articulate desired patterns. These may also be reviewed and adopted at the end of this step if the strategic planning process is relatively simple, small-scale, and involves a single organization. (Such a process would merge this step and Step 7.)

There are numerous approaches to strategy development (Bryson & Anderson, 2000; Holman, Devane, & Cady, 2007; Niven, 2008; Mintzberg, Ahlstrand, & Lampel, 2009). I generally favor either of two approaches. The first is a five-part, fairly speedy process based on the work of the Institute of Cultural Affairs (Spencer, 1996). The second can be used if there is a need or desire to articulate more clearly the relationships among multiple options, to show how they fit together as part of a pattern.

A Five-Part Strategy Development Process. The first part of the five-part process begins with identification of practical alternatives, and dreams or visions for resolving the strategic issues. Each option should be phrased in action terms; that is, it should begin with an imperative, such as "do," "get," "buy," "achieve," and so forth. Phrasing options in action terms helps make the options seem more "real" to participants.

Next, the planning team should enumerate the barriers or constraints to achieving those alternatives, dreams, or visions (that is, possible goals), and not directly on how to achieve these things. Focusing on barriers at this point is not typical of most strategic planning processes, but doing so is one way of assuring that any strategies developed deal with implementation difficulties directly rather than haphazardly (Goldratt, 1999).

Once alternatives, dreams, and visions, along with barriers to their realization, are listed, the team develops major proposals for achieving these goals directly, or else indirectly through overcoming the barriers. (In a variant to this step, the team might solicit proposals from key organizational units, various stakeholder groups, task forces, or selected individuals.) For example, a major Midwest city government did not begin to work on strategies to achieve its major ambitions until it had overhauled its archaic civil service system. That system clearly was a barrier that had to be changed before the city government could have any hope of achieving its more important objectives. As another example, a major West Coast city fire department did not begin strategic planning until many of its employees had visited excellent fire departments elsewhere, so that their views were less parochial, their imaginations were enhanced, and their sights were raised about what was possible.

After major proposals are submitted, two final tasks remain in order to develop effective strategies. Actions that must be taken over the next two to three years to implement the major proposals must be identified. And finally, a detailed work program for the next six months to a year must be spelled out to implement the actions. These last two tasks shade over into the work of Step 9 of the Strategy Change Cycle, but that is good, because strategies always should be developed with implementation in mind, including necessary resource requirements (Hill & Hupe, 2009). As Mintzberg (1994, p. 25) argues (but overstates), "Every failure of implementation is, by definition, also a failure of formulation." In some circumstances, Steps 6 and 9 may be merged—for example, when a single organization is planning for itself. In addition, in collaborative or community settings, implementation details must often be worked out first by the various parties before they are willing to commit to shared strategic plans (Innes, 1996; Huxham & Vangen, 2005; Innes & Booher, 2010). In situations such as these, implementation planning may have to precede strategy or plan adoption.

Action-Oriented Strategy Mapping. The second method is called *action-oriented strategy mapping* (or sometimes causal mapping) and based on the Strategic Options Development and Analysis (SODA) method developed by Colin Eden, Fran Ackermann, and their associates (Eden & Ackermann, 1998, 2010; Bryson, Ackermann, Eden, & Finn, 2004; Ackermann & Eden, 2011). The method involves listing multiple options to address each strategic issue, where each option is written in imperative action terms. The options are then linked by arrows indicating which options cause or influence the achievement of other options. An option can be a part of more than one chain. The result is a "map" of action-to-outcome (cause-effect, means-to-an-end) relationships; those options toward the end of a chain of arrows are possible goals or perhaps even mission statements. Presumably, these goals can be achieved by accomplishing at least some of the actions leading up to them, although additional analysis and work on the arrow chains may be necessary to determine and clearly articulate action-to-outcome relationships. The option maps can be reviewed and revised and particular action-to-outcome chains selected as strategies. (See Resource D for more information on how to develop maps of this sort. Additional detail and numerous examples will be found in Bryson, Ackermann, Eden, & Finn, 2004; Ackermann & Eden, 2011).

An effective strategy must meet several criteria. It should be technically workable and administratively feasible, politically acceptable to key stakeholders, and results-oriented. It also must fit the organization's philosophy and core values, even if the purpose is to change them. In addition, it should be ethical, moral, and legal, and should further the creation of public value. It must also deal with the strategic issue it was supposed to address and create significant public value at reasonable cost. All too often I have seen strategies that were technically, administratively, politically, morally, ethically, and legally impeccable, but did not deal with the issues they were presumed to address, nor did they create much public value. Effective strategies thus meet a rather severe set of tests. Careful, thoughtful deliberation—and often bargaining and negotiation—among key decision makers who have adequate information and are politically astute are usually necessary before strategies can be developed that meet these tests. Some of this work typically must occur in this step; some is likely to occur in the next step.

Step 7: Reviewing and Adopting the Strategies and Plan

Once strategies have been formulated, the planning team may need to obtain an official decision to adopt them and proceed with their implementation. If the strategies are part of a formal strategic plan, a formal decision to adopt and proceed will almost certainly be needed. This decision will help affirm the desired changes and move the organization toward *refreezing* in the new pattern (Lewin, 1951; Dalton, 1970; Fiol, 2001), where the knowledge exploration of the previous steps can be exploited (March, 1991). When strategies and plans are developed for a single organization, particularly a small one, this step actually may merge with Step 6. But a separate step will likely be necessary when strategic planning is undertaken for a large organization, collaboration, or community. The SPCC will need to approve the resulting strategies or plan, while relevant policy- and decision-making bodies and other implementing groups and organizations are also likely to have to approve the strategies or plan, or at least parts of it, in order for implementation to proceed effectively.

In order to secure passage of any strategy or plan, it will be necessary to continue to pay attention to the goals, concerns, and interests of all key internal and external stakeholders. Finding or creating inducements that can be traded for support can also be useful. But there are numerous ways to defeat any proposal in formal decision-making arenas. So it is important for the plan to be sponsored and championed by actors whose knowledge of how to negotiate the intricacies of the relevant arenas can help assure passage (Crosby & Bryson, 2005).

Step 8. Establishing an Effective Organizational Vision

In this step, the organization develops a description of what it should look like once it has successfully implemented its strategies and achieved its full potential. This description is the organization's *vision of success*. Few organizations have such a description or vision, yet the importance of these descriptions has long been recognized by well-managed companies, organizational psychologists, and management theorists (Collins & Porras, 1997; Kouzes & Posner, 2008; Latham, Borgogni, & Petitta, 2008). Such descriptions can include the organization's mission, its values and philosophy, basic strategies, its performance criteria, some important decision rules, and the ethical standards expected of all employees.

The description, to the extent that it is widely circulated and discussed within the organization, allows organization members to know what is expected of them, without constant managerial oversight. Members are free to act on their own initiative on the organization's behalf to an extent not otherwise possible. The result should be a mobilization of members' energy toward pursuing the organization's purposes, and a reduced need for direct supervision (Nutt, 2001).

Some might question why developing a vision of success comes at this point in the process rather than much earlier. There are two basic answers to this question. First, it does not have to come at this point for all organizations. Some organizations are able to develop a clearly articulated, agreed-upon vision of success much earlier in the process. Communities, in fact, often start with visioning exercises in order to develop enough of a consensus on purposes and values to guide issue identification and strategy formulation efforts (Chrislip, 2002; Wheeland, 2004). Figure 2.1 therefore indicates the many different points at which participants may find it useful to develop some sort of guiding vision. Some processes may start with a visionary statement. Others may use visions to help them figure out what the strategic issues are or to help them develop strategies. And still others may use visions to convince key decision makers to adopt strategies or plans, or to guide implementation efforts. The further along in the process a vision is produced, the more likely it is to be more fully articulated.

Second, most organizations typically will not be able to develop a detailed vision of success until they have gone through several iterations of strategic planning—if they are able to develop a vision at all. A challenging yet achievable vision embodies the tension between what an organization wants and what it can have (Senge, 2006; Scharmer, 2009). Often, several cycles of strategic planning are necessary before organizational members know what they want, what they can have, and what the difference is between the two. A vision that motivates people will be challenging enough to spur action, yet not so impossible to achieve that it demotivates and demoralizes people. Most organizations, in other words, will find that their visions of success are likely to serve more as a guide for strategy implementation than strategy formulation.

Further, for most organizations, development of a vision of success is not necessary in order to produce marked improvements in performance. In my experience, most organizations can demonstrate a substantial improvement in effectiveness if they simply identify and satisfactorily resolve a few strategic issues. Most organizations simply do not address often enough what is truly important; just gathering key decision makers to deal with a few important matters in a timely way can enhance organizational performance substantially. For these reasons the step is labeled optional in Figure 2.1.

Step 9: Developing an Effective Implementation Process

Just creating a strategic plan is not enough. The changes indicated by the adopted strategies must be incorporated throughout the system for them to be brought to life and for real value to be created for the organization and its stakeholders. Thinking strategically about implementation and developing an effective implementation plan are important tasks on the road to realizing the strategies developed in Step 6. For example, in some circumstances direct implementation at all sites will be the wisest strategic choice, whereas in other situations some form of staged implementation may be best (Crosby & Bryson, 2005). In all cases, implementation plans should include ways of building capacity for sustained implementation, goal achievement, and ongoing learning and readjustment based on that learning (Simons, 1995). The process should also include building capacity for the next round of strategic planning.

Again, if strategies and an implementation plan have been developed for a single organization, particularly a small one, or if the planning is for a collaborative, or community, this step may need to be incorporated into Step 7, Strategy Formulation. On the other hand, in many multiunit or intergovernmental situations, a separate step will be required to assure that relevant groups and organizations do the action planning necessary for implementation success.

Action plans should detail the following:

- Implementation roles and responsibilities of oversight bodies, organizational teams or task forces, and individuals
- Expected results and specific objectives, requirements, and milestones
- Specific action steps and relevant details
- Schedules
- Resource requirements and sources
- A communication process
- Review, monitoring, and mid-course correction procedures to build in capacity for ongoing learning
- Accountability procedures

It is important to build into action plans enough sponsors, champions, and other personnel—along with enough time, money, attention, administrative and support services, and other resources—to ensure successful implementation. You must "budget the plan" wisely to ensure that implementation goes well. In collaborative or community situations, it is almost impossible to underestimate the requirements for communications, the nurturance of relationships, and attention to operational detail (Huxham & Vangen, 2005).

It is also important to work quickly to avoid unnecessary or undesirable competition with new priorities. Whenever significant opportunities to implement strategies and achieve objectives arise, they should be taken. In other words, it is important to be opportunistic as well as deliberate. And it is important to remember that what actually happens in practice will always be some blend of what is intended with what emerges along the way (Mintzberg, Ahlstrand, & Lampel, 2009).

Successfully implemented and institutionalized strategies result in the establishment of a new regime, a "set of implicit or explicit principles, norms, rules, and decision-making procedures around which actors' expectations converge in a given area" (Krasner, 1983, p. 2; see also Lauria, 1996; Crossan, Lane, & White, 1999; and Crosby & Bryson, 2005). Regime building is necessary to preserve gains in the face of competing demands. Unfortunately, regimes can outlive their usefulness.

Step 10: Reassessing Strategies and the Strategic Planning Process

Once the implementation process has been under way for some time, it is important to review the strategies and the strategic planning process as a prelude to a new round of strategic planning. Much of the work of this phase may occur as part of the ongoing implementation process. However, if the organization has not engaged in strategic planning for a while, this will be a separate phase. Attention should be focused on successful strategies and whether they should be maintained, replaced by other strategies, or terminated for one reason or another. Unsuccessful strategies should be replaced or terminated. The strategic planning process also should be examined, its strengths and weaknesses noted, and modifications suggested to improve the next round of strategic planning. Effectiveness in this step really does depend on effective organizational learning, which means taking a hard look at what is really happening, being open to new information, wisely assessing the situation, and acting *mindfully,* where mindfulness is defined by Weick and Sutcliffe as "a rich awareness of discriminatory detail [which involves] the combination of ongoing scrutiny of existing expectations, continuous refinement and differentiation of expectations based on newer experiences, willingness and capability to invent new expectations that make sense of unprecedented events, a more nuanced appreciation of context and ways to deal with it, and identification of new dimensions of context that improve foresight and current functioning" (2007, p. 32).

Learning and mindfulness of this sort also involve capacity building. Recall that strategic learning was defined as any change in a system which, by better adapting the system to its environment, produces a more or less permanent change in its capacity to pursue its purposes. Viewing strategic planning as a kind of action research or utilization-focused evaluation can help embed learning into the entire process and make sure the kind of information, feedback, dialogue, and deliberation necessary for learning occur (Eden & Huxham, 1996; Patton, 2008; Bryson, Patton, & Bowman, 2011).

TAILORING THE PROCESS TO SPECIFIC CIRCUMSTANCES

The Strategy Change Cycle is a general approach to strategic planning and management. Like any planning and management process, strategic planning therefore must be tailored carefully to specific situations if it is to be useful (Christensen, 1999; Alexander, 2000). A number of adaptations—variations on the general theme—are discussed in this section. Before proceeding, however, it is useful to clarify what *kind* of process the Strategy Change Cycle is and how it might be useful (I am grateful to Michael Barzelay, personal communication, for many ideas in this and the subsequent three paragraphs). As noted, the SCC is a generic *reference approach*—and not the specific strategic planning process *design* that will be negotiated during the initial agreement step. Instead, the SCC presents the central abstract case for what strategic planning is about as a *kind* of response to challenges. I believe the SCC is the best way of exemplifying the argument, and though the SCC includes quite a few elements and links, the detail is needed to ground the argument in a reasonable way. The detail helps clarify what is important and requires deliberation. In short, the SCC provides an idealized conceptual process—a *reference approach*—and I will make suggestions about how to use it as a reference point in particular circumstances.

The most important thing about the SCC is that it sets up a way of thinking about the logic and requirements of a successful strategy change process. In general, the requirements typically flow from the *end* of the process *toward* the beginning and especially the initial agreement—meaning that what is required at the end should affect what you do at the beginning. For example, successful strategy implementation requires workable strategies that will be supported by key internal and external stakeholders; this need (among other requirements) should have an influence on the process of negotiating the initial agreement and its content. More generally, the SCC causal logic is as follows: (1) *desired outcomes* (including creating public value) (2) can be produced or facilitated by *actions* (for example, issue identification, strategy formulation, and implementation activities), (3) whose production or facilitation in turn is guided by *process design features* (for example, the design of forums for deliberation, choices regarding stakeholder engagement, guidelines and limits on analysis, connection to decision points, and specific planning steps), (4) which are tailored to *process context features* (relevant aspects of the internal and external environment). This means that upstream process design—and particularly that which is embodied in the initial agreement to proceed—should be tailored to context and informed by downstream requirements for success, including those linked directly to achieving desired outcomes.

Thus, there are implications in the SCC about the basic logic of how to start, what to do next, and why. The logic is always there; it doesn't get weaker as the nature of the situation changes. Situations create challenges that require a response—and responses vary because situations vary. The SCC as a reference approach can help leaders, managers, and planners think about what might be done in any particular situation to gain the advantages of the SCC logic. Said differently, there are a variety of ways and degrees of meeting the requirements for a successful strategy change process, but they are still requirements and the SCC can be used to help think about what they are and how to meet them.

The SCC is therefore not a recipe, cookbook, computer program, or auto repair manual. It is more like a guide to collaboratively and deliberatively designing a vehicle and the journey you will take using the vehicle, including deciding (ultimately, if not initially) exactly where you want to go. The SCC is also not a take-it-or-leave-it proposition. Instead, it is a referent approach (or conceptual artifact as presented in Figure 2.1) that will help you keep in mind the logic of strategic planning so that you can adapt and make use of that logic in specific situations as circumstances demand and warrant. The SCC as an abstract approach helps you work deliberatively with other people to make change; what the approach means *in practice* will be worked out via participation and deliberation with others over the course of the process (Wenger, 1998).

Specifically, the SCC will help remind you of the importance of:

- Having a process sponsor or sponsors and a process champion or champions
- Carefully designing and using a series of settings for deliberation— formal and informal forums, arenas, and courts
- Emphasizing the development of the initial agreement(s)
- Intensely attending to stakeholders via careful analysis and effective engagement
- Gaining clarity about mission and mandates and knowing the difference between the two
- Understanding the organization's internal and external environments
- Focusing on the identification and clarification of strategic issues and knowing there is an array of available approaches for doing so
- Seeing strategies as a response to strategic issues and knowing there are many approaches to formulating strategies, including incorporating useful aspects of existing or emerging strategies
- Attending to the requirements for successful strategy implementation and evaluation
- Building capacity for ongoing implementation, learning, and strategic change
- Periodically reassessing strategies and the strategic planning process as a prelude to the next round of strategic planning
- Remaining flexible throughout the process, while still paying attention to all necessary requirements that must be met along the way and the logic that links them

Sequencing the Steps

Although the steps (or occasions for deliberation and decision) are laid out in a linear sequence, it must be emphasized that the Strategy Change Cycle, as its name suggests, is iterative in practice. Participants typically rethink what they have done several times before they reach final decisions. Moreover, the process does not always begin at the beginning. Organizations typically find themselves confronted with a new mandate (Step 2), a pressing strategic issue (Step 5), a failing strategy (Step 6 or 9), or the need to reassess what they have been doing (Step 10) and that leads them to engage in strategic planning. Once engaged, the organization is likely to go back and begin at the beginning, particularly with a reexamination of its mission. (Indeed, in my experience, it does not matter where you start, you always end up back at mission.)

In addition, implementation usually begins before all of the planning is complete. As soon as useful actions are identified, they are taken, as long as they do not jeopardize future actions that might prove valuable. In other words, in a linear, sequential process, the first eight steps of the process would be followed by implementing the planned actions and evaluating the results. However, implementation typically does not, and should not, wait until the eight steps have been completed. For example, if the organization's mission needs to be redrafted, then it should be. If the SWOC/T analysis turns up weaknesses or threats that need to be addressed immediately, they should be. If aspects of a desirable strategy can be implemented without awaiting further developments, they should be. And so on. As noted earlier, strategic thinking *and* acting *and* learning are important, and all of the thinking does not have to occur before any actions are taken. For one thing, often action is necessary so that real learning can occur (Weick, 1995). Or as Mintzberg, Ahlstrand, and Lampel (2009, p. 76) note, "Effective strategy making connects acting to thinking which in turn connects implementation to formulation. We think in order to act, to be sure, but we also act in order to think. We try things, and the ones that work gradually converge into patterns that become strategies." Strategic planning's iterative, flexible, action-oriented nature is precisely what often makes it so attractive to public and nonprofit leaders and managers.

Making Use of Vision, Goals, and Issues

In the discussion of Step 8, I noted that different organizations and communities may wish to start their process with a vision statement. Such a statement may foster a consensus and provide important inspiration and guidance for the rest of the process, even though it is unlikely to be as detailed as a statement developed later in the process. As indicated in Figure 2.1, there are other points at which it might be possible to develop a vision statement (or statements). Vision thus may be used to prompt the identification of strategic issues, guide the search for and development of strategies, inspire the adoption of strategic plans, or guide implementation efforts. For example, the 2020 vision statement in the Minneapolis Park and Recreation Board's *2007–2012 Strategic Plan* (2007, p. 5) is used in these ways and states:

In 2020, the Minneapolis park system is a premier destination that welcomes and captivates residents and visitors. The park system and its beauty are part of the daily life and shape the character of Minneapolis. Natural, cultural, artistic, historical, and recreational resources cultivate outstanding experiences, health, enjoyment, fun, and learning for all people. The park system is sustainable, well-maintained, and safe. It meets the needs of individuals, families, and communities. The focus on preserving land continues, with a strong emphasis on connecting people to the land and to each other. Aware of its value to their lives, residents are proud stewards and supports of an extraordinary park and recreation system.

The decision to develop a vision statement should hinge on whether one is needed to provide direction to subsequent efforts; whether people will be able to develop a vision that is meaningful enough, detailed enough, *and* broadly supported; and whether there will be enough energy left after the visioning effort to push ahead.

Similarly, as indicated in Figure 2.1, it is possible to develop goals in many different places in the process (Borins, 1998; Mulgan, 2009). Some strategic planning processes will begin with the goals of new boards of directors, elected policy bodies, chief executive officers, judges, or other top-level decision makers. These goals embody a reform agenda for the organization (or network, or community). Other strategic planning processes may start with goals that are part of mandates. For example, legislation often requires implementing agencies to develop plans that include results and outcome measures that will show how the intent of the legislation is to be achieved. A *starting* goal for these agencies, therefore, is to identify results and outcomes they want to be measured against that also are in accord with legislative intent. The goal thus helps these agencies identify an important *strategic issue*—namely, what the results and outcomes should be. Subsequent strategic planning efforts are then likely to start with the desired outcomes the organization thinks are important.

Still other strategic planning processes will articulate goals to guide strategy formulation in response to specific issues or to guide implementation of specific strategies. Goals developed at these later stages of the process are likely to be more detailed and specific than those developed earlier in the process. Goals may be developed any time they would be useful to guide subsequent efforts in the process *and* when they will have sufficient support among key parties to produce desired action.

In my experience, however, strategic planning processes generally start neither with vision nor with goals. In part, this is because in my experience strategic planning rarely starts with Step 1. Instead, people sense something is not right about the current situation—they face strategic issues of one sort or another, or they are pursuing a strategy that is failing, or about to fail—and they want to know what to do (Borins, 1998; Nutt, 2001; Ackermann and Eden, 2011). One of the crucial features of issue-driven planning (and political decision making in general) is that you do not have to agree on goals to agree on next steps (Innes, 1996; Bryant, 2003; Innes and Booher, 2010). You simply need to agree on a strategy that will address the issue and further the interests of the organization (or collaborative, or community) and its key stakeholders. Goals are likely to be developed once viable strategies have been developed to address the issues. The goals typically will be strategy-specific.

Articulating goals or describing a vision may help provide a better feeling for where a strategy or interconnected set of strategies should lead (Nutt, 2001; Mulgan, 2009). Goals and vision are thus more likely to come toward the end of the process than the beginning. There are clear exceptions—and process designers should think carefully about why, when, and how—if at all—to bring goals and vision into the process.

Applying the Process Across Organizational Subunits, Levels, and Functions on an Ongoing Basis

Strategic thinking, acting, and learning depend on getting key people together, getting them to focus wisely, creatively, and deliberatively on what is really important, and getting them to do something about it. At its most basic, the technology of strategic planning thus involves deliberations, decisions, and actions. The steps in the Strategy Change Cycle help make the process reasonably orderly to increase the likelihood that what is important is actually recognized and addressed, and to allow more people to participate in the process. When the process is applied to an organization as a whole on an ongoing basis (rather than as a one-shot deal), or at least to significant parts of it, usually it is necessary to construct a *strategic management system* (see Exhibit 1.1). The system allows the various parts of the process to be integrated in appropriate ways, and engages the organization in strategic management, not just strategic planning (Poister & Streib, 1999). In the best circumstances, the system will include the actors and knowledge necessary to act wisely, foster systems thinking, and prompt quick and effective action, given that inclusion, systems thinking, and speed are increasingly required of public and nonprofit organizations (Linden, 2002; Behn, 2008; Mulgan, 2009; Innes & Booher, 2010).

The process might be applied across subunits, levels, and functions in an organization as outlined in Figure 2.2. The application is based on an *integrated units of management* (or layered or stacked units of management) system used by many corporations. The system's first cycle consists of "bottom up" development of strategic plans within a framework established at the top, followed by reviews and reconciliation at each succeeding level. In the second cycle, operating plans are developed to implement the strategic plans. Depending on the situation, decisions at the top of the organizational hierarchy may or

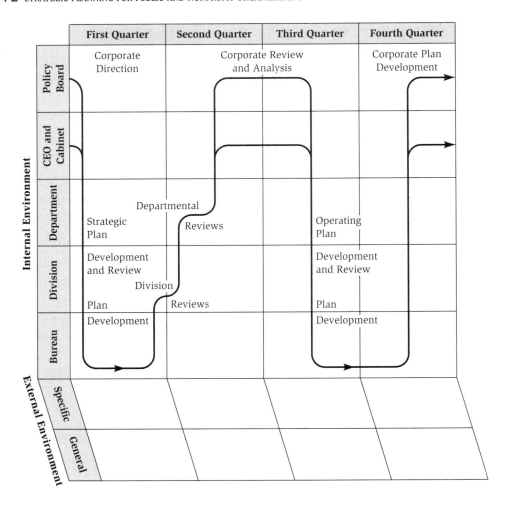

Figure 2.2. Strategic Planning System for Integrated Units of Management.

Source: Adapted from Bryson & Roering, 1987, p. 16.

may not require policy board approval (which is why the line depicting the process flow diverges at the top).

The system may be supported by a set of performance indicators and strategies embodied in a Balanced Score Card (BSC) (Kaplan & Norton, 1996, 2004; Niven, 2008). A famous BSC comes from the City of Charlotte, North Carolina, and is presented in Figure 2.3. The theory behind a balanced scorecard is that learning and growth outcomes should enhance the effectiveness of internal processes, which in turn should facilitate achievement of desirable financial outcomes. Achieving desirable outcomes in all three areas should produce

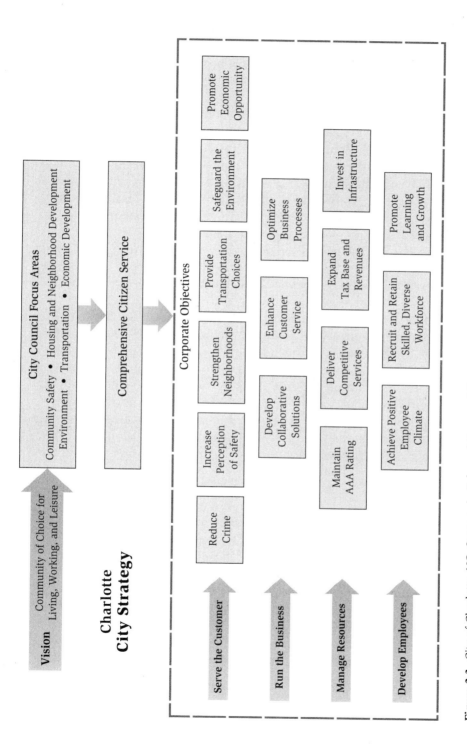

Figure 2.3. City of Charlotte, NC, Strategy in Balanced Scorecard Form.

Source: City of Charlotte, 2009, p. 6. Reprinted with permission from the City of Charlotte, North Carolina.

better customer outcomes. The theory implies that an organization that has gone through the process of developing an organization-wide balanced scorecard and supporting departmental and "line of business" scorecards should be more effective in meeting its mandates, fulfilling its mission, and creating public value.

Strategic planning systems for public and nonprofit organizations usually are not as formalized and integrated as the one outlined in Figure 2.2 (although that may be changing). More typical is a *strategic issues management* system, which attempts to manage specific strategic issues without seeking integration of the resultant strategies across all subunits, levels, and functions (Roberts & Wargo, 1994; Hendrick, 2003; Mulgan, 2009). Tight integration is not necessary because most issues do not affect all parts of the organization, are subject to different politics, and are on their own time frame.

Baltimore, Maryland; Minneapolis, Minnesota; and a number of other cities have institutionalized strategic issues management through use of a *CitiStat* or *PerformanceStat* system (Schachtel, 2001; Behn, 2008). In these systems a central analysis staff uses geographically coded data to spot trends, events, and issues that need to be addressed by line departments. The heads of the relevant units meet regularly with the mayor and his or her key advisers, including the heads of finance, human resources, and information technology, to examine the data and address the issues face-to-face. Actions and follow-up procedures are agreed to on the spot. Notable successes have occurred that produced better outcomes, saved money, enhanced teamwork and competence, or all three. Other common public and nonprofit strategic planning systems include *contract models*, *portfolio approaches*, *collaboration models*, *goal or benchmark models,* and *hybrid models* combining two or more of the above approaches. These will be discussed in more detail in Chapter Ten.

If the organization is fairly large, then specific linkages will be necessary in order to join the process to different functions and levels in the organization so that it can proceed in a reasonably orderly and integrated manner. One effective way to achieve such a linkage is to appoint the heads of all major units to the strategic planning team. All unit heads can then be sure that their units' information and interests are represented in strategy formulation, and can oversee strategy implementation in their unit.

Indeed, key decision makers might wish to form themselves into a permanent strategic planning committee or cabinet. I certainly would recommend this approach, if it appears workable for the organization, as it emphasizes the role of line managers as strategic planners and the role of strategic planners as facilitators of decision making by the line managers. Pragmatic and effective strategies and plans are likely to result. Temporary task forces, strategic planning committees, or a cabinet can work; but whatever the arrangement, there is no substitute for the direct involvement of key decision makers in the process (Borins, 1998; Mulgan, 2009).

Applying the Process to Functions that Cross Organizational Boundaries, Collaborations, and Communities

When applied to a function or collaboration that crosses organizational boundaries, or to a community, the process probably will need to be sponsored by a committee or task force of key decision makers, opinion leaders, "influentials," or "notables" representing important stakeholder groups. Additional working groups or task forces probably will need to be organized at various times to deal with specific strategic issues or to oversee the implementation of specific strategies. Special efforts will be needed to engage traditionally underrepresented groups (Innes & Booher, 2010). Because so many more people and groups will need to be involved, and because implementation will have to rely more on consent than authority, the process is likely to be much more time-consuming and iterative than strategic planning applied to an organization. On the other hand, more time spent on exploring issues and reaching agreement may be made up later through speedy implementation (Innes, 1996; Bardach, 1998; Bovaird, 2008; Innes & Booher, 2010). Strategic planning in an organization typically involves a mixture of lateral collaboration and vertical hierarchy. In interorganizational collaborations, lateral collaborative processes overshadow hierarchy, yet attention to the hierarchical structure and power differences that exist within the collaboration and in its participating organizations will be vital in developing and implementing a strategic plan (Bryson, Crosby, & Stone, 2006).

In addition, when a community is involved, special efforts will be necessary to make sure that important connections are made, and incompatibilities resolved, between strategic plans and the community's comprehensive plan and the various devices used to implement it, such as the government's capital improvements program, subdivision controls, zoning ordinance, and official map. The fact that these connections should be made, however, should not unduly hamper the process. Strategic planning and comprehensive planning can be complementary, and efforts should be made to ensure that they are, if the community's best interests and those of its various stakeholders are to be advanced (Innes, 1996; Burby, 2003; Wheeland, 2004).

Roles for Planners, Decision Makers, Implementers, and Citizens

Planners can play many different roles in a strategic planning process. In many cases, the planners are not people with the job title of planner, but are in fact policymakers or line managers (Mintzberg, Ahlstrand & Lampel, 2009). The people with the title of planner often act primarily as facilitators of decision making by policymakers or line managers, as technical experts in substantive areas, or both. In other cases, planners operate in a variety of different roles. Sometimes the planner is an "expert on experts" (Bolan, 1971) who eases different people with different expertise in and out of the process for different purposes at different times. At other times, planners act as technicians, politicians, or hybrids (Howe, 1980). At still other times, they are finders of strategy, who do their job by interpreting existing actions and recognizing important patterns in the organization and its environment; analysts of existing or potential strategies; catalysts for promoting strategic thought and action; or, finally, strategists themselves (Mintzberg, 1994, pp. 361–396).

Since the most important thing about strategic planning is the development of strategic thought, action, and learning, it may not matter much which person does what. However, it does seem that the strategic planning most likely to be implemented is that done by policymakers, line managers, or both. (Line managers in government are not usually charged with making important political trade-offs—politicians are. Therefore an effective government strategic planning process probably needs participation by both line managers and policymakers.)

Public organizations involved in strategic planning—including as part of multiorganizational collaborative efforts—often have little citizen participation in the planning process other than that of elected or appointed policy board members, although clearly there are exceptions (Wheeland, 2004; Epstein, Coates, Wray, & Swain, 2005), including the Minneapolis Park and Recreation Board. One reason may be that the organization may already possess the necessary knowledge and expertise in-house and therefore citizen involvement may be redundant and excessively time-consuming. In addition, insiders typically are the chief implementers of strategies, and thus their ownership of the process and resultant decisions may be what is most crucial. Further, citizen participation may not be necessary to legitimize the process because an elected or appointed policy board already is directly involved, in keeping with the idea that the United States is a representative, rather than direct, democracy. The absence of participation by ordinary outsiders would parallel much of corporate planning practice. However, it is easy to be wrong about how much one knows, or needs to know, and how much perceived legitimacy the process needs (Suchman, 1995; Nutt, 2002). Interviews, focus groups, and surveys of outsiders, including citizens, and external sounding boards of various sorts, often are worth their weight in gold when they open insiders' eyes to information they have missed, add legitimacy to the effort, and keep them from reaching the wrong conclusions or making the wrong decisions (Feldman & Khademian, 2000; Holman, Devane, & Cady, 2007). So a word of caution is in order, and that is to remember, as the Greeks believed, that nemesis always walks in the footsteps of hubris!

Program-focused strategic planning—including multiorganizational collaborative efforts—appears to be much more likely to involve citizens, particularly in their capacity as "customers." Citizen involvement in program planning thus is roughly analogous to extensive consumer involvement in private sector marketing research and development projects. For example, transportation planning typically involves a great deal of citizen participation. Citizens may provide information concerning travel needs and desires, reactions to various transportation system design alternatives, and advice on ways to resolve conflicts that arise during the process. Planning for individual parks also typically involves substantial citizen participation. Unfortunately, because the use of transportation systems or parks by citizens is generally broad based, users and the citizen-at-large are often equated. This is hardly ever justified, however, as it probably masks great variety in stakeholder concerns about and contributions to the process (Eden & Ackermann, 1998). A careful stakeholder analysis can help keep the various citizen interests and contributions analytically separate.

Finally, planning on behalf of a community almost always involves substantial citizen participation. Unfortunately, community-focused strategic plans often treat all citizens alike and assume that all citizens are interested in the community as a whole—two assumptions at odds with most studies of political participation (for example, Putnam, 2000). Application of the stakeholder concept to community strategic planning would help avoid some of these errors. Beyond that, broad citizen involvement usually results in better plans and implementation processes (Chrislip, 2000; Burby, 2003; Wheeland, 2004).

SUMMARY

This chapter has outlined a process called the Strategy Change Cycle for promoting strategic thinking, acting and learning in governments, public agencies, nonprofit organizations, networks, communities, or other entities. Though the process is presented in a linear, sequential fashion for pedagogical reasons, it proceeds iteratively as groups continuously rethink connections among the various elements of the process, take action, and learn on their way to formulating effective strategies. In addition, the process often does not start with Step 1 but instead starts somewhere else and then cycles back to Step 1. The steps also are not steps precisely, but instead occasions for deliberation, decisions, and actions as part of a continuous flow of strategic thinking, acting, and learning; knowledge exploration and exploitation; and strategy formulation and implementation. Mintzberg, Ahlstrand, and Lampel (2009, p. 204) assert that "All real strategic behavior has to combine deliberate control with emergent learning." The Strategy Change Cycle is designed to promote just this kind of strategic behavior.

Figure 2.4 shows how the Strategy Change Cycle is designed to help create the desired outcomes noted in Figure 1.4 by helping orchestrate the major

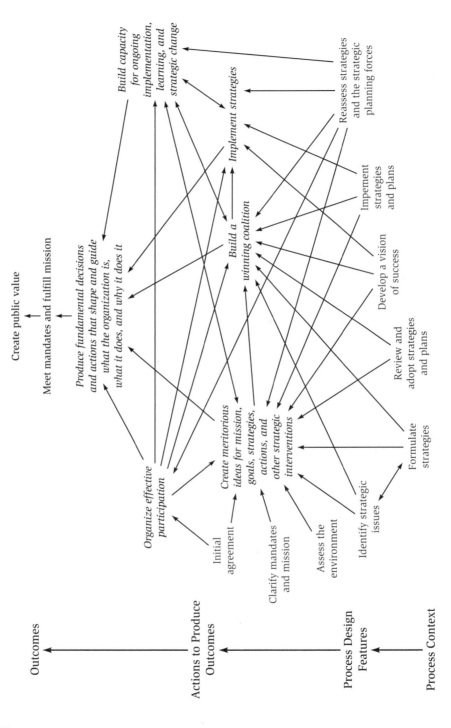

Figure 2.4. Strategic Planning Outcomes, Actions, Design Features, and Context.

categories of action (or functions) needed to accomplish the outcomes. Figure 2.4 also helps demonstrate graphically the likely iterative nature as advocates work to organize participation, create ideas of strategic significance, build a winning coalition, implement the ideas so that the organization meets its mandates, fulfills its mission, creates real public value, and also builds the knowledge and competence for ongoing implementation and the next round of strategic planning.

At first glance, Figures 2.1 and 2.4 may make the Strategy Change Cycle seem overwhelming. But let me assure you that you have been doing strategic planning—at least on an individual level—most of your life, so you already know much of what you need to know and understand. For example, for much of your life you have engaged in thinking, acting, and learning about:

- Your situation, purpose, and things you must do
- Your strengths and competencies, weaknesses, opportunities, and challenges or threats
- The big issues you face and what might be done about them
- What strategies have worked for you and which have not
- What success might mean for you

My purpose in this book is to scale that kind of thinking up to the group, organizational, collaborative, and community level to help you understand more about what works and why, and how to make things work better for you, your colleagues, and the people you serve. I want to add to your understanding by bringing to bear a common language and some of what social science has to offer, along with what I take from my own practical experience. With this approach the tension between science and practice lessens; they move closer together (Simon, 1996; Romme, 2003; Mulgan, 2009). The book and the Strategy Change Cycle are meant to help people deliberate with others using a common language and orienting framework to guide a strategic planning and strategy change journey.

As previously mentioned, my colleague Farnum Alston and I have prepared a strategic planning workbook designed to help individuals, teams, groups, and organizations work through the process and in particular work on developing a strategic plan (Bryson & Alston, 2011). The workbook should not be used without this book, however, because the process typically requires careful tailoring to specific circumstances. Owing to space limitations, the workbook contains little advice on how to adapt the process to different situations, whereas this book offers a great deal of the advice and guidance necessary to design and manage a successful process. In addition, my colleague Sharon Anderson and I, along with Farnum, have developed a new workbook to help organizations sustain implementation of their strategies (Bryson, Anderson, & Alston, 2011).

In Chapter Three, I will discuss how to negotiate an initial agreement among key internal (and perhaps external) decision makers or opinion leaders on the purpose and process of a strategic planning effort. The agreement will shape the nature and direction of deliberations, decisions, and actions designed to deal with what is truly important to the organization or community.

PART TWO

KEY STEPS
IN THINKING AND
ACTING STRATEGICALLY

The ten-step strategic planning process is presented in detail in Part Two. It is a reasonably orderly, deliberative, and participative approach to facilitating strategic thought, action, and learning by key decision makers. Chapter Three covers the initial agreement phase, the *plan for planning.* Chapter Four focuses on clarifying organization mandates and mission. Chapter Five describes how to assess an organization's strengths and weaknesses, as well as the opportunities and challenges it faces. Chapter Six discusses strategic issues—what they are, how they can be identified, and how to critique them. Chapter Seven is devoted to formulating and adopting effective strategies and plans.

The final three chapters in Part Two move from planning to management. Chapter Eight covers development of the organization's "vision of success," a description of what the organization should look like as it fulfills its mission, meets its mandates, and achieves its full potential for creating public value. Chapter Nine focuses on implementing strategies and plans, and Chapter Ten on reassessing them.

An organization that completes this Strategy Change Cycle should be well on its way toward improving and maintaining its effectiveness, pursuing its mission, meeting its mandates, creating genuine public value, and building its capacity for continuing to do so in the future. It should be clearly focused on satisfying key stakeholders in ways that are politically acceptable, technically and administratively workable, and legally and ethically defensible.

CHAPTER THREE

Initiating and Agreeing on a Strategic Planning Process

The beginning is the most important part of the work.
—Plato, *The Republic*

The *purpose* of the first step in the Strategy Change Cycle is to develop an initial agreement about the overall strategic planning effort and main planning steps among key internal decision makers or opinion leaders (and, if their support is necessary for the success of the effort, key external leaders as well). This agreement represents a plan for planning—or specific *process design*—intended to point the way toward the ultimate end of creating significant and enduring public value. As Nobel Prize winner Herbert Simon (1996, p. 111) says, "Everyone designs who devises a course of action aimed at changing existing situations into preferred ones."

The support and commitment of key decision makers are vital if strategic planning and change in an organization are to succeed. But the importance of their early involvement goes beyond the need for their support and commitment. They supply information vital to the planning effort: who should be involved, when key decision points will occur, key requirements for a successful process, and what arguments are likely to be persuasive at various points in the process. They can provide critical resources: legitimacy, staff assignments, a budget, and meeting space.

Every strategic planning effort is in effect a drama that must have the correct setting; themes; plots and subplots; actors; scenes; beginning, middle, and conclusion; and interpretation (Mangham & Overington, 1987; Bryant, 2003). Only key decision makers will have access to enough information and resources to allow for the effective development and direction of such a drama. But unlike

83

a normal play, the end is not known to anyone in advance. The end may well be as much "emergent" as it is intentional. Indeed, strategic planning and management at their best involve "real learning [that] takes place at the interface of thought and action, as actors reflect on what they have done; in other words, strategic learning must combine reflection with result . . . [They] involve crafting the subtle relationships between thought and action, control and learning, stability and change" (Mintzberg, Ahlstrand, & Lampel, 2009, pp. 205–217).

PLANNING FOCUS AND DESIRED IMMEDIATE OUTCOMES

The initial agreement will outline the important design features of the planning process. Ideally, the step will produce agreement on several issues:

1. The purpose(s) and worth of the strategic planning effort

2. Project organization, including who the sponsors and champions are

3. The organizations, units, groups, or persons who should be engaged, and in what ways

4. The specific steps to be followed, how the Web and information and communication technologies will be used, and the way ongoing feedback and learning will occur

5. The form and timing of reports

6. Resource commitments to begin the effort

7. Key requirements for a successful effort

Finally, a strategic planning coordinating committee and a strategic planning team probably should be formed and given a charge statement or charter.

As a general rule, the strategic planning effort should focus on that part of the organization (or function, collaboration, or community) controlled, overseen, or strongly influenced by the key decision makers interested in engaging in strategic planning. In other words, only under unusual circumstances would it make sense to develop strategic plans for organizations or parts of organizations over which the key decision makers involved in the effort have no control, or for which they have no responsibility.

The exception to this rule is externally initiated reform programs designed to demonstrate how an organization might conduct itself if it took the reformers' aims seriously. For example, candidates running for elective office often include in their campaign platforms proposed new strategies for the governments they wish to lead. Editorial and opinion pages of newspapers, public affairs books and magazines, and think tank reports also often include what are in effect reformers' strategic plans for public or nonprofit organizations.

The agreement also should make clear what the "givens" are at the beginning of the process. In other words, what is it about the organization's history, arrangements, and practices that will be off-limits, at least for the time being, and what is open for revision? On the one hand, if everything is a candidate for far-reaching change, potential participants may be scared off and resistance to change within the organization may harden. On the other hand, if everything is sacred, then there is no reason for strategic planning. There should be enough tension to prompt change and make it worth the effort, but not so much that it paralyzes potential participants with fear and anxiety (Nutt, 2001; Fiol, 2002; Eden & Ackermann, 2010).

The process of reaching an initial agreement is straightforward in concept, but often rather circuitous in practice. It usually proceeds through the following stages:

1. Initiating the process
2. Introducing the concept of strategic planning
3. Developing an understanding of what it can mean in practice
4. Thinking through some of its more important implications in terms of necessary commitments and other requirements for success
5. Developing a commitment to strategic planning
6. Reaching an actual agreement

The more numerous the decision makers who must be involved and the less they know about strategic planning, the more time-consuming the process will be, and the more indirect the route to agreement. Indeed, typically a series of agreements must be reached before the strategic planning process can begin in earnest.

DESIRED LONGER-TERM OUTCOMES

A number of significant longer-term outcomes flow from a good initial agreement (Benveniste, 1989; Janis, 1989; Nutt, 2002). These longer-term outcomes involve laying the groundwork for what Innes and Booher (2010, pp. 36–39) call "system adaptations," meaning changes that help the organization or collaboration create a better fit with its environment, including the possibility of changing the environments in important ways. The first is simply that the purpose and worth of the strategic planning effort are likely to be widely recognized by the affected parties, leading to broad sponsorship and legitimacy. Broad sponsorship dispels any suspicion that the effort is a power play by a small group. And it ensures that the results of the efforts are likely to be seen as objective (that is, as not manipulated to serve narrow partisan interests). Broad sponsorship also is a source of *psychological safety* that can help people address what otherwise might be highly threatening, anxiety- or guilt-producing prospects for change (Heifetz, 1994; Fiol, 2002; Schein, 2010; Scharmer, 2009).

Legitimacy justifies the occasions, content, and timing of the discussions and ensuing actions in the next stages of the planning process (Suchman, 1995; Innes & Booher, 2010). Such discussions—particularly when they involve key decision makers across functions, levels, and organizational boundaries of various sorts—are unlikely to occur without prompting. And they are unlikely to be prompted without authorization. As Borins (1998, p. 47) notes, "Collaboration across boundaries does not happen naturally, it must be made to happen."

Authorization of such discussions is an enormous resource to the planners who organize them because they gain considerable control over the forums in which they occur, the agenda, the information provided, and how the issues to be discussed are framed. The planners gain control because the deliberations typically will be cross-functional rather than under the control of any unit or department. As facilitators of cross-functional deliberations, planners gain leverage. Control of this sort is not manipulative in a partisan sense; instead, it ensures that the organization as a whole is looked at and discussed, rather than only its separate parts (Bryson & Crosby, 1996; Crosby & Bryson, 2005).

The Loft case was the most straightforward of the three cases focused on in this book. As noted in Chapter One, there was general agreement that the time had come for the next strategic planning process. The time period of the existing plan was running out and most of the goals had been achieved. There was the prospect that the executive director, Linda Myers, might retire within the next five years. And there were some concerns about the emergence of a more challenging competitive, financial, and technological environment. Broader understanding of these issues was sharpened in the winter of 2006 when board member Steve Wilbers led a committee of Loft board and staff members to identify strategic issues affecting the Loft. This work resulted in a Spring 2006 conference exploring how technology might influence literary life in the future. The conference involved around 150 writers, teachers, librarians, parents, and students in discussions about digital access, changing forms of writing and reading, youth education, the role of libraries, and the work of the Loft. The conference helped set much of the context for the upcoming strategic planning process.

In the summer of 2006 a strategic planning team was charged by the board with leading an eighteen-month, participatory process, with regular reports back to the board. The group consisted of two members of the board of directors, Steve Wilbers and Jocelyn Hale, and the staff managing director, Nancy

Gaschott. The group consulted with and received frequent guidance from executive director Linda Myers and the executive committee of the board (Hale, 2007, p. 10).

The Park Board's process for establishing the initial agreement was organizationally more complicated, reflecting in part its much larger size, government status, and somewhat conflicted recent history. After an initial attempt at strategic planning in 2001, the process progressed slowly. The hiring of a new superintendent in 2003 resulted in some organizational and administrative restructuring that positioned the organization to launch an organization-wide, cross-functional, and community-involving strategic planning process in October 2005 that was sponsored by the elected board and new superintendent.

The MetroGIS case was by far the most complicated of the three because it involved creating a voluntary agreement among scores of individuals and organizations. First, in 1995 Rick Gelbmann, head of the Metropolitan Council (MC) GIS Unit, convinced Richard Johnson, the MC's deputy regional administrator, that they should convince the Council members (the formal MC policymakers) that the MC should do two things: (1) authorize an exploration of what the MC should do about fostering creation of a regional GIS system that included parcel data; and (2) hire someone to help with the exploration. Randall Johnson (no relation), a planner with suburban Shoreview who had experience with MC data and projections that did not effectively take into account carrying capacity of the land, was hired and became the process champion. Since the counties produced parcel data—which are a critical component to harmonizing projections with actual capacity—Johnson received permission from the MC to explore with the seven regional counties what incentives would be needed: (1) to establish a means by which the MC would have ongoing access to county-produced parcel data; and (2) to gain county approval to participate in the development and use of standards to normalize parcel data across the seven counties. These discussions lead to a substantially more ambitious concept: broadening the stakeholders to include all local and other governmental units that served the metropolitan area and collaborating to address a host of shared geospatial information needs beyond parcel data. The MC was willing to put $1.1 million on the table to gain access to data produced by others in a form it could readily use.

Randall Johnson took the lead on organizing a series of formal and informal discussions and two major forums of 75-plus stakeholders each to explore the issue of whether to pursue a regional GIS system and whether the MC should lead the initiative. Each forum involved creating or maintaining and reinforcing existing relationships among actors. A general consensus emerged from these discussions for the idea that there should be a regional GIS system and the MC should take the lead in this case—although tension continued to exist between the MC and local governments on other issues, which is partly a consequence of the way regional and local governments are organized constitutionally and legislatively in Minnesota.

The MC officially accepted responsibility for sponsoring a formal strategic planning effort. Randall Johnson was process champion and was assisted by a strategic planning team consisting of Johnson; MC GIS Unit Coordinator Rick Gelbmann; MC Learning and Development Director Shelly Bergh Gardner; and MC Learning and Development Assistant Director Marcy Syman. Part of their job was to use the process to figure out how to organize and govern a collaborative approach to accomplishing metrowide sharing of geospatial data. In other words, in new, large, and voluntary collaboration efforts, often the collaboration's governance structure is itself a strategic issue that must be resolved as part of the process, not settled at its beginning.

As part of the unfolding series of "initial agreements," Richard Johnson, the MC's Deputy Regional Administrator, agreed to allow the Council to sponsor the December 14, 1995, Strategic Planning Forum. The forum planning team, together with the facilitators John Bryson and Charles Finn, decided on the critical stakeholder categories that needed to participate and candidates to invite to represent each critical stakeholder interest. The primary purpose of the forum was to reach agreement on strategic issues and statements of intent to guide the work of creating a metrowide mechanism to improve organizational effectiveness through collaborative use of geospatial technology. The resulting session achieved these purposes and set in motion a four-month process that yielded an agreed mission statement, five initial strategic design projects, an initial organizational structure, and a road map that guided MetroGIS's efforts for nearly a decade. The participants (with the exception of the NSDI Framework Coordinator, who deferred to the U.S. Geological Survey's Minnesota liaison) agreed to continue to serve in an advisory capacity that evolved into the MetroGIS Coordinating Committee. As noted in Chapter One, MetroGIS also engaged in a second major strategic planning effort in 2007. That process will be discussed in more detail in subsequent chapters. For now it is important to note that the "initial" agreement in that process as well involved a number of agreements, including fending off a concerted challenge to the organization's existence and subsequent endorsement of its continued existence by the MC. In sum, those involved in multiorganizational collaborative strategic planning should expect that a rather lengthy series of such "initial agreements" will be involved as part of the process of initiating a strategic planning effort.

A well-articulated initial agreement also provides a clear definition of the network to be involved and the process by which it is to be maintained. A good network management process will provide involved or affected stakeholders with a sense of *procedural justice*—that is, with the sense that both the procedures used to reach decisions and the decisions themselves are fair (Eden

& Ackermann, 1998, pp. 53–55; Page, Eden, & Ackermann, 2010). For example, adopting a *doctrine of no surprises* can be a good idea when developing a network and moving toward major decisions. The doctrine means that major stakeholders are at least kept informed of progress, events, and impending decisions, and perhaps consulted or even involved in decision making. Nothing is dropped on them "out of the blue." This would appear to be particularly necessary when the need for cooperation and the risks of failure are high (Janis, 1989; Weick and Sutcliffe, 2007). The doctrine of no surprises may be the best in other situations as well—even when there seem to be good reasons for keeping certain stakeholders in the dark. In an era when a basic characteristic of information seems to be that it leaks (Cleveland, 1985), full and prompt disclosure may be advisable. As Ben Franklin used to say, "Three people can keep a secret if two of them are dead."

A good initial agreement also will include an outline of the general sequence of steps in the strategic planning effort, the way the Web and information and communication technologies will be used to facilitate the process, and the way in which ongoing feedback and learning will be incorporated. Ongoing feedback and learning are crucial since they are indispensable means of keeping the process on track in pursuit of desired purposes. As management guru Ken Blanchard famously said, "Feedback is the breakfast of champions." In a more academic vein, Herbert Simon (1996, p. 172) asserts, "Feedback control shows how a system can work toward goals and adapt to a changing environment, thereby removing the mystery from teleology."

The sequence should contribute to stakeholders' sense that the process is *procedurally rational.* According to Eden and Ackermann (1998, p. 55), procedural rationality means that "the procedures used for strategy making make sense in themselves—they are coherent, follow a series of steps where each step is itself understood (not opaque) and relates to prior and future steps." They add that a procedurally rational process needs to be "sensible and reasonably thorough going, but neither too time-consuming nor too hurried," and the process must allow for "cognitive and emotional commitment." As a result, any decisions made are seen to be the outcome of appropriate deliberation. To be effective, the sequence of steps must ensure that the process is tied to key decision-making points in arenas such as, for example, budget decisions, elections, and the rhythm of the legislative cycle. Time in organizations is partly chronological, but key junctures also matter (Bryson & Roering, 1988; 1989; Albert & Bell, 2002; Mulgan, 2009). And the most important junctions are decision points.

To return to our drama metaphor, a good initial agreement will name the actors and their roles, describe the general character of the story and themes to be followed, spell out as much of the plot as it is possible to know in advance, specify the way the drama will be broken into acts and scenes, state how interactions among the actors will be designed and governed, designate the stage on which it will be played, and clarify who the audience is. Thus, the initial agreement step is extremely important because what follows depends significantly on the specifics of the beginning. The opening epigraph captures the fatefulness embodied in this early work, particularly in systems prone to unpredictable or at least partly chaotic behavior (Kingdon, 2002; Innes & Booher, 2010). As Gleick (1988, p. 23) notes, chaotic systems demonstrate a "sensitive dependence on initial conditions."

Moreover—and this will dramatically affect the story that develops—the agreement should specify exactly what is to be taken as given—at least at the start. For example, an organization's existing legal commitments, mandates, personnel complements, organizational designs, mission statements, resource allocations, job descriptions, or crucial aspects of its culture may need to be taken as a given in order to gain agreement. It is very important to be clear from the start what is off-limits for the exercise; otherwise, several key decision makers are unlikely to participate. With too much up for grabs the process will be too threatening or dangerous, will result in unconstructive or downright damaging conflict, or will produce a strategic plan that is useless because it lacks adequate support. On the other hand, the more that must be taken as given, the less useful strategic planning is likely to be (Scharmer, 2009). It is important, therefore, to find the right tension between what is given and what is possible. A good agreement also provides mechanisms, such as a strategic planning task force or coordinating committee, for deliberation, buffering, consultation, negotiation, or problem solving among units, groups, or persons involved in or affected by the effort. Without these mechanisms, conflicts are likely to stymie or even destroy the effort (Ury, Brett, & Goldberg, 1988; Borins, 1998). These mechanisms also will allow errors to be detected and corrected as the process proceeds. A strategic planning task force or coordinating committee can make needed midcourse corrections. A task force also will be a valuable sounding board for ideas. An important function of such a group will be to keep attention focused on strategic concerns while referring operational matters to appropriate groups and individuals.

A good initial agreement guarantees the necessary resources. Money typically is not the most needed resource for strategic planning; the time and attention of key decision makers are more important. Staff time will also be needed to gather information and provide logistical and clerical support (probably one part-time staff person in a small organization, several people in a larger organization).

A good agreement should provide useful preparation for any major changes that may be forthcoming. For example, if initiators envision pursuing a *big win* of some sort—ultimately, if not initially—rather than a series of *small wins*, the groundwork will probably need to be laid in this phase. A big win may mean changing the conceptual frame underpinning current strategy, dramatically changing goals or guiding visions, changing basic technologies, altering dominant coalitions, or some other fundamental change. Needed groundwork may involve having people other than the "usual suspects" on the planning committee or planning team; highlighting or separating off the planning effort in such a way that its power and influence are increased; gaining authorization for a range of background studies, such as benchmarking analyses, reengineering studies, or system analyses; arranging for visits to, and interviews at, innovative organizations; and so forth. Such groundwork can lead to undesirable fear and rigidity among stakeholders, so how it is undertaken must be thought through carefully. Consider the words of novelist Amy Tan in *The Bonesetter's Daughter* (2001, p. 153): "And Precious Auntie flapped her hands fast: '*A person should consider how things begin. A particular beginning results in a particular end*'" (italics in original).

Finally, a good initial agreement signifies the political support of key decision makers or opinion leaders at several levels in the organization, and it helps maintain that support at different points in the process. For strategic planning to work, a coalition must develop that is large enough and strong enough to formulate and implement strategies that deal effectively with key strategic issues. Such coalitions typically do not develop quickly (particularly in interorganizational or community planning efforts; see Denis, Lamothe, & Langley, 2001; Huxham & Vangen, 2005; Innes & Booher, 2010). Instead, they coalesce around the important strategic ideas that emerge from the sequence of deliberations, consultations, mutual education, and reconceptualization that are at the heart of any strategic planning effort (Mintzberg & Westley, 1992; Sabatier & Weible, 2007; Crosby & Bryson, 2005; Innes & Booher, 2010).

DEVELOPING AN INITIAL AGREEMENT

So far we have covered the purpose and desired short- and longer-term outcomes of this first step in the strategic planning. Now we can go into greater depth on specific aspects of the process of developing an initial agreement.

Whose Process Is It, and Who Should Be Involved?

Important design considerations include deciding who *owns* the process and who should be involved. Obviously, some individual or some group must initiate and champion the process. This champion will need to make the initial decisions about what the process should focus on and who should be involved. If the strategic planning process is going to affect the entire organization, then the organization's key decision makers (and perhaps representatives of some of the external stakeholders) should be involved. For example, the Loft's strategic planning process included a multitiered system of involvement for its strategic planning effort. The first tier included the board and executive director. The second tier was the strategic planning team consisting of two board members and one senior staff member. The third tier consisted of the board and staff as a whole entity that engaged in a major strategy mapping session (discussed in Chapter Six). The fourth included six task forces to look at six different strategic issue areas (programs for writers, education, new sources of financial support, constituents, technology, and leadership and succession). Finally, the 2,800 Loft members were informed of the process and asked for their ideas.

Those in the first two tiers obviously were the key decision makers, but they chose to involve the other groups—and especially staff—in a consultative role in order to get the necessary strategy-related ideas, other information, support, and commitment to make the strategic planning effort work for the organization as a whole. The group decided not to involve representatives of all key external stakeholder groups (for example, funders, publishers, or broadcasters) in major decision-making roles, although they did include representatives of teachers and students. As the official, legally responsible decision-making body for the organization, the board could not really share this responsibility. However, various outsiders were consulted or did serve on the advisory task forces created to make recommendations for addressing the strategic issue areas identified by the board and staff. Each task force had external stakeholders involved and some community topic experts who were not necessarily Loft stakeholders.

If the strategic planning focus is on an organizational subunit, collaboration, or community, then the key decision makers (and possibly other stakeholders) for those entities should be involved. For example, key decision makers or stakeholders for a community, such as the owners of major businesses, may not actually live in the community. The initial agreement for the Park Board strategic planning effort—which focused both on the organization and its connections within the community it served—included the Park Board Commissioners elected by that community, and Jon Gurban, the superintendent. Again, legally and politically the board and superintendent were the key formal decision makers, but particular staff members played vital roles in helping develop elements of the agreement and in carrying it out. Ultimately, more than a hundred staff members were involved in the process, especially through membership on one or more of nine different staff teams (infrastructure, demographics, programs and services, information management, sustainability, planning, community outreach and research, evaluation, and art and history). Some three thousand more people were involved at various points in the process via town meetings, a questionnaire mailed to all Minneapolis households, focus groups, community leader workshops, and a telephone survey.

For organizations, it may be advisable to involve insiders from three levels of the organization, as well as key outsiders. (Note that elected or appointed policy board members can be outsiders as well as insiders.) These include top policy and decision makers, middle management, and technical core or frontline personnel (Thompson, 1967; Nutt & Backoff, 1992). Top policy and decision makers should be involved for several reasons. First, they are formally charged with relating the organization to its domain. Second, because of their responsibilities they are often highly effective boundary spanners, with links to many organizations and people both inside and outside the organization. Third, they often are among the first to perceive mismatches between the organization and its environment, and therefore the most responsive to external threats and opportunities affecting the organization (Schein, 2010; Kettl & Fesler, 2008). Finally, they control the resources necessary to carry out the strategic planning effort and implement the recommendations that grow out of it. It is simply very difficult to plan around these people, so they should be included from the start, if at all possible (Fernandez & Rainey, 2006).

In governments and public agencies, this initial group is likely to include members of an elected or appointed board as well as high-level executives. In council-manager cities, for example, the initial agreement typically is negotiated among council members, the city manager, and key department heads. As noted earlier, the initial agreement that framed the Park Board's effort involved the elected board, the appointed superintendent, and key managers. In nonprofit organizations, the key decision-making group is likely to include the senior managers and board of directors. The initial agreement for the Loft's effort was negotiated among the organization's board, executive director, and senior managers.

Middle management personnel should be included because of their vital role in translating policies and decisions into operations. Further, middle management personnel are likely to bear the brunt of any managerial changes that result, and therefore should be involved to reduce unnecessary resistance and make transitions smoother (Block, 1987; Fernandez & Rainey, 2006).

Technical core or frontline personnel also may need to help fashion an initial agreement. Again, there are several reasons to consider involving them or their representatives (Benveniste, 1989; Cohen & Eimicke, 1998). First, they are in charge of the day-to-day use of the core technologies contributing to, or affected by, strategic change. As a result, they are likely to be the most knowledgeable about how the organization's basic technologies work in practice, and also are most likely to be immediately helped or hurt by change. Their early involvement may be necessary to ensure that needed changes can be understood, wise changes are implemented, and resistance to change can be minimized. Second, technical or frontline personnel are likely to be asked for their opinions by key decision makers anyway, so anything that can make them receptive to strategic change is a plus. Finally, because of their technical knowledge or their daily contact with customers, clients, or users, these personnel can severely hamper strategic changes they do not support. In extreme cases they might undermine or even sabotage change efforts. Co-opting these groups early on can be an important key to strategic planning success.

An important caveat is in order. If it is clear from the start that strategic planning will result in the elimination of certain positions, work groups, or departments—such as in major reengineering efforts—then it may be both unnecessary and downright harmful to involve people in those positions. The effective and humane approach may be to involve these people in planning for their transition to new jobs, including retraining, placement, and severance arrangements (Behn, 1983; Nutt, 2001; Holzer, Lee, & Newman, 2003; Nutt & Hogan, 2008).

Finding the Right People

Typically, some initial stakeholder analysis work will need to be done before the "right" group of people can be found to forge an effective initial agreement. The purpose of a stakeholder analysis at this point is to help process sponsors decide who should be involved in negotiating an initial agreement either because they have information that cannot be gained otherwise, or their support is necessary to assure successful implementation of initiatives built on the analyses (Thomas, 1993, 1995).

But a prior strategic question involves first figuring out who should be involved in doing the stakeholder analyses, and how. Again, in general, people should be involved if they have information that cannot be gained otherwise, or if their participation is necessary to assure a successful strategic planning process. Fortunately, the choice actually can be approached as a sequence of choices, in which an individual or small planning group begins the effort and then others are added later as the advisability of doing so becomes apparent (Bryson, 2004b).

One way to approach the task is as a five-step process in which a decision can be made to stop any time after the first step. Stopping might be advisable, for example, because enough information and support to proceed has been gained, time lines are short, the analyses are too sensitive, or for some other good reason. The steps are as follows:

1. Someone or some small planning group needs to initiate the process by doing a preliminary stakeholder analysis, for example, using the Basic Analysis Technique (discussed in more detail in Chapter Four), Power Versus Interest Grid, Stakeholder Influence Diagram, Bases of

Power—Directions of Interest Diagram, and Participation Planning Matrix (discussed in Resource A). This step is useful in helping sponsors and champions of the change effort think strategically about how to create the ideas and coalitions needed for the effort to reach a successful conclusion. This step typically is "back room" work. Necessary informational inputs may be garnered through the use of interviews, questionnaires, focus groups, or other targeted information-gathering techniques in this and subsequent steps, or in conjunction with the other techniques outlined in Resource A.

2. After reviewing the results of this analysis, a larger group of stakeholders can be assembled. This meeting can be viewed as the more public beginning of the change effort. The assembled group should be asked to brainstorm the list of stakeholders who might need to be involved in the change effort. Again, the Basic Analysis Technique, Power versus Interest Grid, Stakeholder Influence Diagram, Bases of Power—Directions of Interest Diagram, and Participation Planning Matrix might be used as a starting point.

3. After this analysis has been completed, the group should be encouraged to think carefully about who is not at the meeting but should be at subsequent meetings. The group should consider actual or potential stakeholder power, legitimacy, and urgency (defined as a composite of the stakeholder's time sensitivity to an organizational response, and the importance of the claim or relationship to the stakeholder) (Mitchell, Agle, & Wood, 1997). The group should carefully think through the positive and negative consequences of involving—or not—other stakeholders or their representatives, and in what ways to do so.

4. After these conversations have been completed, the "full" group should be assembled—the group that includes everyone who should be involved in the stakeholder analyses. The previous analyses may need to be repeated, at least in part, with the full group present, in order to make any needed corrections or modifications to prior analyses and get everyone on board and committed to moving forward.

5. Finally, after the full group has met, it should be possible to finalize the various groups who will have some role to play in the change effort: sponsors and champions, coordinating group, planning team, and various advisory or support groups (Chrislip, 2002; Linden, 2002; Friend & Hickling, 2005). It probably makes sense to fill out a Participation Planning Matrix, found in Resource A.

Note that this staged process embodies a kind of technical, political, administrative, and ethical rationality. The process is designed to gain needed information, build political acceptance, make sure appropriate administrative concerns are taken into account, and address at least some concerns about legitimacy, representation, and credibility of the process. Stakeholders are included when there are good and prudent reasons to do so, but not when their involvement is impractical, unnecessary, or imprudent. A certain amount of collective wisdom is used to inform these choices. Clearly, the choices of whom to include, how, and when are freighted with questions of value, and are perhaps fraught as well, but there is no way of escaping the need for wise and ethical judgments if an organization's or collaboration's mission and the common good are to be advanced (Vickers, 1995; Frederickson, 1997; Forester, 2009; Innes & Booher, 2010).

An Opening Retreat

For an organization, often the best way to reach initial agreement is to hold a retreat (Weisman, 2003). Begin the retreat with an introduction to the nature, purpose, and process of the proposed strategic planning effort. Often key decision makers need such an introduction before they are willing fully to endorse a strategic planning effort. For organizations that have not done strategic planning before, or not for some time, or have new leadership with little strategic planning experience, orientation and training methods might include a lecture and discussion; presentations by representatives of organizations that have used strategic planning, followed by group discussion; analysis by key decision makers of written case studies, followed by group discussion; circulation of reading materials; strategy films; and so on. Because strategic planning means different things to different people, such an introduction can be useful even if many key decision makers have considerable experience with strategic planning. The discussions can help people reach a common agreement on what the process might mean in practice for the organization and a common language with which to discuss it.

A possible format for the first day of a strategic planning retreat is:

Morning. Presentation and discussion about the nature, purpose, and process of the strategic planning effort.

Lunch. Presentation from a representative of a similar organization that engages in strategic planning, highlighting the benefits and liabilities of the process.

Afternoon. Analysis and discussion of a written case study, as well as instruction in any special techniques necessary for successful strategic planning, such as brainstorming, the snow card technique (see Chapter Five; Spencer, 1996), or the use of the action-oriented strategy mapping process (see Resource D).

By the end of the first day it should be clear whether or not the key decision makers wish to proceed. If so, the second day might be organized as follows:

Morning. Basic stakeholder analysis, power versus interest grid, and stakeholder interest diagram (see Resource A), review of mandates, review of the existing mission statement, or development of a draft mission statement.

Lunch. A speaker presents another case example.

Afternoon. SWOC/T analysis, preliminary identification of strategic issues, and next steps.

Organizations that lack experience with strategic planning, but are committed to it nonetheless, may skip the activities outlined above for the afternoon of the first day in order to begin the second day's activities earlier. Organizations that have used strategic planning before may spend much of the first morning identifying the strengths of their previous processes and modifications that would improve the processes. They would then begin the second day's activities in the afternoon of the first day.

The retreat may conclude at the end of the second day, after next steps have been consensually mapped out, or it may continue for a third day. The morning of the third day can be devoted to further identifying and discussing strategic issues, establishing priorities among them, and developing possible strategies for addressing them. The afternoon can carry this discussion further and outline possible next steps in the process. The retreat should not end until agreement is reached on what the next steps in the process will be and who will be responsible for what in each step. (Unfortunately, the regrettable fact is that it is increasingly hard to get any group of participants to commit two, let alone three, continuous days to any process. The difficulty seems to have two parts: people simply do not think they can delay the urgent to attend to the important; nor do they find it easy to justify the cost of retreats that are held off-site, no matter how important they know them to be.)

If a group can reach quick agreement at each point, fewer than three days might be sufficient. If quick agreement is not possible, more time may be necessary to complete the various tasks, and sessions may have to be spread out over several weeks. For one thing, it can take time to do needed analyses of the organization and its situation and what can be done about it. Beyond that, quick agreement is particularly unlikely if the strategic issues imply the need for a major change. It takes a group time to cope with the anxiety, fear, anger, and denial that may accompany profound change, particularly if it senses that its culture and basic beliefs about the world are being threatened (Fiol, 2002; Bryant, 2003; Scharmer, 2009; Schein, 2010).

A retreat also might be helpful for a network or community engaged in strategic planning to help decision makers reach agreement about the nature of the planning effort. Such a retreat, however, might be very difficult to organize. More groundwork will probably be necessary to build trust and to gain agreement from decision makers on the purposes, timing, and length of the retreat. The retreat itself probably would have to be less than three days, and post-retreat logistics, coordination, and follow-through would probably take more time and effort. Nonetheless, a retreat can provide an important signal and symbol that the network community is about to address its most important issues and concerns; can provoke desirable media attention and pressure to continue; and can prompt other stakeholders, who might have been more lukewarm about the process, to participate (Chrislip, 2002; Ray, 2002; Wheeland, 2004; Innes & Booher, 2010).

How Many "Initial" Agreements?

Sequential agreements among successively larger groups of key decision makers may be necessary before everyone is on board. For example, the Park Board initiated a strategic planning effort in 2001, when it contracted with a planning consultant to begin the process. The consultant conducted initial interviews with Park Board commissioners, but the process was delayed by budgetary and administrative changes. Then in 2003 the board decided not to renew the then-superintendent's contract. The ensuing hiring process was contentious. After a national search, the field was narrowed to two candidates, both of whom dropped out, possibly because of worries about troubled relations among the commissioners. The situation was only resolved when Superintendent Jon Gurban was hired by a 5–4 vote in late 2003. The board chair had made the unusual move of nominating Gurban for the position—for which he had neither applied nor interviewed. Four of the commissioners knew nothing of him prior to the meeting. According to a local media story, "the vote and the chaotic meeting solidified the board's reputation for dysfunction and disregard for the usual measure of public notice and process" (Olson, 2003). But in hindsight, Gurban's hire can be viewed as a second agreement toward what ultimately became a formal, participative, and very effective strategic planning process.

Once hired, Gurban obviously had a difficult challenge trying to guide the organization toward a new beginning with a divided board, significant budget shortfall, and questions about the way he was hired. He knew strategic planning was needed, but also knew that significant reorganization and administrative improvements were needed before an organization-wide, cross-functional, and community-involving formal effort was likely to succeed. He proceeded in a very strategic manner to address long-standing management issues. He started by restructuring the organization into cross-functional teams and reorganized the park district into three newly delineated subdistricts with a district administrator for each. Work was streamlined and each of the three new subdistricts was assigned a planner, maintenance foreman, support specialist, and liaisons from the park police and forestry. Operating procedures were put in place to standardize management of the various divisions and functions (Enke, Nguy, Sullivan, & Zenk, 2009, p. 8). The changes at the senior management level have already been noted. By August 2005, the stage was set for a highly participative and deliberative strategic planning effort that had a good chance of succeeding, and an agreement was outlined and approved by the board and senior management team (Enke et al., 2009). The strategic planning efforts of the Loft and MetroGIS also began with more than one "initial" agreement. In short, strategic planning in collaborative settings will almost certainly require a series of initial agreements (Chrislip, 2002; Linden, 2002; Innes & Booher, 2010).

Indeed, it is worth keeping in mind that forging agreements of various sorts will go on throughout the Strategy Change Cycle. Coalitions are built incrementally by agreement, and strategies and plans also are typically adopted and implemented incrementally, through various agreements. These agreements may be signaled by various means, including handshakes, letters or memoranda of agreement, contracts, formal votes, and celebrations.

It is important for sponsors and champions to keep in mind that throughout a Strategy Change Cycle there are a number of tangible and intangible, process- and content-oriented outcomes that are likely to be needed if the process is to succeed. Figure 3.1 classifies outcomes according to these dimensions. The process versus content dimension is probably quite familiar—at least in a negative way—as, for example, when people will complain that "process is getting in the way of substance." Less obvious, because it is less frequently discussed, is the distinction between tangible versus intangible outcomes (Innes & Booher, 1999; Friend & Hickling, 2005, p. 100). Here I have subcategorized the dimension according to my interpretation of Schein's three levels of culture (2010). The most obvious aspects of culture are what we can see; namely, artifacts, plans, documents, or other symbolic representations of the less visible values, beliefs, and interpretive schemes that shape them. Even less obvious, but in many ways the most important of all, are the basic assumptions and worldviews that underpin the values, beliefs, and interpretive schemes. They are most important because they serve as the (almost) invisible underpinnings of what is above them; they are the platform on which the rest is built. As Innes (1998, p. 54) notes, *"When information is most influential, it is also most invisible"* (italics in original). Strategic planning and management grow out of organizational or community culture, and thus any outcomes produced must tap into that culture, even if the purpose—as it usually is—is to change the culture in some ways, including possibly some of its basic assumptions (Schein, 1997; Khademian, 2002; Scharmer, 2009).

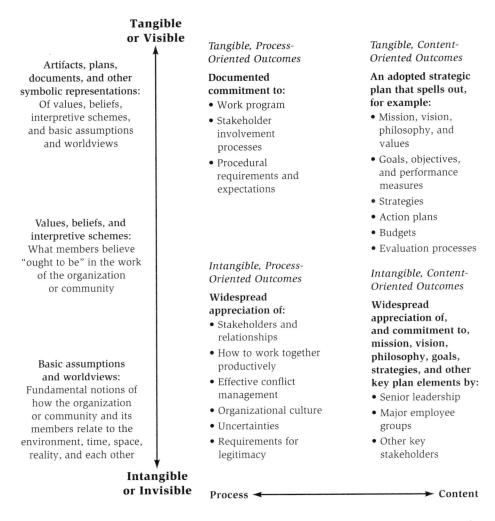

Figure 3.1. Outcomes Likely to Be Needed if the Strategic Planning Process Is to Succeed.

Source: Bryson, 2004a.

The entries in Figure 3.1 show that the most obvious outcome—but in some ways the least important one—is the *tangible, content-oriented outcome* represented by a strategic plan. Recall that earlier I said the purpose of strategic planning was to produce fundamental decisions and actions that shape and guide what an organization is, what it does, and why it does it—and not to produce a strategic plan. Often a strategic plan can help, but strategic plans will sit on the shelf if they are not based on positive outcomes in the other three quadrants of the figure.

The initial agreement is primarily about developing *tangible, process-oriented outcomes*; specifically, a commitment—probably in the form of a written agreement—to project organization; process steps, procedures, and requirements; a general work program for carrying out those steps; stakeholder involvement processes; and requirements for success. The initial agreement will be meaningless, however, unless it is based on some *intangible, process-oriented outcomes.* These would include some appreciation of: stakeholders and stakeholder relationships, how to work together productively, effective approaches to conflict management, organizational culture, uncertainties surrounding the process and the organization, and requirements for perceived rationality and legitimacy. If these appreciations are not deepened and widened over the course of the process, the process will fail. If they are enriched and spread throughout relevant networks, then crucial *intangible, content-oriented outcomes* will be produced. These include a widespread appreciation of and commitment to—on the part of senior leadership, major employee groups, and other key stakeholders—the organization's mission, mandates, vision, philosophy, core values, goals, strategies, and other key elements of a successful change effort.

If these last outcomes are in place, then the strategic plan will basically implement itself when a small organization is involved; in the case of a larger organization, collaboration, or community, implementation will be far easier than it would be otherwise. The plan will simply record the changes that have *already* occurred in the hearts and minds of key stakeholders. Said differently, if the intangible elements are in place, then the tangible outcomes will follow. As Mintzberg (1994, p. 252) observes, "Organizations function on the basis of commitment and mindset. In other words, it is determined and inspired people who get things done." Commitment, mindset, determination, and inspiration are not directly visible. What matters most in strategic planning thus is what is *not visible*, so sponsors, champions, and facilitators must pay very careful attention to the production of those *intangible* but highly consequential outcomes; if they do not, the plan will be mostly worthless. It may satisfy certain mandates or reporting requirements, but it certainly will not be a living document.

What Should the Initial Agreement Contain?

The initial agreement should cover the immediate desired outcomes listed at the beginning of this chapter: agreement on the purpose of the effort (including by implication what it will not achieve) and its worth; project organization, including sponsors and champions; the organizations, units, groups, or persons who should be involved, and how; a shared understanding about the nature and sequence of the steps in the process and how the Web and information and communication technology will be used to facilitate the process; agreement on the form and timing of reports; commitment of necessary resources to begin; and articulation of key requirements for a successful process. Next, a committee or task force probably should be established to oversee the strategic planning effort. The committee should be headed by someone with enough standing and credibility in the organization to assure that the effort is given visibility and legitimacy. Ideally, this person will be trusted by all or most factions in the organization so that the effort will not be seen as a narrow partisan affair. The committee can be an existing group, such as a board of directors or city council, that adds strategic planning oversight to its responsibilities, or it can be a committee or task force established for the specific purpose. In the Loft case, the official overseers of the process were the board and the executive director, although the executive committee and a three-person board and staff strategic planning team also shared responsibility for the strategic planning effort. The Park Board's process was overseen officially by the board and superintendent; however, in addition, a team consisting of staff from multiple disciplines (planning to forestry) and levels within the organization (management to the front line) played a key role in guiding and managing the process. As the process proceeded, a subcommittee of the board was delegated the responsibility for overseeing and promoting the process, and communicating to all board members information about progress on the plan's development. And in the MetroGIS case, the MC and deputy regional administrator were the formal overseers, but day-to-day oversight and management of the process were the responsibility of Randall Johnson, MetroGIS staff coordinator, in regular consultation with Rick Gelbmann, Council GIS unit coordinator, and occasionally with Richard Johnson, deputy regional administrator, and Shelly Berg-Gardner and Marcy Syman, director and assistant director of the Council's Learning and Development Unit. The oversight committee probably will be the body with whom the initial agreement is formulated, although it may be necessary to work out agreements first with various groups and factions who then send representatives to sit on the oversight body.

Next, a team to carry out the staff work probably will be necessary. The team should include planners and change advocates, but also helpful critics, to make sure that difficulties arising over the course of the process are recognized and constructively addressed (Janis, 1989). The teams assisting with the Loft's, Park Board's, and MetroGIS's processes were mentioned above. In the MetroGIS case, some consultants, including myself, were *de facto* team members while preparing for and during the December 1995 forum, and for several weeks following the forum, when the newly formed MetroGIS Coordinating Committee was acting on the forum's products. In the Loft case, I was occasionally a *de facto* team member via consultations with Jocelyn Hale and Nancy Gaschott. In all three cases, task forces were assigned to look at specific issue areas and report back to the teams with recommendations.

The necessary resources to begin the endeavor must be committed. Obtaining needed financial resources may not be difficult as they will be relatively minor in comparison with an organization's overall budget. The more important—and typically scarce—resources needed for a successful effort are the attention and involvement of key decision makers (Light, 1998; Van de Ven, Polley, Garud, & Venkataraman, 1999; Mulgan, 2009). Depending on the scale of the effort, strategic planning may demand from five to twenty-five days of attention from an organization's key decision makers over the course of a year—in other words, up to 10 percent of ordinary work time. Is this too much? Not for what is truly important for the organization. If there is not enough time for everything, then something else—not strategic planning—should go. Recall the great German philosopher Goethe's admonition: "Things which matter most must never be at the mercy of things which matter least."

Finally, there should be an understanding of the likely requirements for success. Start listing requirements by first asking: Who has to say yes to this process and the resulting plan? And who—as best we can know at present—has to say yes to implementing approved strategies? And what would it take for these persons, groups, or organizations to say yes? Beyond that, there are almost certainly additional administrative, financial, legal, ethical, and not least, political considerations to be taken into account. Being clear about likely requirements is not the same as accepting the list as rigid and nonnegotiable constraints. Instead, it is a way of helping to clarify what specific process design features and activities may be necessary as a response to requirements in order to ensure overall success.

The end of this first step typically is the first major decision point in the process if the organization (collaboration, community) is large, the situation is complex, or many people need to be involved. (If the organization is small, few people are involved, and the situation is simple, the first major decision point will come later, although precisely when will depend on the particular details.) If agreement is reached on the various content items, then it makes sense to go ahead with the process.

If agreement is not reached, then either the effort can go on anyway—with little likelihood of success—or else this step should be repeated until an effective agreement can be worked out. It usually makes sense to repeat the step, or to scale down the effort to focus on a smaller area where agreement is possible. Part of the scaled-down effort might be to develop effective strategies to involve the other parts later. Recall that in the Park Board case the first attempt at strategic planning in 2001 was slowed because of budgetary and administrative challenges. When the board decided not to renew the superintendent's contract, a targeted effort at hiring a replacement ensued. Once a new superintendent was hired, his initial focus was on reorganizing and streamlining the organization in such a way that it was prepared to undertake an organization-wide, cross-functional, and highly participative process involving the board and large numbers of staff and members of the community. These changes involved a fair amount of conflict, but through the process awareness grew of how strategic issues might be addressed effectively, including the challenge of rebuilding the Park Board's image, credibility, and sustained capacity for fulfilling its mission and mandates in the community and with key external stakeholders. In effect, over a number of years agreement widened and deepened on how best to approach strategic planning and what its benefits might be.

PROCESS DESIGN AND ACTION GUIDELINES

The following process design guidelines may be helpful in developing an initial agreement:

1. *Some person or group must initiate and champion the process.* Strategic planning does not just happen—involved, courageous, and committed people make it happen. In each of our cases the process worked in large part because there were people involved—usually key decision makers and leaders—who acted as *process champions* (Kanter, 1983, p. 296; Bryson & Roering, 1988, 1989; Crosby & Bryson, 2005). These people believed in the process and were committed to it—but not to any preconceived solutions. They may have had good hunches about what might emerge, but their main belief was that following the process would produce good answers. Indeed, the champions were willing to be surprised by the answers that emerged. The champions were not necessarily the initiators, but they often were. For example, in the MetroGIS case, the main champion was MetroGIS Staff Coordinator Randall Johnson, but the initiator was technically Rick Gelbmann, the head of the MC MetroGIS Unit. He made the case to Richard Johnson, deputy regional administrator, that a collaborative approach to geospatial data acquisition and sharing was needed and received permission in turn to hire Randall Johnson to pursue the effort. In the Park Board case, the initiator was the superintendent, but the main champion was Jennifer Ringold, the citywide planner. And the initiator of the Loft's effort was Executive Director Linda Myers, but the ongoing champions were the team of board members Jocelyn Hale and Steve Wilbers and Administrative Director Nancy Gaschott.

2. *It may be desirable for the initiators to do a quick assessment of the "readiness" of the organization to engage in strategic planning.* The

assessment should cover the organization's current mission; its budget, financial management, human resources, information technology, and communications systems; leadership and management capabilities; expected costs and benefits of a strategic planning process; and how to overcome any anticipated barriers. Based on the assessment, the initiators may decide to push ahead, focus on improving the organization's readiness, or drop the effort. Readiness assessment worksheets will be found in Bryson and Alston (2011).

3. *Some person or group must sponsor the process to give it legitimacy.* Sponsoring a strategic planning process is different from championing it—even though sponsors and champions may be the same people. Sponsorship is necessary to provide legitimacy to the process; championing the process provides the energy and commitment to follow through. In the Loft, Park Board, and MetroGIS cases, the most senior administrators and the boards were the sponsors, although in the MetroGIS case the effort was mainly sponsored by the deputy regional administrator. The strategic planning coordinating committee or task force (discussed in guideline 6) often serves as the legitimizing, sponsoring body.

4. *Some initial stakeholder analysis work is likely to be needed before the "right" group of people can be found to forge an effective initial agreement.* The purpose of a stakeholder analysis at this point is to help process sponsors decide who should be involved in negotiating an initial agreement either because they have information that cannot be gained otherwise, or their support is necessary to ensure successful implementation of initiatives built on the analyses. The five-step process outlined earlier is a useful way to figure out who should be involved.

5. *Decide whether or not a detailed, jointly negotiated initial agreement is needed.* An informal understanding may suffice when the organization is small, few people need to be involved in the process, and the situation faced is relatively straightforward. Conversely, a detailed, jointly negotiated initial agreement is likely to be needed if the organization is large, many people need to be involved, and the situation is complex, or if a strategic plan for a collaboration or community is to be developed.

   A formal contract is probably unnecessary (except, of course, contracts with outside consultants), but someone should prepare a written memorandum that outlines the content of the agreement, including statements on the following items: the purpose and worth of the effort; project organization; organizations, units, groups, or persons who should be involved; steps to be followed; the way the Web and information and communication technologies will be involved; form and timing of reports; role, functions, and membership of a strategic planning coordinating committee; role, functions, and membership of the strategic planning team; commitment of necessary resources to begin the effort; and key requirements for a successful process. The agreement might be summarized in a chart and distributed to all planning team members. Two examples outlining the basics of an initial agreement are presented in Exhibits 3.1 and 3.2. Exhibit 3.1 outlines the process followed by a small, community-based development organization in St. Paul called North End Area Revitalization (N.E.A.R.). Exhibit 3.2 shows the initial agreement used to organize the strategic planning effort of a large human service organization. The process is considerably more lengthy and involved than N.E.A.R.'s process because many more people need to be involved in various ways.

Exhibit 3.1. N.E.A.R.'s Strategic Planning Process.

Steps	Responsible	By When
1. Select a steering group. (The board's executive committee and executive director will serve in this role.)	Board chair and executive director	Feb. 1
2. Select a consultant to assist in design and facilitation of the process.	Steering group	Feb. 15
3. Get agreement on the planning steps, responsibilities, and resources required.	Steering group, consultant	Feb. 25
4. Gather information via a questionnaire from board members, staff, other neighborhood representatives, and others familiar with N.E.A.R.—regarding our image, strengths, weaknesses, opportunities, and critical issues or choices. Also conduct focus group discussions with staff, the Neighborhood Housing Agenda Committee, and Community Building Initiative Committee about their hopes for the future and issues that need attention in the planning process. Summarize this information.	Consultant, staff, steering group	March 20

Steps	Responsible	By When
5. At a six-hour planning retreat with board and staff:	Participants, consultant	April 1
• Review N.E.A.R.'s history and accomplishments since inception; note when participants got involved and what lessons they've learned. Use time line.		
• Review progress toward our mission and goals over the past year.		
• Review summary of questionnaire responses and information on neighborhood changes. In small groups, identify key issues or choices for N.E.A.R.		
• Determine N.E.A.R.'s future direction		
• Review steps to complete the strategic plan.		
6. Summarize the retreat.	Consultant, executive director	April 12
7. At two follow-up meetings (approximately two hours each), develop a draft of the strategic plan. The executive director will develop the initial draft for discussion and refinement with the steering group.	Steering group, consultant as needed	May 15
8. Review the draft with staff, board, other community representatives, and a key funder. Make needed revisions based on these reviews.	Steering group, consultant as needed	June 10
9. Approve the plan.	Board	June 25
10. Implement the plan.	Those indicated	July 1
11. Monitor progress at six months and update the plan yearly.	Steering group	Feb. 1

Meeting Time Required

Approximately eighteen to twenty hours for Steps 1 through 8 plus staff work in preparing for the retreat and drafting the plan.

Source: Adapted from Barry, 1997, p. 30.

Exhibit 3.2. Longer Planning Process of a Large Human Service Organization.

Steps	Responsible	By When
1. Get agreement on planning steps, responsibilities, and time lines. Review the planning process with the board and staff.	Executive director and board chair	Feb. 1
2. Meet informally with neighborhood groups, user groups, other nonprofits, public officials, funders, and others to solicit ideas on how our organization might better serve this community. Summarize this information.	Executive director and designated staff	May 1
3. In preparation for the board/ management planning retreat, summarize information on: (1) the organization's mission, success, and limitations over the past twenty years; (2) human service and community trends; and (3) several options and scenarios for how the organization might have the greatest impact in coming years.	Executive director with staff support	July 1
4. At a two-day board/management retreat, review and discuss the summarized information and determine the organization's future focus and emphasis. Use a scenario approach. Invite two resource people with knowledge of these issues to participate in the retreat.	Participants, guests, facilitator	Aug. 1
5. Summarize the retreat, develop a proposed focus statement for the organization, and discuss implications with staff.	Executive director, management staff	Sept. 15
6. Review implications and approve the focus statement.	Board	Oct. 15
7. Draft strategic plans for each of the organization's three divisions describing how they will implement the new focus over the next five years. Involve potential partner groups in developing these plans.	Executive director, management staff	Jan. 1

Steps	Responsible	By When
8. Review division plans. Note any recommended changes in areas that require coordination across the organization, and implications for administrative support services.	Executive director, management staff	Jan. 15
9. Draft overall strategic plan for the organization.	Executive director	March 1
10. Review draft plan with staff, the board, and six to eight community representatives. Make revisions based on these reviews.	Executive director	April 1
11. Approve strategic plan.	Board	May 1
12. Implement the plan. Review progress and update the plan yearly.	Executive director and those indicated	

Meeting Time Required

Sixty to sixty-five hours for Steps 1 through 10 (includes strategic planning for each division), plus staff time for informal meetings with community representatives, development of background materials for the retreat, and drafting the plan.

Source: Adapted from Barry, 1997, p. 31.

6. *Form a strategic planning coordinating committee or task force, if one is needed.* Again, if the organization is small, few people need to be involved, and the situation is easy to comprehend, then such a task force or committee probably won't be needed. But if the organization is large, many people need to be involved, and the situation is complex, then a task force or committee should probably be appointed.

Such a group should not be formed too early, however. It is easier to include someone later, after the committee is formed, than it is to drop a troublesome participant who is already a member. Consult with trusted advisers before inviting people to participate. Also keep in mind that there is a big difference between giving people a seat on a committee and consulting with them as part of the process. People can supply a great deal of information and advice—and legitimacy for the process—without actually having a vote on a committee. Unless membership in the committee is limited, it may balloon in size and become unmanageable and unproductive.

If an organization is the focus of attention, the coordinating committee might include: top-level decision makers, mid-level managers, technical and professional opinion leaders, outside resource persons, representatives of key stakeholder groups, process experts, and critics. Remember, however, that there may be a trade-off between having a broadly representative committee (which may be very large) and an effective one (which probably should number no more than nine). Two groups may in fact be necessary: a large representative and legitimizing body, and a small executive committee that engages in the most extensive discussions and makes recommendations to the larger group. For a collaboration or community, a large, representative legitimizing body could coordinate the process and smaller representative bodies could attend to specific issue areas.

7. *If a coordinating committee is formed, use it as a mechanism for deliberation, consultation, negotiation, problem solving, or buffering among organizations, units, groups, or persons involved.* The committee is likely to be the body that officially legitimizes the initial agreement and makes subsequent decisions, although the committee also may serve in an advisory body to the "official" decision makers. For example, the Loft's strategic planning team (acting in this committee role) served in an important mediating role among groups and interests and advised the executive director and board. The same is true of the Park Board's strategic planning team, which advised the superintendent and board. In the MetroGIS case, the participants in the December 1995 strategic planning session (with the exception of the NSDI Framework Coordinator, who deferred to the U.S. Geological Survey's Minnesota liaison) agreed to continue to serve in an advisory capacity. This group evolved into the MetroGIS Coordinating Committee, which advises the MetroGIS Policy Board, which was also created as a result of the session.

Committee decisions should be recorded in writing and probably should be circulated to key stakeholder groups. (For example, in the MetroGIS case, Randall Johnson diligently documented the results of each meeting and made them publicly available.) It is possible that the committee should include more than one representative from each key stakeholder group, so that a clearer picture can emerge of stakeholder preferences, interests, and concerns. Also, if the group is to be a standing committee that oversees annual strategic planning efforts, it probably is wise to rotate membership to keep new ideas flowing and widen involvement in the process.

You will not necessarily be asking for a major commitment of time from committee members, but they should expect to spend from five to twenty-five days on strategic planning over the course of a year. And that time must be "quality" time, typically away from the office, and concentrated in blocks of one to three days. The group should focus its attention on strategic concerns and refer operational matters to appropriate individuals and groups.

8. *The process is likely to flow more smoothly and effectively if the coordinating committee and any other policy board that is involved are effective policymaking bodies.* Recall that strategic planning has been defined as a deliberative, disciplined effort to produce fundamental decisions and actions that shape and guide what an organization (or other entity) is, what it does, and why it does it. It is hard to produce those decisions unless the process is overseen by effective policymaking bodies. In other words, the work of strategic planning forums, no matter how good, will not be worth much unless it is linked to arenas in which effective policies and strategies can be adopted and decisions made. Also note that a strategic issue in many cases is how to foster more effective policy- and decision making; the process thus must be a design for improving policymaking and also typically must embody it as well.

Effective policymaking bodies (Houle, 1989; Bryce, 1999; Chait, Ryan, & Taylor, 2004; Cornforth, 2004; Carver, 2006):

- Discipline themselves to focus most of their attention on their policymaking role.
- Have a mission statement that clearly states their purposes as a policymaking body.
- Establish a set of policy objectives for the organization, function, collaboration, or community that they oversee.
- Concentrate their resources to be more effective as policymakers.
- Control managers primarily through the questions they ask. The general form of these questions is, "How does this recommendation [whether a proposal, strategy, or budget] serve our purposes, values, or policies?"
- Have staff help them become better policymakers.
- Rely on various media (press releases, newsletters, television, Web sites, and so forth) to transmit information to key stakeholders and the general public.
- Hold periodic retreats to foster learning and to develop strategic plans and work programs for subsequent years.

- Monitor appropriate performance data in appropriate ways and deliberate wisely on its meaning and what to do in response. Not many public or nonprofit organizations, collaborations, or communities are governed by effective policymaking bodies (see, for example, Gurwitt, 2003). A strategic issue that often arises, therefore, is how to make the governing bodies more effective policymaking bodies. The Loft used its strategic planning process to help the board better exercise its responsibilities as a board. The Park Board's process also was intended to enhance the elected board's ability to fulfill its responsibilities and be an effective policymaking body. The MetroGIS process was intended, in part, to develop effective governance arrangements for a regional GIS capability.

9. *Form a strategic planning team if one is needed.* In theory, a team would be assigned the task of facilitating decision making by the strategic planning committee. The team would gather information, advice, and produce recommendations for committee action. The committee would legitimize the process, provide guidance to the team, and make decisions on team-produced recommendations. In practice, a team may or may not be formed and may or may not serve as facilitator of decision making by the coordinating committee. In the three cases used to illustrate this book, there was an overlap between strategic planning committees and teams.

   A team may not be needed if the organization or community is small, few people need to be involved in the effort, and the situation is relatively easy to handle. In these cases, a single planner, perhaps with the assistance of an outside consultant, will probably suffice. However, if the organization is large, many people need to be involved, and the situation is complex, a team will probably be necessary. Most of the team members probably will not need to work full-time on the effort, except for brief periods. But formation of a team will allow many different skills to be brought forward at important times. The team should be headed by an organizational diplomat and should include members skilled in boundary spanning, process facilitation, technical analysis, synthesis of diverse views, advocacy, and self-criticism. Such a team will almost certainly be needed for a large community effort.

   Whether or not the team actually does much of the strategic planning itself or, instead, facilitates strategic planning by key decision makers will depend on a number of factors. On the one hand, if team members actually possess most of the information needed to prepare the plan, and if they hold positions of substantial power, then they may go ahead and prepare the plan themselves. In this situation the planners themselves are the key decision makers. On the other hand, if there are a number of key decision makers who already possess much of the necessary information, and if the planners are not themselves powerful by virtue of their position or person, then the planners will need to serve primarily as facilitators of the process.

In my experience, planners typically find that they can be of greatest service by serving as facilitators of cross-functional, cross-level, and deliberative planning, policymaking, and decision making by key decision makers (Bryson & Crosby, 1996; Crosby & Bryson, 2005). Nevertheless, planners typically must have at least some substantive knowledge of the topic areas under discussion in order to be good facilitators. Thus, a blend of process skill and content knowledge is typically required of strategic planners and strategic planning teams; however, the specific proportions vary by situation.

Once you have decided that a strategic planning team is needed, you can turn your attention to procedures that will make the team more effective. First, to recruit skilled, committed team members, you may need to use special personnel hiring, transfer, or compensation procedures. People must see how their careers could be helped by joining the team, or they are not likely to join voluntarily. If the assignment is to be temporary, people must be assured that they can return to their old jobs—or better ones—when the effort is completed. Second, clear and positive working relationships need to be negotiated among team members and supervisors. Third, the team should meet frequently and communicate effectively to foster sharing of information and joint learning.

In the case of strategic planning for a community, the team or teams may have many volunteer members. Personnel hiring, transfer, and compensation procedures may not be an issue for volunteers, but clear and positive working relationships and effective communication are likely to be very important.

10. *Key decision makers may need orientation and training about the nature, purpose, and process of strategic planning before they can negotiate an initial agreement.*

11. *A sequence of "initial" agreements among a successively expanding group of key decision makers may be necessary before a full-scale strategic planning effort can proceed.* In expanding the circle, sponsors, champions, planners, and facilitators need to be attentive to the need for, and slow process of, building trust among involved stakeholders (Huxham and Vangen, 2005; Innes & Booher, 2010).

They also need to be attentive to the range of tangible and intangible content and process outcomes that are necessary for a successful effort (see Figure 3.1). Remember that the outcomes that are not visible are considerably more important than those that are.

12. *Recognize that things will change over the course of the Strategy Change Cycle.* Note, for example, what Berger and Vasile (2002, p. 25) concluded about the strategic planning efforts of the many nonprofit organizations they studied: "Decisions regarding plan breadth and detail, the mechanics of how it would be written, and the look of its final form were made as the process unfolded."

13. *Keep in mind that a good initial agreement should provide useful preparation for any major changes that may be forthcoming.* For a strategic planning process to be successful, the process itself must be thought about strategically. The initiators of the planning process should play out various scenarios about how it might unfold and then use them to understand the requirements to which the initial process design must respond. (This same kind of strategic thinking about the process itself should then occur throughout the process.) For example, if a major transformation of some kind is envisioned, a successful process is likely to be different than if a series of incremental changes is imagined (see Chapter Seven; Scharmer, 2009). Similarly, if major data collection and analysis efforts are likely to be needed, the groundwork should be laid in this step. Try to be as clear as possible about the requirements for success—and be open to the possibility that those requirements will change as the process unfolds.

14. *In complex situations, development of an initial agreement will culminate in the first big decision point. If an effective agreement cannot be reached among key decision makers, then the effort should not proceed.* The initiators may want to try again or focus on areas in which key decision makers can reach agreement. In relatively simple situations, the first major decision points are likely to be reached later in the process, although precisely when will depend on the particular situation.

HAVE REALISTIC HOPES FOR THE PROCESS

The initiation of strategic planning primarily involves a series of three simple activities for many organizations: (1) gathering key actors (preferably key decision makers); (2) working through a strategic thinking, acting, and learning process; and (3) getting people to do something practical about what is truly important for the organization. Although these activities may be simple in concept, they are quite difficult to implement because strategic planning is a process deliberately designed to produce change.

Organizations prefer to program, routinize, and systematize as much as they can (Thompson, 1967; Bolman & Deal, 2008). Strategic planning, however, is designed to question the current routines, along with the treaties that have been negotiated among stakeholders to form a coalition large enough and strong enough to govern the organization. The process therefore is inherently prone to fail because it is *deliberately disruptive* (although that doesn't mean it must be ungraciously, undiplomatically, or nastily so). Only strong sponsors, champions, skillful planners and facilitators, a supportive coalition, and a clear view of the potential benefits it can bring can make the process succeed. Even then, the best efforts still can be derailed by unexpected events, changes, crises, or intractable conflicts. Initiating strategic planning can be worth the effort, but the process will not necessarily be a smooth or successful one. As Bette Davis says in *All About Eve* (1950), "Fasten your seatbelts—it's going to be a bumpy night!" Potential sponsors and champions should go into it with their eyes open (Bryson & Roering, 1988, 1989; Nutt, 2001, 2002; Weick & Sutcliffe, 2007). You can choose to work hard to make good things happen— which is the approach I advocate; you can step aside and just watch what happens; or you can really be out of touch and then wonder what happened. You and your colleagues must choose—and the easy choice—at least in the short term—is to do nothing. As the famous British businessman Sir John Harvey-Jones allegedly said, "The nicest thing about not planning is that failure comes as a complete surprise, rather than being preceded by a period of worry and depression."

In part because of the disruption that strategic planning can cause during strategy formulation (as opposed to implementation), Mintzberg argues (1994) that the *only* role for strategic planning is strategic *programming*, by which he means the codification, articulation, and elaboration of strategies that are already in place. As he asserts, "planning works best when the broad outlines of a strategy are already in place, not when significant change is required from the process itself" (p. 176). I do not adopt so extreme a view, although I can empathize with it. I obviously think strategic planning can play an important role in strategy formulation, but I also think no one should expect that the process will succeed automatically. One way to develop reasonable hopes for the process is to have the sponsoring group and planning team explicitly discuss together or separately their hopes and concerns (or fears) for the process. The hopes can be a source of goals for the organization or community, at least for the process, and the process can be designed in such a way that it deals effectively with the concerns and fears.

SUMMARY

The initial agreement is essentially an understanding among key internal (and perhaps external) decision makers or opinion leaders concerning the overall strategic planning effort. The agreement should cover the purpose and worth of the effort; project organization, including who the sponsors and champions are; the persons, units, groups, or organizations to be involved; steps to be followed; the form and timing of reports; the role, functions, and membership of strategic planning committee members, if such a committee is formed; the role, functions, and membership of strategic planning team members, if one is formed; the commitment of necessary resources to begin the effort; and key requirements for success.

The importance of an initial agreement is highlighted by viewing every strategic planning effort as a drama in which the most important questions the organization faces are raised and resolved. For the drama to have a successful ending, the agreement needs to sketch out the setting, the actors, their roles, and how the actor's interactions will be designed and governed; the themes, perhaps the plots and subplots, the acts and scenes; and the beginning, the climax, and the desired conclusion. As the tale itself unfolds, content and detail will be added to this sketch, along with surprise twists and turns, making it a rich, instructive, and emotional drama that is lived by the actors. In the absence of such an agreement, the story may never reach a climax or conclusion. Instead, it might be what Macbeth called "a tale told by an idiot, full of sound and fury, signifying nothing" (William Shakespeare, *Macbeth*, act 5, scene 5)—or it could just be wasteful and boring theatre of the absurd.

An effective initial agreement ultimately helps leaders, managers, and planners raise and resolve key issues. Deliberation concerning these issues helps effective political coalitions coalesce (Riker, 1986; Mulgan, 2009). Otherwise, issues and answers are likely to flow randomly through the organization disconnected from the resources and decisions necessary for effective action (Cohen, March, & Olsen, 1972; Kingdon, 2002). Organizational survival, let alone effectiveness, will itself become random, and key decision makers will have abdicated their responsibility to focus on organizational purposes and their pursuit (Selznick, 1957; Terry, 2001; Hill & Lynn, 2009).

In the next chapter we will move to Steps 2 and 3 in the Strategy Change Cycle: the identification of mandates and the clarification of mission and values. Together, these two steps stipulate the organizational purposes to be strategically pursued.

CHAPTER FOUR

Clarifying Organizational Mandates and Mission

*Three outstanding attitudes—obliviousness to the growing
disaffection of constituents, primacy of self-aggrandizement,
and the illusion of invulnerable status—are persistent aspects of folly.*
—Barbara Tuchman, *The March of Folly*

This chapter covers Steps 2 and 3 of the Strategy Change Cycle, identifying mandates and clarifying mission and values. Together mandates, mission, and values indicate the *public value* the organization will create and provide the social justification and legitimacy on which the organization's existence depends.

Public and nonprofit organizations are *externally justified.* This means that they are chartered by the state to pursue certain public purposes (Rainey, 2009), and their legitimacy is conferred by the broader society (Suchman, 1995; Frederickson, 1997). These organizations must find ways to show that their operations do indeed create public value, or they risk losing the social justification for their existence, legitimacy, and any tax-exempt status they have.

Democratic governments can create public value through a number of overlapping activities, some of which are more appropriate to one level or type of government than another (Moore, 1995; Bozeman, 2002; Weimer & Vining, 2010). These activities include:

- Providing a constitutional framework of laws and supporting the rule of law—not least by the government itself.
- Creating open, transparent government.

- Fostering and relying on the democratic process, including making sure that mechanisms for articulating and aggregating values function in a democratic way.
- Protecting human rights, human dignity, and the core of subsistence.
- Ensuring that a long-term, holistic view is taken, and that stewardship of the public interest and the common good are seen as crucial functions of government, albeit shared with other actors and usually subject to contest.
- Inspiring and mobilizing the government itself and other key entities and actors to undertake individual and collective action in pursuit of the common good (Crosby & Bryson, 2005), which includes promoting both within-group social connections (or what Robert Putnam calls "bonding social capital") and across-group social connections (what he calls "bridging social capital") (Putnam, 2000), and catalyzing *active* citizenship in which diverse groups of citizens create programs, projects, products, or services of lasting public value (Boyte & Kari, 1996; Boyte, 2004).
- Maintaining a stable economy with reasonable levels of growth, unemployment, inflation, debt, savings, investment, and balance of payments figures.
- Relying on markets when they can be expected to work, including correcting market imperfections, and freeing, facilitating, and stimulating markets; and not relying on markets when they cannot be expected to work (Bryson & Crosby, 2008). Serving this purpose might include:
  - Providing needed public goods that private markets will not provide on their own, or else will provide badly (for example, defense, large infrastructure projects, common spaces, free parks), and ensuring that the benefits of publicly provided goods and services are not inappropriately captured by some subset of the population for whom they are not intended (for example, unnecessarily restricting public access to public lands).
  - Subsidizing activities with positive spillover effects for the general public (for example, K–12 and higher education, basic research, certain economic development activities, block clubs).
  - Taxing or regulating activities with actual or potential negative spillover effects for the general public (for example, commercial and investment banking, food and drug production and distribution, building construction, automobile operation).

- Addressing problems created by asymmetries in information availability, distribution, or use (for example, licensing or certification programs, product labeling requirements).
- Addressing problems of loss and uncertainty (for example, governmentally organized or subsidized insurance schemes, the Strategic Petroleum Reserve).
- Making sure that conservation of resources is emphasized rather than assuming substitutable resources will be found or invented (for example, conserving oil and fossil fuels instead of assuming replacements will be found).
- Protecting a common heritage when it otherwise might be lost (for example, historic and architectural preservation programs, protecting areas of outstanding natural beauty, memorials to outstanding public service).
- Providing public goods and services in a cost-effective way (for example, transportation infrastructure and systems, health and social services, police and criminal justice services).
- Using information and cost-benefit and cost-effectiveness analyses that are as objective as possible to inform public decisions.
- Making use of civic-minded public servants and professional expertise (Frederickson, 1997).

Nonprofit organizations in the United States can create public value by a number of means. The array of types of nonprofit organizations and their specific purposes is extraordinary. Section 501(c)(3) of the Internal Revenue Service code contains the largest number of tax-exempt organizations. They are granted tax concessions because they are presumed to create public value when they:

- Express the First Amendment right of assembly
- Promote public welfare directly, rather than privately, as in the case of firms, or of a definable subgroup, as in the case of associations
- Promote public welfare in a manner that goes beyond government, as in the case of religion, or in a way that substitutes for government, as in the cases of housing and health
- Serve public purposes at a cost less than government would incur, and therefore there is a savings in taxes foregone
- Serve public purposes in a charitable way, so that public or community welfare rather than individual welfare is served (Bryce, 1999, pp. 32, 40)

There are three tests that an organization must pass to be granted 501(c)(3) status (Bryce, 1999, pp. 40–41, 49–50). The *organizational test* requires that the nonprofit be organized to improve public welfare, rather than to benefit individuals or owners, by pursuing one or more of eight specific purposes: educational, religious, charitable, scientific, literary, testing for public safety, fostering certain national or international sports competitions, or preventing cruelty to children or to animals. The *political test* requires that the organization's charter forbid the nonprofit from participating in any political campaign on behalf of a candidate. And the *asset test* requires that the charter prohibit any distribution of assets or income to benefit individuals as owners or managers, except for fair compensation of services rendered, and must forbid the use of the organization for the personal benefit of founders, supporters, managers, their relatives, or associates.

Nonprofit organizations also can fail in a variety of ways; thus public value can be created by working to avoid the failures. Salamon (1995, pp. 44–48) identifies four categories of voluntary failure:

- Philanthropic insufficiency—or the sector's "inability to generate resources on a scale that is both adequate enough and reliable enough to cope with the human service problems of an advanced industrial society" (p. 45)

- Philanthropic particularism—which refers to "the tendency of voluntary organizations and their benefactors to focus on particular subgroups of the population. . . . As a result, serious gaps can occur in the coverage of subgroups by the existing voluntary organizations" (pp. 45–46)

- Philanthropic paternalism—in which the "nature of the sector comes to be shaped by the preferences not of the community as a whole, but of its wealthy members" (p. 47)

- Philanthropic amateurism—in which care that requires professional training and expertise is "entrusted to well-meaning amateurs" (p. 48)

Communities can create public value by promoting a sense of individual and collective identity, belonging, recognition, and security; by providing people a place to live, work, learn, enjoy, and express themselves; by building and maintaining physical, human, intellectual, social, and cultural capital of various sorts; and by fostering a civically engaged, egalitarian, trusting, and tolerant democratic society (Boyte & Kari, 1996; Chrislip, 2002). Social capital in particular has been shown to have a broad range of positive effects on health, education, welfare, safety, and civic activism (Putnam, 2000). Communities are necessary for our existence as human beings, and serving communities provides a justification for our existence as humans (see, for example, Friedmann, 1982; Becker, 1997; McKnight & Block, 2010).

As public problems have increasingly been defined in such a way that they are beyond the competence of single organizations or sectors to solve, collaboration has been looked to as a way to pool competence to mount an effective response. Cross-sector collaboration specifically is seen as a way to systematically harness each sector's unique strengths, while minimizing or overcoming its characteristic weaknesses, in order to ensure that the joint response to challenges is competent to successfully do the job at hand (Bryson, Crosby, & Stone, 2006; Bryson & Crosby, 2008).

MANDATES

Although Step 3, clarifying mission, is usually more time-consuming than Step 2, clarifying organizational mandates, Step 2 is no less important. Before an organization can define its mission and values, it should know exactly what it is formally and informally *required* to do (and not do) by external authorities. Formal requirements are likely to be codified in laws, regulations, ordinances, articles of incorporation, charters, and so forth, and therefore may be easier to uncover and clarify than the organization's mission. In addition, organizations typically must meet a variety of informal mandates that may be embodied in norms or the expectations of key stakeholders, such as the electorate or duly elected representatives. These informal mandates may be no less binding. For example, newly elected officials often talk about the "mandate" they have received from the voters—and if the mandate is real and strong, woe unto those who ignore it. Real clarity, however, about these informal mandates may have to await a stakeholder analysis, discussed in a subsequent section.

An interesting example is provided by the British National Health Service (NHS). The NHS is a national, publicly financed health care system covering everyone within its borders, not just citizens; there are no "uninsureds." Since the Citizen Charter initiative begun by John Major's Conservative government in the 1990s, the NHS for the various countries and provinces that comprise the United Kingdom (England, Scotland, Wales, and Northern Ireland) has prepared a number of documents that outline rights and responsibilities of patients, the public, and staff and offer a number of commitments. In effect, these statements are both government- and self-imposed mandates of varying force. The idea that patients, clients, customers, or citizens have both rights and responsibilities is worth emphasizing in any situation, such as health care, education, or public safety, where *coproduction* is a central feature of effective service provision (Osborne & Plastrik, 1997, 2000; Normann, 2000).

The latest version of the NHS mandates for England is found in the NHS Constitution, the short version of which is presented in *The Handbook to the NHS Constitution for England, 8 March 2010*. The constitution restates and reaffirms principles and values on which the NHS had been built (it was founded in 1948) and emphasizes the idea of partnership between the NHS, patients, staff, and the public. The constitution sets out rights to which patients, the public, and staff are entitled; "pledges" which the NHS makes (that is, self-imposed mandates); and responsibilities that the public, patients, and staff owe to one another "to ensure that the NHS operates fairly and effectively" (National Health Service for England, 2010, p. 2). All NHS bodies and private and nonprofit providers supplying NHS services "are required by law to take account of the constitution" when making decisions and taking action (p. 2). Patients are strongly encouraged to assume the responsibilities outlined for them. (The new coalition Conservative–Liberal-Democratic government is proposing major changes to the NHS, so it is not clear what will happen to its constitution.)

The NHS Constitution for England *Handbook* begins with what is essentially a statement of mission (National Health Service for England, 2010):

> The NHS belongs to the people. It is there to improve our health and well-being, supporting us to keep mentally and physically well, to get better when we are ill and, when we cannot fully recover, to stay as well as we can to the end of our lives. It works at the limits of science—bringing the highest levels of human knowledge and skill to save lives and improve health. It touches our lives at times of basic human need, when care and compassion are what matter most.

The principles that guide the NHS are as follows (pp. 3–4):

- The NHS provides a comprehensive service, available to all.
- Access to NHS services is based on clinical need, not an individual's ability to pay.
- The NHS aspires to the highest standards of excellence and professionalism.
- NHS services must reflect the needs and preferences of patients, their families, and their caregivers.
- The NHS works across organizational boundaries and in particular with other organizations in the interest of patients, local communities, and the wide population.
- The NHS is committed to providing the best value for taxpayers' money and the most effective fair and sustainable use of finite resources.
- The NHS is accountable to the public, communities, and patients that it serves.

The document goes on to outline a set of patient rights and NHS promises to patients in the areas of: access to health services; quality of care and environment; nationally approved treatments, drugs, and programs; respect, consent, and confidentiality; informed choice; involvement in one's own health care; and the NHS generally in terms of planning, service provision, and decision making, and complaint and redress (pp. 5–8). For example, in terms of access to health services, patients have the right to:

- Receive NHS service free of charge, apart from certain limited exceptions sanctioned by Parliament
- Access NHS services
- Expect your local NHS to assess the health requirements of the local community and to commission and put in place the services to meet those needs as are considered necessary
- Go to other European Union countries or Switzerland for treatment that would be available to you through your NHS commissioning body
- Not be unlawfully discriminated against in the provision of NHS services
- Access services within maximum waiting times

In the same domain, the NHS also commits to:

- Provide convenient, easy access to services within the waiting times
- Make decisions in a clear and transparent way
- Make the transition as smooth as possible when you are referred between services, and to involve you in relevant discussions

In terms of patient and public responsibilities, the constitution argues that since the NHS belongs to everyone, there are things everyone should do to help it work effectively and responsibly. These responsibilities include admonitions to (p. 9):

- Recognize that you can make significant contributions to your own, and your family's, good health and well-being, and to take some personal responsibility for it
- Register with a general practitioner's practice, the main point of access to the NHS
- Treat NHS staff and other patients with respect
- Provide accurate information about your health, condition, and status
- Keep appointments or cancel within a reasonable time
- Follow the course of treatment to which you have agreed and to talk to your clinician if you find this difficult

- Participate in important public health programs
- Ensure that those closest to you are aware of your wishes about organ donation
- Give feedback—both positive and negative—about the treatment and care you have received, including any adverse reactions you may have had

Next the document sets out staff rights and NHS pledges. These are intended to help assure high-quality care and a high-quality workplace (p. 10). This is followed by an articulation of staff responsibilities to the public, patients, and colleagues (p. 11). The document concludes with a statement of NHS values (p. 12). These include valuing:

- Respect and dignity
- Commitment to quality of care
- Compassion
- Improving lives
- Working together for patients
- And the idea that everyone counts

Purpose and Immediate Desired Outcomes

The purpose of Step 2 is to identify and clarify the nature and meaning of the externally imposed mandates, both formal and informal, affecting the organization. Four outcomes should be sought from this step:

1. Identification of the organization's formal and informal mandates, including who is mandating what and with what force

2. Interpretation of what is required as a result of the mandates (leading perhaps to explicit goals or performance indicators)

3. Clarification of what is forbidden by the mandates (which also might lead to explicit goals or performance indicators)

4. Clarification of what is not ruled out by the mandates (that is, the rough boundaries of the unconstrained field of action)

It is very important to clarify what is explicitly required, explicitly forbidden, and not explicitly ruled out. Attending to the first two can alert organizational members to what they *must* or *must not* do, the key elements of what Simons (1995, p. 6) defines as an organization's "boundary system" meant to set limits on behavior tied to defined sanctions and credible threat of punishment. For example, research on state-imposed local government planning mandates in Florida indicates that much of the variation in local compliance is directly attributable to which mandates the state's department of community affairs has chosen to emphasize (Deyle & Smith, 1998). Clearly, not all mandates are of equal interest to both the state and local governments. Whether or not more public value would have been created if they were is unclear. In a time of constrained resources and competing demands, choices no doubt must be made about which mandates to emphasize and which to downplay or try to change, but doing either is not without risk.

By considering what the organization *might* or *should* do, organizational members and other key stakeholders can engage in valuable discussions about which mandates are useful, in that they allow for "the responsible exercise of discretion" (Lynn, 2003, p. 16; Hill & Hupe, 2009) and "allow desirable creativity within defined limits of freedom" (Simons, 1995, p. 178); which mandates may need to be changed; and what the organization's mission ought to be. Too many organizations think they are more constrained than they actually are and, indeed, make the fundamental error of assuming that their mandates and mission are the same. They may be, but leaders and planners should not start out with that assumption.

The Minnesota Department of Transportation (MNDOT) offers an interesting example of the interplay of mandates and mission. In the late 1990s, a vocal state legislator was strongly criticizing the use of existing ramp meters to govern access to freeways in the Twin Cities area. Many professionals in MNDOT thought the organization's mission could be served by studying the impact that turning off the existing ramp meters would have on travel times and accidents in the Twin Cities area. But they did not think they *could* turn off the meters because of the state's liability laws. Victims of accidents might sue MNDOT on the supposition that turning off the meters had led to the accidents. A 2000 state law mandating MNDOT to do such a study allowed them to turn the meters off, study the results, and then make several readjustments when the meters finally were turned back on (Krause & Milgrom, 2002). As a result of a carefully designed study in which ramp meters were turned off for 30 days, MNDOT in fact did make several adjustments to the system. The change in mandates helped MNDOT better pursue its mission and create more public value.

MetroGIS provides another interesting example. Recall that prior to MetroGIS's first formal strategic planning effort, Randall Johnson took the lead on organizing a series of formal and informal discussions and two major forums of seventy-five-plus stakeholders each to explore the issue of whether to pursue a regional GIS system and whether the MC should lead the initiative. A general consensus emerged from these discussions for the idea that there should be a regional GIS system and the MC should take the lead. The discussions and forums in effect created a strong informal mandate to proceed both with strategic planning and with the creation of a regional GIS system.

Desired Longer-Term Outcomes and Process Design and Action Guidelines

There are two potential longer-term desired outcomes of Step 2. First, clarity about what is mandated—what must be done and not done—will increase the likelihood that mandates will actually be met and public value created (Nelson & French, 2002; Piotrowski & Rosenbloom, 2002). Research on goal setting indicates that one of the most important determinants of goal achievement is the clarity of the goals themselves. The more specific the goal, the more likely it will be achieved (Nutt, 2002; Latham, Borgogni, & Petitta, 2008). Second, the possibility of developing a mission that is not limited to mandates is enhanced. It helps people examine the *potential* purposes of organizational action for creating public value if they know what is not explicitly forbidden.

The process guidelines for this step are straightforward:

1. *Have someone compile the formal and informal mandates faced by the organization.* A straightforward summary in plain English should be produced. If the organization is governmental in nature, it is important not to forget the democratic-constitutional values that legislatures and the courts have been trying to enforce for decades, such as representation, participation, transparency, and individual rights (Piotrowski & Rosenbloom, 2002; Hill & Lynn, 2009).

2. *Review the mandates in order to clarify what is required, what is forbidden, and what is allowed.* Part of this exercise may include gaining clarity about who is mandating what and with what force. This can provide a major clarification of organizational goals or performance indicators. These goals can then be used, along with goals that might be derived from stakeholder analyses and the mission statement, to identify issues.

3. *Regularly remind organizational members what the organization is required to do, and forbidden to do, as a way of ensuring conformity with the mandates.* In other words, institutionalize attention to the mandates. Certainly strategic plans, annual reports, staff retreats, and orientation sessions for new employees should include a section (perhaps a very brief one) on mandates. Other methods might prove useful as well. Failure to do so can *diminish* public value and undermine legitimacy. For example, research on federal annual performance plans required by the Government Performance and Results Act has indicated a disturbing failure of those plans to attend to some important mandates, specifically requirements under the Freedom of Information Act. This leads one to wonder if other

important mandated elements of creating public value are being ignored (Piotrowski & Rosenbloom, 2002).

4. *Undertake a regular review of the mandates and discuss which seem to be current, which may need to be revised, and which should be dropped.* In a review of state-imposed mandates in Minnesota, local government respondents saw a need for dialogue with the state to ensure mandates are reasonable, flexible, adequately funded, and less burdensome in terms of their cumulative impact (Grossback, 2002).

MISSION

Yogi Berra, the famous New York Yankees baseball player and manager, once said, "You've got to be very careful if you don't know where you're going, because you might not get there." His maxim emphasizes that without a sense of purpose we are quite literally lost. Mission provides that sense of purpose. In addition, it can be very helpful (although not always necessary or possible) to expand an organization's mission into an early vision of success, which may then guide subsequent efforts at issue identification and strategy development (see Figure 2.1). Without a vision of success, organizational members may not know enough or see enough about how to fulfill the mission. Communities, in particular, may find it useful to develop a guiding vision that embodies important purposes and values. They are unlikely to have a mission statement as such, but a guiding vision can provide the sense of purpose, values, and common ground that enables disparate and essentially independent groups and organizations to strive together for the common good (Wheeland, 2004).

Mission, in other words, clarifies an organization's purpose, or *why* it should be doing what it does; vision clarifies *what* the organization should look like and *how* it should behave in fulfilling its mission. Chapter Eight discusses constructing a vision of success; for now it is enough to note simply that the foundation of any good vision of success is an organization's mission statement, or a community's statement of purpose and values.

Note the contrast between Yogi Berra's maxim and J.R.R. Tolkien's observation in *The Fellowship of the Ring* (1965, p. 182), "Not all those who wander are lost." Tolkien was speaking of people who may look like they are wandering, but who do have a clear sense of purpose. Purposeful wandering is quite different from the mindless wandering to which Yogi Berra alludes. Purposeful wandering also is what Daniel Boone is alluding to in the epigraph opening Chapter Two.

The statement from Barbara Tuchman (1984) quoted as the epigraph to this chapter makes a different point: any organization that becomes an end in itself is doomed to failure. The collapse of the former Eastern Bloc nations and the Soviet Union twenty-some years ago illustrates how self-aggrandizement, illusions of invulnerability, and disregard for constituents' desires can lead to disaster. More recent illustrations are provided by the rapid collapses of dictatorships in Tunisia and Egypt (events propelled in part by advances in information and communication technology that made it easier for opponents to unite and coordinate their actions). Indeed, most planning disasters probably meet Tuchman's criteria for folly (Hall, 1980; Nutt, 2002).

Purpose and Immediate Desired Outcomes

Ultimately strategic planning is about purpose, meaning, values, and virtue. Nowhere is this more apparent than in the clarification of mission and the subsequent development of a vision of success. The aim of mission clarification is to specify the purposes of the organization and the philosophy and values that guide it. Unless the purposes focus on socially useful and justifiable ends, and unless the philosophy and values are themselves virtuous, the organization cannot hope to command indefinitely the resources needed to survive, including high-quality, loyal, committed employees (Selznick, 1957; Burns, 1978; Collins & Porras, 1997; Rainey, 2009). Unfortunately, as Paul Light (1998) points out, some organizations can plod in ignorance and inertia for some time: "One of the great mysteries of organizational life is how agencies survive year after year without a clue as to their mission" (p. 187).

Step 3 has two main immediate desired outcomes: a stakeholder analysis (if one has not been completed already) and a mission statement. A stakeholder analysis provides useful information and valuable preparation for a mission statement. Agreement on the stakeholder analysis and mission statement by key decision makers should clarify the organization's arenas of action, many of the basic rules of the game within these arenas, the implicit if not explicit goals of the organization, and possible performance indicators. In addition, the agreement on mission—particularly if it is consensual—will itself be a source of power for the organization that can have positive effects on performance (Pfeffer, 2010). Much of the power comes from framing and communicating the mission (including through measurable goals) in such a way that employees and other actors can commit to and identify with the organization and its mission (Weiss & Piderit, 1999; Wright & Davis, 2003). The mission in this case provides a deep source of meaning to those who pursue it (Delbecq, 2010). Finally, agreement on an organizational mission that embraces socially desirable and justified purposes should produce legitimacy internally and externally for the organization (Suchman, 1995), as well as enthusiasm, and even excitement, among organizational members (Kouzes & Posner, 2008).

Longer-Term Desired Outcomes

A number of additional desirable outcomes flow from clarifying and agreeing on the organization's mission. Perhaps the most important is simply that agreement helps fosters a habit of focusing deliberations on what is truly important. Too often key decision makers in a public or nonprofit organization never come together to discuss cross-functional issues or, more important, the organization as a whole. The boards and senior staff of the Minneapolis Park and Recreation Board and the Loft wanted to find time to focus on what was important for their organizations and used strategic planning specifically for this purpose. Similarly, the activists supporting creation of MetroGIS used the first round of MetroGIS strategic planning to create the organization's mission and the main outlines of the organization's architecture and starting initiatives. The organization's policy board used the second round of strategic planning to focus anew on the organization's mission and what was most important for it to do.

Often, if key decision makers do gather—for example, at a staff meeting—most of their time is taken up with announcements or else with discussion of relatively trivial matters. Although such discussions may serve to introduce key decision makers to one another and may provide some of the social glue necessary to hold any organization together, they are relatively useless and may in fact be a colossal waste of everyone's time.

When important issues are not being addressed, it is important to know *why*. Participants simply may not know how to do so, particularly if serious conflicts might be involved, in which case targeted training might help. Or they may not be comfortable with one another—for example, they may be unsure of one another's motives—and therefore may be fearful of the consequences of raising difficult issues. Team building might be used to build trust and address these fears. Or, avoiding discussing real issues can be a way for senior decision makers to control the agenda and enhance their own power (Benveniste, 1989). In this last case, senior personnel might be persuaded of the benefits of more participatory decision making, or else might somehow be persuaded to leave. As Scharmer (2009, p. 415) observes, "The underlying principle here is that *energy follows attention* [italics in original]. This means that the biggest leverage we have is what we pay attention to and how we attend to a situation." To be blunt: If you are not paying attention to what is important, what good are you as a leader or follower?

The second important longer-term desired outcome, of course, is the clarification of organizational (or community) purpose, or its *strategic intent* (Hamel & Prahalad, 1994; Eden & Ackermann, 2010; Ackermann & Eden, 2011). Depending on how this is done, the performance payoffs can be significant. For example, quantitative evidence from public schools in Michigan demonstrates that the existence of a mission statement that is focused and activist and that emphasizes a commitment to measurable achievement is linked to a measurable positive effect on students' math and reading achievement (Weiss & Piderit, 1999). There is case evidence to indicate similar positive measurable impacts of similarly worded mission statements in a number of other public and nonprofit organizations (for example, Bryson, 1999; Sawhill & Williamson, 2001).

Because defining the mission may be thought of as the central function of leadership, more effective leadership is another outcome (Selznick, 1957). Clarity of organizational purpose helps leaders in other ways as well. In particular, it helps articulate the purpose of organizational structures and systems, including the resource allocation system. Agreed-upon purpose provides a kind of *premise control* (Perrow, 1986; Bryant, 2003, p. 36), or *control lever* (Simons, 1995, p. 7) that serves as a criterion against which organizational structures and systems and actions will be judged. In addition, leaders will be helped to guide internal conflict, so that it furthers organizational ends. Leaders are required to guide the play of the game within the structure of the rules, but they also need to change the rules on occasion. Clarity of purpose provides a valuable basis for guiding conflict productively and for understanding which rules help with that task and which need to be changed (Schein, 2010).

A key point about managing conflict is that organizational conflicts typically are about something other than what is nominally in dispute. For that reason, their resolution requires the conflict to be reframed at a higher level of abstraction (Watzlawick, Weakland, & Fisch, 1974; Schön & Rein, 1994; Nadler & Hibino, 1998). Terry (1993, 2001), for example, describes a hierarchy of human action. *Fulfillment* is at the top, and is the embodiment of all that is underneath. Then comes *meaning*, or why people act; then *mission*, which guides one in a meaningful direction; then *power*; *structures and systems*; *resources*; and finally the *givens* of existence. He argues that disputes at any level in this hierarchy are usually really about what is at the next level up. Thus, power struggles in general are usually about the purposes the power is to serve. Arguments about organizational structures and systems are really about who is empowered or disempowered by different designs. Disputes over resources are typically about how the use of those resources should be regulated in structures and systems. Conflicts over givens are about what counts as a resource and what is to be discounted, devalued, or ignored. A focus on the purpose and ultimate meaning of organizational efforts—to the extent that there is agreement on them—therefore can frame most of these conflicts in such a way that they facilitate the pursuit and fulfillment of organizational ends.

Agreement on purpose can also help the parties in a conflict to disconnect ends from means and thus be clear about what goals are to be pursued, or problems addressed, prior to exploring solutions. The advantage of doing so is that most conflicts are about solutions; that is, there usually is no agreement or clear understanding about what problems the solutions are to meant to solve (Nadler & Hibino, 1998; Nutt, 2002; Bryant, 2003). Further, the organization cannot really know what problems it ought to address without some sense of the purpose it serves. Once an organization understands its purpose, it can define the problems it is meant to solve and can better understand how to choose among competing solutions. David Osborne and Ted Gaebler based their best-selling book *Reinventing Government* (1992) in part on this very point: if governments stick to *steering*—as noted in Chapter One, the word *government* comes from the Greek for steering, which means focusing on purpose (and problem definition)—then they are less likely to be a captive of any one approach to *rowing* (solutions) (see also Osborne & Plastrik, 1997, 2000; Osborne & Hutchinson, 2004; Hill & Hupe, 2009, pp. 123–131, 193–195).

Agreement on purpose therefore gets the organization to pursue what is often a normatively preferable sequence of conflict resolution activities: to agree on purposes, identify problems or issues, and then explore and agree on solutions. The likelihood that successful solutions will be found is increased because the sequence narrows the focus to fulfillment of the mission, but broadens the search for acceptable solutions to include all that would further the mission (Nadler & Hibino, 1998). The dangers of *jumping to solutions* and thereby producing a blunder or debacle are minimized (Nutt, 2002).

Agreement on purpose provides a very powerful means of social control. To the extent that the purposes are socially justified and virtuous, agreement will invest organizational discussions and actions with a moral quality that can constrain self-serving and organizationally destructive behavior on the part of organizational members. Said differently, agreement on purpose can lead to a mobilization of organizational energies based on pursuit of a morally justifiable mission beyond self-interest (Suchman, 1995; Lewis & Gilman, 2005).

Another desired outcome of this step is the explicit attention given to philosophy, values, and culture. Organizations rarely discuss these matters directly. As a result, they are likely to misread their strengths and weaknesses and thus will make mistakes in the internal assessment step to come. Also, without understanding their philosophy, values, and culture, organizations are likely to make serious errors in the strategy formulation step. They may choose strategies that are not consonant with their philosophy, values, and culture and that therefore are doomed to fail unless a well-conceived strategy for culture change is pursued as well (Hampden-Turner, 1990; Schein, 2010; Johnson, Scholes, & Whittington, 2008).

Finally, as a result of answering the six questions that follow, the organization will be well on its way to development of a clear vision of success. Indeed, answers to these questions may provide organizational members with the conception that must precede any actual perceptions of success. In other words, it is conceiving and believing that make seeing possible (Weick, 1995).

STAKEHOLDER ANALYSES

A stakeholder analysis is a valuable prelude to a mission statement, a SWOC/T analysis, and effective strategies. Indeed, I usually argue that if an organization has time to do only one thing when it comes to strategic planning, that one thing ought to be a stakeholder analysis. Stakeholder analyses are so critical because the key to success in the public and nonprofit sectors—and the private sector, too, for that matter—is the satisfaction of key stakeholders. If an organization does not know who its stakeholders are, what criteria they use to judge the organization, and how the organization is performing against those criteria, there is little likelihood that the organization (or community) will know what it should do to satisfy its key stakeholders (Rainey, 2009).

An example may prove instructive at this point. The example shows how a misreading of who the key stakeholders are can cause serious trouble for an organization, how a better reading can improve things dramatically, and how building on a series of stakeholder analyses can lead to far greater fulfillment of the mission. The story plays out over almost twenty-five years and comes from the Division of Fish and Wildlife of the state Department of Natural Resources in a Midwestern state. The department (as the state's agent) is one of the major landowners in the United States. It manages a vast area, including water, forests, mineral and land resources, and huge populations of fish and wildlife. The fish and wildlife resources are important to in-state and out-of-state anglers and hunters and to the large recreational and tourist industry that depends on them. A large fraction of the state's people identify themselves as anglers and hunters, while a large number of others enter the state each year to fish and hunt.

You would think that the Division of Fish and Wildlife would be one of the most protected and supported units of this state's government, that legions of interest groups—from the National Rifle Association, to resort-industry groups, to recreational equipment dealer associations—would be continually lobbying state legislators and the governor to maintain, if not increase, public financial support for the division. When our story begins, however, such was most emphatically not the case. Indeed, quite the opposite. The division had been under frequent attack from some key stakeholders—hunters and anglers. They argued that the division saw itself primarily as a regulator and naysayer to these stakeholders. They felt it was completely uninterested in their satisfaction.

The division decided to engage in strategic planning to turn around an increasingly bad situation. One of the first steps was a stakeholder analysis. The most important piece of information to emerge from that analysis was that the professionals in the division operated under the mistaken assumption that, in effect, their prime stakeholders were fish and deer! They felt their job was to regulate anglers and hunters, so that the state's fish and wildlife resources could be protected and managed over the long term.

There would have been little problem with this view if the fish and deer could vote, spend money, and pay taxes. But they cannot. But anglers, hunters, and their families do, along with the owners of resorts and sporting goods establishments. Though the division's maintenance of fish and wildlife resources was obviously one criterion that anglers and hunters used to judge its performance, there were many more as well (such as its ability to provide enjoyable recreational opportunities), and the division was failing in many instances to perform well against them. The result was hostility on the part of these stakeholders and attempts in the legislature to cut the division's budget and curtail its powers. As a result of insights gained from its stakeholder analysis, the division began pursuing several strategies to manage fish and wildlife resources effectively in the long term, while increasing the satisfaction of hunters and anglers (and not simultaneously alienating environmentalists!). The division has in fact dramatically increased support from the sports groups.

But the division and its encompassing department did not stop there. The department embraced strategic planning and began to work at issues that mattered to the department's key stakeholders and developed a synthesis of divisional missions and mandates. By taking a bigger-picture view the department developed a new mission focused on what is now called ecosystem-based management, including working with citizens to protect and manage the state's natural resources (not just those that are state owned), to provide outdoor recreation opportunities, and to provide for commercial uses of natural resources in a way that creates a sustainable quality of life. The new mission has the support of all the major stakeholders (although they certainly do not all support the department on every issue) because it took their interests into account. The mission and the strategies used to pursue it have won the department accolades nationally and internationally for innovative approaches to involving the public and to pursuing the common good. And it all began—at least in part—with a simple stakeholder analysis almost twenty-five years ago.

Resource A presents a variety of stakeholder analyses. In general, the three that are most useful for developing a mission statement are the Basic Analysis Technique, Power Versus Interest Grid, and Stakeholder Influence Diagram. These analyses may have been produced as part of developing an initial agreement, in which case they should be revisited. If these analyses have not been conducted, then now is the time. Here we present them in brief.

The Basic Analysis Technique consists of a minimum of three steps. The first step is to identify exactly who the organization's stakeholders are. Figure 4.1 presents a typical stakeholder map for a government. The stakeholders are numerous (although many organizations have even more).

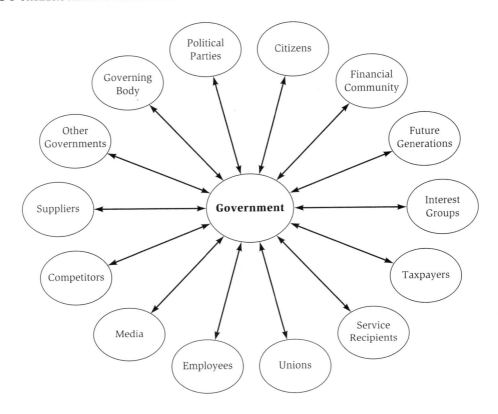

Figure 4.1. A Stakeholder Map for a Government.

Five additional points should be made about this figure. First, the diagram makes clear that any organization (and especially a government), network, or collaboration is an arena in which individuals and groups contest for control of its attention, resources, and output (Crosby & Bryson, 2005; Innes & Booher, 2010). A major purpose of a stakeholder analysis is to get a more precise picture of the players in the arena.

Second, it is important to identify stakeholders at the right level of aggregation. For example, in the Park Board case, it is certainly true that citizens are a key stakeholder. In the Loft case, writers are a key stakeholder. And in the MetroGIS case, local governments are a key stakeholder. But saying so does not help much because the citizenry, writers, and local governments as stakeholders really consist of a host of different stakeholders with different stakes or interests in the Park Board, Loft, and MetroGIS, respectively. There is an art to knowing what level of aggregation to pick, and the choice can influence subsequent analyses about how well the organization is doing with its stakeholders and what it needs from specific stakeholders. In general, stakeholders should be differentiated if doing so would make a difference in expectations placed on the organization and the responses it might make (Eden & Ackermann, 1998; Ackermann & Eden, 2011).

Third, special note should be made of future generations. I believe strongly that organizations (and especially governments) have an obligation to leave the world in as good shape as they found it, if not better. It is important in this era of special interest groups and a strong lurch to the political right that seems to devalue the stewardship function of government to keep this public trust in mind. As Theodore Roosevelt said, "We do not inherit the earth from our ancestors, we borrow it from our children."

Fourth, it is very important for key employee groups to be explicitly identified. Not all employees are the same. There are different groups with different roles to play who will use different criteria to judge organizational performance. Clarity about these groups is necessary to ensure that organizational responses are sufficiently differentiated to satisfy each group. I worked with a public library that presents an interesting example in this regard. It took considerable encouragement on my part to get the librarians to identify themselves as key stakeholders. Their self-effacing and altruistic view of themselves as public servants was admirable, but misplaced. By definition they are key stakeholders of the organization and their own satisfaction is important to the success of their services. Indeed, one of the issues driving the strategic planning process for the library was the fact that the librarians were experiencing increased stress and even "burnout" as a result of heightened demands on their services. Something had to be done to alleviate the stress. Furthermore, several of the key criteria they use to judge organizational performance relate to the professional standards the library does or does not meet (including, for example, guaranteeing First Amendment protections). In other words, it is usually the professional librarians themselves, not other stakeholders, who hold the organization to exacting professional standards of service.

Fifth, key stakeholders for many organizations and communities actually are likely to be quite distant physically, yet nonetheless must be considered carefully. For example, federal and state governments and distant corporate headquarters of local establishments typically have a significant impact on local communities.

The second step in the analysis is to specify the criteria the stakeholders use to assess the organization's performance. There are two approaches to this task. One is to guess what the criteria are; the second is to ask the stakeholders themselves. The strategic planning team should always make its own guesses, but at some point it may prove instructive and politically useful to ask stakeholders (for example, through surveys, interviews, or group discussions) to state their professed criteria.

The compatibility of strategic planning with many newer governance and management approaches is directly related to the emphasis on addressing key stakeholder needs, particularly of those that might be called "customers." For example, a hallmark of government reinvention (Osborne & Gaebler, 1992; Osborne & Plastrik, 1997, 2000), reengineering, and continuous quality improvement (Cohen, Eimicke, & Heikkila, 2008; Berman, 2006; Osborne & Hutchinson, 2004) is their emphasis on meeting customer expectations. And nonprofit organizations are exhorted by the Drucker Foundation (Stern, 1998) to clearly identify their *primary* and *supporting* customer needs as part of their organizational assessment efforts.

Why should the team always make its own guesses? First, it is faster. Second, the stakeholders may not be completely honest. In the case of city council members, for example, city employees will usually say a key criterion for this important stakeholder group is whether the performance of city departments enhances their reelection prospects. Council members are unlikely to declare this criterion in public, even though it is important to them. On the other hand, asking stakeholders what their criteria are can be instructive, because the team's own guesses can be wrong (Nadler & Hibino, 1998; Normann, 2000).

The third step in the process is to make a judgment about how well the organization performs against the stakeholders' criteria. The judgments need not be very sophisticated. Simply noting whether or not the organization does poorly, okay, or very well against the criteria is enough to prompt a very useful discussion. Topics of discussion should include areas of organizational strength and weakness; overlaps, gaps, conflicts, and contradictions among the criteria; and opportunities and challenges or threats posed by the organization's current performance.

These three steps should help set the stage for a discussion of the organization's mission (or a community's purposes and values). In particular, a stakeholder analysis forces team members to place themselves in the shoes of others—especially outsiders—and make a rather dispassionate assessment of the organization's performance from the outsiders' points of view. Such activity is one of the best possible ways to avoid the attributes of folly that Tuchman describes. It is also likely to be a necessary precursor of ethical action (Lewis & Gilman, 2005). In addition, the stakeholder analysis provides a valuable prelude to the SWOC/T analysis (Step 4), strategic issue identification (Step 5), and strategy development (Step 6).

If time permits, or circumstances demand it, three additional steps may be advisable. The strategic planning team may wish to discuss exactly how the various stakeholders influence the organization (Eden & Ackermann, 1998). Many members of the team may not know precisely how the organization is influenced, and the discussion may also highlight the really important stakeholders. The Power Versus Interest Grid and Stakeholder Influence Diagram techniques can help move this discussion forward.

Second, the strategic planning team may wish to discuss what the organization needs from each stakeholder group. I have emphasized the need for the organization to satisfy key stakeholder groups, but it may also be very important to focus attention directly on what the organization needs to survive and prosper. The usual assumption is that if the organization satisfies key stakeholders, it can survive and prosper. But that may not be the case, especially when there is a difference between funders and service recipients (as is often the case for public and nonprofit organizations). A direct focus on what the organization needs to survive may reveal an important strategic issue to address: how can the organization secure the resources necessary to continue pursuit of its mission when it does not already receive those resources from the key stakeholders?

Finally, the team may wish to establish a rough ordering among the stakeholders according to their importance to the organization. The order, of course, might vary with different issues, but the rough ordering will give the team an idea of which stakeholders demand the most attention.

A Power Versus Interest Grid arrays stakeholders according to their power to place a claim on the organization's attention, resources, or output, and according to their interest in the organization's attention, resources, or output. Four categories of stakeholders result: Those with high power and high interest are called *players*; those with high power and low interest are called *context setters*, because their power helps set the context, but they are not interested enough to be players. Those with high interest and lower power are called *subjects*, as they are subject to the power of others. And those with low interest and low power form the *crowd* (Eden & Ackermann, 1998). The mission certainly must take the players and context setters into account in some way, even if the organization's ultimate purpose is to serve the subjects or crowd (Bryson, Cunningham, & Lokkesmoe, 2002).

A Stakeholder Influence Diagram begins with a Power Versus Interest Grid. Once stakeholders are located on the grid, arrows can be drawn in to show which stakeholders influence whom. (In tandem, a Power Versus Interest Grid and Stakeholder Influence Diagram can be used to help facilitate and formalize completion of the three final steps in the Basic Analysis Technique.)

The team will have to decide whether or not to circulate the stakeholder analysis (or analyses) outside the strategic planning team. It is primarily just an input to other steps in the process (mission statement, SWOC/T analysis, strategic issue identification, strategy development, implementation), so there may be no good reason for more public discussion of it (especially if a major purpose of the strategic planning effort is to change the power, interest, influence, or other aspects of the organization's current stakeholders).

THE MISSION STATEMENT

A mission statement is a declaration of organizational purpose. Mission statements vary in length depending on their intended use, but they are typically short—no more than a page, and often not more than a punchy slogan. They should also be targeted, activist in tone, and inspiring. And they should lead to measures that will indicate whether or not the mission is being achieved.

The actual statement should grow out of discussions aimed at answering six questions (a process that is often highly informative, as the late movie mogul Sam Goldwyn clearly realized when he said, "For your information, let me ask a few questions"). The statement should at least touch on most answers, though for some purposes it may be distilled into a slogan. Answers to the six questions (outlined below) will provide the basis for developing a vision of success later in the process.

Developing answers to these questions is a valuable but very demanding process. Several hours (and in some cases days) of discussion by the strategic planning team may be required to reach consensus on the answers, and perhaps additional time for reflection may be necessary. The Park Board, Loft, and MetroGIS all revisited and refined their missions in a deliberative and productive way. The deliberations took time but were ultimately highly consequential in terms of clarifying organizational purposes in light of changed circumstances.

Sometimes the discussions may seem too philosophical or academic to be of much use. If discussions start to get bogged down in grand abstractions or minutiae, by all means move ahead. Assign someone the task of writing up what has been covered so far, including points of agreement and disagreement, and come back for further discussions when the time seems right or when decisions must be reached. Strategic planning should not be allowed to get in the way of useful action. However, it is important to remember that strategic planning *is* ultimately about purpose, meaning, value, and virtue, and therefore is philosophical at its base. To paraphrase management guru Peter Drucker, strategic planning involves responding to a series of Socratic questions. The six questions that follow structure one of the most important parts of that Socratic dialogue:

1. *Who are we?* If your organization were walking down the street and someone asked it who it was, what would the answer be? The question is one of identity, defined as what organizational members believe is distinct, central, and enduring about their organization (Dutton & Dukerich, 1991; Ackerman, 2000; Rughase, 2007). The answer certainly may need to be more than just what appears on the organization's letterhead, as the name there may not mean much.

Clarity about identity is crucial because often the most effective way to influence a person is not to tell them what to *do*, but to communicate who they *are*. So, too, with organizations. Because of their strong cultures, traditions, and reputations, to say that we are the Internal Revenue Service, the Federal Bureau of Investigation, or the United States Marine Corps carries a great deal of meaning, and implies a great deal about what the organization can and ultimately will do (Ashforth & Mael, 1989; Alvesson & Wilmott, 2002; Rughase, 2007; Goodsell, 2010).

It is also important to ask a question about identity in order to help the organization draw a distinction between what it is and what it does. Too many organizations make a fundamental mistake when they assume they are what they do (Osborne & Plastrik, 1997), meaning they conflate mission and strategy. Although it can be hard to know what something is without seeing what it does, it is still important not to assume that something is only what it appears to do. If that mistake is made, important avenues of strategic response to environmental conditions can be unwittingly sealed off. At best the organization may fail to create as much public value as it can; at worst, it becomes irrelevant. Collins and Porras (1997) in their influential work on companies that were "built to last" (such as 3M, Johnson & Johnson, and Sony) argue that, "The only truly reliable source of stability is a strong inner core and the willingness to change and adapt everything but that core" (p. xx). They define inner core as the combination of the organization's guiding purpose and fundamental values. And one of the important values has to be to appreciate and embrace change in pursuit of the purpose (Brown & Starkey, 2000). Paul Light (1998) found much the same thing in his research on public and nonprofit organization. The organizations in his sample that have been able to sustain innovation over long periods of time hold fast to their missions (although they may tinker with them around the edges), but are willing to change many other things.

Finally, if collaboration is important to the organization, it is also important to note that the organization's identity may well change at least some as collaborative relationships and the identity of the collaboration itself develop. This is to be expected and should be acknowledged as part of the process (Stone, 2000; Fiol, 2002; Innes & Booher, 2010). The fact that cycles of identity change typically occur in collaborative relationships underscores the need for the partners to value change in the pursuit of their missions (Brown & Starkey, 2000). It also emphasizes the need to honor the previous identity while partially estranging people from it (Bryson, Ackermann, Eden, & Finn, 1996), in keeping with the idea that if you want change you should emphasize stability (Collin & Porras, 1997; Johnson 1996).

2. *What are the basic social and political needs we exist to meet or what are the basic social or political problems we exist to address?* The answer to this question, along with the organization's mandates, provides the basic social justification for the organization's existence, and much of the source of its legitimacy. The purpose of the organization is to meet the needs or address the problems. The organization can then be seen as a means to an end, and not as an end in itself; the real end is to create public value in areas that need it. This question may need to be asked stakeholder by stakeholder.

3. *In general, what do we do to recognize, anticipate, and respond to these needs or problems?* This question prompts the organization to actively stay in touch with the needs it is supposed to fill, or the problems it is supposed to address, typically through continuing informal and formal research. Left to their own devices organizations generally will talk primarily to themselves, not to the outside (March & Olsen, 1989; Wilson, 1989). When we see individuals talking mainly to themselves in the absence of an iPod or smartphone with ear buds, we often suspect mental illness. When we see organizations talking primarily to themselves, we should suspect some sort of pathology as well. In order to remain "healthy," organizations must be encouraged to stay in touch with the outside world that justifies their existence and provides the resources to sustain them. Furthermore, constant attention to external needs or problems is likely to prompt the necessary adjustments to the organization's mission (though these would probably be rare), mandates, or product or service level and mix, costs, financing, management, and structure necessary for it to remain effective. Successful innovations typically are a response to real needs or problems; mere technological feasibility is not enough (Van de Ven, Polley, Garud, & Venkataraman, 1999). Furthermore, most of the information critical to the creation of innovations usually comes from outside the organization. The more people in the organization as a whole who attend to external needs and problems, the more likely a climate conducive to innovation and effectiveness will prevail and the easier it will be to justify desirable innovations to internal audiences (Light, 1998; Osborne & Plastrik, 1997; Rainey, 2009). Finally, people often need to be reassured that they will not be punished for returning from the outside world with bad news. We all have seen messengers shot down because key decision makers didn't like the message. An explicit endorsement of contact with the outside

world is likely to make the organization a safer haven for messengers who carry bad news that should be heard (Nutt, 2002).

4. *How should we respond to our key stakeholders?* This question asks the organization to decide what relations it wishes to establish with its key stakeholders and what values it seeks to promote through those relations. For example, it almost always pays to be open to what people have to say (King, Felty, & Susel, 1998), to listen (Stivers, 1994), and to engage in constructive dialogue (Roberts, 2002; Scharmer, 2009). The question also focuses on what the stakeholders value and what the organization does or might do to provide stakeholders what they value. If the key to success in the public and nonprofit sectors is the satisfaction of key stakeholders, what will the organization do to understand and satisfy those stakeholders? Obviously, a really detailed discussion of what the organization could do may have to wait until Step 6, but discussions of this sort can be pursued usefully throughout the process. In this step it is particularly important to encourage people to talk and think in terms of creating public value.

5. *What are our philosophy, values, and culture?* The importance of reflecting on and clarifying an organization's philosophy, core values, and culture becomes most apparent in the strategy development step. Only strategies that are consonant with the philosophy, core values, and culture are likely to succeed; strategies that are not are likely to fail unless culture change is a key part of the strategy (Hampden-Turner, 1990; Johnson, Scholes, & Whittington, 2008; Schein, 2010). Unfortunately, because organizations rarely discuss their philosophies, values, and culture, they often adopt strategies that are doomed to failure. Clarity about philosophy and values in advance of strategy development is one way to avoid this error. Perhaps even more important, however, clarity about philosophy, core values, and culture will help an organization maintain its integrity. If an organization can be clear about its philosophy and core values, it will be able to more easily refuse any proposals or actions that are likely to damage its integrity and to accept those that maintain or enhance its integrity. In a time when public confidence in most institutions is low, it is vital to maintain organizational integrity. Once this integrity is damaged, it is very difficult to reestablish public confidence in the organization. The difficult but successful turnaround in the 1990s at the Federal Emergency Management Administration (FEMA) demonstrates how hard creating or rebuilding integrity is (Abramson & Lawrence, 2001); the damage done to FEMA when the George W. Bush administration treated it (as it had been historically) as a dumping ground for

political hacks showed up with a vengeance when it failed utterly to respond effectively to the Hurricane Katrina disaster (Brinkley, 2006). The FEMA case clearly demonstrates how important it is for government organizations (and their political masters) to explicitly embrace virtuous philosophy, core values, and culture; and how much effort must be expended on building and maintaining an organization that reflects them (Khademian, 2002; Goodsell, 2010).

A caution is in order at this point, however. It might be argued that relatively open discussion of philosophy, values, and culture actually could damage an organization's effectiveness in some cases. Because only publicly acceptable aspects of philosophies, values, and culture are likely to be discussed in public, an organization whose success depends in part on pursuit of publicly unacceptable values could suffer. For example, a local economic development agency may in effect further the ends of wealthy land developers as part of its strategy of encouraging private development and investment to boost the local economy. No matter how beneficial such a strategy ultimately is to the community, it is probably unacceptable in most parts of the country for a government agency to say publicly that as a byproduct of successful pursuit of its mission, it helps the rich get richer. Public discussion of the agency's philosophy and values therefore might require the agency to change its strategy and, as a result, perhaps become less effective. At the very least, the agency may need to engage in some public education about the virtues of private markets and the fact that there is no guarantee that private developers and investors will survive in those markets. Key decision makers will have to decide whether to go public with a discussion of the organization's philosophy, values, and culture. Those persons interested in "reform" are likely to favor public discussion; those against are not. The point to be made, of course, is that *any* discussion of philosophy, values, and culture, whether public or not, will have political consequences (Stone, 2002).

6. *What makes us distinctive or unique?* There was a time in the not-too-distant past when it seemed public organizations were, in Herbert Kaufman's term (1976), *immortal.* Not anymore. *Cutback management* or *downsizing* are now terms familiar to most public managers, and many public organizations or parts of organizations have disappeared, and the number of public functions that are being carried out by private or nonprofit organizations has increased. Privatization is here to stay and its domain may increase (Light, 1997; Osborne & Plastrik, 1997; Peters & Pierre, 2003; Osborne &

Hutchinson, 2004). Public organizations must be quite clear about what makes them or the functions they perform distinctive or unique, or they will be likely candidates for privatization. Indeed if there is nothing distinctive or unique about a public organization or function, then perhaps it should to be privatized. Nonprofit organizations also need to be clear about what makes them distinctive or unique or they, too, may find themselves at a competitive disadvantage (Light, 1998; Bryson, Gibbons, & Shaye, 2001). The world has become increasingly competitive and those organizations that can't point to some distinct contribution they make may lose out.

Some Examples

Some examples can help illustrate how these mission questions might be answered, or at least touched upon. The mission statements for the Park Board, Loft, and MetroGIS are presented in Exhibits 4.1, 4.2, and 4.3. Though all are relatively short, each grew out of extensive discussions, emphasizes important purposes to be served, and articulates what many employees would see as a *calling* worthy of their commitment (Delbecq, 2010; Goodsell, 2010). Note that MetroGIS changed its mission statement after the 2007 strategic planning exercise. The first mission statement focused on establishing the organization and

---

Exhibit 4.1. Minneapolis Park and Recreation Board Mission Statement.

The Minneapolis Park and Recreation Board shall permanently preserve, protect, maintain, improve, and enhance its natural resources, parkland, and recreational opportunities for current and future generations.

The Minneapolis Park and Recreation Board exists to provide places and recreation opportunities for all people to gather, celebrate, contemplate, and engage in activities that promote health, well-being, community, and the environment.

Source: Minneapolis Park and Recreation Board, 2007. Reprinted with permission of The Minneapolis Park and Recreation Board.

Exhibit 4.2. The Loft Mission Statement.

The mission of the Loft is to support the artistic development of writers, to foster a writing community, and to build the audience for literature.

Source: The Loft Literary Center, n.d. Reprinted with permission of The Loft Literary Center.

Exhibit 4.3. MetroGIS Mission Statements.

1996–2007

To provide an ongoing, stakeholder-governed, metro-wide mechanism through which participants easily and equitably share geographically referenced graphic and associated attribute data that are accurate, current, secure, of common benefit and readily usable.

2007 to date

The mission of MetroGIS is to expand stakeholders' capacity to address shared geographic information technology needs and maximize investments in existing resources through widespread collaboration of organizations that serve the Twin Cities metropolitan area.

Source: MetroGIS, 2007a. Reprinted by permission of the Metropolitan Council of the Twin Cities.

---

the GIS. The second mission statement emphasizes the new purposes of expanding stakeholders' capacities.

Another example comes from the Amherst H. Wilder Foundation, a large nonprofit operating foundation located in St. Paul, Minnesota. It provides a wide range of effective and often quite innovative social services and programs. Its mission statement, presented in Exhibit 4.4, is somewhat lengthy, but also clearly authorizes and prompts the foundation to seek the biggest impact it can in its chosen domain. Wilder has been guided by virtually the same mission for over one hundred years.

A final example comes from Miami-Dade County, Florida (see Exhibit 4.5). The county is one of the largest local governments in the United States. Its approach to strategy making and strategic management systems will be discussed in Chapters Seven and Ten, respectively.

PROCESS DESIGN AND ACTION GUIDELINES

Several process guidelines should be kept in mind as a strategic planning group works at clarification of mission and mandates:

1. *Someone should be put in charge of compiling the organization's formal and informal mandates.* The group should then review and

Exhibit 4.4. The Wilder Foundation Mission Statement.

Our mission: To promote the social welfare of persons resident or located in the greater Saint Paul metropolitan area by all appropriate means, including:

- Relief of the poor
- Care of the sick and aged
- Care and nurture of children
- Aid of the disadvantaged and otherwise needy
- Promotion of physical and mental health
- Support of rehabilitation and corrections
- Provision of needed housing and social services
- Operation of residences and facilities for the aged, the infirm and those requiring special care

And in general the conservation of human resources by the provision of human services responsive to the welfare needs of the community, all without regard to, or discrimination on account of, nationality, sex, color, religious scruples or prejudices.

Source: http://www.wilder.org/aboutus.0.html; accessed February 5, 2011.

discuss this list and make any modifications that seem appropriate. The group should pay particular attention to what is required, what is not ruled out, and what mandates the organization should try to change.

2. *The group should complete a stakeholder analysis using the worksheets found in Bryson and Alston (2011) (the worksheets take the group through the Basic Analysis Technique and Power Versus Interest Grid; other techniques are discussed in Resource A).* Public and nonprofit organizations typically consist of shifting coalitions involving networks of internal and external stakeholders. Organizational purpose should be crafted at least in part out of a consideration of these stakeholders' interests. Otherwise, successful agreement on organizational purposes is unlikely (Fisher & Ury, 1991; Thompson, 2008).

3. *After completing the stakeholder analysis, the group should fill out the mission statement worksheets also found in Bryson and Alston*

Exhibit 4.5. Miami-Dade County Mission Statement and Guiding Principles.

Miami-Dade County's Mission Statement

Delivering excellent public services that address our community's needs and enhance our quality of life.

Miami-Dade County's Guiding Principles

- Customer-Focused and Customer-Driven
- Honest, Ethical and Fair to All
- Accountable and Responsive to the Public
- Diverse and Sensitive
- Efficient and Effective
- Committed to Development of Leadership in Public Service
- Innovative
- Valuing and Respectful of Each Other
- Action-Oriented

Source: http://www.miamidade.gov/manager/mission.asp; accessed on February 5, 2011.

(*2011*). Group members should fill them out as individuals first, and then discuss their answers as a group. Extra time must be reserved for a "culture audit," which is necessary to identify organizational philosophy, values, and culture. (Guidelines for performing a culture audit will be found in Khademian, 2002, pp. 108–123; Schein, 2010, pp. 315–325; Johnson, Scholes, & Whittington, 2008, pp. 178–206).

4. *After answering the questions and discussing the answers, the group should turn the task of developing a draft mission statement (and perhaps a separate values statement) over to an individual.* It is very important to allow sufficient time for deliberation about the draft mission statement, particularly if any changes in mission are contemplated by the draft. Quick agreement may occur, but should not be expected. It is particularly important that the mission either be directly measurable or measurable indirectly through closely associated measurable goals or performance indicators. Otherwise, the mission may

well be a "mission impossible" and the satisfaction of employees and other key stakeholders may suffer (Wright & Davis, 2003; Poister, 2003; Patton, 2008). Sawhill and Williamson (2001) found that the nonprofit organizations they studied had the most success with the indirect measurement approach, although the direct approach could work as well. The best of the measurable missions or goals: "(1) set the bar high, (2) helped focus the organization on high-leverage strategies, (3) mobilized the staff and donors, and (4) served multiple purposes, such as setting the larger public agenda about a certain issue" (p. 383). Further, organizations found that it was best to keep measures simple and easy to communicate, that the measures and performance against them made the organization "marketable" to boards of directors and donors interested in effectiveness and accountability; and the measures made management easier (pp. 384–385).

After an agreed-upon mission statement is developed, the group also may wish to brainstorm a slogan that captures the essence of the mission, or run a contest among organizational members or stakeholders for an appropriate slogan. For example, a public library with which I worked came up with the wonderful slogan, "Mind of the City," which emphasizes intelligence, learning, information and information technology, community, and wholeness, rather than an older view of libraries as book warehouses.

5. *It is important not to get stalled by development of a mission statement.* If the group hits a snag, record areas of agreement and disagreement, and then move on to the next steps. Return later to discuss the mission based on any additional information or solutions that turn up in future steps.

6. *Strategic planning teams should expect to have to reexamine their draft mission statement as they move through the process, either to reaffirm the statement or to redraft it in light of additional information or reflection.* Even if the organization has a satisfactory mission statement, it still should expect to reexamine the statement periodically during the process. Steps 4 through 6 provide additional opportunities to discuss the mission. As the process continues, more detail may be added to the mission statement in terms of types of programs, products, services, or relationships that will be offered to stakeholders, particularly those who are customers.

7. *Once agreement is reached on a mission statement, it should be kept before the strategic planning group as it moves through the planning process.* The group should refer to the statement as it seeks to formulate goals, identify strategic issues, develop effective strategies,

prepare a vision of success, and in general resolve conflicts among the team. The organization's mission provides a basis for resolving conflicts based on purposes and interests, not positions (Fisher & Ury, 1991; Schwarz, 2002; Thompson, 2008).

8. *Once general agreement is reached, the mission should be visibly before all organizational members.* It should be referred to in preambles to official organizational actions and posted on walls and in offices; it should become a *physical* presence in the organization. Otherwise, it is likely to be forgotten at the very times it is most needed. Explicit reference to the mission should be the standard first step in resolving conflicts. The organization that forgets its mission will drift, and opportunism and the loss of integrity are likely to spread and perhaps become rampant. Organizational survival itself— or at least the survival of its leadership—will then be in serious question (Selznick, 1957; Kouzes & Posner, 2008).

9. *Adoption of the organization's mission should mark an important decision point.* Agreement may not occur at the end of this step, however, as the draft mission may be revised over the course of the strategic planning process. Formal agreement on the organization's mission definitely should be reached by the end of the strategy development step or review and adoption step.

10. *Organizations not engaged in a full-blown strategic planning process may still want to hold mission retreats periodically to reaffirm and/or revisit and modify their mission.* Retreats that prompt organizational members to focus on mission (and vision) may be helpful during the organization's formative period and at multiyear intervals after that (Angelica, 2001, pp. 11–12; Weisman, 2003). The dialogue at such retreats may bring to light the need for some organizational tinkering that can be dealt with promptly, or perhaps highlight a strategic issue to be addressed later.

SUMMARY

This chapter has discussed the identification of mandates an organization faces and clarifying the mission it wishes to pursue. Mandates are typically imposed from the outside and may be considered the "musts" that the organization is required to pursue (although it may want to do them as well). Mission is developed more from the inside; it identifies the organization's purposes. Mission may be considered what the organization "wants" to do. Rarely is an organization so boxed in by mandates that its mission is totally limited to meeting the mandates. Mandates and mission jointly frame the domain within which the organization seeks to create public value. Jointly they articulate the boundaries for desirable search and action in pursuit of organizational purposes, on the one hand, and the territory of prohibited actions, on the other hand. In other words, a consideration of mandates and mission forces organizations to examine "the cost both of failure to do what is required of them and of failure to do what they want to do" (Hill & Hupe, 2009, p. 72). Creating lasting public value requires that the enduring benefits of what the organization does do and does not do must significantly outweigh the costs.

CHAPTER FIVE

Assessing the Environment to Identify Strengths and Weaknesses, Opportunities and Challenges

You wouldn't think that something as complexly
busy as life would be so easy to overlook.
—Diane Ackerman, *A Natural History of the Senses*

So it is said that if you know others and know yourself,
you will not be imperiled in a hundred battles; if you do
not know others, but do know yourself, you win one
and lose one; if you do not know others and do not
know yourself, you will be imperiled in every single battle.
—Sun Tzu, *The Art of War*

To respond effectively to changes in their environments, public and non-profit organizations (collaborations and communities) must understand the external and internal contexts within which they find themselves, so that they can develop effective strategies to link the two in such a way that significant and long-lasting public value is created. The word *context* comes from the Latin for "weave together," and that is exactly what well-done external and internal environmental assessments help organizations do: weave together their understandings and actions in a sensible way so that organizational performance is enhanced. As Weick (1995, p. 104) observes, "Sensemaking is about context. Wholes and cues, documents and meanings, figures and ground, periphery and center, all define one another. Sensibleness derives from relationships, not parts." Sensemaking is needed to weave hindsight, foresight, and insight into sensible action.

The sheer pace of change in the world at large heightens the need for effective assessments. It seems as if the future is hurtling toward us more quickly, dramatically, and disruptively than ever—and this can be alternately confusing, pleasing, or downright scary. There are disputes about whether or not the pace of change is accelerating (Mintzberg, 1994; Barkema, Baum, & Mannix, 2002; Ball, 2004). Whether it is or not, there is enough change all around that wise organizational leaders feel compelled to pay attention. In part this is because change so often occurs where, when, how, and in a form that is least expected—which, of course, is exactly what you should *expect* in a complex, richly interconnected world (Kelly, 1994; Ball, 2004; Senge, 2006). In other words, the pace of change may or may not have increased, but the complexity of the systems that make up the world almost certainly has. A complex system is:

> One made up of a large number of parts that have many interactions. . . . [In] such systems the whole is more than the sum of the parts in the weak but important pragmatic sense that, given the properties of the parts and the laws of their interaction, it is not a trivial matter to infer the properties of the whole (Simon, 1996, pp. 184–185).

As a result, change anywhere can result in unpredictable results elsewhere as the behavior of complex systems often demonstrates a sensitive and unpredictable dependence on initial conditions (Gleick, 1988, 1999; Weick and Sutcliffe, 2007).

Some of these changes might be what Taleb (2007, p. xxii) calls Black Swan events, where the term *black swan* refers to exceedingly rare events in a world where it is assumed all swans must be white. Black Swan events are high-impact events that are both unusual—statistically extreme outliers—and highly consequential. Taleb cites World War I, the rise of the personal computer, the Internet, and the events of September 11, 2001, as examples. More recently we might add the global financial meltdown of 2007–2009; the eruption of Iceland's *Eyjafjallajökull,* which means "island mountain volcano," that stranded millions of travelers worldwide (including yours truly); and the allegedly impossible destruction of British Petroleum's *Deepwater Horizon* oil platform resulting in one of the worst environmental disasters in U.S. history. Some may dispute the unpredictability of these occurrences, but the fact is that most people were taken by surprise as much of their world changed dramatically around them, temporarily in some cases and profoundly in others. Not all of this is new, of course. Around 400 BCE, Plato observed in the dialogue *Cratylus,* "Everything changes and nothing remains still" (paragraph 402, section a, line 8). But the sheer scope and scale of hard-to-predict changes emanating from unexpected sources probably is new.

PURPOSE

The purpose of Step 4 in the strategic planning process, therefore, is to provide information on the strengths and weaknesses of the organization in relation to the opportunities and challenges or threats it faces. This information can be used, as Figure 2.3 indicates, to create ideas for strategic interventions that would shape and guide organizational decisions and actions designed to create public value. Strengths and weaknesses are usually internal and refer to the present capacity of the organization, whereas opportunities and challenges are typically external and refer to future potentials for good or ill. The distinctions, however, between internal and external and present and future orientations are fluid and people should not worry too much about whether they have drawn them properly.

In addition, collaborations and communities may wish to focus not on strengths, weaknesses, opportunities, and challenges, but on their hopes and concerns for the community. The reason is that the distinction between internal and external ceases to be very meaningful when applied to collaborations or communities, because what is internal and external for groups and organizations who will be key implementers is not the same as what is internal and external for the collaboration or jurisdiction. Beyond that, attention to hopes and fears is more likely to elicit value concerns (Weick, 1995, pp. 30, 127), which may be more central to collaboration or community-oriented strategic planning than to strategic planning for organizations (Provan & Milward, 2001; Stone, 2002; Agranoff, 2007). (Interestingly, delineation of hopes often may lead directly to the articulation of goals and strategic issues; enumerating fears helps identify strategic issues that must be addressed in order to achieve the goals, in part by avoiding what might be called *negative goals*, or serious outcomes to be avoided; see Bryson, Ackermann, Eden, & Finn, 2004, pp. 161–163. The desire to avoid negative outcomes is often more motivating than the desire to achieve more positive outcomes; see Eden & Ackermann, 2010.)

The approach to external and internal environmental assessments outlined in this chapter will set the stage for the identification of strategic issues in Step 5. It will also provide valuable information for use in the following step, strategy development. Strategic issues typically concern how the organization (what is inside) relates to the larger environment it inhabits (what is outside). Every effective strategy will take advantage of strengths and opportunities at the same time it minimizes or overcomes weaknesses and challenges. In other words, a good strategy will link inside and outside in effective ways.

Chapter One highlighted several major trends and events that are currently forcing often-drastic changes on governments, public agencies, and nonprofit organizations. Unfortunately, for various reasons, public and nonprofit organizations typically are not very savvy about perceiving such changes quickly enough to respond effectively (Light, 1998, p. 66; Weick & Sutcliffe, 2007). Instead, a crisis often has to develop before organizations respond (Wilson, 1989). This may open up significant *opportunity spaces*, but for the unprepared organization many useful avenues of response typically will be closed off by the time a crisis emerges (Bryson, 1981, pp. 185–189; Mitroff & Anagnos, 2005).

Also, in crisis situations people typically stereotype, withdraw, project, rationalize, oversimplify, and otherwise make errors likely to produce unwise decisions (Janis, 1989). The result can be colossal errors and debacles (Tuchman, 1984; Nutt, 2002). A major purpose of any strategic planning exercise therefore is to alert an organization to the various external or future-oriented threats and challenges that may prompt or require an organizational response in the foreseeable future. In other words, a major purpose of strategic planning is to instill the kind of "mindfulness" (Weick & Sutcliffe, 2007, p. 32) or "support for sensemaking" (Weick, 1995, p. 179) that prompts timely learning and action and prepares an organization to respond effectively to the outside world either before a crisis emerges or when one cannot be avoided. Even in a crisis, however, organizations can use many of the concepts, procedures, and tools of strategic planning to help them think and act strategically (Mitroff & Anagnos, 2005).

But any effective response to potential challenges or opportunities must be based on an intimate knowledge of the organization's competencies and the strengths and weaknesses they entail. Strategic planning, in other words, is concerned with finding the best or most advantageous fit between an organization and its larger environment based on an intimate understanding of both. Finding that fit may involve changing the organization, affecting the environment, or both.

DESIRED IMMEDIATE OUTCOMES

Step 4 produces documented lists of external or future-oriented organizational opportunities and challenges or threats and internal or present strengths and weaknesses. Ordered differently, these four lists comprise a SWOC/T analysis, a popular strategic planning tool. Note that traditionally challenges have been called *threats,* but experience and research indicate that talking about threats may be *too threatening* to many strategic planning participants. Characterizing things as threats can lead to rigidity in thinking or, alternatively, excessively risky behavior in response to the threat (see, for example, Staw, Sandelands, & Dutton, 1981; Dutton & Jackson, 1987; Chattopadhyay, Glick, & Huber, 2001). My own experience and that of other consultants with whom I work indicates that the more neutral label *challenges* seems to open people up more to considering a range of possible futures and actions. If the threat category alone is used, the SWOC/T analysis becomes a SWOT analysis, a more commonly used term (see Bryson, 2001, 2003).

The SWOC/T analysis, in conjunction with a stakeholder analysis, can help the team to identify what the organization's *critical success factors* (CSFs) (also called *key success factors*) are (Johnson, Scholes, & Whittington, 2008). These are the things the organization must do, criteria it must meet, or performance indicators it must do well against (because they matter to key stakeholders) for it to survive and prosper. Key success factors, in other words, function as important performance requirements that the organization's strategies as a set must meet. In addition, the team should be encouraged to clarify the organization's *distinctive competencies* (Selznick, 1957; Prahalad & Hamel, 1990; Van der Heijden, 2005; Eden & Ackermann, 2010). Here some definitions are helpful: a *competency* is an *ability*, sets of actions or processes that an organization can manage and that ideally help it perform well (the desired outcome) against important goals, desired competency outcomes, or CSFs (which should also be desired outcomes) (Eden & Ackermann, 2010). In other words, an organization may have a competency, but if it does not help the organization do well against a goal or CSF, it is not much of a competency—unless stakeholders can be convinced to change what their CSFs are. Competencies usually arise and are perfected through "learning by doing" (Joyce, 1999, p. 35). A *distinctive competency* is a competency that is very difficult for others to replicate, and so is a source of enduring organizational advantage. A *core competency* is really central to the success of the organization, that is, crucial to its doing well against goals or CSFs. A *distinctive core competency* is not only central to the success of the organization, but helps the organization add more public value than alternative providers. Examples of distinctive core competencies might be what goes into providing outstanding customer service, maintaining a strong reputation and the trust of key stakeholders, or being resilient in the face of crises. Note that a competency indicates *an ability to do something*, so providing outstanding service is not a competency *per se*, but the specific abilities that make it possible to do so are. Outstanding service is the *competency outcome* of making use of the competencies needed and being available to do so. Usually distinctive core competencies arise from the interrelationships of a set of competencies and core competencies. It is the interrelationships that are particularly hard for others to replicate, for example, because they are based on tacit knowledge and long-term relationships (Eden & Ackermann, 1998; Eden & Ackermann, 2010). Guidance on identifying competencies will be found in Resource C.

A particularly useful outcome is the creation of the organization's current *livelihood scheme* (Bryson, Ackermann, & Eden, 2007; Eden & Ackermann, 2010) that shows how competencies are directly related to aspirations, including helping to do well against key success factors necessary to achieve the aspirations. A livelihood scheme represents the core logic of a strategic plan; namely, mission, goals, key success factors or performance indicators, and the necessary competencies to do well against each. Each aspiration and key success factor must be supported by a competency, or else it is not achievable. As Hill and Hupe (2009, p. 195) argue, "among possibly the most relevant factors" for fostering effective implementation is directly linking "ambition ('willing') and competence ('being able')." Guidance on developing a livelihood scheme will also be found in Resource C. Note that the current livelihood scheme may well be changed as a result of further strategic planning work.

Before completing a SWOC/T analysis, it may be necessary to prepare various background reports on external forces and trends; on key resource controllers, such as clients, customers, payers, or dues-paying members; and on competitors and collaborators (Stone and Sandfort, 2009); with additional reports on internal resources, present strategy, and performance. It may also be necessary to prepare various *scenarios*, or stories, that capture important elements of possible futures for the organization—delineating strengths, weaknesses, opportunities, and challenges, as well as key success factors and competencies, which are then assessed in relation to these possible futures (Schwartz, 1996; Van der Heijden, 2005; Marcus, 2009). Further, once the lists of SWOC/Ts, key success factors, and competencies is prepared (with or without the help of scenarios), it may be necessary to commission careful analyses of some listed items in relation to the overall strategic posture of the organization.

Another important early outcome of these two steps may be specific, relatively immediate actions to deal with challenges, threats, and weaknesses; build on strengths (including especially distinctive core competencies); and take advantage of opportunities (including improving performance against key success factors). As soon as appropriate moves become apparent, key decision makers should consider taking action. It is not only unnecessary, but probably also undesirable, to draw a sharp temporal distinction between planning and implementation. As long as the contemplated actions are based on reasonable information, have adequate support, and do not foreclose important strategic options, serious consideration should be given to taking them. The feedback arrows in Figure 2.1 try to capture this continuous blending and interplay of thinking and acting, doing and learning, planning and implementation, and strategic and operational concerns. This kind of prompt action in response to a rich appreciation of the interconnectedness of the organization's operations and its environment is the essence of "mindfulness" (Weick & Sutcliffe, 2007).

Short, thoughtful deliberations among key decision makers and opinion leaders concerning strengths, weaknesses, opportunities and challenges, key success factors, distinctive competencies, and immediate desirable short-term actions are one of the most important outcomes of this step. Such deliberations— particularly when they bridge various intra- and interorganizational boundaries—provide important quantitative and qualitative insights into the organization and its environment, and also prepare the way for the identification of strategic issues in the next step. Strategic issues will stem from the convergence of these factors. Discussions such as these are absolutely crucial in order to move from what individuals do (intuit and interpret) to what groups do (integrate information) to what organizations do (institutionalize information) (Crossan, Lane, & White, 1999). To paraphrase marketing guru Paco Underhill (1999), such discussions provide a way to make apparent what perhaps *ought* to be obvious, but is not, and then to act on it. Paying attention to the obvious is one important key to success in a competitive world. As Isaac Asimov supposedly said, "Pay attention to the obvious—no one else will."

But be aware that getting key stakeholders to engage in these sorts of analyses and deliberation is not necessarily easy. People can find many more reasons not to engage in a SWOC/T analysis than they can to participate. The reasons are familiar: participants may argue that they have no time or that they already know the answers. Other opinions may not be voiced, but nonetheless be strongly held. People may be afraid of discussing weaknesses and threats. They may not want to know what a SWOC/T analysis will reveal. Or they may simply not know how to do one and feel embarrassed by their lack of knowledge. Whatever the reasons, process sponsors and champions should strongly encourage engaging in a SWOC/T analysis. The deliberations can be extremely helpful and actually should result in some very direct positive change. That said, it is possible to do SWOC/T analyses at various places in the process, and sometimes the most effective places to do the analyses are in relation to specific strategic issues (Step 5) or strategies (Step 6). In those steps the analysis will seem more grounded and specific to many people.

LONGER-TERM DESIRED OUTCOMES

An effective external and internal environmental assessment should result in several longer-term benefits to the organization. Among the most important is that it will produce information that is vital to the organization's survival and prosperity. It is difficult to imagine that an organization can be truly effective over the long haul unless it has an intimate knowledge of its strengths and weaknesses in relation to the opportunities and challenges it faces, as Sun Tzu observed over 2,500 years ago.

Said somewhat differently, Step 4 allows the strategic planning team to develop the habit of seeing the organization as a whole in relation to its environment. This is usually one of the singular accomplishments of strategic planning. An ability to see the organization as a whole in relation to its environment keeps the organization from being victimized by the present. Instead, the organization has a basis for *reasoned* optimism, in that difficulties may be seen as specific rather than pervasive, temporary rather than permanent, and the result of factors other than irremediable organizational incompetence (Seligman, 1998; Kouzes & Posner, 2002). The organization thus prepares itself to follow Hubert Humphrey's advice: "Instead of worrying about the future, let us labor to create it" (Humphrey, 1959).

Step 4 clarifies for the organization the nature of the *tension fields* within which it exists. Backoff and his coauthors (Wechsler & Backoff, 1987; Nutt & Backoff, 1992, 1996) argue that every organization must manage the tensions among its capacities and intentions in relation to the opportunities and challenges it faces. A SWOC/T analysis clarifies the nature of these tensions by juxtaposing two fundamental dimensions of existence: good (strengths and opportunities) and bad (weaknesses and challenges or threats), as well as present (strengths and weaknesses) and future (opportunities and challenges). A SWOC/T analysis in conjunction with an understanding of key success factors and distinctive competencies helps clarify the tensions that arise when trends and events juxtapose concerns for equity, productivity, preservation, and change.

External and internal assessments also develop the boundary-spanning skills of key staff, especially key decision makers and opinion leaders. Assessments draw attention to issues and information that cross internal and external organizational boundaries. In effect, key decision makers and opinion leaders are prompted to move beyond their job descriptions in their thinking and discussions, increasing the opportunities for them to produce creative and integrative insights and actions that bridge functions and levels of the organization and link it to its environment (Ford & Ford, 1995).

In large organizations, completion of Step 4 may be an impetus for establishing a formal environmental scanning operation, if one does not exist already (Pflaum & Delmont, 1987; Johnson, Scholes, & Whittington, 2008). It will need adequate staff—typically an in-house coordinator, plus volunteer in-house scanners, including, ideally, persons with major decision-making responsibility. Added staff may be needed for special studies. Scanning should result in periodic meetings to discuss what people are learning, plus a newsletter or some other form of regular report distributed widely within the organization. Special studies that produce detailed analyses may also need to be distributed widely. Environmental scanning, however, never should be allowed to become a bureaucratic, paper-pushing exercise. It should be kept simple and relatively informal; otherwise it will deaden strategic thought and action, not promote it. One important way of staying on track is to always let purpose—in terms of meeting mandates, fulfilling mission, and creating public value—be your guide. Paying attention to purpose can help you engage in limited, rather than overwhelming and useless, information collection (Nadler & Hibino, 1998).

The most effective scanning operations will be part of a network of scanners or boundary spanners from several organizations who exchange information and mutually develop scanning and boundary-spanning skills and insights. If this network does not exist, it may be possible to create it through regular meetings and the use of electronic support. The point is for people to keep their eyes open and to talk about what they see—rather than overlook what might be important, as this chapter's opening epigraph by Diane Ackerman indicates may happen. Paying attention also means not being blinded by existing categories or expectations, because they will reveal some things and hide others. Categories are a necessary part of sensemaking; they help trim the amount of information that must be absorbed. But what is trimmed and then hidden may turn out to be what is most important (Weick & Sutcliffe, 2007; Mintzberg, Ahlstrand, & Lampel, 2009). So paying attention also means staying open to surprises. As J.R.R. Tolkien says in *The Hobbit* (1982 [1937], p. 58), "You certainly find something if you look, but it is not always quite the something you were after."

Completion of Step 4 also should prompt development or refinement of an effective management information system (MIS) that includes input, process, and output (and outcome, if possible) categories, if one does not already exist. An effective MIS system usually is expensive and time-consuming to develop, but without it the organization may be unable to assess, relatively objectively and unambiguously, its strengths, weaknesses, efficiency, and effectiveness. If an organization is using a Balanced Score Card (discussed in Chapters Two and Seven), the MIS should support the use of the scorecard. Again, the MIS system should not be allowed to become excessively bureaucratic or cumbersome. And in no circumstances should the MIS system drive out attention to the kinds of qualitative information so vital to real understanding and so useful to effective managers (Mintzberg, 1973; Innes, 1998). As Mintzberg (1994, p. 266) notes, "While hard data may inform the intellect, it is largely soft data that generates wisdom." Beyond that, the MIS system should be designed to serve organizational purposes, and if they change, or the strategies for achieving them change, the MIS system should change, too.

If reasonably routine, formal environmental scanning and MIS operations are established, along with regular dialogues on what the information means, then the organization will have routinized attention to major and minor external trends, issues, events, and stakeholders, and to internal inputs, processes, and outputs (Emmert, Crow, & Shangraw, 1993). The chances of encountering major surprises are reduced and the possibilities for anticipatory actions enhanced—particularly if the systems themselves are the subject of mindful scrutiny.

But even if external scanning and MIS systems are not institutionalized, the organization will have become more externally oriented if it engages in periodic assessments, and will gain a better understanding of its internal strengths and weaknesses in relation to what is outside. In my experience, organizations tend to be rather insular and parochial and must be forced to face outward.

Unless they face out, they are virtually certain not to satisfy key external stakeholders and to be overwhelmed by the unexpected.

In addition, people should never assume that the existence of any formalized systems of environmental assessment and management information relieve them of the need to constantly pay attention to what is going on in the outside world and to talk about it. For one thing, as noted, systems are designed around categories—and the categories may be outdated or simply wrong. The categories may make it hard or impossible to see important new developments that do not fit the categories (Mintzberg, 1994; Weick & Sutcliffe, 2007). So the best advice may come from Yogi Berra, who once aptly observed, "You can observe an awful lot just by watching." Beyond that, perhaps writer Salmon Rushdie is right: most of what matters in our lives takes place in our absence (Rushdie, 1981, pp. 19, 236). But that does not mean one has to be taken completely by surprise.

As noted above, an important immediate outcome of this step is that timely actions may be taken based on the analyses and conversations. But the outcome has a longer-term aspect as well; whenever appropriate actions become apparent at any point throughout the process, they should be taken, as long they are based on reasonable information, have adequate support, and do not prematurely close off important strategic avenues. Indeed, the organization should work to make this habit of prompt, informed action a distinctive core competency (Weick & Sutcliffe, 2007).

EXTERNAL ENVIRONMENTAL ASSESSMENTS

The purpose of the first part of Step 4 is to explore the environment outside the organization in order to identify the opportunities and challenges the organization faces (and ideally, in conjunction with stakeholder analyses, to identify key success factors). Figure 2.1 identifies three major categories that might be monitored in such an exploration: (1) forces and trends, (2) key resource controllers, and (3) actual or potential competitors or collaborators, important forces affecting competition and collaboration, and the competitive and collaborative advantages available to the organization. The three categories represent the basic foci for any effective environmental scanning system.

Forces and trends are often broken down into political, economic, social, technological, environmental, and legal categories (Johnson, Scholes, & Whittington, 2008). Organizations may choose to monitor additional categories that are particularly relevant. For example, colleges and universities usually add education, and public health care organizations monitor health outcomes. Strategic planners must be sure they attend to both threats and challenges in whatever categories are used.

What are the recent issues and trends affecting public and nonprofit sector organizations? Innumerable reviews and forecasts are available, but it is hard to know what to make of them (for example, Huntingdon, 1998; Glassner, 2010; Schwartz, 2004; Friedman, 2007; Watson, 2008; Stiglitz, 2010; World Future Society, 2008). For example, Schwartz, Leyden, and Hyatt's 1999 book *The Long Boom*, published at the height of the economic and stock market boom of the 1990s, seems decidedly optimistic as of 2010, after the sharp recession of 2001 and the worst economic downturn since the Great Depression of the 1930s in 2007 through 2009, sometimes called the Great Recession. But they are looking twenty-five years ahead and, who knows, they may be right. I hope they are. On the other hand, as W. S. Gilbert said, in *H.M.S. Pinafore*, "Things are seldom what they seem, skim milk masquerades as cream," and the trick is to figure out which is which. What follows is a quick review of much of this literature focused particularly on the United States in the form of ten interconnected categories of forces or trends of particular importance to the public and nonprofit sectors:

1. *Social and organizational complexity.* The complexity is driven by a number of forces, including technological change, the globalization of information and economies, and the consequent interconnectedness of almost everything (Ball, 2005; Mulgan, 2009). Meanwhile, many of our most important institutions were designed for a world that was more stable and simple. As a result, there are serious institutional mismatches between the problems or issues that need to be addressed and the institutional arrangements for doing so (Schön, 1971; Kettl, 2005, 2008; Abramson, Bruel, & Kamensky, 2006; Innes & Booher, 2010). We can expect serious interventions in selected areas, such as financial regulation, health care and educational reform, environmental protection, and homeland security to alleviate some of the mismatches (Mulgan, 2009). In other words, in contrast to the backing off from government interventions in the 1980s and 1990s, we can expect more of what Hill and Hupe call "neo-interventionism" involving forceful, concerted, but very selective government interventions to address important public problems, (2009, pp. 91–101).

2. *Reform and redirection of governments and increased interaction among public, private, and nonprofit sectors.* Citizens in the developed nations around the world have been asking for more effective, and often smaller and cheaper, governments. Given the massive debts run up by the United States, United Kingdom, and other governments in order to stave off global depression, this means that in very practical terms there will be limited economic growth and public-sector

resources and interventions will therefore need to be very targeted. Specifically, this means that the size of government is not likely to increase in relation to gross domestic product (GDP) although the overall cost of public problems almost certainly will (Osborne & Hutchinson, 2004). On the other hand, citizens have also asked for more programs and better services. In order to resolve this paradox, governments are experimenting with numerous ideas to be more productive, to improve performance, and to reduce costs (Light, 1998, 2005; Pollitt & Bouckaert, 2000; Kettl, 2008). Ultimately, this means changing the focus on *government* to resolve public problems to emphasizing *governance* as a shared phenomenon in which the institutions of public, private, and nonprofit sectors and civil society share the effort and responsibility for the common good (Osborne, 2010). Effective governance will place a premium on inclusion of multiple organizations and perspectives, systems thinking, and speed of analysis, synthesis, and response, which are quite hard to do simultaneously (Bryson, 2003). As outlined by David Osborne and his associates (Osborne & Gaebler, 1992; Osborne & Plastrik, 1997; Osborne & Hutchinson, 2004), government's principal role is to steer, not row, but steering can also involve very direct and forceful intervention when needed. Governments of the future—and not just in the United States—will rely far more on the nonprofit and for-profit sectors to do much of the actual rowing (Kettl, 2008). Opportunities for increased effectiveness will be opened to organizations in each sector, but numerous challenges will arise as well through heightened competitive pressures, uncertainty, and revenue instability.

3. *Continuation of technological change.* Many futurists and economists see technological innovation as *the* major force driving change (Cleveland, 2002; Ruttan, 2003). Nanotechnology, biotechnology, materials science, and information technology, among other areas, will alter many aspects of our lives in unforeseeable ways. Public and nonprofit organizational personnel will need new skills to utilize new technologies, while their organizations will need to adapt their processes, structures, and resource allocation patterns. Information technologies, in particular, are driving major changes likely to have dramatic impacts on organizational performance, accountability, stakeholder empowerment, and issues related to data use and privacy (Yang & Melitski, 2007; Behn, 2008). For many organizations moving into e-commerce or e-government, making use of information technology is of paramount importance.

4. *Diversity of workforce, clientele, and citizenry.* The diversity will take many forms, including racial, ethnic, gender, and cultural, but also in almost any other category you can imagine, including those related to knowledge, expertise, and competence. The result will be a *demassified* version of the *mass society* of the 1950s and early 1960s (Toffler, 1971). In addition, as people live longer the numbers of senior citizens will increase dramatically in most advanced economies, increasing the need for many public services while simultaneously increasing the fraction of people out of the taxpaying workforce. In the jargon of strategic planning, the number of stakeholders is increasing, each with its own ideas, interests, and needs. This differentiation will complicate the quest for public value, governance, service design and delivery, and workforce recruitment, retention, training, and management.

5. *Individualism, personal responsibility, and civic republicanism.* Most futurists envision a move away from reliance on large institutions, particularly governmental institutions, and toward self-reliance and greater personal responsibility. U.S. welfare reform initiatives of the 1990s emphasized these values, as do reforms of the U.S. tax code to favor saving rather than spending. Critics of the recent expansion of health insurance in the United States see it as a big-government program, but the fact is most of the insurance will be provided by the private sector and will make it easier for individuals to take responsibility for themselves and their families. There are also signs that citizenship is being reinvigorated to emphasize active citizen involvement in public problem solving and governance—the kind of "civic republicanism" favored by Jefferson and the Anti-Federalists, Jacksonian Democrats, the Populists, John Dewey and many of the Progressives, and the present-day communitarians (Dewey, 1927/1954; Gastil & Levine, 2005; Leighninger, 2006; Jacobs, Cook, & Delli Carpini, 2009). But citizen action is going against the tide at present, when *social capital* of many kinds has been in decline for decades (Putnam, 2000). Social capital formation is the antidote to excessive individualism (Putnam, Feldstein, & Cohen, 2004).

6. *Quality of life and environmentalism.* Concern for the quality of life is likely to increase. The sources of these concerns are numerous, including the emergence of an era when time is more scarce than money for many people (Gleick, 1999). There also is a search for meaning beyond work, fears for the long-term viability of the planet, and worry about health and physical safety issues. The increased influence of women in the workplace is bringing with it demands for changes in the workplace. Flexibility and workplace improvements

are likely to be needed and demanded, further health care reform will be necessary to get costs down and quality of care up, crime prevention and control will be called for (yet difficult to provide), and "green" policies and practices will be preferred by a majority of the population.

7. *Struggles for legitimacy and the changing American dream.* Governments at all levels, churches of many kinds, a host of nonprofit organizations (for example, the Red Cross, United Way, Boy Scouts), and many corporations (for example, Goldman Sachs, Toyota, British Petroleum) have seen their legitimacy undermined as a consequence of poor performance, scandals, or sometimes concerted ideological attack. There are not many icons left to topple and legitimacy is increasingly difficult to attain as much of what was previously taken for granted is questioned (Suchman, 1995). In the midst of all this, the American Dream has been changing. Andrew Delbanco (1999) argues that in the Colonial era, the dream involved doing or realizing God's will in the New World. From the early republic to Lyndon Johnson's Great Society, the dream was secularized as an ideal of the sacred nation state—smaller than God, but larger and more enduring than the individual American citizen. Abraham Lincoln's *Second Inaugural* captures perfectly this sense of transcendence through national union (Wills, 2006). Now, however, "hope has narrowed to the vanishing point of self alone" (Delbanco, 1999, p. 103). Delbanco goes on to argue, however, that ironically "the most striking feature of contemporary culture is the unslaked craving for transcendence" (p. 114; see also Aburdene, 2005). This is very dangerous for the United States, for as University of California, Berkeley, social scientist Robert Reich has argued, "Unlike the citizens of most other nations, Americans have always been united less by a shared past than by the shared dreams of a better future. If we lose that common future, we lose the glue that holds the nation together" (quoted in Glassner, 1999, p. xviii). The big worry, at least in the foreign policy arena, is that the glue that holds us together will be a legitimate fear of terrorism coupled with a quite irrational xenophobia and perhaps zeal for our own ideals that are used by ambitious politicians and others to muster the will to impose our will abroad by force—no matter what the precedents, legality, costs, and destruction left in its wake (Monbiot, 2003). The War in Iraq is Exhibit A for this kind of misadventure (for example, Ricks, 2006; Packer, 2006). If there is a silver lining to the massive federal debt, it is that we can't afford another so-called *war of choice* anytime soon.

8. *Culture of fear.* It should not be surprising that we have developed what University of Southern California sociologist Barry Glassner (2010) calls a "culture of fear" in a our very diverse culture in which so many icons have been toppled, social capital is in decline, a transcendent faith in the purpose of life has diminished, and the American Dream is increasingly focused on the self. Mainly what we fear is individuals of many kinds—black males, pedophiles, single mothers, teenagers, drug dealers, and so on. We also fear plane crashes. What is so striking about all these fears—media hype notwithstanding—is how truly small the risks really are. Take plane crashes for example: even when you take terrorism into account, you are far more likely to be struck by lightning than to die in a plane crash. Or crime: while press coverage of crimes went *up* in the 1990s and 2000s, crime typically was going *down*. As Glassner notes, "In just about every American scare, rather than confront disturbing shortcomings in society the public discussion centers on disturbed individuals" (p. 6). As individuals we have become a market for fears, and there are plenty of media sources, pundits, and politicians to supply them. As communities and as a nation we have the wherewithal to address those fears, but we have to relearn how to be the vibrant civil society and democracy we once were if we are to succeed. Meanwhile, things we really ought to fear and do something about include the ill effects of poverty; an extraordinarily expensive health care system that underperforms the much cheaper systems in many other developed countries; poor education; the almost 18,500 homicides and 34,500 suicides that occur each year; and the untold misery resulting from the almost unbelievable proliferation of handguns (National Center for Health Statistics, 2007). We also should fear the serious decline in social capital, as the loss makes us more vulnerable to fear mongers and less able to respond wisely and collectively to what we genuinely should fear. Finally, we should fear the media that sensationalizes the unusual, plays to our fears, seriously distorts our perceptions of risk, and overemphasizes personal rather than systemic causes of behavior.

9. *An emphasis on learning.* Individuals, jobs, organizations, and communities cannot stand still, given the pace of change. People, organizations, and communities must constantly be learning how to do their work better and how to make the transitions they are likely to face if they are to play constructive roles in shaping the future (Crossan, Lane, & White, 1999; Light, 2005; Senge, 2006; Weick & Sutcliffe, 2007).

10. *Transitions with continuity, not revolution.* The American tradition emphasizes *disjointed incrementalism* involving *partisan mutual adjustment* among actors (Braybrooke & Lindblom, 1963; Lindblom, 1965). We had an American Revolution, and many major convulsions such as the Civil War and Great Depression, but generally *muddling through* (Lindblom, 1959) has been our preferred strategy as a nation. As the French observer Alexis de Tocqueville observed in the mid-1830s in *Democracy in America*, "They like change, but they dread revolutions" (quoted in Damrosch, 2010, p. 205). The good news is that continuous improvement in institutions is possible; the bad news is that typically it is very difficult to stimulate major institutional change in the absence of a crisis (Kingdon, 2002; Baumgartner & Jones, 2009). Clearly it is a leadership challenge to inspire and mobilize others to undertake collective action in pursuit of the common good—producing wise small or big changes in response to the situation at hand (Crosby & Bryson, 2005).

In addition to various trends, public and nonprofit sector organizations might monitor important stakeholder groups, especially actual or potential clients, customers, payers, or members (for voluntary organizations), as well as competitors and collaborators and the forces driving competition or collaboration.

In my experience, members of a public or nonprofit organization's governing board, particularly if they are elected, are often better at identifying and assessing external threats and opportunities than are the organization's employees. Partly this is a reflection of differing roles; unlike most employees, a governing board typically has formal responsibility for relating an organization to its external environment (Thompson, 1967; Carver, 2006). In the public sector, there is a further reason. Employees get their mandates from laws, rules, and policies. Elected officials and politicians get their mandates primarily from elections. There can be a major difference between legal or quasi-legal mandates and political mandates. Politicians mostly pay attention to political mandates, because they must. Indeed, they typically employ *external environmental assessors* (pollsters, that is) to keep them informed about likely externally imposed mandates. So it actually may be easier to sell external scanning to elected officials than to planners and public administrators, given that politicians live or die by how well they scan.

Even though the board may be better than staff members at identifying external opportunities and threats, typically neither group does a systematic or effective job of external scanning. Thus, both groups should rely on a more or less formal and regular process of external assessment. The technology is fairly simple, and allows organizations to keep tabs cheaply, pragmatically, and effectively on outside trends and events that are likely to have an impact on the organization and its pursuit of its mission. A simple process is outlined later in this chapter.

In addition to performing external scanning, organizational members can construct scenarios to help them pinpoint possible opportunities and challenges (as well as the organization's internal strengths and weaknesses). A simple method of scenario construction is outlined in Resource D. More complicated, yet still relatively simple, methods will be found in Schwartz (1996), Van der Heijden (2005), and Marcus (2009).

INTERNAL ENVIRONMENTAL ASSESSMENT

The purpose of the second part of Step 4 is to assess the organization's internal environment in order to identify its strengths and weaknesses; that is, those aspects of the organization that help or hinder accomplishment of the organization's mission and fulfillment of its mandates. (Note also that communities are more likely to think in terms of assets rather than strengths—see Kretzmann & McKnight, 1997.) This step may also lead to the clarification of the organization's competencies, distinctive competencies, and distinctive core competencies. The three major categories that should be assessed (see Figure 2.1 in Chapter Two) are the basic elements of a simple systems model: resources (inputs), present strategy (process), and performance (outputs). Not only are these categories basic to any internal organizational assessment, they also are the fundamental categories around which any effective management information system (MIS) should be built (Kearns, 1996; Niven, 2008). Indeed, organizations with effective MIS systems should be in a better position to assess their strengths and weaknesses than organizations without such systems. The caveat, of course, is that no MIS system can provide all the information the organization needs—especially qualitative information, which is absolutely crucial. Culture, for example, is largely qualitative and rarely shows up in an MIS system, and yet culture is a crucial bridge across inputs, process, and outputs, and the inside and outside worlds (Khademian, 2002; Schein, 2010).

In my experience, most organizations have plenty of quantifiable information about inputs—salaries, supplies, physical plant, full-time equivalent (FTE) personnel, and so on—readily available. They typically have far less of a command of qualitative information about inputs, such as the nature of their culture—even though culture typically is crucial to their performance (Khademian, 2002; Johnson, Scholes, & Whittington, 2008).

Also, organizations generally cannot say succinctly what their present strategy is, either overall, by business process, or by function. One of the most important things a strategic planning team can do is simply to articulate clearly what the organization's current strategies-in-practice are. This role of *finders of strategy*—codifying the organization's apparent *logic model* (Knowlton & Phillips, 2009; McLaughlin & Jordan, 2010) or *value chain* (Porter, 1985; Williams & Lewis, 2008)—is a very useful role for planners (Mintzberg, Ahlstrand, & Lampel, 2009). The pattern recognition involved, and the discovery of pockets of innovative strategies in various parts of the organization, can be immensely instructive and provide a better-informed basis for assessing strengths and weaknesses. Additionally, clarifying the current strategy helps people understand exactly what the *value proposition* is that the organization offers its stakeholders—that is, precisely how the organization is going about converting inputs into outputs intended or presumed to meets its mandates, fulfill its mission, satisfy its stakeholders, and create public value (Moore, 2000, p. 197). As noted in Chapter Two, being clear about what *is* can be an extraordinarily helpful prelude to discerning what *ought* to be (Weick, 1995). As psychiatrist Fritz Perls once observed, "Nothing changes until it becomes what it is" (quoted in Ashner & Meyerson, 1997, p. 6).

Organizations also typically can say little, if anything, either historically or in the present about outputs, let alone about the effects those outputs have on clients, customers, or payers. For example, social welfare agencies can say a lot about their budgets, staff, physical facilities, and so on, but often they can say very little about the effects they have on their clients, and schools typically can say little about how educated their students are (Behn, 2001).

The relative absence of performance information presents problems both for the organization and for its stakeholders. Stakeholders will judge the worth of an organization by how well the organization meets the criteria for success that the stakeholders have chosen. For external stakeholders in particular, these criteria typically relate to performance. If the organization cannot demonstrate its effectiveness against the criteria, then stakeholders are likely to withdraw their support. Public schools, for example, are now finding their management, budgets, staffing patterns, and curricula judged by how well the schools' pupils score on standardized educational achievement tests. Schools that fail to produce *educated* students may be forced to do better or close their doors (Behn, 2003). If educational voucher schemes become widespread, public schools may even have to compete directly with one another for revenues, students, and staff, in the same way that private and nonprofit schools must compete with each other and with the public schools. In fact, some voucher schemes allow public monies to be spent on education delivered in private and nonprofit schools, including religiously affiliated ones, so that *all* schools, regardless of legal status, might need to compete with one another. This kind of competition is prompting many school districts to engage in strategic planning, because they want to be winners in the competition for students. As another example, nonprofit organizations that rely on government financing, foundation support, or charitable contributions to provide social services are likely to find their funding sources drying up unless they can demonstrate effective performance against relatively objective measures (Sawhill & Williamson, 2001; Ebrahim, 2010).

The absence of performance information may also create, or harden, major organizational conflicts. This is because without performance criteria and information, there is no way to judge the relative effectiveness of different resource allocations, organizational designs, and distributions of power. Without such judgments, organizational conflicts are likely to occur unnecessarily, be more partisan, and be resolved in ways that undermine the organization's mission.

The difficulties of measuring performance in the public and nonprofit sectors are well known (Poister, 2003; Niven, 2008). Nevertheless, stakeholders will continue to demand that organizations demonstrate effective performance and thereby justify their existence. Indeed, the Government Performance and Results Act of 1993 and similar acts by states across the nation—and indeed around the world—mandate strategic plans and annual or multiyear performance plans geared to key criteria held by external stakeholders (Frederickson, 2001). The *managerialist* push goes by different names—for example, strategic management, performance management, managing for results, results-oriented budgeting, and so on—but regardless, the push is in large part a response to stakeholders demanding demonstrably better performance and value for money (Abramson, Bruel, & Kemensky, 2006).

THE ASSESSMENT PROCESS

Here are two techniques for carrying out a SWOC/T analysis. The first is often a useful prelude to the second.

The Organizational Highs, Lows, and Themes Exercise

Often it is helpful for organizations to look forward by first looking backward. Indeed, organizations will find it easier to look forward for any period of time (five, ten, twenty years) if first they look backward for an equivalent period of time. An extremely useful technique for helping organizations assess strengths, weaknesses, opportunities, and challenges in a historical context is the "Organizational Highs, Lows, and Themes" exercise. The exercise is patterned after one for individuals outlined in Crosby and Bryson (2004, p. 50), which in turn is based on a more elaborate charting exercise described by Kouzes and Posner (2002), and consists of the following steps:

1. Reserve a room with a large wall. A room with a whiteboard that covers a whole wall is ideal. Alternatively, you might wish to cover a

wall with sheets of flip chart paper taped together (two rows of eight each), so that the results of the exercise may be saved intact.

2. Divide the wall into top and bottom halves. This can be done by drawing a line on the whiteboard or flip chart sheets with a flip chart marker or by using a long strip of masking tape.

3. At the right-hand end of the line, write in the current year. At the left-hand end, write in the date that is as far *back* as you wish the strategic planning team to ultimately look *forward* (typically five or ten years).

4. Ask group members to individually and silently brainstorm, on a sheet of scratch paper, all of the organizational "highs" and "lows" they can recall that occurred within the agreed timeframe. These might include the organization's founding, arrivals or departures of respected leaders, successful or unsuccessful management of crises, particularly useful or disastrous innovations, and so on. Participants should date each item and label it as a high or low.

5. Have participants transcribe their highs and lows onto half sheets of paper, one high or low per sheet. Once this is done, a piece of tape rolled sticky side out or a small bit of self-adhesive putty is attached to the back of each sheet.

6. Have participants stick their cards to the wall at the appropriate place on the time line. The height of each card above or below the line should indicate just how high the "high" was or how low the "low" was.

7. Ask the group to identify the themes that were common to the highs, to the lows, and to both.

8. Then ask the group to analyze the data and themes by answering these questions:

   What opportunities have we had? Which have we taken advantage of, which were we unable to take advantage of, and which have we ignored?

   What challenges have we had to deal with? Which have we handled successfully, which have we handled unsuccessfully, and which have we ignored?

   What strengths have we relied upon to deal with threats and take advantage of opportunities? Which have we ignored?

   What weaknesses have we had in dealing with threats and opportunities? What have we done about them?

9. Identify patterns in the way strengths, weaknesses, opportunities, challenges, and themes have interrelated over the relevant organizational history. In particular, identify what the organization's strategies have been *in practice*—what has actually happened, as

opposed to what might be voiced in official pronouncements. Ask what the organization seems to be particularly good at doing; probe for ambitions and competencies and how they have been linked.

10. Have the group move the time line forward an equivalent distance and discuss what their previous analyses might imply for the future. In particular, have the group speculate about future opportunities and challenges and the strengths and weaknesses the organization might have to address them. What themes, patterns, and strategies from the past would the group like to see projected into the future? Which would the group not like to see projected? What new themes would the group like to see?

One example of the usefulness of this exercise is provided by a generally quite successful nonprofit organization in the United Kingdom devoted to addressing the needs of children (and whose patron is a member of the Royal Family). Their management team realized as a result of this exercise that the organization almost always performed better when they did careful planning, attended to key stakeholder interests, and took advantage of opportunities. Conversely, they did less well when they got caught in crisis management, failed to attend to key stakeholder interests, and failed to deal with important challenges. The exercise thus renewed their commitment to strategic planning and helped them focus on some key strengths, weaknesses, opportunities, and challenges related particularly to stakeholder concerns. Mintzberg, Ahlstrand, and Lampel (2009, p. 217) capture this interplay of past, present, and future well when they say, "Strategies appear first as patterns out of the past, only later, perhaps, as plans for the future, and ultimately, as perspectives to guide overall behavior."

The Snow Card Technique

The *snow card* technique (Greenblat & Duke, 1981; Spencer, 1996) is a very simple yet effective group technique for developing a list of strengths, weaknesses, opportunities, and challenges or threats. Also referred to as the *snowball* technique (Nutt & Backoff, 1992), the method combines brainstorming—which produces a long list of possible answers to a specific question—with a synthesizing step in which the answers are grouped into categories according to common themes. Each of the individual answers is written on a white card (a snow card): for example, a half-sheet of inexpensive photocopy paper, a five-by-seven-inch card, or a large self-stick note. The individual cards are then stuck to a wall with masking tape or self-adhesive putty according to common themes, producing several snowballs of cards.

The technique is extremely simple in concept, very easy to use, speedy, and productive. The technique is particularly useful as part of a SWOC/T analysis and as part of the strategy development step. In a SWOC/T analysis the technique would be used four times in order to focus on the questions:

- What major external or future opportunities do we have?
- What major external or future challenges or threats do we face?
- What are our major internal or present strengths?
- What are our major internal or present weaknesses?

This quickly produces four lists for the strategic planning team to discuss, compare, and contrast, both to determine actions that should be taken immediately and to prepare for the identification of strategic issues in the next step. The SWOC/T analysis also will help the team prepare effective strategies in response to the issues.

Here are the guidelines for using the snow card technique:

1. Select a facilitator.

2. Form the group that will use the technique. The ideal size for the group is five to nine persons, but the technique can still be effective with as many as twelve to fifteen. Even larger numbers of participants can be involved if subgroups are formed.

3. Have the members of the group seat themselves around a table in a room that has a nearby wall onto which the snow cards can be attached.

4. Focus on a single question, problem, or issue. Typically the entire process will be repeated four times in a SWOC/T analysis, once each for strengths, weaknesses, opportunities, and challenges. Alternatively, you may choose to do strengths and weaknesses in one round, and opportunities and challenges in another round.

5. Have the participants silently brainstorm as many ideas as possible in response to the question, and record them on their personal worksheets.

6. Have individuals pick out their five to seven best items on their personal worksheets and transcribe them onto separate snow cards. Make sure people write legibly enough and large enough so that items can be read when posted on a nearby wall. Have group members attach a rolled piece of tape or bit of self-adhesive putty to the back of each of their snow cards.

7. Collect the cards (shuffle them if anonymity is important) and attach them one at a time to the wall, clustering cards with similar themes together. The tentative label for each cluster should be selected by the group. As an alternative, the group may wish to tape all of the cards to the wall at once, and as a group rearrange the cards into thematic clusters.

8. Label each cluster with a separate card. These label cards should be differentiated in some way from regular snow cards, perhaps by using paper or ink of a different color, or by drawing a box around the category name.

9. Once all items are on the board and included in a cluster, rearrange the items and tinker with the categories until the group thinks the results make the most sense. Categories might be arranged in logical, priority, or temporal order. New items may be added and old ones deleted as necessary. Subcategories should be added as needed. In addition, structuring within categories may be advisable to highlight any linkages among items (see Resource D).

10. When the group members are satisfied with the categories and their contents, they should discuss, compare, and contrast the results.

11. The group's collective opinion of the importance of the categories (or individual items) may be visually accentuated with colored stick-on dots. For SWOC/T analyses, I usually give each participant seven dots per list and ask them to place one dot on each of the seven most important categories or items in the list. The pattern of the dots graphically displays the pattern of group opinion.

12. When the session is over, collect the cards in order, have them typed up in outline or spreadsheet form, and distribute the results to the group. Having a notebook computer and secretary at the session will speed up this process. It may also be advisable to take digital photographs of the display, both as a backup and to provide a pictorial reminder of the process.

A fascinating variation of this exercise is the "camera exercise" used on occasions in East St. Louis, Missouri, by a community planning group (Khademian, 2002). Community members are given an inexpensive disposable camera holding at least twenty-seven shots. Members are asked to bring back at least nine shots of things that represent community strengths, nine shots of things that represent community weaknesses, and nine shots of potential assets or opportunities for the future. The photographs are then clustered as they would be in the snow card exercise and discussed.

SWOC/T ANALYSES: AN EXAMPLE

Simply creating lists of strengths, weaknesses, opportunities, and challenges or threats is not enough. The list must be carefully discussed, analyzed, compared, and contrasted; that is, a SWOC/T *analysis* must be performed. Planners should note specific implications for the formulation of strategic issues and effective strategies, as well as actions that may be necessary (and that could be taken) before the end of the strategic planning process.

One of the fascinating features of most SWOC/T analyses is that strengths and weaknesses are often highly similar to one another. That is, an organization's greatest strengths may also be its greatest weaknesses. Likewise, the opportunities and challenges an organization faces are also often similar to one another. Strategic planning team members should not be surprised to see such relationships. Indeed, they should expect that every organization will carry the weaknesses of its strengths and face the challenges of its opportunities (and vice versa). The trick is to take advantage of the strengths and opportunities without being disadvantaged by the related weaknesses and challenges (Johnson, 1996).

The team also should not be surprised to find internal opportunities and challenges and external strengths and weaknesses. Figure 2.1 indicates that opportunities and challenges are primarily external and strengths and weaknesses are internal; meanwhile, Nutt and Backoff (1992) argue that strengths and weaknesses are primarily in the present and opportunities and challenges are primarily in the future. As a result, SWOC/Ts may arise either inside or outside the organization, in the present, or in the future.

The Minneapolis Park and Recreation Board provides an elaborated example of a SWOC/T analysis. The Park Board engaged in an extensive internal and external environmental assessment process. There were citizen surveys, town meetings, community leader workshops, and detailed interviews of each of the nine commissioners. The assessment tools were meant both to gather information and to build relationships. The commission interviews are particularly interesting, as the commissioners are on the boundary between inside and outside and are in extensive contact with all the key stakeholder groups. Exhibit 5.1 presents the summary of findings of the commissioner interviews prepared by staff that became part of the public record and helped guide the next steps in the process. The questions the commissioners were asked focused on mission and goals, organizational effectiveness, needs and concerns (another name for immediate and longer-term strategic issues), strengths, challenges, board-staff relations, collaboration, community engagement, and vision. The summary concludes by posing another set of questions for the commissioners focused on the next steps in the Strategy Change Cycle of honing in on strategic issues and considering possible strategies.

A few observations about the Park Board commissioners' interview responses are in order. First, the summary provides a very succinct statement of the situation the organization faces and the challenges it will need to address in the next steps of the planning process. The holistic assessment is one of the most important outcomes of a SWOC/T analysis. Second, the Park Board clearly has strengths on which it can draw, but it also needs to work constantly at

Exhibit 5.1. Minneapolis Park Board Summary of Findings from Commissioner Interviews, May 2006.

Overview

Starting in January 2006, all nine Minneapolis Park and Recreation Board (MPRB) commissioners were interviewed to gain a better understanding of their collective perspectives of the organization and the questions or issues that need to be addressed in the comprehensive planning process.

As leaders, the commissioners will set the direction of the MPRB through the development of the mission, vision, and values statements for the organization. These guiding documents will be the cornerstone of the future planning. To achieve and uphold the mission, vision, and values, staff will develop strategic initiatives and strategies on a regular basis.

The information shared in the interviews and compiled below is intended to assist commissioners in creating the guiding documents. Below you will find a summary of those interviews and questions for consideration during the planning process. Note that the summaries do not represent every response given, but rather the main themes of the interview responses.

Summary of Commissioner Interviews

Mission

"How would you define the organization's mission and primary goals?"

- Commissioners were quick to express their high regard and passion for the park system and respect for its legacy. Commissioners also see the system as a focal point of the city's identity.

- Through examples and experiences commissioners articulated that the mission of the organization currently focuses on the environment, recreation (especially programming for youth) and service to the community. Many also indicated that the system seems to strike a good balance between the environment and recreation.

- Commissioners tended to express the need to build stronger relationships with the community and to implement measures that will allow staff to better discern the needs of the community.

Effectiveness

"How effective is the organization in accomplishing its mission (on a scale of 1, not very effective, to 5, highly effective)?"

- On average, commissioners felt that the organization is very effective (4) at meeting its mission. While most commissioners think that park visitors and residents as a whole would find the work of the organization to be highly effective, they felt there is still room for improvement and cautioned against complacency.

- Some commissioners felt that the discord in the working relationship among commissioners over the past couple of years made it difficult to accomplish goals. Others felt that unclear priorities and communication with the public has had an impact on effectiveness. Another perspective was that the effectiveness improved over the past couple of years due to initiating changes, reorganization, and addressing difficult problems that had been lingering.

Needs/Concerns

"What do you see as the short- and long-term needs and concerns of your constituents and the community as a whole? What specific items must be addressed for this plan to be successful?"

Short Term

- In the short term many commissioners indicated the desire to improve programming for specific user groups (that is, young girls, skate boarders, seniors, and dog owners), and a need to solve problems (that is, 201 Building, youth sports uniform controversy, publishing of the Wirth book and removal of invasive species).

- Building stronger relationships with park users and partners was a short-term need expressed by commissioners.

- Commissioners articulated a need for increased communication with residents and partners. This includes better, faster response to concerns, more community dialogues, faster response to resident inquiries and clear articulation of how residents can be involved in decision making.

- Identifying new funding or better management of existing funding was a clearly expressed need of commissioners.

(Continued)

Exhibit 5.1. Minneapolis Park Board Summary of Findings from Commissioner Interviews, May 2006, Continued.

Long Term

- When looking to the future, commissioners tended to focus on the built structure of the system and the needs of the environment. Creating a well-kept, sustainable system is broadly desired among commissioners. Many commissioners articulated specific needs for improved athletic fields, water quality, recreation center buildings, shoreline and wetland restoration, and removal of invasive plants from the land and water of Minneapolis.

- Commissioners focused significantly on the needs of youth when looking into the future. Many wanted the MRPB to make a significant impact in the life and well-being of children, whether it is physical activity, jobs, or social interaction.

- Commissioners felt that articulating a vision for the system and long-term land use planning were important.

- As with the short-term needs, identifying new funding or better management of existing funding was a clearly expressed need of commissioners.

Strengths

"What do you see as the current strengths of the organization and the park system?"

- Commissioners shared similar perspectives on the strengths of the organization, including:
  - The physical assets that comprise the system
  - The dedication and investment of staff
  - Independence of the organization
  - Strong history and reputation
  - Programs provided through the parks
- Many commissioners also noted the recent reorganization to districts, responsiveness, and innovation of the system as strengths.

Challenges

"What do you consider to be the limitations/weaknesses of the organization? What do you find most frustrating?"

- Commissioners saw lack of funding and limited staff time as limitations of the organization.

- It was also felt that the organization needs to be better in touch with the needs of the community, improve relationships with residents, park visitors, and public agencies, and improve communication on all levels.
- Commissioners noted that the organization does a lot of things for a lot of people and that the expectations placed on it can make it hard to change directions.
- Interest in focusing on the big picture versus individual interests was consistently expressed. Commissioners expressed that many interactions they have with constituents are focused on single-issue concerns and that being able to present a solution in the context of the larger picture would be helpful.

Board/Staff Relationship

"How effective is the Park Board and its relationship with staff and what, if anything, would make it more effective and functional (1, not very effective, to 5, highly effective)?"

- Commissioners indicated the desire to improve the staff/board relationship and on average rated it as a 2 in terms of effectiveness.
- Commissioners expressed a desire to be better informed of the organization so they could more effectively represent it. They also wanted to be known as working fairly and honestly with the superintendent and senior management.
- Many commissioners felt that they need to focus on policy issues and avoid micromanaging, but staff also need to be more proactive in communication.

Collaboration

"Whom do you see as your partners in the community? Competitors? Why?"

- Commissioners articulated a wide range of partners including community groups, city, schools, local and state government agencies and officials, neighborhood organizations, nonprofits, foundations, and constituents.
- Many commissioners could not identify competitors, and those that were mentioned compete for money sources, land, or park visitors.
- Collaboration in general needs to be improved.

(*Continued*)

Exhibit 5.1. Minneapolis Park Board Summary of Findings from Commissioner Interviews, May 2006, Continued.

Community Engagement

"How would you envision community engagement in the comprehensive planning process?"

- Commissioner perspectives on community engagement varied widely. Most commissioners felt information should be gained through multiple methods that allow feedback from all communities (especially those that are difficult to reach). Public meetings, Web site, listening sessions, and roundtable discussions were listed as possible methods.

- Many commissioners indicated a need for making the community engagement fun, creative, and interactive. In addition, translators and good publication of opportunities were considered important to the success of the process.

- Commissioners indicated that the process should be an opportunity for residents and park users to articulate what they would like to see in the system.

Vision

"If you had a magic wand, how would you use it?"

- In general, commissioners envisioned a well-maintained, resource-abundant, clean, green park system that contributes to the health of the city and engages youth. In addition, the system would successfully implement some high-profile projects such as the Grand Rounds missing link.

Questions for Future Consideration

For commissioners, one of the most important actions in the comprehensive planning process will be to set the overall direction of the organization—Mission, Vision, and Values. The interviews provide a glimpse of the collective perspectives of the commissioners. A next step is to consider the questions that need to be answered through the planning process. Below is a list of questions for future consideration as the comprehensive planning ensues:

- Should the park system continue to grow? If yes, what should be the focus of the growth?

- Should public and private partnerships be expanded? If yes, what criteria should be used to evaluate and prioritize potential partnerships?

- How do social and environmental issues such as obesity, emergency preparedness, and climate change relate to the future direction of the organization? How should the park board position itself to effectively respond to these issues?

- Does the board effectively measure progress toward its goals? If not, how will the board do this in the future?

- Is the board addressing its funding needs? If not, what steps need to be taken to fulfill the needs of the system?

- What steps are being taken to reach the desired board and staff relationship?

- Is the board committed to the comprehensive planning process? If not, what actions need to be taken to solidify commitment?

- Does the board feel it leads the organization and community in setting clear direction and priorities? If not, what will help the board in accomplishing these tasks?

- How and when will the board celebrate positive change?

Source: Reprinted with permission from the Minneapolis Park and Recreation Board.

overcoming any weaknesses its opportunities create or expose, in addition to the challenges that can magnify the weaknesses or overwhelm the strengths and opportunities. Third, this needed outward focus is the reverse of what often happens when a group of senior managers (or even elected officials) get together. Typically, most managers are responsible for the day-to-day operation of their departments. Their jobs often virtually preclude paying careful attention to external trends and events. Furthermore, most organizations do not have well-established occasions and forums for line managers, as a group, to discuss external trends and events and their likely impact. Most organizations are thus in danger of being blindsided by external developments, unless they make use of external scanning practices and have organized forums for managers to discuss information developed through external scanning or an invited speakers program.

Fourth, there is good news in the shared perception of needs or concerns and challenges, as that may induce both group cohesion and action, particularly if the culture supports facing rather than avoiding failure, weakness, and threats (Weick & Sutcliffe, 2007). Indeed, as was noted in Chapter Two, most organizations get into strategic planning because they face strategic issues that they do not know how to handle or because they are pursuing strategies that are failing or likely to fail. In either case, it is the perception of serious challenges that prompts strategic planning. There is potential bad news in shared perceptions about strategic issues because without some sense of safety provided by credible leaders, inspiring missions, visions, goals, supportive cultures, or strong facilitators, groups gripped by challenges or actual threats may become paralyzed and unable to think of or take advantage of opportunities (Schwarz, 2002; Weick & Sutcliffe, 2007; Kouzes & Posner, 2008; Schein, 2010).

Fifth, while there are implicit and explicit weaknesses on the list, there are still many strengths on which to build. This is good, as it helps inoculate the group against the natural human tendency to become a captive of action inhibitors (weaknesses) rather than focusing on what facilitates human action (strengths). It also protects them from the equally familiar human tendency to assign blame or find a scapegoat as a way of avoiding action. Whatever the reason, it is important to turn weaknesses into challenges to be overcome (Csikszentmihalyi, 1990; Bandura, 1997; Seligman, 1998).

A final point to be made about SWOC/T analyses is that if a special-purpose government such as the Park Board or a general-purpose government performs a SWOC/T analysis (in contrast to the Loft example), the results will involve both the government as an organization and its jurisdiction as a place or community. This blending should be expected of governments responsible for themselves and for places. The same blending of results for both the organization and its jurisdiction occurred for MetroGIS. This was expected, given the interdependence between MetroGIS and its member governments and its mandated focus on the seven-county metropolitan area.

PROCESS DESIGN AND ACTION GUIDELINES

One of the special features of strategic planning is the attention it accords to external and internal environments. Coupled with attention to its mandates and mission, external and internal assessments give an organization a clear sense of its present situation and lay the basis for identifying strategic issues and developing strategies in the next two steps. As the ancient Chinese military strategist Sun Tzu (1910) might have said, without this kind of in-depth understanding, an organization is likely to be continuously imperiled. And certainly successful major change will be highly unlikely. The following process guidelines may be helpful as an organization looks at its external and internal environments.

1. *Make a point of regularly paying attention to what is going on inside and outside the organization.* Regardless of whether there is a formal

scanning process or not, you should keep your eyes and ears open and pay attention. This guideline isn't a call for some sort of hypervigilance, but it is a call for attending in a thoughtful way to the "complexly busy" world Diane Ackerman describes around you. Numerous sources of good ideas, observations, and reflections abound, including good general newspapers in hard copy and electronic form; Web sites and Web aggregators like Google Alerts; trade journals and newsletters; interest group and professional association meetings, newsletters, blogs, and listserv discussions; Webinars; public lectures in person or online as podcasts; and one of my favorites, browsing in bookshops that also serve coffee.

2. *Keep in mind that simpler is likely to be better.* Highly elaborate, lengthy, sophisticated, and quantified procedures for external and internal assessment are likely to drive out strategic thinking, not promote it. Let purpose be your guide—meaning always keep in mind the mandates, mission, and need to create public value—and search for information related to them. Do not gather information indiscriminately. (One possible way to simplify that process that participants may prefer is to skip doing a SWOC/T analysis for the organization as a whole in this step and instead to do the analysis in relation to specific strategic issues, Step Five, or strategies, Step Six. In those steps the analysis will seem more grounded and specific to many people.)

3. *The organization may wish to review its mission and mandates, stakeholder analyses, existing goal statements, results of the Organizational Highs, Lows, and Themes exercise (if it was used), the Livelihood Scheme Exercise in Resource C (if it was used), cultural audits, relevant survey results, MIS and external scanning reports, possible future scenarios, and other information related to the organization's internal and external environments prior to performing a SWOC/T analysis.* Alternatively, a "quick and dirty" SWOC/T analysis may prompt strategic planning team members to pay attention to what they previously ignored, or it may indicate where more information is needed.

Because an organization's culture can place severe limits on its ability to perceive SWOC/T's as well as constrain strategic responses, an analysis of the culture may be particularly useful. If key decision makers and opinion leaders are willing, a serviceable cultural analysis can be performed in one and a half days, following guidelines provided by Schein (2010, pp. 315–325; see also Hampden-Turner,

1990, pp. 185–207; Khademian, 2002, pp. 108–123; and Johnson, Scholes, & Whittington, 2008, pp. 197–203).

4. *Consider using the snow card technique with the strategic planning team to develop a list of strengths, weaknesses, opportunities, and threats.*

5. *Always try, if possible, to get a strategic planning team to consider what is going on outside the organization before it considers what is going on inside.* Attending to the outside is crucial, because the social and political justification for virtually every organization's existence is what it does, or proposes to do, about external social or political challenges or problems. Organizations, therefore, should focus on those challenges or problems first and on themselves second.

6. *As part of the discussion of its SWOC/T list, the strategic planning should look for patterns, important action that might be taken immediately, and implications for the identification of strategic issues.* Discussants should also see if there are any important requirements emerging from the SWOC/T analysis that will need to be taken into account or addressed in later stages in the process. For example, a requirement of effective strategies is that they must build on strengths and take advantage of opportunities, while minimizing or overcoming weaknesses and threats.

7. *A follow-up analysis of the SWOC/T analysis developed by the strategic planning team is almost always a good idea.* Constructing logic models or action-oriented strategy maps that capture the apparent reasoning and perceived causal chains behind existing organizational processes and strategies can be very instructive (Bryson, Ackermann, Eden, and Finn, 2004; Knowlton & Phillips, 2009; McLaughlin & Jordan, 2010). Mapping the "policy fields" in which the organization finds itself can also be a very good idea (Stone & Sandfort, 2009).

8. *The organization should take action as quickly as possible on those items for which it has enough information.* Doing so is desirable if it does not foreclose important strategic options for the future. It is important to show continuous progress and desirable results from strategic planning if people are to stay with it when the going gets tough.

9. *The organization should consider institutionalizing periodic SWOC/T analyses.* The simplest way to do this is to schedule periodic meetings of the strategic planning team, say, once or twice a year, to engage in a snow card exercise to develop a SWOC/T list as a basis for discussion. A norm should be established that at least some

organizational changes will result from the sessions. In more elaborate form, holding periodic meetings would imply establishing a quasi-permanent external and internal scanning function.

10. *The organization may wish to construct various scenarios in order to help it identify SWOC/Ts.* There are advantages to doing so, in that the stories conjured up by scenarios can help many people better imagine the future. As poet Muriel Rukeyser said, "The world is made of stories, not atoms." The often abstract categories of a SWOC/T analysis may just be vague "atoms" to people when what they need is a tangible story—a scenario—with "real" scenes, events, and actors. The story can help them see the whole rather than just the parts. I have seen effective assessments done with and without scenarios. Not using scenarios can save time, but some of the possible richness of a good assessment exercise can be lost without them. In the 1990s, both the United States Naval Security Group (Frentzel, Bryson, & Crosby, 2000) and, on a much larger scale, the United States Air Force (Barzelay & Campbell, 2003) made effective use of scenarios in order to understand their situations better and to set the stage for strategic issue identification in the next step. Both organizations transformed themselves as a result of their strategic planning efforts. Scenarios can be particularly useful in identifying and assessing the risks surrounding potential Black Swan events (Taleb, 2007).

SUMMARY

Step 4 explores the organization's external and internal environments in order to identify the strengths, weaknesses, opportunities, and challenges or threats that the organization faces. When combined with a greater attention to mandates and mission, these steps provide the foundation for identifying strategic issues and developing effective strategies to create public value in the following two steps. Recall that every effective strategy will build on strengths and take advantage of opportunities while it minimizes or overcomes weaknesses and challenges.

By far the most important strategic planning techniques are individual thinking and group deliberation. Neither may look like useful work—as when poet Wallace Stevens says, "Sometimes it is difficult to tell the difference between thinking and looking out the window." But do not be deceived. The Organizational Highs, Lows, and Themes exercise and the snow card technique, for example, can be used to provide the basic SWOC/T list that will be the focus of the individual thinking and group deliberations to come that will clarify the most important issues and much of what the organization has to work with.

Organizations should consider institutionalizing their capability to perform periodic SWOC/T analyses. To do so, they will need to establish serviceable external and internal scanning operations, develop a good MIS system, and undertake regular strategic planning exercises.

As with every step in the strategic planning process, simpler is usually better. Strategic planning teams should not get bogged down in external and internal assessments. Important and necessary actions should be taken as soon as they are identified, as long as they do not prematurely seal off important strategic options.

CHAPTER SIX

Identifying Strategic Issues
Facing the Organization

Depend upon it, Sir, when a man knows he is to be
hanged in a fortnight, it concentrates his mind wonderfully.
—Samuel Johnson, in James Boswell, *Life of Johnson*

Identifying strategic issues is the heart of the strategic planning process. Recall that a strategic issue is a fundamental policy question or challenge affecting an organization's mandates, mission and values, product or service level and mix, clients or users, cost, financing, organization, or management. The purpose of this step (Step 5) therefore is to identify the fundamental policy questions—the *strategic issue agenda* (Nutt & Backoff, 1992)—facing the organization. The way these questions are framed can have a profound effect on the creation of ideas for strategic action and a winning coalition, along with the associated decisions that define what the organization is, what it does, and why it does it—and therefore on the organization's ability to create public value (see Figure 2.4). If strategic planning is in part about the construction of a new social reality, then this step outlines the basic paths along which that drama might unfold (Mangham & Overington, 1987; Bryant, 2003; Bolman & Deal, 2008, pp. 270–286).

An organization's mission often is explicitly or implicitly identified as an issue during this phase. After lengthy deliberations, the Park Board's elected commissioners decided to modify the existing mission statement to include natural resources and add a second paragraph (see Exhibit 4.1) to highlight the importance of being responsive to Minneapolis's rapidly diversifying population. The Loft's board and staff also revisited their existing mission as part of their strategic planning efforts. The mission did not change in a substantial way but the wording was strengthened. Specifically, the original mission was "to foster a writing community, the artistic development of individual writers, and an audience for literature." The new mission was "to support the artistic development of writers, to foster a writing community, and to build an audience for literature." The board thought the change not only strengthened the statement, but also helped the organization to emphasize and more closely link serving the individual writer and building the writing community and the broader audience for literature. And MetroGIS did not exist in a formal way when it undertook its first strategic planning effort. A key issue in that effort is what the purpose of such an organization should be. During MetroGIS's second strategic planning effort, those involved concluded the organization had outlived its original mission and was in need of a new one (see Exhibit 4.3). In other words, organizational purpose is almost always an issue, at least implicitly, and strategic planning efforts revisit the issue often, if only to reaffirm existing purposes.

The organization's culture will affect which issues get on the agenda and how they are framed, and which strategic options get serious consideration in Step 6, strategy formulation and plan development. The need to change the organization's culture may thus become a strategic issue itself if the culture blinds the organization to important issues and possibilities for action. It is also worth keeping in mind that every major strategy change will also involve a cultural change (Khademian, 2002; Schein, 2010; Mulgan, 2009).

As noted in Chapter Two, strategic issues are important because issues play a central role in political decision making. Political decision making begins with issues, but strategic planning can improve the process by affecting the way issues are framed and addressed. With carefully framed issues, subsequent choices, decisions, and actions are more likely to be politically acceptable, technically workable, administratively feasible, in accord with the organization's basic philosophy and values, and morally, ethically, and legally defensible.

Identifying strategic issues typically is one of the most riveting steps for participants in strategic planning (Ackermann, 1992). Virtually every strategic issue involves conflicts: what will be done, why it will be done, how and how much of it will be done, when it will be done, where it will be done, who will do it, and who will be advantaged or disadvantaged by it. These conflicts are typically desirable and even necessary, as they help clarify exactly what the issues are. As Rainey (1997, p. 304) observes, "In public and nonprofit organizations, one expects and even hopes for intense conflicts, although preferably not destructive ones." As a result, a key leadership task is to promote constructive conflict aimed at clarifying exactly which issues need to be addressed in order to satisfy key stakeholders and create public value. But whether the conflict draws people together or pulls them apart, participants will feel heightened emotion and concern (Ortony, Clore, & Collins, 1990; Weick and Sutcliffe,

2007; Schein, 2010). As with any journey, fear, anxiety, and sometimes depression are as likely to be travel companions as excitement and adventurousness. It is very important, therefore, that people feel enough psychological safety to explore potentially threatening situations, relationships, and ideas; in other words, they need what Ron Heifetz calls a *holding environment* (Heifetz, 1994, p. 103; see also Chrislip, 2002, pp. 45–46) and what Karl Weick (1995, p. 179) calls a "sensemaking support system" to help them through. An effective strategic planning coordinating committee and strategic planning team will provide these necessary supports.

IMMEDIATE AND LONGER-TERM DESIRED OUTCOMES

This step should result in the creation of the organization's strategic issue agenda. The agenda is a product of three prior outcomes. The first is a list of the issues faced by the organization. The items on the list may have many sources, but the list itself is likely to be a product of strategic planning team deliberations. The second is the division of the list into two broad categories: strategic and operational. It often takes focused discussion to discern which issues are really strategic, which are more operational, and which are somewhere in between.

Figure 6.1 shows key differences among strategic issues, operational issues, and those that are a mix of the two (Crossan, Lane, & White, 1999; Heifetz, Grashow, & Linsky, 2009; Scharmer, 2009). Strategic issues are likely to involve more need for knowledge exploration, changes in basic stakeholders or stakeholder relationships, and perhaps radical new technologies. Responses different from the status quo are likely to be required from the system level (for example, changes in basic rules or institutional redesign) or organizational level (for example, changes in mission, vision, and goals). Decision makers involved are likely to be top-level decision makers and decision-making bodies at the system and organizational level. Operational issues, in contrast, are more technical in nature and are likely to involve knowledge exploitation, strategy refinement, and process improvement. Line managers, operations groups and personnel, and service coproducers or recipients will be required to respond. Issues that are partly strategic and partly operational are in between. New strategies are likely to be needed and the strategic planning team will be a key focal point for helping formulate new strategies or codifying effective emergent strategies; each issue's strategic aspects should be examined and resolved first before operational concerns can be settled. And the third is an arrangement of the strategic issues in some sort of order: priority, logical, or temporal. The listing and arrangement of issues should contain information to help people consider the nature, importance, and implications of each issue.

What Type of Issue Is It?	What Type of Response Possibly Is Required?	Who Possibly May Have to Respond?
Strategic (adaptive, developmental, complex) issues, where there is typically a need for: • More knowledge exploration • New concepts • Changes in basic stakeholders and/or stakeholder relationships • Radical new technologies	From the system: • Constitutive governance • Rules for making rules • Institutional redesign From the organization (collaboration, community): • Mission • Vision • Goals	At the system level: • Institutional level decision-making bodies (e.g., law makers, policy-makers, rule and regulation makers) • Other top-level key decision makers At the organization level (collaboration, community): • Governing or policy board • Senior staff • Key stakeholders
Issues that are partly strategic and partly operational (both adaptive and technical, complicated)	Strategies for fulfilling mission, realizing the vision, and/or achieving the goals Strategies for: • Developing strategies • Producing programs, products, projects, services • Controlling strategy delivery in the present • Developing future capabilities Maintaining and enhancing stakeholder relations	Strategic planning team as locus for helping formulate new strategies and/or compiling and codifying emergent strategies
Operational (technical, nondevelopmental, difficult) issues, where there is more of a need for: • Knowledge exploitation • Strategic refinement • Process management • Process improvement • Use of existing technologies • Good relationships with existing stakeholders	• Strategy implementation and fine-tuning • Improvements in ongoing operations • Action planning	• Line managers • Operations groups and teams • Program, product, project or service coproducers and/or recipients

Figure 6.1. Sorting Out the Issues and Their Implications.

Source: Adapted from Ostrom, 1990; Heifetz, 1994; Raisch & Birkenshaw, 2008; Hill & Hupe, 2009; Farnum Alston, personal communication; Michael Barzelay, personal communication.

A number of additional outcomes ensue from the identification of strategic issues. First, attention is focused on what is truly important. The importance of this outcome is not to be underestimated. Key decision makers in organizations usually are victimized by the "80–20 rule." That is, they usually spend at least 80 percent of their time on the least important 20 percent of their jobs (Parkinson, 1957). When this is added to the fact that key decision makers in different functional areas rarely discuss important cross-functional matters with one another, the stage is set for shabby organizational performance.

It also helps to recognize that in terms of the immediacy of required attention, there are three different kinds of strategic issues: (1) issues where no action is required at present, but that must be continuously monitored; (2) issues that can be handled as part of the organization's regular strategic planning cycle; and (3) issues that require an immediate response.

A second desirable outcome is that attention is focused on issues, not answers. All too often serious conflicts arise over solutions to problems that have not been clearly defined (Fisher & Ury, 1991; Janis, 1989). Such conflicts typically result in power struggles, not problem-solving sessions. More important, they are unlikely to help the organization achieve its goals, be satisfied with the outcome of its planning, or enhance its future problem-solving ability (Nutt, 2002).

Third, the identification of issues usually creates the kind of useful tension necessary to prompt organizational change. Organizations rarely change unless they feel some need to change, some pressure or tension—often fear, anxiety, or guilt—that requires change to relieve or release the stress (Light, 1998, p. 66; Fiol, 2002; Ackermann and Eden, 2011). The tension must be great enough to prompt change, but not so great as to induce paralysis. Strategic issues that emerge from the juxtaposition of internal and external factors—and that involve organizational survival, prosperity, and effectiveness—can provide just the kind of tension that will focus the attention of key decision makers on the need for change (Nutt, 2001). These decision makers will be particularly attentive to strategic issues that entail severe consequences if they are not addressed. As Samuel Johnson observed, albeit humorously, frightening situations quickly focus one's attention on what is important.

Fourth, strategic issue identification should provide useful clues about how to resolve the issue. By stating exactly what it is about the organization's mission, mandates, and internal and external factors (or SWOC/Ts) that makes an issue strategic, the team also gains some insight into possible ways that the issue might be resolved. Insights into the nature and shape of effective answers are particularly likely if the team follows the dictum that any effective strategy will take advantage of strengths and opportunities and minimize or overcome weaknesses and challenges (Mintzberg, 1994, p. 277). Attention to strengths and opportunities is likely to promote action-enhancing optimism, as opposed to the inaction, depression, or rigidity of thought associated with attention only to weaknesses and threats (Nadler & Hibino, 1998; Seligman, 2006).

Fifth, if the strategic planning process has not been *real* to participants previously, it will become real for them now. For something to be real for someone there must be a correspondence between what the person thinks, how he or she behaves toward that thing, and the consequences of that behavior (Boal & Bryson, 1987; Hunt, Boal, & Dodge, 1999). As the organization's situation and the issues it faces become clear, as the consequences of failure to face those issues are discussed, and as the behavioral changes necessary to deal with the issues begin to emerge, the strategic planning process will begin to seem less academic and much more real. The more people realize that strategic planning can be quite real in its consequences, the more seriously they will take it. A qualitative change in the tone of discussions among members of the team often can be observed at this point, as the links among cognitions, behaviors, and consequences are established. Less joking and more serious discussion occur. A typical result of this *real-ization* is that the group may wish to cycle through the process again. In particular, the group's initial framing of the strategic issues is likely to change as a result of further dialogue and deliberation among members who come to realize more fully the consequences of both addressing and failing to address the issues. Or, to return to the theatrical metaphor, as the group *rehearses* the various decision and action sequences that might flow from a particular issue framing, they may wish to reframe the issue so that certain kinds of strategies are more likely to find favor (Bryant, 2003; Bolman & Deal, 2008).

A further consequence of the understanding that strategic planning may be all too real in its consequences is that key decision makers may wish to terminate the effort at this point. They may be afraid of addressing the conflicts embodied in the strategic issues. They may not wish to undergo the changes that may be necessary to resolve the issues. The decision makers may fall into a pit where they may experience stress, anger, depression, feelings of powerlessness, and grief. Such feelings are quite common among individuals undergoing major changes until they let go of the past and move into the future with a new sense of direction and renewed confidence (Baum, 1999). A crisis of trust or a test of courage may thus occur, and lead to a turning point in the organization's character. If after completion of this step, the organization's key decision makers decide to push on, a final very important outcome therefore will have been gained: the organization's character will be strengthened. Just as an individual's character is formed in part by the way the individual faces serious difficulties, so too is organizational character formed by the way the organization faces difficulties (Selznick, 1957; Schein, 2010). Strong characters only emerge from confronting serious difficulties squarely and courageously.

EXAMPLES OF STRATEGIC ISSUES

There are many ways to identify strategic issues. The Loft began their strategic planning process by forming six task forces early on. These included programs for writers, education, technology, leadership support and transitions, constituents, and new sources of funding. Naming these task forces may be seen as an early attempt to identify strategic issues, because planners knew there were important questions in each area about what the Loft should do next. The task forces had little to do, however, until after a major strategic planning retreat was held in October 2006. The retreat involved virtually every board and staff member.

As the main focus for the retreat, the planning team decided to use a variant of the goals approach to identifying strategic issues (discussed further below) when they chose to highlight the key issues posed by the three elements of the mission. Recall that, "the mission of the Loft is to support the artistic development of writers, to foster a writing community, and to build an audience for literature." The three strategic issues that flow directly from the mission are:

- How can the Loft support the artistic development of individual writers?
- How can the Loft foster a writing community?
- How can the Loft build an audience for literature?

Note that each strategic issue is phrased as a question that the Loft can do something about and that has more than one answer. Taking an initial stab at answering the questions was the main agenda item at the strategic planning retreat, which moved the Loft into Step Six, Strategy Formulation. But note as well that at least one other strategic issue emerged later in the process when the executive director announced she was retiring by October 2007. The issue was not unexpected, although its precise timing was. The executive director had already said she would be leaving at some point, and there was a leadership support and transitions task force in place, so the Loft actually was well positioned to address the issue. Indeed, the process and plan would help prepare the organization for change and for understanding what it should seek in a new executive director.

The Minneapolis Park and Recreation Board used a cross between the direct and vision of success approaches (also discussed further on). A broadly participative assessment process was undertaken that involved the board, a large portion of the staff organized into nine teams (infrastructure, demographics, programs and services, information management, sustainability, planning, community outreach and research, evaluation, and art and history), and many community members (through town meetings, questionnaires, focus groups, community leader workshops, and a phone survey). Teams got to work on matters related to their focus that could be acted on immediately (meaning the issues were already clear), and also built knowledge and capacity for what needed doing throughout the rest of the strategy change cycle.

The board itself met three times to review assessment results and work on what the mission, vision, and values of the organization were and ought to be. Out of this process came the values articulated and elaborated on in the strategic (also known as comprehensive) plan: sustainability, visionary leadership, safety, responsiveness and innovation, and independence and focus (Minneapolis Park and Recreation Board, 2007, pp. 4–5). A set of vision themes also emerged that became guides for goal formulation and strategy development. In other words, the strategic issues concerned what the Park Board should do in order to bring the themes to life. The themes assert that, "As a renowned and award-winning park and recreation system, the Minneapolis Park and Recreation Board (2007, p. 9) delivers:

- Urban forests, natural areas, and waters that endure and captivate
- Recreation that inspires personal growth, healthy lifestyles, and a sense of community
- Dynamic parks that shape city character and meet diverse community needs
- A safe place to play, celebrate, contemplate, and recreate

The board established goals to support each vision theme. New strategies were developed deliberately in response to themes and existing strategies were also pulled together and organized in accordance with the themes.

A point worth emphasizing when it comes to strategic issue identification is that major issues are always likely to involve information technology, human resources, and financial management aspects. Issues in these three areas are now becoming salient for virtually every public and nonprofit organization (Bryson, Berry, & Yang, 2010). Information technology, in particular, is assuming almost paramount importance for organizations moving into e-commerce and e-government (Cassidy, 2002; Abramson & Morin, 2003; Abramson & Harris, 2003). It is imperative that issues involving information technology, human resources, and financial management be addressed in such a way that they support the organization's overall mission and efforts to meet its mandates and create public value.

How Should Strategic Issues Be Described?

An adequate strategic issue description (1) phrases the issue as a question the organization can do something about and that has more than one answer, (2) discusses the confluence of factors (mission, mandates, and internal and external environmental aspects, or SWOC/Ts) that make the issue strategic, and (3) articulates the consequences of not addressing the issue. A strategic issue description probably should be no longer than a page or two for it to attract the attention of and be useful to busy decision makers and opinion leaders.

There are several reasons why the issue should be phrased as a question the organization can do something about. First, if there is nothing the organization can do about a situation, then there is no strategic issue, at least not for the organization. This apparent issue, in other words, is really a condition or constraint. Having said that, I must point out that a strategic issue may exist if the organization is forced by circumstances into doing something, however symbolic or ineffective, about the condition (Edelman, 2001). Second, effective strategic planning has an action orientation. If strategic planning does not produce useful decisions and actions, then it probably was a waste of time—although it is not a waste of time to consider taking action in response to an issue and then to choose, based on careful analysis, not to act. Third, focusing on what the organization can do helps it attend to what it controls, instead of worrying pointlessly about what it does not. Finally, organizations should focus their most precious resource—the attention of key decision makers—on issues they can do something about. Articulating strategic issues as challenges the organization can do something about, particularly when done on a regular basis, should help the organization strongly influence the way issues get framed and what might be done about them. In the vernacular, this will help the organization get out in front of the issues. If the organization waits until a crisis develops, it may be very difficult to deal with it strategically in wise ways (Heath & Palenchar, 2008). Strategic issues thus typically—or at least ideally—are not *current* problems or crises, although obviously there are almost always strategic implications to the way current problems or crises are resolved, and equally obviously decision makers *should* think strategically about how to address current problems and crises (Mitroff & Anagnos, 2005; Weick & Sutcliffe, 2007). In any event, strategic issues are typically complex and potentially destructive if not satisfactorily resolved.

There are several reasons why the issue should be phrased as a challenge that has more than one solution. If the question has only one answer, it is probably not really an issue, but a choice about whether to pursue a specific solution or not. In addition, if people are forced to frame issues in such a way that there might be more then one answer, the chances are increased that strategic issues will not be confused with strategies, and that innovative or even radical answers to those issues might be considered (Nadler & Hibino, 1998; Nutt, 2002). Innovative or radical answers may not be chosen, but they almost always should be considered, since dramatic performance gains, increases in key stakeholder satisfaction, or public value creation may result.

Attention to the factors that make an issue strategic is important both to clarify the issue and to establish the outlines of potential strategies to resolve the issue (Nutt & Backoff, 1992). Strategic issues arise in three kinds of situations. First, they can arise when events beyond the control of the organization make or will make it difficult or impossible to accomplish basic objectives acceptably and affordably. These situations would certainly be challenges and may even be called threats. Second, they can arise when technology, cost, financing, staffing, management, or political choices for achieving basic objectives change or soon will. These situations might present either challenges or opportunities. Finally, they arise when changes in mission, mandates, or internal or external factors suggest present or future opportunities to (1) make significant improvements in the quantity or quality of products or services delivered, (2) achieve significant reductions in the cost of providing products or services, (3) introduce new products or services, (4) combine, reduce, or eliminate certain products or services, or (5) in general create more public value. Unless the context surrounding the issue is understood clearly, it is unlikely that key decision makers will be able to act wisely in that context, which they must do to improve the chances for successful issue resolution (Janis, 1989; Nadler & Hibino, 1998, pp. 107–126; Crosby & Bryson, 2005).

Finally, there should be a statement of the consequences of failure to address the issue. These consequences may be either exposure to serious threats or failure to capitalize on significant opportunities. If there are no positive or negative consequences, then the issue is not an issue. The issue may be interesting in an academic sense, but it does not involve an important or fundamental challenge for the organization. Again, the resource in shortest supply is the attention of key decision makers, so they should focus on issues that are most consequential for the organization.

Once a list of strategic issues has been prepared, it is possible to figure out just how strategic each issue is. Two methods for doing so, the use of a "litmus test" and construction of an "issue-precedence diagram" are covered later in the process design and action guidelines section.

EIGHT APPROACHES TO STRATEGIC ISSUE IDENTIFICATION

At least eight approaches to the identification of strategic issues are possible: the direct and indirect approaches, the goals approach, the vision of success approach, the action-oriented strategy mapping approach (Eden & Ackermann, 1998; Bryson, Ackermann, Eden, & Finn, 2004), the alignment approach, the issue-tensions approach (Nutt & Backoff, 1993), and the systems analysis approach (Senge, 2006). Which approach is best depends on the nature of the broader environment and the characteristics of the organization, collaboration, or community. Guidelines for the use of the eight approaches will be presented in this section; guidelines for the whole strategic issue identification step will be presented in the following section.

The *direct approach* is probably the most useful to most governments and nonprofit organizations. In it, planners go straight from a review of mandates, mission, and SWOC/Ts to the identification of strategic issues. The direct approach is best if (1) there is no agreement on goals, or the goals on which there is agreement are too abstract to be useful; (2) there is no preexisting vision of success, and developing a consensually based vision will be difficult; (3) there is no hierarchical authority that can impose goals on the other stakeholders; or (4) the environment is so turbulent that development of goals or visions seems unwise, and partial actions in response to immediate, important issues seem most appropriate. The direct approach, in other words, can work in the pluralistic, partisan, politicized, and relatively fragmented worlds of most public (and many nonprofit) organizations, as long as there is a dominant coalition (Thompson, 1967) strong enough and interested enough to make it work. That is, there must be a coalition committed to the identification and resolution of at least some of the key strategic issues faced by the organization, even if they are not committed to the development of a comprehensive set of goals or a vision of success (Bolman & Deal, 2008, pp. 181–238).

In the *goals approach*—which is more in keeping with traditional planning theory—an organization first establishes goals and objectives for itself and then goes on to identify issues that need to be addressed to achieve those goals and objectives, or else goes straight to developing strategies. Increasingly these goals and objectives are likely to be embedded in a balanced scorecard from a prior round of strategic planning; the issues thus concern how best to achieve what is in the scorecard. For the approach to work, fairly broad and deep agreement on the organization's goals and objectives must be possible, and the goals and objectives themselves must be specific and detailed enough to provide useful guidance for developing issues and strategies (but not so specific and detailed that they filter out wise strategic thought, action, and learning). This approach also is more likely to work in organizations with hierarchical authority structures in which key decision makers can impose goals on others affected by the planning exercise, and in which there is not much divergence between the organization's *official goals* and its *operative goals* (Rainey, 1997, p. 127). Finally, externally imposed mandates may embody goals that can drive the identification of strategic issues or development of strategies.

The approach, in other words, is most likely to work in public or nonprofit organizations that are hierarchically organized, pursue narrowly defined missions, and have few powerful stakeholders (Bolman & Deal, 2008, pp. 41–67). In contrast, organizations with broad agendas and numerous powerful stakeholders are less likely to achieve the kind of consensus (forced or otherwise) necessary to use the goals approach effectively—although they may achieve it in specific areas as a result of political appointments, elections, referenda, or other externally imposed goals or mandates. Similarly, the approach is likely to work for communities that are relatively homogeneous and have a basic consensus on values, but is unlikely to work well for heterogeneous communities, or those without agreement on basic values, unless extraordinary efforts are put into developing a real consensus on goals (Chrislip, 2002; Wheeland, 2004). Of course, many city and county governments have put in the effort to develop consensus-based goals for their communities with often impressive results; for example, Edmonton, Alberta, Canada; Miami-Dade County, Florida; Minneapolis, Minnesota; and King County, Washington.

In the *vision of success* approach, the organization is asked to develop a "best" picture of the organization in the future, as it fulfills its mission and achieves success. The issues then involve how the organization should move from the way it is now to how it would look and behave based on its vision of success. The vision of success developed in this step will be sketchier than the more elaborate version called for in Step 8 of the strategic planning process. All that is needed in the present step is a relatively short idealized depiction of the organization in the future (Angelica, 2001). The vision of success approach is most useful when it is particularly important to take a holistic approach to the organization and its strategies—that is, when integration across a variety of organizational boundaries, levels, or functions is necessary (Kotter, 1996; Barzelay & Campbell, 2003; Bolman & Deal, 2008, pp. 214–286). As conception precedes perception (Weick, 1995), development of a vision of success can provide the concepts necessary in times of major change to enable organizational members to see what changes are necessary (Mintzberg & Westley, 1992; Morgan, 2006). Finally, many people understand the utility of beginning with a sense of vision. When enough key actors think that way, it may be the best approach and may lead to truly integrated strategies, assuming the actors will be able to agree on a vision. This approach is more likely to apply to nonprofit organizations than to public organizations, as public organizations are usually more tightly constrained by mandates and conflicting expectations of numerous stakeholders. Public organizations will find the approach particularly useful, however, when newly elected leaders take charge after having campaigned for organizational reform based on their vision for the future, or been appointed because of their vision. In addition, the approach has been shown to be quite successful as a way of helping cope with significant downsizing. The Ohio Department of Public Health used a vision of success to help guide a dramatic downsizing of operations in response to mandated deinstitutionalization of its clients (Nutt & Hogan, 2008). This approach may also work for communities, if they are reasonably homogeneous, share an underlying value consensus, or are willing to take the time to develop a consensus (Chrislip, 2002; Wheeland, 2004).

Next, there is the *indirect approach*, which, as its name implies, is a more indirect way to identify strategic issues than the direct approach. The approach works in the same situations as the direct approach and is generally as useful. In addition, the approach is particularly useful when major strategic redirection is necessary but many members of the planning team and organization have not yet grasped the need, or cannot sense where the changes might lead. The method starts with the participants' existing system of ideas, helps them elaborate on the action implications of those ideas, and then recombines the ideas in new ways, so that participants *socially construct* (Berger & Luckman, 1967) a new reality, which allows them to convince themselves of the need for change (Bryson, Ackermann, Eden, & Finn, 2004). Participation in this process of social reconstruction is a means producing the commitment necessary to pursue new directions (Bolman & Deal, 2008, pp. 111–159). In other words, participants' own ideas, when recombined in new ways, help them see things differently and act accordingly. Innovation thus is more a consequence of recombination than mutation (Kingdon, 2002). When using this approach, the planning team develops several sets of options, merges the sets, then sorts the combined sets into clusters of options having similar themes using the snow card (or affinity diagram) process (discussed in Chapter Five) or the action-oriented strategy mapping process (described in Resource D). Each cluster's theme represents a potential strategic issue. The sets consist of options generated by the team to: (1) make or keep stakeholders happy according to their criteria for satisfaction; (2) build on strengths, take advantage of opportunities, and minimize or overcome weaknesses and challenges; (3) fulfill the mission and mandates and in general create public value; (4) capture existing goals, strategic thrusts, and details; and (5) articulate stated or suggested actions embodied in other relevant background studies.

The *action-oriented strategy mapping* approach involves creation of word-and-arrow diagrams in which statements about potential actions the organization might take, how they might be taken, and why, are linked by arrows indicating the cause-effect or influence relationships between them. In other words, the arrows indicate that action A may cause or influence B, which in turn may cause or influence C, and so on; if the organization does A, it can expect to produce outcome B, which in turn may be expected to produce outcome C. These maps can consist of hundreds of interconnected relationships, showing differing areas of interest and their relationships to one another. Important clusters of potential actions may comprise strategic issues. A strategy in response to the issue would consist of the specific choices of actions to undertake in the issue area, how to undertake them, and why (Bryson,

Ackermann, Eden, & Finn, 2004; Ackermann & Eden, 2011). The approach is particularly useful when participants are having trouble making sense of complex issue areas, time is short, the emphasis must be on action, and commitment on the part of those involved is particularly important. Participants simply brainstorm possible actions, cluster them according to similar themes, and then figure out what causes what. The result is an issue map (see Figure 6.2 later in this chapter). This process of producing word-and-arrow diagrams may also be called *causal mapping*, and it can be used in tandem with the other approaches to indicate whatever logic is being followed.

The *alignment* approach helps clarify where there are gaps, inconsistencies, or conflicts among the various elements of an organization's governance, management, and operating policies, systems, and procedures. The approach is based on the assumption that superior (or even just good) organizational performance requires reasonable (or better) coherence across an organization's governance, management, mission, mandates, stakeholder relations, policies, goals, budgets, human resources, communications, technologies, operations, and other elements (for example, Rainey and Steinbauer, 1999; Kaplan & Norton, 2006). If an organization is to be at least the sum of its parts, then there must be reasonable alignment across these organizational elements and between the organization and what it seeks to do in relation to its environment. Issues related to alignment are very common in all organizations, whether they are well-established, expanding, downsizing, or new start-ups. Indeed, leaders, managers, and planners should always be alert to possible alignment challenges—including throughout a strategic planning process—and should regularly consult with frontline workers about possible misalignments in operations. The approach thus works well in tandem with all of the other approaches. For example, the Hubert H. Humphrey School of Public Affairs at the University of Minnesota (on whose faculty I serve) underwent a major organizational transformation during the previous decade in order to assure its place among the nation's leading schools of public affairs. Throughout the strategy change process participants were alert to issues of alignment, including the need to update the school's constitution and bylaws, revise the mission, create new strategic goals, and assure that all governance, management, and operating systems were in sync with the newly clarified directions (Crosby, Bryson, Eustis, & Goetz, 2010).

The *issue tensions* approach was developed by Nutt and Backoff (1992, 1993) and elaborated in Nutt, Backoff, and Hogan (2000). These authors argue that there are always four basic tensions around any strategic issue. These tensions involve human resources, and especially *equity* concerns; *innovation and change*; maintenance of *tradition*; and *productivity improvement*; and their various combinations. The authors suggest critiquing the way issues are framed using these tensions separately and in combination in order to find the best way to frame the issue. The critiques may need to run through several cycles before the wisest way to frame the issue is found. The tensions approach can be used by itself or in conjunction with any of the other approaches. Taking the extra time to critique an issue statement using the tensions approach is advisable when the costs of getting the issue framing wrong are quite high, or when there is a lot of uncertainty about what the issue actually is.

Finally, *systems analysis* can be used to help discern the best way to frame issues when the issue area may be conceptualized as a system (and they almost always can be) and the system contains complex feedback effects that must be modeled in order to understand the system (Sterman, 2000; Senge, 2006; Mulgan, 2009). Systems analysis can vary in how formal it is and whether or not computer support is needed. Many systems do not require formal modeling in order to be understood, but others do, and it can be dangerous to act on these more complex systems without adequately appreciating what the system is and how it behaves. The more complicated the system, the more difficult it is to model and the more expert help will be needed. But there are limits to systems analysis, because there are systems no one can understand given current methodologies. Considerable wisdom is required to know when it is worth attempting sophisticated analyses, which analysts to use, and how to interpret and make use of the results.

The Direct Approach

The following guidelines may prove helpful to organizations that use the direct approach.

After a review of mandates, mission, and SWOC/Ts, strategic planning team members should be asked to identify strategic issues on their own. For each issue, each member should answer these three questions on a single sheet of paper (sample worksheets will be found in Bryson & Alston, 2011):

- What is the issue, phrased as an issue the organization can do something about and that has more than one answer?
- What factors (mandates, mission, external and internal influences) make it a strategic issue?
- What are the consequences of failure to address the issue?

It may be best to give individuals at least a week to propose strategic issues. The identification of strategic issues is a real art and cannot be forced. People may need time to reflect on what the strategic issues really are. Also, an individual's best insights often come unpredictably in odd moments and not in group settings (Mintzberg, Ahlstrand, & Lampel, 2009; Scharmer, 2009).

Each of the suggested strategic issues should then be placed on a separate sheet of flip chart paper and posted on a wall so that members of the strategic planning team may consider and discuss them as a set. The sheets may be treated as giant snow cards with similar issues grouped together and perhaps recast into a different form on blank sheets held in reserve for that purpose.

Alternatively, ask planning team members to individually brainstorm as many strategic issues as they can—answering only the first question—on individual worksheets. Have each participant place a check mark next to the five to seven most important issues on their individual lists. These items should be transferred to snow cards and then clustered into issue categories. The group (or subgroups) can then answer the three questions in relation to each cluster.

Whichever method is used, it is usually helpful to clarify which issues the group thinks are the most important issues in the short and long term. I usually rely on the use of colored stick-on dots to indicate individuals' views. I ask each person to place an orange dot on the five issues they think are the most important in the short term and a blue dot on the five issues they think are the most important in the long term. (The same issue can be important in both the short and the long term.) The pattern of dots will indicate where the majority opinion lies, if any exists. As with any judgmental exercise, it usually is best to have people make their individual judgments first and record them on a piece of scratch paper before they publicly express their views (by placing colored dots, for example). After individuals have expressed their views, a group discussion should ensue, followed by additional individual "voting" (using the dots) if it appears people have changed their minds. A more reasoned group judgment is likely to emerge via this procedure (Delbecq, Van de Ven, & Gustafson, 1975).

When at least tentative agreement is reached on the list of strategic issues, prepare new single sheets of paper that present each issue and answer the three questions. These new sheets will provide the basis for further dialogue if necessary, or for the development of strategies to resolve the issues in the next step.

The Goals Approach

The following guidelines are for organizations that choose the goals approach.

The goals approach begins with a compilation, review, and update of existing organizational goals or desired outcomes. These goals may be found in a variety of places; for example, prior strategic plans, functional area plans, key performance indicators, balanced scorecards, or mandated outcomes. Remember, however, that there may well be a divergence between an organization's official goals and its operative goals.

If the organization does not already have a current set of goals, then after a review of mandates, mission, and SWOC/Ts, members of the strategic planning team should be asked to propose goals for the organization as a basis for group discussion. Again, the snow card procedure is an effective way to develop and organize a set of possible goals quickly as a basis for further group discussion. More than one session may be necessary before the group can agree on a set of goals that are specific and detailed enough to guide the development of strategies to achieve the goals in the next step.

It may not be necessary to identify strategic issues if this approach is used; rather, the team may move directly to the strategy development step. If strategic issues are identified, they are likely to pose questions such as: "How do we gain the agreement of key decision makers on this set of goals?" "How do we establish priorities among these goals?" "And what are the best strategies for achieving the goals?" The Loft essentially followed this latter approach, although instead of identifying strategic issues in relation to goals, they did so in relation to the key elements of their mission. An alternative way to identify a set of goals for the organization is to assign one or more members of the strategic planning team the task of reviewing past decisions and actions to uncover the organization's implicit goals. (This activity can also be usefully undertaken as part of the previous step, internal assessment.) This approach can uncover the existing consensus in the organization about what its goals are. It also can uncover any divergences between this consensus and the organization's mandates, mission, and SWOC/Ts. Dealing with the divergences may represent strategic issues for the organization.

Whichever approach to the development of goals is used, specific objectives will be developed in the next step, strategy development. Strategies are developed to achieve goals; objectives (as opposed to goals) should be thought of as specific milestones or targets to be reached during strategy implementation.

Vision of Success Approach

New boards or elected or appointed officials may arrive with a vision essentially already worked out. Their main task often will involve spending time selling their vision and incorporating any useful modifications that are suggested (Kotter, 1996). Other organizations wanting to develop a vision of success from scratch may wish to keep in mind the following guidelines.

After a review of mandates, mission, and SWOC/Ts, each member of the strategic planning team should be asked as an individual to develop a picture or scenario of what the organization should look like as it successfully meets its mandates, fulfills its mission, creates public value, and in general achieves its full potential. The visions should be no longer than a page in length, and might be developed in response to the following instructions: "Imagine that it is three to five years from now and your organization has been put together in a very exciting way. It is a recognized leader in its field. Imagine that you are a newspaper reporter assigned to do a story on the organization. You have thoroughly reviewed the organization's mandates, mission, services, person-nel, financing, organization, management, etc. Describe in no more than a page what you see" (Barry, 1997, p. 56; also see Angelica, 2001).

The members of the strategic planning team should then share their visions with one another. A facilitator can record the elements of each person's vision on large sheets. Either during or after the sharing process, similarities and differences among them should be noted and discussed. Basic alternative visions then should be formulated (perhaps by a staff member after the session) as a basis for further discussion.

At a subsequent session, planning team members should rate each alterna-tive vision or scenario along several dimensions deemed to be of strategic importance (such as ability to create public value, fit with mandates and mission, stakeholder support, SWOC/Ts, and financial feasibility) and should develop a list of relative advantages and disadvantages of each vision. The team may also wish to consult internal and external advisers, critics, and pos-sible partners to gain their insights and opinions. Deliberation should follow to decide which vision is best for the organization.

An alternative approach involves asking team members to develop two lists: what the organization is moving *from* (both good and bad) and what it is moving *toward* (both good and bad) (Nutt & Backoff, 1992, pp. 168–177). The approach involves capturing the essence of the organization's past and present and then projecting what it might be into the future. The good and bad aspects inherent in future possibilities can be used to formulate best- and worst-case scenarios. A subsequent sketch of an organizational vision of success would highlight what is good that the organization wants to move toward, and take account of what is bad that the organization wants to avoid.

Once agreement is reached among key decision makers on the best vision, the strategic planning team may be able to move on to the next step: develop-ing strategies to achieve the vision. A major three thousand–member down-town church in Minneapolis, Minnesota, pursued the vision of success approach. Its strategic planning team constructed visions to guide subsequent strategy development in areas covered by its mission statement or other areas where it was clear new strategies were needed. These included:

- Worship
- Nurture (Christian education for member families and their children)
- Global outreach (education and action abroad)
- Local outreach (local social service and community action)
- Children and youth (bringing member youth more into the life of the church and doing more for youth who are not members)

- Ministry of caring (mutual support and comfort for those in need)
- Evangelism (faith sharing and development)
- Stewardship (resource development)
- Communication with the public (electronic broadcasts of services, public forums on timely issues)
- Facilities (redoing the sanctuary and entrances to the building, education, and outreach facilities)

Goals, strategies, and action steps were then formulated within each of these vision areas.

The visions developed with this approach actually may constitute a *grand strategy* for the organization, the overall scheme or plan for how best to "fit" with its environment. The strategy development step then would concentrate on filling in the detail for putting the grand strategy into operation.

The strategic planning team may decide to identify strategic issues first, however, before developing more detailed strategies for implementation. The strategic issues typically would concern how to gain broad acceptance of the vision and how to bridge the gap between the vision and where the organization is at present. It is important not spend all of your energy on visioning so that not enough time, energy, and attention are left for developing detailed strategies, implementation guidance, and vehicles for implementation. Atlanta apparently made this mistake in its *Vision Atlanta* process of the late 1990s (Helling, 1998).

The Indirect Approach

The following guidelines may help organizations identify strategic issues using the indirect approach.

Planning team members should review the organization's current mission, the summary statement of its mandates, the results of the stakeholder and SWOC/T analyses, statements of present goals and strategies, and any other pertinent background studies or discussions. The team then should systematically review these materials to brainstorm sets of possible options for organizational action. Each option should be phrased in action terms—that is, it should start with an imperative (get, acquire, create, develop, achieve, show, communicate, and so on). Each then should be placed on a separate snow card or oval (see Resource D). The following option sets should be created:

1. Create options to keep stakeholders happy where they are happy, or that will make them happy where they are not. (Obviously, the organization may not wish to make certain stakeholders happy. For example, police forces are not likely to pursue options that will make

drug dealers happy by relaxing law enforcement efforts; however, police forces might collaborate with economic development agencies, for example, to find alternative employment for drug dealers.)

2. Develop options that enhance strengths, take advantage of opportunities, and minimize or overcome weaknesses and threats.

3. Identify options tied directly to fulfilling the organization's mission, meeting its mandates, and creating public value.

4. Create options that articulate the goals, thrust, and key details of current organizational strategies.

5. Create cards or ovals for options identified or suggested by any other pertinent background studies or discussions.

The source of each option (stakeholder or SWOC/T analysis, mission or mandates, existing goals and strategies, background reports, or discussions) should be indicated in small print somewhere on the snow card or oval. Knowing the source can help participants assess the potential importance of options.

Once the option sets have been assembled they should be mixed and regrouped by team members into clusters that share similar themes. The theme of each grouping represents a candidate strategic issue. The action-oriented strategy mapping process also can be used to structure the clusters further by showing interrelationships among clusters and the various options that comprise them (see Resource D).

When suitable categories have been identified, and key interrelationships noted, the team should develop one-page descriptions of the strategic issues that answer the three questions discussed earlier. The process of noting the source of each option will help the team answer the second question, about relevant situational factors, and the third question, about the consequences of not addressing the issue.

The Action-Oriented Strategy Mapping Approach

People interested in the action-oriented strategy mapping approach will find detailed process guidelines in Resource D and in Bryson, Ackermann, Eden, and Finn (2004).

MetroGIS used action-oriented strategy mapping in a retreat setting during its first strategic planning process in December 1995 to develop a rough draft mission statement and sets of goals, guiding principles, core services and functions, and strategic issues (Bryson, Crosby, & Bryson, 2009). (The strategy map and the process used to develop it may be seen at http://www.metrogis.org/about/history.) After extensive deliberation involving key stakeholders, the coordinating committee, and the Metropolitan Council, agreement was reached in April 1996 on a formal mission statement, goals, guiding principles, set of core services and functions, and five strategic projects (called Strategic Initiatives) that really were strategic issues because they were then assigned to advisory teams to develop recommended courses of actions. The five Strategic Initiatives (SI) involved the questions of how best to:

- Obtain formal endorsement from key stakeholder organizations of the MetroGIS principles and expectations

- Execute and administer data-sharing agreements with key partners

- Identify and address common priority information needs among the stakeholders

- Implement an Internet-based data search and retrieval tool, now known as MetroGIS DataFinder

- Identify a sustainable long-term financing and organizational structure

MetroGIS's use of action-oriented strategy mapping thus is related to the goals approach discussed earlier. They used mapping to create a potential mission and goals. The strategic issues were bundles of possible actions that might be taken to achieve the goals. The advisory teams were charged with reviewing the bundles of possible actions and other actions they could imagine to determine which they would recommend as a way of achieving the goals and fulfilling the mission. The overall map actually was a composite map created from several separate maps developed by small groups of approximately eight to ten members each. This broadly based process enabled deep understanding and commitment among process participants to the final list of goals and strategic issues. The action-oriented strategy mapping process was used in a similar and just as successful way in MetroGIS's second strategic planning process in 2007–2008 (see Chapter Ten).

The Alignment Approach

The *alignment* approach helps clarify where there are gaps, inconsistencies, or conflicts among the various elements of an organization's governance, management, and operating policies, systems, procedures, financing, and competencies. The approach is based on the assumption that superior (or even good) organizational performance requires reasonable (or better) coherence across an organization's governance, management, mission, mandates, stakeholder relations, policies, goals, budgets, human resources, communications, technologies, operations, competencies, and other elements (for example, Rainey and Steinbauer, 1999; Kaplan & Norton, 2006). If an organization is to be at least the sum of its parts, then there must be reasonable alignment across these organizational elements and between the organization and what it seeks to do in relation to its environment. As noted, issues related to alignment are very common in all organizations, whether they are well-established, expanding, downsizing, or new start-ups. Indeed, leaders, managers, and planners should always be alert to possible alignment challenges. The alignment approach thus works well in tandem with all other approaches.

The following guidelines will help identify alignment issues:

1. Review documents pulled together or specifically prepared for the strategic planning process, looking for alignment challenges. Alignment challenges are often highlighted as a result of comparing and contrasting the results of stakeholder analyses and external and internal assessments of various kinds, including, for example, analytic performance reports, staff surveys, logic modeling, livelihood scheme development, strategy reviews, balanced scorecard use, and so on. Search for gaps, inconsistencies, or conflicts among the various elements of an organization's various governance, management, and operating policies, systems, procedures, financing, and competencies.

2. Pull together insights from these various assessments as a basis for a more encompassing dialogue around what the real alignment challenges are. Many alignment issues are likely to be essentially operational in nature, but the most significant gaps, inconsistencies, and conflicts are highly likely to flag potential strategic issues.

3. Consider using the alignment approach with any of the other approaches.

The Issue Tensions Approach

The following guidelines will help those who wish to explore the tensions surrounding an issue.

The tensions approach begins much like the direct approach. After a review of mission, mandates, and SWOC/Ts, planning team members are encouraged to put forward statements of potential strategic issues. The statements are then categorized according to whether they are essentially a question of human resources, and especially *equity* concerns; *innovation and change*; maintenance of *tradition*; or *productivity improvement*. After the initial categorization, the statements are then explored further to draw out any other tensions that might be involved. Thus, for example, an issue about executive pay (human resources) may also be explored in relation to the other tensions: human resources or equity concerns versus the need to foster innovation and change, versus the need to maintain a culture and tradition, versus productivity improvement. Drawing out these other aspects of the issue may allow for the kind of reframing often necessary to find constructive strategies in response to the issues (Nutt & Backoff, 1992; Bolman & Deal, 2008, pp. 303–333). The critiques may need to run through several cycles before the wisest way to frame the issue is found. The tensions approach can be used in tandem with any of the other approaches to gain additional insight. For example, the tensions related to goals, visions, clusters of actions, or system models may be explored.

Systems Analysis

Modeling a system of any complexity takes considerable skill (Sterman, 2000; Senge, 2006); therefore skilled help and facilitation should be sought if it appears that a system model will be necessary. Modeling is often done in a conference setting in order to elicit needed information and to build understanding of and commitment to the resulting model. Andersen and Richardson (1997) offer detailed guidance, what they call "scripts," for building a model directly with a planning team. Their approach includes the following steps:

1. *Plan for the modeling conference.* This includes goals setting and managing the scope of the work, logistics, and designing and making use of the appropriate groups for specific tasks.

2. *Schedule the day.* This includes a variety of planning guidelines, such as starting and ending with a bang; clarifying expectations and products; mixing kinds of tasks and including breaks frequently; striving for visual consistency and simplicity in model representations; and reflecting frequently on the model as it develops.

3. *Follow specific scripts for specific tasks.* Andersen and Richardson have developed scripts for defining problems; conceptualizing model structure; eliciting feedback structure; supporting equation writing and parameterizing for quantified models; and policy development.

It should be noted that the eight approaches to the identification of strategic issues are interrelated (a point that will be brought out again in the next chapter on strategy development). It is a matter of where you choose to start. For example, an organization can frame strategic issues directly, indirectly, or through action-oriented strategy mapping, and then in the next step can develop goals and objectives for the strategies developed to deal with the issues. Mission, strategies, goals, and objectives then can be used to explore issues of alignment or to develop a vision of success in Step 8 of the process. Or an organization may go through several cycles of strategic planning using the direct or goals approaches before it decides to develop a vision of success. Or the organization may start with the ideal scenario approach in this step and then expand the scenario into a vision of success after it completes the strategy development step. Particular issue areas may require system modeling in order to be understood well enough to guide subsequent strategy development. At various points along the way, the organization may explore issues, goals, visions, system models, or potential strategies further through using the alignment approach or using the tensions framework.

Finally, a planning team may use more than one approach as part of the same strategic planning effort. Differing conditions surrounding different issue areas can prompt the use of multiple approaches to the identification of strategic issues. Where useful goals or visions are already developed, they may be used to help formulate issues. Where they are not available, efforts to develop them or use the direct or indirect approaches should be considered. Whenever sophisticated analyses are needed, they should be undertaken.

PROCESS DESIGN AND ACTION GUIDELINES

The following process guidelines should prove helpful as a strategic planning team identifies the strategic issues its organization faces:

1. *Review the organization's (collaboration's or community's) mandates, mission, strengths, weaknesses, opportunities, and challenges, including any key indicators the organization watches—or should watch.*

2. *Select an approach to strategic issue identification that fits the organization's situation: direct, indirect, goals, vision of success, action-oriented strategy mapping, alignment, tensions, or systems analysis.* Whichever approach is used, prepare one-page descriptions of the resulting strategic issues that (a) phrase the issue as a question the organization can do something about; (b) clarify what it is about mission, mandates, and internal and external factors that make it an issue; and (c) outline the consequences of failure to address the issue. In the process of identifying and articulating issues, do not be surprised if: (a) mission itself is an issue, (b) you need to do issue-specific SWOC/T analyses in order to appropriately understand and frame the issues, and (c) the issues go through considerable reframing as the consequences of one framing versus another become clear.

   Also, no matter which approach you choose, do not be surprised if problems arise involving misalignment between or across the organization's mission, goals, strategies, staffing, technology, resources, and so on. Organizations are chronically out of alignment and issues can be expected to arise at points of mismatch (Schön, 1971). For example, MetroGIS grew out of a mismatch between a fragmented institutional environment in the Twin Cities metropolitan region, on the one hand, and the need for an integrated and functional metro-wide GIS, on the other hand.

The phenomenon of misalignment is so common that I have included the alignment approach as one of eight approaches to identifying strategic issues. In other words, serious misalignments may emerge as strategic issues, and planning team members should be alert to the possibility. (In my experience, misalignments are also quite likely to emerge as operational issues.) Team members also should search for misalignments in Step 7, strategy formulation; Step 9, implementation; and Step 10, strategy and planning process reassessment. There is almost always a need to work on appropriate alignments in those steps.

3. *Once a list of issues has been prepared, try to separate them into strategic and operational issues (see Figure 6.1).* Operational issues should be assigned to an operations group, team, or task force. If an appropriate grouping does not exist, it should be created. Some issues are likely to have both strategic and operational aspects; try to treat the strategic aspects first before assigning operational concerns to an operations group.

4. *It may be helpful to use a "litmus test" to develop some measure of just how "strategic" an issue is.* For example, a litmus test that might be used to screen strategic issues is presented in Exhibit 6.1. A truly strategic issue is one that scores high on all dimensions. A strictly operational issue would score low on all dimensions.

5. *Once strategic issues have been identified they should be sequenced in either a priority, logical, or temporal order as a prelude to strategy development in the next step.* The attention of key decision makers probably is the resource in shortest supply in most organizations, so it is very important to focus that attention effectively and efficiently. Establishing a reasonable order, or agenda, among strategic issues allows key decision makers to focus on them one at a time. (It must be recognized, however, that the issues may be so interconnected that they have to be dealt with as a set.)

An effective tool for figuring out a useful issue order is an issue-precedence diagram (Nutt & Backoff, 1992). An issue-precedence diagram consists of issues and arrows indicating the direction of influence relationships among them (which makes these diagrams a variant of an action-oriented strategy map; see Resource D). Figure 6.2 presents an issue-precedence diagram of the strategic issues facing

Exhibit 6.1. Litmus Test for Strategic Issues.

Issue: Issue is: Operational □   Operational and Strategic □   Strategic □

	Operational ◄————————————► Strategic		
1. Is the issue on—or if put forward, could it be on—the agenda of the organization's policy board (whether elected or appointed)?	No		Yes
2. Is the issue on—or if put forward, could it be on—the agenda of the organization's chief executive (whether elected or appointed)?	No		Yes
3. When will the strategic issue's challenge or opportunity confront you?	Right now	Next year	Two or more years from now
4. How broad an impact will the issue have?	Single unit or division		Entire organization
5. How large is your organization's financial risk and opportunity?	Minor (< 10% of budget)	Moderate (10–15% of budget)	Major (> 25% of budget)
6. Will strategies for issue resolution likely require: a. Changes in the mandates or other rules governing the organization, such as significant amendments in federal or state statutes or regulations?	No		Yes
b. Changes in mission?	No		Yes
c. New institutional or organizational design?	No		Yes
d. Development of new, or elimination of existing, service goals and programs?	No		Yes
e. Significant changes in revenue sources or amounts?	No		Yes

	Operational ◄――――――――► Strategic		
f. Major facility additions or modifications?	No		Yes
g. Significant staff expansion or retraction?	No		Yes
h. Important changes in stakeholder relations?	No		Yes
i. Major changes in technology?	No		Yes
j. Significant new learning?	No		Yes
k. Changes in the way strategy delivery is controlled in the present?	No		Yes
l. Development of significant future capabilities?	No		Yes
7. How apparent is the best approach for issue resolution?	Obvious, ready to implement	Broad parameters, few details	Wide open
8. What is the lowest level of management that can decide how to deal with this issue?	Line staff supervisor		Head of major department
9. What are the probable consequences of not addressing this issue?	Inconvenience, inefficiency	Significant service disruption, financial losses	Major long-term service disruption and large cost/ revenue setbacks
10. How many other groups are affected by this issue and must be involved in resolution?	None	1–3	4 or more
11. How sensitive or "charged" is the issue relative to community, social, political, religious, and cultural values?	Benign	Touchy	Dynamite

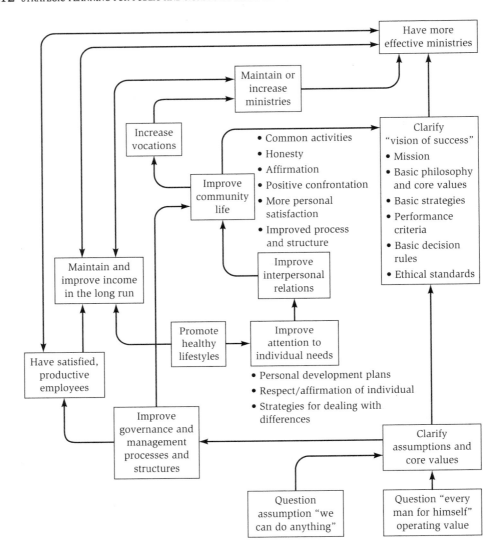

Figure 6.2. Strategic Issues Facing a Roman Catholic Religious Order.

the U.S. province of a Roman Catholic religious order. The order consists of priests and brothers who live in religious communities and work with low-income people and communities. The order employs many laypeople to teach in its schools, work with target communities, produce publications, and assist with fundraising and management.

The diagram indicates that in order to achieve more effective ministries, an issue closely linked with the order's mission, four additional issues must be dealt with first (maintain or increase ministries; clarify vision of success; maintain and improve income in the long run; and have satisfied, productive employees). In order to maintain or increase ministries more members will need to join the order (increase vocations) and income will need to be maintained and improved in the long run. In general, arrows leading to an issue indicate the issues that also must be addressed if the focal issue is to be resolved. Arrows leading from an issue indicate potential consequences of having addressed the issue.

Preparation of this diagram produced two crucial insights for the planning team. First, they were able to see that the key to "increasing vocations" was the sequence of issues flowing into that issue from "improve community life" (key strategy options are indicated by the bullet points), "improve interpersonal relations," "improve attention to individual needs," "promote healthy lifestyles," and "improve governance and management structures and processes." It is this set of issues, in particular, that is tied to the order's community life that prompted members of the planning team to push for strategic planning in the first place. Second, the team was able to make the case to the members of the order who mainly cared about having more effective ministries and increased vocations that the best way to achieve these was to first address the issues tied to improving community life. The diagram thus helped all members of the religious order understand the logical, and probably temporal, relationships among the issues; helped key stakeholder groups understand how their individual agendas might be served by working together on each other's issues; and helped the group decide what its priorities for attention should be.

Of course, the strategic implications of the issue agenda should be considered carefully. For example, it may not be wise to have key decision makers focus first on the top-priority issue, especially if there has been little prior interaction among key decision makers and little experience with constructive conflict resolution. In such circumstances it may be best to start the process of resolving strategic issues by focusing on the least important issue, so that decision makers can gain experience in dealing with one another and with conflict when the consequences of failure are least. Planning team members should talk through the likely implications of different issue agenda orders before deciding on the appropriate sequence for action in the next step, strategy development.

6. *There is a real art to framing strategic issues.* Considerable discussion and revision of first drafts of strategic issues are likely to be necessary

in order to frame issues in the most useful way. The process is likely to seem rather messy at times as people struggle with finding the best way to frame the issues, but out of the struggle wisdom is likely to emerge. If the organization's mission is itself a strategic issue, the organization should expect to develop a second set of issues after the mission is reexamined. Once the new or revised mission is in place, the *real* strategic issues can be identified. The importance of former Vice President Hubert Humphrey's advice—"When in doubt, talk"— should be apparent.

It is important to critique strategic issues to be sure that they really do usefully frame the fundamental policy questions the organization faces. The strategic planning team should ask itself several questions about the issues it identifies before it settles on a set of issues to address. Some useful questions include the following:

- What is the real issue, conflict, or dilemma?
- Why is it an issue? What is it about mission, mandates, or SWOC/Ts that makes it an issue?
- Who says it is an issue?
- What would be the consequences of not doing something about it?
- Can we do something about it?
- Is there a way to combine or eliminate issues?
- Should issues be broken down into two or more issues?
- What issues are missing from our list, including those that our culture might have kept us from recognizing?

It is especially important to remember that strategic issues framed in single-function terms will be dealt with by single-function departments or agencies. Strategic issues that are framed in multifunctional terms will have to be addressed by more than one department. And strategic issues that are framed in multiorganizational, multi-institutional terms will have to be addressed by more than one organization or institution. If one seeks to wrest control of an issue from a single department, then the issue must be framed multifunctionally. If one seeks to wrest control of an issue from a single organization, then it must be framed multiorganizationally. Strategic planners can gain enormous influence over the strategic planning process and its outcomes if the issues are framed in such a way that decision makers must share power in order to resolve the issues. Often, wresting control over the framing of the issue from the *status quo ante* is a crucial step in moving toward dramatic changes, or what will be called *big wins* in the next chapter (Schön, 1971; Baumgartner & Jones, 2009; Barzelay & Campbell, 2003; Crosby & Bryson, 2005).

The importance of this admonition is apparent when one examines organizations' efforts to engage in total quality management, performance budgeting, or new uses of information technology. In my experience, organizations often get into these ventures without thinking through carefully why they wish to do so. Partly this may be the result of particular professionals championing the causes that are the current fashion within their respective professions. Quality management then gets assigned to a *quality czar* of some sort, performance budgeting to the budget director, and information technology improvement strategies to IT professionals. The reform agenda then becomes the captive of these particular units, and the organization-wide perspectives and goals are subverted. The means substitute for the ends and a kind of *goal displacement* occurs in which instrumental values become terminal values (Merton, 1940). Although the power of the subunits may be enhanced, organizational performance is less than it should be. The quality initiative ends up making continuous improvements in unwise strategies; budgets enhance performance in the wrong directions; and IT improvements are led by technology rather than overarching organizational strategies. Convening forums in which the organization-wide perspective is developed is the best way to make sure the means serve the ends and not the reverse.

7. *Remember that there are likely to be at least three kinds of strategic issues in terms of the attention they require; each will need to be treated differently.* The three are (1) those that require no action at present, but must be monitored; (2) those that can be handled as part of the organization's regular strategic planning cycle; and (3) those that require urgent attention and must be handled out of sequence with the organization's regular strategic planning cycle. Do not be surprised if issues in this latter category emerge in the midst of the strategic planning process.

8. *Focus on issues, not answers.* The answers will be developed in the next step, strategy formulation. Those answers will be helpful only if they are developed in response to the issues that actually confront the organization. That is, an answer without an issue is not an answer.

Keep in mind, however, that people can be counted on to put forward favored solutions, whether or not they have much to do with the real issues (Neustadt & May, 1986; Nutt, 2002). Planners can utilize this tendency to their advantage by constantly asking team members what problems or issues their proposed solutions actually address. When this question is asked about several proposed solutions, a useful picture of what the real issues might be is likely to emerge (Eden & Sims, 1978; Nutt, 2002). Issues developed in this fashion have the advantage of emerging from what people actually can imagine doing, and thus may seem more "real" to them.

9. *Reach an agreement among key decision makers that a major fraction of their time together will be devoted to the identification and resolution of strategic issues.* Without an agreement of this sort, it will be too easy to forget that when key decision makers get together one of their most important tasks is to deal with what is most important to the organization. The decision-making bodies in all three organizations highlighted in this book made such a commitment.

10. *Keep it light.* As noted at the beginning of this chapter, this step in the strategic planning process can quickly become very serious and "heavy." It is important for members of the strategic planning team to keep a sense of humor, acknowledge emotions, and release tensions with good-humored mutual solicitude. Otherwise, destructive conflict or paralysis may set in, and the group may find it difficult to agree on a set of strategic issues and move on to developing effective strategies to deal with the issues. Emotions may run high—or low in the case of depression and grief—and the group will have to acknowledge these emotions and deal with them constructively.

11. Notwithstanding efforts to keep things light, remember that participants may fall into the pit or hit the wall (Spencer & Adams, 1990). The walls often consist of what appear to be dilemmas, vicious circles, or paradoxes that cannot be resolved (Hampden-Turner, 1990; Senge, 2006; Scharmer, 2009). For example, a public library with which I worked faced a vicious circle that resulted when its service culture collided with serious budget cuts. Existing strategies had begun to fail, because the system was at its limit and staff stress and burnout were reaching crisis proportions. Given their ethos, the librarians could not yet see what to do about it. They were all deeply committed to giving library patrons what they wanted—almost no matter what it took—but could not continue to do so without increased resources. The obvious need to narrow their role, set priorities among patrons, and adopt a more entrepreneurial and political mentality challenged their professional identifies built up over many years. They felt themselves surrounded by a wall they did

not know how to climb, skirt, tunnel under, or blow up. However, through lots of discussion, emotional venting, mutual support, and consideration of various options for addressing the issues, they did eventually figure out how to knock down the wall.

12. *Agreement on strategic issues to be addressed in the next step is likely to mark an important organizational decision point.* Remember that the identification of strategic issues is the heart of the planning process. Identifying the fundamental challenges the organization faces will have a profound effect on the actual choices made and ultimately on the viability and success of the organization.

13. *Managing the transition to the next step in the process—strategy development—is crucial.* Too often organizations move quickly to the identification of strategic issues and then back off from resolving those issues. The conflicts or choices embodied in the issues may seem too difficult or disruptive to address. Strong leadership and commitment to the strategic planning process must be exercised if the organization is to deal effectively with the basic issues it confronts.

SUMMARY

The purpose of Step 5 is to identify the fundamental challenges facing the organization concerning its mandates, mission, and product or service level and mix; clients, customers, or users; cost; financing; organization; or management. At the end of this step key decision makers should agree on a *strategic issue agenda*—the set of strategic issues to be addressed, arranged in priority, logical, or temporal order. Effectively addressing the issues on this agenda should help the organization satisfy its key stakeholders and create real public value.

The eight approaches to identifying issues are: the direct approach, the indirect approach, the goals approach, the vision of success approach, action-oriented strategy mapping, the alignment approach, the issue-tensions approach, and systems analysis. In general, governments and nonprofit agencies will find the direct and action-oriented strategy mapping approaches most useful, but which approach to use depends on the situation at hand.

To return to the story metaphor, this step constitutes the framing of conflicts (issues). The climax of the story will be reached in the next two steps, when these conflicts are resolved through the construction and adoption of effective strategies. Fear, anxiety, guilt, dread, or grief about how these issues might get resolved can cause people to flee from strategic planning. Faith, hope, courage, and reasoned optimism typically are needed to press forward (Seligman, 2006).

The transition to the next step in the process will require careful management. It is one thing to talk about what is fundamental, quite another to take action based on those discussions. Strong leadership, high morale, and a reasonable sense of psychological safety and optimism will all help the team and organization keep moving ahead. Unless they push on, organizational effectiveness and stakeholder satisfaction are likely to suffer, and the organization will not meet its mandates or fulfill its mission.

CHAPTER SEVEN

Formulating and Adopting Strategies and Plans to Manage the Issues

If you play with the fibers, they suggest possibilities.
—Annie Albers, weaver

This chapter will cover Steps 6 and 7, formulating and adopting strategies and plans. Even though the two steps are likely to be closely linked in practice, they should be kept separate in the planning team members' minds. Both concern creating ideas for strategic action and building a winning coalition (see Figure 2.4), but the dynamics that surround each step may be dramatically different, especially when strategies must be adopted by elected or appointed policy boards. Strategy formulation often involves freewheeling creativity and the give-and-take of dialogue and deliberation, while formal adoption of strategies and strategic plans can involve political intrigue, tough bargaining, public posturing, and high drama. Strategies should be formulated that can be adopted in politically acceptable, technically and administratively workable, results-oriented, and legally, ethically and morally defensible form.

Strategy may be thought of as a pattern of purposes, policies, programs, projects, actions, decisions, or resource allocations that defines what an organization (or other entity) is, what it does, and why it does it. Strategy therefore is the extension of an organization's mission, forming a purpose-driven (and sometimes purpose-revealing) bridge between the organization and its environment. Strategies typically are developed to deal with strategic issues; that is, they outline the organization's response to the fundamental challenges it faces. To follow the bridge metaphor, strategic issues show where bridges are needed, and strategies are the bridges. (If the goal approach to strategic issues is taken, strategies will be developed to achieve the goals; or, if the vision of success approach is taken, strategies will be developed to achieve the vision.)

This definition of strategy is purposely very broad. It is important to recognize patterns that transcend and, ideally, integrate and align organizational policies, decisions, resource allocations, and actions large and small. General strategies will fail if specific steps to implement them are absent. Further, strategies are prone to fail if there is no alignment or consistency between what an organization says, what it pays for, and what it actually does. The definition of strategy offered here—an arrangement to achieve the mission, meet the mandates, and create public value—calls attention to the importance of this alignment.

Good strategies involve creating effective linkages with the organization's environment, even if the purpose is to change the context. As noted in Chapter Five, the word *context* comes from the Latin *to weave together*. The arrows in the strategic planning process outlined in Figure 2.1 may be thought of as the *threads* of communication concerning ideas about the organization's context and what might be done to respond usefully to it (Forester, 1999; Healey, 2006; Innes & Booher, 2010). The possibilities for creating good patterns are suggested if you play with these threads or fibers, as weaver Annie Albers proposes. The *art* of creating an effective response is also highlighted—as it should be, since in my experience decision makers and strategic planning team members often are not creative enough in addressing strategic issues and crafting strategies (see also Mintzberg, 1987; Mulgan, 2009).

The art, however, is typically not without anguish. As psychotherapist-theologian Thomas Moore observes: "Creative work can be exciting, inspiring, and godlike, but it is also quotidian, humdrum, and full of anxieties, frustrations, dead ends, mistakes, and failures" (1992, p. 199). Rosabeth Moss Kanter goes further and asserts that every innovation is a failure in the middle of the change process introducing it (Kanter, 1983, 1989). Innovations are failures in the middle because they *must* be. By definition, they have never been tried before (at least by the organization), and success can only be determined after they are implemented. Thus strategy is intentionally defined in a way broad enough to help ensure that although strategic changes (a kind of innovation) may be failures initially, they are successes in the end.

Also, according to my definition, every organization (or collaboration or community) already *has* a strategy (or strategies). That is, for every organization there is already some sort of pattern—or *logic in action* (Poister, 2003; McLaughlin & Jordan, 2010)—across its purposes, policies, programs, actions, decisions, or resource allocations. The pattern is there—although it may not be a very good one. It may need to be refined or sharpened or (less frequently) changed altogether for it to be an effective bridge between the organization and its environment. The task of strategy formulation typically involves highlighting what is good about the existing pattern; reframing, downplaying, or pruning away what is bad about it; and adding whatever new elements are needed to complete the picture (Nutt, Backoff, & Hogan, 2000; Mulgan, 2009). Culture becomes very important in strategy formulation, as whatever patterns exist are typically manifestations of the organization's culture or cultures. Culture provides much of the glue that holds inputs, processes, and outputs together. The culture affects how strategic issues are framed and placed on the agenda in the first place, and subsequently affects which strategy options are given serious consideration (Khademian, 2002; Schein, 2010). Issues of organizational identity are similarly wrapped up in existing strategies and affect how issues are framed, get on the agenda, and are addressed (Dutton & Dukerich, 1991; Rughase, 2007).

Put differently, every strategy is thus almost always both emergent *and* deliberate, although the balance can vary a good deal (Mintzberg, Ahlstrand, & Lampel, 2009). The world of sports provides two useful examples of this emergent and deliberate quality. Jean-Claude Killy of France, triple gold medal winner in alpine skiing at the 1968 Winter Olympics, was asked why he drank wine for lunch. His reply: "What would you have me do—drink milk and ski like an American?" His unorthodox (some said wild) style of skiing revolutionized alpine ski racing. His style capitalized on his physique and psyche and, he said, was the only way he knew how to ski. In this sense his strategy was at first emergent and then became deliberate. It also became deliberate for many other racers who tried to imitate him. The other example comes from Francis "Fran" Tarkenton, former quarterback of the Minnesota Vikings and New York Giants, member of the National Football League Hall of Fame, and still holder of several NFL records. Tarkenton was known as a *scrambling* quarterback; he drove defenses crazy when he would run around in the open field, buying time until he could run or pass for a big gain. In describing his strategy as it moved from deliberate to emergent, he said, "Whenever things break down completely, I don't hesitate to roam out of the pocket and do the boogaloo."

Borins (1998), in a major study of 217 public sector innovations, explored when innovations were more deliberate or emergent. He found that politicians tended to be the initiators of innovations in times of crisis; agency heads were the initiators when they took over the reins or were overseeing an organizational change effort; and middle-level and frontline public servants were the initiators in response to internal problems or technological opportunities (pp. 48–49). But the extent to which these initiators' strategies involved deliberate comprehensive planning or emergent *groping along* (Behn, 1988) varied considerably. Formal planning was more likely when the changes involved responding to political mandates, large capital investments, coordination of a large number of organizations, or making a well-developed theory operational. Groping (or trying lots of things and learning by doing) was more likely in the absence of large capital investments, when it was not necessary to coordinate several organizations, when there was no well-articulated theory, and no political impetus. Overall, in Borins's sample, planning was more frequent than groping (Borins, 1998, pp. 64–65). A study by Nutt and Hogan (2008) of the downsizing of the Ohio Department of Mental Health through closures and mergers of its mental hospitals supports these findings. The authors found that better results were produced by emphasizing the importance of careful planning—including the use of *strategic waiting* to slow the process down enough so that people could get used to the new reality and work out a way forward (perhaps using some groping)—than were produced by more rushed processes. In other words, speed led to an overemphasis on groping, which resulted in disarray and confusion and did not produce good results; a more deliberate and deliberative approach resulted in better outcomes.

Recall also that most organizations' strategies remain fairly stable for long periods of time, and then may change abruptly. Thus, most of the time strategic planning will focus on adapting and programming strategies whose outlines are already reasonably clear (Mintzberg, Ahlstrand, & Lampel, 2009). At other times, though, strategic planning will be called upon to assist with the formulation of new strategies to deal with quite new and different circumstances. Even in times of rather drastic change, however, an organization is unlikely to discontinue all of its existing strategies, so the task of blending the old with the new and the deliberate with the emergent still remains (Benner & Tushman, 2003). In effect, organizations are always called upon to develop three agendas: what they will keep and improve, what they will initiate that is new, and what they will stop. Of the three, the stop agenda always seems to be the hardest to pursue.

As indicated in Exhibit 6.1, strategic issues and therefore strategies to address them may be focused on:

1. Addressing the need for new or revised high-level rules for making rules; institutional redesign; or adaptations involving new knowledge exploration, new concepts, changes in basic stakeholders and/or stakeholder relationships, or radical new technologies

2. Creating a process (for example, a strategic planning process) to develop mission, vision, and goals and realize them in practice

3. Producing programs, products, projects, and services

4. Controlling strategy delivery in the present

5. Developing future capabilities

6. Maintaining and enhancing stakeholder relations

Strategies also can vary by time frame, from fairly short-term to long-term, and by level. Four basic levels include:

1. Grand strategy for the organization as a whole.

2. Subunit strategies. Subunits may be divisions, departments, or units of larger organizations.

3. Program, service, or business process strategies.

4. Functional strategies (such as financial, staffing, communications, facilities, information technology, and procurement strategies).

Strategies are different from tactics. Tactics are the short-term, adaptive actions and reactions used to accomplish limited objectives. Strategies provide the "continuing basis for ordering these adaptations toward more broadly conceived purposes" (Quinn, 1980, p. 9). One needs to be cautious, however, about drawing too sharp a distinction between the two, given the importance of changing environments and emergent strategies. As Mintzberg (1994, p. 243) observes, "The trouble with the strategy-tactics distinction is that one can never be sure which is which until all the dust has settled."

PURPOSE

The purpose of the strategy formulation and plan development step (Step 6) is to create a set of strategies that will effectively link the organization (or community) to its environment and create significant and enduring public value. Typically these strategies will be developed in response to strategic issues, but they may also be developed to achieve goals or a vision of success. The purpose of the strategy and plan adoption step (Step 7) is to gain authoritative decisions to move ahead with implementing the strategies and plans.

The Loft's 2007–2012 Strategic Plan provides a good example of formulated and adopted strategies (The Loft, 2010). The plan is straightforward, clearly structured, well written, fairly short at fourteen pages with lots of graphics and white space, indicates when it was adopted by the board of directors, and includes contact information. The plan begins on its cover with a statement of the mission (see Exhibit 4.3). The organization's vision and values follow on succeeding pages. Next come seven pages devoted to the Loft's strategies arranged according to three themes: building and sustaining relationships, reaching out, and infrastructure (see Exhibit 7.1). For each strategy the plan lists action steps and an overall success measure. For example, the first strategy under the theme of building and sustaining relationships includes the following action steps:

- Continue ongoing evaluation and improvement of Loft programs, course offerings, activities, events, and overall operation

Exhibit 7.1. The Loft's Strategies, 2007–2012.

Strategic Themes	Building and Sustaining Relationships	Reaching Out	Infrastructure
	The Loft will continue to nurture and develop sustaining relationships with its various constituents—including writers and readers of all ages, at all stages of development, from all ethnic and socio-economic backgrounds—in attending to the values, interests, and needs of the literary community.	The Loft will broaden its outreach to Minnesota's socially, economically, and ethnically diverse communities in order to call forth the many voices in our rapidly changing state and evolving literary culture.	The Loft will strengthen and enhance the key elements of its already solid infrastructure—board, staff, finance, facility, and technology—to provide for the Loft's continued programmatic success.
Strategies	Build on the Loft's array of highly successful programs, courses, and activities.	Build on the Loft's already successful efforts to extend Loft programming to a broad range of communities.	Foster the leadership, creativity, and professionalism of the Loft's staff and board of directors while continuing to be recognized as an exemplary nonprofit employer with an excellent board of directors.

Strategies (continued)	Provide a coherent sequence of activities following a participant's Loft experience to encourage further engagement in Loft activities and to foster the participant's long-term growth and development.	Reinstate the Inroads Program (a mentoring program).	Deepen the Loft's relationships with its existing donors and funders, and welcome new philanthropists to the Loft community to provide the resources needed for the accomplishment of this plan and continued Loft achievement.
	Continue to expand the Loft's programming for children and youth.	Collaborate with new and existing local partners to connect various communities through a shared love of reading and writing.	Explore and pursue innovative mission-based income opportunities within existing programs and investigate the creation of new ones.
	Continue to expand the Loft's services, classes, and programs for accomplished writers.		Invest staff and board time wisely to make the best use of the Loft's beloved home, Open Book, in the nascent arts district along the Mississippi River.
	Provide meaningful opportunities for members to engage in all aspects of the Loft's work.		Employ new technologies to expand the Loft's reach and effectiveness, both locally and globally.

Source: Reprinted with permission of The Loft Literary Center.

- Continue existing collaborative partnerships with other successful literary or artistic organizations to encourage shared vision, consider exchanges, link to one another's Web sites, and copublicize national opportunities for writers and readers

- Expand the use of the Loft's Web site by all Loft departments to modernize and update programs to reach an increasingly Web-based readership.

The overall success measure of these activities is growth in vitality and attendance by people from a variety of backgrounds. The next two pages of the plan discuss the process by which it was developed. Then come two pages that present the outcomes resulting from the prior 2002–2007 plan. The final page of the plan (the back cover) lists the cochairs and members of the task force teams, along with the members of the strategic planning team.

A very different example is provided by the City of Charlotte, North Carolina's, City Strategy (discussed as well in Chapter Two) (City of Charlotte, NC, 2009). The City Strategy represents a statement of grand strategy for the city adopted by the city council (see Exhibit 7.2). The strategy includes a statement of vision and mission and then is organized in a balanced scorecard format. The four main scorecard categories (perspectives) are:

- *Serve the customer.* What are our mission and vision?
- *Run the business.* At what processes must we excel to achieve the mission and vision?
- *Manage resources.* How do we ensure value in achieving the mission and vision?
- *Develop employees.* How do we develop employees to respond to the mission and vision?

The city's current sixteen objectives are organized as responses to the questions presented by these perspectives. The four categories and sixteen objectives apply to all five of the focus areas the city council has identified in its grand strategy statement:

- Community safety
- Housing and neighborhood development
- Environment
- Transportation
- Economic development

Key business units, support business units, and divisions within the city manager's office (from aviation to solid waste services) submit annual business plans that describe how the organization provides services and programs, and

Exhibit 7.2. City of Charlotte, NC, City Strategy.

The City Strategy includes corporate objectives that guide and direct planning, decision making, and the accomplishments of the vision and mission.

City's Vision

The City of Charlotte will be a model of excellence that puts citizens first. Skilled, diverse, and motivated employees will be known for providing quality and value in all areas of service. We will be a platform for vital economic activity that gives Charlotte a competitive edge in the marketplace. We will partner with citizens and businesses to make this a community of choice for living, working, and leisure activities.

City's Mission

The mission of the City of Charlotte is to ensure the delivery of quality public services that promote safety, health, and the quality of life of its citizens. We will identify and respond to community needs and focus on the customer through strategic business planning and creating and maintaining effective partnerships.

Corporate Objectives by Balanced Scorecard Perspective

Serve the Customer

- Reduce Crime
- Increase Perception of Safety
- Strengthen Neighborhoods
- Provide Transportation Choices
- Safeguard the Environment
- Promote Economic Opportunity

Run the Business

- Develop Collaborative Solutions
- Enhance Customer Service
- Optimize Business Processes

Manage Resources

- Maintain AAA Rating
- Deliver Competitive Services

(Continued)

Exhibit 7.2. City of Charlotte, NC, City Strategy, Continued.

- Expand Tax Base and Revenues
- Invest in Infrastructure

Develop Employees

- Achieve Positive Employee Climate
- Recruit and Retain Skilled, Diverse Workforce
- Promote Learning

The four BSC perspectives and sixteen objectives apply to the organization as a whole and to each of Charlotte's focus areas; companion documents show how the objectives are tailored for each of the five main focus areas:

- Community Safety
- Housing and Neighborhood Development
- Environment
- Transportation
- Economic Development

Source: City of Charlotte, NC, 2009, pp. 3, 5. Reprinted with permission from the City of Charlotte, North Carolina.

responds to strategic and organizational initiatives. Each business plan relies on the common BSC format tailored to fit its unique circumstances and showing how the organization contributes to implementing the grand strategy. The city's annual performance report is also organized according to the BSC perspectives (City of Charlotte, NC, 2009).

Unfortunately, not enough governments, nonprofit organizations, collaborations, or communities have thought as long and hard as the Loft or the City of Charlotte about what they want to do, for whom, why, where, when, and how. Nor have most condensed their thinking into a succinct grand strategy, either in text or graphic form. As a result, there is often little more than an odd assortment of goals and policies to guide decision making and action in pursuit of organizational purposes. In the absence of deliberate or emergent overall strategic directions, the sum of the organization's parts can be expected to add up to something less than a whole. Of course, in a period of transition from a deliberate strategy to an emergent one whose contours are not yet clear, or vice versa, perhaps this is acceptable—even good (Lindblom, 1990; Mulgan, 2009; Kay, 2010). In such cases, sometimes the best strategy is sustained exploration, prototyping, trials, and pilot testing (Scharmer, 2009). Franklin D. Roosevelt argued in the midst of the Great Depression for "bold, persistent experimentation." He went on to say, "Try something; if it fails, admit it frankly, and try another" (quoted in Kay, 2010, p. 128). Or the organization may face powerful stakeholders whose expectations are conflicting or contradictory, making it unwise or impossible to develop a coherent grand strategy. In either case, the organization's key decision makers and planning team should be clear at least in their own minds about the legitimate reasons—as opposed to what may be excuses—for not having a grand strategy.

Special note must also be made of the importance for many organizations of having a strategy for technology use, particularly information and communication technology (ICT) use. Note that the Loft's first strategy mentioned earlier takes particular note of the importance of the World Wide Web for pursuit of the Loft's mission. A larger-scale example comes from the Labour Government of the United Kingdom, which published an ICT strategy for the central government in early 2010 (see Exhibit 7.3). Although the Labour government lost the May 2010 election and was succeeded by a coalition of the Conservatives and Liberal-Democrats, it is hard to see how the new

---

Exhibit 7.3. The ICT Strategy for the British Government.

The ICT strategy for government is:

1	The Public Sector Network Strategy	Rationalising and standardising to create a "network of networks," enabling secure fixed and mobile communications for greater capability at a lower price.
2	The government Cloud (g-Cloud)	Rationalising the government ICT estate, using cloud computing to increase capability and security, reduce costs and accelerate deployment speeds.
3	The Data Centre Strategy	Rationalising data centres to reduce costs while increasing resilience and capability.
4	The government applications Store (g-aS)	Enabling faster procurement, greater innovation, higher speed to deliver outcomes and reduced costs.

(Continued)

Exhibit 7.3. The ICT Strategy for the British Government, Continued.

5	Shared services, moving systems to the government Cloud	Continually moving to shared services delivered through the government Cloud for common activities.
6	The Common Desktop Strategy	Simplifying and standardising desktop designs using common models to enhance interoperability and deliver greater capability at a lower price.
7	Architecture and standards	Creating an environment that enables many suppliers to work together, cooperate and interoperate in a secure, seamless, and cost-efficient way.
8	The Open Source, Open Standards, and Reuse Strategy	Levelling the playing field for procurement, enabling greater reuse of existing tools, fewer procurement exercises and enhanced innovation—all at a lower cost.
9	The greening government ICT Strategy	Delivering sustainable, more efficient ICT at a lower price.
10	Information Security and Assurance Strategy	Protecting data (citizen and business) from harm—whether accidental or malicious.
11	Professionalising IT-enabled change	Building capable people and capable organisations with the capacity to deliver and manage fit for purpose IT-enabled projects and services.
12	Reliable project delivery	Using portfolio management and active benefits management to ensure that government undertakes the right projects in the right ways.
13	Supply management	Working together to gain maximum value from suppliers—both for individual organisations and collectively across the public sector.
14	International alignment and coordination	Ensuring that international treaties and directives reflect UK national requirements and that the UK remains at the forefront of delivery.

Source: Her Majesty's Government, 2010, p. 18.

government can avoid embracing all or most of the strategy. Any public or nonprofit organization, collaborative, or community would be wise to attend to the need for an ICT strategy that emphasizes common infrastructure, standards, capability, and implementation approaches and keep the fourteen enumerated "strands of delivery" in mind as strategic planning participants consider which strands might pose issues and which might offer useful strategy components.

DESIRED IMMEDIATE AND LONGER-TERM OUTCOMES

Several immediate desired planning outcomes may emerge from these two steps. First, the organization (or collaboration) might seek a grand strategy statement for itself, perhaps including an accompanying strategy map. It also might want subunit; program, product, project, service, or business process; and functional strategy statements for its constituent parts. It might want to tie all of these statements to balanced scorecards, as the City of Charlotte does. On the one hand, a complete set of these statements may be warranted if the organization has chosen the vision of success approach; the set would be necessary to clarify strategies for achieving the vision. On the other hand, the organization may have more limited aims. If it has chosen the direct or indirect approaches it may simply want a statement of how it will deal with each issue. If it has chosen the goal approach, it may want statements that clarify how it will achieve each goal. Collaborations may be inclined to produce issue-specific plans.

Second, the organization—or at least the strategic planning team and key decision makers—should gain clarity about which parts of current strategies should be kept and improved, what will be initiated that is new, and what should stop. Keeping these three agendas clear and conceptually separate is important; otherwise what is currently being done is likely both to drive out what is new and to make it harder to stop what should be stopped (Benner & Tushman, 2003).

Third, the organization may or may not wish to have a formal strategic plan at the end of Step 6, to be formally adopted in Step 7. The contents of a strategic plan will be discussed later in this chapter.

Fourth, planners may seek formal agreement to push ahead at the conclusion of Step 6. If a strategic plan has been prepared, and the organization (collaboration) is governed by an elected or appointed policymaking body, this agreement likely will mean proposing policy board adoption of the plan (Step 7). Policy board adoption then would be a fifth desired outcome. (It is likely that collaboration- and community-based strategic plans will need to be adopted by several organizations if the plans are to be implemented; see Chrislip, 2002, and Wheeland, 2004.) If the unit doing the planning is the board itself or if the organization does not need the approval of its board (or does not have a board), then Steps 6 and 7 may be collapsed into a single step. Formal agreement by key decision makers may not be necessary, but it usually enhances the legitimacy of strategic actions and provides an occasion for widely communicating the intent and content of such actions.

Finally, as is true throughout the process, actions should be taken when they are identified and become useful or necessary. Otherwise, important opportunities may be lost or threats may not be countered in time. It is also important to ease the transition from an old reality, whatever that may have been, to the new reality embodied in the organization's emerging strategies. If the transition can be broken down into a small number of manageable steps, it will be easier to accomplish than if it requires a major leap. Small steps can result in the equivalent of a big leap.

Ten additional longer-term desirable outcomes of the strategy and plan development steps can be identified. First, a fairly clear picture will emerge—from grand conception to many implementation details—of how the organization can create public value, meet its mandates, fulfill its mission, and deal effectively with the situation it faces. This picture provides the measure of clarity about where an organization is going, how it will get there, and why, which is an important part of most successful change efforts (Kotter, 1996). A new reality cannot be fully realized until it is named and understood (May, 1969; Weick, Sutcliffe, & Obstfeld, 2005).

Second, this new picture should have emerged from a consideration of a broad range of alternative strategies, which in itself should enhance organizational creativity and overcome the usual tendency of organizations to engage in simplistic, truncated, and narrow searches for solutions to their problems (Cyert & March, 1963; Nutt, 2002). Typically, major parts of existing strategies should continue and be improved, some new strategies should be tried, and some things should stop. Considering a variety of options, often via rapid prototyping, helps build the organization's capacity to embrace new approaches (Scharmer, 2009).

Third, if actions are taken as they become identified and useful, a new reality will emerge in fact, not just in conception. If the strategic planning exercise hasn't become *real* for team members and key decision makers prior to this point, it certainly will become real now (Boal & Bryson, 1987; Hunt, Boal, & Dodge, 1999).

Fourth, early implementation of at least parts of major strategies will facilitate organizational learning. The organization will be able to find out quickly whether its strategies are likely to be effective. Thus strategies can be revised or corrected before being fully implemented. Learning of this sort will be facilitated if a *formative evaluation*—designed to help shape implementation as it "forms"—has been included in strategic plans (Patton, 2008).

Fifth, emotional bonding to the new reality can occur as the new reality emerges gradually through early and ongoing implementation efforts. To return to the story metaphor, no drama can reach an effective and satisfying conclusion without a catharsis phase in which the audience is allowed time to break its emotional bonds with an old reality—and perhaps experience confusion, distress, depression, and despair—so that it can forge new emotional bonds to the new reality (Kübler-Ross, 1969; Spencer & Adams, 1990; Fiol, 2002). This bonding process is likely to fail if the gap between old and new realities is too large and not bridged in a series of *acts* and *scenes* (Mangham & Overington, 1987; Rughase, 2007).

Sixth, organizational members will get help working their way through the failure-in-the-middle syndrome identified by Kanter (1983). In many of the strategic planning efforts in which I have been involved, decision makers and planning team members all experienced this sense of failure somewhere between identifying strategic issues and formulating strategies to deal with the issues. The planning groups for the Loft, Park Board, and MetroGIS all worked at coming to grips with what they should do in response to the issues they faced. Each of these organizations had to acknowledge their difficulties, engage in constructive (though not always easy) dialogue and deliberation, offer support, and search for thoughtful responses to the issues before they could see their way through the difficulties and imagine a better and viable future (Roberts, 2002; Scharmer, 2009). In this regard, recall philosopher Jean-Paul Sartre's (1947) observation that "human life begins on the other side of despair."

Seventh, heightened morale among strategic planning team members, key decision makers, and other organizational members should result from task accomplishment and early successes in the resolution of important issues. If the organization is pursuing an important mission and dealing with the fundamental questions it faces, it can expect involvement and excitement on the part of key organizational actors (Selznick, 1957; Kouzes & Posner, 2008).

Eighth, further strategic planning team development (and indeed broader organization, collaboration, and community capacity building, development, adaptability, and resilience) should result from the continued discipline of addressing fundamental questions constructively. Improved communication and understanding among team (and organizational, collaboration, or community) members should occur. Strategic thinking and acting are likely to become a habit.

Ninth, if key internal and external stakeholder interests have been addressed successfully as part of the strategic planning process, a coalition is likely to emerge that is large enough and strong enough to agree on organizational (collaboration, community) strategies and pursue their implementation. If a formal strategic plan is prepared, there is likely to be a coalition large and strong enough to adopt it, implement it, and use it as an ongoing basis for decision making.

Tenth, organizational members will have the permission they need to move ahead with implementation of strategies. Those who wish to preserve the status quo will find themselves fighting a rearguard action as the organization mobilizes to implement adopted strategies.

If all these benefits are realized, the organization will have achieved progress in an effective and artful way. Following Alfred North Whitehead's observation about "the art of progress," the organization will have preserved "order amid change, and change amid order." It will have built new and more effective bridges from itself to its environment, and from its past to its future. And people will be able to cross those bridges relatively easily and painlessly.

TWO APPROACHES TO STRATEGY DEVELOPMENT

In this section I present two approaches to strategy development that I have found to be particularly effective. Participants should be adequately prepared prior to using either approach, as the success of the approaches depends on ideas that can be created, brought forth, and organized by participants. Preparations may include doing relevant background reading (including results of previous planning steps), visiting relevant comparison organizations, attending suitable conferences, being part of cognate online discussion groups, and so on. Recall, for example, that prior to engaging in strategic planning, the Loft held a conference in which members of its community explored the implications of the new information technologies for writing, literature, and audiences. The executive director and key board members knew that technology would have a major impact on the Loft's strategies, whatever they might be, and wanted to open participants up to the issue and its implications. As another example, prior to the 2007–2008 strategic planning process, key MetroGIS stakeholders frequently attended relevant conferences, including two forums hosted by MetroGIS that were well attended by its stakeholders—one to identify potential public-private partnering opportunities and the other to better understand where geospatial technology may be heading in the next five or more years. Participants read and discussed related literature and engaged in regular discussions about what MetroGIS might and should be doing.

The Five-Step Process

One useful approach to strategy development involves a five-step process, in which planners answer five questions about each strategic issue. (The approach is adapted from one developed by the Institute of Cultural Affairs; see Spencer,

1996). The questions themselves should be adjusted depending on which approach to strategic issue identification was used.

1. What are the practical alternatives, dreams, or visions we might pursue to address this strategic issue, achieve this goal, or realize this idealized scenario?

2. What are the barriers to the realization of these alternatives, dreams, or idealized scenarios?

3. What major proposals might we pursue to achieve these alternatives, dreams, or idealized scenarios directly or to overcome the barriers to their realization?

4. What major actions (with existing staff within existing job descriptions) must be taken within the next year (or two) to implement the major proposals?

5. What specific steps must be taken within the next six months to implement the major proposals and who is responsible?

The five-part process begins conventionally by asking strategic planning team members to imagine grand alternatives to deal with the specific issue. Then comes an unconventional step—enumerating the barriers to realizing the alternatives, instead of developing major proposals to achieve them directly. Listing barriers at this point helps ensure that implementation difficulties are dealt with directly rather than haphazardly. The next step asks for major proposals either to achieve the alternatives directly, or else indirectly through overcoming the barriers. Many organizations find that they must spend considerable time overcoming barriers before they can get on with achieving an alternative. For example, the Park Board did some organizational restructuring *prior* to reinitiating the strategic planning process so it could be assured of developing via strategic planning the kind of cross-functional strategies its leadership team wanted to pursue. Before officially launching the Loft's strategic planning effort, a large group of Loft stakeholders examined the possibilities that technology might entail for the organization—in order to make sure people's minds were open to doing things quite differently. And, in order to realize the public value creation potential of sharing data across government units and with other organizations, MetroGIS planners found that they had to deal with resistance within some governmental units to forgoing standard practices for recovering their costs of producing the data they were sharing.

The answer to the fourth question will essentially consist of a one- to two-year work program to implement the major proposals. Note that the work will be done by existing staff within existing job descriptions. This question begins to elicit the specifics necessary for successful strategy implementation. The question also conveys the notion that any journey must begin where one is.

For example, if full-blown implementation of the strategy will require more staff and resources, this question will ask strategists to be clear about what can be done, using existing staff and resources, to procure them. The question also begins to force people to put their money where their mouths are. As the precise shape and content of strategy implementation emerges, it will become quite clear who is willing to go ahead and who is not. The final question asks strategists to be even more specific about what must be done and who must do it. The implications of strategy implementation for organizational members will become quite real at the conclusion of this step. Defining specific actions and assigning responsibilities to particular individuals are requisites of successful strategy implementation (Joyce, 1999; Randolph & Posner, 2002). In addition, such specificity often will determine *exactly* what people are and are not willing to live with. Often such details prefigure the emerging future better than any grand vision. To paraphrase novelist Gustave Flaubert, the divine is in the details.

The fourth and fifth questions involve the group in the work of Step 9 (implementation), but this is desirable, because strategies always should be developed with implementation in mind. Actually, Steps 6 and 9 may be merged in some circumstances: for example, when implementation must be understood clearly before the key decision makers or policy boards within an organization or collaboration are willing to act; or when a small, single-purpose organization is involved.

A strategic planning team can use the snow card process to answer each question. (Alternatively, software or a Web site that supports brainstorming and clustering can be used to create and organize ideas.) The technique allows for great creativity, and it facilitates development of organization-specific categories to hold the individual ideas. Using this five-step process together with the snow card technique has several other advantages. First, relatively large groups of people can be involved (broken into subgroups of five to twelve people). Second, the process keeps people from jumping immediately to solutions, a typical failing of problem-solving groups (Janis, 1989; Nadler & Hibino, 1996; Nutt, 2002). Third, it keeps people from overevaluating their own and others' ideas; it keeps idea creation and evaluation in a reasonable balance. Fourth, it forces people to build a bridge from where they are to where they would like to be. Fifth, it forces people to deal with implementation difficulties directly.

Finally, a particular advantage of the technique is that a great deal of unnecessary conflict is avoided simply because alternatives proposed in answer to one question will drop out if no one suggests a way to handle them in the next step. For example, instead of struggling over the advantages and disadvantages of some major proposal to realize an alternative, the process simply asks the group what has to happen in the next year or two, with existing staff within existing job descriptions, to implement the proposal. If no one can think of a reasonable response, then an unnecessary struggle never happens and strategy remains tied to what people can actually imagine themselves doing. Strategy formulation thus remains more realistic and grounded. Of course, the group needs to make sure that answers in previous steps are linked to answers in subsequent steps to keep some proposals from being unintentionally dropped from sight.

But there is a caveat: The five-part process is very useful for developing the broad outlines of a strategy and for engaging fairly large groups of people, but it does not promote much understanding of the structure of relationships among ideas. Categories of ideas are created in response to the five questions, but the connections among ideas within categories or across responses to the five questions remain unclear. Care should be taken to ensure that important connections are made. It may be necessary to develop logic models to tie together key elements of desirable strategies (Knowlton & Phillips, 2009; McLaughlin & Jordan, 2010).

Some groups may find that it may not be necessary to answer all five questions; they may be able to collapse the last three questions into two questions or even a single question. The important point is that the specifics of implementation must be clarified as much as necessary to allow effective evaluation of options and to provide desired guidance for implementation. Recall that a strategy has been defined as a *pattern* of purposes, policies, decisions, actions, or resource allocations that effectively link the organization to its environment. The purpose of the questions, whether or not all five are used, is to get the organization to clarify exactly what the pattern has to be and who has to do what to make the pattern truly effective.

Some organizations (and collaborations or communities), particularly the larger ones, find it useful to have their strategic planning team answer the first two questions using the snow card technique. The task of developing answers to the last three questions is then delegated to task forces, committees, or individuals. Those answers are then brought back for review and perhaps decisions made by the team. Alternatively, the entire task of answering all five questions may be turned over to a division, department, task force, committee, or individual who then reports back to the appropriate review or decision-making body. Yet another alternative is to use the two-cycle strategic planning process outlined in Chapter Two. In the first cycle, divisions, departments, or smaller units are asked to identify strategic issues (or goals, or visions) and to prepare strategies, using the five-part process (or the action-oriented strategy mapping process described later in this chapter), within a framework established at the top. The strategies are then reviewed by cross-divisional or cross-departmental strategic planning committees, perhaps including a cabinet. Once this committee agrees to specific strategies, detailed operating plans may be developed. These plans would involve a detailed elaboration of answers to the last two questions.

Once answers have been developed to deal with a specific strategic issue, the strategic planning team is in a position to make judgments about what strategies actually should be pursued. In particular, the team needs to ask:

1. What is really reasonable?

2. Where can we combine proposals, actions, and specific steps?

3. Do any proposals, actions, or specific steps contradict each other, and if so, what should we do about them?

4. What (including the necessary resources) are we or key implementers really willing to commit to over the next year?

5. What are the specific next steps that would have to occur in the next six months for this strategy to work?

The process also helps with ongoing strategy implementation efforts. Once specific strategies have been adopted and are being implemented, the organization should, on a regular basis, work its way back up the original set of five questions. Every six months the last question should be addressed again. Every year or two the fourth question should be asked again. Every two or three years the third question should be asked. And every three to five years, the first two questions should be addressed again as well. Both the Park Board and the Loft used aspects of the five-step process as they developed their strategies—although the Park Board in particular paid very little attention to barriers, instead preferring to focus on strengths and what might be achieved by building on them.

The Action-Oriented Strategy Mapping Process

The action-oriented strategy mapping process is a second helpful approach to formulating effective strategies. The approach is based on the Strategic Options Development and Analysis (SODA) method developed by Eden and associates over the past thirty years (Eden & Ackermann, 1998; Bryson, Ackermann, Eden, & Finn, 2004; Ackermann & Eden, 2011). It involves creating options (phrased as actions) to address each issue. (This already will have been done if the action-oriented strategy mapping or indirect approaches to strategic issue identification have been used.) The planning team should be as practical *and* creative as possible when brainstorming options. As with the five-step process, it is important for mapping participants to be prepared.

Specific options can be triggered by any number of considerations relevant to the issue at hand, including mission, mandates, and ideas for creating public value; stakeholder analyses; SWOC/Ts; existing strategies; applicable reports and background studies; and knowledge of what other organizations are doing. Each option is written on a large self-adhesive note, snow card, or separate oval-shaped sheet of paper, 7½ inches long by 4½ inches wide. (Experience indicates this is the best size for capturing one idea per card and allowing cards to be grouped and moved around easily; see Resource D for a pattern for ovals and for detailed instructions in the use of the ovals process; see also Bryson, Ackermann, Eden, & Finn, 2004, and Ackermann and Eden, 2011, for more examples and guidance on the whole process.)

Once a set of options is in hand, they are stuck on a wall covered with flip chart sheets or on a whiteboard—by means of adhesive putty or tape if the options are on snow cards or ovals. The options are then arranged by a facilitator or the team members and linked with arrows indicating which options cause or influence the achievement of other options. An option can be part of more than one influence chain. The result is a *map* of action-to-outcome (cause-to-effect, means-to-end) relationships between the options intended to address the issue at hand. The team is then asked to develop options that outline consequences (desired or otherwise) of effectively address-ing the issue. These options are used to extend the action-to-outcome relation-ships to develop goals for the organization in each issue area. Options toward the end of a chain of arrows (usually placed near the top of the map) are likely to be goals and are likely to be closely related to the organization's mission. Once a draft map has been prepared, it can be discussed further, reviewed, and revised until the full range of options for addressing each issue is articu-lated and the full range of possible goals for each issue area is understood. Particular action-to-outcome sets can then be selected as strategies for address-ing each issue. As with the five-step process, this method also shades over into the work of Step 9.

Maps can get quite large, and computer support may be needed to under-stand, analyze, and manage the resulting complexity. Decision Explorer soft-ware has been specially designed for this purpose (Banxia Software, 2010). (More information on the software is offered in Resource D.)

MetroGIS relied on action-oriented strategy mapping and the Decision Explorer software (among other techniques) to develop the strategies designed to deal with the strategic issues it faced as part of its 1995–1996 and 2007–2008 strategic planning processes (discussed in Chapter Six). The strategies growing out of each process are grouped into *strategic initiatives* (Exhibit 7.4) (Bryson, Crosby, & Bryson, 2009). In the interim between the two processes, efforts concentrated on developing and updating as needed the initial set of strategic initiatives. Of the three main cases discussed in this book, MetroGIS's strate-gic plans have been the most detailed. In part this has had to do with its completely voluntary nature, which means that transparency, clarity, and logic are extremely important, as are the education of members and advocacy of the organization based on the creation of public value. The mapping processes used as part of the strategic planning processes helped build necessary under-standing of what MetroGIS should do, how it should do it, and why.

Exhibit 7.4. MetroGIS Strategic Initiatives.

1996–2001

- Obtain formal endorsement from key stakeholder organizations of MetroGIS principles and expectations.
- Execute and administer data-sharing agreements with critical partners.
- Implement an Internet-based data search and retrieval tool, now known as MetroGIS DataFinder.
- Identify and address common priority information needs among the stakeholders.
- Identify a sustainable long-term financing and organizational structure.

2008–2011

- Develop and maintain regional data solutions to address shared information needs.
- Expand regional solutions to include support and development of application services.
- Facilitate better data sharing.
- Promote a forum for knowledge sharing.
- Build advocacy and awareness.
- Expand MetroGIS stakeholders.
- Maintain funding policies that make the most efficient and effective use of available resources and revenue for systemwide benefit.
- Optimize MetroGIS governance and organizational structure.

Source: MetroGIS, 2010. Reprinted by permission of the Metropolitan Council of the Twin Cities.

STRATEGIC PLANS

Strategic plans can vary a great deal in their form and content. The simplest form of strategic plan may be nothing more than an unwritten agreement among key decision makers about the organization's mission and what it should do given its circumstances. This is the most common form of strategic plan and clearly reflects a basic premise of this book—that shared strategic thinking. acting, and learning are what count, not strategic plans in and of themselves. As Mintzberg (1994, p. 252) notes, "Organizations function on the basis of commitment and mind set."

But coordinated action among a variety of organizational actors over time usually requires some kind of reasonably formal plan so that people can keep track of what they should do and why (Daft, 2009; Bolman & Deal, 2008). For one thing, people forget, and the plan can help remind them of what has been decided. The plan also provides a baseline for judging strategic performance. And the plan serves a more overtly political purpose: it usually amounts to a treaty among key actors, factions, and coalitions. Finally, the plan (perhaps not in all its details) can serve as a communications and public relations document for internal and external audiences.

The simplest form of written strategic plan consists of the final versions of several of the worksheets in Bryson and Alston (2011):

- Mission statement
- Mandates statement
- Vision of success, if one has been prepared
- SWOC/T analysis (perhaps as an appendix)
- Strategic issues (or a set of goals, or scenario outlining the preferred future)
- Strategies—grand; subunit; program, service, product, project, and business process; and functional—including especially information technology, human resources, and financial strategies. (Indeed, for many organizations pursuing e-commerce or e-government strategies, the IT strategy, though functional, is becoming paramount and must be aligned with the organization's fundamental strategies.)

Most organizations will prefer, however, to use the final versions of the worksheets as background material for preparation of a written strategic plan. When this approach is taken, a table of contents for a very complete strategic plan might include the following headings (Barry, 1997; Bryson & Alston, 2011):

- Executive summary
- Introduction (including purpose, process, and participation, as well as a brief organizational history)
- Mission statement (including meeting the mandates)
- Mandates statement (may be presented as an appendix)

- Vision of success (if one has been prepared)
- Values and guiding principles
- Situation analysis, including SWOC/Ts (perhaps as an appendix)
- Goals, overarching performance indicators, and grand strategy statement
- Issue-specific goals, performance indicators, and strategy statements
- Subunit goals, performance indicators, and strategy statements (if applicable)
- Program, service, product, project, or business process plans, including goals, performance indicators, and strategy statements
- Functional strategy statements, goals, and performance indicators
- Implementation plans (perhaps including action plans)
- Staffing plans (including needed full-time staff, part-time staff, and volunteers)
- Financial plans (including operating budgets for each year of the plan, plus any necessary capital budgets or fundraising plans)
- Monitoring and evaluation plans
- Plans for updating all or parts of the plan
- Appendixes

The plan itself need not—and should not—be overly long. If it is, it will be put aside or forgotten by key staff.

Additional sections that might be included, perhaps as appendixes, are the following:

1. A review of needs, problems, or goals to be addressed
2. A description of the organization's structure (current, proposed, or both)
3. Governance procedures (current, proposed, or both)
4. Key organizational policies (current, proposed, or both)
5. Relationships with key stakeholders (current, proposed, or both)
6. Assumptions on which the plan is based
7. Risk assessments
8. Marketing plans
9. Facilities plans
10. Contingency plans to be pursued if circumstances change
11. Any other sections deemed to be important

The task of preparing a first draft of the strategic plan usually should be assigned to a key staff person. Once the draft is prepared, key decision makers, including the strategic planning team, the governing board, and possibly several external stakeholders, should review it. Several modifications are likely to be suggested by various stakeholders, and modifications that improve the plan should be accepted. After a final review by key decision makers the revised plan will be ready for formal adoption. After that occurs, the planning team will be ready to move on to implementation, although many implementing actions may have occurred already as they have become obvious and necessary over the course of the planning process.

PLAN ADOPTION

The purpose of Step 7 is to gain an official decision to adopt and proceed with the strategies and plan prepared and informally reviewed in Step 6. For the proposed plan to be adopted, it must address issues that key decision makers think are important with solutions that appear likely to work. Also, the political climate and stakeholder opinion must be favorable, and the barriers to effective action must be down. There must be a "coupling," in other words, of problems, solutions, and politics (Kingdon, 2002; Crosby & Bryson, 2005).

The planning team should keep Step 6 *conceptually* distinct from Step 7, as the dynamics surrounding the two steps may differ—even though in practice Steps 6 and 7 may merge (for example, when the planning involves small, hierarchically organized, single-purpose organizations). Step 6 may be quite collegial, as the team deliberates in forums about what might be best for the organization. Step 7, however, can be quite conflictual, particularly when formal adoption must take place in legislative arenas such as city councils, multiorganizational confederations, or the various boards and organizations necessary for effective implementation of community plans. (Readers seeking more detailed advice on this step should see Crosby & Bryson, 2005, pp. 290–311).

In order to gain the necessary support, key decision makers and important stakeholders must be open to the idea of change, and they must be offered specific inducements to gain their support. The arguments and inducements likely to produce support must be geared to their targets' values, interests, and frames of reference, as they will choose whether or not to support the proposal according to their own judgment (Bryson, 2004b). Considerable bargaining, negotiation, and invention of items to trade may be necessary in order to find the right combination of exchanges and inducements to gain the support needed without also bargaining away key features of the proposed strategies and plans (Susskind & Cruikshank, 1987; Thompson, 2008).

Formal adoption is likely to occur at a *window of opportunity*, an occasion when action favoring change is possible. There are three kinds of windows: those opened by the emergence of pressing issues, those opened by important political shifts (new elected or appointed policymakers, new executive directors, changed priorities of funding agencies), and those opened by reaching decision points (times when official bodies are authorized and empowered to act). A major purpose of the initial agreement step is to define the network of stakeholders likely to form the basis of a supportive coalition and to map out likely decision points in advance so that the full-blown coalition will be able to act when the specific, viable plan is ready for adoption. Steps 2 through 6 also are designed to prepare the way for formal plan adoption in Step 7, through producing the appropriate array of tangible and intangible process and content outcomes needed to convince enough people to move ahead (see Figure 3.1).

Sometimes formal adoption of a strategic plan occurs in stages over many months. For example, the MetroGIS strategies and strategic plans (what they call business plans) went through weeks of discussions following the strategy mapping sessions before they were ready for adoption. As another example, I worked with a school board that broadly supported most features of a draft plan. But board members had sharply differing opinions about the desirability of selling an old high school and the land on which it sat. The high school was obsolete and did not meet state standards, but was important symbolically as a focus for much of the community. After much discussion, bargaining, and negotiation over the entire facilities section of the plan, deciding and then redeciding, the board finally approved building a new high school on a site adjacent to the old one. The old high school was then to be remodeled to become the district's headquarters. The strategic plan was formally adopted six months after it was presented. The dynamics of this adoption process were often rocky—in sharp contrast to previous steps—except for the final stages of Step 6. When the first-draft strategic plan was formulated for review by the board, the conflicts became clear, as did the challenge of resolving them in a way that would assure a supportive coalition on the board and in the community. The difficulties of that challenge carried all the way through Step 7.

The Minneapolis Park and Recreation Board offers another example of a formulated and adopted strategic plan. The plan is a bit long for a strategic plan at fifty pages (though short for a physically oriented comprehensive plan), but Minneapolitans love their parks and, as with MetroGIS, it was very important for the Park Board's intentions to be transparent, logical, and understandable, and that the process of broad engagement with decision makers and the community be understood. The Park Board had some relationship and trust building to do and used its strategic planning process in part to do just that. The plan starts with the mission and a brief history, along with a letter of introduction of the plan to stakeholders from the president of the board and the park superintendent. An executive summary follows, along with a map of park properties and facilities and a table of contents (see Exhibit 7.5). The bulk of the plan is organized by the four vision themes discussed in Chapter Six. For each theme, the findings from research and engagement with stakeholders that helped shape the goals and strategies are presented, followed by the goals and strategies themselves. Next comes a discussion of the Park Board's values, how the values will be used to guide commissioners, staff, and volunteers in doing their work. The following section presents decision principles that will be considered when making decisions that have district- or systemwide impact. The implementation process is presented next, including, for example, the nature and role of implementation plans, work plans, annual budgets, performance measurement and review, and other guiding documents. The final sections present an outline of opportunities and challenges facing the district, describe the planning process, include a glossary, and offer thanks to all those who contributed to the process.

PROCESS DESIGN AND ACTION GUIDELINES

The following guidelines should be kept in mind as a strategic planning team formulates effective strategies to link the organization with its environment.

1. *Remember that strategic thinking, acting, and learning are more important than any particular approach to strategy formulation or the development of a formal strategic plan.* The way in which strategies are formulated is less important than how good the strategies are and how well they are implemented. Similarly, whether or not a formal strategic plan is prepared is less important than the effective formulation and implementation of strategies. Note as well that you do not have to have the best strategies, you just have to have good ones and stick with them. And good strategies are those that effectively address the specific issues (goals, visions) that require strategic action, meaning in part that they are adequately resourced. In this regard the importance of considering three agendas—the new initiatives, continuing efforts, and stop agendas—becomes clear. The stop agenda may well provide the resources needed to the new initiatives.

2. *It is very important that a variety of creative, even radical, options be considered during the strategy formulation process.* The broader the range of alternative strategies the team considers, the more likely they will find supportable, implementable, and effective strategies (Nutt,

Exhibit 7.5. Minneapolis Park and Recreation Board Vision Themes, Goals, and Strategies, 2007–2020.

Vision Theme 1: Urban Forests, Natural Areas, and Waters That Endure and Captivate

Sound management techniques provide healthy, diverse, and sustainable natural resources.	*Healthy boulevard trees connect all city residents to their park system.*	*Residents and visitors enjoy and understand the natural environment.*	*People and the environment benefit from the expansion and protection of natural resources.*	*Knowledgeable stewards and partners generously support the system's natural resources.*
• Develop and implement a natural area management plan that ensures natural areas (prairies, shorelines, and woodlands) are ecologically diverse, sustainable, and managed with scientifically based methods, giving preference to remnant native plant communities. • Develop and implement management plans for all lakes and water bodies within the Minneapolis park system that ensure these resources will be protected and enhanced. • Outline in the plan the partnerships with cities and watershed organizations that will aid in managing these resources. • Develop and implement a land management plan for the grounds, trees, and gardens of parks and golf courses in the Minneapolis park system.	• Revise and maintain the master planting plan for boulevard trees. • Plant boulevard trees that complement the park system's natural areas and are appropriate for the conditions of the boulevard. • Formalize a boulevard tree management plan that promotes a pleasant and safe street environment and focuses on scientifically based methods of planting and caring for boulevard trees.	• Encourage people to experience the natural environment by providing and maintaining, where feasible, trails and access points that serve people of all ranges of ability. • Provide environmental education and nature-based recreation that encourages all people, especially children and new populations, to explore, protect, understand, and become stewards of natural areas.	• Ensure day-to-day operations and construction do not damage natural resources within parklands, and require replacement when loss or damage occurs. • Within the park system, protect natural resources recognized as significant city, regional, or national resources due to historical, ecological, or aesthetic value. • Enforce leash laws and use of designated trails to protect sensitive ecosystems and wildlife.	• Develop programming to educate residents and park visitors of the importance of preserving and properly managing natural resources for health, water and air quality, and general environmental benefits. • Be a resource for residents and visitors seeking information about the park system's natural resources and urban forests. • Engage volunteers in the restoration, maintenance, and preservation of the system's natural resources.

- Work with and advise the City of Minneapolis as necessary to develop an integrated tree canopy plan that is consistent with the specified roles of each governing unit in existing agreements and policy documents.
- Provide leadership and coordination with area partners and regulatory agencies in monitoring, regulating, and improving water quality and the ecological integrity of water bodies throughout the park system. Enforce regulations and policies as necessary.
- Collaborate with local, state, and federal organizations to plan for and fund ongoing ecological management and restoration.

- Maximize every opportunity to reforest city boulevards.
- Work with the city to ensure that boulevard conditions and designs heighten tree longevity.

- Develop a strong connection between community/neighborhood center programming and the natural areas in the regional parks.
- Provide or support other entities in providing programming that teaches residents to reduce their individual negative impact on the natural environment.

- Balance public access to natural areas throughout the city, giving priority to acquiring, developing, or restoring areas in north and northeast Minneapolis.
- Enhance natural features in neighborhood and community parks to increase residents' awareness and enjoyment of the natural environment.

- Lead efforts to establish public and private partnerships that enhance the Minneapolis Park and Recreation Board's management of natural areas, waters, and urban forests.
- Sponsor programs and events that promote exploring, protecting, and enhancing these resources.
- Strengthen opportunities for research and cooperative exchange of information with universities, state and federal agencies, and recognized experts.
- Participate in efforts sponsored by local partners that enhance the Minneapolis Park and Recreation Board's goals for managing natural areas, waters, and urban forests within the park system.

(Continued)

Exhibit 7.5. Minneapolis Park and Recreation Board Vision Themes, Goals, and Strategies, 2007–2020, Continued.

Vision Theme 2: Recreation That Inspires Personal Growth, Healthy Lifestyles, and a Sense of Community

People play, learn, and develop a greater capacity to enjoy life.	*Residents, visitors, and workers enjoy opportunities to improve health and fitness.*	*People connect through parks and recreation.*	*Volunteers make a vital difference to people, parks, and the community.*	*Parks provide a center for community living.*
• Provide programming, especially for children, youth, and teens, in four key areas—physical, artistic, environmental, and social—at a level where high quality can be ensured. • Adapt programming to busy lifestyles and make it easy for individuals and families to participate. • Enrich physical, artistic, environmental, and social program delivery by partnering with other agencies, professionals, and providers.	• Provide access and encouragement for children and youth to participate in fundamental-level athletics. • Provide team sports for all age groups. • Provide opportunities for self-directed recreation on land and water throughout the park system. • Form or encourage groups and clubs that help motivate individuals to reach their health and fitness goals.	• Offer a culturally rich selection of programs, expanding cross-cultural programming and interpretive opportunities. • Be the source of information about recreation opportunities citywide. • Develop programming partnerships with groups and organizations that provide lifelong learning or work-readiness skills, such as community education.	• Provide volunteer opportunities that are meaningful to individuals of all ages and families and further the work of the Minneapolis Park and Recreation Board. • Promote volunteer opportunities in each park. • Recruit neighborhood adults to be positive role models in the lives of youths through mentoring and coaching.	• Design and implement a community center service model that is relevant to community members, provides a personal touch and easy access for all residents, creates a social gathering space for the community, and is delivered from a sustainable number of community center hubs (also a component of Vision Theme 3). • Provide programs for family members to enjoy within the same location.

• Identify and reduce physical and financial barriers to participation in programming. • Develop connections between programming in the community/ neighborhood park system and the regional park system. • Provide opportunities to interpret the park system's history and historic features through venues that are engaging and fun.	• Explore ways to integrate nontraditional recreation opportunities for all ages into the park system. • Provide recreation opportunities that support active lifestyles for workers before, after, and/or during their workday. • Ensure that recreation opportunities are available for persons with disabilities.	• Encourage opportunities that nurture relationships, develop an understanding of differences, and develop team-building skills. • Encourage the use of parks for public cultural, art, and history events, giving priority to those that support local artists or foster an understanding of local cultures and history. • Create and support events, concerts, festivals, athletic events, and celebrations that can be enjoyed by the entire community. • Tell the story of the park system through interpretive displays and programming, and by celebrating key milestones in park history.	• Encourage and manage large-scale volunteer projects that accommodate the desire of local businesses and corporations to volunteer in the community. • Initiate, sponsor, and support citywide volunteer projects and events.	• Tailor programs and services to the demographics and needs of the community. • Deliver programming that connects individuals to the land and to each other.

(Continued)

Exhibit 7.5. Minneapolis Park and Recreation Board Vision Themes, Goals, and Strategies, 2007–2020, Continued.

Vision Theme 3: Dynamic Parks That Shape City Character and Meet Diverse Community Needs

Parks shape an evolving city.				
Park facility renewal and development respects history and focuses on sustainability, accessibility, flexibility, and beauty.	*Focused land management supports current and future generations.*	*Financially independent and sustainable parks prosper.*	*Through outreach and research, park and recreation services are relevant today and tomorrow.*	*Easily accessible information supports enjoyment and use of the park and recreation system.*
• Continue to expand physical access to the Mississippi River in a manner that is aesthetically compatible with the riverfront and sensitive to ecological function, giving priority to implementing the Above the Falls Master Plan. • Provide a well-maintained, safe, and continuous trail system, giving priority to completing the "missing link" of the Grand Rounds Parkway, and providing trail connections in north and northeast Minneapolis.	• Integrate sustainable practices, ecological design for landscapes, and green building techniques into new construction and renewal of all amenities, giving priority to those practices that meet or exceed established standards, improve ecological function, and minimize long-term maintenance and operating costs. • Design and implement a community center hub model that serves community members, is sustainable, and taps the resources of area neighborhood, community, and regional parks (also a component of Vision Theme 2).	• Maintain a vital park system for city residents with a thoughtful acquisition and disposition plan and practice. • Acquire land that meets one or more of the following criteria (in priority order): fulfills park needs for growing areas or implements adopted park plans, meets the needs of areas underserved due to poor access or insufficient parkland acreage per household, provides trail connections or natural areas, establishes clear park boundaries, eliminates easements and leases, promotes ecological function, and secures unique sites or facilities.	• Increase revenue and develop sustainable spending practices throughout the park system that consider the short- and long-term costs and priorities for projects, programs, or services. • Work with necessary partners to enact and implement a park dedication ordinance to ensure new city development is adequately served with park and recreation facilities.	• Create a community outreach and research plan that focuses on identifying the park and recreation needs of the city's dynamic populations. • Evaluate current facility and program delivery based on key indicators and park visitation to determine the best way to meet the park and recreation needs of residents and visitors.	• Implement communication strategies to provide timely, accurate information to Minneapolis residents and park visitors, including those who do not speak English. • Enhance technology to share information effectively and efficiently across the organization and with the community.

• Balance the distribution of premier park and recreation features across the city, giving priority to adding features to north and northeast Minneapolis. • Help shape the built form of the city by developing and/or implementing park plans to acquire parkland and build amenities in current or projected growth areas of the city: Bassett Creek Valley, Hiawatha LRT Corridor, Downtown, Southeast Minneapolis Industrial, Midtown Greenway Corridor, Upper River, Northeast Industrial, North Loop, and Central Riverfront. • Periodically examine trends in household and population growth or shifts to identify additional study areas.	• Implement a sustainable, long-term renewal plan based on a complete inventory of the system, life-cycle cost analysis, and condition assessment of all park facilities. • Systematically develop activity plans that outline the delivery goals, benefits, facilities, operations, and maintenance required to provide each major recreation activity (or group of similar activities) in the park system. Use these plans to guide capital improvement and facility maintenance programs. • Build or renew facilities to meet or exceed standards for accessibility. • Build quality facilities that can be adapted to new uses as community needs change.	• Ensure parcels considered for disposition meet one or more of the following criteria: removing the parcel does not diminish recreation or environmental function of the park system, the parcel is not accessible by the public, the parcel does not serve the needs of individuals within a growth area of the city or is not part of an adopted park plan, and the parcel is too small for future park or natural area development. • Monitor and update lease and joint-use agreements to meet current and anticipated park and recreation needs.	• Prepare for future opportunities by increasing funding reserves and establishing a park endowment fund. • Obtain grants that further the work of the Minneapolis Park and Recreation Board. • Engage local businesses, corporations, foundations, and individuals in sustainable partnerships that build on the value of the system without jeopardizing aesthetics or over-commercializing the public realm.	• Regularly review social and demographic trends that affect service delivery. Be the first to identify and address new recreational needs and to reposition those recreational facilities that are no longer relevant. • Ensure staff are prepared to engage a diverse public by training staff to be sensitive to the park system's users, recruiting bilingual staff, and recruiting and retaining people of color for staff and volunteer positions.	• Cultivate open communication with the city, county, Metropolitan Council, and other elected officials or appointed groups. • Develop and implement a customer service program, including training, to ensure customer service techniques are applied effectively and consistently across the organization.

(Continued)

Exhibit 7.5. Minneapolis Park and Recreation Board Vision Themes, Goals, and Strategies, 2007–2020, Continued.

Parks shape an evolving city.	*Park facility renewal and development respects history and focuses on sustainability, accessibility, flexibility, and beauty.*	*Focused land management supports current and future generations.*	*Financially independent and sustainable parks prosper.*	*Through outreach and research, park and recreation services are relevant today and tomorrow.*	*Easily accessible information supports enjoyment and use of the park and recreation system.*
• Ensure park access for all residents by providing parks within an easy walk from their homes (no more than six blocks) and achieving a ratio of .01 acres of parkland per household. • Work with the City of Minneapolis and other entities to identify and support multimode transportation corridors between parks, with preference given to routes that encourage nonmotorized linkages between parks.	• Maintain an inventory of historic structures, documents, landscapes, features, and archeological sites that includes site analysis, evaluation of integrity, and historic significance. • Develop a management and interpretive plan for significant historic resources. • Beautify the park system by integrating gardens and art into park designs, and provide strategically placed gardens and art displays throughout city parklands and facilities.	• Pursue public and private partnerships to acquire, or promote access to, land for parks, open space, and recreation. • Pursue land trades when the trade will result in equal or more parkland that will provide greater function to the park system.	• Create opportunities for entrepreneurs, both nonprofit and for-profit, to enrich the park experience and implement innovative approaches to revenue generation. • Work with all levels of government to secure consistent, dedicated funding for park development, maintenance, and operation. • Develop and maintain a five-year financial plan that includes disaster recovery provisions.	• Engage and involve residents in identifying the program, service, and facility needs of their respective communities. • Anticipate and respond to the cultural diversity of the population.	• Effectively utilize technology to make program registration and enjoyment of services easy.

Vision Theme 4: A Safe Place to Play, Celebrate, Contemplate, and Recreate

Positive recreation experiences and welcoming parks prevent crime.	Residents, park visitors, and staff make safe choices in the parks.	Intervention and communication reduce safety concerns.	Parks are safe and welcoming by design.	Communities, public and private partners, and staff cooperate to promote safety.
• Get to know and positively influence youth. • Communicate clear expectations of behavior to park visitors. • Train all staff to recognize and divert dangerous activity within the park system. • Balance the ratio of children to adults at neighborhood, community, and regional parks by engaging all in positive activities. • Implement a safety first policy in which programs are cancelled when established minimum safety standards are not met.	• Educate park visitors on personal safety and actions they can take to avoid being a target of crime. • Install clear signage that instructs park visitors to safely use or access park amenities. • Teach drivers, pedestrians, and bicyclists the rules of the road and path safety.	• Identify recurring safety concerns and devise new prevention plans using available resources. Eliminating a service or facility will happen only when attempts to modify the problematic behavior have failed. • Increase visibility of park police officers. • Modify behavior that may cause harm to persons, the environment, or property within the park system.	• Design parks to meet or exceed safety standards, building codes, and Crime Prevention Through Environmental Design (CPTED) principles. • Develop and implement lighting standards by park amenities to promote a safe, welcoming environment while respecting natural habitats. • Provide access to restrooms, drinking water, bike racks, and shade throughout the park system.	• Ensure at least two adult staff are present during open building hours within neighborhood and community parks. • Support community policing efforts.

(Continued)

253

Exhibit 7.5. Minneapolis Park and Recreation Board Vision Themes, Goals, and Strategies, 2007–2020, Continued.

Positive recreation experiences and welcoming parks prevent crime.	Residents, park visitors, and staff make safe choices in the parks.	Intervention and communication reduce safety concerns.	Parks are safe and welcoming by design.	Communities, public and private partners, and staff cooperate to promote safety.
• Ensure that all staff are visible, welcoming, and positive. • Set park hours to promote safe use of the parks and safety in the community. • Ensure facilities are well-maintained (see park facilities renewal goal of Vision Theme 3).	• Educate residents and park visitors about the negative impacts of feeding or interacting with wild animals. • Dedicate staff time to safety training and risk assessment to prevent accidents that can lead to injuries and lost staff time.	• Warn park visitors and staff of one-time, seasonal, and periodic hazards related to natural occurrences, environment, operating and maintenance practices, and property damage. • Facilitate quick emergency response by installing distinguishable markers and building addresses that are recognized by 911. • Develop and maintain a disaster recovery plan for the park system.	• Monitor park amenities to ensure safety standards and codes are continually met, and develop plans to meet standards or remove facilities that do not meet minimum safety requirements. • Adopt new technology proven to effectively enhance safety throughout the system. • Work with communities and the city to provide safe pedestrian and bicycle routes to and within parks.	• Cooperate with other agencies to develop an integrated approach to chronic issues within and beyond park borders. • Work with communities to identify necessary safety improvements within parks. • Pursue public and private partnerships to promote safety in the parks and expand available resources.

Source: Reprinted with permission from the Minneapolis Park and Recreation Board.

2002; Mulgan, 2009; Scharmer, 2009). Constant awareness of the variety of options available will help ensure that a diverse set of possible strategies is considered before final choices are made. Recall the advice of the late, Nobel Prize laureate Linus Pauling: "The best way to have a good idea is to have lots of ideas." Or consider the advice of the great German philosopher, Johann Wolfgang von Goethe: "When ideas fail, words come in very handy." Keep talking and bouncing ideas off one another; keep your eyes open for nascent, useful, but nonmainstream ideas in the organization; pay attention to what might be going on elsewhere that is good; and do not become a victim of what has been called "hardening of the categories" (Mintzberg, Ahlstrand, & Lampel, 2009, p. 70). Another way of making this point is to argue that an organization should not engage in strategic planning unless it is willing to consider alternatives quite different from business as usual. If the organization is only interested in minor variations on existing themes, then it should not waste its time on a full-blown strategic planning exercise. Instead, it should concentrate on programming existing strategies (the main focus of Chapter Nine), and making process and quality improvements in those strategies. Or the organization may wish to pursue a strategy of logical incrementalism, that is, a number of small changes organized around a general sense of direction (Quinn, 1980; Barzelay & Campbell, 2003; Kay, 2010). Or it may wish to give up on strategic planning altogether and pursue traditional incremental decision making, or muddling through (Lindblom, 1959), as a way of finding an acceptable fit with its environment.

A number of authors provide useful typologies that can help strategic planning teams think broadly about the array of strategy possibilities for governments and nonprofit organizations (for example, Salamon, 2002; Nutt, 2004). For example, Christopher Hood and Helen Margetts (2007) propose a typology that asserts governments use tools for *detection*—to take in information—and to *effect* change outside government. Detectors and effectors can be passively or actively used (or somewhere in between) and aimed at particular individuals or groups, or more broadly. Hood and Margetts argue there are just four broad categories of tools available for detecting information and effecting change. These include: communication tools (*nodality*), the possession of legal or official power (*authority*), money and other fungible assets (*treasure*), and the ability to act directly via people, skills, and materials (*organization*). The typology has the virtue of simplifying what otherwise can be a bewildering array of ways that governments can act in the world. The book is particularly good on discussing the ways information and communication technologies can help or hinder the work of governments. For example, variable road pricing in real time is changing the nature of tolling in many places (London, Singapore, Minneapolis, Miami) and digitized geospatially referenced data permits better ecosystem management, emergency responses, and weapons targeting. On the other hand, cybercrime and cyberterrorism are huge new challenges. The authors conclude that, "In the digital age as in every other, the challenge for government is to find new ways of using a limited basic array of tools effectively and creatively, as technology and social patterns change" (p. 196). So when considering options, be especially attentive to options that information and communication and other technologies make possible.

David Osborne and Peter Plastrik (1997, 2000) offer a range of strategy options for public organizations. Exhibit 7.6 groups these strategies according to type and source of leverage. The *core* strategy focuses on clarifying purpose, direction, and roles. The *consequences* strategy makes use of incentives, forcing reliance on markets, competitive contracting, and benchmarking, and using performance-oriented rewards. *Customer-focused* strategies create accountability to key stakeholders by inducing competition for customers, offering customers choices, and emphasizing service quality. The *control* strategy shifts power away from the top and center by empowering managers, frontline staff, and communities. Finally, the *culture* strategy emphasizes creation of an entrepreneurial and service-oriented culture. Osborne and Plastrik (2000) offer a superb source of practical advice on when and how to pursue these strategies. Bryan Barry (1997) presents an array of strategies typically pursued by nonprofit organizations (See Exhibit 7.7). Unlike Osborne and Plastrik's typology, the strategies are not grouped according to sources of leverage, but there are some clear similarities between the two lists. Barry also identifies the importance of attending to the environment; clarifying purpose, role, and market; doing the job well; being entrepreneurial and innovative when needed; and attending to key stakeholders.

3. *Consider using a three-step search process to find desirable strategies for addressing particularly troublesome issues, especially those involving considerable complexity (Crosby & Bryson, 2005, pp. 252–255).* The process allows the strategic planning team to unearth a range of strategy components and then narrow them down to feasible alternatives that may be assembled into an effective strategy. The process consists of the following steps:

Exhibit 7.6. David Osborne and Peter Plastrik's Typology of Public-Sector Strategies.

Type of Strategy	Source of Leverage	Approaches
Core Strategy	Clarifying purpose	Use strategic management to create clarity of direction
		Eliminate functions that no longer serve core purposes
		Clarify roles by separating policymaking and regulatory roles from service delivery and compliance roles; also separate service delivery from compliance
Consequences Strategy	Making use of incentives	Use markets to create consequences
		Use competitive contracts and benchmarks
		Use performance-oriented rewards as incentives
Customer Strategy	Making public organizations accountable to their key stakeholders	Induce competition
		Offer customers choice
		Emphasize service quality
Control Strategy	Shifting power away from the top and center	Give managers the power to manage
		Give frontline employees the power to improve results
		Give communities the power to solve their own problems
Culture Strategy	Developing an entrepreneurial and service-oriented culture	Change habits by introducing new experiences
		Create emotional bonds among employees
		Change employees' mental models

Source: Adapted from Osborne & Plastrik, 1997, 2000.

Exhibit 7.7. Bryan Barry's Typology of Nonprofit Strategies.

Sharpen the organization	Gain greater clarity about mission and goals, program effectiveness, accountability, funding and resource management, and marketing
Rekindle the fire	Reinvigorate the organization around purpose and mission
Find a niche	Clarify the organization's role and market
Focus on one or two success factors	Be a leader around one or two factors critical for success
Plan the mix of programs and funding	Carefully plan the mix of programs and funding to keep programs fresh and enhance responsiveness to community needs
Gain advantages associated with size	Pursue growth, including through alliances and mergers
Simplify or downsize	Eliminate activities that are not directly related to the core; wisely deploy the remaining resources
Replicate	Build on proven approaches and best practices; do not reinvent the wheel
Balance exploration with getting it done	Balance innovation in new and unproven areas with refining performance in time-tested strategy areas
Make relationships central	Concentrate on building strong relationships with staff, board, and other key stakeholders
Engage the community as an ally	Tap the resources of the community through better working relationships
Focus on root causes of social problems	Focus on prevention, research, advocacy, community organizing, or public policy work to get at root causes
Become entrepreneurial	Undertake new ventures or increase earned income
Become "chaos pilots"	Emphasize responsiveness and adaptability through creating flexible organizational designs and cultures, and hiring people who thrive on ambiguity
Pay attention to your organization's stage of development	Attend to issues of founding, growth, institutionalization, and leadership transition
Note sweeping trends	Focus on big changes and whether the organization is catching the wave, on the crests, or about to be in outwash; decide what to do about it

Source: Adapted from Barry, 1997, pp. 65–69.

a. A broad scan within and outside normal search channels, to gain an understanding of the general area within which strategy components might be found. Information and communication technologies can offer considerable help with such searches, but so can going to conferences and attending to trade publications.

b. A narrow-gauge search within the most promising areas to find specific strategy components likely to be effective, ethical, and acceptable to key stakeholders.

c. Detailed exploration of identified strategy components.

MetroGIS typically uses an informal version of this process as it develops its strategies.

Technologies of various kinds may show up in the search process and care must be taken in assessing them. Francis Bacon in his 1627 book *The New Atlantis* imagined a time when technology would help create the perfect human society. Mary Shelley's 1818 book *Frankenstein* showed what could happen when technology runs amok. Technologies can produce good and ill effects; thus, the use of technologies, particularly unfamiliar ones, must be carefully thought through. Similarly, different kinds of experts may be consulted during the search process and, again, care must be taken in assessing what they say. For one thing, you must make sure you have the right expert for the task at hand. For another, experts can be rather quirky—and just plain wrong—in the application of their knowledge, particularly when asked to think and act quickly (Janis, 1989; Gladwell, 2005; Gawande, 2010). So maintain an independent view of both technologies and experts.

4. *Remember that logical incrementalism can be very effective, but sometimes a big win is the way to go.* Incrementalism guided by a sense of mission and direction can result in a series of small decisions that c.an accumulate over time into major changes. Karl Marx is perhaps the progenitor of this line of thought with his observation that in social systems changes in degree can lead to changes in kind. Indeed, Mintzberg, Ahlstrand, & Lampel (2009) indicate that most strategic changes in large corporations are in fact small changes that are guided by and that result in a sense of strategic purpose. And Neustadt (1990, p. 192) in his study of U.S. presidential power observes, "Details are of the essence in the exercise of power, day by day, and changes of detail foreshadow institutional development; they cumulate and thus suggest the system's future character." In general, realization of a new future is easier if it can be shown to be a continuation of the past and present,

even if the new future ultimately is qualitatively different (Neustadt & May, 1986; Weick, Sutcliffe, & Obstfeld, 2005).

In effect there are two sets of polar opposite strategies—big wins and small wins (Bryson, 1988), and knowledge exploration and knowledge exploitation (March, 1991; Benner & Tushman, 2003). I will consider the big win–small win dichotomy first. A big win is "a demonstrable, completed, large-scale victory" (Crosby & Bryson, 2005, p. 276), while a small win is "a concrete, completed, implemented outcome of moderate importance" (Weick, 1984, p. 43). Because it highlights what is fundamental, the strategic planning process outlined in this book may tempt organizations always to go for the big win. Sometimes big-win strategies can work, but they also can lead to big failure. Julius Caesar had a penchant for big-win strategies, even when his chances of succeeding were not good. As he said, "If fortune doesn't go your way, sometimes you have to bend it to your will" (quoted in Freeman, 2008, p. 267). But we all know what happened to Caesar when he tempted fate once too often on the Ides of March and died in the Roman Senate at the hands of Marcus Brutus (his erstwhile friend and son of his lover Servilia) and other conspirators. The hubris that led him to persistently pursue big wins—often by bending or breaking the rules and needlessly affronting key stakeholders—frequently blinded him to the risks and consequences such strategies often entail, including needlessly making enemies, and led him to minimize the need to effectively manage those risks and consequences.

Although big-win moves should be considered, the organization also should look at how a whole series of small wins might add up to big wins over time. A small-win strategy reduces risk, eases implementation, breaks projects into doable steps, quickly makes change seem real to people, releases resource flows and human energy, empowers people, encourages participation, boosts people's confidence and commitment, provides immediate rewards, and preserves gains (Weick, 1984; Kouzes & Posner, 2008). Indeed, *Financial Times* columnist and Oxford don John Kay (2010) argues that typically our most important personal, organizational, and societal goals are achieved by pursuing them *obliquely* rather than head-on via big-win strategies. Nonetheless, a big-win strategy may be best when a small-win strategy is unworkable or undesirable for some reason. For example, Britain and France did not first try out a tiny tunnel across the English Channel. Big wins might also be pursued when the time is right—for example, when the need is obvious to a large coalition, the proposed strategy will effectively address the issue without any concomitant ill effects, solution technology is clearly understood and readily available, resources are available, and there is a clear vision to guide the changes (Crosby & Bryson, 2005, pp. 274–279). Big wins probably must be controlled by senior decision makers in fairly hierarchical organizations, or else may emerge through the loosely coordinated actions moving in the same direction of many people at the operating level (Mintzberg, Ahlstrand, & Lampel, 2009). Similarly, a big win in a collaborative setting may require the relatively tightly coordinated efforts of senior leaders (Provan & Milward, 1994, 2001; Huxham, 2003), but in a community setting may emerge from the relatively loosely coordinated efforts of many organizations (Wheeland, 2004; Innes & Booher, 2010). The Park Board and the Loft each pursued small-win strategies—each sought significant, but not frame-changing, improvements via a buildup of reasonably coordinated actions. Even so, each still encountered some opposition internally or externally over specific strategy choices. MetroGIS generally has pursued a small-win strategy of accumulating small wins, but it can be argued that these changes have added up to a big win over time. MetroGIS is now a taken-for-granted part of the institutional landscape and has changed the way its member organizations interact and access and utilize geospatial data. Its new mission adopted in 2008 may become frame-changing in its consequences as it calls on the organization to "to expand stakeholders' capacity to address shared geographic information technology needs and maximize investments in existing resources through widespread collaboration of organizations that serve the Twin Cities metropolitan area." The new mission goes well beyond the original mission of building the regional GIS network to focus on facilitating expanding regional capacities for creating public value through use of GIS.

The second pair of opposing strategies is knowledge exploitation and knowledge exploration. *Knowledge exploitation* involves getting the most out of existing technologies (broadly conceived). Major repositioning is not required in terms of the core business, major stakeholders, basic strategies, or key practices. Most of the decision premises can be inferred from much of current practice. Strategy improvement in these circumstances depends primarily on systematic pursuit of process and quality improvements via better process management—meaning mapping processes, improving the processes, and adhering to systems of improved processes (Benner & Tushman, 2003). Issues of knowledge exploitation tend to be more operational than strategic (see Figure 6.1). In contrast, issues requiring *knowledge exploration* tend to be more strategic and involve tensions that pull the organization in many directions (Nutt, 2001; Scharmer, 2009). Changes implied by the knowledge exploration activities of the organization—or provoked by the results of knowledge exploration by other organizations—often require substantial repositioning in terms of the core business, key stakeholders, basic strategies, and important practices (Benner & Tushman, 2003).

Organizations get into trouble when they invest excessively in knowledge exploitation activities to the detriment of knowledge exploration. For example, the U.S. Department of Defense (DoD) knows a great deal about war fighting, as its two military victories in Iraq in 1991 and 2003 demonstrate. What is now quite painfully obvious in the aftermath of the quick 2003 military victory—where DoD exploited the knowledge it had—is that the DoD knew far less about nation building and the creation of vibrant civil societies. In part this was because before the war then-President George W. Bush (in his 2000 campaign and later) said the United States did not "do" nation building; not surprisingly, he later changed his mind and DoD has been playing catch-up—including exploring needed new knowledge—ever since. The fact that senior civilian DoD and White House officials in the Bush Administration failed to appreciate the need for such planning for postwar Iraq and even ignored or under-mined needed planning that was under way prior to the war resulted in thousands of needless deaths and terrible waste of financial and other resources (Rieff, 2003; Fallows, 2006). In other words, needed knowledge exploration did not occur prior to the invasion (outside of what was done under the auspices of the State Department and was subsequently ignored). This was a very serious mistake and there remains considerable reason for caution in predicting what will happen ultimately in the aftermath of that war and in the parallel war in Afghanistan. A key point is that an adaptive organization must preserve a balance between knowledge exploitation and knowledge exploration. Too much knowledge exploitation will blind the organization to impending frame-breaking changes in its environment, and cripple it when the changes do occur. Too much knowledge exploration won't pay the bills fast enough, because almost by definition a lot of effort will be wasted before the effective answers or operational formulas can be found. To paraphrase Benner and Tushman (2003, p. 242), an organization's dynamic capabilities depend on simultaneously exploiting current technologies and resources to gain efficiency benefits and creating new possibilities through exploratory innovation.

5. *Effective strategy formulation can be top-down or bottom-up.* The organizations that are best at strategic planning indeed seem to deftly combine these two approaches into an effective strategic planning system (Mintzberg, Ahlstrand, & Lampel, 2009). Usually some sort of overall strategic guidance is given at the top, but detailed strategy formulation and implementation typically occur deeper in the organization. Detailed strategies and their implementation may then be reviewed at the top for consistency across strategies and with organizational purposes. Chapter Ten contains more information on strategic management systems.

6. *Decide how to link strategy development with the strategic issues identified in Step 6.* Planners need to determine whether strategies should be formulated in response to strategic issues, or to achieve goals, or to realize a vision. Issues also need to be addressed at the appropriate level in the system (see Exhibit 6.1). Most organizations probably will choose to develop strategies in response to strategic issues, at least at first. Smaller, single-function, or hierarchically organized organizations, or organizations that have engaged in strategic planning for some time, or communities with significant value consensus may find it easier to develop strategies to achieve goals or a vision. Nonprofit organizations are more likely than governments or public agencies to be able to develop strategies in response to goals or a vision. But other organizations too may decide that they need more clarity about goals or vision before proceeding very far with strategy development.

It is important to repeat a point made in the previous chapter: the various ways of developing strategies are interrelated. For example, an organization can start by developing strategies in response to strategic issues identified directly or indirectly or through the vision of success approach, action-oriented strategy mapping, the tensions approach, or systems analysis, and then develop goals based on its strategies. Goals then would represent the strategy-specific desired states to result from effective strategy implementation. Mission, goals, and strategies then can be used as the basis for development of a full-blown vision of success. Alternatively, an organization may go through several cycles of strategic planning using various approaches to issue identification and strategy development before it decides to develop a vision of success (if indeed it ever chooses to do so) to guide subsequent rounds of issue identification and strategy development. Or an organization may start with the ideal scenario approach and expand the scenario into a full-blown vision of success after it completes the strategy development step. Or the organization may identify strategic issues using various means and then develop goals or idealized scenarios to guide strategy development in each issue area.

No matter which approach is chosen, the five-part process outlined in this chapter provides an effective way to formulate strategies, particularly if the snow card technique is employed in each step. The questions will change only slightly depending on the approach. The strategic planning team may wish to assign different questions to different groups or individuals. If, for example, the team wishes to identify major alternatives and barriers to their achievement, it could ask task forces to develop major proposals and work programs to achieve the alternatives or to overcome the barriers. The action-oriented strategy mapping process is also an effective way to develop strategies to deal with issues, achieve goals, or realize visions. Again, the questions asked will vary slightly depending on the approach taken. The team may wish to develop the broad outlines of a strategy map and then delegate detailed development of strategies and work programs to individuals or task forces. MetroGIS took this approach when a group of key stakeholders developed a map at a retreat in December 2007 that helped clarify mission, goals, and strategic issues. The contents of the map were then studied by various groups before the current business plan (strategic plan) was adopted in March 2008. Various groups are now working on clarifying and implementing the details of the strategies in the plan.

7. *Describe strategic alternatives in enough detail to permit reasonable judgments about their efficacy and to provide reasonable guidance for implementation.* For example, strategy descriptions may be required to include the following information:

- Intended results or outcomes, along with performance measures
- Principal components or features, including necessary capabilities or competencies
- Timetable for implementation
- Organizations and persons responsible for implementation
- Resources required (staff, facilities, equipment, information technology, training)
- Costs (start-up, annual operating, capital)
- Estimated savings, if any, over present approaches
- Flexibility or adaptability of strategy
- Effects on other organizations, departments, persons, or communities
- Effects on other strategies
- Rule, policy, or statutory changes required

- Procedures for "debugging" the strategy during implementation (that is, formative evaluation plans) and for subsequent evaluations to see whether or not the strategy has worked (summative evaluation) (Patton, 2008)
- Associated risks and how they might be managed
- Other important features

Financial costs and budgets deserve special attention. Readers are encouraged to look at the section on budgets in Chapter Nine.

8. *Evaluate alternative strategies against agreed-upon criteria prior to selection of specific strategies to be implemented.* As a set the criteria should indicate the extent to which possible strategies are:

- *Politically acceptable:* for example, to key decision makers, stakeholders, and opinion leaders, and to the general public
- *Administratively and technically workable:* in terms, for example, of technical feasibility; coordination or integration with other strategies, programs, and activities; cost and financing; staffing, training, information technology requirements, facilities and other requirements; flexibility and adaptability; timing; and risk management
- *Results oriented:* for example, in terms of consistency with mission, values, philosophy, and culture; achievement of goals; relevance to the issue; client or user impact; long-term impact; availability or at least possibility of performance measures; and cost-effectiveness
- *Legally, ethically, and morally defensible:* for example, in accord with all applicable laws, rules, policies, and guidelines; justifiable in terms of commonly held ethical and moral frameworks and standards

The bottom line is that adopted strategies must meet the requirements for effectively addressing the issues, achieving the goals, or realizing the vision, while also satisfying key stakeholders. (For more about criteria, see Joyce, 1999, pp 50–60.) Those involved in strategy formulation or adoption, or both, should probably agree in advance what criteria will be used to judge alternatives. But even if the criteria are agreed in advance, be cognizant of people's ability to ignore them when they want to. As Benjamin Franklin observed, "So convenient a thing it is to be a reasonable creature, since it enables one to find or make a reason for everything one has a mind to do" (quoted in Kay, 2010, p. 90). Being a "reasonable creature" in Franklin's sense can at times be a good thing, but don't count on it!

But keep in mind a very important caveat—which has been emphasized previously—that sometimes you need to take action in order to figure out what the real issues, goals, or vision are. The process of strategy formulation is likely have helped the team and key stakeholders better understand the challenges and opportunities by figuring out what possibly might be done about them. Modifications to issues, goals, and visions are to be expected as a consequence of better understanding strategy possibilities. But occasionally the best you can do is have a conscious strategy of *strategic learning* (or purposeful wandering as described in Chapter Two) involving experiment and discovery that will help reveal what the actual issues, preferred goals, and desired visions should be. As Kay (2010, p. 62) says, "Successes and failures and the expansion of knowledge lead to reassessment of our goals and objectives and the actions that result."

9. *Consider development of a formal strategic plan.* Such a plan may not be necessary, but as the size and complexity of the organization grows, a formal, written strategic plan is likely to become increasingly useful. The members of the strategic planning team should agree on major categories and approximate length so that the actual preparer has some guidance. Indeed, a general agreement on the form of the strategic plan probably should be reached during the negotiation of the initial agreement (Step 1), so that key decision makers have some general sense of what the effort is likely to produce, and surprises are minimized. It is conceivable, of course, that preparation and publication of a formal strategic plan would be unwise politically. Incompatible objectives or warring external stakeholders, for example, might make it difficult to prepare a rational and publicly defensible plan. Key decision makers will have to decide whether a formal strategic plan should be prepared, given the circumstances the organization faces.

10. *Even if a formal strategic plan is not prepared, the organization should consider preparing a set of interrelated strategy statements describing grand strategy; subunit strategies; program, service, product, project, or business process strategies; and functional strategies.* To the extent they are agreed upon, these statements will provide extremely useful guides for action by organizational members from top to bottom. Again, remember that it may be politically difficult or dangerous to prepare and publicize such statements.

11. *Use a normative process to review strategy statements and formal strategic plans.* Drafts typically should be reviewed by planning team

members, other key decision makers, governing board members, and at least selected outside stakeholders. Review meetings need to be structured so that the strengths of the statements or plan are recognized and modifications that would improve on those strengths are identified. Review sessions can be structured around the following agenda (Barry, 1997, p. 70; Crosby & Bryson, 2005 p. 237–238):

1. Overview of plan.
2. General discussion of plan and reactions to it. Is it in the ballpark?
3. Brainstormed list of plan strengths. What do people like?
4. Brainstormed list of plan weaknesses. What are problems, soft spots, or omissions?
5. Brainstormed list of modifications that would improve on strengths and minimize or overcome weaknesses.
6. Agreement on next steps to complete the plan.

All modifications that actually do improve the statements and plans should be accepted. At least by the time the review process is nearing completion, planning team members and key decision makers should make a point of asking themselves what risks are entailed in the plan. They then should ask whether the level of risk is acceptable, what can be done about the risks, and if nothing can be done, whether the plan should go forward.

12. *Discuss and evaluate strategies in relation to key stakeholders.* Strategies that are unacceptable to key stakeholders probably will have to be rethought. Strategies that do not take stakeholders into consideration are almost certain to fail. A variety of stakeholder analysis techniques can help, including Stakeholder Support Versus Opposition Grids, Stakeholder Role Plays, and Ethical Analysis Grids. More information on these techniques will be found in Resource A.

13. *Have budgets and budgeting procedures in place to capitalize on strategic planning and strategic plans.* This may include making sure that monies tied to implementation of strategic plans are *flagged* so that they always receive special attention and treatment. It also can mean attempting to develop a special contingency fund to allow *bridge* funding, so that implementation of all or portions of strategies can begin out of sequence with the normal budgeting process. Having a stop agenda can provide needed funds (but note the need to think through strategically how to stop doing things so that minimal damage occurs). Most important, however, is the need to make sure that strategic thinking precedes, rather than follows, budgeting. This is the key idea behind *performance budgeting, entrepreneurial*

budgeting, and *results-based budgeting* (Osborne & Plastrik, 1997, 2000; Osborne & Hutchinson, 2004; and Cole & Parston, 2006). Unfortunately, the only strategic plans many organizations have are their budgets, and those budgets have typically been formulated without benefit of much focused strategic thought. Attention to creating public value, mission, mandates, situational assessments, strategic issues, and strategies should precede development of budgets.

14. *Be aware that the strategy formulation step is likely to proceed in a more iterative fashion than previous steps because of the need to find the best fit among elements of strategies, among different strategies, and among levels of strategy.* Additional time and iterations are likely to be needed when a collaboration or community-based strategic planning effort is involved (Chrislip, 2002; Linden, 2002; Innes & Booher, 2010). Strong process guidance and facilitation, along with pressure from key decision makers to proceed, probably will be necessary in order to reach a successful conclusion to this step. Process sponsors and champions, in other words, will be especially needed if this step is to result in effective strategies. The issue often is one of appropriately aligning new strategies with existing strategies, and some special planning sessions may be needed to work things out. For example, it is very important that information technology, human resources, and financial strategies support the organization's overall strategy and supporting strategies. Barry (1997, pp. 59–60) suggests a four-step process:

- Provide a written or graphic depiction (such as a logic model or action-oriented strategy map) of existing and proposed strategies in terms of their mission and desired impacts, programmatic elements, and required support and resources.
- Identify what is working well with existing strategies and what needs adjusting, and identify what will need to work well with proposed strategies and what adjustments might be needed. Focus as well on the integration of existing with new strategies.
- Determine how the needed adjustments can be made.
- Incorporate these revisions into the strategy statements or strategic plan.

This same process is often very useful in Step 9, Implementation, when issues of alignment often became apparent.

15. *Allow for a period of catharsis as the organization moves from one way of being in the world to another.* Strong emotions or tensions are

likely to build up as the organization moves to implement new or changed strategies, particularly if these strategies involve fairly drastic changes and challenge the current organizational identity and culture (Rughase, 2007). Indeed, the buildup of emotions and tensions may prevent successful implementation. These emotions and tensions must be recognized, and people must be allowed to vent and deal with them (Spencer & Adams, 1990; Marris, 1996; Schein, 2010). For example, people need time to grieve for the past they are giving up, even if they prefer the future being offered. Such emotions and tensions must be a legitimate topic of discussion in strategic planning team meetings. Sessions designed to review draft strategy statements or strategic plans can be used to vent emotions and to solicit modifications in the statements or plans that will deal effectively with these emotional concerns.

16. *Remember that completion of the strategy development step is likely to be an important decision point.* The decision will be whether to go ahead with strategies or a strategic plan recommended by the strategic planning team. When a formal strategic plan has not been prepared, a number of decision points may ensue. The strategies proposed to respond to various issues are very likely to be presented to the appropriate decision-making bodies at different times. Thus, there would be an important decision point for each set of strategies developed to deal with each strategic issue.

17. *Ensure that key decision makers and planners think carefully about how the formal adoption process should be managed, particularly if it involves formal arenas.* Formal arenas typically have specific rules and procedures that must be followed. These rules must be attended to carefully so that the plan is not held hostage or overturned by clever opponents. Bargaining and negotiation over the modifications and inducements necessary to gain support and minimize opposition are almost certain to be needed. Obviously, any modifications that improve the proposal should be accepted, and agreements reached through bargaining and negotiation should not sacrifice crucial plan components.

18. *Provide some sense of closure to the strategic planning process at the end of the Step 7, or else at the end of Step 6 if no formal plan is prepared.* Formal adoption of a strategic plan provides a natural occasion for developing such a sense of closure. But even without a strategic plan, some sort of ceremony and celebration may be required to give process participants the sense that the strategic

planning effort is finished for the present and that the time for sustained implementation is at hand.

19. *When the strategic planning process has been well designed and faithfully followed, but the strategies and plans are nevertheless not adopted, consider the following possibilities:*

- The time is not yet right.
- The draft strategies and plans are inadequate or inappropriate.
- The issues the strategies and plans purport to address simply are not that "real" or pressing.
- The organization (or collaboration or community) cannot handle the magnitude of the proposed changes, and they need to be scaled back.
- The strategies and plans should be taken to some other arena, or the arena should be redesigned in some way.

SUMMARY

This chapter has discussed strategy formulation and adoption. Strategy is defined as a *pattern* of purposes, policies, programs, actions, decisions, or resource allocations that defines what an organization (or other entity) is, what it does, and why it does it. Strategies can vary by level, function, and time frame; they are the way an organization relates to its environment.

Two approaches to developing strategies were outlined, a five-part process and the action-oriented strategy mapping process. The chapter also offers suggestions for the preparation of formal strategic plans, although once again I emphasize that strategic thinking, acting, and learning are the most important results, rather than any particular approach to strategy formulation or the preparation of a formal strategic plan. Suggestions also were offered to guide the formal adoption of the plan when that step is necessary or desirable.

CHAPTER EIGHT

Establishing an Effective Organizational Vision for the Future

You must give birth to your images. They are the future waiting to be born.
—Rainer Maria Rilke, poet

The purpose of Step 8 in the strategic planning process is to develop a clear and succinct description of what the organization (collaboration or community) should look like as it successfully implements its strategies, achieves its full potential, and creates significant and lasting public value. This description is the organization's *vision of success*. Typically, this vision of success is more important as a guide to implementing strategy than it is to formulating it. For that reason, the step is listed as optional in Figure 2.1, and it comes after strategy and plan review and adoption. However, Figure 2.1 also indicates that under the right circumstances, visioning might occur at many places through a strategic planning process (see also Figure 2.4).

Although many—perhaps most—public and nonprofit organizations have developed clear and useful mission statements in recent years, fewer have a clear, succinct, and useful vision of success. Part of the reason is that a fully developed vision, though it includes mission, goes well beyond mission. A mission outlines the organizational purpose; a vision goes on to describe how the organization should look when it is working extremely well in relation to its environment and key stakeholders. Developing this description is more time-consuming than formulating a mission statement (Angelica, 2001; Senge, 2006). It is also more difficult, particularly because most organizations are coalitional (Bolman & Deal, 2008; Pfeffer, 2010), and thus the vision must usually be a treaty negotiated among rival coalitions.

Other difficulties may hamper construction of a vision of success. People may be afraid of how others will respond to their vision. Professionals are highly vested in their jobs, and to have one's vision of excellent organizational performance criticized or rejected can be trying (Rughase, 2007). People may be afraid of that part of themselves that can envision and pursue excellence. First of all, we can be disappointed in our pursuit, which can be painful. Our own competence can be called into question. And second, being true to the vision can be a very demanding discipline, hard work that we may not be willing to shoulder all the time.

Key decision makers must be courageous in order to construct a compelling vision of success. They must imagine and listen to their best selves in order to envision success for the organization as a whole. And they must be disciplined enough to affirm the vision in the present, to work hard through conflicts and difficulties to make the vision real in the here and now (Collins & Porras, 1997). As novelist Richard Powers (2001, p. 130) says, "The mind is the first virtual reality. . . . It gets to say what the world isn't yet." But saying yes to the vision is only a step—albeit an important one—in the persistent stream of action required to realize the vision.

It may not be possible, therefore, to create an effective and compelling vision of success for the organization. The good news, however, is that although a vision of success may be very helpful, it may not be necessary in order to improve organizational performance. Agreement on strategy is more important than agreement on vision or goals (Bourgeois, 1980; Mintzberg, Ahlstrand, & Lampel, 2009). Simply finding a way to frame and deal with a few of the strategic issues the organization faces often markedly improves organizational effectiveness.

DESIRED IMMEDIATE OUTCOMES AND LONGER-TERM BENEFITS

Even though it may not be necessary to have a vision of success in order to improve organizational effectiveness, it is hard to imagine a truly high-performing organization that does not have at least an implicit and widely shared conception of what success looks like and how it might be achieved (see, for example, Collins & Porras, 1997; Rainey & Steinbauer, 1999; Light, 1998, 2005; Goodsell, 2010). Indeed, it is hard to imagine an organization surviving in the long run without some sort of vision to inspire it—hence the merit of filmmaker Federico Fellini's comment, "The visionary is the only realist." Recall as well the famous admonition in Proverbs 29:18: "Where there is no vision, the people perish." Thus a vision of success might be advantageous.

Assuming key decision makers wish to promote superior performance, the following immediate outcomes might be sought in this step. First, if it is to provide suitable guidance and motivation, the vision should probably detail the following attributes of the organization:

- Mission
- Basic philosophy, core values, and cultural features
- Goals, if they are established
- Basic strategies
- Performance criteria (such as those related to critical success factors)
- Important decision-making rules
- Ethical standards expected of all employees

The vision should emphasize purposes, behavior, performance criteria, decision rules, and standards that serve the public and create public value rather than serve the organization alone. The guidance offered should be specific and reasonable. The vision should include a promise that the organization will support its members' pursuit of the vision. Further, the vision should clarify the organization's direction and purpose; be relatively future oriented; reflect high ideals and challenging ambitions; and capture the organization's uniqueness and distinctive competence as well as desirable features of its history, culture, and values (Shamir, Arthur, & House, 1994; Weiss & Piderit, 1999; Kouzes & Posner, 2008). The vision should also be relatively short and inspiring.

Second, the vision should be widely circulated among organizational members and other key stakeholders after appropriate consultations, reviews, and sign-offs. A vision of success can have little effect if organizational members are kept in the dark about it.

Third, the vision should be used to inform major and minor organizational decisions and actions. Preparing the vision will have been a waste of time if it has no behavioral effect. If, however, copies of the vision are always handy at formal meetings of key decision makers and prominently displayed on the organization's Website, and performance measurement systems are explicitly attuned to the vision, then the vision can be expected to affect organizational performance.

At least a dozen longer-term (and overlapping) desired outcomes can flow from a clear, succinct, inspiring, and widely shared vision of success. First, a fully developed vision of success provides a capsule future-oriented theory of the organization; that is, its theory of what it should do and how it should do it to achieve success by altering the world in some important way (Bryson, Gibbons, & Shaye, 2001). The vision helps organizational members and key stakeholders imagine and create sustainable new circumstances by understanding the *requirements* for success—that is, why and how things should be done. Knowing the basic theory allows organizational members to act effectively without having everything spelled out in detail and without needing rules written to cover every possible situation. As the great psychologist Kurt Lewin observes, "Nothing is as practical as a good theory" (1951, p. 169). Beyond that, the organization's vision (or capsule theory) of success articulates the way in which people can participate in creating a new and more desirable order. In a follow-up to his remarkable study (Krieger, 1996) of some of the world's great entrepreneurs (Moses, Oedipus, Antigone, and Augustine, among others), Martin Krieger (2000) argues that "redemptive order, what we might call theory, allows us to be involved in the world, to have a sense of what we are doing here" (p. 263). Such a theory and actions based on it are designed to "manufacture transcendence"—to excel, surpass, and go beyond the range of current experience (pp. 258–259)—to enact what the world isn't yet. The vision thus represents a kind of "persuasive and constitutive storytelling about the future" (Throgmorton, 2003, p. 146) that starts out as a form of fiction (from the Latin *to shape*) that through concerted action and organizational change may become more factual. The vision doesn't need to be wholly accurate—it is not a street map—it just needs to provide a reasonable basis for action and learning in desired directions (Bryson, Ackermann, Eden, & Finn, 2004, pp. 337–340).

Second, organizational members are given specific, reasonable, and supportive guidance about what is expected of them and why. They see how they fit into the organization's big picture. Too often the only guidance for members—other than hearsay—is a job description (which is typically focused on the parts and not on the whole). In addition, key decision makers are all too likely to issue conflicting messages to members or simply tell them, "Do your best." A widely accepted vision of success records enough of a consensus on ends and means to channel members' efforts in desirable directions while at the same time providing a framework for improvisation and innovation in pursuit of organizational purposes (Collins & Porras, 1997; Osborne & Plastrik, 1997). In this way the vision serves primarily as an aid to strategy implementation, rather than formulation. Specifically, the two things that most strongly determine whether goals are achieved appear to be the extent to which the goals are specific and reasonable and the extent to which people are able and committed to achieving them. In fact, "given ability as well as commitment, the higher the goal, the higher a person's performance" (Latham, Borgogni, & Petitta, 2008, p. 386). It seems reasonable to extend the same argument to a vision of success and claim that the more specific and reasonable the vision, and the more able and committed organizational members are in pursuit of the vision, the more likely the vision will be achieved or realized.

Third, as we noted earlier, conception precedes perception (Weick, 1995). People must have some conception of what success and desirable behavior look like before they can actually see them and thus strive toward achieving them. A vision of success makes it easier for people to discriminate between preferred and undesirable actions and outcomes and thus produce more of what is preferred.

Fourth, if there is an agreement on the vision, and if clear guidance and decision rules can be derived from the vision, the organization will gain an added increment of power and efficiency. Less time will need to be expended on debating what to do, how to do it, and why, and more time can be devoted to simply getting on with it (Weiss & Piderit, 1999; Eisenhardt & Sull, 2001; Pfeffer, 2010).

Fifth, a vision of success provides a way to claim or affirm the future in the present, and thereby to invent one's own preferred future. If the future is at least in part what we make it, then development of a vision outlines the future we want to have and forces us to live it—create it, *realize* it—in the present. Nobel Prize–winning physicist Neils Bohr apparently said, "Prediction is very difficult, especially about the future." What is being said here is different: a vision of success helps not with *predicting* the future, but with *making* it (Gabor, 1964).

Sixth, a clear yet reasonable vision of success creates a useful tension between *is* and *ought*, the world as it is and the world as we would like it. If goals are to motivate, they must be set high enough to provide a challenge, but not so high as to induce paralysis, hopelessness, or too much stress. A well-tuned vision of success can articulate reasonable standards of excellence and motivate the organization's members to pursue them. The vision can provide what Ludema, Wilmot, and Srivastva (1997, p. 1025) call a "textured vocabulary of organizational hope."

Seventh, a well-articulated vision of success will help people implicitly recognize the barriers to realizing that vision. (In this way the vision acts in much the same way as the first step in the five-part strategy formulation process outlined in Chapter Seven.) Recognizing barriers is the first step in overcoming them (Butler, 2009).

Eighth, an inspiring vision of success can supply another source of motivation: clarification of a vocation tied to a calling. When a vision of success becomes a calling, jobs and careers can become *vocations* that release enormous amounts of individual energy, dedication, power, and positive risk-taking behavior in pursuit of the vision of a better future. A vocation creates meaning in workers' lives and fuels a justifiable pride. Noted theologian Frederick Buechner defines vocation as "the place where your deep gladness meets the world's deep need" (quoted in Palmer, 2000, p. 16). Consider, for example, that most remarkable of nonprofit organizations, the Society of Jesus (the Jesuits), founded in 1534 in Paris by Saint Ignatius of Loyola. Their vision was first formulated in Ignatius's *Spiritual Exercises* (Guibert, 1964). The worldwide success (in general) of order members as missionaries, teachers, scholars, and spiritual directors, is a tribute to how much they have been guided by their ideal: to be a disciplined force on behalf of the Roman Catholic Church. The fact that they have succeeded for so long against often incredible odds and trials is in part due to the power of their vision. They clearly have been called for a very long time to their vocation. The references to vocation and calling may seem odd to some, but it is becoming increasingly clear that attention to the broadly spiritual aspects of work matters enormously (Bolman & Deal, 2006). Paul Light (1998) finds that public and nonprofit organizations that are able to sustain innovations give witness to a deep and abiding faith (albeit usually a secular one). In other words it may well be that doubt is overvalued in management thought and guidance, and belief is seriously undervalued. Or as Karl Weick (1995) might say, believing is seeing, not the reverse. A well-crafted vision can provide a shared statement of belief—a creed—that starts out as a fiction and becomes a fact through action.

Ninth, a clear vision of success provides an effective substitute for leadership (Manz, 1986; Kouzes & Posner, 2008). People are able to lead and manage themselves if they are given clear guidance on the organization's direction and behavioral expectations. More effective decision making can then occur at a distance from the center of the organization and from the top of the hierarchy.

Although constructing a vision of success may be difficult in politicized settings, the task may nonetheless be worth the effort, leading to a tenth benefit. An agreed-upon vision may contribute to a significant reduction in the level of organizational conflict. A set of overarching goals can help rechannel conflict in useful directions and make it more manageable (Fisher & Ury, 1991; Thompson, 2008).

Eleventh, depending on its content, the vision can help the organization stay attuned to its environment and develop its capacities to deal with the almost inevitable crises characteristic of organizational life these days. The vision can promote the useful learning and adaptation to a changing environment typically necessary to avoid catastrophic failure (Weick & Sutcliffe, 2007). In particular, a good vision should help the organization distinguish between strategic or developmental issues and operational or nondevelopmental issues (Nutt, 2001; Benner & Tushman, 2003). Catastrophes are perhaps more likely when what are in fact strategic issues are mistaken for operational issues and therefore not brought to the attention of key decision makers soon enough. A good vision, in other words, can help an organization be really clear about what is most important, and therefore help that organization thrive over the long term by being *ambidextrous*—by being good at both strategy implementation and strategy formulation, both knowledge exploitation and knowledge exploration, both making routine changes within the existing architecture and changing the architecture, both maintaining their identity and subtly changing it, both avoiding decision failures and learning from their mistakes, and at both being very serious but not taking themselves too seriously (Bryson, Boal, & Rainey, 2008). A good vision will provide the kind of overarching framework and the detail necessary to allow the organization to purposefully yet flexibly respond to changes in its environment—to hold tightly to the core while being willing to change the rest (Collins & Porras, 1997; Light, 2005).

And twelfth, to the extent that the vision of success is widely shared, it lends the organization an air of virtue. It is not particularly fashionable to talk explicitly about virtue, but most people wish to act in morally justifiable ways in pursuit of morally justified ends (Frederickson, 1997). A vision of success therefore provides important permission, justification, and legitimation to the actions and decisions that accord with the vision at the same time that it establishes boundaries of permitted behavior (Simons, 1995). The normative self-regulation necessary for any moral community to survive and prosper is thereby facilitated (Kanter, 1972; Mandelbaum, 2000), and the legitimacy of the organization in the broader community can be enhanced (Suchman, 1995).

AN EXAMPLE

The Belfast Way outlines the 2008–2013 vision of success for Belfast Health and Social Care Trust (the Trust) of Northern Ireland. The Belfast Way is an excellent example of a vision. It is in effect the Trust's grand strategy for the period and serves as the prime source document for the Trust's annual corporate management (operational) planning cycle and for other major planning initiatives. The Trust was formed out of a government-mandated merger of six National Health Service trusts in 2007; it came into existence on April 1, 2007. The Trust delivers integrated health and social services to the 340,000 citizens of Belfast and an adjoining borough, along with specialist services to all of Northern Ireland. Note that unlike the rest of the United Kingdom, Northern Ireland's health and social services are integrated, an arrangement to be admired and emulated. The Trust has an annual budget of approximately £1.1 billion ($1.69 billion) and a staff of 20,000. It is one of the largest such Trusts in the United Kingdom. Its hospitals treat approximately 117,000 inpatients and 75,000 day patients a year, 700,000 outpatients, and 170,000 people in its four emergency departments (emergency rooms) (Belfast Health and Social Care Trust, 2010).

The Belfast Way consists of a statement of purpose, set of principles for working collaboratively with others as part of a health and social care system, a statement of values (including ethical standards expected of all employees), a set of strategic objectives, and a statement about how decisions are made. Of the items mentioned in the introduction that should be in a vision of success, only one is missing: performance criteria. These do show up in part, however, in quantitative or qualitative targets beginning with the 2009–2010 corporate management plan (Belfast Health and Social Care Trust, 2008b), which is tied directly to the strategic objectives. The vision statement is a glossy sixteen-page document with fifteen pages of text and pictures. The document is also available on the Web (http://www.belfasttrust.hscni.net/pdf/The_Belfast_Way.pdf). The vision serves primarily as a guide for implementation, but it is written in a way that prompts the Trust's staff to attend to their environment, to keep learning, and to stay open to change.

The Belfast Way represents, in part, the next stage in visioning begun in 1994 by one of the Trusts that was merged to form the Belfast Trust. The Royal Group of Hospitals (the Royal) published vision statements in 1994, 1998, and 2003. However, since the Royal now represents only a third of the new Trust, The Belfast Way also represents a significant break from the past. One important continuity across the four visions is that the Royal's chief executive, William McKee, became the chief executive of the Belfast Trust, a post from which he retired in September 2010. He brought with him to the new Trust practices that had worked well in the Royal, including the development and use of visions of success. Note, however, that the process of producing the vision statements changed significantly over time. The 1994 vision statement was written primarily by McKee himself, and was used as an effective, but essentially one-way, leadership and communication tool. The 1998 vision statement was published after it had been reviewed by a substantial number of people and organizations in almost final draft form. The 2003 vision statement was published only after involving far larger numbers of people far earlier in the process—long before a draft of the vision was produced. Extensive consultations occurred internally and with numerous key external partners. The document was produced collaboratively because the health care environment increasingly demanded health and social care delivery through collaborative networks of providers and caregivers in big institutions, clinics, the community, and families. After 2003, the use of a vision of success became an embedded practice to the point that everyone quoted it.

The 2008–2013 vision statement was also produced collaboratively because it had to be. Six major organizations with their own cultures and histories of success were being merged into one. In the midst of everyone's grief at losing their familiar and particular ways of doing things they needed anchoring and direction in a clear sense of purpose and related guidance. They also needed a new sense of identity (Rughase, 2007). A sense of purpose, direction, and identity were particularly needed as the new Trust was to reduce senior management costs by 25 percent and to find £120 million ($185 million) in efficiency savings, or 11 percent in total over three years. Work on the vision started before the Trust began in April 2007. McKee was appointed in the late summer of 2006 and began meeting with people and testing what the new

Trust's purpose should be, clarifying exactly what business the trust was in, and exploring what the new structures of service delivery might be. Staff groups also worked on particular aspects of what became the vision. McKee held sixty staff meetings the first year that all included his nine-minute Belfast Way–related "stump speech" and offered channels for ideas and feedback. Drafts of the vision were sent to the entire community development database, all members of the Local Assembly (the Province now had a devolved government), members of Parliament, all city council members, all general practitioners, trade unions, all managers from the middle on up, and special interest groups. All responses were compiled into a document that went to the board of directors in September 2008. The Belfast Way was launched in November 2008. By that time all of its contents were well known. There were no surprises when the document was published.

The vision begins with an introduction noting the document's purpose. Next comes the Belfast Trust's *purpose*, which is "to improve health and well-being and reduce health inequalities." The statement of purpose is followed by a discussion of how health is dependent on more than the health and social care system—for example, the economy, policies promoting inclusion and social justice, and the broader environment, including the physical environment. The document notes that while *health gain* for the population as a whole is increasing, *health inequalities* are widening. The *business* of the Trust is discussed next, which is "in partnering with others, and by engaging with staff, we will deliver safe, improving, modern, cost-effective health and social care." The business is thus to focus on health and social care in service of the purpose of increasing health and well-being and reducing health inequalities. The section includes what are in effect a set of principles for working in collaboration with others as part of a larger system. These principles include: being a good corporate citizen, emphasizing safety, updating and improving services, providing services closer to people's homes, and listening to people. These principles are a necessary response to several factors: Government policies are mandating major improvements in health and a reduction in health inequalities both geographically and by demographic group. European Union directives are affecting working conditions for health care professionals, especially doctors. The nature of health care delivery is changing. Specifically, the focus is moving away from individual hospitals and toward networks of clinical teams that provide services across a number of locations and closer to people's homes, which means more teamwork and partnership with others. In addition, the focus is increasingly on health, rather than illness. Further, the increased emphasis on service quality means the Belfast Trust will continue to emphasize quality improvement processes. The next section discusses the *values* meant to guide Trust employees' behavior, attitudes, decision making, and relations with one another. The four values include: respect and dignity, accountability, openness and trust, and learning and developing. A set of affirmations is included along with the values. For example, the first listed under respect and dignity is: "We will treat everyone with respect and dignity."

The following major section lists the Trust's *five strategic objectives,* which include these headers: safety and quality, modernization, partnerships, our people, and resources. Again, under each is a set of affirmations. The section on *safety and quality* emphasizes providing safe, high-quality, and effective care. The affirmations, for example, commit the Trust to evidence-based and audited care, benchmarking against best practices, an environment where concerns about safety and care are openly discussed, performance measures that take outcomes into account, use of external assessors to assess quality and suggest improvements in quality, and so on. The *modernization* objective includes affirmations aimed at delivering "the best possible care in the right place at the right time." The broad aim is "to reform and renew our services so we deliver care in a faster, less bureaucratic and more effective way to our citizens." A key affirmation is "to deliver, as far as possible, our services as a single service across Belfast even when it is delivered in different locations." This statement involves capitalizing on the possibilities inherent in integrating the six Trusts. The *partnerships* objective takes seriously the notion that only through working with others can health gains and well-being be improved and health inequalities reduced. Belfast Trust is only a piece of the puzzle and the other puzzle pieces must be engaged for the full vision to be assembled. The strategic objective focused on *our people* recognizes the centrality of staff to health and social care delivery and includes a set of affirmations meant to embrace progressive human resource management practices. The emphasis is on "showing leadership and excellence through organizational and workforce development." Finally, the *resources* objective attends to the need to "make best use of resources by improving performance and productivity." Affirmations focus on, for example, getting the resources necessary to provide needed services, wisely stewarding public monies, providing adequate physical and equipment infrastructure, and eliminating unnecessary costs. The vision's final major section outlines *accountabilities and decision rules.* The roles of the Trust board, chief executive, and service groups are emphasized, along with the role of the executive team. Service groups are an integrative device linking across the previously separate Trusts. There are now four: acute services, cancer and specialist services, social and primary care services and specialist hospitals, and woman and child health services. The document concludes with mail, telephone, and e-mail contact details.

As noted earlier, only one of the items that I suggest may be included in a vision of success is missing: performance criteria. A number of reasons can explain this omission: First, there are likely to be too many to list in a short document. Second, it is hard to develop performance criteria collaboratively across major, previously semi-independent organizations (Huxham, 2003), but that is what Belfast Trust is being called on to do. Third, publishing performance criteria—particularly when they must be met through collaborative work with outsiders—can leave an organization hostage to fortune. Further negotiations with involved and affected stakeholders were necessary before Belfast Trust was willing to own a number of key collaborative performance indicators (Moynihan, 2008). As noted, the 2009–2010 corporate management plan does include several targets expressed in qualitative or quantitative terms, which can be considered performance indicators. Once collaborative performance indicators are developed and agreed on, a logical next step might be to produce a set of complementary scorecards (balanced or otherwise) to further clarify the operational aspects of the vision—that is, to clarify exactly what realizing the vision should mean in terms of performance. Nonetheless, it is important to emphasize that as Belfast Trust embarks on realizing this new vision, it is able to build on the Royal's earlier performance management system (rooted in its visioning efforts), which was widely recognized as one of the best in the United Kingdom public sector.

The vision provides much specific and reasonable advice to employees and other stakeholders and indicates that Belfast Trust will support and reward those who act in accord with the vision. Because much of the Trust's success depends on the actions and decisions of others whom it does not control, including those in government departments and ministries above it, the importance of wide circulation of, and agreement on, this document is hard to overestimate. It is also important to emphasize that the vision is no mere public relations ploy. Key decision makers and opinion leaders are committed to it. The vision codifies much of what Belfast Trust already does, but also charts some new agreed-upon directions necessary to achieve excellence and serves as the basis for its annual management planning cycle. It informs all that the Trust does—its strategic and corporate documents, its performance management system, and its staff appraisal system (known as the Personal Contribution Framework). All the Trust's activities are reported under the key strategic objectives. The chief executive's briefings to senior managers and other staff also use the five key objectives as their template. The heightened emphasis on working in partnerships and focusing on health improvement is particularly noteworthy. In short, the vision is a prime source document for all further efforts at developing a truly integrated and increasingly effective Trust.

PROCESS DESIGN AND ACTION GUIDELINES

The following guidelines are intended to help a strategic planning team formulate a vision of success.

1. *Remember that in most cases a vision of success is not necessary to improve organizational effectiveness.* Simply developing and implementing strategies to deal with a few important strategic issues can produce marked improvement in the performance of most organizations. An organization therefore should not worry too much if developing a vision of success seems unwise or too difficult. Nevertheless, it seems unlikely that an organization can achieve truly superior performance without a widely shared, at least implicit, vision of success—what theologian Teilhard de Chardin called "a great hope held in common" (quoted in Nanus, 1992, p. 15).

2. *In most cases, wait until the organization goes through one or more cycles of strategic planning before trying to develop a full-blown vision of success.* Most organizations need to develop the habit of thinking about and acting on the truly important aspects of their relationships internally and with their environments before a collective vision of success can emerge. In addition, it is likely to require more than one cycle of strategic planning for a consensus on key decisions and an ability to resolve conflicts constructively to emerge, and both are necessary for developing an effective vision of success. Of course, this guideline may not apply if the organization has decided to proceed with strategic planning using the idealized scenario or goals approaches, and if the organization has developed and is implementing effective strategies based on those approaches. If key decision makers have enough capacity for consensus to make either of these approaches possible, then the organization also may succeed in developing a viable, detailed vision of success.

3. *Include in a vision of success the items listed earlier in this chapter as part of the first desired outcome.* The vision itself should not be long, preferably no more than ten double-spaced pages, and ideally less. The vision should also be clearly externally focused—on the better world that will result from the organization successfully implementing its strategies and fully realizing its mission. Organizations should think about making the published versions of their strategic plans serve as a vision of success, as in effect the Park Board, Loft, and MetroGIS do.

4. *Ensure that the vision of success grows out of past decisions and actions as much as possible.* Past decisions and actions provide a record of pragmatic consensus about what the organization is and should do. Basing a vision on a preexisting consensus avoids

unnecessary conflict. Also, the vision should effectively link the organization to its past. Realization of a new future is facilitated to the extent that it can be shown to be a continuation of the past and present (Weick, 1995; Marris, 1996; Fiol, 2001, 2002). However, a vision of success should not be merely an extension of the present. It should be an affirmation in the present of an ideal and inspirational future. It should encourage organizational members to extrapolate backward from the vision to the present; this will help them determine which actions today can best help the organization achieve success tomorrow. A vision of success also should encourage organizational members to keep their eyes open for new knowledge and changes in their environment.

5. *Remember that a vision of success should be inspirational.* It will not move people to excel unless it is. And what inspires people is a clear description of a desirable future backed up by real conviction. An inspirational vision (Shamir, Arthur, & House, 1994; Kouzes & Posner, 2008):

- Focuses on a better future
- Encourages hopes, dreams, and noble ambitions
- Builds on (or reinterprets) the organization's history and culture to appeal to high ideals and common values
- Clarifies purpose and direction
- States positive outcomes
- Emphasizes the organization's uniqueness and distinctive competence
- Emphasizes the strength of a unified group
- Uses word pictures, images, and metaphors
- Communicates enthusiasm, kindles excitement, and fosters commitment and dedication

Just recall Martin Luther King Jr.'s "I Have A Dream" speech and you will have a clear example of an inspirational vision of success, focused on the better future of an integrated society.

6. *Remember that an effective vision of success will embody the appropriate degree of tension to prompt effective organizational change.* On the one hand, too much tension will likely cause paralysis. On the other hand, too little tension will not produce the challenge necessary for outstanding performance (Fiol, 2002; Light, 1998, 2005). If there is not enough tension, the vision should be recast to raise organizational sights.

7. *Consider starting the construction of a vision of success by having strategic planning team members draft visions of success (or at least relatively detailed outlines) individually, using the worksheets in Bryson and Alston (2011).* The team may find it useful to review the discussion of the vision of success approach to strategic issue identification in Chapter Six and visionary leadership in Chapter Eleven before starting their individual drafts. Team members should then share and discuss their responses with each other. After the discussion, the task of drafting a vision of success should be turned over to one individual, because an inspirational document is rarely written by a committee. Special sessions may be necessary to develop particular elements of the vision of success. For example, the organization's performance criteria or success indicators may not be fully specified. They might be developed out of the mandates, stakeholder analyses, SWOC/T analysis, the strategy statements, or the snow card technique or oval mapping activities. Wherever there are gaps in the vision, special sessions may be necessary to fill them.

8. *Use a normative to review the vision of success.* Drafts typically are reviewed by planning team members, other key decision makers, governing board members, and at least some selected outside stakeholders (Nutt, 2001). Review meetings need to be structured to ensure that the vision's strengths and any possible improvements are identified and listed. Review sessions can be structured according to the agenda suggested for the review of strategic plans (see Chapter Seven).

9. *Be aware that consensus on the vision statement among key decision makers is highly desirable, but may not be absolutely necessary.* It is rarely possible to achieve complete consensus on anything in an organization, so all that can be realistically hoped for is a fairly widespread general agreement on the substance and style of the vision statement. Deep-seated commitment to any vision statement can only emerge slowly over time.

10. *Arrange for the vision of success to be widely disseminated and discussed.* This makes it more likely that the vision will be used to guide organizational decisions and actions. The vision statement probably should be published as a booklet, on the organization's Web site, and given to every organizational member and to key external stakeholders. Discussion of the statement should be made a part of orientation programs for new employees, and the statement should be discussed periodically in staff meetings.

A vision of success can become a living document only if it is referred to constantly as a basis for discerning and justifying appropriate organizational decisions and actions. If a vision statement does not regularly inform organizational decision making and actions, then preparation of the statement was probably a waste of time.

SUMMARY

This chapter has discussed developing a vision of success for the organization. A vision of success is defined as a description of what the organization will look like after it successfully implements its strategies and achieves its full potential. A vision statement should include the organization's mission, its basic philosophy and core values, its basic strategies, its performance criteria, its important decision rules, and its ethical standards. The statement should emphasize the important social purposes that the organization serves and that justify its existence. In addition, the statement should be short and inspirational.

For a vision of success to have a strong effect on organizational decisions and actions, it must be widely disseminated and discussed, and must be referred to frequently as a means of determining appropriate responses to the various situations that confront the organization. Only when the statement is used as a basis for organizational decision making and action will it have been worth the effort of crafting it.

CHAPTER NINE

Implementing Strategies and Plans Successfully

You give an order around here, and if you can figure out
what happens to it after that, you're a better person than I am.
—Harry S. Truman

Well-executed implementation (Step 9) furthers the transition from strategic planning to strategic management by incorporating adopted strategies throughout the relevant system. Creating a strategic plan can produce significant value—especially in terms of building intellectual, human, social, political, and civic capital—but that is not enough. Developing effective programs, projects, action plans, budgets, and implementation processes will bring life to the strategies and create more tangible and intangible value for the organization (collaboration or community) and its stakeholders as mandates are then met and the mission fulfilled (see Figure 2.4). Programs, projects, action plans, and budgets are necessary in order to coordinate the activities of the numerous executives, managers, professionals, technicians, and frontline practitioners likely to be involved. The implementation process itself should allow for adaptive learning as new information becomes available and circumstances change. Such learning will lead to more effective implementation and to the cognitive, emotional, and practical basis for emergent strategies and new rounds of strategizing. Recall that *realized* strategies are a blend of what is intended with what emerges in practice (Mintzberg & Westley, 1992; Mintzberg, Ahlstrand, & Lampel, 2009).

DESIRED IMMEDIATE AND LONGER-TERM OUTCOMES

The most important long-term outcome that leaders, managers, and planners should aim for in this step is real *added public value* resulting from the reasonably smooth and rapid achievement of the organization's goals and heightened stakeholder satisfaction. (For balanced scorecard advocates, this means accomplishing what is set out in a scorecard's top-tier aspirations; see Figure 2.3, which shows the Charlotte, North Carolina, balanced scorecard.) To paraphrase Karl Weick (1995, p. 54), a desired order of greater public value becomes a tangible order "when faith is followed by enactment." Following James Throgmorton (2003, p. 130), with effective implementation the enacted strategies and strategic plans become "not only persuasive, but constitutive . . . of community, character, and culture." Or to paraphrase Mark Moore (2000, p. 179, 2003), with effective implementation the value proposition embodied in the strategic plan moves from being a hypothetical story to being a true story. The further and deeper this process reaches, the more a desired strategy change will have become part of people's *assumptive worlds* or *world-taken-for-granted* (Eden, Ackerman, & Cropper, 1992; Kelman, 2005). As Mintzberg, Ahlstrand, and Lampel (2009, p. 17) note, "We function best when we take some things for granted. And that is the major role of strategy in organizations: it resolves the big issues so that we can get on with the little details." Of course, what they call "the details," may not be so little, but their point is still well taken. The reasonably smooth and rapid introduction of the strategies throughout the relevant system typically requires using a broad repertoire of approaches in order to bring all necessary entities on board, or at least to get them to do what needs doing (for example, Light, 1998; Borins, 1998; Peters & Pierre, 2003, pp. 205–256; Bolman & Deal, 2008).

This transition to new order will be achieved via more instrumental outcomes. The most important of these outcomes may well be the creation and maintenance of the coalition necessary to support and implement the desired changes. The coalition may already exist; if not, it will have to be created. The size and shape of this coalition will vary depending on the nature of the changes being sought. As Van de Ven, Polley, Garud, and Venkataraman (1999, p. 57) note, "Fewer hurdles and resistances to change are encountered when a few, presumably easy, components of an innovation are implemented by a few, presumably supportive, stakeholders, than when all, easy and hard, components of a program are implemented in depth with all partisan stakeholders involved."

The second of these subordinate desired outcomes is in many ways the reverse of the most important desired outcome—namely, the avoidance of the typical causes of failure. These causes are legion, but include the following:

- Failure to maintain or create the coalition necessary to protect, support, and guide implementation.

- Resistance based on attitudes and beliefs that are incompatible with desired changes. Sometimes these attitudes and beliefs stem simply from the resisters' not having participated in strategy or plan development.

- Personnel problems such as inadequate numbers, poorly designed incentives, inadequate orientation or training, or people's over-commitment to other activities or uncertainty that involvement with implementation can help their careers.

- Incentives that fail to induce desired behavior on the part of implementing organizations or units.

- Implementing organizations' or units' preexisting commitment of resources to other priorities and a consequent absence of uncommitted resources to facilitate new activities; in other words, there is little "slack" (Cyert & March, 1963).

- The absence of administrative support services.

- The absence of rules, resources, and settings for identifying and resolving implementation problems.

- The emergence of new political, economic, or administrative priorities.

The third subordinate outcome is therefore the development of a clear understanding by implementers of what needs to be done and when, why, and by whom. Statements of goals and objectives, a vision of success, clearly articulated strategies, and educational materials and operational guides all can help. If they have not been created already, they may need to be developed in this step. These statements and guides will help concentrate people's attention on making the changes that make a difference as adopted strategies are reconciled with existing and emergent strategies.

A fourth subordinate outcome is the use of a *debugging* process to identify and fix difficulties that almost inevitably arise as a new solution is put in place. As political scientist and anthropologist James Scott (1998, p. 6) notes, "Designed or planned social order is necessarily schematic; it always ignores essential features of any real, functioning social order." Or to put it in less academic terms, implementers should recall the well-known administrative adage Murphy's Law: "Anything that can go wrong will go wrong." They should also recall the quip, "Murphy was an optimist!" The earlier steps in the process are designed to ensure, as much as possible, that the adopted strategies and plans will outline and help meet the requirements for success and do not contain any major flaws. But it is almost inconceivable that some important difficulties will not arise as strategies are put into practice. Key decision makers should pay regular attention to how implementation is proceeding in order to focus attention on any difficulties and to plan how to address them. *Management by wandering around* (Peters & Waterman, 1982) can help decision makers gather information and solve difficulties on the spot. *Managing by groping along* can help if it leads to useful adaptive learning (Behn, 1991; Borins, 1998). Also, as mentioned briefly in Chapter Seven, a conscious formative evaluation process is needed to help implementers identify obstacles and steer over, around, under, or through them to achieve—or if necessary, modify—policy goals during the early stages of implementation. A good formative evaluation will also provide useful information for new rounds of strategizing (Patton, 2008).

Fifth, successful implementation also is likely to include summative evaluations (Scriven, 1967; Mattessich, 2003; Patton, 2008), to find out whether strategic goals have actually been achieved once strategies are fully implemented. Summative evaluations often differentiate between outputs and outcomes. *Outputs* are the actual actions, behaviors, products, services, or other direct consequences produced by the policy changes. *Outcomes* are the benefits of the outputs for stakeholders and the larger meanings attached to those outputs. In other words, outputs are substantive changes, whereas outcomes are both substantive improvements and symbolic interpretations. Both are important in determining whether a change has been worth the expenditure of time and effort (Lynn, 1987; McLaughlin & Jordan, 2010). (Balanced scorecards can help implementers make the link between outcomes, which are customer oriented, and outputs, which are results produced by internal processes—particularly as customer-oriented outcomes tend to be *lagging* indicators, and internal process outputs are *leading* indicators.) Summative evaluations may be expensive and time-consuming. Further, they are vulnerable to sabotage or attack on political, technical, legal, or ethical grounds. Nonetheless, without such evaluations it is very difficult to know whether things are *better* as a result of implemented changes, and in precisely what ways.

A sixth subordinate desired outcome is retention of important features of the adopted strategies and plans. As situations change and different actors become involved, implementation can become a kind of *moving target*. It is possible that mutations developed during the course of implementation can do a better job of addressing the issues than would the original adopted strategy or plan. In general, however, it is more likely that design distortions will subvert the avowed strategic aims and gut their intent, so it is important to make sure that important design features are maintained, or, if they are not, that such changes are desirable.

Seventh, successful implementation likely requires creation of redesigned organizational (or collaborative or community) settings that will ensure long-lasting changes. These settings are marked by the institutionalization of implicit or explicit principles, norms, rules, decision-making procedures, and incentives; the stabilization of altered patterns of behaviors and attitudes; and the continuation or creation of a coalition of implementers, advocates, and supportive interest groups who favor the changes. For example, MetroGIS has followed a set of guiding principles to govern its decision making and activities virtually since the beginning of its existence in 1995—to the point that they are essentially an internally generated and institutionalized mandate. The Loft has developed a tradition of disciplined focus on its mission and broad consultation with the board (and often other important stakeholder groups) before making important decisions. And the Park Board has moved a long way toward institutionalizing interdisciplinary decision making and broadly based as well as targeted community consultation.

If the redesign of the settings is significant, the result may in fact be a new regime. Regime construction is not easy and, therefore, will not happen unless relevant implementers believe the changes are clearly worth the effort. A variety of new or redesigned settings that allow the use of a range of tools, techniques, and incentives (including positive and negative sanctions) may be necessary in order to shape behaviors and attitudes in desired directions (Osborne & Plastrik, 2000). MetroGIS, for example, created and institutionalized its policy board, coordinating committee, and use of short-term technical teams. Incentives for participation by units of government, businesses, and nonprofit organizations had to be created. Group norms encouraging participation and doing the work operated as both positive reinforcements and negative sanctions when people didn't follow through. And new tools and techniques were developed to facilitate the work of geospatial data acquisition and use. A vision of success (discussed in Chapter Eight) may be highly desirable for outlining what the new regime would look like if the purpose of the changes is realized and strategies are fully implemented.

The eighth and final subordinate desired outcome is the establishment or anticipation of review points during which strategies may be maintained, significantly modified, or terminated. The Strategy Change Cycle is a series of loops, not a straight line. Politics, problems, and desired solutions often change (Kingdon, 2002). There are no once-and-for-all solutions, only temporary victories. Leaders, managers, and planners must be alert to the nature and sources of possible challenges to implemented strategies; they should work to maintain still-desirable strategies, replacing them with better ones when possible or necessary, and terminating them when they become completely outmoded.

If the real public value has been created via these subordinate outcomes, then additional outcomes are also likely to be produced. One of the most important is increased support for, and legitimacy of, the leaders and organizations that have successfully advocated and implemented the changes (Bartlett & Ghoshal, 1994; Crosby & Bryson, 2005). Real issues have been identified and effectively addressed; public value has been created. That is what public and nonprofit organizational or community leadership is all about. In addition, leaders who advocate and implement desired changes may reap career rewards. Their formal or informal contracts may be extended. They may receive pay raises or other perks, as well as attractive job offers from elsewhere. Further, since organizations are externally justified by what they do to address basic social or political problems or needs, the advocating organizations should experience enhanced legitimacy and support (Suchman, 1995).

Second, individuals involved in effective implementation of desirable changes are likely to experience heightened self-efficacy, self-esteem, and self-confidence (Schein, 2010; Kelman, 2005; Scharmer, 2009). If a person has done a good job of addressing real needs and of creating real public value, it is hard for him or her *not* to feel good about it. Effective implementation thus can produce extremely important "psychic income" for those involved. Finally, organizations (or communities) that effectively implement strategies and plans are likely to enhance their capacities for action in the future. They acquire an expanded repertoire of knowledge, experience, tools, and techniques, and an expanded inventory of capital (intellectual, human, social, political, civic)—and therefore are better positioned to undertake and adapt to future changes.

For these various benefits to accrue, a number of implementation vehicles are likely to be necessary. These include performance measurement and management, programs, projects, and budgets.

Performance Measurement and Management

Performance measurement and management are becoming standard practice in public and nonprofit organizations, but not necessarily in the ways their advocates envisioned. The adage that what gets measured gets managed may be true, but more often than not performance information is ambiguous, subjective, and rarely comprehensive. Performance information is part of the politics of strategy change and is embedded in political language and used as a political tool (Stone, 2002; Moynihan, 2008). Actual use of performance information depends on: support from senior leaders; the information being accessible, credible, understandable, and usable; the presence of a culture that values learning and collaboration and is goal-oriented; and routines that encourage people to use performance-related information as part of ongoing learning. It also helps if the implementers have been involved in developing the assessment measures (Lu, 2007; Moynihan, 2008; Patton, 2008; Moynihan & Pandey, 2010). Although meritorious performance can lead to favorable budget outcomes, it is hardly surprising that partisan politics can override the effects of meritorious performance (Gilmour & Lewis, 2005). Even so, there is fairly clear evidence that performance measures can make a positive difference in influencing the direction of change efforts and learning from them (for example, Kelman, 2005; Boyne & Chen, 2006; Moynihan, 2008; Innes & Booher, 2010). Use of performance measures is a key to high performance of individuals, including leaders, organizations, and collaborations (Light, 2005; Boyne & Chen, 2006; Latham, Borgogni, & Petitta, 2008; Innes & Booher, 2010). Increasingly, communities and states are developing performance measures and using them to assess how well they are doing as places and to help produce alignments among the various organizational and citizen efforts to contribute to desirable outcomes (for example, Ho & Coates, 2004; Osborne & Hutchinson, 2004; Epstein, Coates, Wray, & Swain, 2005; and Andrews, Jonas, Mantell, & Solomon, 2008).

Performance information, however, must always be treated with a certain amount of skepticism. Leaders and managers should deliberate carefully about what will be measured, how, and why in order to make sure that indicators help rather than undermine effective performance (Moynihan, 2005, 2008; Patton, 2008). For example, all too frequently indicators fail to take into account a policy's or program's complex feedback effects (Courty, Heinrich, & Marschke, 2005), the problematic mapping of cross-agency programs onto agency budgets, differential policy or program effects on stakeholders by race and gender (Soss, Fording, & Schram, 2008), policy or program effects on citizenship (Wichowsky & Moynihan, 2008), and at least some important regime values (Piotrowski & Rosenbloom, 2002). In addition, leaders and managers must make sure *goal displacement* does not occur in which the means to an end—the measures—become the end (Merton, 1940; Schön, 1971). Indicator use should help clarify what the ends actually are or should be, and the measures should be changed if necessary. Measures are as close as we can get to clearly specifying organization, collaboration, community, policy, program, or project goals and debates about measures are in effect debates about the goals (Kay, 2010). Those debates should be engaged in a deliberative way.

To be effective, performance measures must help inform and guide strategy implementation. Recall the discussion in Chapter One about the links between strategic planning and implementation via an appropriate strategic (or performance management) system (see Exhibit 1.1). Effective implementation involves the effort to realize in practice an organization's (collaboration's or community's) mission, goals and strategies, the meeting of its mandates, continued organizational learning, and the ongoing creation of public value. Doing so requires actually developing a useful strategic management system, including linking mission and vision, performance measurement, budgeting, program and project management, and periodic reviews and reassessments in such a way that the desirable results are produced at reasonable cost and desirable changes in ends and means are allowed to emerge over time. Conceptually, it is useful to view strategic planning as the front end of strategic management, even though most strategic planning efforts begin amid the implementation of previously designed, or currently emerging, strategies.

Specifically, implementation efforts must somehow be accommodated to ongoing circumstances, even as they seek to change those circumstances (Mulgan, 2009).

PROGRAMS AND PROJECTS

New or revised programs and projects are a component of many strategic change efforts (Joyce, 1999; Project Management Institute, 2008; Kassel, 2010; Kwak & Anbari, 2010). The Park Board, Loft, and MetroGIS implemented many aspects of their strategic plans as projects. Creation of programs and projects is a way of *chunking* (Peters & Waterman, 1982, pp. 126–134) changes by breaking them down into smaller pieces to address specific issues. Koteen (1997) refers to program and project management as a form of *bite-sized management* because the creation of programs and projects can help clarify the overall design of a change initiative, provide a vehicle for obtaining the necessary review and approval, and provide an objective basis for evaluation of progress. Programs and projects also can focus attention on strategic initiatives, facilitate detailed learning, build momentum behind the changes, provide for increased accountability, and allow for easier termination of initiatives that turn out to be undesirable (Project Management Institute, 2008; Kassel, 2010). When drawing attention to the changes is unwise for any reason, decision makers can still use a program or project management approach, but they will need an astute public relations strategy to defuse the ire of powerful opponents.

Program and project plans are a version of action plans, and should have the following components:

- Definition of purpose
- Clarification of program or project organization and mechanisms for resolving conflicts
- Articulation of the logic model or strategy-specific map guiding the initiative, that is, clarification of the process by which inputs are to be converted to outputs (Poister, 2003; McLaughlin & Jordan, 2010; Bryson, Ackermann, Eden, & Finn, 2004)
- Calculation of inputs desired, including financial, human resources, information technology, and other resources
- Definition of outputs to be produced
- Identification of target clientele

- A time line of activities and decision points
- Specification of objectively verifiable indicators of key aspects of the logic model
- Indicators of assumptions that are key to the success of the program, including presumed requirements for success

THE SPECIAL ROLE OF BUDGETS

Budget allocations have crucial, if not overriding, significance for the implementation of strategies and plans. Budgets often represent the most important and consequential policy statements that governments or nonprofit organizations make. Not all strategies and plans have budgetary significance, but enough of them do that public and nonprofit leaders and managers should consider involving themselves deeply in the process of budget making. Doing so is likely to be a particularly effective way to have an impact on the design, adoption, and execution of strategies and plans (Lynn, 1987, pp. 191–193; Rubin, 2009).

The difficulty of using budgets for planning purposes results partly from the political context within which budgeting takes place. The hustle, hassle, and uncertainty of politics means that budgeting typically tends to be short-term, incremental, reactive, and oriented toward tracking expenditures and revenues—rather than long-term, comprehensive, innovative, proactive, and oriented toward accomplishment of broad purposes, goals, or priorities. The politicized nature of budgeting is likely to be especially pronounced in the public sector, where adopted budgets record the outcomes of a broad-based political struggle among the many claimants on the public purse (Wildavsky, 1984; Rubin, 2009). But the same difficulties emerge (though perhaps in more muted form and for somewhat different reasons) in the private and nonprofit sectors as well (Mintzberg, 1994).

Another fundamental reason for the gap between budgeting and planning is that planning for control and planning for action are so fundamentally different, as Mintzberg (1994, pp. 67–81) argues, that a *great divide* exists between them. What can be done about the great divide, as both performance control and strategies and programs are important? Several suggestions are possible:

1. Have strategic planning precede the budget cycle (Osborne & Plastrik, 2000, pp. 43–53; Osborne & Hutchinson, 2004). Budgeting is more likely to serve overall organizational purposes if environmental assessments, strategic issue identification, and strategy formulation precede rather than follow it. A number of government organizations

are moving in this direction, including Charlotte, North Carolina; Miami-Dade County, Florida; King County, Washington; and Milwaukee, Wisconsin (Hendrick, 2003).

2. To make this happen, gain control of the *master calendar* that guides formal organizational planning and budgeting efforts. As Lynn argues (1987, pp. 203–205), "the master calendar is the public executive's most important device for gaining ascendancy over the process of budget making in the organization. . . . [because it] puts public executives in a position to spell out the assumptions, constraints, priorities, and issues they want each subordinate unit to consider in developing its program, budget, and policy proposals. In the process, they can define the roles of the various staff offices . . . and indicate when and how they will make decisions and hear appeals."

3. Build a performance budgeting system (using the master calendar and any other available tools and resources). As Osborne and Plastrik (2000, p. 43) note, "performance budgets define the outputs and outcomes policymakers intend to buy with each sum they appropriate. . . . This allows both the executive and the legislature to make their performance expectations clear, then track whether they are getting what they paid for. It also helps them learn whether the strategies and outputs they are funding are actually producing the outcomes they want. If not, they can ask for an evaluation to examine why—and what to do about it." A key point, however, is that in general the policymakers should stop if possible at direction setting, budgeting, and evaluation—that is, performance control (Simons, 1995)—and leave the detailed specification of strategies and actions—action planning—to the managers responsible for producing the outputs and outcomes.

4. Prior strategic planning efforts can provide many of the premises needed to try to influence budgeting in strategic directions (Crosby & Bryson, 2005, pp. 267–289). In addition, the short-term, incremental nature of budgeting actually can be a source of opportunity, rather than constraint, for the strategically minded public and nonprofit leader and manager (Lynn, 1987, p. 203; Rubin, 2009). The system is a natural setting for organizing a series of small wins informed by a strategic sense of direction—especially when some of that direction can come from prior planning efforts.

5. Pick your budget fights carefully. Given the number of players that budgeting attracts, particularly in the public sector, you cannot win every battle. Focus your attention on those budget allocation decisions

that are crucial to moving desired strategies forward. Use the master calendar and preexisting decision premises to anticipate when and how potential budgetary fights are likely to arise. Lynn (1987, pp. 208–209) argues that there are three basic approaches to budgetary allocations. Each has a different effect on the way issues are raised:

- Each budget issue can be treated separately. This typically means that issues are framed and forwarded by subunits. Therefore cross-issue or cross-unit comparisons are avoided, and it may be possible to hide particular choices from broad scrutiny. If resolution of the individual issues leads to exceeding the total resources available, across-the-board cuts or selective comparisons on the margin are possible.
- Particular issues can be selected in advance for detailed consideration during budget preparations. The strategic planning process would be a likely source of candidate strategic issues for careful review. The typical incremental nature of budgeting might be influenced by the general sense of direction that emerges from addressing these issues.
- Budgetary issues can be examined in the light of a comprehensive analytical framework, benchmarks or performance measures, or strategy. Here the attempt is to influence budgetary allocations based on a larger strategic vision. This approach is most likely to work when the strategic planning process can be driven by broadly shared goals, a vision of success, balanced scorecard or another boundary-spanning, integrative device, and there is strong leadership in place to follow through with the more detailed vision of success or balanced scorecard that is likely to result (Osborne & Hutchinson, 2004).

6. Consider implementing *entrepreneurial budgeting* concepts to advance strategic purposes. A number of governments around the world are experimenting with reforms likely to facilitate implementation of intended strategies, help new strategies emerge via innovation, enhance managerial autonomy along with accountability for results, and promote an entrepreneurial culture (Osborne & Plastrik, 1997; Osborne & Hutchinson, 2004). The approach can involve creating *flexible performance frameworks* that split policymaking from implementation and then use written agreements to spell out the implementing organization's or department's purposes, expected results, performance consequences, and management flexibilities (Osborne & Plastrik, 2000, pp. 124–148). Governments using these approaches begin by establishing broad strategic goals, and then set overall expenditure

limits, along with broad allocations for specific functions, such as health, public safety, or roads. Then operating departments are given substantially increased discretion over the use of funds in order to achieve their portion of the strategic goals, "subject to the usual constraints of legality and political prudence" (Cothran, 1993, p. 446). This move significantly decentralizes decision making. In a further shift from traditional practice, departments are allowed to keep a significant fraction of the funds left at the end of the fiscal year without having their budget base cut. Cost savings and wise management can be rewarded, and the phenomenon of foolish buying sprees at the end of the year, spurred by use-it-or-lose-it policies, is avoided. In a further move to enhance cost savings and wise management, some governments add to employees' paychecks a fraction of any savings they produce. The final feature of entrepreneurial budgeting is an emphasis on accountability for results. In return for increased discretion, higher-level decision makers want greater evidence of program achievement and efficiency gains. An almost contractual agreement is negotiated between policymakers or the central budget office and the operating departments in which each department lists and ranks its objectives, specifies indicators for measuring the achievement of those objectives, and quantifies the indicators as much as possible. If objectives are not achieved, serious questioning of managers by policymakers can ensue (Cothran, 1993; Osborne & Plastrik, 2000, pp. 126–128).

Entrepreneurial budgeting thus involves a blend of centralization *and* decentralization. Control over broadscale goal setting and monitoring for results is retained by policymakers, and managerial discretion over how to achieve the goals is decentralized to operating managers. Authority is delegated without being relinquished; policymakers and managers are each therefore better able—and empowered—to do their jobs more effectively (Carver, 2006). In effect, as Cothran (1993, p. 453) observes, "entrepreneurial budgeting, and decentralized management in general, can lead to an expansion of power, rather than a redistribution of power." The changes that entrepreneurial budgeting are intended to induce are so profound that a shift in organizational culture is likely to result. Indeed, a major reason for moving to entrepreneurial budgeting is to create a culture of entrepreneurship, particularly in government (Osborne & Gaebler, 1992). This change in culture itself needs to be thought about in a strategic fashion (Khademian, 2002; Schein, 2010).

7. Make sure you have good analysts and wily and seasoned veterans of budgetary politics on your side. Budgeting is a complicated game, and having a good team and good coaches can help. There is really no

substitute for having a savvy insider who can both prepare and critique budgets effectively. But just as it is important to have good analysts and advisers, it is also important not to become their captive, either (Meltsner, 1990). The wise leader or manager will want to make sure that a sense of the organization's desired strategy informs the analysts' and advisors' work.

8. Develop criteria for evaluating the budgets for all programs— preexisting and new—and then to the extent possible make budgetary allocations on the margin away from lower-priority existing programs (the stop agenda) toward higher-priority new initiatives. This is one way of coping with the enormous difficulty in tight budgetary times of getting adequate budgets for new programs approved without first offering up for sacrifice worthy existing programs—and then running the risk of losing both.

9. Finally, involve the same people in both strategy formulation and implementation if you can. Doing so clearly can help bridge the action-control gap. There are two approaches to doing this, one centralized, the other decentralized (Mintzberg, 1994, pp. 286–287). On the one hand, in the centralized approach, which is most closely associated with strong entrepreneurial or visionary leaders of small organizations, the formulator does the implementing. By staying in close contact with the intimate details of implementation, the formulator can continuously evaluate and readjust strategies during implementation. The decentralized approach, on the other hand, is more suitable for highly complex situations in which many more people are involved and where "strategic thinking cannot be concentrated at one center" (pp. 286–287). In this case, the implementers must become the formulators, as when *street-level bureaucrats* determine a public service agency's strategy in practice (Lipsky, 1980; Vinzant & Crothers, 1998). At the extreme, this becomes what Mintzberg (1994, pp. 287–290) refers to as a "grass-roots model of strategy formation."

PROCESS DESIGN AND ACTION GUIDELINES

Successful implementation of strategies and plans will depend primarily on the design and use of various *implementation structures* that coordinate and manage implementation activities, along with the continuation or creation of a coalition of committed implementers, advocates, and supportive interest groups (Hjern & Porter, 1981; Peters & Pierre, 2003, pp. 205–255; Agranoff, 2007; Hill & Hupe, 2009). These structures are likely to consist of a variety of formal and informal mechanisms to promote implementation-centered deliberation, decision making, problem solving, and conflict management. New attitudes and patterns of behavior must be stabilized and adjusted to new circumstances, particularly through the institutionalization of shared expectations among key actors around a set of implicit or explicit principles, norms, rules, and decision-making procedures; positive and negative sanctions and incentives; and the continuation or creation of a supportive coalition.

The following leadership guidelines should be kept in mind as the adopted strategies or plans move to implementation. After the general guidelines, additional guidelines are offered for managing communication and education, personnel, and direct and staged communication.

General Guidelines

1. *Consciously and deliberately plan and manage implementation in a strategic way.* The change implementers may be very different from the members of the advocacy coalition that adopted the changes. This is often the case when changes are imposed on implementers by legislative or other decision-making bodies. Implementers thus may have little interest in making implementation flow smoothly and effectively (Pressman & Wildavsky, 1973). Further, even if implementers are interested in incorporating adopted changes within their respective systems, any number of things can go wrong. Implementation, therefore, is hardly ever automatic—Harry Truman's discovery quoted at the beginning of the chapter should be kept in mind. Alternatively, consider famous historian Arnold Toynbee's observation that "Some historians think that history is one damn thing after another." Implementation therefore must be explicitly considered prior to the implementation step, as a way of minimizing later difficulties, and it must be explicitly considered and planned for during the implementation step itself. Change implementers, particularly if they are different from the change formulators, may wish to view the changes as a mandate (Step 2) and go through the process outlined in Chapter Two to figure out how best to respond to them. This process should include efforts to understand and accommodate the history and inclinations of key implementing individuals and organizations (Neustadt & May, 1986). After all, as William Faulkner wrote in *Requiem for a Nun*, "The past is never dead. It's not even past." Accommodating history also means fitting efforts into preexisting policy fields of stakeholders and authority and budget flows (Stone & Sandfort, 2009). Performance indicators must be developed that operationalize key change goals. Programs and

projects must be organized carefully in order to effectively implement desired strategies. Budgets will also need to be given careful attention. Additional detailed advice will be found in Elmore (1982), Nutt and Backoff (1992), Barry (1997), Bardach (1998), Borins (1998), Nutt (2002), Bryant (2003), Friend and Hickling (2005), Crosby and Bryson (2005), and Stone and Sandfort (2009). If implementation will occur in a collaborative setting, a great deal of time and effort will be necessary to plan and manage implementation in a strategic way (Huxham & Vangen, 2005; Innes & Booher, 2010).

The MetroGIS leadership—policy board, coordinating committee, and technical advisory team—thought quite strategically about implementation during the strategy and plan formulation and adoption steps leading up to the 2008 business plan. Previously, as part of the first 1995–1996 strategic planning effort, key stakeholders thought very strategically about the functions, structure, processes, and membership of the governance bodies, as well as how to proceed with the first strategic initiatives. The process had to be very participative and consensus-based, as MetroGIS is a completely voluntary organization. Similarly, the Loft had to make sure key implementers—often Loft staff—were engaged throughout the process. And the Park Board planning team pursued their plans in light of anticipated positive and negative stakeholder reactions. Each planning group was willing to deal with resistance in pursuit of desirable ends, but also thought carefully about how to anticipate and accommodate stakeholder concerns in a constructive way, so as not to needlessly undermine the change effort.

2. *Develop implementation strategy documents—including key indicators —and action plans to guide implementation and focus attention on necessary decisions, actions, and responsible parties.* Recall that strategies will vary by level. Below the constitutive level, where the rules for making rules are decided, the four basic levels are the organization's or network's grand or umbrella strategy; strategy statements for constituent units; the program, service, product, project, or business process strategies designed to coordinate relevant units and activities; and the functional strategies, such as finance, human resources, information technology, communications, facilities, and procurement strategies, also designed to coordinate units and activities necessary to implement desired changes. It may not have been possible to work out all of these statements in advance. If not, the implementation step is the time to finish the task in as much detail as is necessary to focus and channel action without also stifling useful learning. Recall also that strategies may be long-term or short-term.

Strategies provide a framework for tactics—the short-term adaptive actions and reactions used to accomplish fairly limited objectives. Strategies also provide the "continuing basis for ordering these adaptations toward more broadly conceived purposes" (Quinn, 1980, p. 9). (Recall, of course, that tactics can embody emergent strategies as well as implement intended strategies, making it difficult at times to know what the difference is between strategies and tactics; see Mintzberg, 1994, p. 243.) Action plans are statements about how to implement strategies in the short term (Frame, 2002; Project Management Institute, 2008; Kassel, 2010). Typically, action plans cover periods of a year or less. They outline:

- Specific expected results, objectives, and milestones
- Roles and responsibilities of implementation bodies, teams, and individuals
- Specific action steps
- Schedules
- Resource requirements and sources
- A communication process
- A review and monitoring process
- Accountability processes and procedures

Without action planning, intended strategies are likely to remain dreams, not reality. The intentions will be overwhelmed by already-implemented and emergent strategies.

3. *Try for changes that can be introduced easily and rapidly.* Implementers may have little room for maneuvering when it comes to the basic design of and requirements for the proposed changes and the accompanying implementation process. Nonetheless, they should take advantage of whatever discretion they have to improve the ease and rapidity with which changes are put into practice, while still maintaining the basic character of the changes. Implementation will flow more smoothly and speedily if the changes (Gladwell, 2002; Rogers, 2003; Tilly, 2006; Heath & Heath, 2007):

- Are conceptually clear.
- Are based on a well-understood theory of cause-effect relations.
- Fit with the values of all key implementers and tap their emotional commitments to those values.
- Can be demonstrated and made "real" to the bulk of the implementers prior to implementation. (In other words, people have a chance to see what they are supposed to do before they have to do it.)

- Are relatively simple to grasp in practice, because the changes are not only conceptually clear, but also are operationally clear.
- Are administratively simple, entailing minimal bureaucracy and red tape, minimal reorganization of resource allocation patterns, and minimal retraining of staff.
- Allow a start-up period in which people can learn about the adopted changes and engage in any necessary retraining, debugging, and development of new norms and operating routines.
- Include adequate attention to payoffs and rewards necessary to gain wholehearted acceptance of implementers. In other words, incentives clearly favor implementation by relevant organizations and individuals.
- Can be summarized in a compelling story.

Of course, some changes will not be implemented very smoothly and will take considerable time. For example, MetroGIS was able to fairly quickly implement tangible programs and actions related to some aspects of geospatial data acquisition. The really crucial strategies, however, involved engaging and influencing key stakeholders and these took many months and even years to implement before the full effects were realized.

4. *Use a program and project management approach wherever possible.* Chunking the changes by breaking them down into clusters or programs consisting of specific projects is typically an important means of implementing strategic changes. It also makes it easier to tie resources to specific programs or projects and therefore gain budget approval for the efforts. Use standard program and project management techniques to make sure the chunks actually add up to useful progress (Project Management Institute, 2008; Kassel, 2010).

5. *Build in enough people, time, attention, money, administrative and support services, and other resources to ensure successful implementation.* If possible, build in considerable redundancy in places important to implementation, so that if something goes wrong—which it no doubt will—there is adequate backup capacity. Almost any difficulty can be handled with enough resources—although these days budgets typically are exceedingly tight unless money can be freed from other uses (back to the stop agenda). Think about why cars have seatbelts, airbags, and spare tires, jetliners have copilots, and bridges are built to handle many times more weight than they are expected to carry: it is to ensure enough built-in capacity to handle almost any unexpected contingency. Tight resources are an

additional reason to pay attention to the earlier steps in the Strategy Change Cycle. In order to garner sufficient resources, the strategic issue(s) must be sufficiently important, the adopted strategies must be likely to produce desirable results at reasonable cost, and the supportive coalition should be strong and stable. If these elements are present, the chances of finding or developing the necessary resources for implementation are considerably enhanced. Nonetheless, those who must supply the resources may resist, and considerable effort may be needed to overcome that resistance. In almost every case, careful attention will need to be paid to budgeting cycles, processes, and strategies. Implementation plans should include resources for:

- Key personnel
- Fixers—people who know how things work and how to "fix" things when they go wrong (Bardach, 1977)
- Additional necessary staff
- Conversion costs
- Orientation and training costs
- Technical assistance
- Inside and outside consultants
- Adequate incentives to facilitate adoption of the changes by relevant organizations and individuals
- Necessary expansions and upgrades of information and communication technologies
- Support of learning forums to understand what is working and what is not and how things might be improved
- Formative evaluations to facilitate implementation, and summative evaluations to determine whether or not the changes produced the desired results (Mattessich, 2003; Patton, 2008)
- Unforeseen contingencies

6. *Link new strategic initiatives with ongoing operations.* Establishing new units, programs, projects, products, or services with their own organizational structures and funding streams is a typical strategy in the public sector. That way, overt conflicts with ongoing operations can often be minimized. But in an era of resource constraints, new initiatives often must compete directly with, and be merged with, ongoing programs, projects, products, services, and operations. Unfortunately, the implications of a strategic plan for an organization's ongoing operations may be very unclear, particularly in the public sector where policymaking bodies may impose rather vague (or even conflicting) mandates on operating agencies (Stone & Sandfort, 2009). Somehow new (and often vague) initiatives must be blended with

ongoing operations in such a way that internal support is generated from those persons charged with maintaining the organization's ongoing activities. However, the people working in existing operations are likely to feel overworked and undervalued already, and they will want to know how the changes will help or hurt them. Typically, they must be involved directly in the process of fitting desired strategic changes into the operational details of the organization, both to garner useful information and support and to avoid sabotage (Kelman, 2005). One effective way to manage the process of blending new and old activities is to involve key decision makers, implementers, and perhaps representatives of external stakeholder groups in evaluating both sets of activities using a common set of criteria. At least some of these criteria are likely to have been developed earlier as part of the strategic planning process; they may include key performance indicators, client and organizational impacts, stakeholder expectations, and resource use. Once new and old activities have been evaluated, it may be possible to figure out how to fit the new with the old, what part of the new can be ignored, and what part of the old can be dropped. Again, recall that *realized* strategy will consist of some combination of the strategic plan, ongoing initiatives, and unexpected occurrences along the way. Worksheets that may help with this process will be found in Bryson and Alston (2011) and Bryson, Anderson, and Alston (2011). Process Guideline 13 in Chapter Seven provides additional guidance on how to align new strategies with existing ones.

7. *Work quickly to avoid unnecessary or undesirable competition with new priorities.* The economy is not very good as I write this, and can always get worse, severely damaging financial support. Those who remember the recessions of the early 1980s, early 1990s, and early and late 2000s know this. In addition, tax revolts, tax indexing, tax cuts, and large state and federal deficits have greatly constricted public funds for new initiatives. For these and other reasons, it is wise to build in excess implementation resources, to provide slack. A poverty budget can turn out to be a death warrant. Cheapness should not be a selling point. Instead, program designers and supporters should sell cost-effectiveness—that is, the idea that the program delivers great benefits in relation to its costs. A change in the policy board or administration also is likely to bring a change in priorities (Kingdon, 2002; Schein, 2010). New leaders have their own conception of which issues should be addressed and how. For example, former Park Board Superintendent John Gurban (he left the post in June 2010) pushed for organizational restructuring and then restarted the strategic planning effort in order to address what he and the

board saw as key issues facing the organization. The Loft's previous executive director, Linda Myers, probably knew she might be retiring soon and enlisted board members Jocelyn Hale and Stephen Wilbers as two of the champions of the strategic planning process. There was no guarantee Myers would leave or that Hale would become executive director, but the process resulted in seamless commitment at the top to strategic planning. MetroGIS leadership has always worked to ensure that there would be continuing commitment to the organization and its strategies at the top. Further, the anticipation of a new administration often paralyzes any change effort. People want to see what will happen before risking their careers by pushing changes that may not be desired by new leaders. Thus, once again, leaders and managers must move quickly to implement new strategies and plans before actual or impending change in the economy or the authorizing environment (Moore, 1995).

8. *Focus on maintaining or developing a coalition of implementers, advocates, and interest groups intent on effective implementation of the changes and willing to protect them over the long haul.* One of the clear lessons from the past three decades of implementation research is that successful implementation of programs in shared-power situations depends upon developing and maintaining such a coalition (Sabatier & Weible, 2007; Baumgartner & Jones, 2009; Innes & Booher, 2010). Coalitions are organized around ideas, interests, and payoffs, so leaders and managers must pay attention to aligning these elements in such a way that strong coalitions are created and maintained. Strong coalitions will result if those involved see that their interests are served by the new arrangements (May, 2003; Crosby & Bryson, 2005). The literature on organizational change in general assumes there will be substantial resistance to any changes. As a result, three general prescriptions are offered for helping align people's sense of their interests with the changes being advocated. First, persuasion and discussion may help. Second, continuous pressure from leaders may be necessary (Kotter, 1996). And third, a sense of crisis or urgency may prompt change if people see not changing as more threatening than changing (Rochet, Keramidas, & Bout, 2008; Kotter, 2008). But Steven Kelman (2005) points out that there may be many people who are *not* resisting, but are instead discontented with the status quo and would welcome changes that make their lives easier, engage them more effectively, and advance the common good. Here the prescription is simply to activate the discontented and work to build momentum by promoting successful experience with the changes and the spreading and strengthening of

pro-change attitudes and behaviors. Kelman's careful study of procurement reform in the Clinton Administration makes a strong case for this hopeful view of what he calls "unleashing change."

9. *Be sure that legislative, executive, and administrative policies and actions facilitate rather than impede implementation.* It is important to maintain a liaison with decision makers in arenas such as state legislatures, governors' offices, and key administrators' offices if their decisions can affect the implementation effort. Leaders and managers must also pay attention to implementers' development and use of supplemental policies, regulations, rules, ordinances, articles, guidelines, and so on that are required for implementation to proceed. Efforts should be made to create *green tape*—rules that facilitate effective implementation—as opposed to the sort of *red tape* that gets in the way (deHart-Davis, 2008). Operational details must be worked out, and many of these ancillary materials will need to pass through specific processes before they have the force of law. For example, before implementing regulations can become official at the federal level, they must be developed following the procedures outlined in the Administrative Procedures Act (Cooper, 1996). States have their own administrative procedures and localities and nonprofit organizations may have analogous routines. Change advocates should seek expert advice on how these processes work and attend to the ways in which supplemental policies are developed. Otherwise, the promise of the previous steps may be lost in practice.

10. *Think carefully about how residual disputes will be resolved and underlying norms enforced.* This may mean establishing special procedures for settling disputes that arise. It may also mean relying on the courts. It is preferable to rely on *alternative dispute resolution methods* if possible, to keep conflicts out of formal courts and to encourage all-gain solutions that increase the legitimacy and acceptance of the policy, strategy, or plan and the outcomes of conflict management efforts (Fisher & Ury, 1991; Thompson, 2008). It is also important to remember that the court of public opinion is likely to be important in reinforcing the norms supporting the new changes.

11. *Remember that major changes, and even many minor ones, entail changes in the organization's culture.* Changes in strategy almost inevitably prompt changes in basic assumptions about how to respond to changes in the internal and external environments. Leaders, managers, and planners should facilitate necessary changes in cultural symbols and artifacts, espoused values, and underlying assumptions,

recognizing that it is far easier to change the first two than it is to change the third. Indeed, heavy-handed attempts to change underlying assumptions are more likely to promote resistance and rejection than acceptance (Khademian, 2002; Schein, 2010; Hill & Lynn, 2009).

12. *Emphasize learning.* The world does not stop for planning. Nor does it stop once the planning is done. Situations change, and therefore those interested in change must constantly learn and adapt if their organizations (collaborations, communities) are to remain vital and of use to their key stakeholders (Schein, 2010). Moynihan (2005) provides guidance and examples of how *learning forums* might be designed and used on a regular basis to foster learning—in other words, how their use might become a habit and part of the culture (Crossan, Lane, & White, 1999). Formative evaluations can also facilitate necessary learning (Patton, 2008). Said differently, strategies are hardly ever implemented as intended. Adaptive learning is necessary to tailor intended strategies to emergent situations so that appropriate modifications are made and desirable outcomes are produced (Mintzberg, Ahlstrand, & Lampel, 2009).

13. *Think carefully about how information and communication technologies can help support implementation and ongoing learning efforts.* Implementation Web sites, blogs, wikis, tweets, e-mail, podcasts, electronic tutorials, and other ICT applications all may facilitate implementation efforts both by transferring information and building and sustaining coalitions. Implementers should carefully think through how best to make use of the potential inherent in ICT.

14. *Create an accountability system that assures key stakeholders that political, legal, and performance-based accountability needs are met.* Efforts to build strong relationships with key stakeholders will help, as will legal advice. So, too is a good performance measurement and management system that includes vertical integration of goals, strong strategic guidance for implementation efforts, a balance between top-down direction and bottom-up efforts and learning, use of performance information in decision making, and strong leadership and commitment such that good results are maintained and better ones produced (Moynihan & Ingraham, 2003; Bryson, Crosby, & Stone, 2006). Of course, accountability may not always be clear-cut— for example, when a collaborative works with other collaboratives. Additionally, collaborating organizations may have their own accountability frameworks that conflict with the collaboration's accountability approach (Sullivan, Barnes, & Matka 2002).

Nonetheless, efforts to demonstrate accountability for results, the wise stewardship of resources, the satisfaction of key stakeholders, and ongoing learning and improvement are typically always in order.

15. *Hang in there!* Successful implementation in complex, multiorganizational, shared-power settings typically requires large amounts of time, attention, resources, and effort (Kingdon, 2002; Nutt, 2001, 2002). Fortunately, as long as on balance positive benefits are being produced, change momentum may build simply as time goes by, supportive norms develop, pro-change attitudes are produced, and the winning coalition is created (Kelman, 2005). Implementers still may need considerable courage to fight resisters. The rewards, however, can be great—namely, effective actions addressing important strategic issues that deeply affect the organization (collaboration or community) and its stakeholders. The result can be the creation of substantial and sustained public value.

Communication and Education Guidelines

1. *Invest in communication activities.* This means attention to the design and use of communication networks and the messages and messengers that comprise them. Particularly when large changes are involved, people must be given opportunities to develop shared meanings and appreciations that will further the implementation of change goals (Barzelay & Campbell, 2003; Crosby & Bryson, 2005; Holman, Devane, & Cady, 2007). These meanings will both guide and flow out of implementation activities. People must *hear* about the proposed changes, preferably hearing the same messages across multiple channels many times, to increase the chances that the messages will sink in. As Andre Gide said, "Everything has been said before, but since nobody listens we have to keep going back and begin all over again." Further, people must be able to *talk* about the changes, in order to understand them, fit them into their own interpretive schemes, adapt them to their own circumstances, and explore implications for action and the consequences of those actions (Trist, 1983; Johnson & Johnson, 2008). Web sites, educational programs, information packets, and guidebooks can help establish a desirable frame of reference and common language for addressing implementation issues. The Park Board, Loft, and MetroGIS have all held numerous workshops and other educational sessions with key implementers, organized information sessions for key stakeholders, and used a variety of other media to build understanding around concepts central to their strategic plans.

2. *Work to reduce resistance based on divergent attitudes and lack of participation.* Actions likely to reduce resistance on the part of implementers include providing those implementers with orientation sessions, training materials and sessions, problem-solving teams, one-to-one interactions, and technical assistance to support strategy implementation and overcome obstacles to it. Ceremonies and symbolic rewards to reinforce desired behaviors are also helpful. Recognize as well that unleashing those who do not like the status quo can help turn the tide.

3. *Consider developing a guiding vision of success if one has not been developed already.* Developing a vision of success is an exercise in *rhetorical leadership* (Doig & Hargrove, 1987). Chapter Eight discusses visions of success and offers guidance on how to develop one.

4. *Build in regular attention to appropriate indicators.* This will ensure attention to progress—or lack thereof—against the issues that prompted the strategic planning effort. The Park Board, Loft, and MetroGIS have all developed measures tied to each of their strategic goals. Many public and nonprofit organizations are creating balanced scorecards to help them pay attention to key performance indicators (Niven, 2008).

Personnel Guidelines

1. *As much as possible, fill leadership and staff positions with highly qualified people committed to the change effort.* As noted, changes do not implement themselves—people make them happen. This is particularly true for major changes. When minor changes are required, systems and structures often can be substitutes for leadership. But when significant changes are involved, there are no substitutes for leadership of many kinds. People—intelligent, creative, skilled, experienced, committed people—are necessary to create the new order, culture, systems, and structures that will focus and channel efforts toward effective implementation. In order to attract and retain such people, at least three things are necessary:

    - The jobs must be designed in such a way that the work is intrinsically motivating, which typically means jobs that are challenging, meaningful, and provide a sense of accomplishment. Alternative work schedules can also help (Light, 1998; Perry, Mesch, & Paarlberg, 2006).
    - People must be adequately compensated for their work. Fortunately, compensation does not always have to mean money.

Psychic income—the rewards that come from doing good and being part of a new and important adventure—can count as well (Perry, Mesch, & Paarlberg, 2006). Such income is traditionally extremely important in parts of the nonprofit world, and the fact that people are often willing to commit themselves to altruistic pursuits is one of its distinguishing features (Light, 2000, 2005).

- People must see how their careers can be advanced by involvement in implementation. The most intelligent and able people are likely to take a long view of their careers and will avoid what may be dead-end jobs. Instead, they are likely to choose jobs that can improve their skills, responsibilities, and long-term job prospects (Dalton & Lawrence, 1993; Raelin, 2003).
- People want to have viable escape routes if things go bad or if they want to leave on their own. Many mechanisms can achieve this end—for example, an option of returning to prior jobs, outplacement services, or generous severance packages.

2. *Give the planning team the task of planning and managing implementation, or establish a new implementation team that has a significant overlap in membership with the planning team.* As indicated, successful implementation typically requires careful planning and management. In complex change situations, a team is likely to be necessary to help with this effort. Including some planning team members on implementation teams ensures that important learning from earlier steps is not lost during implementation. The planners and implementers overlapped in important ways in the Park Board, Loft, and MetroGIS cases.

3. *Ensure access to, and liaison with, top administrators during implementation.* This task is easy when the change advocates themselves are or become the top administrators. But even if this is not the case, the implementation team may find that administrators are interested in maintaining regular contact with them.

4. *Give special attention to the problem of easing out, working around, or avoiding people who are not likely to help the change effort for whatever reason.* Standard practice in the public sector, of course, is to start a new agency rather than give implementation responsibilities to an existing agency whose mission, culture, personnel, and history are antagonistic to the intent of the changes. For example, President Lyndon Johnson insisted on a new Office of Economic Opportunity rather than turn over implementation responsibilities for many of his Great Society programs to established agencies such as the depart-

ments of Labor or Health, Education, and Welfare (now Health and Human Services). He remarked at one point, "The best way to kill a new idea is to put it in an old line agency" (Anderson, 1990, p. 180). Or, as management theorist Frederick Herzberg often says, "It is easier to give birth than to resurrect." But even if a new organization is started, leaders and managers may still be stuck with personnel who might be detrimental to achievement of the policy goals. For example, in the aftermath of September 11, 2001, President George W. Bush supported a Democratic proposal for a new Department of Homeland Security (DHS). DHS was formed out of twenty-two previously separate domestic agencies. According to the department's home page, creation of the department is "the most significant transformation of the U.S. government since 1947, when Harry S. Truman merged the various branches of the U.S. Armed Forces into the Department of Defense to better coordinate the nation's defense against military threats." DHS represents a similar consolidation, both in style and substance. Formation of DHS represented a dramatic change involving over 200,000 employees and other stakeholders and a host of different structures, systems, and cultures (DHS, 2011). Presumably, not everyone involved was or is happy with the change—and the federal government's responses to Hurricanes Katrina and Rita and to the Deepwater Horizon oil spill indicate there is still work to do.

There are several options for dealing with people who will not help the change effort. First, help them get jobs to which they are more suited. This may take considerable time initially—for establishing people's skills, ascertaining their goals, and writing favorable letters of recommendation—but the resulting increase in the remaining staff's morale and productivity is likely to be worth the effort. Second, have a policy of awarding merit pay only to people who actively implement policy goals. Third, place them in jobs where they cannot damage the change effort. Fourth, buy them off with early retirement or severance packages. And finally, if all else fails, work around them or ignore them.

Direct Versus Staged Implementation Guidelines

There are two basic approaches to implementation, direct and staged. Direct implementation incorporates changes into all relevant sites essentially simultaneously, whereas staged implementation incorporates changes sequentially into groups of sites (Bryson & Delbecq, 1979; Joyce, 1999, pp. 81–82; Crosby & Bryson, 2005).

1. *Consider direct implementation when the situation is technically and politically simple, immediate action is necessary for system survival in a crisis, or the adopted solutions entail some lumpiness that precludes staged implementation.* When situations are simple, direct implementation can work if enough resources are built in to cover costs and provide sufficient incentives and if resistance to change is low. Therefore, leaders and managers must try to reduce any resistance to change based on divergent attitudes and lack of earlier participation, while also unleashing those already supportive of desired changes. A crisis can simplify a situation politically in that people become more willing to defer to top positional leaders and accept centralized decision making (Hunt, Boal, & Dodge, 1999; Rochet, Keramidas, & Bout, 2008). Thus a crisis often makes direct implementation feasible. However, strategies adopted to address crises must still be technically feasible, or at least practical enough so that difficulties can be worked out without weakening people's support for change. Unfortunately, few organizations have effective crisis management policies and systems in place (Weick & Sutcliffe, 2007; Heath & Palenchar, 2008). Finally, "lumpy" solutions may demand direct implementation. For example, new buildings, information technology systems, and products or services often must be created all at once rather than piecemeal.

2. *In difficult situations, consider staged implementation.* Staged implementation presumes that implementation will occur in waves, in which initial adopters will be followed by later adopters, and finally, even most of the laggards will adopt the changes. The result is the familiar S-shaped curve associated with the adoption of most innovations over time. Early on there are few adopters, so the area under the curve is small. As time progresses and more and more adoptions occur, the area under the curve increases geometrically, and it begins to assume an S shape. Later fewer and fewer adoptions occur, partly because there are fewer people, units, or organizations left to adopt the changes and partly because of deep-seated resistance on the part of the laggards. The curve levels off as the top of the S is completed (Gladwell, 2002; Rogers, 2003).

   The exact nature of the staged process will depend on the difficulties faced. Sometimes various efforts at *prototyping* are necessary in order to develop something that *can* be implemented (Scharmer, 2009). Prototyping involves producing various ideas, sketches, models, or other early versions of what might be implemented. When facing technical difficulties after a prototype has been developed, consider beginning with a pilot project designed to discover or prove cause-effect relations between particular solutions and particular effects. The more technically difficult the situation is, the more necessary it is to have a pilot project to figure out what interventions do and do not work. Once the technical difficulties are resolved, transfer of the implementation process to the remaining potential implementers can be pursued. For example, in the United States, pilot tests of new agricultural products and services occur regularly at experiment stations that involve universities, the U.S. Department of Agriculture, and often businesses in cooperative partnerships. When facing political difficulties after a prototype has been developed, consider beginning staged implementation with demonstration projects to make it clear that solutions known to work in benign and controlled conditions can work in typical implementation settings. Once the applicability of the changes is demonstrated, transfer to remaining implementers can be pursued. Demonstration projects are most likely to work when existing or potential opposition is not well organized; changes can then be put in place before effective opposition can materialize. When there is organized opposition to the proposed changes, demonstration projects may work as a way of convincing at least some opponents of the merits of the changes and thereby dividing the opposition. But when there is a well-organized *and* implacable opposition, direct and massive implementation efforts may be warranted to expand the front and overwhelm opponents, rather than giving them a limited number of smaller targets to oppose (Bryson & Delbecq, 1979; Benveniste, 1989). For example, in World War II the D-Day invasion of Normandy was postponed for two years in order to gather the overwhelming force and material needed make a successful assault—and even then victory was not ensured (Brewer, 2009). Although trying to overwhelm opponents—the so-called *shock-and-awe* approach—may be the best choice, the chances of success in such situations still may not be great (Bryson & Bromiley, 1993). When facing both technical and political difficulties, consider beginning with a pilot project, followed by demonstration projects, followed by additional efforts to transfer the changes to the rest of the pool of implementers. In general, the more difficult the situation, the more important it is to promote education and learning, offer incentives for desired changes, and develop a shared sense of commitment to successful implementation and long-term protection of the changes among all interested parties.

3. *Design pilot projects to be effective.* Consider doing the following:

- Test the scientific validity of the proposed changes, probably using experimental or quasi-experimental designs. In other words, test whether the proposed changes actually produce the desired effects. The classic source of advice for such testing is Campbell and Stanley (1966), but any good contemporary evaluation text will provide the necessary information (for example, Rossi, Lipsey, & Freeman, 2003).

- Perform the test in a safe and controlled environment with access to a rich set of resources. The ideal test for causation matches a control group against an experimental group that differs from the control group *only* in that it will experience the policy change, or *treatment*, being tested. Only with such controlled trials can plausible rival hypotheses be ruled out.
- Test several possible changes and search for their different strengths and weaknesses.
- Use skilled technical specialists to evaluate cause-effect relations. If the specialists' credibility is a concern, consider using outside experts, or an inside-outside team whose objectivity will not be questioned.
- Design tests that are concerned with the effectiveness of the changes, not their efficiency. In other words, tests should measure whether the changes produce the desired effects or not, not whether they do so cheaply. Attention should be on both outputs and outcomes (as defined earlier in this chapter).

4. *Design demonstration projects to be effective by employing the following procedures:*

- Test for the applicability of the proposed changes to typical implementer settings, probably through the use of quasi-experimental designs. True experiments are rarely possible in the field, but it is still important to have some sort of control group, if possible, in order to determine what works under what circumstances and why. Quasi-experimental designs can make it possible for such learning to occur.
- Test in easy, average, and difficult implementation settings in order to gauge the robustness of the changes and the possibilities for handling a range of implementation difficulties.
- Test several possible changes in order to determine their comparative strengths and weaknesses.
- Use a two-cycle process, in which implementers learn how to work with the changes in the first cycle, and the effects of the changes are monitored in the second cycle.
- Include a qualitative evaluation (Patton, 2001), along with quantitative studies, to show different solution strengths and weaknesses. Pay attention to outcomes as well as outputs.

- Remember that what is being tested in the demonstration stage is a process that is already known to work in a technical sense; that is, it can produce the desired effects.
- Assemble a special monitoring team, if necessary, to carry out the monitoring task.
- Provide opportunities for future implementers to witness the demonstrations.
- Develop a media strategy to communicate the desirability of the changes and the best way they might be implemented.

5. *Carefully transfer tested changes to other implementers.* Follow these steps:

- Commit substantial resources to communication tactics, including cycling in observers likely to influence subsequent implementer adoptions and to facilitate word-of-mouth information exchanges.
- Promote the visibility of the demonstration projects.
- Produce, emphasize, and disseminate educational materials and operational guides designed to make adoption and implementation easier.
- Develop credible and easily understood models that show clearly how the desired changes work and how they can be implemented.
- Provide additional resources for technical assistance and problem solving.
- Provide incentives for adopting the changes.
- Be flexible.

6. *Finally, when the implementation process is staged, give special attention to those who will implement changes in the early stages.* In the early stages, when the practical nature of the changes still needs to be worked out, it is important to attract people with enough experience, skill, and desire to make the changes work. People who are likely to do so will have firsthand experience with the issue and the need for an adequate response; above-average ability; and experience with prior major change efforts. Further, later adopters will be watching to see whether or not they wish to embrace the changes or resist them. Therefore, early implementers should be valued and persuasive role models—*connectors,* to use Malcolm Gladwell's term (2002)—who can draw others into the change effort. They are more likely to be effective salespersons for change if they do not mindlessly charge after every new whim and fad that comes over

the horizon. Instead, they should be seen as courageous, wise, able, and committed to addressing the issue in a reasonable way. Further, they should be able to describe their experience to effectively educate the next wave of adopters.

SUMMARY

Desired changes are not completed with the formal adoption of strategies and plans. Without effective implementation, important issues will not be adequately addressed and lasting tangible public value will not be created. Implementation, therefore, should be viewed as a continuation of the Strategy Change Cycle toward the ultimate goal of addressing the issues that prompted change in the first place in such a way that real public value is produced.

Implementation must be consciously, deliberately, and strategically planned, managed, and budgeted. Further, if major changes are involved, successful implementation typically involves creation of a new regime to govern decisions and behavior. Elements of the new regime will include new or redesigned settings; implicit or explicit principles, norms, rules, and decision-making procedures; supportive budgets, including both substantive and symbolic incentives promoting the new arrangements; institutionalization of altered patterns of behavior and attitudes; and a supportive coalition of implementers, advocates, and interest groups. The new regime may incorporate a widely shared vision of success.

Successful implementation introduces desired changes quickly and smoothly, and overcomes the typical causes of implementation failure. These strategies may involve either direct or staged implementation. Direct implementation works best when the time is right, the need is evident to a strong coalition of supporters and implementers, critical issues and adopted strategies are clearly connected, solution technology is clearly understood, adequate resources are available, and a clear vision guides the changes. (These are also the conditions that favor big-win strategies.) Staged implementation is advisable when policymakers, leaders, and managers are faced with technical or political difficulties. It often involves pilot projects, to determine or to prove the cause-effect relations between particular solutions and desired effects, or demonstration projects, to show the applicability of adopted solutions to typical implementer settings and to diffuse knowledge to later waves of adopters. Staged implementation involves organizing a series of small (or relatively small) wins.

Learning is a major theme underlying successful implementation efforts. It is not possible or desirable to plan everything in advance. People must be given the opportunity to learn new procedures and adapt them to actual situations. More effective implementation is likely to result, and the next round of strategizing is likely to be better informed.

CHAPTER TEN

Reassessing and Revising Strategies and Plans

What's past is prologue.
—William Shakespeare

The strategy change cycle is not over once strategies and plans have been implemented. Ongoing strategic management of strategy implementation must ensue to take account of likely changes in circumstances—in part in order to ensure that strategies continue to create public value and in part as a prelude to the next round of strategic planning (see Exhibit 1.1). Times change, situations change, and coalitions change. Strategies that work must be maintained and protected through vigilance, adaptability, and updated plans. Stability matters and is an important determinant of organizational success (Meier & O'Toole, 2009). Stability is particularly important when networks are needed for successful strategy implementation. For example, Milward and Provan (2000, p. 253) found that "human service systems that are stable are more likely to perform well than systems in a state of flux." Thus, ironically, changes of some sort are probably in order if you want things to remain the same. But not all strategies continue to work as well as they should. These strategies must be bolstered with additional resources; significantly modified or succeeded by a new strategy; or else terminated. In each case, "What's past is prologue." In addition, ongoing strategic management these days also often means building and maintaining an organization-wide strategic management system (Poister & Van Slyke, 2002).

Strategies cease to work for four main reasons. First, a basic strategy may be good but have insufficient resources devoted to its implementation, and therefore insufficient progress is made toward resolving the issue it was meant to resolve. The Minneapolis Park and Recreation Board, the Loft, and MetroGIS have all had to worry about making sure their strategies were sufficiently well resourced to succeed. Second, problems change, typically prompting a need for new strategies, on the one hand, and making what was once a solution itself a problem, on the other hand. The Park Board developed a new strategy of engaging citizens in its planning efforts in order to make sure the strategies were well formulated and to ensure sufficient support for the organization and its strategies. The Loft had to find ways of deliberately and aggressively dealing with the changes wrought in audiences and literature by advances in online education and publishing, communication, and social networking technology. Third, as substantive problem areas become crowded with various policies and strategies, their interactions can produce results that no one wants and many wish to change. Indeed, the need to sort out the various inconsistencies, misalignments, and unintended consequences of crowded policy and strategy areas is one of the compelling reasons for creating an organization-wide performance management system.

And fourth, the political environment may shift. As strategies become institutionalized, people's attention may shift elsewhere. Or supportive leaders and managers may be replaced by people who are uninterested or even hostile to the strategy, and they may change elements of it or appoint other people who undermine it. Or people may reinterpret history, ignoring the facts to support their position; in this case, as Voltaire apparently said in a 1757 letter to a friend, "History is nothing but a pack of tricks we play on the dead" (quoted in Hirst, n.d.). For example, the United States clearly has one of the least cost-effective health care systems in the developed world, and yet any proposals for major government interventions, or creation of a single-payer system, or establishment of a national health service are quickly labeled *socialized medicine*—like the British system, for example—by their opponents, and "we all know socialism doesn't work." Meanwhile, the British in 2009 allocated only 9 percent of their GDP for health care and cover everyone, whereas the United States spent more than 17 percent of its GDP on health care and, prior to the 2009 health care reforms taking effect, had over 45 million people without health care insurance. The British system spends $3,150 per capita on health care each year ($2,600 of which is public money); we spend $7,500 per capita ($3,500 of which is public money). Administrative costs are about twice as large in the United States (about 12 percent of total health care spending versus about 6 percent). But in spite of all this spending and administration, the infant mortality rate is higher in the United States than in Britain—6.4 versus 4.8 per 1,000 live births—and our average life expectancy at birth is lower—78.2 versus 79.4 years. In addition, cancer and heart disease mortality rates, as well as many other population-level outcome statistics, are about the same in both countries, or are often better in Britain. My own conclusion, based on having used the British system as a patient for four years, and on having been a management consultant to it for over two decades, is that we should be cautious about letting ideologically loaded labels get in the way of the facts. And the facts are that the British system at the population level does as well or better than ours in most cases at a fraction of the cost. Consider the following *thought experiment*: If we could simply replace our system with theirs we would have virtually the same population-level health outcomes and at least 8 percent of our GDP of $14.5 trillion left over *every year*—or about $1.15 trillion each year—to fix every problem with the system and still have money left to give back to employers, employees, and taxpayers. Note that I am *not* saying we *should* have an NHS or even a single-payer system; instead, I am simply suggesting an exercise in imagination (the kind that strategic planning encourages). What I *am* saying explicitly as a result of this thought experiment is that citizens in the United States in the twenty-first century deserve a health care system that covers everyone, costs less, reduces employer burdens, and produces better outcomes, and we shouldn't let ideology and distorted facts get in the way of creating such a system (Frederickson, 2003; Bryson, 2010b). For any of these four reasons, therefore, policy and strategy can become their own cause—the proximate reason for the initiation of a new round of strategy change (Wildavsky, 1979).

Many organizations now are building and maintaining an organization-wide *strategic management system* (SMS) as a way of fostering greater rationality, coherence, and cost-effectiveness in their strategies and operations. (Strategic management systems are often called *performance management systems* or *results management systems*.) An SMS may be thought of as an *organizational design* for strategically managing the implementation of agreed-upon strategies, assessing the performance of those strategies, reconciling inconsistencies and misalignments, and formulating new or revised strategies. An SMS in practice will describe the organization and its possibilities or capabilities for the future. The focus should be on increasing the overall technical rationality *and* political reasonableness of the organization as a whole and its constituent parts—no easy task in the best of circumstances. And the SMS should ensure that maximum public value is and continues to be created. There are many different kinds of SMSs and these are discussed here.

PURPOSE AND DESIRED OUTCOMES

The *purpose* of this phase of the strategy change cycle is to review implemented policies, strategies, plans, programs, or projects and to decide on a course of action that will ensure that public value continues to be created. Desired outcomes include maintenance of good strategies, modifications of less successful ones through appropriate reforms or plan revisions, and elimination of undesirable strategies. In many cases a second desired outcome is construction and maintenance of a strategic management system to ensure ongoing effective strategic management of the organization. A third desired outcome is often the mobilization of energy and enthusiasm to address the next important strategic issue that comes along.

Several additional desired outcomes flow from successful action in this phase. The first is the assurance that institutionalized capabilities remain responsive to important substantive and symbolic issues. Organizations often become stuck in permanent patterns of response to *old issues*. When the issues change, the institutions often do not, and therefore become a problem themselves (Schön, 1971; Wilson, 1989). A sort of goal displacement occurs, in which the institutions cease to be a means to an end and instead become an end in themselves (Merton, 1940; Schön, 1971). Ensuring that organizations remain responsive to real issues and problems—and therefore produce better services and get better results—takes considerable effort. Periodic studies, reports, conferences, hearings, fact-finding missions, on-site observation, and discussions with stakeholders are necessary to stay in touch with the "real world" (Zollo & Winter, 2002; Weick & Sutcliffe, 2007; Mintzberg, Ahlstrand, & Lampel, 2009).

The second is the resolution of residual issues that occur during sustained implementation. Even if implemented strategies remain generally responsive to the issues that originally prompted them, inevitably there will be a host of specific difficulties that must be addressed if the strategies are to be really effective. Attention and appropriate action over the long haul are necessary to ensure that strategies in practice remain as effective and efficient as they were in concept.

The third is the continuous weeding, pruning, and shaping of crowded strategy areas (Wildavsky, 1979). Although there may be an appropriate *micro-logic* to individual strategy elements, element-piled-upon-element often creates a kind of unintended and unwanted *macro-nonsense* (Peters & Waterman, 1982). Complaints about excessive bureaucracy and red tape often have their source in the foolishness that results from the interaction of individual rules that make sense individually, but do not collectively (Barzelay, 1992; Bozeman, 1999). Public and nonprofit leaders and managers must discover how to talk about the system as a whole in order to figure out what should stay, what should be added, and what should be dropped, so that greater alignment results between desired public value, mission, mandates, strategies, and operations (Senge, 2006; Scharmer, 2009).

The fourth is improved organizational knowledge and collaboration across all levels of the organization. Information on progress and achievement should result in better identification of remaining or new issues, better networks of interaction among key actors, more effective decision making, and generally increased organizational learning that should be useful in this step and in the next round of strategic planning. A fifth and related benefit is increased ability to tell the organization's story to internal and external audiences about what it does, how it does it, and what the results are.

Finally, this step should foster development of the energy, will, and ideas for significant reform of existing strategies. Minor difficulties can be addressed through existing administrative mechanisms, such as regular staff meetings, *management by exception* routines, administrative law courts, periodic strategy review and modification exercises, and routine access channels to key decision makers for advocates and advocacy groups. Major change, however, will not occur without development of a substantial coalition in favor of it. And such a coalition will not develop unless there are real issues to be addressed, and the energy, will, and ideas for doing so can be harnessed. However, this is the step in which the beginning of such a coalition is likely to emerge; in other words, this *end* to the Strategy Change Cycle is often the *beginning* of the next Strategy Change Cycle.

Of the three cases followed in-depth in this book, MetroGIS provides perhaps the clearest illustration of how things can change over time. As described previously, the MetroGIS planning effort of 1995–1996 produced an internationally and nationally award-winning spatial data infrastructure (SDI) that involved a truly remarkable and effective voluntary collaboration of approximately three hundred units of government, businesses, and nonprofit organizations. MetroGIS also survived a major challenge to its existence when a program evaluation audit in response to severe criticism revealed that the organization produced public benefits far in excess of its public costs. In June 2006 the Metropolitan Council endorsed MetroGIS and ensured its continued existence for the foreseeable future. That endorsement, along with a continuing series of awards and recognition, increased perceptions of MetroGIS's efficiency, effectiveness, and legitimacy (Bryson, Crosby, & Bryson, 2009).

Dealing with the program evaluation audit postponed development of the 2004–2006 business plan, but surviving the audit in even stronger shape set the stage for the second round of strategic planning (MetroGIS, 2007b). After considerable background work in the form of numerous meetings with numerous stakeholders stretching over many months, the strategic planning effort was formally launched with a second strategy mapping exercise, using the same methodology as before, on February 8, 2007. The mapping process involved approximately forty key stakeholders and directly resulted in a new mission, goals, and strategies for the organization that respond to the new circumstances it faces. Some revisions to the guiding principles were also suggested. Details of the mapping process, including photographs and the maps themselves, will be found via the following Web site and its embedded links:

http://www.metrogis.org/about/business_planning/sdw/workshop_ summary_07_0626.pdf. After further consultations and meetings, the new mission, goals, and strategies were adopted by the policy board and incorporated into the new strategic plan for 2008–2011 adopted in October 2007. The new mission (presented in Exhibit 4.4) is stated as follows: "The mission of MetroGIS is to expand stakeholders' capacity to address shared geographic information technology needs and maximize investments in existing resources through widespread collaboration of organizations that serve the Twin Cities Metropolitan Area" (MetroGIS, 2007a).

The new mission represents a significant change from the previous mission and helps MetroGIS "go to the next level," according to MetroGIS Staff Coordinator Randall Johnson. Previously the purpose of the organization was to create a mechanism for sharing GIS information. The new mission states the purpose is to expand stakeholders' capacities to address GIS needs, maximize investments in existing resources, and foster widespread collaboration of organizations—not just governments—that serve the metropolitan area. The organization's key stakeholders believed that MetroGIS had outgrown its previous mission.

The strategic planning process also resulted in a focus on eight major activity areas for the next three to five years, beginning in 2008. The activities are as follows:

- Develop and maintain regional data solutions to shared information needs
- Expand endorsed regional solutions to include support and development of application services
- Facilitate better data sharing through making more data available, having more uses, and improving processes
- Promote a forum for knowledge sharing
- Build advocacy and awareness of the benefits of collaborative solutions to shared needs
- Expand MetroGIS stakeholders
- Maintain funding policies that get the most efficient and effective use out of available resources and revenue for systemwide benefit

MetroGIS did not list these major activity areas in priority order, as simultaneous work on some aspect of each will be important to successfully achieving the mission and desired outcomes. There are additional changes on the horizon not dealt with in the 2008–2011 strategic plan. Some MetroGIS founders have moved on; others may soon, and thus there is an ongoing issue around leadership transitions.

Significant additional public value potential exists if building address and street centerline data produced by upwards of 190 communities serving the Minneapolis–St. Paul metropolitan area can be efficiently integrated into standardized regional datasets. To do so, significant logistical and policy challenges have to be overcome, challenges that MetroGIS leadership has acknowledged as high priorities to address. Equally important to MetroGIS leadership is defining geospatial needs of the nonprofit and for-profit communities that are shared by the government community and defining sustainable cross-sector solutions to collectively address these needs. Finally, because MetroGIS is not a membership organization, but rather is designed to serve the broad community, defining an equitable balance of benefits and contributions remains a challenge with respect to securing funding to sustain MetroGIS's efforts.

BUILDING A STRATEGIC MANAGEMENT SYSTEM

Strategic management systems (or performance management systems or results-based management systems) are ongoing organizational designs or arrangements for strategically managing the implementation of agreed-upon strategies, assessing the performance of those strategies, and formulating new or revised strategies. These systems, in other words, are themselves a kind of organizational (or interorganizational) strategy for implementing policies and plans, reassessing those strategies, and coming up with new policies and plans. As Poister and Streib (1999, p. 311) assert,

Strategic management requires the following:

- continual monitoring of the "fit" between the organization and its environment and tracking external trends and forces that are likely to affect the organization

- shaping and communicating to both internal and external audiences a clear vision of the type of organization the unit is striving to become

- creating strategic agendas at various levels, and in all parts of the organization, and ensuring that they become the driving force in all other decision making, and

- guiding all other management processes in an integrated manner to support and enhance these strategic agendas.

Poister and Streib go on to assert that the strategic management process is organized around mission, vision, and values and includes strategic planning, results-oriented budgeting, performance management, and strategic measurement and evaluation (pp. 316–319).

There appear to be six main types of systems, although any strategic management system in practice probably will be a hybrid of the six types, which I am therefore calling a seventh type (Bryson, 2010a). The types, or designs, thus refer to dominant tendencies. The types are:

- Integrated units of management approaches (or layered or stacked units of management approaches)
- Strategic issues management approaches
- Contract approaches
- Collaboration approaches
  - Lead organization
  - Shared governance
  - Partnership administrative organization
- Portfolio management approaches
- Goal or benchmark approaches
- Hybrid approaches

Before describing each approach I must express the ambivalence I have about attempts to institutionalize strategic planning and management. Though it often is important to create and maintain a performance management system, it also is important to guard against the tendency such systems have of driving out wise strategic thought, action, and learning—precisely those features that strategic planning (at its best) promotes. In practice the systems often become excessively formal and bureaucratic, driven by the calendar and not by events or issues, numbers-oriented, captured by inappropriate forecasts, and conservative. The reader therefore is advised to recall my admonition in Chapter Two: whenever any strategic management system (or strategic planning process) threatens to drive out wise strategic thought, action, and learning, you should scrap the system (or process) and get back to promoting effective strategic thought, action, and learning.

It is also important to realize that each system embodies a set of arrangements that empowers particular actors, makes particular kinds of issues more likely to arise than others, and makes particular strategies more likely to be pushed rather than others.

Integrated Units of Management Approach (or Layered or Stacked Units of Management Approach)

The purpose of this approach is to link inside and outside environments in effective ways through development and implementation of an integrated set of strategies across levels and functions of the organization. Figure 2.2 outlines a possible two-cycle integrated performance management system. It represents the classic, private sector, corporate-style top-down bottom-up strategic planning process. In the first cycle, there is a bottom-up development of strategic plans within a framework of goals, objectives, and other guidance established at the top, followed by reviews and reconciliations at each succeeding level. In the second cycle, operating plans are developed to implement the strategic plans. In each cycle efforts are made to relate levels, functions, and inside and outside environments in effective ways. The process is repeated each year within the general framework established by the organization's grand or umbrella strategies. Periodically these overarching strategies are reviewed and modified based on experience, changing conditions, and the emergence of new strategies that were not necessarily planned in advance.

Public and nonprofit organizations also have used variants of this approach to advantage (for example, Hendrick, 2003; Barzelay & Campbell, 2003). Nevertheless, it is precisely this sort of system that is most prone to driving out strategic thought and action when it is excessively formal and also underpinned by a belief that the future can actually be predicted accurately—a belief detached from the messiness of operational reality (Roberts & Wargo, 1994; Mintzberg, Ahlstrand, & Lampel, 2009). Such systems are very likely to be blindsided by unpredictable events. They therefore must be used with extreme caution, because they can take on a life of their own, promote incremental change when major change might be needed, and serve only the interests of the planners who staff them and the leaders and managers who wish to resist—not promote—major change.

With those caveats in place, consider the useful example of Miami-Dade County, Florida. The county in 2010 had 2.4 million residents and an amazingly diverse population, including 61 percent Hispanic, 18 percent white, 18 percent black, and 3 percent other. Approximately 50 percent of the residents are foreign born. The government has a strong mayor and 13 county commissioners elected by district. The government has two tiers: 55.5 percent live in cities (for example, Miami and Miami Beach), while 45.5 percent live in unincorporated areas. The county had a 2009–2010 budget of $7.8 billion. There are 60 county departments and approximately 29,000 employees.

The Miami-Dade County strategic management system is sketched out in Figure 10.1, which indicates the process for implementing the county's first strategic plan, launched on September 21, 2004. The plan is summarized in Exhibit 10.1. The plan includes a vision, mission, guiding principles, and six strategic themes. The vision is "Delivering excellence every day." The mission is "Delivering excellent public services that address our community's needs and enhance our quality of life." The guiding principles are: customer-focused and customer-driven; honest, ethical, and fair to all; accountable and responsive to the public; diverse and sensitive; efficient and effective; committed to development of leadership in public service; innovative; valuing and respectful of each other; and action-oriented. The six strategic themes are: economic development, health and human services, neighborhood and unincorporated area municipal services, public safety, recreation and culture, and transportation.

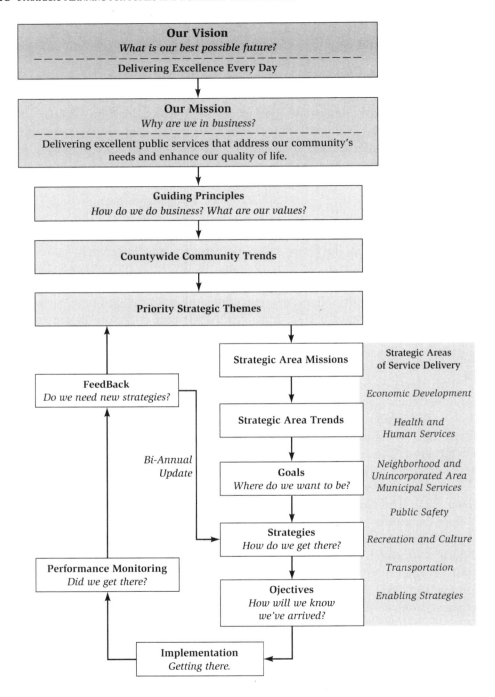

Figure 10.1. Miami-Dade County Strategic Management System.

Source: Miami-Dade County 2003 Strategic Plan.

Exhibit 10.1. Miami-Dade County Strategic Plan Summary.

Mission

Delivering excellent public services that address our community's needs and enhance our quality of life →

Countywide Priorities

Fiscally responsible and stable →	Quality of life for all →
Technology, innovation, access and information →	Planning for land use, transportation, and growth
Transportation →	Environment →
	Safety and quality of neighborhoods
	A healthy economy
	Cooperation and coordination →

Priorities by Area

Economic Development	Health and Human Services	Neighborhood and Unincorporated Area Municipal Services	Public Safety	Recreation and Culture	Transportation
→	→	→	→	→	→

Strategic Area Missions—*Link to Countywide Mission.* **Goals**—*Where do we want to be?* **Strategies**—*How do we get there?*

Economic Development	Health and Human Services	Neighborhood and Unincorporated Area Municipal Services	Public Safety	Recreation and Culture	Transportation
• Targeted industries • Job skills • Low- and moderate-income home ownership	• Reduce rate of uninsured • Transportation access • Child care	• Urban infill and decreased sprawl • Protection of viable agricultural and environmentally sensitive lands	• Facilities and resources • Reduced response time	• Well-maintained, safe facilities and assets • High-quality green space	• Integrated land use development • Roadway level-of-service

(Continued)

Exhibit 10.1. Miami-Dade County Strategic Plan Summary, Continued.

Priorities by Area					
• Coordinated economic development • Community involvement • Organizations with technical and management capacity • Infrastructure and redevelopment	• Intervention and prevention • Basic education and skills • Healthier community • Affordable and special needs housing	• Community design • Strengthened bond with community • Access to information and services • Well-trained, customer friendly • Compliance and remediation	• Reduction in property loss and destruction • Homeland security strengthened • Juvenile assessment center • Information availability and involvement • Facilities and resources	• More programs and services for varied needs • Coordination • Customer service • Facilities located where needed • Reduction in unmet needs	• Successful implementation of "The People's Transportation Plan" (reduced wait time; convenient and clean; improved access; safe and reliable; expanded bus and rail; management and oversight) • Ports of movement of people, baggage, and cargo

Supporting Priorities

• Customer-friendly to entities doing business with Miami-Dade County	• Customer service • Reduction in unmet needs	
• Neighborhood and rights-of-way aesthetics • Neighborhood roadways, sidewalks, drainage and reduced flooding		
• Reduced response time • Reduction in property loss and destruction		
• Awareness and access • Well-maintained, safe facilities and assets		
• Integrated land use development • Roadway level-of-service		

Supporting Priorities		
Defined performance standards	Accessible public information	"Best Value" goods and services
User friendly e-government	Process improved through technology	Motivated, dedicated workforce team aligned with organizational priorities
Workforce skills	Safe, convenient and accessible facilities to meet needs	Safe and reliable vehicles to meet needs
Sound asset management and financial investments	Resources to meet current and future needs	Cohesive, standardized financial system and process
Alignment of services with community's needs and desires	Achievement of performance targets	Accountability to the public
Continuous improvement	Opportunities for every registered voter to conveniently vote	

Source: Miami-Dade County Government, 2004.

The plan was developed out of a number of complementary efforts: A broadly consultative process was pursued involving interviews with elected officials, community workshops, focus groups by county commission districts, community surveys, and employee focus groups. There was a broadly based community visioning effort pushed by a group of engaged citizens meeting with community leaders. A "Core Community Planning Team" worked with Miami-Dade County managers to help guide the project through to completion. A SWOC/T analysis was performed by insiders. The planning process and the plan also took into account existing plans and other initiatives. The plan provides countywide priorities with measurable performance objectives to which department objectives and annual operating plans are to be aligned. Indeed, achieving better alignment of countywide strategic goals and objectives with departmental efforts is a major purpose of the developing strategic management system: "Priorities established in the Strategic Plan and reflected in departmental business plans will be the basis for the County's resource allocation process" (Miami-Dade County Government, 2004, p. 37).

The six strategic themes or areas each have their own strategic plans. The process of developing these plans was guided by the assistant county manager responsible for the area, the appropriate department directors, and a "strategic area community planning team." Each strategic area plan includes goals, strategies, objectives, and performance measures. The overall strategic plan and strategic area plans drive the annual budget process, monthly operational reviews, and individuals' performance evaluations. Development and institutionalization of the system is still a work in progress. It takes time to change a large organization with multiple stakeholders, systems, structures, processes, and cultures (Hill & Lynn, 2009). It also is important to incorporate as much as possible of what already exists into the new system; change thus becomes manageable in part because so much is familiar. Successful change is more likely to result from recombination than mutation (Kingdon, 2002). The Miami-Dade experience demonstrates that it takes time to create a good performance management system and that ongoing learning and error detection and correction must be a part of the process.

Some of the most important features of the system include the following:

- The system is guided by the county's vision, mission, and goals.
- The system is meant to encompass the entire organization, which is seen holistically as consisting of interdependent parts.
- The system emphasizes *strategic themes* or *strategic areas*, which in other settings might be called *lines of business.* Based on similar services with common customers, lines of business may cross departmental lines and even sector boundaries.

- Scorecards (but not balanced scorecards) are used throughout the county government to assess and manage performance.

- The county focuses strategic and operational planning on identifying and achieving the most important results that the county, its departments, and constituencies believe they should focus on.

- The meaning of accountability is intended to shift toward accountability for results. The idea is to hold areas, programs, departments, and individuals accountable for the best possible performance while ensuring that their performance is aligned with and supports overall efforts of the county as a whole.

Strategic Issues Management Approach

Strategic issues management systems are the most common form of institutionalized strategic management system in public and nonprofit organizations. These systems do not attempt to integrate strategies across levels and functions to the extent that integrated units of management approaches do. The reason is that the various issues are likely to be on different time frames, involve different constituencies and politics, and need not be considered in the light of all other issues.

Figure 10.2 provides a schematic of a fairly standard strategic issues management system (Eckhert, Haines, Delmont, & Pflaum, 1993). In this system, strategic guidance is issued at the top, and units further down are asked to identify the issues they think are strategic. Leaders and managers at the top then select which issues they wish to have addressed, perhaps reframing the issues before passing them on to units or task forces. Task forces then present strategic alternatives to leaders and managers, who select which ones to pursue. Strategies are then implemented in the next phase. Each issue is managed relatively separately, although it is necessary to make sure that choices in one issue area do not cause trouble in other issue areas.

As noted, in Chapter Two, Baltimore, Minneapolis, and a number of other cities have institutionalized strategic issues management through use of a *CitiStat* or *PerformanceStat* system (Schachtel, 2001; Behn, 2008). In these systems a central analysis staff uses geographically coded data to spot trends, events, and issues that need to be addressed by line departments. The heads of the relevant units meet regularly with the mayor and his or her key advisers, including, for example, the heads of budgeting, finance, human resources, and information technology, to examine the data and address the issues face-to-face. Actions and follow-up procedures are agreed on the spot. Notable successes have occurred in cities using these systems in which better outcomes were produced, money was saved, teamwork and competence were enhanced, or all three.

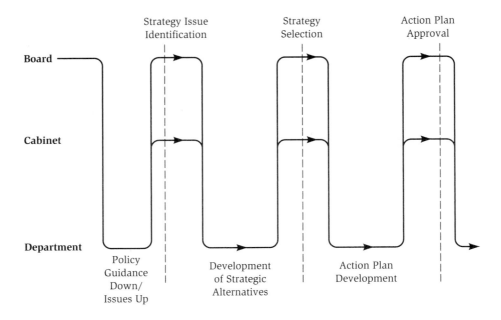

Figure 10.2. Strategic Issues Management Model.

Although many public and nonprofit organizations have several task forces in operation at any one time, fewer go the next step to design and use a strategic issues management system. They do not establish an overall framework of organizational goals or policy objectives; nor do they seek out issues to address or make sure that their various issues management activities add up to increased organizational effectiveness. To make this approach work, organizational leaders and managers should consider taking this last step, keeping in mind that the resulting centralization of certain key decisions at the top is likely to draw the attention and resistance of those who do not want to see power concentrated in that way or who dislike the resulting decisions. Developing a strategic issues management system is often a prelude to creation of an integrated units of management system.

Contract Approach

The contract approach is another popular system of institutionalizing strategic planning and management, especially in simple to moderately complex shared-power environments (see Figure 10.3). The contract model is employed for much of the planning and delivery of many publicly financed social services in the United States via either public or nonprofit service providers (Milward & Provan, 2003; Sandfort & Milward, 2008). The system is also used to insti-

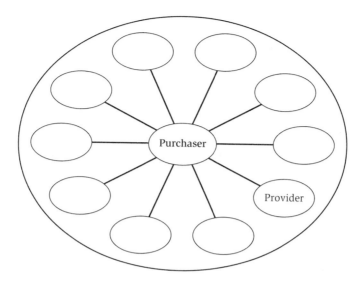

Figure 10.3. Purchaser-Provider Contract Model.

tutionalize strategic planning and management in school districts with site-based management.

In this system there is a *center* that establishes strategic objectives for the jurisdiction or organization as a whole, negotiates contracts with individual units of management, monitors performance, and ensures the integrity of the system. In the language of economics and *principal-agent models*, the center is the *principal* and the individual units of management are the *agents*. In the language of reinventing government, the center *steers* while the units *row* (Osborne & Plastrik, 1997). The contract between the center and a unit outlines the unit's expected performance, defines its resources, lists other support the unit can expect from the center, and describes a review and renegotiation sequence. Within the framework and legal strictures of the contract, general managers of individual units and their staffs are free to do whatever they think is necessary or desirable to ensure adequate performance. At its best, this approach allows both the center and the individual units to focus on what is important for them—both are empowered to do their jobs better. In such a system, there would be a strategic plan for the center and one for each of the units. Key system concerns would include the content and approach embodied in the center's plan, the center's difficulties in acquiring adequate information, the proper alignment of incentives for the principal and the agents, the difficulties the center may have in exercising control in the face of a large number of contractors, and ways to ensure adequate investments by the units if they cannot be sure of a long-term contract.

Collaboration Approach

Collaboration represents a fourth type of strategic management system. Like contracting, collaboration is increasingly being used to govern and manage in shared-power environments. In fact, the contract system represents a classic form of collaboration, but there are many different (and often more complicated) approaches to collaboration that are more suitable than competitive contracting for situations involving moderate to high levels of complexity and ambiguity (Alexander, 1995; Agranoff & McGuire, 2004; Agranoff, 2007). Human service systems often embody contracting and additional collaboration approaches—contracts for what can be specified and governed with reasonable ease, and supplemental collaboration for those situations involving higher levels of complexity and ambiguity, and therefore requiring greater reliance on trust, shared norms, professionalism, and learning-by-doing for effective governance and management (Romzek, 1996; Huxham & Vangen, 2005).

Collaboration is particularly useful when addressing problems for which no organization is fully in charge. Situations of this sort occur when, for example, there is a marked degree of separation between the source and use of funds; services are jointly produced (that is, service recipients are at least partly responsible for effective production, as in mental health services); or the key governance and management task is arranging networks rather than managing hierarchies (Milward & Provan, 2003).

Collaboration involves varying degrees of sharing power and resources (such as information, money, clients, and authority) between units to achieve common ends that could not be achieved separately. The gain beyond what could be achieved separately is called *collaborative advantage* (Huxham, 2003), and the often-elusive pursuit of this advantage is behind persistent calls for more collaboration. We will consider three different archetypal approaches to network collaboration (Provan & Kenis, 2005): the *lead organization*, *shared governance*, and *partnership administrative organization*.

In the *lead organization* approach a single partner organization coordinates the major collaboration activities and key decisions. The lead organization has more power than the other partners, who typically are moderate in number (Stadtler, 2010). Milward and Provan (2003), in their longitudinal study of mental health service delivery networks, have found that network effectiveness is greatest when there is a strong central integrating unit; clear and consistent lines of authority and accountability embodied in contracts; aligned incentives that give everyone a stake in the success of the network; system stability; and munificent resources. These factors allow constructive norms, social capital, and network learning capabilities to develop, and needed incremental investments and changes to be made. Interestingly, the contracts in these situations are what economists call *relational contracts*, as opposed to *competitive con-*

tracts (Milward & Provan, 2003, p. 10). Relational contracting involves infrequent rebidding and instead focuses on maintaining an effective relationship between buyer and seller—because there are only a few sellers to begin with, the production function is ambiguous, and effective performance by the seller depends on trust, collaboration, and long-term investment in the network's infrastructure.

A key system concern with the lead organization approach is how to achieve the right balance between network stability and adaptability. Milward and Provan (2000, 2003) found that the highest-performing mental health networks were the most stable, in the sense that there were no significant changes in any structural feature or funding relationships. On the one hand, stability allows the all-important trust, shared norms, expertise, productive relationships, learning-by-doing, and long-term investments to occur (Huxham, 2003). On the other hand, if a network is too stable, learning and responsiveness to environmental changes will diminish and the network will be unlikely to respond effectively to unexpected changes (Zollo & Winter, 2002; Weick & Sutcliffe, 2007; Scharmer, 2009). Because of the importance of stability to performance, Milward and Provan (2000, p. 258) assert that, "We believe that if a system must be changed, it must be done infrequently and, if possible, incrementally." Another key concern will be the continual need to make sure incentives are aligned properly so that participants have an incentive to maintain the network and high performance levels.

The *shared governance* approach is likely when no partner has significantly greater power and resources than the others and no external governance organization is formed or mandated (Stadtler, 2010). The viability of the approach depends on each organization's involvement and commitment, as the partners are responsible for managing the internal and external relations (Provan & Kenis, 2008). Viability also depends on reasonable goal consensus; exit is always an option for member organizations. If the number of organizations participating in shared governance becomes too large, trust levels decline, goal consensus becomes a bit shaky, and the collaborators have limited collaboration abilities and may create a separate administrative entity—a *partnership administrative organization* (PAO)—to govern the collaboration and its activities and decision. The PAO is a separate organization whose purpose is to manage the collaboration.

Portfolio Management Approach

In the portfolio management approach entities of various sorts (programs, projects, products, services, or providers) are arrayed against dimensions that have some strategic importance. The dimensions usually consist of the attractiveness or desirability of the entity (from high to low) and the capability of the organization or community to deliver what is needed (also from high to low). Portfolio methods are quite flexible, in that any dimensions of interest may be arrayed against one another and entities mapped on to the resulting matrix. Portfolio methods also can be used at sub- and supraorganizational levels as well to assess options against strategically important factors (Nutt & Backoff, 1992; Bryson, 2001, 2003). Unfortunately, few public and nonprofit organizations or communities utilize portfolio models in a formal way, even though many probably use portfolio methods in an informal way. The problem with using this method in a formal way, of course, is that it creates comparisons that may be troubling for politically powerful actors.

Goal or Benchmark Approach

In general, the goal or benchmark approach is much looser than the integrated units of management models and is generally applied at the community, regional, or state level. It is designed to gain reasonable agreement on overarching goals, indicators, or benchmarks toward which relatively independent groups, units, or organizations might then direct their energies. This consensual agreement on goals and indicators can function somewhat like the corporate control exercised in integrative models, although it is of course weaker. This system's looseness means that calling it a strategic management system may be an overstatement. Nonetheless, when agreement can be reached and support for implementation can be generated, this approach can work reasonably well. Besides, in the fragmented, shared-power environments in which most public problems occur, the approach may be the only viable approach. For example, most community strategic plans are implemented via goal or benchmark models (Wheeland, 2004). Typically, large numbers of leaders and citizens are involved in the process of goal setting and strategy development. Then action plans outline what each organization might do to help implement the strategies and achieve the goals on a voluntary basis.

Virginia Performs provides a state-level example (Council on Virginia's Future, 2011). Virginia Performs is a system initiated by the Council on Virginia's Future, which is chaired by the governor and includes state, business, and community leaders. The Council was established by the 2003 General Assembly to advise Virginia's leaders on development and implementation of a *road map* for the state's future. The road map includes: a long-term focus on high-priority issues; creating an environment for improved policy and budget decision making; increasing government performance, accountability, and transparency; and engaging citizens in dialogue about Virginia's future. The logic of the system is outlined in Figure 10.4. The Council helps establish the vision and goals for the state and makes assessments of progress. The State's executive branch is responsible for performance, efficiency, and effectiveness. The vision and high-level goals established by the Council and championed by the governor are meant to serve as guides for state government decisions and actions,

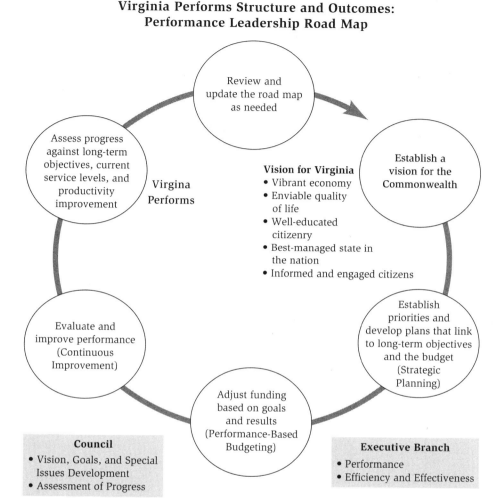

**Virginia Performs Structure and Outcomes:
Performance Leadership Road Map**

Figure 10.4. Road Map for Virginia's Future

Source: Council on Virginia's Future, *The Virginia Report 2010*, p. 79. Reprinted with permission of the Council on Virginia's Future.

but are also intended to influence the thinking and actions of other actors in the state.

The Council's *Vision for Virginia* includes:

- Responsible economic growth
- Enviable quality of life
- Educated citizens prepared for a successful life
- The best-managed state government

- Informed and engaged citizens helping to shape the Commonwealth's future

The Council's long-term goals for the state include:

- Being recognized as the best-managed state in the nation
- Being a national leader in the preservation and enhancement of our economy
- Elevating the levels of educational preparedness and attainment of Virginia's citizens
- Inspiring and supporting Virginians toward healthy lives and strong and resilient families
- Protecting, conserving, and wisely developing Virginia's natural, historical, and cultural resources
- Protecting the public's safety and security, ensuring a fair and effective system of justice, and providing a prepared response to emergencies and disasters of all kinds
- Ensuring that Virginia has a transportation system that is safe, enables easy movement of people and goods, enhances the economy, and improves our quality of life

Progress toward accomplishing the vision and long-term goals is measured by a set of approximately fifty overall indicators broken down into seven goal areas (see Exhibit 10.2). State agencies are expected by the governor and legislature to plan and budget in light of the long-term goals and indicators and related and relevant indicators specifically connected to the agency's work. Agency performance measures are organized into four categories: key measures tied to the long-term goals and mission, service area effectiveness measures, administrative measures meant to assess management quality and effectiveness, and productivity measures indicating efficiency levels. The Virginia Performs Web site provides a useful and visually appealing compendium of performance for the state as a whole, by goal area, and by agency (http://vaperforms.virginia.gov). The attempted linkage of state agency goals, plans, and budgets to the state's long-term goals is the tightest part of the system. The success of the state's system depends on continued broad-based, bipartisan political support.

Cities, counties, communities, and others throughout the state are also encouraged to do their part by making use of the state-level goals and indicators to develop their own indicators linked to the state goals and indicators. Hampton Roads, Virginia, provides a well-known example of a performance management system that is compatible with the Virginia Performs system and in fact is hot-linked to the Virginia Performs Web site (http://

Exhibit 10.2. State of Virginia Agency Key Objectives at a Glance.

Virginia Performs: Vision, Focus, Results

Economy	Education	Health	Public Safety
Goal: Be a national leader in the preservation and enhancement of our economy.	**Goal:** Elevate the educational preparedness and attainment levels of our citizens.	**Goal:** Inspire and support Virginians toward healthy lives and strong, resilient families.	**Goal:** Protect the public's safety and security, ensure a fair and effective system of justice, and provide a prepared response to emergencies and disasters of all kinds.
• Assist companies that are making investments and creating jobs in Virginia	• Increase number of at-risk four-year-olds served by preschool initiatives	• Secure safe, permanent families for children in foster care	• Decrease reoffense and recidivism
• Increase international sales	• Increase third-grade reading proficiency	• Prevent child maltreatment	• Promote successful offender reentry and compliance
• Build additional educational and innovation capacity in Southside and Southwest Virginia	• Increase high school graduation rate	• Reduce infant mortality, obesity, smoking, and teenage pregnancy	• Decrease traffic fatalities
• Reduce economic disparity and increase housing affordability	• Increase career readiness of high school students	• Increase immunization rates	• Increase emergency and disaster response capability
• Increase employment among Virginians with low income and/or disabilities	• Increase enrollment in GED and postsecondary degree programs	• Increase service delivery in community- and family-based settings	• Ensure secure confinement and supervision of offenders
• Increase financing for small businesses	• Maximize higher education access and affordability	• Improve birth outcomes for Medicaid recipients	• Increase compliance with underage alcohol and tobacco use laws
• Increase market value of Virginia food, agricultural, and forestry products		• Help individuals maintain employment and independence	
		• Increase children's access to health services	

(Continued)

Exhibit 10.2. State of Virginia Agency Key Objectives at a Glance, Continued.

Natural History and Cultural Resources	Transportation	Government and Citizens	Virginia's Secretariats
Goal: Protect, conserve, and wisely develop our natural, cultural and historic resources. • Improve and protect air and water quality. • Conserve and enhance resource lands • Increase access to safe and affordable drinking water • Recognize and help protect historic resources • Increase capacity and public attendance at arts events • Improve museum exhibits and educational programs	**Goal:** Ensure that Virginia has a transportation system that is safe, allows the easy movement of people and goods, enhances the economy, and improves our quality of life. • Increase public transportation use • Maintain, improve, and develop railways • Preserve, manage, and securely operate transportation system • Increase the amount of cargo shipped through the Port of Virginia • Increase aviation awareness and use • Increase percentage of on-time, on-budget construction and maintenance projects	**Goal:** Be recognized as the best-managed state in the nation. • Develop a fiscally sound budget and enhance compliance with internal controls • Support increase in voter participation • Achieve best bond rates • Issue timely tax refunds and responses to taxpayer inquiries • Achieve timely resolution of consumer complaints • Achieve cost savings and improve program effectiveness through innovative technology solutions and oversight	Administration Agriculture & Forestry Commerce & Trade Education Finance Health & Human Resources Natural Resources Public Safety Technology Transportation

Source: Council on Virginia's Future, 2011. Reprinted with permission of the Council on Virginia's Future.

hamptonroadsperforms.org). The desire to make progress against individual indicators or sets of indicators provides the basis for collaborative efforts throughout the state involving public, private, and nonprofit sectors.

As I suggested earlier, although there are six general types of strategic management systems, any actual system is likely to be a hybrid of all six types, which I am calling a seventh type. For example, MetroGIS is a collaboration that relies extensively on self-governance, but also has a partnership administrative organization consisting of MetroGIS staff. The Park Board relies primarily on an integrated units of management approach, but some issues are handled on an issue-by-issue basis using a strategic issues management approach. Other issues affecting specific park sites fit more with the contract approach, in which there is an agreement between the headquarters and individual sites that outlines performance expectations; resource allocations; basic rules, regulations, and procedures; and a review schedule. Within the envelope provided by the agreement, individual sites have considerable freedom to manage their own affairs. The district is engaged in a variety of collaborative efforts with other local government units, businesses, and nonprofit organizations. Park Board staff utilize an informal portfolio approach to assess what their program offerings should be based on their desirability and the district's ability to deliver. And finally, the Park Board establishes an overall set of goals toward which everyone is expected to contribute, and around which the board hopes cross-sector collaborations will develop.

PROCESS DESIGN AND ACTION GUIDELINES

The following guidelines should be kept in mind as leaders and managers review implemented strategies and ponder what to do about them. General guidelines are presented first, and then specific suggestions are offered for strategy maintenance, succession, and termination (for additional details, see Hogwood & Peters, 1983; Baumgartner & Jones, 2009; Kingdon, 2002). A final section presents guidelines for building a strategic management system.

General Guidelines

1. *Stay focused on what is important.* Pay attention to the organization's mission and mandates and the social needs and political problems that justify its existence. Think about how to create public value. Pay attention to the fundamental challenges—strategic issues—that the organization faces as it tries to meet its mandates, pursue its mission, and create public value. Never let the organization and its strategies or plans become ends in themselves. Instead, leaders and managers

should focus on key stakeholders and the leaders' own ideals, and how best to serve them.

2. *Focus on signs or indicators of success and failure.* Attention should be paid to changes in signs or indicators that were used to argue for strategy changes in the first place, to new indicators that are important to key stakeholders and that shed light on implementation effectiveness, and to results of any formative or summative evaluations. To the extent that any or all of these indicators provide valid signs of strategic progress or failure, they can provide support for deciding to maintain, reform, or terminate a strategy or plan.

3. *Review the issue framings used to guide strategy formulation in the first place.* Are they still accurate and useful interpretations of reality? Have they led to constructive issue descriptions, strategies, and plans? Or has some reality—political, economic, social, technological, internal, external, or otherwise—changed, making these issue framings into distortions that suggest unhelpful strategies and plans?

4. *Use existing review opportunities or create new ones.* Periodic policy reauthorization sessions, strategic issue identification exercises, and annual budget review periods, for example, provide regular review opportunities (Feldman & Khademian, 2000). Election campaigns and changes in top political or executive leadership provide predictable occasions for strategy reviews in public organizations. Similarly, board turnover or new executive appointments in nonprofit organizations provide occasions for review. However, leaders and managers can create strategy review opportunities almost anytime they wish. Conferences, hearings, study sessions or commissions, media events, investigative reporting, discussion groups, and so on can be arranged whenever leaders and managers wish to promote discussion and critique of strategies.

5. *Create a review group.* The composition of this group may vary considerably depending on the nature of the review. Legislation and policies requiring scheduled reviews may specify a particular group—for example, a legislative committee, city council, or nonprofit board of directors. Often, however, flexibility is possible in choosing participants, and it can be wise to include outsiders who do not have a vested interest in the status quo. They may be counted on to focus on important issues and can offer constructive suggestions for change.

6. *Challenge institutional and organizational rules that favor undesirable inertia.* Institutions have an uncanny ability to take on a life of their own, making constructive change extremely difficult (Wilson, 1989;

Osborne & Plastrik, 1997; Scharmer, 2009). There are many political routines that challenge anything new but do not subject what is already in place to a searching critique. These routines and other rules—embedded in the design and use of existing forums, arenas, and courts—often make present arrangements the *taken-for-granted way things are.* This can make a different future unlikely. If the future is to be what we want, these rules must be confronted and set aside when the need arises (Osborne & Plastrik, 1997; Osborne & Hutchinson, 2004). For example, the decision of the Park Board to engage in strategic planning was a signal to key stakeholders and the community that many of the existing rules and routines would be examined, and innovative strategies would be explored.

7. *Remember that organizations usually have greater staying power than their strategies* (Hogwood & Peters, 1983). Typically, therefore, it is easier to change the strategies than the organizations. Also typically, it is more productive to call into question or attack the strategies than the organizations. In other words, it is likely to be more effective to praise the intentions and goodwill of an organization while attacking its strategies than to attack its motives and goodwill directly. Further, from a strategic standpoint, it is often wise to figure out whether problems can be solved with existing organizational or network strategies, because strategies may be created or changed more easily than organizations and networks. Moreover, it is wise to figure out how existing organizations and their adherents might benefit from possible changes in strategy, so that allies can be created, rather than opponents (Neustadt & May, 1986; Bryson, Cunningham, & Lokkesmoe, 2002). Sometimes this simply means organizing support for new units or programs within existing organizations. But given the distressing inertia of many organizations, change advocates may ultimately conclude that new organizations and networks are required to solve important issues (Osborne & Hutchinson, 2004). Community planning efforts, for example, often involve developing at least partially new networks to frame and address key issues (Wheeland, 2004).

8. *Finally, stay fresh.* Build energy and enthusiasm for continuing with good strategies and addressing new strategic issues. Avoid letting efforts go stale. Issues will not be formulated and addressed effectively unless leaders and managers take responsibility for doing so. To paraphrase Edmund Burke, all that is necessary for the triumph of evil is for good people to do nothing.

Strategy Maintenance Guidelines

1. *To maintain existing strategies, seek little change in current organizational (interorganizational or community) arrangements.* Any significant change is likely to undermine the regime established in the previous phase. It is important, however, to find occasions in forums to recall or reinvigorate the organization's mission and the vision that originally inspired it and to validate the results of previous strategy formulation efforts.

2. *To maintain or marginally modify existing strategies, rely on implementers and focused input from consumers, and involve supportive advocates.* The Loft made use of various stakeholder involvement mechanisms to evaluate its work and suggest possible changes. Its large board of directors was involved in and kept fully informed of the strategic planning process. These groups contained a number of community notables and representatives, but no one likely to propose radical and damaging changes, given the ongoing success the Loft has had and its substantial support in the community. Broader involvement of elites and the public is likely to raise issues and conflicts that may require more fundamental policy changes (Hogwood & Peters, 1983; Baumgartner & Jones, 2009).

3. *Invest in distinctive competencies and distinctive assets necessary for the success of the strategies.* Continual investment is required to maintain the competencies and assets necessary for successful ongoing strategy implementation. Depending on the strategy, this may mean, for example, staff education and professional development, investment in physical infrastructure, nurturing networks of providers, or bolstering fundraising and marketing capabilities. If the organization must compete for resources, it is particularly important to invest in *distinctive competencies* and *distinctive assets*—that is, those that differentiate the organization from its competitors (Johnson, Scholes, & Whittington, 2008; Eden & Ackermann, 2010) (see Resource C).

Strategy Change or Succession Guidelines

1. *To facilitate a move to new strategies, significantly alter existing arrangements.* A new set of issues, decisions, conflicts, and policy preferences are then likely to emerge. The emergence of GIS technology and inexpensive high-speed computing in an environment lacking an effective means to leverage existing public investments in

geospatial data and technology provided an important impetus for the creation of MetroGIS.

2. *Create occasions to challenge existing meanings and estrange people from them, and to create new meanings and facilitate their enactment.* Leaders and managers may wish to estrange people from the missions, mandates, policies, and strategies that support particular ways of being in the world for their organizations, networks, or communities (Mangham & Overington, 1987; Marris, 1996; Scharmer, 2009). New ways of interpreting reality may supply the seed from which a different configuration of policies, plans, programs, projects, products, services, or resource allocations can grow. For example, a strategy reassessment may imply that a different set of external or internal categories, stakeholders, value judgments, signs or indicators, or comparisons is relevant. Change advocates may articulate a new or revised vision that inspires action. Leaders and managers must use available occasions and settings to estrange people from existing meanings, because "estrangement creates a circumstance in which *givenness* becomes *possibility*" (Mangham, 1986, p. 144). Often the estrangement will occur as a result of altering the way in which issues are formulated so that they highlight certain features of the internal and external environments and not others.

Even when change advocates are successful in challenging existing strategies on intellectual grounds, they should not expect new strategies to be adopted without a change in the political circumstances surrounding the strategy, particularly in public organizations. As Kingdon (2002) notes, these changes may include public opinion swings, election results, administrative changes, ideological or partisan redistribution in legislative bodies, and interest group pressure campaigns. Before new proposals for strategies can be adopted, key decision makers in arenas must be receptive, and changes in politics may be necessary before this is likely to occur. The 2009 U.S. health care reform bill would not have happened without health care becoming a major political issue in the 2008 campaign, the election of Barack Obama, and major Democratic gains in both houses of Congress. Even so, the final bill contains a host of problematic features that were required as the price of passage. The Republican resurgence in the 2010 elections, in which they regained control of the House of Representatives, has put implementation of health care reform in serious jeopardy. Major change may also depend on a successful search for important ideas and methods for operationalizing them. For example, MetroGIS is continually exploring in detail the conceptual and practical meaning of a number of the concepts, software, and applications. The Loft is exploring in detail what online instruction and enhanced use of the Web means for its programs. Ongoing workshops and discussions are necessary to figure out what changes might mean in practice (Roberts, 2002).

3. *Be aware that strategy succession may be more difficult than the adoption of the initial strategy was because existing strategy is now likely to have a coalition of supporters in place.* Hogwood and Peters (1983) add that the concessions and compromises embedded in the existing strategy are likely to prevent major reforms, and reformers are likely to be disappointed with the gains achieved in relation to their efforts.

4. *Remember that both implementers and beneficiaries of existing policies are more likely to be concerned with strategy implementation details than with policy innovation* (Hogwood & Peters, 1983; Roberts & King, 1996). Policies themselves are often more symbolic than real. What counts is how they are implemented—what they mean in practice. That is where the real action is for implementers and beneficiaries. There is good news and bad news here. The good news for change advocates is that if the issues they are tackling stem mainly from existing policies, policy changes may be adopted before implementers and beneficiaries of the status quo know what is happening. The bad news is that implementers and beneficiaries may be able to kill any policy they don't like during implementation. More good news for change advocates is that if the problem is not caused by existing policy, only policy implementers may need to be convinced of the virtues of the changes. The bad news is they may not be convinced. MetroGIS's principal stakeholders pay careful attention to any administrative, financial, technical, and technological reforms. Their support has to be nurtured every step of the way, as they can successfully torpedo almost any major change.

5. *To make major strategy changes, rely on key decision makers, along with policy implementers and beneficiaries.* In all likelihood, to make substantial changes, leaders and managers will need the support of a coalition different from the one that adopted and implemented existing strategies. A new constellation of ideas, stakeholder interests, and agreements will need to be worked out (Sabatier & Weible, 2007).

6. *To achieve strategy succession, consider a move either to split aspects of the strategy or to consolidate strategies.* Splitting means carving off and eliminating, revising, or phasing in aspects of a strategy.

Consolidation means joining together previously separate strategies. Reframing the way issues and strategies are viewed can facilitate policy splitting or consolidation. Moreover, key stakeholders will favor consolidation or splitting if it is in their interest. Splitting or consolidation can also resolve conflicts over areas of political influence by making either separate or combined budgetary allocations and, depending on the circumstances, making ambiguous or clear allocations of jurisdiction. For example, a move to budgeting depending on site-based management will sharpen some conflicts between a school district's headquarters and individual schools, particularly those related to the fairness of allocations across the district, but will redirect others to individual schools, particularly those conflicts involving allocations within each school. Conflicts over ideas are less easily resolved, although good analysis may help. However, there may be strong coalitions in support of each position, and no amount of analysis may convince them to reassess their positions (Sabatier & Weible, 2007; Thompson, 2008).

7. *Consider building a new system without dismantling the old system.* The result is parallel, redundant, or competing systems, but often there are overall net social gains through better market segmentation and the benefits of competition (Bendor, 1985). For example, the move to voucher systems and the creation of charter schools is a way to create a new educational system without directly taking apart the traditional public school system.

8. *Invest in distinctive competencies and distinctive assets that continue to be relevant, and build the new competencies and assets that are needed.* For example, the Loft is having to invest in information and communication technology and the skills of its staff to use it. Put simply, you cannot get to where you are going without the ability to get there.

Strategy Termination Guidelines

1. *Think of strategy termination as an extreme version of strategy change.* Many of the strategy change or succession guidelines outlined are applicable to strategy termination as well. And a new coalition organized around new ideas, stakeholder interests, and agreements is likely to be necessary. Given the probable resistance of current implementers and beneficiaries, leadership will be a crucial component of all strategy termination efforts; a fundamental leadership task will be to estrange important stakeholders from strategies to be terminated (Mangham & Overington, 1987; Scharmer, 2009).

2. *Engage in cutback management when programs need to be eliminated or severely reduced.* A substantial literature has developed on how to manage cutbacks in general. Behn (1983) argues that there are typically two stages to cutback efforts in public organizations. In the first stage, the organization typically borrows against the future to cover the gap between current revenues and needed expenditures. Yet if revenues are not increased in the future, this tactic merely makes the adjustments to retrenchment worse by postponing the second stage, or day of reckoning, when major cuts and redesigns are made. The following steps would appear to be important cutback management tasks; although useful, they obviously provide no panacea or quick fix (Behn,1983; Nutt, 2001; Holzer, Lee, & Newman, 2003; Nutt & Hogan, 2008):

- Take a long-term view
- Dramatically slow down the pace of change if possible by *strategically waiting* (Nutt & Hogan, 2008) for opportunities to pursue downsizing and make changes wisely without making big mistakes
- Develop the support of key leaders, decision makers, and constituencies, including legislators, if necessary, in the public sector
- Emphasize the mission, vision, and values to be adhered to, but also attend to the need to create at least a partially new identity for the downsized organization
- Develop clear guidelines and goals for making reductions
- Emphasize the importance of focusing on results, accountability, and integrity
- Use strategic assessments and performance measures in order to know what to cut and what to reward
- Rely on transparent communications to help build understanding of the problems to be faced and to build cooperation among affected units, unions, employees, and other stakeholders
- Maintain morale, in part by indicating what is off-limits to cuts
- First accommodate people being let go before taking steps to assimilate those left to operate the scaled-down system—but still attract and keep quality people, which may be particularly difficult when people think the ship is sinking
- Reinvest and redeploy staff based on a strategic vision; create opportunities for innovation; emphasize continuous improvement in what remains
- Create incentives for cooperation
- Avoid mistakes
- Be compassionate

Guidelines for Building a Strategic Management System

Building an effective strategic management system is an evolutionary process and typically builds on several successful cycles of strategic planning. The following guidelines are adapted from those followed by Hennepin County, Minnesota (the county that contains Minneapolis), as they went about constructing their strategic management system (Hennepin County, Minnesota, 2000, pp. 8–9):

1. *Apply the system to the whole organization.* The system should provide a framework for linking strategic goals and performance indicators to operational results. It should provide a way to cascade high-level measures down to more specific operational measures, and allow the roll up of operational results to higher levels where they can be analyzed and used to support strategic decision making.

2. *Build on performance measurement and management approaches already in use in the organization.* Don't reinvent any more wheels than you need for an effective vehicle.

3. *Focus on a small number of key results and indicators.* A few key indicators should be identified at each level of the organization. Using balanced scorecards is one way to do this, as they also typically rely on a few key indicators. Development of the indicators should make use of stakeholder input, facilitate the identification of strategic issues, and allow for the measurement of success.

4. *Use a common set of categories for performance measures.* Again, use of a balanced scorecard can facilitate adoption of a common set of performance indicators because of the scorecard's emphasis on learning and growth, internal process, financial, and customer and constituent categories of indicators. A common set of categories will help the organization measure short- and long-term progress toward results and how best to allocate resources across strategies, functions, and levels.

5. *Connect performance measures to specific programs, services, and activities.* The performance measures should tell a story about the purpose of the activity, its implementation, and the effect on or benefit to the user.

6. *Support linking organizational performance and individual performance.* The use of a consistent and complementary set of performance indicators helps promote alignment throughout the organization, and facilitates the linkage of individual goals and performance to the organization's strategic goals and performance.

7. *Use the strategic management system to support planning, decision making, budgeting, evaluation, and learning.* A good system should provide a stream of strategic and operational data for planning, decision making, and budgeting purposes. The data should be available to inform regularly scheduled as well as ad hoc management processes and events. The system, in other words, should become a part of the way the organization does business and should underpin a culture of excellent performance. This will happen more quickly and effectively if the system is easy to use and makes ongoing evaluation and learning possible.

8. *Review and update the system on a regular basis.* The system should be adjusted as necessary based on experience, changes in the organization, and changes in the environment.

SUMMARY

In the last step in the Strategy Change Cycle, leaders, managers, and other stakeholders review strategies that have resulted from previous steps or emerged along the way to determine whether they should be maintained, significantly altered, or terminated. This chapter has discussed why strategies cease to work and outlined the benefits of moving successfully through this review step. The most important benefits are assurance that strategies remain responsive to important issues, resolution of residual implementation difficulties, generation of needed energy for strategic renewal, and pruning of areas that are overcrowded with bits and pieces of assorted strategies. The step also includes attention to building an effective strategic management system.

In this step leaders and managers should focus on the issues that prompted the strategy under review and decide whether those issues are still relevant. They should rely on indicators of strategy success or failure to help them decide whether strategies should be maintained, reformed, or terminated. If the strategies have not been effective or the situation has changed, it may be necessary to identify new strategic issues and modify or eliminate particular strategies. Whatever the cause of this changed approach, it may also be necessary to revise the understandings that underlie the adopted strategies. Leaders and managers also must recognize that working within existing organizational structures, rather than trying to change or replace them, may be very productive at this point. A review group and review opportunities must be established and institutional inertia must be overcome, however, in order to review and perhaps revise existing strategies.

The design and use of forums, arenas, and the like in this step will vary, depending on whether the new strategy is to be maintained, reformed, or terminated. In order to maintain and incrementally improve the strategy, leaders and managers should seek little change in the existing settings. They may be able to involve mainly implementers and beneficiaries in the strategy review. If significant change is needed, the design and use of the pertinent forums, arenas, and such will have to be significantly altered. Leaders and managers will have to create or redesign forums to allow challenges to existing meanings and enactment of new meanings. Once again, implementers and beneficiaries are the most likely participants in the review, although some key decision makers and probably a new supportive coalition will have to be enlisted as well. Possible approaches to strategy succession involve splitting or consolidating strategy elements or developing a parallel system. Strategy termination is an extreme version of strategy succession. Leaders and managers will need to employ cutback management and strategies and techniques to minimize the resulting pain and dislocation, and to make sure the organization continues to create public value. Finally, leaders and managers should renew their own energy for working on the important issues their organizations or communities face.

Strategic management systems (or performance management systems or results-based management systems) are organizational arrangements meant to ensure ongoing strategic management of organizations and their strategies. There are a variety of types of strategic management systems, but virtually every system in practice is some hybrid version of two or more of the types. Construction, maintenance, and revision of a strategic management system is almost always an evolutionary process that unfolds as the organization gains more experience with strategic planning, results-based budgeting, performance management, and strategic measurement and evaluation. It usually takes years of experience to build a really effective and vital system and to build the culture of outstanding performance that goes along with it.

PART THREE

MANAGING THE PROCESS AND GETTING STARTED WITH STRATEGIC PLANNING

Strategic planning is in no way a substitute for leadership. Nor does strategic planning implement itself. It is simply a set of concepts, procedures, tools, and practices designed to help an organization's (collaboration's or community's) leaders, managers, planners, staff, and other stakeholders to think, act, and learn strategically. People who want to use strategic planning must attend to a wide range of leadership concerns. This section focuses on these needs.

Chapter Eleven addresses the leadership tasks in making strategic planning work. These include the need to understand the context; understand the people involved; sponsor and champion the process; foster collective leadership; design and use formal and informal settings for discussion, decision making, and conflict management; and put it all together over the course of the Strategy Change Cycle. Many different people will need to lead and follow at different times to accomplish these tasks. When strategic planning does work, it is a collective achievement.

In Chapter Twelve, the book's final chapter, the three major examples of strategic planning used throughout this book—the Minneapolis Park and Recreation Board, The Loft Literary Center, and MetroGIS—are summarized and discussed. Then a number of process guidelines are presented to help organizations (collaborations and communities) get started with their own strategic planning process.

CHAPTER ELEVEN

Leadership Roles in Making Strategic Planning Work

Barbara C. Crosby and John M. Bryson

Leaders perform political, spiritual, and intellectual
functions as well as managerial and group-maintenance
tasks. These range from providing vision and strategies
for change, to mobilizing a constituency, to facilitating
group decisions or creating coalitions.
—Charlotte Bunch, *Passionate Politics*

As has been pointed out before, strategic planning is *not* a substitute for effective leadership. There is *no* substitute for effective leadership (and committed followership) when it comes to planning and implementation. Instead, strategic planning is simply a set of concepts, procedures, and tools designed to help executives, managers, and others to think, act, and learn strategically on behalf of their organizations and their organizations' stakeholders. At its best, strategic planning and strategic management help leaders pursue virtuous ends in desirable ways so that significant public value is created and the common good is advanced. At its worst, strategic planning drives out strategic thought, action, and learning; makes it more difficult for everyone to do their job; and keeps organizations from meeting their mandates, fulfilling their missions, and creating public value. Whether strategic planning helps or hurts depends on how formal and informal leaders and followers at all organizational levels use it—or misuse it.

In each of the cases detailed in this book, executives, managers, and others had the ability to think, act, and learn strategically. They used strategic planning to tap this ability, canvass diverse views, build coalitions and commitment, and identify and address key organizational issues in order to enhance organizational performance in the eyes of key stakeholders. They used strategic planning to help their organizations proceed with some certainty amid plenty of ambiguity, unpredictability, and complexity. Without inclusive, collaborative leadership focused on both content *and* process concerns, strategic planning simply would not have happened.

So what is leadership? We define it as "the inspiration and mobilization of others to undertake collective action in pursuit of the common good" (Crosby & Bryson, 2005, p. xix). This definition suggests that *leadership* and *leaders* are not the same thing. Effective leadership in public and nonprofit organizations and communities is a collective enterprise involving many people playing different leader and follower roles at different times, as the opening quotation from Charlotte Bunch emphasizes. Often the word *leader* is applied to individuals in formal, and top, positions of authority—for example, CEO, board chair, senior manager, president, executive director—within an organization. We apply the term to people who use both formal and informal authority, as well as other assets, to help achieve worthy outcomes and contribute to societal well-being. Indeed, the same people will be leaders and followers at different times over the course of a strategy change cycle. This view harmonizes with the Belfast Health and Social Care Trust's Leadership and Management Strategy intended to help implement the Trust's vision of success that was discussed in Chapter Eight (see Exhibit 11.1).

Exhibit 11.1. The Leadership and Management Strategy of the Belfast Health and Social Care Trust.

The strategy is contained in a visually appealing document that outlines requirements of leaders and managers as well as the Trust's commitment to leadership and management development (Belfast Health and Social Care Trust, 2009). Elements of the strategy are very directly linked to the strategic objectives articulated in *The Belfast Way* (Belfast Health and Social Care Trust, 2008a):

- Safety and quality
- Modernization
- Partnerships
- People
- Resources

In her introduction to the leadership and management strategy document, the Trust's human resources director Marie Mallon emphasizes, "This is not just a strategy for those in the most senior posts within the

Trust, but is a plan which has relevance for all of our community of leaders as well as those who aspire to obtain managerial posts" (Belfast Health and Social Care Trust, 2009, p. 3).

The strategy was developed through extensive internal consultation and a literature review. Distinguishing between leadership and management behaviors and emphasizing the importance of both, it offers the following definition: "Leadership is an interpersonal relationship and process of influencing, by employing specific behaviors and strategies, the activities of an individual or organized group towards goal setting and goal achievement in specific situations. Management, in contrast, refers to the coordination and integration of resources through planning, organizing, directing and controlling to accomplish specific work-related goals and objectives" (p. 8).

The underlying philosophy is that some people in the organization have management responsibilities by virtue of their job titles, but everyone can lead in his or her sphere of influence or knowledge domain. Indeed, the document declares that "every member of staff can and should be a leader and demonstrate leadership qualities" (p. 10).

The document includes specific plans for providing leaders and aspiring managers a range of development opportunities and declares: "Leadership and management development must be a priority activity to which all leaders/managers will be expected to commit sufficient time and effort concentrating on developing their own talents and those of other leaders/managers. Senior leaders/managers must lead by example to demonstrate their commitment to lifelong learning and development" (p. 12).

Finally, the document includes a plan for assessing the strategy's effectiveness and promises a full review in 2013.

The following interconnected leadership tasks are important if strategic planning and implementation are to be effective:

- Understanding the context
- Understanding the people involved, including oneself
- Sponsoring the process
- Championing the process
- Facilitating the process
- Fostering collective leadership

- Using dialogue and deliberation to create a meaningful process, clarify mandates, articulate mission, identify strategic issues, develop effective strategies, and possibly develop a vision of success
- Making and implementing policy decisions
- Enforcing rules, settling disputes, and managing residual conflicts
- Putting it all together and preparing for ongoing strategic change

UNDERSTANDING THE CONTEXT

Leaders should help constituents view their organization and organizational change in the context of relevant social, political, economic, technological, and ecological systems and trends. They should take a long view backward over the organization's history and even its prehistory in order to help people in the organization think more wisely about the future. At the same time, they must avoid being captured by that history (Burns, 1978). They must see history as the interplay of continuity, or stability, and change, and recognize how best to balance these forces in a given context. They will need insight about how today's major global developments—such as the global marketplace, the information revolution, climate change, the push for democratization and human rights, and attention to multiculturalism—affect their organizations (Lipman-Blumen, 1996; Rifkin, 2000; Friedman, 2000, 2007; Cleveland, 2002; Hawken, 2007). They also must have an intimate knowledge of their organizations in order to make sense of the organizations in relation to the broader context (Mintzberg, Ahlstrand, & Lampel, 2009).

Leaders' understanding of the external and internal context of their organizations is important for recognizing emergent strategies, understanding how strategic planning might help their organizations, tailoring the process to the organizations' circumstances, negotiating the initial agreement, framing issues effectively, developing viable strategies for addressing them, and getting those strategies adopted and implemented. The leaders in each of our three cases were very attentive to their organization's internal and external contexts, their historical roots, and the possibilities for change presented by the context.

External and internal organizational assessments, stakeholder analyses, and special studies all are designed to attune strategic planning participants to important specifics of the context within which the organization exists. Those explorations typically occur *after* the process has started. Leaders also need some understanding of the context *before* the process begins—in order to know when the time is right to initiate strategic planning, how to organize it, and how to promote it. When an organization is beset by an immediate crisis or severe internal conflicts, immediate actions—for example, responding to an opportunity, curtailing a service, or reassigning people—may be needed. If the organization's internal culture has strong currents of unfair treatment and disrespect, leaders may need to take immediate steps to establish a more procedurally and interpersonally just workplace (Page, Eden, & Ackermann, 2010). At the same time, crisis and conflict may help leaders make the case that strategic planning is urgently needed if the organization is to thrive because of its participatory nature, future orientation, and focus on the common good. Leaders can stay attuned to the organization's external and internal environment through personal contacts and observation, attention to diverse media, continuing education, use of the organization's monitoring systems, and reflection. Leaders at the top of an organization or organizational unit should ensure that accurate information is flowing upward from frontline experts who typically know important things about the environment that top managers do not.

Leaders should be especially attentive to the possibilities for rather dramatic strategic change. Pressures and opportunities for significant change can come from the political context (for example, a change of government), social context (for example, a demographic shift), economic context (for example, loss of a funding stream), technological context (for example, opportunities and threats embedded in the Internet), or ecological context (for example, a natural or man-made disaster). Additionally, major shifts within the organization—for example, an anticipated wave of retirements—can signal the need for rethinking. Organizational strategies typically remain stable over reasonably long periods, and then can suddenly change all at once in response to cumulative changes in their environments (Gersick, 1991; Baumgartner & Jones, 2009; Kingdon, 2002; Mintzberg, Ahlstrand, & Lampel, 2009). Leaders should be in touch with the possibilities for significant change in order to know whether strategic planning should be used to help formulate major intended strategy changes—typically through raising the visibility and priority of particular strategies already present in nascent form—or whether it will be primarily a tool to program improvements in stable strategies. Without some intuitive sense of whether big or small changes are in the cards, strategic planning could be used quite inappropriately; hopes for big changes may be raised when they are not possible, or time may be wasted in programming strategies when drastic change is needed.

Understanding the People Involved, Including Oneself

Understanding oneself and others is particularly important for developing the strength of character and insight that invigorates leadership and increases the chances that strategic planning and implementation will help the organization. Leaders should seek to understand the strengths and weaknesses of the people who are or should be involved in strategic planning and implementation, including themselves. Perhaps the most important strength is a passion for fulfilling the organization's mission and contributing to the well-being of multiple stakeholders. Yet this strength must be coupled with a degree of humility and open-mindedness if a leader is to avoid the descent into self-righteousness and rigidity (Crosby & Bryson, 2005; Delbecq, 2006). In the case of the Loft, leaders such as Jocelyn Hale, Stephen Wilbers, Nancy Gaschott, and Linda Myers all cared deeply about the development of writers and creative writing and had a powerful sense of stewardship for their organization. Randall Johnson (MetroGIS coordinator), Richard Johnson (deputy regional administrator), Victoria Reinhardt (Ramsey County commissioner), and Randy Johnson (Hennepin County commissioner) all had a long-standing commitment to public service and believed that geographic information technology could make a vital contribution to more effective governance; Randall Johnson, in particular, had a burning desire to build a better data system to serve his region. At the Park Board, Jennifer Ringold and colleagues were sincerely devoted to sustaining a prized urban park system and citizen engagement in the board's planning process.

In addition to passion tempered by humility and open-mindedness, personal strengths include professional or technical competencies, interpersonal skills and networks, and a feel for complexity—that is, the ability to view the organization from multiple perspectives and choose from a repertoire of appropriate behaviors (Cleveland, 2002; Bolman & Deal, 2008). In strategic planning, the personal qualities of moral integrity, self-efficacy, compassion, and courage are especially important in helping participants develop the trust and determination to take risks, explore difficult issues and new strategies, and pursue what might be unpopular causes. Additional personal leadership assets include a sense of humor, awareness of one's habitual ways of learning and interacting with people, commitment to continual learning, power and authority, supportive personal networks, ability to balance competing demands, and awareness of how leadership is affected by one's location in major social hierarchies (based on race/ethnicity, class, gender, age, religion, physical ability, and the like). Of these, a sense of humor, supportive networks, and balance may be especially important for the persistence and resilience needed to cope with the often protracted ups and downs of a strategic planning effort. Leaders should remember that understanding and marshaling personal assets is perhaps the most powerful instrument of all (Lipman-Blumen, 1996).

Helpful approaches to understanding oneself and others range from formal assessments in leadership development programs, to deep study and reflection, to informal storytelling. Feedback from others, especially skilled coaches and mentors, is often highly useful. The process of understanding oneself and others can be used to establish personal development plans, choose team members, and gear messages and processes to different styles of learning and interacting.

Effective strategic thinking, acting, and learning seem to depend a great deal on intuition, creativity, and pattern recognition, none of which can be programmed, although they may be recognized, facilitated, and encouraged (Gardner, 2009; Mintzberg, Ahlstrand, & Lampel, 2009). Thus, finding people who are effective strategists is not an exact science; gathering information about potential leaders from a variety of sources and betting on the basis of past performance may be the most reliable approach.

SPONSORING THE PROCESS

Process sponsors typically are top positional leaders. They have enough prestige, power, and authority to commit the organization to undertaking strategic planning and to hold people accountable for doing so. Sponsors are not necessarily involved in the day-to-day details of making strategic planning work—the champions do that—but they do set the stage for success and pay careful attention to the progress of the process. They have a vested interested in a successful outcome and do what they can to make sure it happens. They also typically are important sources of knowledge about key strategic issues and effective strategies for addressing them. The information they have about the organization and its environment is invaluable. They also are likely to be especially knowledgeable about how to fit the process to key decision points, so that strategic planning dialogue and discussion can inform decisions in the relevant arenas. As Kelman (2005) points out, when organizations are under pressure to change, some people within the organization may already be discontented with the status quo and thinking strategically about needed changes, but these latent supporters for strategic planning may only be activated when a powerful sponsor endorses the change process.

In the Loft case, Linda Myers and the executive committee of the board engaged the organization in the strategic planning process in order to help the organization carry out its mission in the digital age. In the MetroGIS case, Richard Johnson in his position as Metropolitan Council deputy administrator provided legitimacy, political protection, and funding to help launch and sustain the development of the GIS network. Victoria Reinhardt and Randy Johnson ensured that county commissioners' perspectives were represented in the process and that the process was legitimate in commissioners' eyes. At the Minneapolis Park Board, Superintendent Jon Gurban authorized the strategic planning process and promoted Jennifer Ringold to oversee it.

Leaders interested in sponsoring a strategic planning process should consider the following guidelines:

1. *Articulate the purpose and importance of the strategic planning effort.* Many participants will need some convincing about why the

organization should undertake a strategic planning effort. Leaders can start by outlining their views of the organization's past, present, and future. They should invoke powerful organizational symbols as they link the strategic planning effort to the organization's mission and values and to the best aspects of the organization's culture (Schein, 2010; Bolman & Deal, 2008). They also can highlight core organizational competencies, key changes in the environment, significant strategic issues that the organization faces or will face, the importance of creating public value, possible actions the organization will need to consider, and the likely consequences of failure to engage in strategic planning. Based on this sketch, leaders should outline in general how they want the organization to engage in strategic planning and what they hope the outcomes and benefits of doing so will be. These leaders will demonstrate a concern for the content, process, and outcomes of strategic planning. Emphasizing the importance and potential payoffs of the strategic planning effort is vital at the outset, but also at points along the way, when participants' enthusiasm is dwindling and their spirits need to be raised and their energies restored.

2. *Commit necessary resources—time, money, energy, legitimacy—to the effort.* A crucial way of making the process real is through allocating resources to it. Nothing will demonstrate leaders' seriousness (or lack of it) about strategic planning more than that.

3. *Emphasize at the beginning and at critical points that action and change will result.* This is another crucial way of making the process real for participants and getting them to take it seriously. If they see that strategic planning has real consequences, they will invest the necessary effort in the process.

4. *Encourage and reward creative thinking, constructive debate, and multiple sources of input and insight.* Sponsors should emphasize the importance of creativity, constructive debate, and the value of strategically significant ideas no matter what their origin. They should identify the people who are ready to change, authorize champions, and reward those who supply creative ideas. Otherwise, the leaders will be viewed as hypocrites, and important sources of energy and new ideas and information will be cut off. The reward for creative participation is often simply evidence that a wide range of stakeholders' contributions are included in the strategic plan. In the Loft case, for example, the plan approved by the board of directors clearly built on the conclusions of the six task forces that focused on specific issue areas; the task forces and their membership were listed on the final page of the plan.

Encouraging constructive debate and deliberation also means anticipating where conflicts might develop and thinking about how those conflicts might be addressed productively. In particular, leaders must think about which conflicts can be addressed within the existing rules of the game and which can be managed effectively only if the rules of the game are changed. For example, in the case of MetroGIS, sponsors needed to convince county commissioners to change the rules that permitted each county's staff to set prices for sharing local data with other governments.

In an organization in which past strategic planning efforts have failed, coleaders and followers are likely to require signals from sponsors that this time will be different. Especially if people contributed their time and ideas to previous processes only to see no real effect, they will need assurances that the new process will be not only be participatory but will produce outcomes that reflect their efforts.

5. *Be aware of the possible need for outside consultants.* Outside consultants may be needed to help design the process, facilitate aspects of it, do various studies, or perform other tasks. It is a sign of strength to ask for help when you need it. Enough money must be budgeted to pay for any consultants you may need.

6. *Be willing to exercise power and authority to keep the process on track.* Strategic planning is inherently prone to break down (Bryson & Roering, 1988, 1989). For one thing, effective strategic planning is a nonroutine kind of activity and, as March and Simon (1958, p. 185) have pointed out, there is a sort of "Gresham's Law of Planning" at work in organizations: "Daily routine drives out planning." Sponsors use their authority to provide continuous support for change to the point that enough momentum is built that important tipping points are passed and desired changes take on a life of their own and become a part of the organization's culture (Kelman, 2005).

Another danger with strategic planning is that people are likely to fight or flee whenever they are asked to deal with tough issues or failing strategies, serious conflicts, or significant changes. Sponsors have a key role to play in keeping the process going through the difficult patches; they can provide a *holding environment* (Heifetz, Grashow, & Linsky, 2009) that provides a measure of safety for participants as they are encouraged to face unpleasant challenges or dilemmas. How these difficulties are handled will say a lot about the leaders' and participants' characters. As Csikszentmihalyi (1990, p. 24) points out, "The ability to persevere despite obstacles and setbacks is the quality people most admire in others, and justly so; it is probably the most important trait not only for succeeding in life, but for enjoying it as well." In the case of the Loft, for example, the board was surprised partway through the strategic planning process when Myers announced her plan to retire in a few months. Board members discussed the possibility of altering or halting the planning process, but decided that proceeding with the plan was the best way to ensure a successful transition to a new executive director. Thus, challenges are an opportunity to demonstrate courage, forge strong characters, and end up with a more effective organization to boot (Selznick, 1957; Terry, 1993). Wise dispute resolution and conflict management strategies are called for, but they also may need to be backed up by sufficient power and authority to make them work well.

CHAMPIONING THE PROCESS

The champions are the people who have primary responsibility for managing the strategic planning process day to day. They are the ones who keep track of progress and also pay attention to all the details. They model the kind of behavior they hope to get from other participants: reasoned, diligent, committed, enthusiastic, and good-spirited pursuit of the common good. They are the cheerleaders who, along with the sponsors, keep the process on track and push, encourage, and cajole the strategic planning team and other key participants through any difficult spots. Champions, especially, need the interpersonal skills and feel for complexity noted earlier. Sometimes, it is they who actually see the need for strategic planning and must convince sponsors to endorse the process. Sometimes the sponsors and champions are the same people, but usually they are not. In the Loft case, Jocelyn Hale and Stephen Wilbers were sponsors (as members of the board's executive committee) who joined staff director Nancy Gaschott as champions of the process. In organizing MetroGIS, Randall Johnson persisted in championing strategic planning and implementation over fifteen years. At the Minneapolis Park Board, Jennifer Ringold managed a complex two-year process, including staff teams, town meetings, community surveys, focus groups, and community leader workshops.

Champions should keep the following guidelines in mind:

1. *Keep strategic planning high on people's agendas.* Daily routine easily can drive out attention to strategic planning. Blocking out time in people's calendars is one way to gather participants together and focus their attention. Another is calling on sponsors to periodically emphasize the importance of the process. Yet another is to publish updates on the process in special memoranda or regular newsletters.

One more way is to circulate think pieces, special reports, relevant CDs, podcasts, and Web sites that encourage strategic thought and action. By whatever means, people will need to be reminded and shown on a regular basis that something good will come from getting together to talk about what is important and then doing something about it.

2. *Attend to the process without promoting specific solutions.* Champions are far more likely to gain people's participation and constructive involvement if they are seen more as advocates for the process rather than for specific solutions. If the champions are seen as committed partisans of specific solutions, then other participants may boycott or torpedo the process rather than seek to find mutually agreeable strategies to address key issues.

3. *Think about what has to come together (people, tasks, information, reports) at or before key decision points.* When it comes to strategy formulation and strategic planning, time is not linear; instead, it involves important junctures. The best champions think like theatre directors, orchestrators, choreographers, or playwrights. They think about stage setting, themes, acts and scenes, actors and audiences, and how to get the right people with the right information on stage at the *right time*—and then get them off the stage.

4. *Organize time, space, materials, and participation needed for the process to succeed.* Without attention to the details of the process, its benefits simply will not be achieved. The *trivialities* of the process matter a great deal—in fact, they are not trivial at all (Huxham, 1990). Effective champions and their assistants arrange the retreats, book the rooms, make sure any necessary supplies and equipment are handy, send out the meeting notices, distribute the briefing papers and minutes, maintain relevant social networking and collaborative working Web sites, oversee the production details of draft and final plans, and keep track of the work program.

5. *Pay attention to the language used to describe strategic planning and implementation.* One function of strategic planning is to provide a vocabulary and format that allows people to share views and deliberate about what is fundamental for the organization (Mintzberg, 1994, p. 352). At various points in the process, therefore, participants are likely to wonder about the meaning of particular planning concepts and how they relate to substantive matters of concern. An introduction to strategic planning, often in a retreat setting, is typically a useful way to begin developing a common vocabulary of concepts with which to organize efforts to plan strategically. As the

process proceeds further, at various points the discussion will almost invariably focus anew on the meaning of planning concepts (mission, vision, goals, issues, strategies) and how they relate to the subjects of group discussion and specific products of group work. Champions should be prepared to discuss similarities and differences among various concepts and how they do or do not relate to substantive concerns, products, and outcomes. The specific vocabulary a group uses to label things does not matter as much as development of a shared understanding of what things mean.

6. *Keep rallying participants and pushing the process along.* Successful strategic planning processes can vary from a few weeks or months to two or more years (Bryson & Roering, 1988, 1989). Some processes must fail one or more times before they succeed. Some never succeed. Champions should keep the faith and push until the process does succeed, or until it is clear that it will fail and there is no point in continuing. At the same time, it is important to remember that strategic planning is likely to feel like a failure in the middle, as Kanter (1983, 1989) has said of innovations. Champions keep pushing to help the strategic planning team and organization move through the failure stage toward success. Rallying the troops will be easier if they can show some early wins and continued small (and occasionally big) wins along the way (Weick, 1984; Kelman, 2005). Remember a point made earlier that strategic action does not have to, and usually should not, wait until the strategic planning process is complete.

7. *Develop champions throughout the organization.* A champion-in-chief may oversee the entire strategic planning process, but he or she should seek out champions throughout the organization (collaboration, community) to oversee parts of the process—for example, by chairing task forces or working groups. Otherwise, the central champion can be in danger of burning out, and in the position of having no one else to take over if he or she has to drop out of the process. Having multiple champions is especially important when the planning is in multiorganizational or community settings (Bardach, 1998; Huxham & Vangen, 2005).

8. *Be sensitive to power differences.* Differences in status, authority, and access to resources are likely to be pronounced in more hierarchical organizations and within inclusive collaborations like MetroGIS. In the cases of MetroGIS and the Minneapolis Park Board, the champions were mindful that elected officials would determine the fate of their plans, but they also used inclusive structures—such as the MetroGIS

Coordinating Committee and Technical Advisory Group and the Park Board staff teams—along with community engagement methods to balance the power of the officials. They made special efforts to engage groups of people who might not readily respond to surveys or attend town meetings.

FACILITATING THE PROCESS

Process facilitators are often helpful in moving a strategic planning process along because of their group process skills, the attention they can give to structuring and managing group interactions, and the likelihood that they have no stake in the substantive outcomes of the process, particularly if they are outsiders (Schwarz, 2002; Chrislip, 2002). The presence of a facilitator means that champions can be free to participate in substantive discussions without having to worry too much about managing group process. A skilled facilitator also can help build trust, interpersonal skills, and conflict management ability in a group. Building trust is important because the members of a strategic planning team often come from various parts of the organization and have never worked together before, let alone on fundamental strategic questions facing the organization.

Skilled facilitation usually depends on the establishment of a successful partnership among facilitators, sponsors, and champions. To do their work well, facilitators must learn a great deal very quickly about the organization, its politics, issues, culture, and secrets. They must quickly gain the trust of the sponsors and champions, learn the lay of the land, and demonstrate their ability to further the strategic planning effort. Their efforts will be thwarted, however, unless the sponsors and champions commit themselves to working closely with the facilitators. The sponsors, champions, and facilitators usually form the core group that moves the process forward with the help of the strategic planning team that is a part of most planning efforts (Schwarz, 2002; Friend & Hickling, 2005)

Facilitators should come to any process with a well-developed set of group process skills (Schwarz, 2002; Johnson & Johnson, 2008), along with skills especially applicable to strategic planning for public and nonprofit organizations (Nutt & Backoff, 1992; Friend & Hickling, 2005). The initiators of a complex strategic planning process may wish to provide facilitator training for some staff and community participants so that (1) the facilitation tasks can be widely shared and (2) the organization or community will have numerous members with valuable group process skills. The Park Board used its process as an important opportunity to build its staff's strategic planning process facilitation skills.

Strategic planning facilitators should consider following these guidelines:

1. *Know the strategic planning process and explain how it works at the beginning and at many points along the way.* Participants often will be experiencing a new or different process at the same time that they work on issues of real importance to the organization. Thus participants can easily get lost. Facilitators play a key role in explaining to participants where they are, where they can head, and how they might get there.

2. *Tailor the process to the organization and the groups involved.* Planning processes must be fit to the unique circumstances in which organizations (collaborations, communities) and groups find themselves (Christensen, 1999; Alexander, 2000). Facilitators, along with sponsors and champions, are the ones who are in the best position to design the process so that it fits the organization, its circumstances, and the participants. Facilitators must pay careful attention to both the *tasks* of strategic planning and the *socioemotional maintenance* of the groups and teams involved in the process. Both content and process dimensions are crucial to effective group functioning and, indeed, are the basic elements of effective team leadership (Johnson & Johnson, 2008).

3. *Convey a sense of humor and enthusiasm for the process and help groups get unstuck.* Sponsors and champions can express humor and enthusiasm for the process, but not the same way that a facilitator can. Strategic planning can be alternately tension ridden and tedious. Good facilitators can help manage the tensions and relieve the tedium. Facilitators also can help groups confront the difficulties that arise over the course of a strategic planning process. By helping groups reframe their situations imaginatively, invent new options, channel conflict constructively, and tap hidden sources of courage, hope, and optimism, facilitators can provide or find important resources to help groups move forward (Terry, 1993; Seligman, 1998; Schwarz, 2002; Bolman & Deal, 2008; Innes & Booher, 2010).

4. *Ensure that participants rather than the facilitators are doing the work.* Skilled facilitators give participants many chances to interact in small groups, to produce idea-covered flip chart sheets and walls, stakeholder diagrams, strategy maps, reports, and presentations.

5. *Press groups toward action and the assignment of responsibility for specific actions.* Part of keeping the process moving is to make sure that participants engage in timely action. If the whole process is

devoted entirely to thinking and strategizing, without taking action, people will quickly quit participating. Facilitators should emphasize that not all of the thinking has to take place before any of the acting can occur. Further, much effective learning only occurs in the aftermath of action. Whenever useful and wise actions become apparent—as a result of attention to mission and mandates, stakeholder analyses, SWOC/T analyses, strategic issue identification, and various strategizing efforts—they should be taken, as long as they do not jeopardize possible choices that decision makers might want to make in the future. There are limits to thinking things out in advance. Often people can only know what they think by acting first, and often important strategies can only emerge by taking small steps and using adaptive learning to figure things out as one goes along (Weick, 1995; Mintzberg, Ahlstrand, & Lampel, 2009). Huxham and Vangen (2005) point out that especially in multiorganization collaborations, participants may need to jointly undertake some small steps in order to build the trust and sense of shared purpose that are necessary for the collaboration to function effectively.

Pushing people toward action does raise the danger of inducing premature closure. People may act on what is immediately at hand without thinking creatively about other options, or simply waiting until the time is right. A good facilitator will have a well-developed intuitive sense about when to push for action and when to hold back. He or she will also be good at probing people and groups about the merits of options and the advisability of taking specific actions.

6. *Congratulate people whenever possible.* In our experience, most people in most organizations suffer from chronic—and sometimes acute—positive reinforcement deprivation. Yet people respond very favorably to kind words and praise from people who are important to them. Indeed, many excellently managed organizations are known for the praise and emotional support they provide their employees (Collins & Porras, 1997; Kouzes & Posner, 2008). Facilitators are in an excellent position to congratulate people and say good things about them in a genuine and natural way.

FOSTERING COLLECTIVE LEADERSHIP (AND FOLLOWERSHIP)

When strategic planning is successful for public organizations it is a collective achievement. Many people contribute to its success, sometimes by leading, other times by following. Collective leadership may be fostered through the following approaches:

1. *Rely on teams.* The team is the basic vehicle for furthering strategic planning. Champions, in particular, will find that much of their time will be focused on making sure strategic planning teams or task forces perform well and make effective contributions. There are two reasons why teams are so important. The first is that no one person can have all the relevant qualitative or quantitative information, and thus forming a team is one way to increase the information available for strategic planning. The second reason is political. To be viable, strategic planning and strategies will need support at many points throughout the organization and from external stakeholders. A strategic plan and intended strategies will need the support of a critical coalition when they are adopted and during implementation. A wisely constructed strategic planning team or teams can provide the initial basis for such a coalition and team members can do much of the work leading to formation of the necessary coalition. In the case of the Loft, each strategic planning task force was co-led by a staff member and a board member, thus strengthening ties among board and staff and facilitating the formation of a strong board-staff coalition for change.

Team leaders naturally must focus on the accomplishment of team goals or tasks, but they also must attend to individual team members' needs and consciously promote group cohesion (Johnson & Johnson, 2008). Team leadership balances direction, mentoring, and facilitation so that everyone can make useful contributions. Leaders should help team members:

- Communicate effectively face-to-face and at a distance (including promotion of active listening, dialogue, and other conflict management methods)
- Balance unity around a shared purpose with diversity of views and skills
- Define team mission, goals, norms, and roles
- Establish an atmosphere of trust
- Foster group creativity and sound decision making
- Obtain necessary resources
- Develop leadership and followership competencies
- Celebrate achievement and overcome adversity

Although the role of team leaders typically receives attention in books like this one, we also want to highlight follower roles. Active, committed followers play vital roles in keeping leaders in check and on track, contributing knowledge and ideas, promoting change, and carrying out and shaping agreed-upon tasks (Riggio, Chaleff, & Lipman-Blumen, 2008).

2. *Focus on network and coalition development.* Coalitions basically organize around ideas and interests that allow people to see that they can achieve together what they could not separately. The way issues, goals, or visions—and strategies for achieving them—are framed will structure how stakeholders interpret their interests, how they assess the costs and benefits of joining a coalition, and the form and content of winning and losing arguments. Therefore, leaders should use the insights gained from various stakeholder analysis exercises to gain a sense of where stakeholders' interests overlap and how issues, goals, visions, and strategies could be framed to draw significant support from key stakeholders. The worldview that public, nonprofit, and community leaders should seek is one likely to evoke widely shared notions of what constitutes the public interest and the common good (Bryson, Cunningham, & Lokkesmoe, 2002; Chrislip, 2002; Crosby & Bryson, 2005).

A strategic plan's or strategy's political acceptability to key stakeholders is enhanced as the benefits of adopting and implementing it increase and the costs of doing so diminish. As Light (1991) notes in relation to presidential agenda setting, it is primarily the issues with the greatest potential benefit for key stakeholders that get on the agenda, whereas those that are the least costly for key stakeholders are the ones that receive prime consideration. Moreover, any proposal likely to be adopted and implemented will be a carefully tailored response to specific circumstances, rather than an off-the-shelf solution imported from somewhere else (Nadler & Hibino, 1998; Kingdon, 2002; Nutt, 2002). Typically, not every member of a winning coalition will agree on every specific aspect of an entire plan or set of strategies, and that is okay.

Leaders should recognize that coalition development depends on following many of the same guidelines that help develop effective teams. In particular, coalitions are probably more likely to be formed if organizers employ strategies for valuing the diversity of coalition members and their various ideas and special gifts. Acquiring the necessary resources is also vital to coalition development, and the coalition itself can become a major source of resources for implementing a strategic planning process. Rewarding and celebrating collective achievements and sharing credit for them broadly are also likely to help (Bardach, 1998). The Loft demonstrates the sharing of credit for a successful strategic planning effort; for example, the booklet presenting the plan lists every member of the strategic planning task force team and includes a photograph of all Loft board members and staff.

In a broader sense, public leaders should work to build a sense of community—that is, a sense of relationship, mutual empowerment, and common purpose—within and beyond their organizations. This is desirable because so many of the problems that public and nonprofit organizations are called on to address require multi-organizational, or community, responses (Chrislip, 2002; Linden, 2002). Community may be tied to a place or be what Heifetz and Sinder (1988) and others have called a *community of interest*, an interorganizational network that often transcends geographic and political boundaries and is designed to address transorganizational problems, Leaders contribute to community building by facilitating communal definition and resolution of issues, fostering democratic leader-follower relations (Boyte & Kari, 1996; Boyte, 2004, 2008), providing resources, and using their knowledge of group process to help people work together. Most important, as Palmer (2000, p. 138) suggests, leaders build community by "making space for other people to act."

3. *Make leadership and followership development an explicit strategy.* Many organizations invest in leadership development, but may not directly tie leadership development to the organization's strategic change processes. One that does is the Belfast Health and Social Care Trust through its Leadership and Management Strategy (see Exhibit 11.1). Community leadership programs such as those conducted by university extension services are often intended to help communities pursue new visions and regenerate themselves (Scheffert, Horntvedt, & Hoelting, 2011). We don't know of followership development programs, though suggestions abound (Riggio, Chaleff, & Lipman-Blumen, 2008). Some elements of good followership may be included in organizations' orientation programs or in citizen engagement processes (Gastil & Levine, 2005).

4. *Establish specific mechanisms for sharing power, responsibility, and accountability.* Authority is not usually shared by policymaking bodies or chief executives—and often cannot be by law—but that does not mean power, responsibility, and accountability cannot be shared. Doing so can foster participation, trigger information and resource flows, and help build commitment to plans and strategies and their implementation (Linden, 2002). The use of strategic planning teams, strategic issue task forces, and implementation teams are typical vehicles for sharing power. Action plans should spread out responsibilities while also establishing clear accountability.

USING DIALOGUE AND DELIBERATION
TO CREATE A MEANINGFUL PROCESS

Creating and communicating meaning is the work of visionary leadership. Sometimes visionary leadership results in a vision of success for the organization (collaboration or community), but in the present discussion visioning covers a broader range of outcomes; it is meant more as a verb than as a noun. Leaders become visionary when they play a vital role in interpreting current reality (often in light of the past), fostering a collective group mission, articulating desirable strategies, and shaping a collective sense of the future (Denhardt, 1993; Hunt, Boal, & Dodge, 1999; Crosby & Bryson, 2005; Senge, 2006). Furthermore, visionary leaders must understand important aspects of their own and others' internal worlds, and they must also grasp the meaning of related external worlds. As truth tellers and direction givers, they help people make sense of experience, and they offer guidance for coping with the present and the future by helping answer the questions: What's going on here? Where are we heading? What traditions should we preserve? And how will things look when we get there? They frame and shape the perceived context for action, and they manage important stakeholders' perceptions of the organization, its strategies, and their effects (Neustadt, 1990; Boal & Schultz, 2007; Hill & Lynn, 2009). In order to foster change, particularly major change, they become skilled in the following methods of creating and communicating new meanings.

1. *Understand the design and use of forums.* Forums are the basic settings we humans use to create shared meaning through dialogue and deliberation (Crosby & Bryson, 2005). Much of the work of strategic planning takes place in forums, where fairly free-flowing consideration of ideas and views can take place before proposals are developed for adoption and action in decision-making arenas. The tasks of sponsoring, championing, and facilitating strategic planning are primarily performed in forums. Strategic planning retreats, team meetings, task force meetings, focus groups, strategic planning newsletters and Internet notices, conference calls, e-mail and social networking exchanges, and strategic plans themselves—when used as educational devices—are all examples of the use of forums. These forums can be used to help develop a shared understanding about what the organization is, what is does or should do, and why. All of the three cases featured in this book included diverse, participatory forums for developing and implementing the strategic plan. In the

MetroGIS case, for example, Randall Johnson and his staff organized numerous discussion forums and intensive strategic planning workshops. Meetings of the technical advisory group, the coordinating committee, policy board, and various working groups were used to hash out the best ways to implement the plan. Reports and a Web site helped solidify the network's developing identity and made progress on the strategic plan highly visible.

2. *Seize opportunities to be interpreters and direction givers in areas of uncertainty and difficulty.* Leadership opportunities expand in times of difficulty, confusion, and crisis, when old approaches clearly are not working, and people are searching for meaningful accounts of what has happened and what can be done about it (Heifetz, 1994; Hunt, Boal, & Dodge, 1999; Schein, 2010; Kouzes & Posner, 2008). Focusing on strategic issues or failing strategies therefore provides opportunities for exercising leadership, for inspiring and mobilizing others to figure out what might be done to improve the organization's performance in the eyes of key stakeholders. Turning dangers, threats, and crises into manageable challenges is an important task for visionary leaders (Chattopadhyay, Glick, & Huber, 2001; Rainey, 2009). Doing so not only promotes optimism and resilience, but also is more likely to free up the necessary thinking, resources, and energy to confront the challenges successfully. At the Loft, the explosion in publishing opportunities on the Internet and corresponding effects on traditional print outlets presented considerable ambiguity and concern for Linda Myers and the Loft board. They launched their strategic planning process in part to respond to the effects of the digital revolution. In the case of MetroGIS, Randy Johnson focused on the opportunities that geographic information systems presented for dealing with the mounting frustrations of local planners trying to obtain accurate predictions of population growth, employment, and public service needs. The Park Board undertook strategic planning to take on the uncertainties and difficulties created by population changes, constricted public budgets, and the need to rebuild its image.

3. *Reveal and name real needs and real conditions.* New meaning unfolds as leaders encourage people to see the "real" situation and its portents. To illuminate "real" conditions, leaders may use observation and intuition as well as integrative and systems thinking (Cleveland, 2002; Mintzberg, Ahlstrand, & Lampel, 2009; Heifetz, Linsky, & Grashow, 2009). They formally or informally scan their environment, consider multiple perspectives, and discern the patterns emerging

from local conditions, or they accept patterns and issues identified by other people, such as pollsters or planners. Simply articulating these patterns publicly and convincingly can be an act of revelation. As the poet Wallace Stevens (1990 [1954], p. 344) notes, "Description is revelation. It is not/ The thing described, nor false facsimile." However, leaders cannot just delineate emerging patterns and issues; they must also explain them (Neustadt, 1990). They must relate what they see to their knowledge of societal systems and to people's experience. Going further, leaders alert followers to the need for action by their "uncovering and exploiting of contradictions in values and between values and practice" (Burns, 1978, p. 43).

4. *Help co-leaders and followers frame and reframe issues and strategies.* In revealing and explaining real conditions, leaders are laying the groundwork for framing and reframing issues facing the organization and strategies for addressing them (Stone, 2002; Bolman & Deal, 2008). The *framing* process consists of naming, characterizing, and explaining the issue, opening the door to alternative ways of addressing it, and suggesting outcomes. The *reframing* process involves breaking with old ways of viewing an issue or strategy and developing a new appreciation of it (Mangham & Overington, 1987; Scharmer, 2009). As noted earlier, framing and reframing should be connected to stakeholder views and interests.

5. *Offer compelling visions of the future.* Leaders convey shared visions through stories rooted in shared history yet focused on the future. These stories link people's experience of the present (cognitions), what they may do about the situation (behaviors), and what they may expect to happen as a result (consequences); in other words, the stories help people grasp desirable and potentially real futures (Boal & Bryson, 1987; Boal & Schultz, 2007). Effective stories are rich with metaphors that make sense of people's experience, are comprehensive yet open-ended, and impel people toward union or common ground (Gabriel, 2000; Terry, 2001). Leaders transmit their own belief in their visionary stories through vivid, energetic, optimistic language (Shamir, Arthur, & House, 1994; Kouzes & Posner, 2008). To be effective, the visions and the symbols they incorporate should be enacted through organizational rituals that honor what is to be preserved from the past, celebrate new activities, and leave behind (and even mourn) what is to be discarded (Bridges, 2004; Bolman & Deal, 2008).

6. *Champion new and improved ideas for dealing with strategic issues.* Championing ideas for addressing issues is different from

championing the process of strategic planning, but is nonetheless important. Astute leaders gather ideas from many sources (Burns, 1978; Mintzberg, Ahlstrand, & Lampel, 2009). Within organizations and political communities, they foster an atmosphere in which innovative approaches flourish (Crossan, Lane, & White, 1999; Kouzes & Posner, 2008; Mumford, Eubanks, & Murphy, 2007). Acting in the mode of Schön's *reflective practitioner* (1983), these leaders champion *improved* ideas, those that have emerged from practice and have been refined by critical reflection, including ethical analysis. In analyzing ideas, leaders keep strategic planning participants focused on the important outcomes they seek (Nutt, 2002).

7. *Articulate desired actions and expected consequences.* Pragmatic visionary leaders ensure that actions and consequences are an integral part of organizational, collaboration, or community visions, missions, and strategies. These naturally will become more detailed as implementations proceed (Mintzberg & Westley, 1992) and should include things the organization, collaboration, or community will stop doing. Crises, however, can necessitate reversing this sequence. When old behaviors are not working and disaster is imminent, followers may wish leaders to prescribe new behaviors and may be willing to try those behaviors even before they can develop a clear vision of the outcome for the organization, collaboration, or community as a whole or its specific strategies. At some point, though, leaders must link the recommended actions to organizational or communal purposes (Boal & Bryson, 1987; Hunt, Boal, & Dodge, 1999).

MAKING AND IMPLEMENTING DECISIONS IN ARENAS

Public and nonprofit leaders are also required to be political leaders—partly because all organizations have their political aspects (Bolman & Deal, 2008), and partly because public and nonprofit organizations are inherently involved in politicized decision making much of the time. The key to success, and the heart of political leadership, is understanding how intergroup power relationships shape decision making and implementation outcomes. Particularly important is understanding how to affect outcomes by having some things never come up for a decision. Specifically, political leaders must undertake the following responsibilities:

1. *Understand the design and use of arenas.* Politically astute leaders must be skilled in designing and using formal and informal arenas, the basic settings for making decisions about which policies,

programs, and projects will be adopted and implemented (Crosby & Bryson, 2005). For government organizations, these arenas may be legislative, executive, or administrative. The Park Board's governing board, for example, functions as an arena in setting policies for the park system, yet it also is affected by decisions made in the Minneapolis mayor's office (an executive arena) and in the City Council and the Metropolitan Council (other legislative arenas). It also may have to comply with decisions made by administrative arenas, such as the Minnesota department that promulgates rules about accommodations for citizens with disabilities. For nonprofit organizations, internal arenas will include the board and management meetings; they too will be affected by a variety of government arenas. Collaborations and communities will be dependent on many relevant arenas. A collaboration may include its own policymaking body—for example, the policy board in the MetroGIS case—but may also depend on decisions by boards of member organizations and be affected by various other government arenas. It is in arenas that the products of forums—such as strategic plans and important aspects of strategies—are adopted as is, altered, or rejected.

A major issue in any strategic planning process is how to sequence the move from planning forums, particularly planning team meetings that include key decision makers, to decision-making arenas. A large fraction of the necessary strategic thinking will occur as part of the dialogue and deliberation in forums. Once viable proposals have been worked out, they can move to arenas for any necessary revisions, adoption, and implementation—or else rejection. At a minimum, managing the transition from forums to arenas depends on figuring out when key decision points will occur and then designing the planning process to fit those points in such a way that decisions in arenas can be influenced constructively by the work done in forums.

A further issue is how to handle any residual conflicts or disputes that may arise during implementation. Some advance thinking, therefore, is almost always in order about how these residual or subsidiary conflicts might be handled constructively, either in arenas or through the use of formal or informal courts. In the case of MetroGIS, Randy Johnson insisted on having a direct link to the deputy administrator of the Metropolitan Council in order to ensure that recommendations emanating from the strategic planning process had a good chance of endorsement by the Metropolitan Council and its top administrators. By establishing a policy board that would consist of county commissioners, the early collaborators in MetroGIS also ensured that recommendations secured county boards' endorsement when needed.

2. *Mediate and shape conflict within and among stakeholders.* Conflict, or at least recognizable differences, are necessary if people are to be offered real choices in arenas (Burns, 1978; Bryant, 2003), and if decision makers are to understand the choices and their consequences (Janis, 1989). Further, political leaders must possess transactional skills for dealing with followers, other leaders, and various key stakeholders who have conflicting agendas. To forge winning coalitions, they must bargain and negotiate, inventing options for mutual gain so that they can trade things of value that they control for others' support (Thompson, 2008).

3. *Understand the dynamics of political influence and how to target resources appropriately.* The first requirement for influencing political decision making may be knowing whom to influence. Who controls the agenda of the relevant decision-making body, which may be a city council, a board of directors, or some other group? Who chairs the group and any relevant committees? The next requirement is knowing how to influence. What forms of providing information, lobbying, vote trading, arm twisting, and so on are acceptable? Should change advocates try to alter the composition of the decision-making bodies? Given the available time, energy, and other resources, how might they best be spent (Benveniste, 1989; Bryson, 2004b)? Essentially, political leaders manipulate the costs and benefits of actions, so supporters are more motivated to act in desired directions and opponents are less motivated to resist.

Leaders can affect outcomes in arenas dramatically by *agenda control*—influencing what items come up for decision in the first place, and which do not, thereby becoming a *nondecision* in the latter case (Bachrach & Baratz, 1962; Crosby & Bryson, 2005). Decision outcomes also can be affected by *strategic voting* in which participants use their knowledge of voting rules and manipulation of their vote resource to steer outcomes in directions they favor. *Issue framing*—reshaping the way issues are viewed—also can have dramatic effects on how people vote (Riker, 1986). For example, in the case of MetroGIS, the advocates of creating cross-region public databases were able to help county commissioners see information about local land parcels in a new way. County officials and administrators had tended to view the information as a proprietary asset; now they were being persuaded to see it as a resource that could be vastly improved if it were pooled with other counties' information and organized with geospatial technology.

4. *Build winning, sustainable coalitions.* For strategic planning to be effective, a coalition of support must be built for the process and its outcomes (Bolman & Deal, 2008). The coalition in place must be strong enough to adopt intended strategies and to defend them during implementation. Building winning coalitions can be pretty gritty work. As Riker (1986, p. 52) notes, "Politics is winning and losing, which depend, mostly, on how large and strong one side is relative to the other. The actions of politics consist in making agreements to join people in alliances and coalitions—hardly the stuff to release readers' adrenaline as do seductions, quarrels, or chases." Finding ideas (visions, goals, strategies) that people can support that further their interests is a large part of the process, but so is making deals in which something is traded in exchange for that support.

5. *Avoid bureaucratic imprisonment.* Political leaders in government, particularly, may find their ability to make and implement needed decisions severely constrained by the bureaucracies in which they serve. Those bureaucracies usually have intricate institutionalized rules and procedures and entrenched personnel that hamper any kind of change. Leaders committed to change must continually challenge the rules, or else find their way around them. Whenever possible, they should try to win over members of the bureaucracy—for example, by appealing to shared goals (Behn, 1991)—or by enlisting insiders distressed by the inhibiting aspects of rules (Kelman, 2005). When necessary, they should appeal over the heads of resistant bureaucrats to high-level decision makers or to key external stakeholders (Burns, 1978; Kouzes & Posner, 2008; Hill & Lynn, 2009).

ENFORCING NORMS, SETTLING DISPUTES, AND MANAGING RESIDUAL CONFLICTS

Leaders are always called upon to be ethical, not least when they are handling conflict. Disputes and residual conflicts are likely to arise during the implementation of strategies. The decisions made in arenas are unlikely to cover all of the details and difficulties that may come up during implementation. These residual or subsidiary conflicts must be handled constructively, either in other arenas or through the use of formal or informal courts, both to address the difficulty at hand *and* to reinforce or change important norms governing the organization. The following tasks are vital to exercising ethical leadership.

1. *Understand the design and use of formal and informal courts.* Courts operate whenever two actors having a conflict rely on a third party (leader, manager, facilitator, mediator, arbitrator, judge) to help them address it. Managing conflict and settling disputes not only take care of the issue at hand, but also reinforce the important societal or organizational norms used to handle it. Leaders must be skilled in the design and use of formal and informal courts, the settings for enforcing ethical principles, constitutions, and laws, and for managing residual conflicts and settling disputes (Crosby & Bryson, 2005). Formal courts theoretically provide the ultimate social sanctions for conduct mandated or promoted through formal policymaking arenas, but in practice the informal court of public opinion can be even more powerful. In the MetroGIS case, for example, Randall Johnson and his staff must be sure to honor licensing arrangements that are backed up by formal courts. They also rely on the court of public opinion to sanction the conduct of data suppliers and users. As the Loft promotes increased use of Web-based technologies to foster creative writing, its leaders must worry about breaches of privacy that can lead to formal court action and think about how to use the court of public opinion to sanction misuse of electronic forums.

2. *Foster organizational (collaboration, community) integrity and educate others about ethics, constitutions, laws, and norms.* In nurturing public organizations, collaborations, and communities that advance the common good, leaders must adopt practices and systems that align collective actions with espoused principles (Frederickson, 1997). Such leaders make a public commitment to ethical principles and then manifest them in their own behavior. They involve stakeholders in ethical analysis and decision making, inculcate a sense of personal responsibility in followers, and reward ethical behavior.

3. *Apply constitutions, laws, and norms to specific cases.* Constitutions are usually broad frameworks establishing basic organizational purposes, structures, and procedures. Laws, though much more narrowly drawn, still typically apply to broad classes of people or actions; moreover, they may emerge from the legislative process containing purposeful omissions and generalities that were necessary to obtain enough votes for passage (Posner, 1985). Therefore, both constitutions and laws require authoritative interpretation as they are applied to specific cases. In the U.S. judicial system, judges, jurors, and attorneys, and even interest groups filing *amicus curiae* briefs, all contribute to that authoritative interpretation. Outside the formal courts, leaders typically must apply norms, rather than laws.

4. *Adapt constitutions, laws, and norms to changing times.* Judicial principles endure even as the conditions that prompted them and the people who created them change dramatically. Sometimes public leaders are able to reshape the law to current needs in legislative, executive, or administrative arenas; often, however, as Neely (1981) suggests, leaders must ask formal courts to mandate a change because vested interests that tend to oppose change hold sway over the executive and legislative branches. In other words, sometimes strategic issues involve the need to change the rules for making rules (Hill & Hupe, 2009) (see Exhibit 6.1).

5. *Resolve conflicts among constitutions, laws, and norms.* Ethical leaders working through the courts must find legitimate bases for deciding among conflicting principles. This may mean relying on judicial enforcement, or on reconciliation of constitutions, laws, and norms. Conflict management and dispute resolution methods typically emphasize the desirability of finding principles or norms that all can support as legitimate bases for settling disputes (Fisher & Ury, 1991; Thompson, 2008). Obviously, these principles and norms should be applied in such a way that the public interest is served and the common good is advanced.

   One of the best tests for discerning the public interest or common good is asking whether respect for future generations is implied in an outcome, which, as Lewis and Gilman (2005, p. 47) point out, typically requires an understanding of the context and "accommodating rather than spurning the important values, principles, and interests at stake." Another test is to look for empathy: are public and nonprofit leaders to act as stewards of the vulnerable, dependent, and politically inarticulate—meaning those mostly likely to be left out of deliberations (Lewis & Gilman, 2005; see also Block, 2009)?

SUMMARY: PUTTING IT ALL TOGETHER AND PREPARING FOR ONGOING STRATEGIC CHANGE

The tasks of leadership for strategic planning are complex and many. Unless the organization is very small, no single person or group can perform them all. Effective strategic planning is a collective phenomenon, typically involving sponsors, champions, facilitators, teams, task forces, and others in various ways at various times. Over the course of a strategy change cycle, leaders of many different kinds must put together the elements we have described in such a way that enhances organizational collaboration, or community effectiveness—thereby making some important part of the world noticeably better. Personal and collective reflection and deliberation are warranted at many points along the way to consider whether the right people are in the right roles at the right time; whether the content and pace of change, and the approach to it, should be modified; what has been accomplished so far; and what remains to be done. By maintaining awareness of progress, celebrating resilience in the face of setbacks, publicizing the tangible and intangible benefits of the planning process, and continually developing collective leadership and followership, leaders can help their organizations, collaborations, and communities become places in which strategic thinking, acting, and learning simply become the way things are done. In short, for strategic planning and management to be effective, caring and committed leadership and followership are essential. As Dr. Seuss (1971, p. 52) points out in *The Lorax:*

> UNLESS someone like you cares a whole awful lot,
> nothing is going to get better.
> It's not.

CHAPTER TWELVE

Getting Started with Strategic Planning

With hope it is, hope that can never die,
Effort, and expectation, and desire,
And something ever more about to be.
—William Wordsworth, *The Prelude*

Previous chapters presented an overview of strategic planning, an introduction to the Strategy Change Cycle, detailed guidance on working through the process, and a discussion of the leadership roles in strategic planning. This chapter will present a number of guidelines on how public and nonprofit organizations and communities interested in strategic planning might proceed with the process.

THE THREE EXAMPLES REVISITED

How have our three examples—one government organization, one nonprofit organization, and one cross-sector collaboration—fared with strategic planning? Each has achieved notable successes, and each also has encountered challenges to its ability to think, act, and learn strategically. A number of lessons can be drawn from each organization's experience. The lessons have been discussed before, particularly in Chapters Two through Ten, but they become more concrete in relation to specific cases.

MetroGIS

The first MetroGIS strategic plan was adopted in 1996 and was followed by subsequent plans (virtually all of which have been implemented) up to the present plan (Bryson, Crosby, & Bryson, 2009); The most recent MetroGIS

2008–2011 Business Plan (strategic plan) was adopted by the MetroGIS Policy Board on October 17, 2007. The main elements of the plan were outlined in Chapter Ten. By the end of 2010 a great deal of progress had been made on implementing the plan, but a number of challenges must still be dealt with. Progress has been made in the following ways: First, MetroGIS successfully passed leadership of the policy board from the longtime chair, county commissioner Victoria Reinhardt, to suburban mayor Terry Schneider. The change recognizes that to date counties have been the major contributors of GIS data and solutions, but that now cities will be critical for addressing the next-generation shared information and application needs (for example, for property transaction–based address data and street centerline–based regional data solutions). Second, *framework Web services* (Geocoder Service, Best Image Service, Proximity Finder Service, and Data Synchronizer for Address Point Dataset) have been produced to facilitate accessibility and usefulness of numerous GIS data solutions. Third, MetroGIS gained needed political and technical support to develop a nationally unprecedented regional address points dataset that will eventually involve some eight million discrete address points in a seamless, seven-county dataset, updated on a property transaction-by-transaction basis by local address authorities (mainly cities) as they create and modify addresses. Fourth, after considerable debate and dialogue, geospatial data managers across the region decided that it made sense to clearly define shared information needs across sectors as a prelude to successfully defining needed cross-sector partnerships, which is a priority of the policy board. For much of 2009, the managers believed that defining shared Web service needs was the way to define needed cross-sector partnerships, but that approach did not work. Ultimately they decided that the best way to approach cross-sector collaboration was to start at the more basic level of shared information needs. Fifth, MetroGIS has placed a renewed emphasis on defining the benefits it provides to the public as a result of having organizations collaborate to address shared information needs—because attaining sufficient and stable funding has been an ongoing challenge, and because state and local governments are under serious pressure to cut costs. Progress on this front has included projects to define performance measures for all areas of the MetroGIS agenda and a federally funded study to create a replicable model indicating how it is possible to create public value when parcel data are placed in the public domain. Sixth, four members of the MetroGIS Policy Board and the chair of the coordinating committee accepted appointments to the Statewide Geospatial Coordinating Committee representing MetroGIS, the Metropolitan Council (MC), local government, and nonprofit organizations. Finally, Randall Johnson was named one of two regional representatives to the National Geospatial Advisory Committee in part as an acknowledgement of the success of MetroGIS. His work on the governance subcommittee appears to have had an impact on shaping the objectives for the next generation National Spatial Data Infrastructure—now known as the National Geospatial Platform.

There also are substantial challenges. The first is the need to sustain commitment to MetroGIS from new policymakers to enable the organization to continue to aggressively pursue collaborative solutions to shared information needs. The champions for MetroGIS at the Metropolitan Council on the council itself and among senior executives will all be leaving soon as a result of state elections and retirements. The MC's regional administrator and all of the council members are gubernatorial appointees and the vast majority will be replaced as a result of the 2010 state elections. The second is the need to find a financially sustainable governance structure that is also an integral component of state and national geospatial information platforms. Because MetroGIS is a voluntary organization, acquiring an adequate and reliable financial base has always been problematic. The third challenge is related to the second, and that is the need to clearly articulate the public benefit that MetroGIS provides in a way that justifies the public costs. This is a challenge facing most public and nonprofit organizations these days, but the challenge is particularly acute for MetroGIS as a completely voluntary cross-sector collaboration. The challenge of defining public benefit was made more difficult by the current strategic plan's emphasis on shared geospatial applications, the defining of which proved daunting because MetroGIS leadership did not have a solid understanding of current shared information needs. This problem is in the process of being rectified. Finally, sustaining the support and commitment from all important stakeholder communities is essential to MetroGIS's continued viability.

MetroGIS is clearly a strategic planning success story. In its first and second strategic planning efforts the organization mapped out its mission, goals, and key issue areas, developed strategies to address them, adopted the best ones, and then worked hard to ensure that the plan was implemented. MetroGIS staff housed at the Metropolitan Council and hundreds of other people were the implementers. Prior plans have been implemented and the goals and initiatives of the current strategic plan are on their way to being fully achieved. All the advocates along the way were inspired by a hope of "something ever more about to be." William Wordsworth would be proud of them.

The lessons from the MetroGIS experience seem clear. First, unless the top decision makers are fully committed to strategic planning, it is unlikely to succeed in the organization as a whole. Again, there simply is no substitute for that kind of leadership. Second, one of the biggest innovations that strategic planning promotes is the habit of focusing key decision makers' attention on what is truly important. Both strategic planning processes helped the key decision makers and staff identify the key issues, figure out what to do about them, and follow through. There is simply no substitute for that kind of often quite time-consuming (especially in MetroGIS's case) dialogue and deliberation.

Third, if strategic planning is to be really effective in an organization that has a governing board, the board itself must understand and *own* the process. Fourth, the board must understand what it means to be an effective policymaking body and must act the part (Chait, Ryan, & Taylor, 2004; Carver, 2006). The strategic planning process can help policy boards be better policymaking bodies. Fifth, strategic planning is an iterative process that can lead to surprising understandings—and to new and more effective rounds of strategic thought and action. The 1995–1996 strategic planning effort resulted in a new organization that went on to win national and international awards. The 2007 strategic planning effort resulted in a new mission for the organization.

Sixth, staff must be assigned to work on what is truly important. A good plan would not have been prepared and adopted and the plan's contents would not have been implemented had not Randall Johnson and others followed through. Here is a place where process champions are again critical. The most important champion in this case was Randall Johnson, without whose single-minded efforts MetroGIS would not have been created and sustained. He diligently and faithfully followed through and made sure that what was necessary occurred—no matter how overworked, tired, or frustrated he became. Strong support from further up the MC hierarchy, among key local government officials, and the staffs of numerous government, business, and nonprofit organizations also helped. The strategic planning consultants also provided support, encouragement, and needed insights at key points. And facilitators were often used to help various groups work through difficult issues.

Seventh, if strategic discussions precede budgeting efforts, budgets may be prepared and reviewed in light of their consequences for the public or nonprofit organization or collaboration as a whole. These days it is becoming increasingly important to demonstrate that the organization creates significant public value at reasonable cost. If the demonstration can be made, then even in an era when public officials and the citizenry are quite opposed to new spending in general, it may be possible to create a persuasive case for needed funding. Eighth, advocates of strategic planning and plans must be prepared for disruptions, delays, and unexpected events, because they are almost bound to happen. The slowdown that resulted from the challenge to MetroGIS's existence that in turn prompted a program evaluation audit is an example.

Ninth, strategic planning by itself is not enough. The key decision makers in the system (in this case the policy board members and MC officials) must be willing to take effective political action to promote strategic thought, action, and learning. Policy board chair Victoria Reinhardt in particular stands out in this regard. To my mind she is clearly a public sector heroine. Though it didn't happen in the MetroGIS case, I have certainly seen instances where some decision makers may need to be sacrificed in order to get needed changes introduced. Hope and courage are necessary—but not costless—civic virtues. Public leaders must be willing to pay the price when necessary.

The Loft Literary Center

In 2007, the Loft embarked on a new five-year strategic plan to carry it through 2012. By the end of 2010 most of what was in the plan had been accomplished, but not without considerable pain along the way. The economic crisis affected fundraising, and a local foundation that for years had provided operating funds announced that it would quit funding the arts. Nonetheless, the Loft stayed focused on its priorities and moved forward. While the staff was reduced from nineteen to sixteen employees through layoffs of support staff, and the remaining staff took pay cuts and worked longer hours, important programs continued and new ones were added. But by 2010 the executive director and board also believed that the world had changed enough that it was important to revisit the plan's priorities. A broadly consultative process involving a member survey and work with the board and staff was undertaken to come up with a new set of ranked priorities by the end of 2010 to guide the organization through the financially unpredictable next several years.

Many noteworthy accomplishments have occurred since adoption of the 2007–2012 strategic plan. First, the Loft celebrated its thirty-fifth anniversary in June 2010 and remains the nation's premier comprehensive literary center and a model for similar organizations across the country. Second, in spite of the financial hardships, the Loft won a national award as a psychologically healthy workplace. Third, writing mentorship and apprenticeship series have continued, expanded, or been initiated. Fourth, program outreach has expanded, including to Minnesota's socially, economically, and ethnically diverse communities (for example, Latino, African American, African, Asian, and Native American communities). Fifth, programs for youths and seniors have been expanded. Sixth, in the 2009–2010 fiscal year there were 6,500 class enrollments and 78 new course instructors. Classes offered included, for example, poetry, fiction, memoir, mystery and thriller writing, graphic novels, blogging, and screenwriting. Seventh, the Loft is moving into offering online courses, in part in recognition of the significant interest in its Web site to which hits increased by 30 percent in the 2009–2010 fiscal year. The Loft's first online class pilot program sold out immediately. And finally, the Loft's blog *Writers' Block* has become an increasingly lively Web space for sharing ideas.

Many of the lessons from the MetroGIS case apply to the Loft (and to the Minneapolis Park and Recreation Board). Rather than repeat them, however, we will focus on five particularly apparent ones. First, leadership counts (Crosby & Bryson, 2005). The Loft's senior administrators and board members are and have been thoughtful, service-oriented professionals deeply committed to the organization's mission. They are dedicated to providing high-quality, cost-effective programs that create substantial public value. They understand how to be effective sponsors and champions and know when to involve stakeholders, consultants, and facilitators. And they have tried to be wise about which projects to pursue, how to build support, and how to garner needed resources. Former executive director Linda Myers and current executive director Jocelyn Hale have made good use of their well-developed social and political skills.

Second, strategic planning and strategy change are almost always about culture change. The dramatic changes under way in information and communication technology are starting to have major effects on the process of writing, on teaching writing, and on the creation and maintenance of writing communities. The frequency of online instruction is increasingly making it possible to do asynchronously what previously had to happen synchronously and vice versa. Essentially costless videoconferencing technology (for example, Skype) makes it possible to have "face-to-face" tutorials while the parties are thousands of miles apart. YouTube and podcasts offer new avenues of instruction. Communities of interest can be maintained via Facebook. And so on. All of these changes have involved culture changes of some sort. The Loft's board and executive director realize they are behind the technology curve, particularly in comparison with their younger existing and potential audiences. Without paying attention to the culture—what is good about it and what needs changing—strategy change is unlikely to succeed. And productive culture changes only happen when leaders are committed to it over long periods of time.

Third, it takes times and effort to gain widespread appreciation of an organization as a whole—and when the organization is involved in a host of collaborative relationships, or relies extensively on volunteers and voluntary contributions, it takes even longer. (This lesson also applies with special force to MetroGIS.) A great deal of dialogue and deliberation was necessary before a fuller understanding of the Loft, its varied stakeholders and relationships, and strategies likely to be effective emerged and ultimately were synthesized in the strategic plan. There is no substitute for this kind of conversation; people must reach their own conclusions in their own time through conversation with others—and it all takes time.

Fourth, it is important to blend what is ongoing with what is new. The Loft has kept many programs while it added or phased out others. In other words, the strategic planning effort had to be about what was existing and working, not just about what was new and what should stop. Finally, it really helps to have a governing board that is also an effective policy board. The Loft's board was essentially an effective policy board when the process began, and they used the process to become more effective.

The Minneapolis Park and Recreation Board

In 2007, the Park Board adopted its first strategic plan in almost forty years. A very participative process was used to develop the plan. As noted in Chapter Seven, the plan is organized according to four vision themes and a set of values. The *Superintendent's Annual Report 2009* is organized according to these themes (see Exhibit 7.5) and values, which are: sustainability, visionary leadership, safety, responsiveness and innovation, and independence and focus. An impressive list of accomplishments is presented. For example, in a city of approximately 390,000 inhabitants, visits to the larger Minneapolis parks (termed *regional* parks by the Metropolitan Council) increased over 15 percent from 2007 to 15.4 million park visits. Six of the seven most visited regional parks were in the Minneapolis park system. As another example, the Park Board oversaw 600 youth sports teams attracting over 8,000 youths, and over 1,900 adult sports teams attracting 32,000 participants. Plus there were many significant investments in park infrastructure and management.

But the gains were made in a difficult financial and political environment. The 2007–2009 financial, banking, and housing crisis resulted in significant cuts in state funding to local governments, including the Park Board, and several Minneapolis City Council members began a concerted effort to amend the City Charter to have the Park Board become a city department. A major effort on the part of Park Board commissioners and a grassroots campaign in support of Park Board independence defeated the effort. The Park Board was helped by the results of a survey commissioned by the Minneapolis Parks Foundation that found massive majorities (well over 90 percent) among city residents supporting the parks and the various benefits and activities they offer, 75 percent in favor of maintaining the current governance structure, and almost 50 percent not able to think of anything they disliked about the parks. The company doing the survey said that there was an overwhelming perception among residents that the parks and lakes were "the jewel in the crown of the city and the current governance structure should be preserved" (Minneapolis Park and Recreation Board, 2009, p. 15).

But while there is major support for the parks and the governance structure, Jon Gurban the park superintendent proved far more controversial (Kaiser, 2010). Although he oversaw a successful planning process and helped maintain the Park Board's independence, he was also seen as a controversial leader to a number of people, including a few Minneapolis City Council members. Opponents felt he was not consulting widely enough about key projects, he lacked diplomacy, and he had a bad temper. With the election of three new members, and the reelection of one after a four-year break, to the Park Board in 2009, a majority on the board was in favor of not renewing Gurban's contract, which ran out at the end of June 2010. Previous superintendent David

Fisher was brought back on an interim basis and a permanent superintendent, Jayne Miller, was hired in October to begin work in November 2010. Miller has extensive experience in park management and appears to have many of the skills Gurban lacked.

The new superintendent will confront a number of major challenges (Brandt, 2010). For example, the number of full-time workers who maintain and staff the city parks has dropped from over 600 to approximately 450. A number of management positions have also been lost. If there are additional cuts in state aid, as is likely, these numbers may drop more. Meanwhile, there are also many opportunities. For example, the Mississippi riverfront will be getting renewed attention, in part because there are additional state funds for that. Some important parks are in need of redevelopment. And there is a continued need to respond to the many multicultural immigrants arriving in Minneapolis, an aging population, and other demographic changes while continuing to keep the parks safe.

There are lessons to be drawn from the Park Board case as well. First, it is tempting to speculate that a decisive, strong-willed superintendent like Jon Gurban was necessary to really get the Park Board moving again. He clearly shook things up and sponsored a major, highly participative, highly successful strategic planning process. The resident survey results reported earlier also speak well of his tenure. But the commissioners always seemed to be fairly split in their support for him, ranging from the 5–4 vote in favor of hiring him to the 6–3 vote refusing to renew his contract. His strengths may well have also been his weaknesses. The organization gained, but he ultimately lost his job.

Second, a highly participative process can help build coalitions of support that are needed not just to implement the plan, but to protect the organization. The Park Board's ability to triumph over a challenge to its independent existence, if not without anxiety and pain, may have been possible, in part, because it had worked so diligently to engage its various stakeholders in its strategic planning process. If the process had alienated key stakeholders, the challenge to the Park Board's independence might have gone further.

There are some added lessons not tied to any of the cases in particular that should be emphasized. The first lesson is that strategic planning can proceed in an evolutionary way and still have revolutionary consequences. You might consider the establishment and now institutionalization of MetroGIS over the last fifteen years as a kind of slowly occurring revolutionary change that is institutionalizing collaborative solutions to shared information needs in a way that accomplishes MetroGIS's vision that "organizations serving the Twin Cities Metropolitan Area are successfully collaborating to use geographic information technology to solve real-world problems" (www.metrogis.org/about/#what). Second, surprises should be expected (as happened in the MetroGIS case). In other words, if everyone already knows what should be done strategically, then there is no need for strategic planning. If people do not know the answer, and are open to new learning and possibilities, strategic planning can be of use. Furthermore, strategic planning can help create the organization's own desirable surprises, rather than having it need to respond to surprises sprung on it by someone else (Frentzel, Bryson, & Crosby, 2000, pp. 420–421). In other words, strategic planning can facilitate an important shift in a group's thinking to the point that some things that once were only possibilities become givens (Mangham and Overington, 1987). Here is an example—and fourth lesson— that fits de Gues's (1988, p. 71) observation that "the real purpose of strategic planning is not to make plans but to change the mental models decision makers carry in their heads." Recall Mintzberg's observation (1994, p. 252), noted earlier, that "Organizations function on the basis of commitment and mindset." Strategic planning can help alter the premises and binding choices that govern behavior. Fifth, all of the cases strongly emphasize a lesson about the importance of forums in any strategic planning process that bridges organizational boundaries. Sixth, a very important lesson concerns the need to fit strategic planning to other ongoing processes in an organization.

Seventh, operational detail can overwhelm strategic planning efforts. Even though each organization has been successful at strategic planning, it still took each one a fairly long time to get through the process. Often attention to the day-to-day simply drove out attention to the long term. It takes a real commitment to find the time to attend to what is fundamental on a regular basis. This may well be the most important discipline that strategic planning is designed to promote. Without it, strategic thinking, acting, and learning among a group of senior decision makers is not likely to occur. Strategic planning cannot be simply an add-on to already overworked leaders, managers, and staff. Eighth, quicker really can be better. If the challenges are serious and imminent— bankruptcy, for example—a lengthy and elaborate strategic planning process can doom the organization to an early death. Ninth, simpler can be better, too. Focusing on the most critical issues in a direct and timely way and developing effective strategies to address them may be all that is needed. Such a process would not be data heavy, although some key quantitative and qualitative data is likely to be necessary. Instead, it will be heavy on strategic thinking, acting, and learning. Finally, if there is no real reason to plan strategically—no major threats or important opportunities—then *perhaps* strategic planning is a waste of time. "Muddling through" may work acceptably until strategic planning does become necessary.

GETTING STARTED

These three cases along with the others cited in the book indicate that strategic planning can help public and nonprofit organizations and communities fulfill their missions, meet their mandates, create public value, and satisfy their key

stakeholders more effectively. These cases also indicate that a number of difficulties and challenges must be overcome if strategic planning is to fulfill its
promise for organizations. Let me conclude with some advice about how to
get started with strategic planning:

1. *Start where you and the other people who might be involved in or
   affected by the process currently are.* This is one of the most
   important principles for organizing collective action (Rubin & Rubin,
   2007; Kahn, 2010). You can always undertake strategic planning for
   the part of the organization you control. Whatever you are in charge
   of—a unit, department, division, or a whole organization—you can
   always start there. But wherever you start, you must also keep in
   mind where the participants currently are. Other involved or affected
   parties are likely to need some education concerning the purposes,
   processes, and products of strategic planning. If they are important
   for the formulation or implementation of strategies, you will need to
   bring them along so that they can be effective supporters and
   implementers.

2. *Have a compelling reason to undertake strategic planning.* Otherwise,
   the process is not likely to be worth the effort, or to reach a
   satisfactory conclusion. The obverse of this lesson is that people can
   create an infinite number of reasons *not* to engage in strategic
   planning, even when it would be the best thing for the organization
   or community; such reasons may be nothing more than excuses. The
   reasons that might be compelling are numerous. The organization or
   community may be performing well, but key decision makers may be
   fully aware of important strategic issues that must be addressed if the
   organization is to continue to do well. That was the case for the Loft,
   which had essentially accomplished everything in its prior strategic
   plan—but key decision makers knew that advances in information
   and communication technology were beginning to have profound
   effects on writing, education, and management, and that the Loft was
   facing the prospect of a major leadership transition sometime in the
   foreseeable future. MetroGIS had also accomplished virtually
   everything in its prior strategic plan, which focused primarily on
   achieving collaborative regional solutions to several geospatial data
   needs shared by core stakeholders and instituting an effective
   Internet-based means to discover and access existing geospatial data.
   During the second strategic planning process, MetroGIS leadership
   expanded the initial data-centric focus to include pursuing solutions
   to shared Web service and geospatial application needs that were not
   considered during the initial process, because the technology did not

exist. MetroGIS leadership also agreed to seriously seek out solutions important to addressing needs shared not just by governments, but by nonprofits and businesses as well.

An organization may feel threatened by the emergence of strong rivals. Periodically over its history the Park Board had had to fight for its independence against arguments that the public would be better served by fully integrating the organization with the City of Minneapolis. The fractious relationships at the beginning of the strategic planning process among Park Board commissioners and the difficulties of hiring a new superintendent raised concerns among some stakeholder groups and in the mainstream press, the Minneapolis mayor's office, and the Minneapolis City Council. While it is true there is no direct connection between the initiation of strategic planning by the Park Board and challenges to its independence, it is also true that the successful strategic planning process probably helped the Park Board defend itself against the serious challenge to its independence once it occurred.

In another scenario, an organization may be confronting a real turning point in its history—a point that could lead to success or extermination. Recall that organizational strategies are usually fairly stable for rather long periods of time during which strategic planning is usually more concerned with programming strategy implementation than with formulation of whole new strategies. That was the case for the Park Board, the Loft, and MetroGIS. But then, after long periods of stability, come significant shifts—either as a result of changes in the environment or new leadership visions. At such times strategic planning is much more concerned with enhancing strategy formulation (Gersick, 1991; Mintzberg & Westley, 1992; Mintzberg, Ahlstrand, & Lampel, 2009). Such was the case with MetroGIS, which faced a serious threat to its existence from the program evaluation audit. Once the audit was passed with flying colors and MetroGIS's substantial return on investment was verified, MetroGIS was again endorsed by the Metropolitan Council. The stage was set for the second round of strategic planning in which the mission was changed from a more data-centric approach to institutionalizing use of geospatial technology and collaborative solutions to shared geospatial needs and spreading use of geospatial technology to enhance the capabilities and performance of the organizations serving the Minneapolis–St. Paul metropolitan area. As the new strategies unfold it is entirely possible that a *quantum change* in the organization may occur (Miller & Friesen, 1984)—although that result was clearly not anticipated at the beginning of the process or fully appreciated at the end of the process. Yet another reason is that the organization may feel the need for strategic planning but not engage in the process until ordered to do so by decision makers further up the hierarchy. That was not the case with any of the three organizations, but it can happen; indeed, federal legislation and many states now require certain organizations to engage in strategic planning. But whatever the compelling reason, organizational or community members—especially key decision makers—must see some important benefits to be derived from strategic planning, or they will not be active supporters and participants. And if they do not support and participate, the process is bound to fail.

3. *Remember there is no substitute for leadership.* The concepts, procedures, tools, and practices that strategic planning comprises cannot think, act, or learn by themselves. Nor can they inspire and mobilize others to act on behalf of what is best for an organization (collaboration or community). Only concerned and committed people—leaders and followers—can do that. Broad-based, collective leadership spread throughout an organization is necessary to assure that it fulfills its mission, meets its mandates, creates real public value, and satisfies the expectations of its key stakeholders. And when the organization succeeds, it is a collective accomplishment.

Two leadership roles are especially important to the success of any strategic planning effort: *sponsoring* and *championing.* Unless the process is sponsored (ultimately, if not initially) by important and powerful leaders and decision makers, it is likely to fail. Only key decision makers who are also effective leaders will be able to motivate and guide their organizations through a successful strategic thinking, acting, and learning process. Leadership from the key decision makers is absolutely necessary if the organization itself must be changed as a result of strategic planning. A strategic planning process will not succeed unless it is championed by someone. This person should believe in the process and see his or her role as promoting effective thinking, acting, and learning on the part of key decision makers. A process champion does not have a preconceived view of what the key issues are facing the organization or a preconceived set of answers to those issues, but he or she pushes a process that is likely to produce effective answers. It certainly helps if the process champion is near the top of the organization chart. That was the case for Jennifer Ringold at the Park Board and Jocelyn Hale at the Loft. Randall Johnson was the champion of the MetroGIS process and was four levels down from the top of the Metropolitan Council, but he had the support of senior managers in the MC and of the MetroGIS policy board. But it does not hurt to have other champions from other levels. Indeed, the process is likely to be more effective if more than one champion is involved. A third leadership role—*facilitating*—also can be very important, though I would not place it in the same category as the first two. Facilitation is a special skill and can be very important at particular points, especially during the design of the process and as groups of participants learn how to work effectively together (Schwarz, 2002; Kaner & Associates, 2007).

4. *When designing a strategic planning process, always be attentive to the requirements for success in the situation at hand and tailor the process according to the needs of the organization, collaboration, or community and situation.* As noted in Chapter Two, the Strategy Change Cycle highlights the need to have a strategic planning process design that includes:

- Having a process sponsor or sponsors and a process champion or champions
- Carefully designing and using a series of settings for deliberation—formal and informal forums, arenas, and courts
- Emphasizing the development of the initial agreement(s)
- Intensely attending to stakeholders via careful analysis and effective engagement
- Gaining clarity about mission and mandates and knowing the difference between the two
- Understanding the organization's internal and external environments
- Focusing on the identification and clarification of strategic issues and knowing there is an array of available approaches for doing so
- Seeing strategies as a response to strategic issues and knowing there are many approaches to formulating strategies, including incorporating useful aspects of existing or emerging strategies
- Attending to the requirements for successful strategy implementation and evaluation
- Building capacity for ongoing implementation, learning, and strategic change
- Periodically reassessing strategies and the strategic planning process as a prelude to the next round of strategic planning
- Remaining flexible throughout the process, while still paying attention to all necessary requirements that must be met along the way and the logic that links them

Strategic planning efforts clearly must fit the situation at hand, even if the ultimate aim of the process is to change the situation (Mintzberg, Ahlstrand, & Lampel, 2009). The roles that official planners play in the process also will depend on the situation. In most cases involving strategic planning across units or levels within an organization or a community, planners will need to facilitate strategic thought, action, and learning by key decision makers. In other situations, planners also will be called upon to serve as technical experts. Another key situational factor concerns the presence or absence of the necessary formal and informal forums (for discussion), arenas (for decision making and implementation), and formal or informal courts (for managing residual conflicts and enforcing underlying norms). These are the settings within which strategic planning and implementation will occur, and the ways they are designed and used are important to the success of the process (Crosby & Bryson, 2005, 2010). For example, if it is clear that key strategic issues bridge organizational boundaries, then it is probably necessary to create forums to discuss the issues that also bridge the boundaries. Forums may include strategic planning teams, task forces, or discussion groups. Similarly, if implementation will require coordinated action across boundaries, some sort of arena-like mechanism to manage the process across those boundaries may be necessary. Appropriate mechanisms could include a policy board, cabinet, interagency coordinating council, project management group, or community leadership council. Court-like vehicles to manage residual conflicts also are likely to be needed. Referral procedures up administrative hierarchies, alternative dispute-resolution mechanisms, administrative tribunals, or access to the formal courts may be needed.

The strategic plans themselves must also be tailored to fit the situation. It may be important, for example, not to prepare a written strategic plan. Indeed, some of the best strategic "plans" I have seen were unwritten agreements among key decision makers about what was important and what actions they would take. In other cases, plans will consist of informal letters, memoranda of agreement, issue-specific strategy documents, or full-blown glossy publications and Web sites intended for public consumption. It all depends on the purposes to be served by the plan. A final area of needed situational sensitivity concerns the evaluative criteria used to assess strategies and plans. Viable strategies and plans will need to be politically acceptable, technically and administratively workable, and legally and ethically justifiable—a severe test, given the many stakeholders who are likely to be involved or affected. To find strategies that can satisfy the various stakeholders means that leaders, managers, and planners will need to be willing to construct and consider arguments geared to many different evaluative criteria.

5. *Remember that the big innovation in strategic planning is having key decision makers talk with one another about what is truly important for the organization, collaboration, or community as a whole.* A strategic planning process is merely a way of helping key decision makers think, act, and learn strategically. In no way can the process substitute for the presence, participation, support, and commitment of key decision makers to raise and resolve the critical issues facing the organization, collaboration, or community. The initiation and institutionalization of the process, however, can provide the occasions, settings, and justification for gathering key decision makers together to think, act, and learn strategically on behalf of the organization, collaboration, or community. In all too many cases, such occasions, settings, and justifications do not exist, and organization, collaboration, and community performance and stakeholder satisfaction suffer accordingly.

6. *Be aware that the resource most needed to undertake strategic planning is not money but the attention and commitment of key decision makers.* Strategic planning is not expensive in dollar terms, but it is expensive when you consider the resources that typically are most scarce—the attention and commitment of key decision makers. For organizations, strategic planning may involve having key decision makers spend up to 10 percent of their ordinary work time working together to identify and address fundamental policy questions. That may not seem like much. Indeed, one might argue that decision makers unwilling to devote up to 10 percent of their work time to what is truly important for the organization are either incompetent or disloyal and ought to be fired! But realistically, for a variety of reasons it is hard to persuade key decision makers to commit more than 10 percent of their time to strategic planning. The reasons include the fact that the urgent often drives out the important and what is routine drives out what is nonroutine. But beyond that, because major strategy changes are relatively rare, many decision makers realize that strategic planning usually focuses on strategy implementation rather than strategy formulation. Thus, strategic planning may seem redundant to them, repeating what they are already doing, or it may appear less glamorous and important than its sponsors and champions think. In addition, decision makers may be justifiably concerned that strategic planning will drive out strategic thought, action, and learning or may unreasonably or unwisely limit their own discretion. Or they may simply be afraid of the

consequences, conflictual or otherwise, that may result from focusing on particular strategic issues. For whatever reason, it is simply hard to get much attention for the process in most situations. And it may even be more difficult to get substantial blocks of time from community leaders for community strategic planning. Strategic planning processes are also likely to be thrown off track by various disruptions and delays. Strategic planning processes in which I have been involved have been thrown off course by elections, promotions, firings, crises, scandals, deaths and life-threatening illnesses, planned and unplanned pregnancies, horrible public gaffes, and chance events both favorable and unfavorable of numerous sorts. Such eventualities are normal, and sponsors and champions should expect them. Also, strong sponsors and champions are necessary to keep key decision makers focused on what is important, so that wise strategic thought, action, and learning are not lost in the disruptions and delays.

Given the difficulties of getting key decision makers' attention, an effective strategic planning process is therefore likely to be one that is fairly simple (simpler is better), quick (quicker is better), and treated in a special and sensitive way so that key decision makers will give the time and attention it needs when needed. In addition, it is important that sponsors and champions think of *junctures* (or timing) as a key temporal metric. Time in strategic planning is generally not linear (*chronos*) or characterized by peaks or optimal experiences (*kyros*). Instead, it is *junctural:* key people must come together at the right time with the right information in order to discuss what is important and do something effective about it (Albert & Bell, 2002). The ability to think juncturally, to think about timing, is a special skill that must be cultivated (particularly by sponsors and champions) if the strategic planning process is to be successful (Bryson & Roering, 1988, 1989).

7. *Remember that the biggest payoffs from strategic planning may come in surprising ways or from surprising sources.* For example, organizations often find that organizational development, team building, and heightened morale throughout the organization are among the greatest benefits derived from a strategic planning process. The Park Board found it had to concentrate on new and enhanced ways of engaging its many stakeholders. The Loft has found it must continually engage with issues involving information and communication technology (ICT) and major gaps in ICT skill levels across generations. MetroGIS stakeholders were surprised to find themselves endorsing a change in the organization's mission at the

end of the 2007 strategy mapping session that marked the public launch of the most recent strategic planning process. There is no telling what will happen as a result of the strategic planning process. But the organization, collaboration, or community that is open to surprises may create and take advantage of its own opportunities. As Louis Pasteur said, "Fortune favors the prepared mind."

8. *Outside consultation and facilitation can help.* Often organizations, collaborations, and communities need some consultation, facilitation, and education from outsiders to help with the design and management of the strategic planning process. The Park Board, the Loft, and MetroGIS each relied on outside help of various kinds at various points throughout the strategic planning process. If help is needed, try to get it.

9. *If the going gets tough, keep in mind the potential benefits of the process.* Recall that strategic planning can help organizations, collaborations, and communities in a number of ways. For example, strategic planning can help organizations and communities:

- Think, act, and learn strategically and develop effective strategies
- Clarify future direction and establish priorities
- Improve decision making by:
  - Making today's decisions in light of their future consequences
  - Developing a coherent and defensible basis for decision making, and
  - Making decisions across levels and functions
- Exercise maximum discretion in the areas under organizational control
- Solve major organizational and community problems
- Improve organizational, community, or broader system performance
- Deal effectively with rapidly changing circumstances
- Develop capacities to address future problems or challenges
- Build teamwork and expertise

But it may not be easy to achieve these benefits. The faith of process sponsors and champions is often sorely tried, particularly if the organization or community is engaged in strategic planning for the first time. For example, the process seems particularly prone to disintegration in the middle—the strategic issue identification and strategy development steps. And the big payoffs may take a long time to achieve. For instance, it may take several years to know whether some important strategy has worked or not. In the meantime, therefore, try to label as much as possible that comes out of the process a success—count every small win and work hard to improve the process along the way. In order to maintain enthusiasm for the process until successes tied directly to implemented strategies began to appear, the Loft emphasized—even celebrated—the achievements and benefits of the process as they occurred. Thus, the process was managed so that it was "successful" long before any strategies were implemented. It also is useful for sponsors and champions to do what they can to maintain an optimistic stance toward the world—to see difficulties as specific rather than pervasive, temporary rather than permanent, and as something that can be changed (Seligman, 2006). They should do what they can to build their own and others' psychological hardiness through building commitment to the organization's mission, building a sense of control over the organization's future, and seeing difficulties as manageable challenges (Kouzes & Posner, 2008). Sponsors and champions also should be realistic—at least with themselves—about what strategic planning might achieve. They might keep in mind, for example, what Sigmund Freud (Bruer and Freud, 2000 [1957]) told doubting patients: "Much will be gained if we succeed in transforming your hysterical misery into common unhappiness." Strategic planning will not lead to perfection, but it can result in useful, implementable strategies for addressing a few key issues—and that is something worth pursuing. By organizing hope, strategic planning can make the courageous organization's hopes reasonable. Recall also Maya Angelou's observation that "Courage is the most important of all the virtues, because without courage you can't practice any other virtue consistently. You can practice any virtue erratically, but nothing consistently without courage." Creating lasting public value almost always take committed, courageous, hopeful people—and strategic planning is a set of concepts, procedures, tools, and practices that can help such people make the world a better place.

10. *Finally, keep in mind that strategic planning is not right for every organization or community.* In the following situations, strategic planning perhaps shouldn't be undertaken (Barry, 1997):

- The roof has fallen.
- The organization or community lacks the necessary skills, resources, or commitment of key decision makers to produce a good plan.
- Costs outweigh benefits.
- The organization or community prefers to rely on the vision, intuition, and skill of extremely gifted leaders.

- Incremental adjustments or muddling through in the absence of a guiding vision, set of strategies, or plan are the only processes that will work.
- Implementation of strategic plans is extremely unlikely.

And yet, though there may be *reasons* not to undertake strategic planning, those reasons all too easily become *excuses* for not paying attention to what is really important for the organization or community. An organization or community that gives in to excuses has suffered a failure of hope and courage. Wordsworth reminds us that "our destiny, our being's heart and home" are with hope, effort, expectation, and desire. And Maya Angelou reminds us that only courage will consistently get us there.

Strategic planning can help public and nonprofit organizations and collaborations fulfill their missions, meet their mandates, and create real public value; it also can help communities serve important purposes, including the creation of public value. Said differently, strategic planning can help organizations, collaborations, and communities create a better, more productive, more effective, more satisfying value proposition for their key stakeholders. But strategic planning will only work if people want it to work. This book was written to help all those who want their organizations, collaborations, and communities to survive, prosper, and serve noble purposes. I hope it will prompt more than a few of these organizational and community citizens to proceed with strategic planning, because then significant change can occur. As Woodrow Wilson said long ago, "There is no higher religion than human service. To work for the common good is the greatest creed" (quoted in Bowman, West, & Beck, 2010, p. 1).

RESOURCES

Four resources are included. The first presents an array of stakeholder identification and analysis techniques. The second describes how Web-based tools could be used as part of a strategic planning process. The third shows how to create a *livelihood scheme* linking organizational aspirations to distinctive competencies and distinctive assets. The final resource shows how to use the *action-oriented strategy mapping process* to identify strategic issues and formulate effective strategies.

A Guide to Stakeholder Identification and Analysis Techniques

This resource focuses on how and why leaders, managers, and planners might go about using stakeholder identification and analysis techniques in order to help their organizations meet their mandates, fulfill their missions, and create public value. A range of stakeholder identification and analysis techniques is reviewed. The techniques cover the functions presented in Figure 2.4: organizing effective participation; creating meritorious ideas for mission, goals, strategies, actions, and other strategic interventions; building a winning coalition around proposal development, review, and adoption; implementing, monitoring, and evaluating strategic interventions; and building capacity for ongoing implementation, learning, and change. Wise use of stakeholder analyses can help frame issues that are solvable in ways that are technically and administratively feasible and politically acceptable, legally and morally defensible, and that create public value and advance the common good.

Figure A.1 shows how the stakeholder identification and analysis techniques fit with the simplified public and nonprofit sector strategic management theory summarized in Figure 2.4. Note, however, that there is an elaboration of one function in Figure 2.4—namely, that creating ideas for strategic interventions consists of the two connected subfunctions of formulating problems (identifying issues) and searching for solutions (developing strategies).

AN ARRAY OF TECHNIQUES

Two techniques have already been discussed in detail: Choosing Stakeholder Analysis Participants in Chapter Three and the Basic Stakeholder Analysis

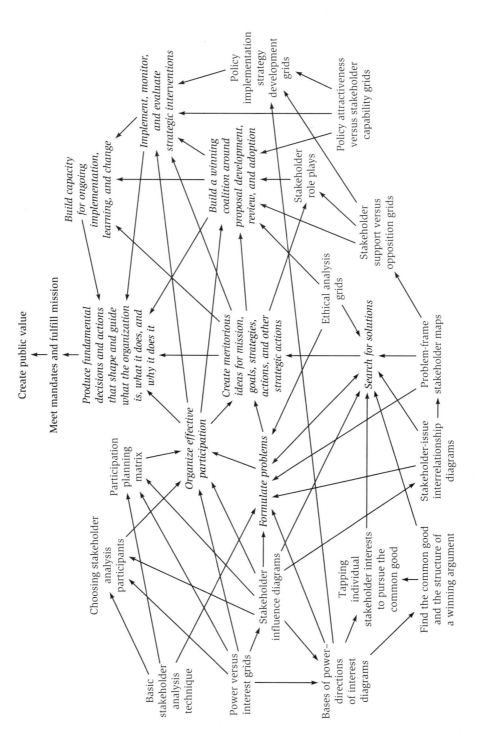

Figure A.1. Strategic Management Purposes and Functions and Stakeholder Analysis Techniques to Assist in Fulfilling Them.

Technique in Chapter Four. This resource presents an additional thirteen stakeholder identification and analysis techniques. The techniques are grouped according the functions presented in Figure A.1. All of the techniques are fairly simple in concept and rely on standard facilitation materials such as flip charts, marking pens, tape, colored stick-on dots, and so on. All it takes to do them is some time and effort—an expenditure of resources that typically is minuscule when compared with the opportunity costs of less-than-adequate performance, or even disaster, that typically follow in the wake of failing to attend to key stakeholders, their interests, and their information (Nutt, 2002).

Techniques for Organizing Participation

Stakeholder analyses are undertaken for a purpose and that purpose should be articulated as clearly as it can be before the analyses begin—while also understanding that purposes may change over time. The purpose should guide the choices concerning who should be involved in the analyses and how. Different analyses will be needed at different stages in the Strategy Change Cycle.

Deciding who should be involved, how, when, and why is a key strategic choice in doing stakeholder analyses. In general, people should be involved if they have information that cannot be gained otherwise, or if their participation is necessary to assure successful adoption and implementation of initiatives built on the analyses (Thomas, 1993, 1995). There is always a question of whether there can be too much or too little participation. The general answer to this question is, yes, of course. But the specific answer depends on the situation, and there are no hard-and-fast rules, let alone good empirical evidence, on when, where, how, and why to draw the line. There very well may be important trade-offs between early and later participation in analyses and one or more of the following: representation, accountability, analysis quality, analysis credibility, analysis legitimacy, the ability to act based on the analyses, or other factors, and these will need to be thought through. Fortunately, "the choice" actually can be approached as a sequence of choices, in which first an individual or small planning group begins the effort, and then others are added later as the advisability of doing so becomes apparent (Finn, 1996).

Five stakeholder identification and analysis techniques are particularly relevant to helping organize participation: a process for choosing stakeholder analysis participants (discussed in Chapter Three); the basic stakeholder analysis technique (discussed in Chapter Four); power versus interest grids; stakeholder influence diagrams; and the participation planning matrix.

Power Versus Interest Grids. The power versus interest grid is described in detail by Eden and Ackermann (1998, pp. 121–125, 344–346) (see Figure A.2). This grid arrays stakeholders on a two-by-two matrix where the dimensions

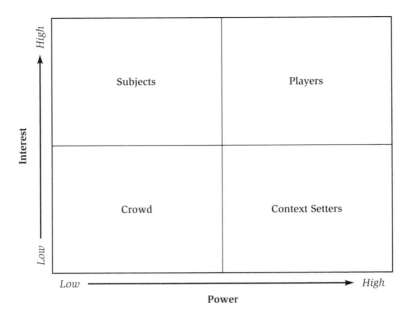

Figure A.2. Power Versus Interest Grid.

Source: Eden & Ackermann, 1998, p. 122. From *Making Strategy: The Journey of Strategic Management,* by C. Eden and F. Ackerman. Copyright © 1998 by Sage Publications, Inc. Reproduced with permission of Sage Publications via Copyright Clearance Center.

are the stakeholder's interest (in a political sense as opposed to simple inquisitiveness; see Campbell & Marshall, 2002) in the organization or issue at hand, and the stakeholder's power to affect the future of the organization or issue. Four categories of stakeholders result: players who have both an interest and significant power; subjects who have an interest but little power; context setters who have power but little direct interest; and the crowd, which consists of stakeholders with little interest or power.

The power versus interest grid helps determine the players, the people whose interests and power bases *must* be taken into account in order to address the problem or issue at hand. It also highlights coalitions to be encouraged or discouraged, behavior that should be fostered, and people whose buy-in should be sought or who should be co-opted. Finally, it provides some information on how to convince stakeholders to change their views. Interestingly, the knowledge gained from this grid can be used to help advance the interests of the relatively powerless (Bryson, Cunningham, & Lokkesmoe, 2002). Note that in some cases it may make sense to construct a *power versus identity* grid, for identity as well as interest can motivate stakeholder action; see Rowley & Moldoveanu, 2003.

A power versus interest grid is constructed as follows:

- The facilitator tapes four flip chart sheets to a wall to form a single surface two sheets high and two sheets wide.

- The facilitator draws the two axes on the surface using a marking pen. The vertical axis is labeled *interest* from *low* to *high*; the horizontal axis is labeled *power* from *low* to *high.*

- Planning team members brainstorm the names of stakeholders by writing the names of different stakeholders as they come to mind on a 1½ × 2-inch (2½ × 5-cm) self-adhesive label, one stakeholder per label. Alternatively, if the Basic Analysis Technique has been performed, the names should be taken from that list.

- The facilitator places each label in the appropriate place on the grid, guided by the deliberations and judgments of the planning group members. Labels should be collected in round-robin fashion, one label per group member, until all labels (other than duplicates) are placed on the grid or eliminated for some reason.

- Labels are moved around until all group members are satisfied with the *relative* location of each stakeholder on the grid.

- The group should discuss the implications of the resulting stakeholder placements.

- The facilitator records the results of the discussion on flip chart sheets.

Stakeholder Influence Diagrams. The *stakeholder influence diagram* indicates how the stakeholders on a power versus interest grid influence one another. The technique is taken from Eden and Ackermann (1998, pp. 349–350; see also Bryson, Cunningham, & Lokkesmoe, 2002) and begins with a power versus interest grid. The steps in developing such a diagram are as follows:

- The planning team should start with a power versus interest grid and then, for each stakeholder on the grid, suggest lines of influence from one stakeholder to another.

- The facilitator draws in the lines with a soft-lead pencil. Two-way influences are possible, but an attempt should be made to identify the primary direction in which influence flows between stakeholders.

- Team members engage in a dialogue to determine which influence relationships exist, which are most important, and what is the primary direction of influence.

- Once final agreement is reached, the pencil lines should be made permanent with a marking pen.

- Team members discuss the results and implications of the resulting diagram, including identifying who are the most influential or central stakeholders.

Participation Planning Matrix. In a sense, all the techniques considered thus far are relevant to planning for stakeholder participation. The *participation planning matrix*, however, is specifically designed for this purpose. The matrix adapts contributions from the International Association for Public Participation (2007), specifically the association's notion of a spectrum of levels of public participation and the strategic management functions identified in Figures 2.1 and A.1. The levels of participation range from a minimum of ignoring stakeholders through to empowerment, giving stakeholders or some subset of them final decision-making authority. Each level has a different objective and makes a different kind of promise—implicitly if not explicitly (see Exhibit A.1).

The matrix prompts planners to think about responding to or engaging different stakeholders in different ways over the course of a strategy change effort. As a result, planners may reap the benefits that arise from taking stakeholders seriously yet avoid the perils of responding to or engaging stakeholders in inappropriately. The process for filling out the matrix is as follows:

- Begin using this matrix relatively early in any change effort, but not before some prior stakeholder analysis work has been done

- Place stakeholders' names in the appropriate boxes and then develop action plans for how to follow through with each stakeholder

- Revise the matrix as the change effort unfolds

Techniques for Creating Ideas for Strategic Actions

Creating ideas for strategic interventions involves strategic issue identification and strategy development, but also depends on understanding political feasibility. In other words, creating ideas that are worth implementing and also implementable depends on clearly understanding stakeholders and their interests, both separately and in relation to each other, so that issues can be formulated in such a way that they have a chance of being addressed effectively in practice (Wildavsky, 1979). Therefore, the techniques relevant to organizing participation also have something to contribute to the process of issue identification and strategy development. In turn, issue identification in conjunction with strategy development can have an impact on organizing participation. Six additional techniques are particularly relevant to creating ideas for strategic interventions. They are the bases of power and directions of interest diagram; the technique of finding the common good and the structure of a winning argument; the technique of tapping individual stakeholder interests to pursue the common good; stakeholder-issue interrelationship diagrams; the problem-frame stakeholder maps; and ethical analysis grids.

Bases of Power–Directions of Interest Diagrams. This technique, building on the power versus interest grid and a stakeholder influence diagram, involves looking more closely at each of the stakeholder groups, including the most influential or central stakeholders. A *bases of power–directions of interest diagram* can be created for each stakeholder. The technique is an adaptation of Eden and Ackermann's "star diagrams" (1998, pp. 126–128, 346–349; see also Bryson, Cunningham, & Lokkesmoe, 2002). A diagram of this kind indicates the sources of power available to the stakeholder, as well as the goals or interests the stakeholder seeks to achieve or serve (see Figure A.3). Power can come from access to or control over various support mechanisms, such as money and votes, or from access to or control over various sanctions, such as regulatory authority or votes of no confidence (Eden & Ackermann, 1998, pp. 126–127). Directions of interest indicate the aspirations or concerns of the stakeholder. Typically the diagrams focus on the stakeholder's bases of power and directions of interest in relation to a focal organization's purposes or goals; that is, they seek to identify the powers that might affect achievement of the focal organization's purposes.

There are three reasons for constructing the diagrams for each stakeholder, or at least for all key stakeholders. The first is to help the planning team find the common ground—especially in terms of interest—across all of the stakeholder groups. After exploring the power bases and interests of each stakeholder, the planning group will be in a position to identify commonalities across the stakeholders as a whole, or across particular subgroups. Second, this search will allow the group to find the common good and the structure of a winning argument (see the next technique). Third, the diagrams are intended to provide background information on each stakeholder in order to know how to tap into stakeholders' interests or make use of their power to advance the focal organization's agenda as well as the common good. For example, background information can be used in stakeholder role plays (discussed later in this resource) to help planners further understand stakeholder reactions to specific problem frames or proposals for change.

A bases of power–directions of interest diagram may be constructed as follows:

- The facilitator attaches a flip chart to a wall and writes the stakeholder's name in the middle of the sheet.

Exhibit A.1. Participation Planning Matrix.

Strategic Management Function, Major Activity Category, or Specific Planning Step	Which Stakeholders to Approach by Which Means					
	Ignore	Inform	Consult	Involve	Collaborate	Empower
		Promise: We will keep you informed.	Promise: We will keep you informed, listen to you, and provide feedback on how your input influenced the decision.	Promise: We will work with you to ensure your concerns are considered and reflected in the alternatives considered, and provide feedback on how your input influenced the decision.	Promise: We will incorporate your advice and recommendation to the maximum extent possible.	Promise: We will implement what you decide.
Organize effective participation						
Create meritorious ideas for mission, goals, strategies, and other strategic interventions						

Build a winning coalition around proposal development, review, and adoption		
Implement, monitor, and evaluate strategies		
Build capacity for ongoing implementation, learning, and strategic change		

Source: Adapted from International Association for Public Participation, 2007, and Bryson, 2010, p. S256. See also Figure 1.4.

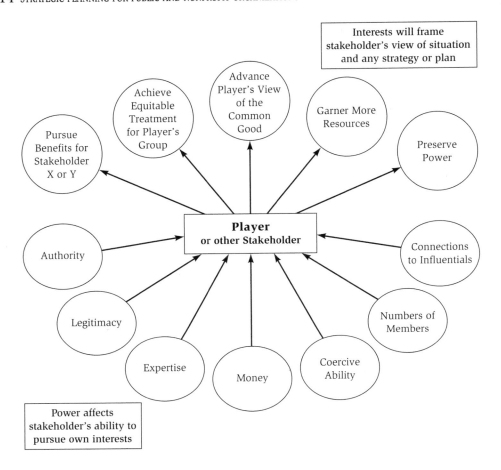

Figure A.3. Bases of Power–Directions of Interest Diagram, with Examples of Power Bases and Interests.

Source: Adapted from Eden & Ackermann, 1998, p. 127, and Bryson, Lokkesmoe, & Cunningham, 2002.

- The planning team then brainstorms possible bases of power for the stakeholder (particularly as they affect the focal organization's purposes or interests) and the facilitator writes these on the bottom half of the sheet.

- Following team discussion, the facilitator draws arrows on the diagram from the power base to the stakeholder, and between power bases to indicate how one power base is linked to another.

- The planning team then brainstorms goals or interests they believe the stakeholder has (particularly those relevant to the focal organization's purposes or interests). The facilitator writes these on the top half of the sheet and draws arrows from the stakeholder to the goals or interests and, when appropriate, arrows linking goals or interests.

- A thorough discussion of each diagram and its implications should occur.
- The facilitator records the results of the discussion on flip chart sheets.

Finding the Common Good and the Structure of a Winning Argument.
Bryson, Cunningham, and Lokkesmoe (2002) created this technique and used it successfully to help develop a viable political strategy for producing better outcomes for young African American men in a large county in the United States. The technique builds on the bases of power–directions of interest technique; such diagrams can be explored in depth to determine which interests or themes appear to garner support from a significant number of stakeholders. Members of the planning team will need to search for these common themes, which are called *super-interests*. For each theme, the team should construct a label that appears to capture or integrate the specific interests that make up the theme. The identification of common themes is a subjective exercise calling for creativity, discernment, and judgment. After identifying these themes, the team should then construct a map that identifies all of the super-interests that tie together the individual stakeholders' interests and that indicates what appear to be the relationships among the super-interests.

The map is called *finding the common good and the structure of a winning argument* because it indicates—at least in part—what the common good (or the creation of real public value) *is* for this group of stakeholders and suggests how arguments probably will need to be structured to tap into the interests of enough stakeholders to create a winning coalition. In other words, if persuasive arguments can be created that show how support for specific policies and programs will further the interests of a significant number of important stakeholders, then it should be possible to forge the coalition needed to adopt and implement the policies and programs. Being relatively clear about goals or interests—though not always necessary (Crosby & Bryson, 2005; Huxham & Vangen, 2005; Innes & Booher, 2010)—does help when it comes to producing successful programs and projects (Nutt, 2002). Any difficulties that then arise are likely to concern the means to achieve specific ends rather than the ends themselves. Conflicts over means can be resolved through interest-based bargaining and through the creation of prototypes, pilot projects, or small experiments to identify the most effective approaches (Nutt, 1992). In addition, the structure of a winning argument outlines a *viable political rhetoric* around which a *community of interests* can mobilize, coalesce, and co-align to further the common good (Majone, 1989; Stone, 2002).

Tapping Individual Stakeholder Interests to Pursue the Common Good. Developing a viable political rhetoric is a key visionary leadership task (Crosby & Bryson, 2005) and should help public leaders, managers, staff, and their collaborators understand how they might "pursue significance" for themselves and their organizations (Denhardt, 1993). What still remains is the task of understanding how *specific stakeholders*—either separately, in coalitions, or in co-aligned groups—might be inspired and mobilized to act in such a way that the common good is advanced. A further analysis therefore is needed in order to understand how *each stakeholder's interests* connect with the *super-interests.*

Specifically, a set of diagrams is needed that shows how each individual stakeholder's bases of power–directions of interest diagram links to the super-interests (Bryson, Cunningham, & Lokkesmoe, 2002). Once the diagrams are constructed, it is possible to see how policies, programs, and projects would need to be found, tailored, or sold in such a way that individual stakeholders perceive that their own interests are advanced. Developing these diagrams is a kind of research intended to help create and market social programs successfully (e.g., Kotler & Lee, 2007). This research is designed to help the team understand the organization's audiences well enough to satisfy both their interests and to advance the common good. Strategy, program, and project design will be enhanced as a result of more clearly understanding stakeholder interests, and effective one- and two-way communication strategies may be created through developing and testing out these diagrams with key informants in the target audiences.

The techniques discussed thus far have at least implicitly if not explicitly approached strategic issue identification and strategy formulation in terms of the common good or creating public value by searching for themes, concerns, or goals shared by key stakeholders. The analyses have tended to downplay the significance of opposition—including opposition to a specifically defined common good. The techniques that follow begin to address the ways in which opposition might need to be taken into account.

Stakeholder-Issue Interrelationship Diagrams. The *stakeholder-issue interrelationship diagram* helps the planning team understand which stakeholders have an interest in which issues, and how some stakeholders might be related to other stakeholders through their relationships with the issues (see Figure A.4). (Bryant [2003, pp. 190–197] calls this diagram the *preliminary problem structuring diagram.*) This diagram helps provide some important structuring of the issue areas, in which a number of actual or potential areas for

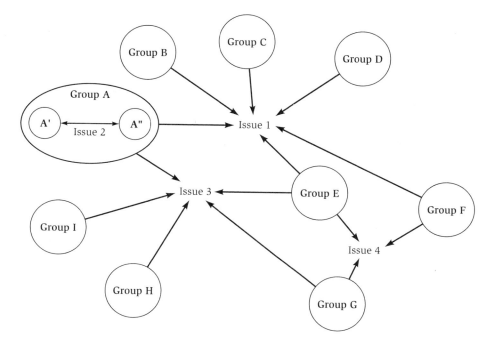

Figure A.4. Stakeholder-Issue Interrelationship Diagram.
Source: Adapted from Bryant, 2003, pp. 196, 264.

cooperation—or conflict—may become apparent. An arrow on the diagram indicates that a stakeholder has an interest in an issue, though the specific interest is likely to differ from stakeholder to stakeholder, and those interests may well be in conflict. The arrows therefore should be labeled to indicate exactly what the interest is in each case. In Figure A.4, stakeholders A, B, C, D, E, and F all have an interest, or stake, in Issue 1, whereas subgroups of stakeholder A have a further issue between them, Issue 2. Stakeholder A is also related to stakeholders E, G, H, and I through their joint relationship to Issue 3. Again, in an actual case, the arrows should be labeled, so it is clear exactly what the interests are, and whether they are in conflict.

A stakeholder-issue interrelationship diagram may be constructed as follows:

- The planning team starts with a power versus interest grid and stakeholder influence diagram, and perhaps with the basic stakeholder analysis technique.

- The facilitator tapes four flip chart sheets to a wall to form a single surface two sheets high and two sheets wide.

- Planning team members should brainstorm the names of stakeholders by writing the names of different stakeholders as they

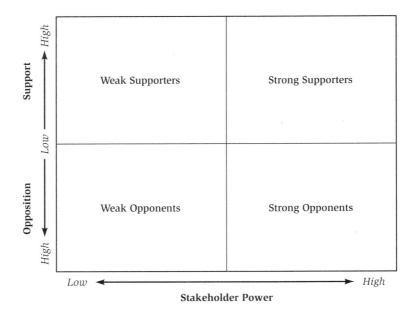

Figure A.5. Problem-Frame Stakeholder Map.

Source: Anderson, Bryson, & Crosby, 1999; adapted from Nutt & Backoff, 1992, p. 198.

come to mind on a 1½ × 2-inch (2½ × 5-cm) self-adhesive label, one stakeholder per label. Alternatively, the names may be taken from one of the previous analyses.

- Planning team members also brainstorm issues that appear to be present in the situation at hand. These also are placed on self-adhesive labels, preferably of a different color.

- The facilitator places the issues on the flip chart surface and, following team discussion, arrays stakeholders around the issues. A stakeholder may be involved in more than one issue.

- The facilitator draws arrows indicating which stakeholders have a stake in which issues; the content of each arrow—that is, the stake or interest involved—should be identified.

- The team thoroughly discusses each issue, stakeholder, and arrow, and any implications for the framing or reframing of issues and management of stakeholder relationships should be noted.

Problem-Frame Stakeholder Maps. The *problem-frame stakeholder mapping technique* was developed by Anderson, Bryson, and Crosby (1999) and is adapted from a technique developed by Nutt and Backoff (1992). It is especially useful in developing problem (or issue) definitions likely to lead to a winning coalition. Careful analysis is usually necessary to find desirable problem definitions that can motivate action by a coalition of stakeholders large enough to secure adoption of preferred solutions and to protect them during implementation (Rochefort & Cobb, 1994; Jacobs & Shapiro, 2000; Crosby & Bryson, 2005). A crucial first step in this analysis is to link stakeholders to alternative problem definitions through a problem-frame stakeholder map (see Figure A.5). Ideally, once a "winning" frame has been identified, specific policy proposals can be developed within that framing.

The following steps may be followed to construct a problem-frame stakeholder map:

- The facilitator tapes four flip chart sheets to a wall to form a single surface two sheets high and two sheets wide.

- Draw a two-by-two matrix on the surface using a marking pen. The vertical axis on the left is labeled *problem frame*. The vertical axis above the horizontal line in the middle is labeled *support* from *low* at the horizontal line to *high* at the top of the axis. The vertical axis on the left below the horizontal line in the middle is labeled *opposition* from *low* at the horizontal line to *high* at the bottom of the axis. The horizontal axis across the bottom is labeled *stakeholder power* from *low* on the left-hand side to *high* on the right-hand side.

- On a second set of flip chart sheets the planning group should brainstorm and write down the various problem frames or definitions that might apply to the case at hand. The whole range of frames or definitions should be recorded, including those favored by known critics or opponents. The snow card technique, nominal group technique, or other brainstorming method can be used.

- On a third set of flip chart sheets the planning group should brainstorm the list of potential stakeholders likely to be implicated by the range of problem definitions. Alternatively, if the basic analysis technique has been performed, the names should be taken from that list.

- These stakeholders' names are placed on 1½ × 2-inch self-adhesive labels, one stakeholder per label.

- For each problem frame or definition, consider the likely policy changes based on the definition.

- Next, for each problem frame or definition, a facilitator—guided by the deliberations and judgments of the planning group members— should array the stakeholders on the matrix that was created at the beginning of the process, placing each label in the appropriate spot on the grid.

- Labels are moved around until all group members are satisfied with the *relative* location of each stakeholder on the grid.

- The group should discuss the implications of the resulting stakeholder placements. Particular attention should be given to the stakeholders who show up in the right-hand quadrants for all definitions of the problem. In other words, attention should be devoted to the more powerful stakeholders. Emphasizing a problem frame that increases the number of strong supporters and reduces the number of strong opponents facilitates formation of a winning coalition.

- The facilitator records the results of the discussion on flip chart sheets.

Ethical Analysis Grids. Attending to stakeholders and to the common good certainly can be thought of as contributing to ethical behavior. But more is required in order to assure the ethical appropriateness of whatever actions are ultimately taken. Lewis (1991; see also Lewis and Gilman (2005) proposes use of a grid to clarify and prompt a dialogue around *who* and *what* counts. Use of the grid helps the organization fulfill both deontological (duty-based) and teleological (results-oriented) obligations. Results of the analysis should indicate which proposals or options should be eliminated or altered on ethical grounds. A modified version of the grid they propose will be found in Exhibit A.2. The planning team members simply work together to fill it out and then discuss the results. It may be wise to involve others in this discussion as well. In general, Lewis's admonition would be to pursue the common good *and* avoid doing harm.

Techniques for Plan Development, Review, and Adoption

Once stakeholders and their interests have been identified and understood, it is typically still advisable to do additional analyses in order to develop proposals that can garner adequate support in the plan review and adoption process. Three techniques will be considered here: the stakeholder support versus opposition grid, stakeholder role plays, and policy attractiveness versus stakeholder capability grid.

Stakeholder Support Versus Opposition Grids. The *stakeholder support versus opposition grid* builds on the problem-frame stakeholder map, using the same grid and process. But this time specific proposals—rather than problem frames or definitions—are assessed in terms of stakeholder support, opposition, and importance. Nutt and Backoff (1992) developed the technique. The steps are simple. For each proposal:

Exhibit A.2. Ethical Analysis Grid.

Stakeholder (S/H) Name and Category		Description of Stake			
Internal s/h					
External s/h and direct					
External s/h and indirect					
Factors and Score		**High (3)**	**Medium (2)**	**Low (1)**	**None (0)**
Dependency of s/h on government (for example, inaccessible alternative services)					
Vulnerability of s/h (for example, potential injury					
Gravity (versus triviality) of s/h's stake					
Likelihood remedy or relief will be unavailable					
Risk to fundamental value					
Policy impact on s/h					
Total scores: Do they indicate obligatory action or relief?					

Source: Adapted from Lewis, 1991, p. 122.

- The facilitator constructs a separate grid.
- The planning team members brainstorm stakeholders' names and place them on self-adhesive labels, one name per label.
- The facilitator places the labels on the grid in the appropriate places.
- The team discusses the results in terms of the viability of specific proposals and of stakeholders requiring special attention.

- Specific tactics should be discussed and deployed based on the analysis to build a stronger coalition in support of changes and weaken any opposition coalition.

- The facilitator records the results of the discussion on flip chart sheets.

A serious question concerns how large a winning coalition should be. On the one hand, the political science literature on policy adoption tends to emphasize the idea of a *minimum* winning coalition (that is, the smallest size feasible for victory), because creating a larger coalition is likely to entail having to make so many concessions or trades that the proposal gets so watered down to the point that it cannot achieve its original purpose (Riker, 1962, 1986). On the other hand, the literature on collaborative planning argues that a larger coalition probably should be pursued, since sustained implementation requires broadscale support and the minimum winning coalition may not provide it (Margerum, 2002; Bryant 2003; Bryson, Crosby, & Stone, 2006). Obviously, in any specific case a thoughtful discussion should focus on answering this question.

Stakeholder Role Plays. Eden and Ackermann (1998, pp. 133–134) show how role plays—in which members of the planning team play the roles of different stakeholders—can be used to develop plans that are likely to address stakeholder interests, effectively build a supportive coalition, and ensure proper implementation. Role plays have the special benefit of really enhancing the planning group's capacity to understand how other stakeholders think. Role plays build on the information revealed in bases of power–directions of interest diagrams, as well as, perhaps, the problem-frame issue maps and stakeholder support versus opposition grids. In some cases, it may be wise to use role plays to inform the issue identification and strategy development steps.

A stakeholder role play involves the following steps:

- Each member of the planning team reviews the bases of power–directions of interest diagrams, the problem-frame stakeholder maps, and the stakeholder support versus opposition grids, if they have been prepared.

- Each member of the planning team assumes the role of a different stakeholder.

- With the stakeholder's bases of power–directions of interest diagram as a guide, each team member should answer, from the stakeholder's point of view, two questions about each proposal:

  - How would I react to this option?

  - What could be done that would increase my support or decrease my opposition?

- The facilitator uses flip chart sheets to record the responses.
- Team members do the exercise more than once as they repeatedly modify proposals to increase proposal robustness and political viability, testing each modification with role plays until they are satisfied with the result.

Policy Attractiveness Versus Stakeholder Capability Grid. The *policy attractiveness versus stakeholder capability grid* is discussed in Bryson, Freeman, and Roering (1986, pp. 73–76) and involves assessing the attractiveness of policies, plans, proposals, or options in general against stakeholder capacities to implement them (see Figure A.6). The grid reveals the proposals that are likely to be implemented successfully because they match stakeholder capabilities and those that are likely to fail because of lack of capability. The technique is therefore especially useful in shared-power, no-one-in-charge situations where planners are necessarily led to focus on the proposals that are likely to be implemented successfully. Proposals that are high in attractiveness and capability certainly should be pursued. Proposals that are otherwise attractive but do not match up well with stakeholder capabilities will require a substantial buildup of stakeholder capabilities in order to be implemented. Where the

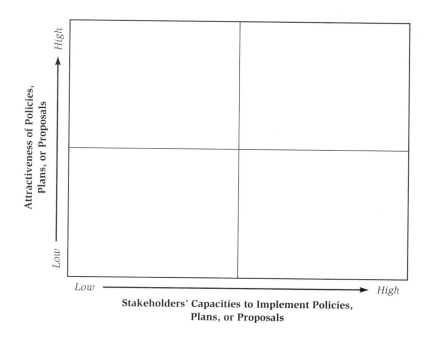

Figure A.6. Policy Attractiveness Versus Stakeholder Capability Grid.

Source: Bryson, Freeman, & Roering, 1986, pp. 73–76; see also Bryson, 1995, pp. 197–198, 283–284.

organization might find the resources for the buildup should be explored and discussed during the proposal development, review, and adoption process. Low-attractiveness proposals are best discarded.

The process for constructing one of these grids is:

- The facilitator constructs an attractiveness versus capability grid on flip chart(s) and has a list of proposals and a list of stakeholders ready.

- The planning team develops criteria to assess the *attractiveness of proposals* from *low* to *high* (in terms of mission, goals, results, outcomes, or stakeholder-related criteria) and *capabilities necessary for successful implementation* from *low* to *high*.

- Team members write proposals on self-adhesive labels, one proposal per label, and the facilitator places each label on the grid in the appropriate position after the team has considered both the proposal's attractiveness and the various stakeholders' capacities to implement it.

- The team discusses the results and any implications for building necessary capacity among stakeholders and for getting unattractive proposals off the agenda.

- The facilitator records the results of the discussion on flip chart sheets.

Techniques for Policy Implementation

In a sense, all of the techniques considered thus far are relevant to policy implementation, as they are concerned with helping develop proposals likely to garner significant stakeholder support. But it is still important to focus directly on stakeholders during implementation (Nutt, 2002; Hill & Hupe, 2009). Developing a *policy implementation strategy development grid* can give planners and decision makers a clearer picture of what will be required for implementation and help them develop action plans that will tap stakeholder interests and resources. The technique is adapted from Meltsner (1972), Coplin and O'Leary (1976), Kaufman (1986), and Christensen (1993) and builds on information revealed by previously created bases of power–directions of interest diagrams, stakeholder support versus opposition grids, stakeholder role plays, and policy attractiveness versus stakeholder capability grids (see Exhibit A.3).

The process for filling out one of the grids is fairly simple:

- The facilitator creates a grid on a wall covered with flip chart sheets and assembles the results of previously done bases of power–directions of interest diagrams, stakeholder support versus

Exhibit A.3. Policy Implementation Strategy Development Grid.

Stakeholders	Stake or Interest	Resources	Action Channels Open to Stakeholder	Probability of Participation and Manner of Doing So	Influence— as a Product of Resources and Participation	Implications for Implementation Strategy	Action Plan Elements
Supportive Stakeholders							
Opposing Stakeholders							

Source: Adapted from Meltsner, 1972; Coplin & O'Leary, 1976; Kaufman, 1986; and Christensen, 1993.

425

opposition grids, stakeholder role plays, and policy attractiveness versus stakeholder capability grids.

- The planning team members fill out the policy implementation strategy grid.
- The team discusses the next steps and prepares action plans.
- The facilitator records the results of the discussion on flip chart sheets.

The final strategic planning function of building capacity for ongoing implementation, learning, and change is also well served by diligent use of all or most of the stakeholder analysis techniques. Using the techniques helps organizational members stay attuned to their stakeholders; to think, act, and learn strategically; and to keep the need for ongoing responsiveness clearly in mind.

CONCLUSIONS

As can be seen, a wide variety of techniques are available for performing the basic functions of strategic management. Each technique provides a different kind of information that can at times be of tremendous assistance.

Some might argue that stakeholder analyses involve a lot of rigmarole that produces not too surprising results. For example, Mintzberg, Ahlstrand, and Lampel (2009, pp. 250–251) put little faith in such analyses, although their criticism seems to be based on a very limited understanding of the full range of available stakeholder analysis techniques. However, Nutt's (2002) masterful study of four hundred strategic decisions indicates that a failure to attend carefully to stakeholder interests and information can easily lead to disaster. Given Nutt's evidence, and given how relatively simple and cheap the technology is, doing stakeholder analyses certainly would appear to be a wise practice. Indeed, I would go further and assert that *not* doing stakeholder analyses would often appear to be a *dumb practice.*

But whether the practice is as wise as it can be depends on which techniques are used for what purposes and when, where, how, by whom, and with what results. Each of the techniques has a different purpose and reveals some things while hiding, or at least not highlighting, others. Like any other technique designed to aid strategic thinking, acting, and learning, stakeholder analyses must be undertaken skillfully and thoughtfully, with a willingness to learn and revise along the way (Lynn, 1996; Bardach, 1998). For some smaller change efforts, a one-time use of one or two techniques may be all that is necessary; for larger change efforts, a whole range of techniques will be needed at various points throughout the process. Hybrid techniques or new techniques may need to be invented along the way. The key point is the importance of thinking strategically about why, when, where, how, and with whom the analyses are to be undertaken, and how to change direction when needed.

It is also worth noting that stakeholder analyses can be used to advance causes that many people would believe do not serve the common good or create public value. Stakeholder analysis never should be seen as a substitute for virtuous and ethical practices, although it may be a part of promoting such practices. One way to avoid outcomes that do not create public value is to begin with an inclusive definition of stakeholders, so that the net of considerations about who and what counts is cast widely from the beginning. Another step appears to be undertaking enough stakeholder analyses to prompt the kind of strategic conversations needed to discover a morally and ethically sound version of the common good to pursue. In the end, the analyses certainly do not guarantee that public value will be created, but they may well provide information that guides the organization toward creating such value.

Using the Web in the
Strategic Planning Process

Peter Fleck and John M. Bryson

The Internet has already changed strategic planning. The use of e-mail, file attachments, strategic planning Web sites, Web-based searches, file storage, and collaborative word processing are now a part of many, if not most, strategic planning efforts. More Internet-based tools are being used each day in a tailored way to facilitate strategic planning processes and, in particular, information generation, information sharing, participation, and collaborative aspects of the process. Judicious use of Web-based tools can foster assembly of the relevant people, perspectives, expertise, and local knowledge that are generally unevenly distributed across the population. The tools can also engage multiple participants in such a way that noticeably better judgments, coordination, and collaboration occur (Surowiecki, 2005).

This resource has four sections in addition to the introduction. The first examines the challenge of creating an organizational culture open to the use of Web-based information and communication technology beyond e-mail and simple Google searches. The second presents an array of Web-based tools that may contribute to the effectiveness of strategic planning efforts. The third section discusses which tools may be of particular use in each of the ten steps of the Strategy Change Cycle. The resource ends with a short concluding section.

ENHANCING ORGANIZATIONAL USE OF TECHNOLOGY

The success of using the Internet and Internet-based tools rests on building a technology-embracing culture that extends across the organization and out from it to important external stakeholders. The issue of Internet use—especially in terms of openness, outside support, and commitment—therefore often becomes a strategic issue to be dealt with as part of the design of the strategic planning process and of the strategic plan itself. (Mentoring organizations exist that can help this process along. One is NetSquared, which sponsors local information-sharing meetings for *social innovators* working with the Web and technology; see NetSquared, 2009). The simple truth is that organizations that respond effectively to the challenges of using the Internet are the ones most likely to survive; those that do not, will not.

A particularly significant cultural shift for many organizations is the notion that transparency should become the default mode of operation for the organization. The Obama administration has made a point of emphasizing open government, although perhaps the rhetoric has been stronger than the practice. Nonetheless, the *Innovations Gallery* page on the *White House Open Government Initiative* (http://www.whitehouse.gov/open/innovations) showcases several interesting examples of how technology can be used to enhance government performance, for example, the federal chief information officer's *IT Dashboard*, the Department of Health and Human Services' *IdeaLab*, the Department of Homeland Security's *IdeaFactory*, and perhaps most surprisingly, the Army's *Wikified Army Field Guide*, which allows soldiers to collaboratively update Army practices from the field!

Transparency means sharing internally and externally all the data the organization is producing unless there are strong reasons not to share—for example, reasons involving privacy and security concerns. Technology makes this sharing easier. Meetings are easy to record—both audio and video—and then push to a Web site for easy access. Besides allowing stakeholders and collaborators to hear and see what took place, this site will become an archive for future evaluation and research, and can also aid in finding new stakeholders. The technology exists to make the planning process transparent to stakeholders, the public, funders, and government agencies (although the extent to which the process should be transparent is always a matter of judgment).

What is technologically possible and desirable can collide with the reality that many public and nonprofit organizations are a mix of generational cultures with some ready and willing to use any and all new technologies and others bent on avoiding anything beyond e-mail and a Google search. Creating an enhanced technology and Web-based culture within the organization is an important part of moving toward more participative and collaborative strategic planning practices using Web-based technologies. Initial costs of building a technology-embracing culture must be considered and include such items as adequate hardware and high-speed, dependable, and preferably wireless Internet connections. Web collaboration requires people who are comfortable with their computers, hand-held devices, and a variety of Internet tools. If you are engaging stakeholders outside the organization, it may be necessary to provide them with some kind of technical support or training. All of this will require a commitment over time to increased technology support and training, but the end result will be a much better fit for collaborative Web-based work both internally and with outside groups. Unfortunately, many public and non-profit organizations do not provide much training beyond establishing basic skills for word processing and spreadsheet software. Employees are often left on their own to figure out how to use their e-mail and Web clients efficiently. Even more unfortunate is the fact that training budgets are likely to be extraordinarily tight in the face of current budget challenges.

Another concern for those interested in creating a technology-embracing culture has to do with the accessibility of Web tools and sites by people with disabilities. Challenges facing those with various disabilities should be taken into account when choosing tools for collaborative work. Stakeholders and constituents are likely many and varied and some may have problems with vision, hearing, or use of computers. The choice of tools should take this into account or provide alternative formats that give equal access to information generation, analysis, and use. Reviews are generally available that rate the accessibility of tools, or else do your own testing. Many Web resources on accessibility are available (one of the best is the Worldwide Web Consortium's site, http://www.w3.org/WAI), or contact a local agency that works with people with disabilities.

Various challenges to the use of technology should not mask the long-term trend toward dramatic impacts on organizational performance, accountability, and stakeholder empowerment brought about by technological change. Dameri (2005, p.107) lists the problems in prioritizing information and communication technology (ICT) investments due to "lack of a direct relation between the investments amount and the financial returns." But Allee (2002) states that models need to be reconfigured to understand knowledge and intangible benefits as a type of currency. Because we are venturing into new territory with collaborative tools there is potential disruption, which will take time and money to work through but almost certainly will bring substantial rewards. But even if you don't believe in the rewards part, you should understand that there will be no dialing back to the pre-Internet days and that the longer you hesitate to move on embracing the Internet and the tools it enables, the harder it is likely to be. The tools are getting easier to use all the time, and savvy organizations are learning how to use them wisely.

The Tools

The Web-based tools we recommend here have five attributes. They are:

- **Web-based.** The tool is based on the Web and accessible from anywhere if you can find access to the Internet.

- **Easy to use.** The tools do not require extensive training sessions. They utilize standard Web browser features like the next and back button.

- **Popular.** The tools have a following that has chosen the tool rather than other alternatives. Generally, popularity will also increase longevity.

- **Low-friction at the interface.** This means that the tool has good usability, intuitive and logical navigation, fast response, and a level of design elegance.

- **Free or low-cost.** There are many tools in the free and open source category. In most cases, they work as well or better than proprietary solutions. A potential trade-off is that with local server installations, you will need a resource to manage the server and application. Proprietary solutions can be problematic no matter how wonderful they sound. Often companies have difficulty keeping up with the latest technologies and protocols, or there are security issues.

Web collaborative tools considered in this section are: social networks, Google Docs and Applications, blogging, wikis, discussion groups, social bookmarking, ideation, knowledge mapping, DebateGraph, and online file storage. Exhibit B.1 presents a list of Web sites where examples of the tools or the tools themselves may be found.

Exhibit B.1. Web Sites Where Web-Based Tools May Be Found.

Blogs

Posterous.com
   http://posterous.com
   This is the new kid on the block and an incredibly easy site to use and update. All posting can be done via e-mail.
Tumblr
   http://www.tumblr.com
Google's Blogger
   http://www.blogger.com
WordPress hosted blogging
   http://en.wordpress.com/signup
Google Docs
   http://docs.google.com

(Continued)

Exhibit B.1. Web Sites Where Web-Based Tools May Be Found, Continued.

Wikis

WetPaint
http://www.wetpaint.com
PBWorks
http://pbworks.com
PBWorks has a free offering with very basic features.
Google Sites
http://www.google.com/sites/help/intl/en/overview.html
Google incorporates wikis as part of its sites offering.
Ideation
http://data.govloop.com/Government/Ideation-Tools/bvr7-twnp?
IdeaScale
http://www.ideascale.com
MixedInk
http://www.mixedink.com

Mapping

DebateGraph
http://www.debategraph.org
Decision Explorer
http://www.banxia.com/dexplore

Mapping Links

Howard Rheingold is the author of several books on the Internet and virtual communities including *Smart Mobs: The Next Social Revolution* (2003). He maintains a Delicious social bookmarking account with mind mapping links:
http://delicious.com/hrheingold/mindmapping
Mind Mapping Listing at the GO2WEB20 Site
http://www.go2web20.net/#tag:mindmap
IHMC Cmap Tools for Concept Mapping
http://cmap.ihmc.us/conceptmap.html
Fifteen Great Mind Mapping Tools
http://spyrestudios.com/15-great-mindmapping-tools-and-apps

Online File Storage

Drop.io
Dropbox.com

Social Networks

The social network Web is composed of a large number of new Web applications, including Twitter, Facebook, MySpace, Plaxo, and LinkedIn. Wikipedia (2010) lists 189 social networking sites (excluding dating Web sites). Facebook has over 500 million user accounts, MySpace 130 million, and Twitter 75 million. All continue to grow. According to the Pew Internet & American Life Project's December 2008 tracking survey, "The share of adult Internet users who have a profile on a social networking site has more than quadrupled in the past four years—from 8 percent in 2005 to 35 percent now" (Lenhart, 2009).

When using a social networking application, you make *virtual friends* with people you may or may not know. Some of the tools—Facebook for example—require reciprocity: your request for a connection must be approved. Others, like Twitter, allow anyone to *follow* you, letting you choose whether to follow her or him, or not. Often you *friend* or follow people you know in the *real* world, but you can also connect with people of similar interests you may or may not know and who live anywhere on the globe. Organizational use of social networking should be guided by the mission statement. Ideally, the organization can trust employees to engage responsibly with the social network using the mission statement for guidance. Social networking is also a way to engage a community and find new community members. The social Web offers new and easy ways to open portals on the work that you are doing. This could bring in new financial supporters, new ideas about how to plan, and successful stories of other groups' strategic planning.

The best approach to the social Web is probably a gentle and casual one that encourages personal voices. Rigid *social media plans* drafted by social media experts to ensure proper *branding* grate against the very nature and philosophy of the social Web itself. Social networking streams of communication move quickly, and any embarrassing moments that occur are soon forgotten and even if not, they simply make your organization look human.

In general, organizations should plan to have a Facebook page and to use Twitter to broadcast updates to followers. These tools can also be used to invite followers to events. Organizations can also use these tools to ask people for their opinions about Web tools that you are considering using. Twitter can be especially valuable for this and can generate answers quickly.

Google Docs

Google Docs are becoming the most comprehensive way to address collaboration and archiving on the Web. Crunchbase (2009) calls it a "free web-based word processor, spreadsheet, and presentation application" that "allows users to easily share documents and collaboratively work on them in real-time."

Quantcast (2010) estimates that as of March 2010, roughly 5.5 million people are browsing the Docs site. The Google Doc system is available at no cost when you sign up for a free Google account. Recently, Google added a drawing program, online form generator for gathering information into a spreadsheet, and the ability to upload, store, and share any type of file. Google Docs will import and export from and to popular formats including Microsoft Office files and Adobe PDF, so there is no problem with sharing files with people not using Google Docs. Docs has excellent sharing capabilities allowing you to share with one person or a group easily. All documents can also be published to the Web for public viewing. Google provides version control; you can access and even roll back to previous versions of a document. The system is "cloud-based," meaning storage is "in the Internet cloud" and your files are available from any computer that can access the Internet.

The Google Docs system allows for full collaboration on the three major document types: word processing, spreadsheets, and presentations. If participants use Microsoft's Office applications (Word, Excel, PowerPoint), they should have no trouble using Google Docs with little or no training. Collaboration simply requires that users have a Google account. Google Docs can be published on the Web to a limited group of collaborators or published to the public Web. Unlike wiki documents (discussed later), Google Docs can usually be published as is and are good enough for presentations. They are also convertible to Microsoft-style documents for compatibility with groups that don't use Google Docs. And Microsoft documents can be converted to Google Docs. (There are potential conversion issues for which your staff should research and prepare. One is that Google word processing docs add a *soft* return to the end of each paragraph when converted to a Microsoft Word document. This may or may not be an issue in sharing or publishing, but it is not too difficult to convert the soft returns to standard hard returns if necessary.)

Google also has Google Apps available, which will allow your organization access to Google tools including Docs and Gmail and to run them under your own domain. For example, instead of using yourname@gmail.com as your e-mail address, you could use yourname@your_organization.com instead. Google offers this service free to nonprofits. Google Docs is an excellent solution for smaller organizations that do not have the money to invest in maintaining their own site and a server. Docs compares favorably to wikis and can serve close to the same functions without participants needing to learn new skills or markup languages as you would with the wiki systems.

In spite of Google's functionality, groups may hesitate in using Google due to privacy issues concerning Google's *mining* of personal data for advertisers and the fact that Google does serve up ads in Gmail. (Ads are *not* visible in the Docs system.) It should be noted that although Google does *look* at your e-mail and search data and tries to target ads to your preferences, it does not *see* you as an individual or link the data directly to you. Nonetheless, planting your information in the Internet cloud means that you are dependent on the Internet being available whenever you need to access a document. Connectivity can often vary for individuals. Google does provide methods for mirroring your documents locally for editing offline. Note as well that working online works best with faster Internet access speeds. Participants working from home could have slower access speeds and be frustrated when editing documents.

Blogs

A blog (or Weblog) is "a hierarchy of text, images, media objects and data, arranged chronologically [typically in reverse chronological order], that can be viewed in an HTML browser" (Winer, 2003). The hierarchy is centered on the sequence of blog *posts*, which are the individual *articles*. Blogs usually allow readers to comment on individual posts. Blogs are often thought to be anchored in a personalized journaling style but in reality go far beyond that with most major journalism sites—the *New York Times*, for example—using blogs to inform readers.

When applied to strategic planning, ideally the strategic planning process itself will be narrated by regular blog posts for both documentation and reflection by participants or observers. The blogs can serve as an engagement tool for stakeholders and the public by reporting on strategic planning progress. Allowing open commenting on blog posts can generate public discussion. The blog can also be used to inform what occurs in the future, providing a historical record and possibly analysis of the process. Blogging of this sort can help assure that the strategic planning effort does not become some kind of rigid recipe for producing standardized objects called strategic plans. The capacity of blogs to document is also useful for helping the organization and others better understand how what works in one situation may or may not be transferable to other situations.

Wikis

Benkler (2005, p. 14) describe a wiki as "a program that allows many people . . . to edit the main document online, through a simple web interface, and save their edits to what becomes the single canonical, updated version of the collectively authored text." Wikis are a staple of online collaborative work. Wikipedia is one of the best examples with its over three million user-contributed articles. Kendall, Nino, and Staley (2008) looked at wikis creating a dynamic online workspace with an informal, community-building capability and found that it benefited the strategic planning process among library employees at San Jose State University. Wikis are based on the assumption that "groups of people who want to collaborate also tend to trust one another" (Shirky, 2008, p. 111).

Wikis feature "collaborative authoring with lightweight content management features such as lists of changed pages, author tracking, and locking" (Wood, 2005). Wiki systems also have version control and rollback and make it very easy to add new pages and create links. The ease of editing—including page deletions—could be an issue for hierarchically structured organizations, although wikis can be secured to smaller groups for writing and a larger group for reading, and doing so could help solve the problem.

Although wikis are fairly simple to use, they do require some training, especially if the intent is to use them for actual file storage of documents in addition to collaborative writing and editing. Wiki pages are often not formatted for final publication, requiring that text be moved to a word processing application like Microsoft Word before final publishing.

Discussion Groups

Strategic planning processes can benefit from an ongoing method for discussing all aspects of the strategic planning process. Mailing lists can work well for this if everyone has e-mail access and knows how to use the mail client to at least read and send e-mail. In the past, mailing lists required a server software installation at your site. Today both Google and Yahoo provide free *groups* that double as a mailing list, and Yahoo has the added functionality of storing files online. DeSanctis, Fayard, Roach, and Jiang (2003, p. 572) attribute the success of online group discussions to "regular use of the group discussion space, their development of organized and efficient routines for interaction, a tone of mutual respect and challenge in their discourse, and a willingness to modify routines over time." Attaining this kind of success may require some degree of leadership and moderation within the group.

The decision concerning who should participate in the discussion area will be based on the level of transparency the organization desires or can tolerate. On the one hand, there are certainly arguments for providing a delimited space for staff and consultants to be open about the process without worrying about hurting anyone's feelings. On the other hand, greater participation by all interested parties and stakeholders could be beneficial to the strategic plan itself in bringing all to consensus.

One issue with an online forum or group is the newness of the form for delivering and sharing information and whether participants feel comfortable in that space. Anderson and Kanuka (1997) point out in their study that participants felt information exchanged in the forum was not as good as information that could be exchanged face-to-face and that they felt limited in their ability to communicate. This concern may be changing, however, as online forums become more standard practice. Nonetheless, concerns like this can lead to a reluctance to participate or to participants initiating discussions via private e-mails, subverting the purpose of the group.

Another issue is the lack of nonverbal cues, which reduces the richness of the information transmitted by virtual team members (Warkentin, Sayeed, & Hightower, 2007). This can mean it takes "more time and effort by group members to achieve the same level of mutual understanding in a lean medium" like e-mail or a discussion forum (Warkentin et al, 2007, p. 978).

Social Bookmarking

"Social bookmarking is a method for Internet users to store, organize, search, and manage bookmarks of Web resources" with the help of user-generated metadata to create a "grassroots community classification of digital assets" (Mathes, 2004, p. 2). The bookmarking tool Delicious utilizes user-added keywords—*tags*—as a fundamental organizational construct.

Delicious (http://www.delicious.com), founded in 2003 by Joshua Schachter and purchased by Yahoo in 2005, is one of the oldest social bookmarking sites (Wikipedia, 2010). It is a free service. After creating an account, Delicious provides browser-based tools (basically buttons on your browser's toolbar) that make saving bookmarks to your account very simple. When you find a site you wish to bookmark, you click the button and a window pops up onscreen giving you the chance to add extra metadata including tags and a description. In many cases, Delicious will suggest tags that you've used in the past for similar sites or that others have used for that particular Web page in the Delicious system. Once you have saved the bookmark to your account, the window disappears and you can continue your Web browsing. By default, all Delicious bookmarks are public and anyone (whether they have a Delicious account or not) can access them. (There is a private option available if you're not comfortable with sharing.) Your bookmarks exist on the Delicious network (in the *cloud*) but can be downloaded to your computer in a format compatible with most browser bookmarking systems.

Delicious allows you to subscribe to other user's accounts or to a particular tag or tag grouping. This allows easy sharing of Web sites among a group. Tags could be agreed upon beforehand to aggregate content of interest. An organization could create a special tag utilizing an abbreviated form of its name. Using Delicious encourages exploration and serendipitous discovery. You can explore tags of interest on topics relevant to your organization, then tag them with your custom tag to easily share with your collaborators. Delicious indicates how many have saved a particular page in the system, creating a kind of popularity gauge.

Mathes (2004, p. 5) points out problems with ambiguity of the tags as different users apply different meanings to the same tags. Using a custom tag—based on an organization's name, for example—for collaboration would help with this as the tag would represent a *trusted source.* Mathes also mentions (p. 6) the lack of synonym controls that leads "to tags that seemingly have similar intended meanings, like 'mac,' 'macintosh,' and 'apple' all being used to describe materials related to Apple Macintosh computers."

Ideation

Casabar, Henkel, Hervey, & Lewandowski (2006, p. 3) describe ideation as a concept that:

> has evolved from the combination of science, creativity, and innovation. Ideation is a structured approach to thinking or forming ideas for the purpose of solving a problem. Ideation forces us to focus and open our minds to explore and generate new ideas and accept new ideas from others in the process of concept/product development. This type of divergent thinking can generate a large number of ideas where a group can eliminate, narrow, and merge ideas to come up with the right solution.

The ideation process lends itself well to the strategic planning process, especially in identifying strategic issues and strategies to deal with the issues. The snow card process is a kind of ideation tool. One of the vendors in this space, Ideascale, has designed a platform for ideation that allows you to "submit ideas, discuss and refine others' ideas, and vote the best ones to the top" (National Academy of Public Administration, 2009, Web page). Users at the site "post ideas and comments to your community, others vote them up or down. The best ideas/suggestions float up to the top, guiding you towards the most optimal decisions. . . ." (Ideascale, 2009). Ideascale Web software is free to use at a basic level of voting and discussing ideas. More sophisticated features such as reports and data analysis are available for monthly fees starting at $15.

Ideascale was put to use by the federal government as a three-phase project to help in discussing and constructing proposals to make government more transparent. In all, 4,205 ideas were submitted for discussion and ranked and voted on by the public (National Academy of Public Administration, 2009). After the ranking and voting, the MixedInk site was used to draft recommendations. MixedInk is a free collaborative writing site that also supports a ranking system (MixedInk, 2009).

The federal government under the Obama administration has used ideation extensively. The Centers for Disease Control and Prevention launched a project called Idealab in 2009 to promote communication outside of the chain-of-command structure and apply collective problem solving (Open Government Initiative, 2009). According to the Web site, "Employees may post their 'Ideas' or 'Help Wanted' requests, comment on other users' posts, and vote on the quality of the posts and comments" (http://www.whitehouse.gov/open/innovations/idealab).

Public participation levels were not as great when the Office of Science and Technology Policy (OSTP) requested ideas and comments from the public on its draft "open government plan," as only twenty-three commenters posted twenty-nine ideas. OSTP states that they did not "effectively advertise this opportunity to participate" and to reach new audiences. Also mentioned is the need for OSTP staff to participate by responding to the posted ideas in a timely manner. Staff participation time in these efforts could be a limiting factor for any group (Open Government Initiative, 2010).

Knowledge Mapping

Vail (cited in Folkes, 2004, p. 2), defines knowledge mapping "as the process of associating items of information or knowledge, preferably visually, in such a way that the mapping itself also creates additional knowledge." Maps typically involve statements linked to one another by lines or arrows in such a way that relationships among the statements are made clear. Relationships may be logical, temporal, associational, or causal, meaning that one thing causes or leads to the other. Different types of mapping organize information differently and therefore produce different kinds of knowledge. Action-oriented strategy mapping is a kind of knowledge management tool (see Chapters Two and Seven and Resource D). As Eppler (2003, p. 194) notes, "Each way that one organizes information can create new knowledge and understanding." Web-based knowledge mapping may be used to assist strategic planning in a variety of ways that supports brainstorming, information sharing, and dialogue around stakeholder analyses, environmental scanning, strategic issue identification, strategy formulation, organizational visioning, and the implementation process. The types of knowledge mapping most directly relevant to strategic planning go by different names, including cognitive mapping, concept mapping, causal mapping, action-oriented strategy mapping, oval mapping, and mind mapping (Bryson, Ackermann, Eden, & Finn, 2004).

A basic distinction is between mapping done by individuals and mapping done by groups. *Cognitive mapping* is the term reserved for mapping by individuals. Siau and Tan (2005, p. 276) describe cognitive mapping "as a technique to elicit an individual's belief systems regarding a problem domain" with "great potential in overcoming some cognitive problems and facilitating understanding among stakeholders." Scavarda et al. (as cited in Folkes, 2004, p. 4) says cognitive mapping "is a representation of an individual's perception of a particular topic" using nodes and links:

> The nodes represent a concept, variable, issue, entity, or attribute and can be represented by a single word, phrase or paragraph. Nodes can include hyperlinks to additional information such as web pages or to other nodes. The links represent the relationships between the nodes.

The terms *mind map* and *concept map* are often used interchangeably but usually a *mind map* has one central concept whereas a *concept map* can have several. Additionally, mind maps are more about creative note taking while concept maps are typically used to explore knowledge (or misperceptions) (Folkes, 2004, p. 7). *Causal mapping* is a term that includes action-oriented strategy mapping and oval mapping (causal mapping using oval-shaped cards). As noted earlier, action-oriented strategy mapping is John Bryson's preferred approach to developing strategies; the approach was discussed briefly in Chapters Two and Seven and is presented in much more detail in Resource C and Bryson, et al. (2004).

There are many online tools for knowledge mapping and most are free. Several allow both private online spaces for internal collaboration and the ability to engage the public in the process. When evaluating knowledge mapping software, keep in mind the following criteria:

1. Is it Web-based and compatible with all standard Web browsers (Internet Explorer, Google Chrome, Firefox, and Safari) and computer operating systems (Windows, Mac OS X)?

2. Is it easy and intuitive to use with the ability to easily restructure your map?

3. Is it free or low-cost? Some Web mapping tools have a free version as well as an expensive premium version.

4. Is there a choice of public or closed-group collaboration? There should be the ability to have accounts and restrict access and the option to allow anyone to view it.

5. Is there the ability to export to standard formats for republishing? For example, the JPEG image format is recommended as the most compatible with multiple software applications like Microsoft Word, Web pages, e-mail, and so on.

6. Are there customizable features such as font choices and sizes and colors of nodes?

Using knowledge mapping software can require some training. Interfaces can be complex with many options and almost hidden features. Someone will need to read the manual and practice using the software. It may also require staff time to follow up on the process if it's not done as a team.

DebateGraph

DebateGraph is a special kind of mapping tool described by Philippe Boukobza as involving "Web-based, argument visualization with collaborative wiki editing to make the best arguments on all sides of complex public debates" (DebateGraph, 2008). The DebateGraph site notes that it is a "kind of public

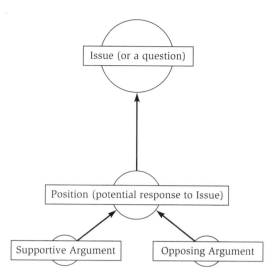

Figure B.1. Basic DebateGraph Structure.

Source: Reprinted by permission of Debategraph.

service that enables local and global communities of people to think together by collaboratively building and editing comprehensive and succinct maps of complex debates that accurately present all sides of the debate from a neutral standpoint, free of repetitive clutter and 'noise.'" In terms of knowledge mapping it is related to a concept map, allowing multiple concepts and a remarkable ability to drill down on questions (called *debate topics*). The basic logic structure of a DebateGraph is presented in Figure B.1. A DebateGraph map of the Obama White House's Open Government Initiative focused on transparency is presented in Figure B.2. DebateGraph has an extensive array of tools for color coding and grouping responses to issues. Although established to facilitate debate on complex topics—abortion, peace in the Middle East, the global financial crisis—DebateGraph can be used as a more traditional concept map to explore ideas relating to strategic planning. Each point on the maps can be rated, facilitating decision making. E-mail alerts are available to let you know when the map changes. Debate maps can be made public (even embedded in Web sites) or kept private to a selected group.

Online File Storage

All important documents, minutes, relevant legislation, policies, and so forth used in the strategic planning process should probably find a home in an Internet archive that is accessible to everyone directly involved if not to the public. Access to the archive area can be controlled, but absent compelling reasons to the contrary, it is probably best to keep the archive as transparent

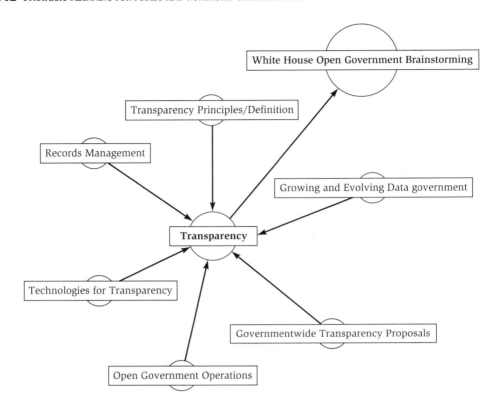

Figure B.2. DebateGraph Map of the Ideascale Transparency Project.

Source: White House Open Government Brainstorming, n.d. Reprinted by permission of Debategraph.

and open as possible, including possibly allowing the public to view and access files. (If knowing who among the public accesses the file is important, members of the public could be required to create an account for access and at least e-mail addresses could be verified.) The document storage and archiving structure should make it easy to find relevant materials. Google Docs can make an excellent repository and also provides control of archives to a group level. Documents can be both stored and read online via Docs. Google Docs files can also be made available to the public for download or as published Web pages. Two other sites for free online storage should also be mentioned: Drop.io and Dropbox.

APPLICABILITY OF WEB-BASED TOOLS TO THE STRATEGY CHANGE CYCLE

In this section examples are presented of the applicability of Web-based tools in each step of the Strategy Change Cycle. Exhibit B.2 summarizes the presentation by matching tools with strategic planning steps and indicating what the tool is good for in the step.

Step 1: Initiating and Agreeing on a Strategic Planning Process

A wiki or the Google Docs system can be used for testing initial agreement statements and to put in place a reference copy of the final agreement. Both systems will archive and allow retrieval of all older versions. This can be useful for comparison and also documents the evolution of the agreement. A discussion group can be initiated to help with developing and evaluating the agreement.

The initial agreement should address the issue of how much transparency and engagement with the larger community should be part of the process at each step, including Step 1. Too much transparency can make some stakeholders uncomfortable. The benefits and costs of transparency should be discussed

---

Exhibit B.2. Matching Web-Based Tools to the Strategy Change Cycle.

Key Indicating Purposes These Tools May Serve

- A. Communication: one-way or two-way
- B. Assisting with searches (for sources, solutions, people, resources, and so on)
- C. Facilitating coordination (helping things happen in the right place at the right time in the sequence)
- D. Facilitating collaboration (as in developing a shared definition of issues, creating strategies, getting alignments worked out)
- E. Facilitating judgment (for example, ranking and voting)
- F. Facilitating deliberation (analysis, synthesis, and choice)
- G. Acting as an external memory or library
- H. Helping with modeling of problems and solutions
- I. Facilitating organizing large groups independent of geography

   The capital letters in the table below correspond to the purposes listed above. For example, Google Docs can act as an external memory or library (G) while you are initiating and agreeing on a strategic planning process (Step 1).

(Continued)

Exhibit B.2. Matching Web-Based Tools to the Strategy Change Cycle, Continued.

Strategic Planning Step (Bryson, 2004)	Google Docs	Blogging	Wikis	Discussion Groups	Social Bookmarking	Ideation	Knowledge Mapping	DebateGraph	Online File Storage
1. Initiate and agree on a strategic planning process.	D, G	A, D	A, C, D, I	A, C, D					G
2. Identify organizational mandates.	G	A	A, G	A, D	C, D, G	E, F	D, E, F	D, E, F	G
3. Clarify organizational mission and values.	D, G	A, D	D	A, D		D, E, F	D, E, F	D, E, F	G
4. Assess the external and internal environments to identify strengths, weaknesses, opportunities, and threats (SWOT).	D, B, G	A	D, I	D, E, F	B	D, E, F	D, E, F	D, E, F	G
5. Identify the strategic issues facing the organization.	D, G	A	D	D, E, F	B	D, E, F	D, E, F	D, E, F	G

Strategic Planning Step (Bryson, 2004)	Google Docs	Blogging	Wikis	Discussion Groups	Social Bookmarking	Ideation	Knowledge Mapping	DebateGraph	Online File Storage
6. Formulate strategies to manage the issues.	D, G	A	D	D, E, F	B	D, E, F	D, E, F	D, E, F	G
7. Review and adopt the strategies or strategic plan.	D, G	A	D	D, E, F		D, E, F	D, E, F	D, E, F	G
8. Establish an effective organizational vision.	D, F, G	A, D, E, F	D, F	A, D, E, F	B	D, E, F	D, E, F	D, E, F	G
9. Develop an effective implementation process.	A, B, D, I	A, C, D, I	A, C, D, I	A, C, D, I	B	C, D, E, F	C, D, E, F	C, D, E, F	G
10. Reassess the strategies and the strategic planning process.	A, C, D, G	A, C, I	A, C, I	A, D, E, F, I	B	D, E, F	D, E, F	D, E, F	G

by those fashioning the initial agreement. One suggestion would be to have both a blog and wiki or Google area for the process, including Step 1; the blog can be public and used to document the process, while the wiki or Google area can be kept private.

Steps 2 and 3: Clarifying Organizational Mandates and Mission

The Strategy Change Cycle draws attention to the *public value* created by an organization's mandates, mission, and values and how they provide the social justification and legitimacy on which the organization's existence depends. The transparency of blogging and the brainstorming, reflection, dialogue, and participation it can encourage can help increase the legitimacy of the process and the desirability—and public value—of the resulting choices and actions. Another benefit is the storage of pertinent documents in a public download space (accomplished via Google Docs or an archive space). Interested parties (including the public, and other stakeholders) can leave comments and even carry on a discussion of sorts via the blog comments.

A central online archive (in the Google Docs system, wiki, or archive site) of both formal and informal mandates will assist a large group in reviewing, discussing, and helping to clarify the meaning of mandates and identify any needed changes. Discussions can take place in a Google or Yahoo group. If this area is open to the wider Web, similar organizations—local, national, or global—could engage in the discussion. An online archive may also help institutionalize attention to and a regular review of the mandates.

The social bookmarking tool Delicious can be used for bookmarking formal mandates codified in laws, regulations, ordinances, articles of incorporation, charters, and so forth. An added benefit of the bookmarks is the creation of an archive for future reference outside of the planning process itself.

Developing the mission statement or a vision can benefit from internal work groups using private discussion spaces (Google or Yahoo groups, for example) to formulate mission and value statements and then share these with a larger group or the public. The discussion could also start with the public and then move to the inner group for evaluating and formulating statements that are then returned to the public area for more discussion. This process is facilitated by the efficiencies realized from previously discussed technologies such as voting features in software like IdeaScale (http://ideascale.com) or the creation and ranking of linked ideas in DebateGraph (http://debategraph.org). Structured and facilitated online discussions could also be used and based on the six questions about mission presented in Chapter Four, in the section on the mission statement.

Some stakeholder analyses (such as stakeholder influence diagrams, bases of power–directions of interest diagrams, and stakeholder-issue interrelationship diagrams) could be attempted using the DebateGraph system to sketch out the stakeholders and to gain an understanding of the relationships that help define the organization's context and business and to identify clues for determining strategic issues and developing effective strategies. DebateGraph also has a ranking system for ideas. This process can be especially useful for the team in making guesses at which criteria stakeholders use in assessing an organization's performance.

Step 4: Assessing the External and Internal Environments to Identify Strengths, Weaknesses, Opportunities, and Challenges (or Threats) (SWOC/Ts)

The Web can help with searching for, ordering, and evaluating information related to SWOC/Ts. Web-based tools can help monitor mentions of your organization or key words in the external environment related to your mission, mandates, and plans. Google Alerts, part of Google News, is an excellent tool for this, providing "email updates of the latest relevant Google results (web, news, etc.) based on your choice of query or topic" (Google, 2009). The social network tool Twitter can also be searched for organizational and key word mentions. Searches like this are wide-reaching nets that can be cast across the Internet relatively easily and analyzed internally. The hits you get from your searches can also lead to connections with other groups doing similar work. Searching can also be done collaboratively with other organizations. The Google Docs system can support SWOC/T analysis work with shared data folders with permissions easily established for cross-organizational use. SWOC/T analyses can also be tried online using an ideation tool and perhaps also tied to some real-time meetings that first show participants how to use the software and then bring people together to discuss results.

For monitoring internal strengths and weaknesses in an objective manner, a combination of online discussion and an ideation (IdeaScale) or mapping tool like DebateGraph can be helpful. Allowing for an agencywide effort with an ideation tool can reveal both unknown strengths and weaknesses that might not have come to light with more traditional meetings. This can be especially useful if employees can post ideas and comment anonymously. Success factors and competencies can also be identified.

Step 5: Identifying the Strategic Issues Facing the Organization

DebateGraph can be used to describe strategic issues. As mentioned, the tool has an extensive array of options for color coding and grouping responses to issues. Ideation software such as IdeaScale can be used to simply list and rank issues and request comments, then draft the issues with the collaborative writing tool, MixedInk. Delicious (social bookmarking) can be useful for identifying articles that support or oppose potential strategic issue framings or analyses. Previous bookmarks that were used to define external conditions could now be tagged with special tags ("stratissue" and a specific tag relating to an issue). Some of these bookmarks could be tagged early on as pointing to a potential strategic issue and then reviewed during this step.

Steps 6 and 7: Formulating and Adopting Strategies to Manage the Issues

DebateGraph or Ideascale and MixedInk can be used to help support strategy formulation, perhaps following the five-step process outlined in Chapter Seven. Web-based collaboration tools can be particularly effective when there is a desire to consider a variety of creative, even radical options during the strategy formulation process. Ideation and mapping tools (DebateGraph especially) have the ability to easily add and rank options. A simpler process would involve using Google Docs. Regardless of the approach, drafts and final documents can be posted to an archive where they can be downloaded for review. The same archive can be used for support if action-oriented strategy mapping is used (see Resource D). The archive creates a place where drafts and final versions of strategies and the strategic plan can be kept, where viewing is allowed, and where changes may be made over time—first to drafts of the plan and then to the adopted plan, thereby making the strategic plan a living document. The transparency of using Web tools can help keep stakeholders honest and potentially limit some of the political intrigue and public posturing that can accompany some strategic planning efforts.

Step 8: Establishing an Effective Organizational Vision

If the organization has been using Web-based collaboration tools, there should be ample content and ideas online by the time this step is reached to begin drafting and testing versions of potential visions of success. Blogging, Google Docs, wikis, discussion groups, and ideation and mapping tools can all be incorporated in a variety of ways to support drafting a vision. For example, a wiki might be established to support collaborative work on vision creation. Or a simpler approach might use multiple single-document visions stored in a Google Docs folder that is shared with everyone in the organization and possibly with the public. Final drafting of the vision is likely to be the responsibility of one person, although the review of the vision will likely involve many people.

Step 9: Developing an Effective Implementation Process

Collaborative work using Web-based tools can help in identifying and recruiting sponsors and champions for implementation efforts at all levels of the organization, as long as the process has been open and allowed for bottom-up influence. Using a wiki or Google Docs the organization can make sure everyone is aware of the plan and can utilize associated discussion groups for communicating information about the plan and its implementation. Those in charge should make sure that everyone with proper access rights knows how to find the background work archive of the strategic plan. Time should be spent organizing the archive in such a way that it is easily comprehensible and people can find what they need. The archive's architecture should be clear. Google Docs, which utilizes Google's own search engine, can help people quickly navigate within the architecture.

Step 10: Reassessing the Strategies and the Strategic Planning Process

The well-organized archive mentioned previously will enhance the review process. This archive can include not only final documents but all the ideation and mapping processes. Additionally, online discussion groups can be used for reviewing the strategic planning process and implementation results as a prelude to the next round of strategic planning.

CONCLUSION

In this resource we have looked at using Web-based tools to support a strategic planning process. Some organizations will be ready to embrace the collaborative Web, but others will have to take time to prepare and shift to a more technology-enabled, collaborative organizational culture. Some training may be necessary and digital inclusion and accessibility issues should be taken into account. The issue of transparency should also be examined with a probable bias toward more openness. As Shirky (2008, p. 20) notes, because of the Internet "we are living in the middle of a remarkable increase in our ability to share, to cooperate with one another, and to take collective action."

The tools covered in this Resource included blogs, wikis, Google Docs, ideation and IdeaScale, discussion groups, social bookmarking, and knowledge-mapping applications (with special consideration of DebateGraph). We touched on social networking (Facebook and Twitter particularly) as a way to engage the public but not necessarily for direct use with strategic planning. (That time is coming.) We have also stressed the need for an online and networked archive where an organization can store according to a good taxonomy all relevant documents and files that are part of that particular strategic planning cycle.

The Web and its tools for search, collaboration, and communication can enhance the strategic planning process. As in pre-Internet days, the final goal is a plan that has the mutual support of staff, board, and stakeholders and that is implemented. What the Internet and Web tools offer are more efficient and democratic methods for sustaining the conversation that leads to the plan.

Developing a Livelihood Scheme That Links Aspirations, Distinctive Competencies, and Distinctive Assets

Colin Eden, Fran Ackermann, and John M. Bryson

An important key to success for public and nonprofit organizations is identifying and building strategic capacities to produce the greatest public value for key stakeholders at a reasonable cost (Bryson, Ackermann, & Eden, 2007). Without continued attention to these capacities, public and nonprofit organizations will find it difficult to achieve their goals, create real public value, respond effectively to changes in their environments, or justify their continued existence. Therefore, dynamic organizational capacities for producing public value are necessary to achieve a desirable fit with the environment (Eisenhardt & Martin, 2000; Kraatz & Zajac, 2001; Eden & Ackermann, 2010). An exploration of these capacities may lead to new goals, performance indicators or criteria for stakeholder satisfaction, efforts to develop new competencies, or creation of new or different resource arrangements.

Sociologist Philip Selznick (1957) was the first to identify and label *distinctive competence* as a particularly valuable capacity and resource for organizations. He believed that a key role for organizational leaders was to identify, invest in, and protect such competencies and the resources underlying them. Early business-oriented strategy theorists, such as H. Igor Ansoff (1965)

Source: This resource is an adaptation of Bryson, Ackermann, & Eden (2007). Changes involve relabeling and minor rewording of the original figures based on the authors' further experience with livelihood schemes.

and Kenneth Andrews (1971), also emphasized the importance of resource differences, especially in their promotion of doing a SWOT analysis (strengths, weaknesses, opportunities, and threats). In recent years, another major school of thought has developed in strategic management. Called the *resource-based view* of the firm, it describes the crucial importance of resources generally and of competencies specifically for organizational survival, growth, and overall effectiveness (Barney, 1991; Peteraf, 1993; Wernerfelt, 1984). The resource-based view is arguably the dominant approach to strategy research and teaching in North America and Europe—explicitly for businesses and implicitly for government and nonprofit organizations (Barney, 2001a, 2001b; Bovaird, 2005). The key insights of the resource-based view are that "scarce, valuable, and imperfectly imitable resources are the only factors capable of creating sustained performance differences among competing firms, and that these resources should figure prominently in strategy making" (Kraatz & Zajac, 2001, p. 632). Distinctive competencies are one such resource. Although public strategic management theorists have been strongly influenced by this body of thought, either explicitly or implicitly (for example, Barry, 1997; Bozeman & Straussman, 1990; Bryson, 2004; Bryson & Roering, 1987; Denhardt, 1993; Joyce, 1999; Moore, 1995; Nutt & Backoff, 1992), they have not focused on the importance of developing a *livelihood scheme*—that is, the government and nonprofit organizational equivalent of a *business model*—to show how distinctive competencies are directly linked to meeting organizational *aspirations*—defined for purposes of this resource as an umbrella term that, depending on the situation, may include mandates, mission, goals, outcome indicators, or key stakeholder requirements that the organization chooses to meet. This shortcoming is unfortunate, to say the least, because a livelihood scheme provides the fundamental logic underlying any effective strategic plan. Said differently, a strategic plan should articulate how the livelihood scheme is to be taken advantage of and deployed in practice.

In this resource we present a method—based principally on the work of Eden and Ackermann (1998, 2000, 2010)—for identifying distinctive competencies for public and nonprofit organizations and showing how patterns of distinctive competencies can be used as the basis for articulating a public or nonprofit organization's overall *livelihood scheme*. The livelihood scheme articulates the rationale that links the organization's aspirations, its distinctive competencies, and its distinctive assets; in other words, the scheme summarizes how, or on what basis, the organization is uniquely able to achieve its mission, meet its mandates, accomplish its goals, do well against outcome indicators, and create public value—an expression, in other words, of its "right" to earn a livelihood. We illustrate the process using the case of a major public sector training and consultancy unit that is part of the United Kingdom's National Health Service.

DEFINITIONS

We discuss and define the following interconnected key terms: critical success factors, distinctive competency outcomes, resources, competencies, distinctive competencies, core competencies, core distinctive competencies, threshold competencies, and distinctive assets. All organizations have aspirations, whether explicit or implicit (Scott, 1987). Organizations also have what are termed *key success factors* or *critical success factors* (CSFs), which are the things the organization must do, the criteria it must meet, or the performance indicators it must do well against—because they matter to key stakeholders—in order to survive and prosper (Johnson, Scholes, & Whittington, 2008). These factors may also be explicit or implicit. Organizations that do well against their CSFs presumably achieve a better "fit" with their environment, enhancing their chances of survival (Drazin & Van de Ven, 1985). Goals and CSFs may be the same when managers and stakeholders agree about the nature of success. Alternatively, goals may support CSFs when stakeholder views are dominant, or CSFs may support goals when stakeholders are less dominant. *Distinctive competency outcomes* (DCOs) are what distinctive competencies (defined in following paragraphs) produce. DCOs may support doing well against a CSF, may essentially be the same as the CSF, or may be disconnected from CSFs (in which case the DCOs actually produce little of value to key stakeholders). DCOs in turn require having or developing the distinctive competencies needed to produce them.

Resources, broadly construed, are any assets that an organization might draw on to help it achieve its goals or perform well on its CSFs. For example, the items considered strengths in a typical SWOC/T analysis would all be resources. *Competencies* (Cs) connote a subset of resources and consist of *abilities*, sets of actions, or processes that an organization can manage and that ideally help it perform well (the desired outcome) against important aspirations, distinctive competency outcomes, or CSFs (which should also be desired outcomes) (Eden & Ackermann, 2010). For example, Sony's competence in miniaturization has allowed it to manufacture a wide range of useful and highly profitable products. Canon's competencies in optics, imaging, and microprocessors have allowed it to enter diverse markets for copiers, printers, cameras, and scanners (Prahalad & Hamel, 1990). The University of Minnesota's Department of Chemical Engineering and Materials Science has process competencies in recruiting and departmental management that have helped it remain one of the top-ranked departments (a competency outcome) in its field in the United States for decades (Bland, 2004). In particular circumstances, public organizational competencies may include the ability to tax and spend wisely (wise results are the competency outcome), the ability to engage citizens constructively (actual constructive engagement is the outcome), the ability to handle emergencies (a well-handled emergency is the outcome), the ability to maintain legitimacy (legitimacy maintenance is the outcome), achieve service-delivery excellence (excellent service is the outcome), and so on. Competencies are less flexible than resources and usually arise through *learning by doing* (Joyce, 1999; Christensen & Overdorf, 2000).

Distinctive competencies (DCs) are competencies that are very difficult for others to replicate and therefore are a source of enduring advantage. They "are the features of the organization that underpin long-term success" (Eden & Ackermann, 1998, p. 103). What makes them distinctive is their uniqueness or lack of substitutability, rarity among competitors or collaborators, difficulty of imitation, value in terms of exploiting opportunities or warding off threats, and the resulting provision of competitive or collaborative advantage (Barney, 1991). They may involve considerable ambiguity and tacit knowledge, which makes them difficult to imitate, let alone codify (Johnson, Scholes, & Whittington, 2008; Murnane & Nelson, 1984). It is especially important to note that distinctive competencies may arise from the *pattern* of links among competencies (Eden & Ackermann, 1998, 2010). In other words, none of the individual competencies may be unique, but the pattern of links among them is. Note as well that the competencies and links among them do not all need to be internal to the organization; instead, linked competencies across organizational boundaries can be a source of distinctive competence (Schroeder, Bates, & Junttila, 2002). The development and exploitation of such cross-boundary competencies is a major argument for seeking collaboration to achieve jointly what cannot be achieved separately (Huxham & Vangen, 2005). A *core competency* (CC) is one that is really crucial to the organization doing well against its aspirations or CSFs. It is core because of its location in the linkages of competencies to aspirations: remove the competency, and achievement or the aspiration or meeting of the CSF is unlikely. A CC, however, will not be *distinctive* if it easy for others to emulate, and thus it will not provide a basis for long-term success. A *core distinctive competency* (CDC) is a distinctive competency whose presence is crucial to achieving organizational aspirations precisely because it is hard to emulate and critical to the long-term success of the organization. CDCs are a necessary element of any viable, sustainable livelihood scheme. There is one final category of competencies worth noting and that is *threshold competencies* (TCs), which are those competencies that must be present in order to be a viable organization in the first place, such as having accounting, financial management, HR, IT, and procurement systems that work.

Distinctive assets (DAs) are a particular resource that may be drawn on or exploited by a competency. Competencies of all sorts require resources to run; if the resources in question are also distinctive, meaning not easily available to others, it will be easier to sustain the competency over the long term. Finally, a *core distinctive asset* (CDA) is a distinctive asset that is core to the achievement of the organization's business aspirations.

Eden and Ackermann argue that "the strategic future of an organization, or division, or business unit, or department, whether private, public, or third sector, depends totally on its ability to exploit competencies in relation to its aspirations. The security and stability of that future depends on the distinctiveness of the competencies and their sustainability" (1998, p. 108). The way in which distinctive competencies and distinctive assets are linked to and support the distinctive competency outcomes and aspirations of a public organization constitutes its livelihood scheme. As noted, aspirations may include mandates, mission, goals, outcome indicators, CSFs, or other key stakeholder requirements that the organization chooses to meet. Though some public and nonprofit organizations have little choice about their aspirations, others have a great deal of choice. The scheme is a shorthand description of how the organization believes it can create real public value in a sustainable way. The scheme says, "Here is our purpose and our goals and what we believe we must do to succeed. Here as well are the distinctive competencies and distinctive assets on which we can draw (or must create) to achieve success. We believe the scheme, if implemented, will allow us to achieve the success, legitimacy, financing, and other necessary long-term support needed to sustain our continued existence" (adapted from Ackermann & Eden with Brown, 2005, p. 202). Thus, distinctive competencies are crucial to a viable livelihood scheme. The livelihood scheme is not the same as a strategic plan, but it provides the crucial underpinning for one. The sustenance and exploitation of distinctive competencies and particularly core distinctive competencies must be an important aspect of a strategic plan. The plan provides more detail and operational content to the livelihood scheme.

A PROCESS FOR DEVELOPING A LIVELIHOOD SCHEME

The process for developing a livelihood scheme presented here is based principally on the work of Eden and Ackermann (1998, 2010). The process is illustrated with an example from the Beeches Management Centre (BMC), a major training and consultancy organization that is part of the health and personal social service system for Northern Ireland in the United Kingdom (see http://www.beeches-mc.co.uk). Causal mapping is used throughout as a technique for structuring strategic ideas by explicating beliefs and indicating the influence relationships among them (and thus being able to illustrate how, for example, competencies can support aspirations). Causal mapping uses statement-and-arrow diagrams to show that statement A may lead to statement

B, which, in turn, may lead to statement C (that is, A → B → C). Causal mapping is described in detail in Bryson et al. (2004).

The BMC was established in 1993 to provide a range of management and organizational support to health and personal social services organizations and individuals in Northern Ireland. The BMC is a government organization that is owned by most of the health and social service boards, trusts, and agencies of Northern Ireland, all of which are also public organizations. In Northern Ireland, the vast majority of health and social services organizations are public. In U.S. terms, the BMC is a governmental unit that exists and operates through a joint powers agreement. At the time of the exercise (June 2004), the BMC identified eighteen major health and personal social service organizations in Northern Ireland as its "core clients" (this number has since dropped considerably due to mergers), but it also has expanded its client base to include many other public and nonprofit organizations, including several outside the United Kingdom. The BMC is organized into three units: management development, which is the focus of the process outlined here; nursing and midwifery education; and financial services. Thus, the BMC is clearly an unusual public organization: it is the result of a collaboration among other public organizations, and most of its funding comes from service and performance contracts with these organizations. But the BMC is not so unusual in that it represents an increasingly common form of public enterprise whose funding and continued existence is wholly dependent on providing good service to its customers (Barzelay, 1992; Osborne & Plastrik, 1997).

The process of developing and using a livelihood scheme involves several steps. The nature and order of these steps has changed over time as experience with developing a livelihood scheme has accumulated. The steps are as follows (see Exhibit C.1):

- Do the necessary preparation work
- Identify critical success factors (CSFs) and potential distinctive competency outcomes (DCOs)
- Identify competencies (Cs), distinctive competencies (DCs), threshold competencies (TCs), and distinctive assets (DAs)
- Identify a tentative aspiration system (including, for example, mission, mandates, goals, and critical success factors)
- Build a draft livelihood scheme
- Create a full livelihood scheme
- Develop a multiyear strategic plan based on the underlying logic of the livelihood scheme
- Develop a first-year business plan

Exhibit C.1. Identifying Distinctive Competencies, Distinctive Assets, and Aspirations and Creating a Livelihood Scheme to Support the Strategic Plan and Annual Business Plans.

Do Necessary Background Work

- The process champion should assemble necessary background materials and distribute them to group participants prior to the meeting.
- The process champion should assemble the right group to develop a livelihood scheme.
- The process champion should acquire the services of a skilled group process facilitator, if necessary.
- The process champion should secure adequate physical facilities for the exercise, including a conference room with:
  - Comfortable chairs, a supply of beverages, and easily accessible restrooms
  - Uninterrupted wall space covered with flip chart sheets— two rows of paper, eight sheets wide, with each sheet overlapping the next by one inch
- The process champion or facilitator assembles:
  - Two hundred 5- by 7-inch self-stick notes, cards, or ovals (see Resource D)
  - Black, bullet-tipped, water-based marking pens for each participant and the facilitator
  - Self-adhesive putty or masking tape for mounting the cards or ovals on the flip chart sheets
  - Soft-lead pencils for marking in tentative links among statements

Identify Critical Success Factors (CSFs) and Potential Distinctive Competency Outcomes (DCOs)

- The facilitator starts by having the group as individuals brainstorm answers to the question, "From the key stakeholders' perspectives, what must we do especially well to succeed—now and in the future?"
- Individuals should transcribe their responses onto self-stick notes, cards, or ovals using marking pens

- The facilitator attaches the statements to a flip chart–covered wall and, with the assistance of the group, links (maps) the statements into a causal network; the map indicates how the statements are causally linked to one another by using arrows that show, for example, how A $\rightarrow$ (causes or leads to) B $\rightarrow$ (which causes or leads to) C, and so on.

- The facilitator asks the group to identify ideas that appear to be actual CSFs and those which are likely to be actual or potential DCOs—meaning outcomes that support doing well against the CSF, or else are the same as the CSF; DCOs in turn require having or developing the distinctive competencies (DCs) needed to produce the DCOs (see next step).

- The facilitator uses marking pens or stick-on dots of different colors to highlights CSFs and DCOs.

- The group should note which statements support meeting or achieving the CSFs or DCOs directly or indirectly and which do not.

Identify Competencies (Cs), Distinctive Competencies (DCs), Threshold Competencies (TCs), and Distinctive Assets (DAs)

- The facilitator asks the group as individuals to brainstorm potential competencies (either already in existence or needing to be created)—including threshold competencies (TCs) necessary for being in the business in the first place, for example, having accounting, financial management, HR, IT, and procurement systems that work.

- Again, individuals should transcribe their responses onto self-stick notes, cards, or ovals using marking pens.

- The facilitator helps the group map the resulting statements into a causal network.

- The facilitator helps the group identify which statements appear to be DCs (that is, those that are in existence and are difficult for others to replicate), Cs, TCs, and DAs (that is, hard-to-replicate resources necessary to be in place for the distinctive competency

(Continued)

Exhibit C.1. Identifying Distinctive Competencies, Distinctive Assets, and Aspirations and Creating a Livelihood Scheme to Support the Strategic Plan and Annual Business Plans, Continued.

to operate). DCs, Cs, TCs, and DAs that need to be created should also be noted.

- Again, the facilitator uses marking pens of different colors or different colors of stick-on dots to highlight DCs, Cs, TCs, and DAs.

Identify the Tentative Aspiration System (Mission and Goal System)

- The facilitator asks the group to think about aspirations that might be achieved with the DCs—not all of which are likely to be official organizational aspirations at present.
- The facilitator asks the group to brainstorm actual or potential purposes, goals, aims, aspirations, and outcome indicators on cards (or ovals), many of which may already be given.
- Individuals should transcribe their responses onto self-stick notes, cards, or ovals using marking pens.
- The facilitator helps the group create a purpose network or expansion (that is, build a causal network or hierarchy from more specific aspirations to most general and abstract aspirations).
- The facilitator helps the group identify tentative mission and goal statements that are a part of the purpose network; note that some statements may indicate performance indicators.
- Again, the facilitator uses marking pens of different colors or different colors of stick-on dots to highlight mission-related statements, goal-related statements, and performance indicators.

Build Initial Parts of Livelihood Scheme

- The facilitator helps the group link aspirations to CSFs, DCOs, DCs. DAs, and TCs; the facilitator encourages the group to add statements as necessary.

- The facilitator helps the group identify what appear to be crucial linkages, and especially loops, that are at the core of the livelihood scheme.

Create the Full Livelihood Scheme

- The facilitator helps the group review and discuss the full map.
- The facilitator helps the group:
  - Note which are existing aspirations and which are new
  - Check to see that every aspiration is supported directly or indirectly by a DC
  - Check to make sure that assets are in place to resource each DC, C, and TC
  - Note which competencies do not support any goal
  - Note competencies that need to be developed
  - Note which assets need to be developed
  - Decide which aspirations refer to mission, which are goals, and which are outcome or performance indicators
- The facilitator helps the group finalize the livelihood scheme.

Use the Livelihood Scheme to Help Develop a Strategic Plan

- The strategic planning team should use the livelihood scheme to help provide the basic logic for the strategic plan.
- The team should develop a livelihood scheme consultation document for review by key stakeholders.
- The team should make sure the process of developing the strategic plan draws on and reinforces distinctive competencies wherever possible.

Develop an Annual Business Plan

- The strategic planning team or those with operational responsibilities should develop an action plan for each goal and subgoal.
- Action plan developers should provide measurable targets for each goal and subgoal.
- Action plan developers should make sure there is a clear logic linking the livelihood scheme, strategic plan, and annual business plan.

Draft livelihood schemes are typically developed in a one-day workshop that involves minimal physical requirements. Development of a multiyear strategic plan takes longer. The BMC's policy board adopted the organization's 2005–2008 strategic plan in June 2005, twelve months after the livelihood scheme was developed. The BMC's 2005–2006 business plan was adopted shortly thereafter. Twelve months is reasonable given the amount of consultation with key stakeholders that a multiorganization collaboration requires.

General Requirements for the Process, Including Preparation Work

The specific process to be followed depends on the situation. Almost always, though, some advance planning is necessary in order to make sure the needed participants are available and committed to working on the process. Outside facilitation may also be necessary. Important background information needs to be available, either on demand or as background reading for participants. The venue must be booked and necessary materials must be assembled. The most important requirement, of course, is an agreement among the participants to work together constructively. In the BMC case, the preparation work included deciding who should participate. The decision was made by the chief executive to assemble a group consisting of the senior management team of the management development unit (three people), plus the BMC business manager and herself. The chief executive also contracted with John Bryson to provide the necessary facilitation. In all, six people participated in the process, which clearly is a small group; the purpose of the session, however, was enhanced strategic thinking, not broad engagement.

Preparation work in this case also included having key staff revisit previous strategic planning efforts in which the need to develop new products and services had been highlighted. The ensuing discussion crystallized a realization that new product and service development was not occurring fast enough, in large part because the BMC was finding it difficult to stop delivering *old* products and services that were in demand by some clients in order to free up time to develop *new* products and services. A stakeholder analysis exercise was then undertaken in which a two-by-two matrix of clients was created. One dimension captured how much the client used the BMC's consultancy and training products and services, while the other dimension represented how much the clients pushed the BMC to develop new products and services more responsive to new or emerging client demands and conditions. The decision was made to focus on CSFs related to working with the clients who pushed BMC the hardest to stay on the cutting edge and who also made the most use of BMC products and services. If this group—the *key* stakeholders—was not attended to closely, they might quit using BMC's consulting and training services and use alternative sources instead, which would cut off important revenues and the stimulus and partners with which to develop new products and services.

Identify Critical Success Factors (CSFs) or Potential Distinctive Competency Outcomes (DCOs)

The next step in the process is to identify CSFs or potential DCOs. The following steps are suggested: The facilitator should start with the question, "From the key stakeholders' perspectives, what must we do especially well to succeed—now and in the future?" Participants should then brainstorm possible responses to this question on cards, one response per card. Responses should be phrased as actions starting with the imperative form of a verb (get, provide, enhance, create, and so on). At this point it will probably be hard to tell the difference between a CSF and a potential DCO. The key distinction is that CSFs are what matter to key stakeholders, while a potential DCO (the outcome produced by a DC) may not be important to key stakeholders. The question is phrased to get at key outcomes (CSFs or DCOs) because experience has shown that it is easier for managers to identify CSFs and DCOs than DCs, mainly because managers often confuse the outcome of a DC with an actual DC (Eden & Ackermann, 2010).

The facilitator next helps the group map the resulting statements to indicate links among CSFs and potential DCOs and any supporting concepts, indicating how the CSFs and DCOs might be achieved. The mapping should be in the top half of a flip chart sheet–covered wall. Many statements are likely to surface in the process, and quite a few will be incorporated into the final livelihood scheme linking DCs (yet to be identified) to DCOs and CSFs. In the BMC case, three CSFs were identified that ultimately ended up being synonymous with DCOs. These were thought to be crucial in satisfying the demands of key stakeholders—the organizations that use BMC services the most and push the BMC the hardest to stay on the cutting edge. The CSFs were to "develop the clients' capacities," "help clients manage critical business issues," and "enhance clients' performance profiles and image." The first CSF means helping to develop clients' capacities to be well managed and to deliver high-quality health and social care. The second CSF means helping clients to effectively address immediate and challenging difficulties affecting management and health and social care delivery. The final CSF means helping the clients inform others of their successes for political, financial, and public relations reasons. The BMC staff agreed to incorporate these CSFs as the functional equivalent of goals in the final livelihood scheme. After distinctive competencies (DCs) were identified in the next step, the group decided that the CSFs were identical to what the Beeches should want as DCOs produced by the DCs—suggesting the group should explore direct or indirect existing or potential links between the DCs and the CSFs/DCOs, as these links would be an important part of the developing livelihood scheme.

Identify Competencies (Cs), Distinctive Competencies (DCs), Threshold Competencies (TCs), and Distinctive Assets (DAs)

The next step involves the facilitator asking the group to identify distinctive competencies. Again, the group is first asked to brainstorm possible competencies (in general) on cards. Second, the cards are attached to the bottom half of the flip chart–covered wall, leaving space between them and the CSFs, potential DCOs, and other supporting statements already on the wall above them. Clusters of related cards are established and redundant items are removed. Third, relevant causal links are added to indicate influence relationships among the statements. What appear to be distinctive competencies are noted by placing a blue dot on them after the group has reached agreement. Similarly, needed but not-yet-developed or underdeveloped competencies are identified with an orange dot after the group has reached agreement. Eden and Ackermann (1998, p. 108) note that this process can be particularly difficult for public organizations because they are rarely expected to explore distinctive competencies.

In the BMC case, the ultimate result of this exercise appears in Figure C.1, which presents the map of BMC competencies and distinctive competencies. Figure C.1 indicates six DCs (in rounded rectangles), five DAs, and two Cs that need to be developed (TCs are not included). The DAs include funds or stocks of knowledge, skills, and relationships that are difficult for any competitors to emulate. The two Cs needing to be developed include competency in rigorous market research and partnering skills with other providers for product development. Because these would be skills many organizations might have they are unlikely to be *distinctive* competencies. The DCs are linked to the very specific DAs that BMC staff members have in relation to health and social care knowledge, policies, services, organizations, and clients. These abilities and the assets on which they are based are hard to replicate. In addition, the relationships help the BMC maintain a secure resource base, including its facilities. In exploring the resulting network, a number of patterns emerge. There are, in total, eleven self-reinforcing positive loops, or *virtuous circles* (Senge, 2006), within this linked set of statements. The loops support each other to the BMC's benefit. The DA, "Good relationships with key actors in the service" appears in all of these loops. If this DA did not exist and link to others, all of the loops would disappear; for this reason alone, it is likely to be a core distinctive asset. If the BMC wishes to stay "in business," the loops should be diligently maintained and perhaps new ones promulgated.

Identify Aspiration System (such as Mission, Mandates, Goals, and CSFs in Relation to One Another)

The next step in the process is to identify the organization's aspiration system (including, for example, mission, mandates, goals, CSFs). The BMC participants were familiar with the organization's then-current mission statement:

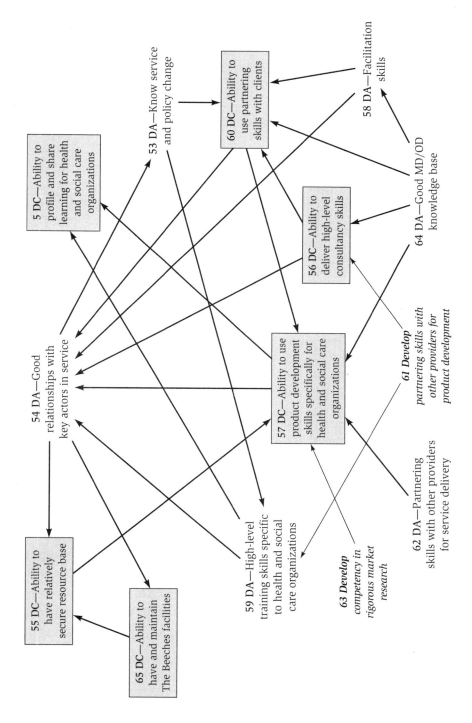

Figure C.1. BMC Competencies, Distinctive Competencies, and Distinctive Assets.

Note: Numbers merely indicate when an idea was entered into the supporting computer program Decision Explorer; see Resource D.

463

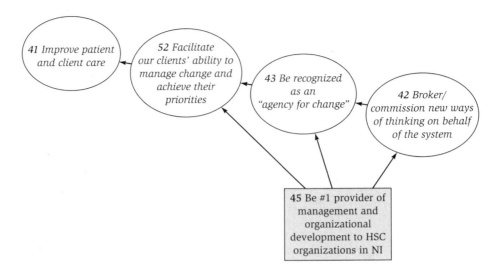

Figure C.2. BMC Goal and Broader Purposes.

The Beeches Management Centre is committed to providing management, education and organizational support to health and social services organizations. We will work in partnership with our clients to enhance their capacity to achieve their objectives. This will be achieved by the effective deployment and use of our staff and other resources at our disposal.

The participants also knew, however, that they needed to add detail to the mission in terms of high-level purposes or public value to be pursued and goals to be achieved.

The purpose-network or expansion technique was used to help identify the BMC's aspirations beyond its current mission (Nadler & Hibino, 1998, pp. 127–159; Nutt, 2002, pp. 124–130). First, the group was asked to brainstorm, as individuals, possible aspirations (purposes, mandates, goals, CSFs already identified, outcome indicators) on cards. Second, the cards were attached to a second wall covered by flip chart sheets, and a causal network was constructed indicating influence relationships among the statements. The ultimate result of this exercise is presented in Figure C.2. The rounded rectangle shows a somewhat shortened version (because of software limitations) of the BMC's overall goal, which in its full form is as follows:

To be recognized as the main regional provider of education, learning and organization development to the Health and Personal Social Services organizations and a leading provider to the wider public, voluntary, and independent sectors within Northern Ireland and beyond.

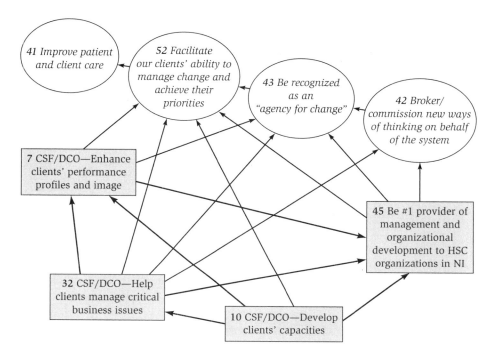

Figure C.3. BMC Goal, Broader Purposes, and Critical Success Factors (CSFs)/ Distinctive Competency Outcomes (DCOs).

The four statements in ovals represent broader health and social care system-level outcomes to which the BMC expects to contribute. These higher-level outcomes are mission-like statements in that they articulate ultimate purposes. It is unlikely, however, that the BMC would choose to be held directly accountable for the ultimate purpose—"improving patient and client care"—as it has no direct responsibility or capacity for doing so. Figure C.3 combines the CSFs and DCOs previously identified with the overall goal and broader purposes. Figure C.3 represents the public value that the BMC seeks to create and captures what was now placed on the flip chart–covered wall used to identify the BMC's DCs, DAs, and Cs.

Create Draft Livelihood Scheme

In order to create a livelihood scheme, the aspiration system—what is desired— must be supported by the competencies, distinctive competencies, and distinctive assets (that is, what can be reliably drawn on to achieve the aspirations). For the BMC, then, the next step in the process was to link the statements in Figure C.1 to those in Figure C.3 and thereby attempt to construct a valid BMC livelihood scheme. After considerable reflection and discussion, mapping and remapping, final agreement was reached on the aspirations, distinctive competencies, distinctive assets, needed competencies, and links among them. Together, these elements composed the draft livelihood scheme for the BMC, which is presented in Figure C.4. The livelihood scheme indicates that the aspiration system is strongly supported either directly or indirectly by distinctive competencies and distinctive assets.

The final steps involve using the livelihood scheme as a guide to developing a strategic plan and annual business plans. The livelihood scheme provides the basic logic that the plans need to embody.

CONCLUSIONS

The argument being made in this resource may be summarized in the form of four assertions. First, it seems reasonable to argue that public and nonprofit organizations that perform well over long periods of time will draw on distinctive competencies and distinctive assets that consist of linked competencies and assets and self-reinforcing loops of competencies and assets. This is the key proposition of the resource-based view of strategy, especially as elaborated by Eden and Ackermann (1998, 2010; Ackermann & Eden, 2011), who emphasize the importance of linked competencies and self-reinforcing positive loops (virtuous circles) of competencies. The BMC example illustrates how competencies, distinctive competencies, core distinctive competencies, and distinctive assets can provide an important basis for sustained performance and the creation of public value.

Second, it also seems reasonable to argue that public and nonprofit organizations that develop a valid livelihood scheme and formulate and implement their strategies based on that scheme will achieve a better fit or alignment with the demands and opportunities of their environments—and will perform better in those environments—than organizations that do not. The meaning of *valid*, of course, is open to debate. Valid in this case means a livelihood scheme that (1) takes aspirations (mission, mandates, goals, key performance indicators, stakeholder demands, and so forth) into account and that (2) is tested with key actors in the environment. Effort of this kind is crucial for actually mobilizing public and nonprofit organizational power for public purposes. As the famous political scientist James McGregor Burns notes, "The two essentials of power are motives and resources. The two are interrelated. Lacking motives [aspirations], resources diminish; lacking resources, motives lie idle. Lacking either one, power collapses" (1978, p. 12). One reason why strategic planning is often less successful than it might be otherwise is probably that strategic planning exercises typically do not take distinctive competencies, distinctive assets, and their links to aspirations into account. In other words, many stra-

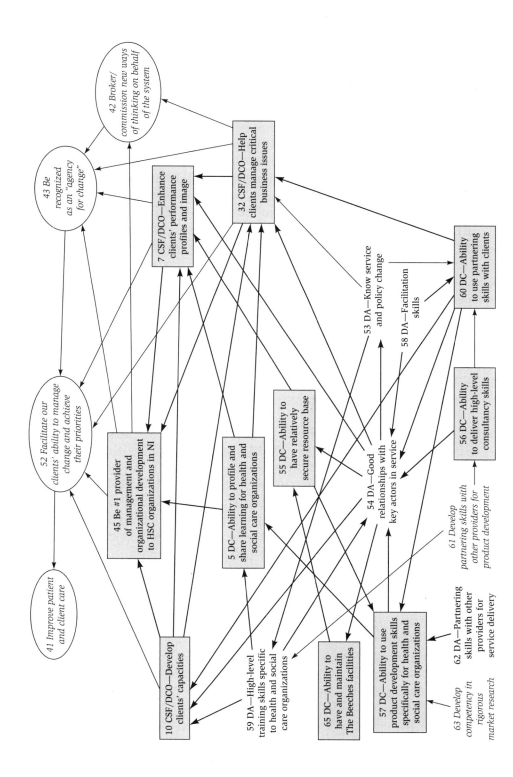

Figure C.4. BMC Livelihood Scheme.

467

tegic planning efforts miss a key component of effective strategizing and performance measurement and management.

Third, successful collaborations involving public and nonprofit organizations must be underpinned by linked competencies and assets across organizations in the service of the organizations' shared aspirations. A key feature of the linked competencies is their contribution to the building and maintenance of network-based intellectual, human, social, political, and cultural capital (Nahapiet & Ghoshal, 1998; Putnam, Feldstein, & Cohen, 2004) and the extent to which they allow participating organizations to achieve together what could not be achieved separately—in other words, to achieve *collaborative advantage* (Huxham & Vangen, 2005). The BMC process did not directly identify the competencies and assets of the clients with whom it collaborates, but the BMC livelihood scheme focused directly on collaborators who use the BMC the most and push it the hardest. The livelihood scheme acknowledges the need to exploit existing knowledge, products, and services, but it also highlights the need to explore and develop new knowledge, products, and services in partnership with these collaborators if the BMC is to continue to produce collaborative advantage and survive. A crucial feature of the BMC's linked competencies appears to be their ability to build on intellectual, human, social, political, and cultural capital tied to the BMC's collaborative role in the health and personal social service system.

Fourth, success for public organizations is likely to be based on the exploitation, sustenance, and protection of existing distinctive competencies and distinctive assets, as well as the development of new distinctive competencies and distinctive assets. The point is typically made with regard to for-profit organizations (Zollo & Winter, 2002). However, there is no reason to suppose that exploiting existing distinctive competencies and assets and developing new ones are any less significant for public and nonprofit organizations. Finally, the day a public or nonprofit management team spends on developing a livelihood scheme is typically one of the best days they will ever spend sharpening their strategic thinking, acting, and learning abilities.

Using Action-Oriented Strategy Mapping to Identify Strategic Issues and Formulate Effective Strategies

John M. Bryson, Fran Ackermann, Colin Eden, and Charles B. Finn

A crucial strategic planning task is to create strategic ideas that are worth implementing and can be implemented (see Figure 2.4). In order to create these ideas, it is useful to think in terms of at least four subtasks:

1. *Brainstorming ideas.* Techniques such as straight brainstorming (Johnson & Johnson, 2008) or the nominal group technique (Delbecq, Van de Ven, & Gustafson, 1986) can be used to create lots of ideas.

2. *Clustering the resulting ideas into categories.* Brainstorming can produce numerous ideas, but usually it is important to provide some clustering and categorization of the ideas in order to start understanding their strategic significance. The snow card process (see Chapter Five) can provide some structure to brainstormed ideas through grouping them into categories, which then can be organized into logical, priority, or temporal order. *Mind mapping* (Buzan & Buzan, 1996), *affinity diagramming* (Bauer, Duffy, & Westcott, 2006), and various *ideation* tools do much the same thing (see Resource B).

3. *Clarifying the specific action-outcome relationships among ideas.* Creating and categorizing ideas is typically not enough. It is also important to identify the causal relationships among ideas—in other words, what leads to what both within and across categories. A process therefore is needed to capture and map these relationships. The resulting causal map, or statement-and-arrow diagram,

consists of concepts (phrased as actions) recorded on self-adhesive labels or special oval-shaped pieces of paper linked by directional arrows indicating the cause and effect or influence relationships among them—such as A may cause or influence B, which in turn may cause or influence C (Bryson, Ackermann, Eden, & Finn, 2004). These maps can consist of hundreds of interconnected relationships, showing different areas of interest and their relationships to one another.

4. *Using the resulting map to inform strategic thinking, acting, and learning.* The maps should help the group using it gain a more holistic understanding of what is going on in an area, what might be done about it, and why. As actions are taken they can be assessed in light of the predicted outcomes the map suggests, and new actions can be taken or the map can be redone, or both.

The *action-oriented strategy mapping* (AOSM) process (or *oval mapping technique*, as it was called in the last edition of this book), which is a causal mapping technique, was developed and refined over a number of years by Colin Eden and a large number of associates (Eden, Jones, & Sims, 1983; Eden & Huxham, 1996; Eden, Ackermann, & Cropper, 1992; Eden & Ackermann, 1998; Bryson, Ackermann, Eden, & Finn, 2004; Ackermann & Eden with Brown, 2005; Ackermann & Eden, 2011). The process was developed as part of an approach to strategic management called *strategic options development and analysis* (SODA) (Eden, 1989; Eden & Ackermann, 2001) that has strongly influenced my own approach to strategic planning (outlined in Chapter Two). Bryson, Ackermann, Eden and Finn (2004) summarize much of this work for practitioners and provide a key source of material for this resource section.

AOSM can be used with individuals or with groups. Normally we suggest that groups have no more than ten members, as in groups larger than ten, participants can be lost in the crowd and not feel they are part of the group. But groups of more than ten are possible, especially if there is a strong group facilitator, or when maps are created by subgroups and then merged. Actually, having subgroups is advantageous; dividing the team into subgroups can produce different interpretations of an issue area, along with subsequent insights gained from comparing and contrasting these interpretations. Subgroups can all be assigned the same question or issue, or each can consider a different aspect of an issue. Subgroups may be homogeneous, representing a single class of stakeholder or organizational level, or heterogeneous, representing diverse interests. The simplicity of the basic process means it can be adapted to a number of uses, including stakeholder analyses (discussed later in this resource and in Resource A), scenario development (see Ackermann &

Eden, 1998), clarification of distinctive competencies (see Resource D), strategic issue identification, strategy development (see Ackermann & Eden, 2011), and clarifying the meaning of symbolically or substantively important concepts. Several of these applications are discussed below.

PURPOSE AND DESIRED OUTCOMES

The purpose of the AOSM process is to make sense of an area of concern by capturing and structuring the ideas that compose it. The meaning of any particular idea is embedded in its context—that is, the ideas that influence it ("arrows in") and the ideas that flow from it as consequences or outcomes ("arrows out"). Comparing and contrasting ideas and elaborating their connections establishes a rich context that makes understanding easier (Kelly, 1963; Weick, 1995). As ideas are explored, different interpretations are identified, leading to a more complete picture. The most important desired outcome of using the oval process thus is increased understanding of an important problem or issue area.

For example, a small nonprofit college was facing a serious financial crisis (see Bryson, Ackermann, Eden, & Finn, 2004, pp. 153–180, for more detail on this composite case synthesized from other real cases). A team of fifteen persons was assembled to develop the basics of a strategic plan (mission, goals, and basic strategy areas) using the oval mapping process. The team included representatives of the board, faculty, administration, students, alumni, potential donors, and townspeople, among others. The group (which was led by a strong facilitator and was not divided into subgroups) constructed a map of about a hundred unique ideas, all linked by arrows, in the space of a few hours. As the map was created, each idea was given a unique number in a sequence beginning with 1. The numbers have no meaning other than to indicate the sequence in which the ideas were created and to allow a special computer software called Decision Explorer to keep track of each idea. In other words, the numbers served as a placeholder for the software, which is discussed further later.

One of the issue areas the group identified was "generate more income, for example, tuition and fee income" [2] (see Figure D.1). This issue was affected directly by one other issue, "increase student enrollment" [28] and indirectly by five others, including "increase academic standards" [82]. There is a negative link between "increase academic standards" and "increase academic enrollment," because increasing academic standards might lower, not increase, student enrollment unless the process is carefully managed. (Such management might include "convening meetings with teachers" [46] and "having meetings with parents" [14]—items not shown in the figure). Generating more

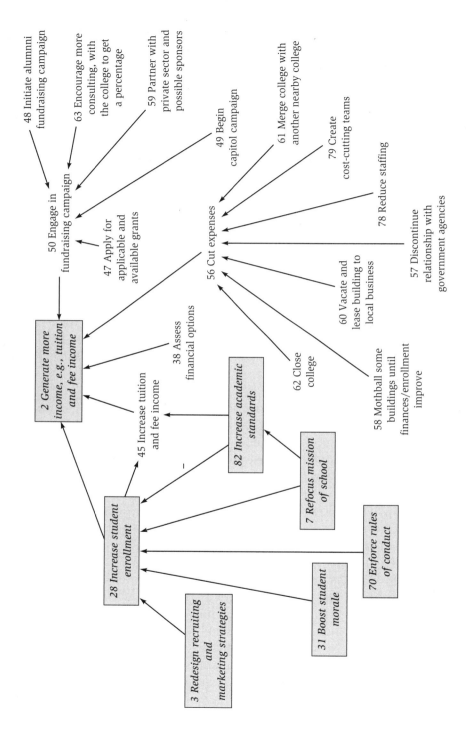

Figure D.1. Small College Strategic Issue: Generate More Income.

Note: Strategic issues are shown in boxes; unboxed entries are options for addressing the issues.

Source: Bryson, Ackermann, Eden, & Finn, 2004, p. 167.

income would also require "increasing tuition and fee income" [45], "assessing financial options" [38], two bundles of actions, "cut expenses" [56] and "engage in a fundraising campaign" [50]. Cutting expenses might involve "closing the college" [62], "mothballing some buildings until finances/ enrollment improve" [58], "vacating and leasing buildings to local businesses" [60], "discontinuing relationships with government agencies" [57], "reducing staffing" [78], "creating cost-cutting teams" [79], or "merging the college with another nearby college" [61]. Engaging in a fundraising campaign could include "applying for applicable and available grants" [47], "beginning a capital campaign" [49], "partnering with the private sector and possible sponsors" [59], "encouraging more consulting, with the college getting a percentage" [63], and "initiating an alumni fundraising campaign" [48].

The issue of generating more income fits into a wider network of issues and goals and mission in somewhat complex ways (see Figure D.2). Generating more income, for example, tuition and fee income [2] would allow the college to "Pay teachers well" [55] and to "Seek to have excellent classroom and physical facilities" [53]. Paying teachers well would help "Ensure morale at the college is high" [51], which in turn would help achieve the mission, "To make lasting positive educational and civic contributions to our students, partners, and the community" [25]. Having excellent classroom facilities would also help directly ensure that morale is high at the college, and also would help ensure morale is high indirectly through "ensuring our students achieve outstanding results" [30], a result that would also contribute directly to the mission. Other goals and other issues also contribute directly and indirectly to the mission.

There are a number of important desired outcomes from using the AOSM process, including generally enhancing participants' capacity to reason effectively, engage in constructive dialogue, manage complex issue areas, and build teamwork within the group. The process, in other words, offers an excellent technique for achieving many of the outcomes indicated in Figure 3.1 that are likely to be needed for a successful strategic planning process. Other desired outcomes are as follows:

1. Making efficient use of a group's time. The process is easy to understand, teach, and use, and thus, complex maps can be developed relatively quickly.

2. Helping people figure out what they can do about an area of concern by structuring plausible action-outcome relationships. This makes the process very useful to leaders and managers, who typically have an action orientation and often are uncomfortable with vague abstractions. It also promotes understanding through working out what is necessary to make something happen.

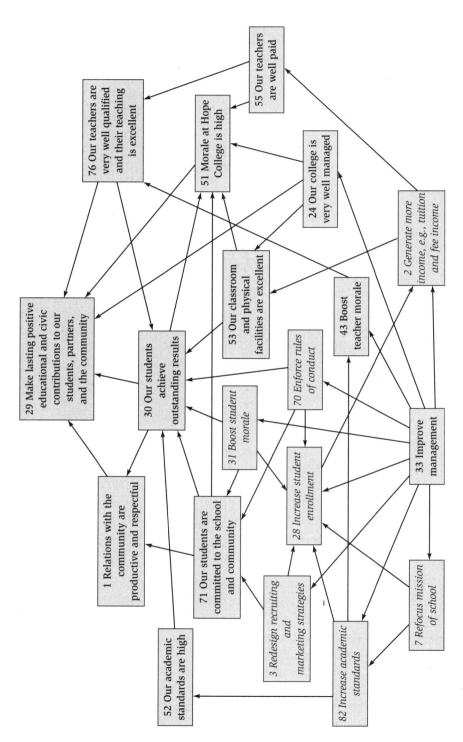

Figure D.2. Small College's Issues and Goals.

Note: Strategic issues are in italics; goals are not.

Source: Bryson, Ackermann, Eden, & Finn, 2004, p. 176.

3. Achieving fuller understanding of an area of concern and thereby helping to ensure that any actions taken are constructive rather than short-sighted, foolish, or downright damaging.

4. Fashioning the fuller understanding that comes from the inclusion of many people's views. The process helps to create a *shared* view of the area of concern and what might be done about it. The process thus promotes intra- and interorganizational, as well as intra- and interdisciplinary, understanding and creativity. In most cases, the shared view represents a reconstruing of reality (Kelly, 1963); that is, participants see the world differently than they did before they came together—not as a result of arguments—but through the way statements come to be linked together.

5. Giving more effective attention to the social aspects of group work by being highly participative and engaging. This promotes participants' understanding of each other's ideas and roles. It also means the process can build cohesion and generate commitment to, and ownership of, subsequent actions. The process thus is an effective team-building tool.

6. Creation of a forum for discussion and dialogue around important areas of concern, a fundamental feature of effective strategic planning, and a crucial precursor of effective action (Crosby & Bryson, 2005; Moynihan & Landuyt, 2009).

7. Creation of a tangible product—a map—that provides a record of the participants' merged contributions. To the extent that the map represents a shared and agreed-upon view, it serves as a *transitional object* (de Gues, 1988; Carlile, 2002; Kellogg, Orlikowski, & Yates, 2006), or bridge, to the next step in the strategic planning process. The map and the shared understanding of what it means can strongly influence mission formation, strategy development, and implementation.

8. The process and the maps that result provide a specific and useful way of managing complexity. The maps can incorporate broad and abstract general statements of desired states (goals) as well as clusters of more specific strategic options (issues) and agreed-upon portfolios of actions (strategies and work programs). The general form and logic of a map intended for use as an action-oriented strategy map is presented in Figure D.3. Goals are at the top, issues are below goals, options to achieve the issues are below issues, and statements of fact or assertions are at the very bottom. Typically, a workshop process is used to convert a draft map to an agreed-upon set of goals, strategies, actions, and assertions. MetroGIS made

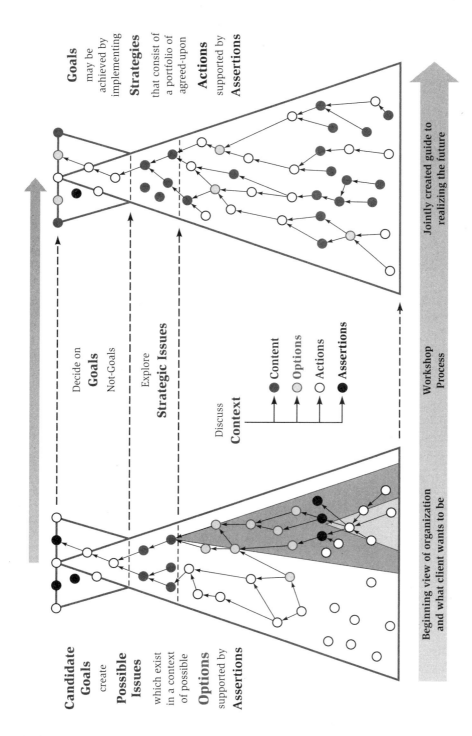

Figure D.3. General Shape and Logic of an Oval Map Intended for Use as an Action-Oriented Strategic Map.

Note: Large shaded triangle within left-hand shape represents an issues area; smaller triangle within it represents a subissue.

Source: Bryson, 2004, p. 362, © 1989 Fran Ackermann, 1995 by Real-izations, Inc. Reprinted with permission.

extensive use of AOSM in both of its strategic planning efforts. The Loft made use of a simplified version of mapping in its strategic planning process.

9. The final desired outcome is enhanced group productivity. Everyone can both "speak" (write on self-adhesive labels or on ovals) and "listen" (read the labels or ovals) in their full and broad context rather than having to hear one person's views at a time and in sequence. Further, participants can come and go without necessarily negatively affecting the process in significant ways.

PROCESS GUIDELINES

Persons wishing to use the process may find the following guidelines useful.

Equipment Needs

A large, smooth, unbroken wall space is needed for each map that will be constructed. The wall space should be approximately twenty feet wide and six to eight feet high. It is often difficult to find suitable wall space without some advance reconnaissance (and do not take someone else's word that a wall will work—go see for yourself!). This space will be papered over with flip chart sheets in two or three rows, one above the other. Each row should be six to nine flip chart sheets wide, depending on how many ideas are likely to be included on the map. The sheets should be hung with masking tape or self-adhesive putty so that they overlap each other by about an inch and the entire assembly is taped to the wall only on the top row. In other words, the top row of flip chart sheets should be taped to the wall at the top of the sheets; the next row should be taped to the top row, and if there is a third row it should be taped to the second row. When all the sheets are hung, the seams should be closed with masking tape so that the map can be taken off the wall in one piece when completed and easily transported. It is also advisable to photograph the map before taking it down; in order to make sure the text and arrows may be seen clearly, it may be advisable to take a photograph of each flip chart sheet. If the map does not need to be transported, it can be constructed on a large whiteboard (although it may be difficult to find one large enough), using whiteboard markers to indicate links among ideas.

It helps if the room is spacious, well-lit, handicapped accessible, and with easily accessible refreshments and restrooms. In addition, the following materials and equipment will prove useful:

- *A full flip chart pad.* Remember each map will take twelve to eighteen sheets or more, so do not get caught short.

- *Masking tape or self-adhesive putty, such as Blu-Tack.* This is to affix the flip chart sheets to the walls. Architect's drafting tape usually does not work as well because it is not as sticky.

- *Pads of self-adhesive labels, half-sheets of letter-sized paper, three-by-five-inch cards, or a stack of ovals.* If ovals are used, cut out or have made oval-shaped pieces of paper for use in the exercise, approximately 7½ inches (180 mm) long and 4½ inches (110 mm) wide. Typically, they are the same weight as construction paper. A template is provided in Exhibit D.1. Ovals should be yellow or some other light color so that they contrast with the background of the flip chart sheets yet allow any writing in marking pens on them to be read easily. Twenty to thirty ovals per participant should be available. Pre-cut, self-adhesive ovals may be purchased from http://www.banxia.com. Ovals are actually the best choice because when self-adhesive labels, half-sheets of paper, or cards are used, the resulting map usually consists of fairly rigid rows and columns rather than a more free-form and realistic organization of ideas that makes fuller and more creative use of a map's two dimensions.

- *A bullet-tipped, water-based marking pen for each participant.* Bullet-tipped, water-based marking pens may be harder to find than chisel-point pens, but they are easier to use and the results are more legible. The pens should be the same color—usually black—to promote anonymity and to contrast with the color of the ovals. Some additional marking pens in different colors should be available to highlight particular features of the map (links, titles, key observations) during group discussions. Do not use regular ballpoint writing pens, as the resulting writing likely will be impossible to read from a distance.

- *Self-adhesive putty (such as Blu-Tack) for attaching the ovals, half-sheets of paper, or three-by-five-inch cards to the flip chart sheet.* You need only a small amount of putty to attach an oval. Larger amounts are a waste and make it harder to move the ovals around. Alternatively, have participants attach a tape roll to the back of each oval. A tape roll is made of tape rolled sticky side out. Drafting tape is better than masking tape for this purpose; masking tape is too sticky and will likely tear the flip chart sheets if you try to move the the ovals around.

- *A sharpened, soft-lead pencil with attached eraser, or else a mechanical pencil with an eraser, for each participant.* These will be used for tentatively linking ovals via arrows and for making notes on the map.

Exhibit D.1. Template for an Oval.

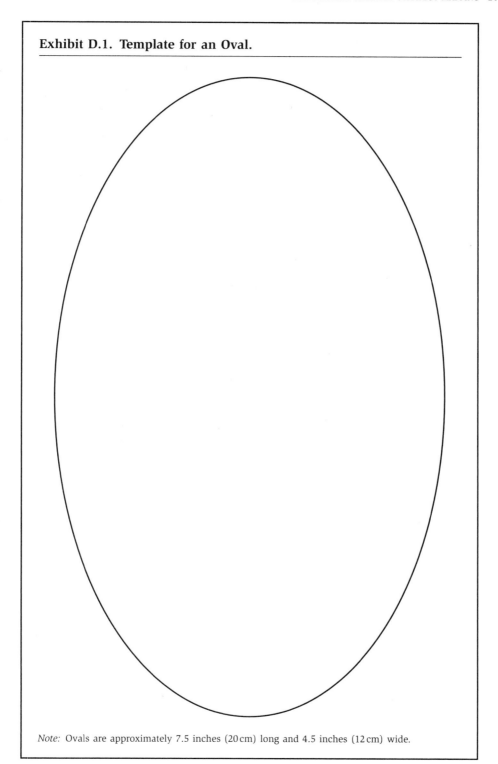

Note: Ovals are approximately 7.5 inches (20 cm) long and 4.5 inches (12 cm) wide.

- *Large erasers for use with lead pencils.* These will be used for larger erasing jobs.

- *Self-adhesive dots in various colors to identify the nature of particular ovals or clusters of ovals and for straw polls.* Have on hand packets of at least one hundred red, purple, blue, green, and orange dots three-quarters of an inch in diameter. (Larger dots cover too much space, particularly when used for straw polling, and smaller dots are harder to see.)

- *Suitable refreshments.* Have a supply of coffee, tea, soft drinks, mineral water, fresh fruit, nuts, cookies, and pastries, if possible.

- *A fully automatic digital camera.* This is to photograph the final map, each separate flip chart sheet, and the group as the process proceeds. The photographs can be used to remind participants of what happened, and to indicate to others the nature of the process. The photographs also provide a backup copy of the map in case anything happens to the original or to an electronic version of the map.

Preparing a Starter Question

Have a "starter" question (or set of questions) written out and clearly visible to participants. *Starting with the* right *question is very important* since it will have a dramatic impact on the answers. The question should be reasonably broad without being ambiguous. It should not be so narrow as to invite only yes or no answers. The planning team probably will need to devote considerable time to developing and pilot-testing the starter question(s), including consultations with key informants. Consider: "What should we do in the next three to five years?"

Introducing the Process

Participants will want information about the purpose of the session and the process to be used. For example, if the purpose of the session is to develop a sense of the strategic issues that face the organization and possible strategies that might address them, then the session might begin with this information:

1. Introduce the session by saying that the purpose of the session is to gather opinions about the issues the organization faces and what might be done about them. All of the information created will be used to inform the strategic planning process. Be as specific as you can be about what will happen to the information and how it will be used; typically, this means that the information will influence decisions rather than creating them directly.

2. All ideas must be written down on ovals (self-adhesive labels, half-sheets of paper, three-by-five-inch cards) or else they will get lost. This is an important opportunity for participants to have a significant influence on the identification of issues and development of strategies. Note that the process will result in a very efficient use of participants' time, since they can all "speak" simultaneously when writing on ovals—thus increasing each person's air time—and they can "listen" simultaneously when reading the ovals.

3. Ideas should be expressed in action terms, preferably starting with a verb, such as *do, buy, get, formulate, implement, achieve,* or some other imperative.

4. This process does not necessarily seek consensus or attempt to resolve conflict. Instead, the purpose is to clarify and understand how individuals and the group view the organization and its environment. If there are disagreements, it is important to clarify the rationales behind them and record them on separate ovals. It is *not* acceptable to remove other participants' ovals, to edit them without the author's consent, or to disparage the ovals or their authors. For example, in one exercise designed to address the needs of students with disabilities on a national basis, one group thought an oval labeled "have inclusive educational environment" meant having visually and hearing-impaired children in regular classrooms with sighted and hearing students. Another group thought it meant having separate schools for visually and hearing-impaired children so that they could experience being in a majority. Each view was placed on a separate oval and had an arrow going into the "have inclusive educational environment" oval.

5. Put ideas up on the wall as soon as they have been written down, rather than allowing participants to hoard them, so that others may see the ideas and build ("piggyback" or "hitchhike") on them.

6. Either the facilitator or the participants themselves should sort the ovals into clusters that make sense. Clusters should be organized according to common themes or subjects. The advantage of using a facilitator is that all participants can observe and join in the discussion of where each idea belongs. A shared group understanding of what all the ideas are may therefore emerge more quickly than if participants work in subgroups of two or three. If a facilitator does do the sorting, however, all participants should be encouraged to offer advice on where ovals should go. If participants do not know where they should go, the ovals should be placed to one side, to be revisited by the group after all the clusters have been examined, or else the

facilitator should sort them into the appropriate clusters as they become apparent. (Often, some combination of small-group and large-group work is desirable. For example, small groups may do the initial clustering and then a facilitator may help the large group make sense of the initial clusters and do any regrouping that is necessary.)

7. Keep the statement of each idea to around eight to ten words. This will encourage participants to write only one idea per oval, as well as make it easier for participants to read each other's ideas. The facilitator should encourage participants to lengthen short statements so that their meaning is clearer.

Facilitating the Process

1. Some participants may grasp the process quickly, start writing and displaying their ideas, and actively participate in structuring clusters of ideas. Others may take longer before they feel comfortable with the process and actively engage in it. It usually takes no more than twenty minutes to half an hour for everyone to be on board.

2. Ideas are first sorted into clusters that make sense. The next step in structuring the clusters involves placing ideas that are more general, abstract, or goal-oriented near the top of clusters. Ideas that are more concrete, specific, and detailed are placed toward the bottom. Also, assertions or statements of fact ("our budget will be cut 10 percent"; "client numbers are growing 20 percent per year"; "the executive director will retire in one year") are placed toward the bottom.

3. Encourage participants to elaborate on the ideas and emergent issue clusters by asking questions. Say, for example, "I do not really understand this, could you say more?" or "How would you make this happen?" or "What would you hope to get out of doing this?" Questions also prompt other participants to add alternative perspectives as they discover that their interpretation is different from the proponent's.

4. Make sure that ideas are worded in the imperative to suggest an action orientation.

5. Make sure each oval contains only one idea. If an oval contains more than eight to ten words, it usually means two separate ideas are present.

6. Keep encouraging people to write their ideas down, especially those participants who are less verbally dominant. One way to do this is to write a person's ideas on ovals as he or she is speaking and then place the ovals on the wall, to give the person confidence that his or

her ideas are worth including. Groups who are discussing or debating ideas can be encouraged to capture their views on ovals and attach them to the wall.

7. It can be helpful to number each oval as it is put up, to help participants locate ideas on the wall. Numbering also helps if computer support (discussed later) is used.

Further Structuring the Clusters

1. Tentatively title the clusters. Once fairly stable clusters appear and the number of new ideas diminishes, review each cluster and give it a name that describes the theme or subject of the ovals inside it. Write the name, phrased in action terms ("get our finances sorted out," "improve board-staff relations") on a new oval and place it at the top of the cluster. The cluster label typically will be the name of a potential strategic issue—indicated by the content of the cluster—and all of the ovals beneath it will consist of options for addressing the issue.

2. With the help of participants, pencil in links within clusters and across clusters. Arrows *to* an idea indicate causes, influencers, or something that has to happen first (the rules do not need to be absolutely precise). Arrows *from* an idea indicate effects, outcomes, or consequences. Using a pencil is a good idea, because the placement of arrows can change based on dialogue. Use an eraser to get rid of unwanted arrows. The placement of arrows shows participants which clusters or ideas are more important or "busy"— they are the ones with the largest numbers of cross-links to other clusters or ideas.

3. Decide whether the idea on an oval is an issue label, possible option, assertion, assumption, or statement of fact. Assertions, assumptions, or statements of fact are not directly actionable (except that they may call for further research) and should be placed at the bottom of clusters. Typically, they provide premises for subsequent strings of possible actions. For example, if "the executive director will retire in one year" (a statement of fact), then the job description may need to be reviewed, a search committee may need to be established, and a choice made whether to search for a replacement outside the organization as well as inside. Assertions or statements of fact also may lead to research (to find out whether they are true), or else may be converted to options by highlighting any implied actions.

Options are those ideas that contribute to achieving the purpose of a cluster (as indicated by the cluster's title). They are actionable ("update organization's Web site," "conduct focus groups," "use a telephone bank for fundraising"), rather than being assertions or statements of fact.

Issues, the label for a cluster of options, are more complex. An issue is usually stated in the top oval in a cluster, although dialogue may indicate that some other existing or new oval better captures the essence of the issue. Issues usually are broad-based, long-term, and highly consequential in terms of associated challenges or opportunities, effects on stakeholders, resource use, or irreversibility of possible strategies to address them. An asterisk or colored stick-on dot may be used to identify issues.

4. Once ovals are arranged hierarchically as issues, options, and assertions, decide on the relative importance of the issues. (This step may come after the following step if that change in order is thought desirable.) Colored stick-on dots may be used to graphically indicate the group's views of the issues' relative importance. For example, give each participant five dots and ask him or her to place a single dot on each of the five most important issues. Alternatively, participants might be allowed to put more than one dot on an issue label to provide a measure of intensity of feeling. It may also be helpful to straw poll participants directly on the relative *unimportance* of the issues. Often it is important to know which issues participants think are most important in the short term and which are most important in the long term. Dots of one color can be used to identify important short-term issues, and another color can be used for long-term issues.

5. Identify goals by asking "so what?" questions about the issue clusters. In other words, query participants about what they would hope to achieve ("arrows out") by addressing the issues effectively. Usually this line of questioning (or "laddering") leads participants to additional issues or options before the set of goals is fully specified. Ideas that are obviously good things in their own right and do not seem to need any further elaboration are candidates for goals. Typically, goals are morally virtuous and upright and tap the deepest values and most worthy aspirations of the organization's (or community's) culture. For example, pursuing this line of questioning around the strategic issues facing it led the small college to the goals outlined in Figure D.2. Goals may be identified with a new color of stick-on dots or self-stick note to highlight their significance. Again, straw polling procedures may be useful to indicate what participants believe are the most important goals.

Formulating and understanding a goal system involves identifying linkages among goals, issue labels, and options that compose issues. When working in a large group divided into subgroups, it is often useful to have subgroups switch the map they are working on after strategic issues have been identified—that is, groups should try to figure out the goal system implied by some other group's strategic issues. This procedure can open groups up to one another's thinking, promote creativity, and lead to a convergence across groups on goals, issues, options, and assertions.

The superordinate goals in a strategy map usually outline the organization's mission. If there is little connection between these goals and the organization's existing mission statement, then what the organization's mission should be is probably a strategic issue.

6. Decide on actions for the immediate future to address the issues and achieve the goals. The group should review the options (and their resource implications) and the ones already being done and the new ones that should be pursued over the course of the next six months to a year. Options that help address more than one issue (*potent options*) are particularly desirable ones to choose. A straw polling exercise—typically using green dots for "go"—may be used to pool participants' opinions about which items should be included in the action set. The group may wish to place two dots on items it wishes to take responsibility for itself and single dots on items it wishes to delegate to others outside the group. Once actions to address an issue have been chosen, the broad outlines of a strategy should be reasonably clear from looking at the map. The action set also typically comprises the basic tasks to be included in a work program that names the responsible parties, reporting dates, resources needed, and expected products or outcomes (see Chapter Nine).

7. Provide closure to the session. Groups of five to approximately thirty participants (in several subgroups) can often get through the process of constructing a draft map (including identifying goals, strategic issues, options, assertions, and actions) in a retreat setting over the course of a long day—or as part of a two- or three-day retreat that includes other activities, such as stakeholder analyses and SWOC/T analyses. At the end of the mapping exercise, some sort of closure is desirable, usually in the form of a review of what the group has done, what understandings or agreements have been reached, and a statement of what the next steps in the strategic planning process will be. For example, individuals or task forces may be assigned specific action items, or the task of developing the issues further and recommending strategies for dealing with them.

Recording the Work of the Map Construction Session

There are several ways to record the group's work:

1. The map can simply be taken off the wall and saved. Before doing so, however, it is advisable to run long strips of drafting tape across all of the ovals so that they do not come loose. The saved map can be posted wherever it is convenient so that its contents can be recorded in outline form, or for use as a focus in follow-up sessions.

2. The contents of the map may be recorded with the aid of a computer as the group discusses them, either in map form using software especially designed for the purpose (such as Decision Explorer, discussed at the end of this resource), or in outline form.

3. The map also may be photographed. A high-resolution digital camera with built-in flash can be used to photograph each flip chart sheet separately. As long as participants have written legibly on their ovals, the map's contents can be read from the photographs. Photographs thus provide a useful backup, in case the map itself gets lost. They also can be a reminder to participants of what the day was like, and can help nonparticipants understand how the process progressed. The photographs can be imported into a text document and distributed electronically or can be mounted on sheets of letter paper (four to a page), inserted into transparent holders, and put into a three-ring binder. A title page, date of the process, and a list of those who attended should precede the photographs. Alternatively, there are photocopying machines that can copy full flip chart sheets, reducing them to a smaller size if desired.

Useful Variations on the Mapping Process

The mapping process is very flexible and can be used in various ways over the course of a strategic planning process. For example, Resource C shows how mapping can be used to develop a livelihood scheme. Chapters Two and Six discussed the indirect approach to identifying strategic issues. In that approach, options are identified that might make or keep stakeholders happy; build on strengths, take advantage of opportunities, and minimize or overcome weaknesses and challenges; capture action-oriented features of mission and mandates, existing strategies, and background studies or reports; and in general create public value. These options are then arranged into clusters in an effort to find issues that emerge indirectly via the options. The mapping process obviously can be used to provide additional structure to the issues and options and to clarify the goal system that might be pursued by addressing them.

Mapping applications to stakeholder analyses, unpacking loaded concepts, and scenario construction are discussed in the following sections.

Stakeholder Analyses. Mapping may be used to develop a more integrated picture of an organization's stakeholders and how they relate to each other and to the organization. Many of the techniques presented in Resource A are forms of causal maps. For example, stakeholder influence diagrams are causal maps. Bases of power–directions of interest diagrams are also causal maps, in which the planning team tries to articulate each stakeholder's goal system and bases of power. The team can expand the map for each stakeholder by placing the team's own organization's goals on the map and indicating what the stakeholder does or can do to effect achievement of the organization's goals. Next, the team can identify what its own organization does or can do to meet the stakeholder's goals (or criteria or expectations regarding the team's organization). The pattern of influences and outcomes can then be explored and elaborated. The resulting map should help the team be clear about what the organization wants or needs from the stakeholder; what the stakeholder can do to give or withhold the wanted item (and why); and what the organization can do, if anything, about it.

These and other causal maps involving stakeholders should help highlight potential strategic issues and the elements of useful strategies. They also can be used for strategic planning team role plays aimed at developing strategic options most likely to address stakeholder interests effectively, build a supportive coalition, and ensure effective implementation. Resource A provides more information on how to conduct such a role play. The maps also are helpful in clarifying areas of potential collaboration with different stakeholders. In particular, the maps can highlight any potential collaborative advantages, which occur when it is clear that two or more stakeholders can achieve desirable outcomes jointly which they cannot achieve alone (Huxham & Vangen, 2005; Innes & Booher, 2010).

Unpacking Loaded Concepts. Often strategic planning is temporarily stymied by the need to deal with issues that carry extraordinary emotional freight for various stakeholders. The need to address issues of gender, race, disability, or political ideology, for example, has given headaches (sometimes heartaches) to teams with which I have worked. Such issues are highly emotional because of the negative consequences people have already suffered or think they may suffer depending on how the issues are resolved (Ortony, Clore, & Collins, 1990; Goleman, 2007). Reasonable dialogue usually becomes difficult or impossible. For example, to return to a case mentioned briefly earlier, a large group of seventy stakeholder representatives working under the auspices of the U.S. Department of Education was interested in developing a national agenda for better addressing the needs of students with disabilities. The group became stymied by what *inclusive* education meant for students with disabilities. The emotional temperature was high, and many people were willing to accuse others of pretty awful things. There was a certain humorous irony in the situation, in that what *divided* people was *inclusion*, but few present saw anything at all funny about it. Group members imagined the worst about each other, partly because in the absence of real dialogue no one really knew what others thought, and therefore many were prone to stereotype, project, and rationalize in inaccurate and unhelpful ways (Roberts, 2002). Eventually, the group was unwilling to proceed further until the facilitators helped them deal directly with this issue of inclusion. In response, the facilitators invented a variant of the mapping process employing the following guidelines:

1. Write the "loaded concept" on an oval and place it in the middle of a wall covered with flip chart paper. In the case of the education group, the loaded concept was "inclusive education for students with disabilities."

2. Have participants seat themselves in a semicircle in front of the wall (or more than one semicircle if the group is large).

3. Ask each person to take out a sheet of scratch paper and draw a line down the middle, dividing it into two columns of equal size. Label the left column "How?" and the right column "Why?" Then have each person individually and silently brainstorm as many answers to the two questions as possible. In the case of the education group it meant brainstorming as many possible *means* to achieving inclusive education as each person could imagine (how), and as many possible *ends* (outcomes, consequences, goals) of inclusive education (why) as they could imagine.

4. Have each person select a specified number of the most important means and an equivalent number of the most important ends and write each one on a separate oval. In the education case, participants were asked to select one item from each list, because with seventy people in the group, a greater number would have drawn the process out too much and probably generated redundant ideas.

5. Cluster the *means* ovals below the loaded concept, and cluster the *ends* ovals above it. Add structure if necessary to indicate how the various ideas within and across clusters are related.

6. Lead participants in a conversation about the resulting clusters. Add ovals, linkages, and clusters as necessary. As the precise nature of the disagreements become more clear, people are better able to discuss them and discover additional options or goals along the way. Keep

asking how and why questions to help participants clarify their reasoning and keep them from coming to blows over particular options. In other words, help people to be reason-*able*. Record key points right on the flip chart–papered wall or on a separate flip chart.

In most cases, the major disagreements will be over means and not ends. The map will make this graphically clear. When people realize they actually *share* some important goals, they are far more likely to engage in constructive dialogue about how to achieve them, and are also less likely to stereotype, project, and rationalize in destructive ways (Fisher & Ury, 1991; Thompson, 2008). In the educational group, many participants were surprised to find out that the entire group really did share most of the goals even though people differed on the far more numerous means. Heightened respect emerged, along with a less fraught atmosphere and a commitment to problem solving. After a number of months, the project ultimately resulted in a valuable report and sense of direction for the future (U.S. Department of Education, 1994).

Scenario Construction. The mapping process also can be used to develop the elements of scenario story lines. The main benefit of constructing scenarios is to promote learning by the planning team; sensitize team members to plausible though perhaps unlikely futures; and develop strategies better able to handle most eventualities (Schwartz, 1996; Van der Heijden, 2005; Marcus, 2009). The following guidelines may be used:

1. For each team member prepare a set of ovals that embodies the organization's mission, mandates, and existing goal system stated in action terms. The writing on these ovals should be in a different color from that used by participants to create their ovals following guideline 3 here.

2. Have the planning team consider the three *external* assessment categories outlined in Chapter Five: forces and trends (political, economic, social, technological, educational, physical); stakeholders who control key resources (clients, customers, payers, members of nonprofit organizations); and competitors, collaborators, and competitive and collaborative forces and advantages. Using three sheets of scratch paper, one for each category, each person brainstorms as many trends or events as he or she can imagine happening in each category. The team should consider trends and events that might affect the *internal* assessment categories as well— resources, present strategy, and performance. An additional three sheets of paper may be needed for this purpose. By looking externally and internally, the organization and all of its stakeholders are likely to be considered.

3. Each participant places ten to twenty brainstormed entries onto ovals, one entry per oval. Each oval should indicate the source of the idea (forces and trends; resource controllers; competitors, collaborators, and competitive or collaborative forces or advantages; resources; present strategy; performance).

4. The facilitator merges the participant-created ovals into a single set and shuffles them. Each participant (or small group) should be given up to twenty ovals. The participants are then asked to arrange their ovals into a map on a flip chart–covered wall in a way that indicates a plausible (though not necessarily likely) set of influence relationships and that connects the ovals positively or negatively to the ovals indicating the organization's mission, mandates, and goal system. Extra ovals may be added as necessary. In other words each participant should construct a *story* that links the ovals together and indicates influence chains that would either help or hinder achievement of the organization's goals.

5. The team should then review each story and answer the following questions:

   - What opportunities or challenges are highlighted?
   - Which stakeholders are affected by this story, and would they be happy or unhappy if it happened?
   - What strengths might we draw on to deal with this scenario, and what weaknesses would hinder us from dealing with it?
   - In the case of challenging scenarios (and especially those that are really threatening), what, if anything, could we do to keep this story from happening?
   - If we cannot do anything to stop it, what should we do to defend against it? Or is there any way to turn it into an opportunity?
   - What can we do, if anything, to make sure that desirable stories happen?

The answers to these questions should be recorded. If the team uses the indirect approach to strategic issue identification, many of the answers can be placed on ovals and used to construct issue clusters. Similarly, if the team develops a strategy map, many of the ovals can be included in the map.

Computer Support

Computer support becomes increasingly helpful as the number of ideas to be mapped, managed, and analyzed increases. Decision Explorer, developed by Colin Eden, Fran Ackermann, and associates, is an extremely powerful and useful software designed to help record, manage, and analyze maps. The software can handle maps containing thousands of concepts and their associated links. The concepts and links are stored in a central database and can be displayed in a similar format to the maps on walls. The software operates in a Windows environment and can draw on Windows for program management, color graphics, printing, and data storage and transfer. The software can be obtained from http://www.banxia.com. Training in the use of the software can be found through the same Web site.

REFERENCES

Abramson, M. A., Bruel, J. D., & Kamensky. J. M. (2006). *Six trends transforming government*. Washington, DC: IBM Center for the Business of Government.

Abramson, M. A., & Harris, R.S.I. (2003). *The procurement revolution*. Lanham, MD: Rowman & Littlefield.

Abramson, M. A., & Lawrence, P. R. (2001). *Transforming organizations*. Lanham, MD: Rowman & Littlefield.

Abramson, M. A., & Means, G. E. (2001). *E-government 2001*. Lanham, MD: Rowman & Littlefield.

Abramson, M. A., & Morin, T. L. (2003). *E-government 2003*. Lanham, MD: Rowman & Littlefield.

Aburdene, P. (2005). *Megatrends 2010: The rise of conscious capitalism*. Charlottesville, VA: Hampton Roads.

Ackerman, L. D. (2000). *Identity is destiny: Leadership and the roots of value creation*. San Francisco: Berrett-Koehler.

Ackermann, F. (1992). Strategic direction through burning issues: Using SODA as a strategic decision support system. *OR Insight*, *5*(3), 24–28.

Ackermann, F., & Eden, C. (2011). *Making strategy: Mapping out strategic success*. London: Sage.

Ackermann, F., Eden, C., with Brown, I. (2005). *The practice of making strategy*. London: Sage.

Agranoff, R. (2007). *Managing within networks: Adding value to public organizations*. Washington, DC: Georgetown University Press.

Agranoff, R., & McGuire, M. (2004). *Collaborative public management*. Washington, DC: Georgetown University Press.

Albert, S., & Bell, G. G. (2002). Timing and music. *Academy of Management Review*, *27*(4), 574–593.

Alexander, E. R. (1995). *How organizations act together: Interorganizational coordination in theory and practice*. Sydney, Australia: Gordon and Breach.

Alexander, E. R. (2000). Rationality revisited: Planning paradigms in a post-postmodernist perspective. *Journal of Planning Education and Research*, *19*, 242–256.

Allawi, A. A. (2008). *The occupation of Iraq: Winning the war, losing the peace*. New Haven, CT: Yale University Press.

Allee, V. (2002). Reconfiguring the value network. *Journal of Business Strategy*, *21*(4), 36–39.

Alvesson, M., & Wilmott, H. (2002). Identity regulation as organizational control: Producing the appropriate individual. *Journal of Management Studies*, *39*(5), 619–644.

Andersen, D. F., & Richardson, G. P. (1997). Scripts for group model building. *System Dynamics Review*, *13*(2), 107–129.

Anderson, J. E. (1990). *Public policymaking*. Boston: Houghton Mifflin.

Anderson, S. R., Bryson, J. M., & Crosby, B. C. (1999). *Leadership for the common good fieldbook*. St. Paul: University of Minnesota Extension Service.

Anderson, T., & Kanuka, H. (1997). *Evaluating the workplace center on-line forum: Knowledge construction and learning communities*. Canada: Office of Learning Technologies, Human Resources.

Andrews, C., Jonas, H. C., Mantell, N., & Solomon, R. (2008). Deliberating on statewide energy targets. *Journal of Planning Education and Research*, *28*(1), 6–20.

Andrews, K. R. (1971). *The concept of corporate strategy*. Homewood, IL: Dow Jones-Irwin.

Andrews, R., Boyne, G. A., Law, J., & Walker, R. M. (2009). Strategy formulation, strategy content, and performance: An empirical analysis. *Public Management Review*, *11*(1), 1–22.

Angelica, E. (2001). *Crafting effective mission and vision statements*. St. Paul, MN: Amherst H. Wilder Foundation.

Ansoff, H. I. (1965). *Corporate strategy*. New York: McGraw-Hill.

Ashforth, B. E., & Mael, F. (1989). Social identity theory and the organization. *Academy of Management Review*, *14*(1), 20–39.

Ashner, L., & Meyerson, M. (1997). *When is enough, enough? What you can do if you never feel satisfied*. Center City, MN: Hazelden.

Bachrach, P., & Baratz, M. S. (1962). Two faces of power. *American Political Science Review*, *56*, 947–952.

Bakewell, S. (2010). *How to live: A life of Montaigne in one question and twenty attempts at an answer*. London: Charro & Windus.

Ball, P. (2004). *Critical mass: How one thing leads to another*. London: Random House.

Ball, P. (2005). *Elegant solutions: Ten beautiful experiments in chemistry*. Cambridge, UK: Royal Society of Chemistry.

Bandura, A. (1997). *Self-efficacy: The exercise of control*. New York: Freeman.

Banxia Software. (2010). *Decision Explorer software*. Retrieved February 23, 2011, from www.banxia.com/dexplore.

Bardach, E. (1977). *The implementation game: What happens after a bill becomes law*. Cambridge, MA: MIT Press.

Bardach, E. (1998). *Getting agencies to work together*. Washington, DC: Brookings Institution Press.

Barkema, H. G., Baum, J.A.C., & Mannix, E. A. (2002). Management challenges in a new time. *Academy of Management Journal, 45*(5), 916–931.

Barney, J. B. (1991). Firm resources and sustained competitive advantage. *Journal of Management, 17*(1), 99–120.

Barney, J. B. (2001a). Resource-based theories of competitive advantage: A ten-year retrospective on the resource-based view. *Journal of Management, 27*(6), 643–650.

Barney, J. B. (2001b). Is the resource-based "view" a useful perspective for strategic management research? *Academy of Management Review, 26*(2), 25–42.

Barry, B. W. (1986). *Strategic planning workbook for nonprofit organizations*. St. Paul, MN: Amherst H. Wilder Foundation.

Barry, B. W. (1997). *Strategic planning workbook for nonprofit organizations* (revised and updated edition). St. Paul, MN: Amherst H. Wilder Foundation.

Bartlett, C. A., & Ghoshal, S. (1994, November–December). Changing the role of top management: Beyond strategy to purpose. *Harvard Business Review*, 79–88.

Barzelay, M. (1992). *Breaking through bureaucracy: A new vision for managing in government*. Berkeley: University of California Press.

Barzelay, M. (2001). *The new public management: Improving research and policy dialogue*. Berkeley & New York: University of California Press & Russell Sage Foundation.

Barzelay, M. B. (2009, December 9). Lecture on public management, deliberative pathways, design, and mechanism-based explanation in course LSE MG 419. London: London School of Economics and Political Science.

Barzelay, M., & Campbell, C. (2003). *Preparing for the future: Strategic planning in the U.S. Air Force*. Washington, DC: Brookings Institution Press.

Bauer, J. E., Duffy, G. L., & Westcott, R. T. (Eds.). (2006). *The quality improvement handbook* (2nd ed.). Milwaukee, WI: ASQ Quality Press.

Baum, H. S. (1997). Social science, social work, and surgery: Teaching what students need to practice planning. *Journal of the American Planning Association, 63*(2), 179–188.

Baum, H. S. (1999). Forgetting to plan. *Journal of Planning Education and Research, 19*, 2–14.

Baumgartner, F. R., & Jones, B. D. (2009). *Agendas and instability in American politics* (2nd ed.). Chicago: University of Chicago Press.

Becker, E. (1997). *The denial of death*. New York: Free Press.

Beckett, S. (1983). *Worstward ho*. New York: Grove Press.

Behn, R. D. (1983). The fundamentals of cutback management. In R. J. Zeckhauser & D. Leebaert (Eds.), *What role for government?* Durham, NC: Duke University Press.

Behn, R. D. (1988). Management by groping along. *Journal of Public Analysis and Management, 7*(4), 643–663.

Behn, R. D. (1991). *Leadership counts: Lessons for public managers from the Massachusetts Welfare, Training, and Employment Program*. Cambridge, MA: Harvard University Press.

Behn, R. D. (2001). *Rethinking democratic accountability*. Washington, DC: Brookings Institution Press.

Behn, R. D. (2003). Rethinking accountability in education. *International Public Management Journal, 6*(1), 43–74.

Behn, R. D. (2008). Designing PerformanceStat. *Public Performance and Management Review, 32*(2), 206–235.

Belfast Health and Social Care Trust. (2008a). *The Belfast way*. Belfast, Northern Ireland, U.K.: Belfast Health and Social Care Trust.

Belfast Health and Social Care Trust. (2008b). *Corporate management plan, 2008–2009*. Belfast, Northern Ireland, U.K.: Belfast Health and Social Care Trust.

Belfast Health and Social Care Trust. (2009). *Leadership and management strategy, 2009–2012*. Belfast, Northern Ireland, U.K.: Belfast Health and Social Care Trust.

Belfast Health and Social Care Trust. (2010). *Annual report 2009–2010*. Belfast, Northern Ireland, U.K.: Belfast Health and Social Care Trust.

Bendor, J. B. (1985). *Parallel systems: Redundancy in government*. Berkeley: University of California Press.

Benkler, Y. (2005, September 30). *Common wisdom: Peer production of educational materials*. Paper presented at Advancing the Effectiveness and Sustainability of Open Education, Utah State University, Logan, UT. Retrieved September 5, 2009, from http://www.lulu.com/items/volume_3/162000/162436/1/print/162436.pdf.

Benner, M. J., & Tushman, M. L. (2003). Exploitation, exploration, and process management: The productivity dilemma revisited. *Academy of Management Review, 28*(2), 238–256.

Benveniste, G. (1989). *Mastering the politics of planning: Crafting credible plans and policies that make a difference*. San Francisco: Jossey-Bass.

Berger, P. L., & Luckman, T. (1967). *The social construction of reality*. New York: Doubleday Anchor Books.

Berger, R. A., & Vasile, L. (2002). *Strategic planning: A review of grantee practices*. Los Altos, CA: David and Lucile Packard Foundation.

Berman, E. (2006). *Performance and productivity in public and nonprofit organizations* (2nd ed.). Armonk, NY: M. E. Sharpe.

Berman, E. M., & West, J. P. (1998). Productivity enhancement efforts in public and nonprofit organizations. *Public Productivity and Management Review*, *22*(2), 207–219.

Berry, F. S., & Wechsler, B. (1995). State agencies' experience with strategic planning: Findings from a national survey. *Public Administration Review*, *55*(2), 159–168.

Bland, C. J. (2004). The research-productive department: Strategies from departments that excel. Bolton, MA: Anker.

Block, P. (1987). *The empowered manager*. San Francisco: Jossey-Bass.

Block, P. (2009). *Community: The structure of belonging*. San Francisco: Berrett-Koehler.

Boal, K. B., & Bryson, J. M. (1987). Charismatic leadership: A phenomenological and structural approach. In J. G. Hunt, B. R. Balinga, H. P. Dachler, & C. A. Schriescheim (Eds.), *Emerging leadership vistas* (pp. 11–28). Elmsford, NY: Pergamon.

Boal, K. B., & Schultz, P. L. (2007). Storytelling, time, and evolution: The role of strategic leadership in complex adaptive systems. *Leadership Quarterly*, *18*, 411–428.

Bolan, R. S. (1971). Generalist with a specialty—still valid? Educating the planner: An expert on experts. ASPO National Planning Conference, New Orleans.

Bolman, L. G., & Deal, T. E. (2006). *The wizard and the warrior: Leading with passion and power*. San Francisco: Jossey-Bass.

Bolman, L. G., & Deal, T. E. (2008). *Reframing organizations: Artistry, choice, and leadership*. San Francisco: Jossey-Bass.

Borins, S. (1998). *Innovating with integrity: How local heroes are transforming American government*. Washington, DC: Georgetown University Press.

Bourgeois, L.J.I. (1980). Performance and consensus. *Strategic Management Journal*, *1*, 227–248.

Bovaird, T. (2005). Public governance: Balancing stakeholder power in a network society. *International Review of Administrative Sciences*, *71*(2), 217–228.

Bovaird, T. (2008). Emergent strategic management and planning mechanisms in complex adaptive systems. *Public Management Review*, *10*(3), 319–340.

Bowman, J. S., West, J. P., & Beck, M. A. (2010). *Achieving competencies in public service: The professional edge*. Armonk, NY: M. E. Sharpe.

Boyne, G. A., & Chen, A. A. (2006). Performance targets and public service improvement. *Journal of Public Administration Research and Theory*, *17*, 455–477.

Boyne, G. A., & Gould-Williams, J. S. (2003). Planning and performance in public organizations: An empirical analysis. *Public Management Review*, *5*(1), 115–132.

Boyte, H. C. (2004). *Everyday politics: Reconnecting citizens and public life*. Philadelphia: University of Pennsylvania Press.

Boyte, H. C. (2008). *The citizen solution: How you can make a difference*. St. Paul, MN: Minnesota Historical Society Press.

Boyte, H. C., & Kari, N. N. (1996). *Rebuilding America: The democratic promise of public work*. Philadelphia: Temple University Press.

Bozeman, B. (1999). Bureaucracy and red tape. Upper Saddle River, NJ: Prentice Hall.

Bozeman, B. (2002). Public-value failure: When efficient markets may not do. *Public Administration Review, 62*(2), 145–161.

Bozeman, B., & Straussman, J. D. (1990). *Public management strategies: Guidelines for managerial effectiveness*. San Francisco: Jossey-Bass.

Bracker, J. (1980). The historical development of the strategic management concept. *Academy of Management Review, 5*, 219–224.

Brandl, J. (1998). *Money and good intentions are not enough*. Washington, DC: Brookings Institution Press.

Brandt, S. (2002, August 15). Park board overrides Rybak's veto of plan for headquarters. *Minneapolis/St. Paul Star Tribune*, p. 3B.

Brandt, S. (2010, October 13). New Minneapolis park chief will face full agenda. *Minneapolis/St. Paul Star Tribune*. Retrieved February 7, 2010, from http://www.startribune.com/local/104830644.html.

Braybrooke, D., & Lindblom, C. E. (1963). *A strategy of decision: Policy evaluation as a social process*. New York: Free Press.

Brewer, G. A. (2009, November/December). Drafting the BOLERO plan. *Public Administration Review*, 1162–1171.

Bridges, W. (2004). *Transitions: Making sense of life's changes*. New York: Perseus/Da Capo Press.

Brinkley, D. (2006). *The great deluge: Hurricane Katrina, New Orleans, and the Mississippi Gulf Coast*. New York: William Morrow.

Broom, C. A. (1995). Performance-based government models: Building a track record. *Public Budgeting and Finance, 15*(4), 3–17.

Brown, A. D., & Starkey, K. (2000). Organizational identity and learning: A psychodynamic perspective. *Academy of Management Review, 25*(1), 102–120.

Bruer, J., & Freud, S. (2000). *Studies in hysteria* (reissued edition). New York: Basic Books. (Originally published in 1957.)

Bryant, J. (2003). *The six dilemmas of collaboration: Inter-organizational relationships as drama*. New York: Wiley.

Bryce, H. J. (1999). *Financial and strategic management for nonprofit organizations* (3rd ed.). San Francisco: Jossey-Bass.

Bryson, J. M. (1981). A perspective on planning and crises in the public sector. *Strategic Management Journal, 2*, 181–196.

Bryson, J. M. (1988). Strategic planning: Big wins and small wins. *Public Money and Management, 8*(3), 11–15.

Bryson, J. M. (1995). *Strategic planning for public and nonprofit organizations* (2nd ed.). San Francisco: Jossey-Bass.

Bryson, J. M. (1999). *Strategic management in public and voluntary services*. Oxford, England: Elsevier Sciences.

Bryson, J. M. (2001). Strategic planning. In N. J. Smelser & P. B. Bates (Eds.), *International encyclopedia of the social and behavioral sciences* (pp. 15145–15151). New York: Pergamon Press.

Bryson, J. M. (2003). Strategic planning and management. In B. G. Peters & J. Pierre (Eds.), *Handbook of public management* (pp. 38–47). Thousand Oaks, CA: Sage.

Bryson, J. M. (2004a). *Strategic planning for public and nonprofit organizations* (3rd ed.). San Francisco: Jossey-Bass.

Bryson, J. M. (2004b). What to do when stakeholders matter: A guide to stakeholder identification and analysis techniques. *Public Management Review, 6*(1), 21–53.

Bryson, J. M. (2010a). The future of strategic planning. *Public Administration Review, 70*(Supp. 1), S255–S267.

Bryson, J. M. (2010b, September 16). My experience with British health care. *Minneapolis/St. Paul Star Tribune*, p. A1.

Bryson, J. M., Ackermann, F., & Eden, C. (2007, July/August). Putting the resource-based view of strategy and distinctive competencies to work in public organizations. *Public Administration Review*, 702–717.

Bryson, J. M., Ackermann, F., Eden, C., & Finn, C. B. (1996). Critical incidents and emergent issues in managing large-scale change. In D. F. Kettl & H. B. Milward (Eds.), *The state of public management* (pp. 267–285). Baltimore, MD: Johns Hopkins University Press.

Bryson, J. M., Ackermann, F., Eden, C., & Finn, C. (2004). *Visible thinking: Unlocking causal mapping for practical business results*. New York: Wiley.

Bryson, J. M., & Alston, F. K. (2011). *Creating your strategic plan* (3rd ed.). San Francisco: Jossey-Bass.

Bryson, J. M., & Anderson, S. R. (2000). Applying large-group interaction methods in the planning and implementation of major change efforts. *Public Administration Review, 60*(2), 143–162.

Bryson, J. M., Anderson, S. R., & Alston, F. K. (2011). *Implementing and sustaining your strategic plan*. San Francisco: Jossey-Bass.

Bryson, J. M., Berry, F. S., & Yang, K. (2010). The state of public strategic management research: A selective literature review and set of future directions. *American Review of Public Administration, 40*(5), 495–521.

Bryson, J. M., Boal, K. B., & Rainey, H. G. (2008, December 3–5). *Strategic orientation and ambidextrous public organizations*. Paper presented at the conference on Organizational Strategy, Structure, and Process: A Reflection on the Research Perspective of Raymond Miles and Charles Snow, Cardiff University Business School and the Economic and Social Research Council, Cardiff, Wales.

Bryson, J. M., & Bromiley, P. (1993). Critical factors affecting the planning and implementation of major projects. *Strategic Management Journal, 14*, 319–337.

Bryson, J. M., & Crosby, B. C. (1992). *Leadership for the common good: Tackling public problems in a shared power world.* San Francisco: Jossey-Bass.

Bryson, J. M., & Crosby, B. C. (1996). Planning and the design and use of forums, arenas, and courts. In R. Burchell, S. Mandelbaum, & L. Mazza (Eds.), *Planning theory for the 1990s* (pp. 462–482). New Brunswick, NJ: Rutgers University/CIPR Press.

Bryson, J. M., & Crosby, B. C. (2008). Failing into cross-sector collaboration successfully. In L. B. Bingham & R. O'Leary (Eds.), *Big ideas in collaborative public management* (pp. 55–75). Armonk, NY: M. E. Sharpe.

Bryson, J. M., Crosby, B. C., & Bryson, J. K. (2009). Understanding strategic planning and the formulation and implementation of strategic plans as a way of knowing: The contributions of actor-network theory. *International Public Management Journal, 12*(2), 172–207.

Bryson, J. M., Crosby, B. C., & Stone, M. M. (2006). The design and implementation of cross-sector collaborations: Propositions from the literature. *Public Administration Review, 66*(1), 44–55.

Bryson, J. M., Cunningham, G. L., & Lokkesmoe, K. J. (2002). What to do when stakeholders matter: The case of problem formulation for the African American men project of Hennepin County, Minnesota. *Public Administration Review, 62*(5), 568–584.

Bryson, J. M., & Delbecq, A. L. (1979). A contingent approach to strategy and tactics in project planning. *Journal of the American Planning Association, 45,* 167–179.

Bryson, J. M., & Einsweiler, R. E. (1987). Editors introduction to the strategic planning symposium. *Journal of the American Planning Association, 53,* 6–8.

Bryson, J. M., & Einsweiler, R. E. (1988). *Strategic planning: Threats and opportunities for planners.* Chicago: Planners Press.

Bryson, J. M., Freeman, R. E., & Roering, W. D. (1986). Strategic planning in the public sector: Approaches and future directions. In B. Checkoway (Ed.), *Strategic Approaches to Planning Practice.* Lexington, MA: Lexington Books, 1986.

Bryson, J. M., Gibbons, M. J., & Shaye, G. (2001). Enterprise schemes for nonprofit survival, growth, and effectiveness. *Nonprofit Management and Leadership, 11*(3), 271–288.

Bryson, J. M., Patton, M. Q., & Bowman, R. A. (2011). Working with evaluation stakeholders: A rationale, step-wise approach, and toolkit. *Evaluation and Program Planning, 34,* 1–12.

Bryson, J. M., & Roering, W. D. (1987). Applying private-sector strategic planning to the public sector. *Journal of the American Planning Association, 53*(1), 9–22.

Bryson, J. M., & Roering, W. D. (1988). Initiation of strategic planning by governments. *Public Administration Review, 48,* 995–1004.

Bryson, J. M., & Roering, W. D. (1989). Mobilizing innovation efforts: The case of governments in strategic planning. In A. H. Van de Ven, H. L. Angle, & M. S. Poole (Eds.), *Research on the management of innovation* (pp. 583–610). New York: Harper Collins.

Burby, R. J. (2003). Making plans that matter: Citizen involvement and government action. *Journal of the American Planning Association*, *69*(1), 33–49.

Burns, J. M. (1978). *Leadership*. New York: Harper Collins.

Butler, T. (2009). *Getting unstuck: A guide to discovering your next career path*. Cambridge, MA: Harvard Business Press.

Buzan, T., and & Buzan, B. (1996). *The mind map book: How to use radiant thinking to maximize your brain's untapped potential*. New York: Plume.

Campbell, D. T., & Stanley, J. C. (1966). *Experimental and quasi-experimental designs for research*. Skokie, IL: Rand-McNally.

Campbell, H., & Marshall, R. (2002). Utilitarianism's bad breath? A re-evaluation of the public interest justification for planning. *Planning Theory*, *1*(2), 163–187.

Carlile, P. R. (2002). A pragmatic view of knowledge and boundaries: Boundary objects in new product development. *Organization Science*, *13*(4), 442–455.

Carver, J. (2006). *Boards that make a difference: A new design for leadership in nonprofit and public organizations*. San Francisco: Jossey-Bass.

Casabar, T., Henkel, B., Hervey, L., & Lewandowski, K. (2006). *Techniques and technologies for ideation*. Retrieved September 5, 2009, from http://bhenkel.echoechoplus.com/resumesite/ideation.doc.

Cassidy, A. (2002). *A practical guide to planning for e-business success: How to e-enable your enterprise*. Boca Raton, FL: St. Lucie Press.

Chait, R. P., Ryan, W. P., & Taylor, B. E. (2004). *Governance as leadership: Reframing the work of nonprofit boards*. New York: John Wiley.

Chattopadhyay, P., Glick, W. H., & Huber, G. P. (2001). Organizational actions in response to threats and opportunities. *Academy of Management Journal*, *44*(5), 937–955.

Chrislip, D. D. (2000). Cutting edge: Leadership 2000. In B. Kellerman & L. R. Matusak (Eds.), *The new civic leadership* (pp. 18–24). College Park, MD: James MacGregor Burns Academy of Leadership.

Chrislip, D. D. (2002). *The collaborative leadership fieldbook: A guide for citizens and civic leaders*. San Francisco: Jossey-Bass.

Christensen, C. M., & Overdorf, M. (2000, March–April). Meeting the challenge of disruptive change. *Harvard Business Review*, 67–76.

Christensen, K. S. (1993). Teaching savvy. *Journal of Planning Education and Research*, *12*, 202–212.

Christensen, K. S. (1999). *Cities and complexity: Making intergovernmental decisions*. Thousand Oaks, CA: Sage.

City of Charlotte, NC. (2009). *Charlotte FY2009 year-end corporate performance report*. Charlotte, NC: City of Charlotte Budget and Evaluation Office.

City of Charlotte, NC. (2010). *Charlotte's balanced scorecard: Aligning strategy with government performance*. Retrieved February 1, 2011, from http://charmeck.org/Search/Results.aspx?k = balanced%20scorecard.

Cleveland, H. (1985). *The knowledge executive*. New York: Truman Talley Books/Dutton.

Cleveland, H. (2002). *Nobody in charge: Essays on the future of leadership*. New York: John Wiley.

Coggburn, J. D., & Schneider, S. K. (2003). The quality of management and government performance: An empirical analysis of the American states. *Public Administration Review, 63*(2), 206–212.

Cohen, M. D., March, J. G., & Olsen, J. P. (1972). A garbage can model of organization and choice. *Administrative Science Quarterly, 17*, 1–25.

Cohen, S., & Eimicke, W. (1998). *Tools for innovators: Creative strategies for strengthening public sector organizations*. San Francisco: Jossey-Bass.

Cohen, S., Eimicke, W., & Heikkila, T. (2008). *The effective public manager* (4th ed.). San Francisco: Jossey-Bass.

Cole, M., & Parston, G. (2006). *Unlocking public value: A new model for achieving high performance in public service organizations*. New York: John Wiley.

Collins, J. C., & Porras, J. I. (1997). *Built to last: Successful habits of visionary companies*. New York: HarperBusiness.

Cooper, P. J. (1996). Understanding what the law says about administrative responsibility. In J. L. Perry (Ed.), *Handbook of public administration* (pp. 115–135). San Francisco: Jossey-Bass.

Coplin, W., & O'Leary, M. (1976). *Everyman's prince: A guide to understanding your political problem*. Boston: Duxbury Press.

Cornforth, C. (2004). The governance of cooperatives and mutual associations: A paradox perspective. *Annals of Public and Cooperative Economics, 75*(1), 11–32.

Cothran, D. A. (1993). Entreprenuerial budgeting: An emerging reform? *Public Administration Review, 53*(5), 445–454.

Council on Virginia's Future. (2011). *Virginia performs*. Retrieved February 12, 2011, from http://vaperforms.virginia.gov.

Courty, P., Heinrich, C. J., & Marschke, G. R. (2005). Setting the standard in performance measurement systems. *International Public Management Journal, 8*(3), 321–347.

Crosby, B. C., & Bryson, J. M. (2005). *Leadership for the common good: Tackling public problems in a shared-power world*. San Francisco: Jossey-Bass.

Crosby, B. C., & Bryson, J. M. (2010). Integrative leadership and the creation and maintenance of cross-sector collaborations. *Leadership Quarterly, 21*, 211–230.

Crosby, B., Bryson, J., Eustis, N., & Goetz, E. (2010). A decade of change at the Hubert H. Humphrey School of Public Affairs: A case of organizational transformation. Paper presented at the Annual Conference of the National Association of Public Affairs and Administration, Las Vegas, NV.

Crossan, M. M., Lane, H. W., & White, R. E. (1999). An organizational learning framework: From intuition to institution. *Academy of Management Review, 24*(3), 522–537.

CrunchBase. (2009). Google docs product profile. Retrieved September 6, 2009, from http://www.crunchbase.com/product/google-docs.

Csikszentmihalyi, M. (1990). *Flow: The psychology of optimal experience*. New York: HarperCollins.

Cyert, R., & March, J. (1963). *The behavioral theory of the firm*. Englewood Cliffs, NJ: Prentice Hall.

Daft, R. (2009). *Organizational theory and design* (10th ed.). Dallas, TX: South-Western College Publications.

Dalton, G. W. (1970). Influence and organization change. In G. Dalton, P. Lawrence, & L. Greiner (Eds.), *Organization change and development*. Homewood, IL: Irwin-Dorsey.

Dalton, G. W., & Lawrence, P. H. (1993). *Novations: Strategies for career management*. Salt Lake City, UT: Novations Group.

Dameri, R. P. (2005). Using the balanced scorecard to evaluate ICT investments in nonprofit organisations. *Electronic Journal of Information Systems Evaluation*, *8*(2), 107–114.

Damrosch, L. (2010). *Toqueville's discovery of America*. New York: Farrar, Straus and Giroux.

De Gues, A. P. (1988, April). Planning as learning. *Harvard Business Review*, 70–74.

DebateGraph. (2008). DebateGraph. Retrieved February 12, 2011, from http://debategraph.org.

deHart-Davis, L. (2008). Green tape: A theory of effective organizational rules. *Journal of Public Administration Research and Theory*, *19*, 361–384.

Delbanco, A. (1999). *The real American dream: A meditation on hope*. Cambridge, MA: Harvard University Press.

Delbecq, A. L. (2006). The spiritual challenge of power: Humility and love as offsets to leadership hubris. *Journal of Management, Spirituality and Religion*, *3*(1), 141–154.

Delbecq, A. L. (2010). How spirituality is manifested within corporate culture: Perspectives from a case study and a scholar's focus group. *Journal of Management, Spirituality and Religion*, *7*(1), 51–71.

Delbecq, A. L., Van de Ven, A. H., & Gustafson, D. (1975). *Group techniques for program planning*. Glenview, IL: Scott Foresman.

Delbecq, A. L., Van de Ven, A. H., & Gustafson, D. H. (1986). *Group techniques for program planning*. Middleton, WI: Green Briar Press.

deLeon, L., & Denhardt, R. B. (2000). The political theory of reinvention. *Public Administration Review*, *60*(2), 89–97.

Denhardt, R. B. (1993). *The pursuit of significance: Strategies for managerial success in organizations*. Belmont, CA: Wadsworth.

Denhardt, R., & Denhardt, J. (2000). The new public service: Serving rather than steering. *Public Administration Review*, *60*, 549–559.

Denis, J., Lamothe, L., & Langley, A. (2001). The dynamics of collective leadership and strategic change in pluralistic organizations. *Academy of Management Journal*, *44*(4), 809–837.

Department of Homeland Security. (2011). History. Retrieved February 23, 2011, from http://www.dhs.gov/xabout/history.

DeSanctis, G., Fayard, A., Roach, M., & Jiang, L. (2003). Learning in online forums. *European Management Journal, 21*(5), 565–577.

Dewey, J. (1954). *The public and its problems.* Athens, OH: Swallow Press. (Original work published 1927)

Deyle, R. E., & Smith, R. A. (1998, Autumn). Local government compliance with state planning mandates: The effects of state implementation in Florida. *Journal of the American Planning Association,* 457–469.

Díaz, J. (2008). *The brief wondrous life of Oscar Wao.* New York: Penguin/Riverhead.

Doig, J. W., & Hargrove, E. C. (1987). *Leadership and innovation: A biographical perspective on entrepreneurs in government.* Baltimore: Johns Hopkins University Press.

Drazin, R., & Van de Ven, A. H. (1985). Alternative forms of fit in contingency theory. *Administrative Science Quarterly, 30*(4), 514–539.

Dunn, W. N. (2004). *Public policy analysis: An introduction.* London: Pearson/Longman.

Dutton, J. E., & Dukerich, J. M. (1991). Keeping an eye on the mirror: Image and identity in organizational adaptation. *The Academy of Management Journal, 34*(3), 517–554.

Dutton, J. E., Frost, P., Worline, M., Lilius, J., & Kanov, J. (2002, January). Leading in times of trauma. *Harvard Business Review,* 54–61.

Dutton, J. E., & Jackson, S. E. (1987). Categorizing strategic issues: Links to organizational action. *Academy of Management Review, 12*(1), 76–90.

Eaton, B. C., & Eswaran, M. (2009). Well-being and affluence in the presence of a Veblen good. *The Economic Journal, 119*(539), 1088–1104.

Ebrahim, A. (2010). The many faces of nonprofit accountability. In D. Renz & Associates (Eds.), *The Jossey-Bass handbook of nonprofit leadership and management* (3rd ed., pp. 101–121). San Francisco: Jossey-Bass.

Eckhert, P., Haines, K., Delmont, T., & Pflaum, A. (1993). Strategic planning in Hennepin County, Minnesota: A strategic issues management approach. In R. L. Kemp (Ed.), *Strategic planning for local government.* Jefferson, NC: McFarland.

Edelman, M. J. (2001). *The politics of misinformation.* New York: Cambridge University Press.

Eden, C. (1989). Using cognitive mapping for strategic options development and analysis (SODA). In J. Rosenhead (Ed.), *Rational analysis for a problematic world.* New York: Wiley.

Eden, C., & Ackermann, F. (1998). *Making strategy: The journey of strategic management.* Thousand Oaks, CA: Sage.

Eden, C., & Ackermann, F. (2000). Mapping distinctive competencies: A systemic approach. *Journal of the Operational Research Society, 51,* 12–20.

Eden, C., & Ackermann, F. (2001). SODA: The principles. In J. Rosenhead & J. Mingers (Eds.), *Rational analysis for a problematic world revisited.* New York: Wiley.

Eden, C., & Ackermann, F. (2010). Competences, distinctive competences, and core competences. *Contemporary Perspectives on Competence-Based Management: Advances in Applied Business Strategy, 12*, 3–33.

Eden, C., Ackermann, F., & Cropper, S. (1992). The analysis of cause maps. *Journal of Management Studies, 29*(3), 309–324.

Eden, C., & Huxham, C. (1996). Action research for management research. *British Journal of Management, 7*, 75–86.

Eden, C., Jones, S., & Sims, D. (1983). *Messing about in problems*. Oxford: Pergamon Press.

Eden, C., & Sims, D. (1978). On the nature of problems. *Omega, 7*(2), 119–127.

Eisenhardt, K. M., & Martin, J. A. (2000). Dynamic capabilities: What are they? *Strategic Management Journal, 21*, 1105–1121.

Eisenhardt, K. M., & Sull, D. N. (2001, January). Strategy as simple rules. *Harvard Business Review*, 107–116.

Elmore, R. F. (1982). Backward mapping: Implementation research and policy decisions. In W. Williams (Ed.), *Studying implementation* (pp. 18–35). Chatham, NJ: Chatham House.

Emmert, M. A., Crow, M., & Shangraw, R. F. (1993). Public management in the future: Post-orthodoxy and organizational design. In B. Bozeman (Ed.), *Public management: The state of the art* (pp. 345–403). San Francisco: Jossey-Bass.

Enke, K.A.E., Nguy, L., Sullivan, M., & Zenk, L. R. (2009). *The Minneapolis Park and Recreation Board: A review and analysis of their strategic planning process*. Unpublished manuscript. Minneapolis, MN: University of Minnesota, Hubert H. Humphrey School of Public Affairs.

Eppler, M. J. (2003). Making knowledge visible through knowledge maps: Concepts, elements, cases. In C. W. Holsapple (Ed.), *Handbook on knowledge management: Knowledge matters* (pp. 189–205). New York: Springer-Verlag.

Epstein, P., Coates, P. M., Wray, L. D., & Swain, D. (2005). *Results that matter: Improving communities by engaging citizens, measuring performance, and getting things done*. San Francisco: Jossey-Bass.

Everitt, A. (2003). *Cicero: A turbulent life*. London: John Murray.

Fallows, J. (2006). *Blind into Baghdad: America's war in Iraq*. New York: Vintage Books.

Faragher, J. M. (1992). *Daniel Boone: The life and legacy of an American pioneer*. New York: Henry Holt.

Feiock, R. C., Moon, M. J., & Park, H. J. (2008, January/February). Is the world "flat," or "spiky"? Rethinking the governance implications of globalization for economic development. *American Review of Public Administration*, 24–35.

Feldman, M. (2000). Organizational routines as a source of continuous change. *Organization Science, 11*(6), 611–629.

Feldman, M. S., & Khademian, A. M. (2000). Managing for inclusion: Balancing control and participation. *International Public Management Journal, 3,* 149–167.

Feldman, M. S., & Khademian, A. M. (2002). To manage is to govern. *Public Administration Review, 62*(5), 541–554.

Fernandez, S., & Rainey, H. G. (2006). Managing successful organizational change in the public sector: An agenda for research and practice. *Public Administration Review, 66*(2), 1–25.

Finn, C. B. (1996). Stakeholder influence mapping. In C. Huxham (Ed.), *Creating collaborative advantage.* Thousand Oaks, CA: Sage.

Fiol, C. M. (2001). Revisiting an identity-based view of sustainable competitive advantage. *Journal of Management, 27,* 691–699.

Fiol, C. M. (2002). Capitalizing on paradox: The role of language in transforming organizational identities. *Organization Science, 13*(6), 653–666.

Fisher, R., & Ury, W. (1991). *Getting to yes: Negotiating agreement without giving in.* New York: Penguin.

Florida, R. (2007). *The flight of creative class: The new global competition for talent.* New York: Harper.

Flyvbjerg, B. (1998). *Rationality and power: Democracy in practice* (Rev. ed.). Chicago: University of Chicago Press.

Folkes, C. (2004). Knowledge mapping: Map types, contexts and uses. Milton Keynes, U.K.: Open University Business School, Working Paper Series, KM-SUE 4.

Ford, J. D., & Ford, L. W. (1995). The role of conversations in producing intentional change in organizations. *Academy of Management Review, 20*(3), 541–570.

Forester, J. (1999). *The deliberative practitioner.* Cambridge, MA: MIT Press.

Forester, J. (2009). *Dealing with differences: Dramas of mediating public disputes.* New York: Oxford University Press.

Frame, J. D. (2002). *The new project management: Tools for an age of rapid change, complexity, and other business realities* (2nd ed.). San Francisco: Jossey-Bass.

Frankfurt, H. G. (2005). *On bullshit.* Princeton, NJ: Princeton University Press.

Frederickson, D. G. (2001). The potential of the Government Performance and Results Act as a tool to manage third-party government. In M. A. Abramson & J. M. Kamensky (Eds.), *Managing for results 2002* (pp. 225–254). Lanham, MD: Rowman & Littlefield.

Frederickson, H. G. (1997). *The spirit of public administration.* San Francisco: Jossey-Bass.

Frederickson, H. G. (2003, February). Lessons in comparative health care reform. *Public Administration Review,* 11–12.

Freeman, P. (2008). *Julius Caesar.* New York: Simon & Schuster.

Frentzel, W. Y., Bryson, J. M., & Crosby, B. C. (2000). Strategic planning in the military: The U.S. Naval Security Group changes its strategy, 1992–1998. *Long-Range Planning, 33,* 402–429.

Friedman, T. L. (2000). *The Lexus and the olive tree: Understanding globalization*. New York: Anchor Books.

Friedman, T. L. (2007). *The world is flat 3.0: A brief history of the twenty-first century*. New York: Picador.

Friedmann, J. (1982). *Good society*. Cambridge, MA: MIT Press.

Friend, J. K., & Hickling, A. (2005). *Planning under pressure: The strategic choice approach* (3rd ed.). Oxford, England: Heinemann.

Gabor, D. (1964). *Inventing the future*. New York: Knopf.

Gabriel, Y. (2000). *Storytelling in organizations: Facts, fictions, and fantasies*. New York: Oxford University Press.

Gardner, H. (2009). *Five minds for the future*. Cambridge, MA: Harvard Business Press.

Garsten, B. (2006). *Saving persuasion: A defense of rhetoric and judgment*. Cambridge, MA: Harvard University Press.

Gastil, J., & Levine, P. (Eds.). (2005). *The deliberative democracy handbook: Strategies for effective civic engagement in the 21st century*. San Francisco: Jossey-Bass.

Gawande, A. (2010). *The checklist manifesto: How to get things right*. London: Profile Books.

Gersick, C.J.G. (1991). Revolutionary change theories: A multilevel exploration of the punctuated equilibrium paradigm. *Academy of Management Review, 16*, 10–36.

Giddens, A. (2002). *Runaway world: How globalisation is reshaping our lives*. London: Profile Books.

Gilmour, J. B., & Lewis, D. E. (2005). Assessing performance budgeting at OMB: The influence of politics, performance, and program size. *Journal of Public Administration Research and Theory, 16*, 169–186.

Gladwell, M. (2002). *The tipping point: How little things can make a big difference*. Boston: Little, Brown.

Gladwell, M. (2005). *Blink: The power of thinking without thinking*. Boston: Little, Brown.

Glassner, B. (2010). *The culture of fear: Why Americans are afraid of the wrong things* (Rev. ed.). New York: Basic Books.

Gleick, J. (1988). *Chaos: Making a new science*. New York: Penguin.

Gleick, J. (1999). *Faster: The acceleration of just about everything*. New York: Pantheon Books.

Goffman, E. (1986). *Frame analysis: An essay on the organization of experience*. Boston: Northeastern University Press.

Goldratt, E. M. (1999). *Theory of constraints*. Great Barrington, MA: North River Press.

Goleman, D. (1995). *Emotional intelligence*. New York: Bantam.

Goleman, D. (2007). *Social intelligence: The new science of human relationships.* New York: Bantam.

Goodsell, C. T. (2010). *Mission mystique.* Washington, DC: CQ Press.

Google. (2009). Google alerts. Retrieved 2009 from http://www.google.com/alerts.

Google. (2010). Google maps. Retrieved August 9, 2010, from http://www.maps.google.com.

Gould, S. (1980). *The panda's thumb: Reflections in natural history.* New York: Norton.

Greenblat, C., & Duke, R. D. (1981). *Principles and practices of gaming simulation.* Newbury Park, CA: Sage.

Grossback, L. J. (2002). The problem of state-imposed mandates: Lessons from Minnesota's local governments. *State and Local Government Review, 34*(3), 183–197.

Grow, D. (2003, December 16). Park board's top job goes begging. *Minneapolis/St. Paul Star Tribune,* p. 2B.

Guibert, J. D. (1964). *The Jesuits: Their spiritual doctrine and practice: A historical study* (W. J. Young, Trans.). Chicago: Institute of Jesuit Sources.

Gurwitt, R. (2003, April). Are city councils a relic of the past? *Governing,* 20–24.

Hale, J. (2007). *Documenting the Loft's strategic planning process.* Unpublished manuscript. Minneapolis, MN: University of Minnesota.

Hall, P. (1980). *Great planning disasters.* Berkeley: University of California Press.

Hamel, G., & Prahalad, C. K. (1994). *Competing for the future.* Boston: Harvard Business School Press.

Hampden-Turner, C. (1990). *Corporate culture.* Hutchinson, England: Economist Books.

Hawken, P. (2007). *Blessed unrest: How the largest social movement in history is restoring grace, justice, and beauty to the world.* New York: Penguin.

Hawkins, J. M. (Ed.). (1986). *The Oxford reference dictionary.* Oxford, England: Clarendon Press.

Healey, P. (2006). *Collaborative planning: Shaping places in fragmented societies* (2nd ed.). London: Palgrave Macmillan.

Heath, C., & Heath, D. (2007). *Made to stick.* New York: Random House.

Heath, R. L., & Palenchar, M. J. (2008). *Strategic issues management: Organizations and public policy challenges.* Thousand Oaks, CA: Sage.

Heifetz, R. A. (1994). *Leadership without easy answers.* Boston: Belknap.

Heifetz, R. A., Linsky, M., & Grashow, A. (2009). *The practice of adaptive leadership: Tools and tactics for changing your organization and the world.* Boston: Harvard Business School Press.

Heifetz, R. A., & Sinder, R. M. (1988). Political leadership: Managing the public's problem solving. In R. B. Reich (Ed.), *The power of public ideas.* New York: HarperBusiness.

Heintzman, R., & Marson, B. (2005). People, service, trust: Is there a public sector service value chain? *International Review of Administrative Sciences, 71*(4), 549–575.

Helling, A. (1998). Collaborative visioning: Proceed with caution! Results from evaluating Atlanta's Vision 2020 Project. *Journal of the American Planning Association, 64*(3), 335–349.

Hendrick, R. (2003). Strategic planning environment, process, and performance in public agencies: A comparative study of departments in Milwaukee. *Journal of Public Administration Research and Theory, 13,* 491–519.

Hennepin County, Minnesota. (2000). Summary of strategic framework. Internal document. Office of Planning and Development.

Her Majesty's Government. (2010). *Government ICT strategy: Smarter, cheaper, greener.* London: Crown.

Hill, C. J., & Lynn, L. E., Jr. (2009). *Public management: A three-dimensional approach.* Washington, DC: CQ Press.

Hill, M., & Hupe, P. (2009). *Implementing public policy* (2nd ed.). Thousand Oaks, CA: Sage.

Hirst, K. K. (n.d.). History definition: A collection of the definitions of history. Retrieved February 5, 2011, from http://archaeology.about.com/od/hterms/qt/history_definition.htm.

Hjern, B., & Porter, D. O. (1981). Implementation structures: A new unit of administrative analysis. *Organizational Studies, 2*(3964), 211–227.

Ho, A., & Coates, P. (2004). Citizen-initiated performance assessment: The initial Iowa experience. *Public Performance and Management Review, 27*(3), 29–50.

Hogwood, B. W., & Peters, B. G. (1983). *Policy dynamics.* New York: St. Martin's Press.

Holman, P., Devane, T., & Cady, S. (2007). *The change handbook: Group methods for shaping the future.* San Francisco: Berrett-Koehler.

Holzer, M., Lee, S., & Newman, M. A. (2003). Best practices in managing reductions in force. *Review of Public Personnel Administration, 23*(1), 38–60.

Hood, C., & Margetts, H. Z. (2007). *The tools of government in the digital age* (2nd ed.). New York: Palgrave Macmillan.

Houle, C. O. (1989). *Governing boards: Their nature and nurture.* San Francisco: Jossey-Bass.

Howe, E. (1980). Role choices of urban planners. *Journal of the American Planning Association, 46,* 398–409.

Hughes, O. (2010). Does governance exist? In S. P. Osborne (Ed.), *The new public governance* (pp. 87–104). London: Routledge.

Humphrey, H. H. (1959, September 17). A sense of purpose. Remarks at a meeting of Democratic Party chairpersons, Washington, DC.

Hunt, J. G., Boal, K. B., & Dodge, G. E. (1999). The effects of visionary and crisis-responsive charisma on followers: An experimental examination of two kinds of charismatic leadership. *Leadership Quarterly, 10*(3), 423–448.

Huntingdon, S. (1998). *The clash of civilizations and the remaking of world order*. New York: Touchstone Books.

Huxham, C. (1990). On trivialities in process. In C. Eden & J. Radford (Eds.), *Tackling strategic problems: The role of group decision support* (pp. 162–168). Thousand Oaks, CA: Sage.

Huxham, C. (2003). Theorizing collaboration practice. *Public Management Review*, 5(3), 401–423.

Huxham, C., & Vangen, S. (2005). *Managing to collaborate: The theory and practice of collaborative advantage*. New York: Routledge.

IdeaScale. (2009). *IdeaScale idea management overview: How it works*. Retrieved September 2, 2009, from http://www.ideascale.com/application/ideascale/how/index.html.

Innes, J. E. (1996). Planning through consensus building: A new view of the comprehensive planning ideal. *Journal of the American Planning Association*, 62(4), 460–472.

Innes, J. E. (1998). Information in communicative planning. *Journal of the American Planning Association*, 64, 52–63.

Innes, J. E., & Booher, D. E. (1999). Consensus building and complex adaptive systems: A framework for evaluating collaborative planning. *Journal of the American Planning Association*, 65(4), 412–423.

Innes, J. E., & Booher, D. E. (2010). *Planning with complexity: An introduction to collaborative rationality for public policy*. New York: Routledge.

International Association for Public Participation. (2007). Spectrum of levels of public participation. Retrieved February 12, 2011, from http://www.iap2.org/associations/4748/files/IAP2%20Spectrum_vertical.pdf.

Jacobs, L. R., Cook, F. L., & Delli Carpini, M. X. (2009). *Talking together: Public deliberation and political participation in America*. Chicago: University of Chicago Press.

Jacobs, L. R., & Shapiro, R. Y. (2000). *Politicians don't pander: Political manipulation and the loss of democratic responsiveness*. Chicago: University of Chicago Press.

Janis, I. L. (1989). *Crucial decisions: Leadership in policymaking and crisis management*. New York: Free Press.

Johnson, B. (1996). *Polarity management: Identifying and managing unsolvable problems*. Amherst, MA: HRD Press.

Johnson, D. J., & Johnson, F. P. (2008). *Joining together: Group theory and group skills* (10th ed.). Boston: Allyn & Bacon.

Johnson, G., Langley, A., Melin, L., & Whittington, R. (2007). *Strategy as practice: Research directions and resources*. New York: Cambridge University Press.

Johnson, G., Scholes, K., & Whittington, R. (2008). *Exploring corporate strategy* (8th ed.). London: Prentice Hall.

Joyce, P. (1999). *Strategic management for the public services*. Buckingham, U.K.: Open University Press.

Kahn, S. (2010). *Creative community organizing*. San Francisco: Berrett-Koehler.

Kaiser, E. (2010, March 3). Jon Gurban forced out as Minneapolis Park Board's controversial superintendent. *City Pages*.

Kaner, S., & Associates. (2007). *Facilitator's guide to participatory decision making* (2nd ed.). San Francisco: Jossey-Bass.

Kanter, R. M. (1972). *Commitment and community: Communes and utopia in sociological perspectives*. Cambridge, MA: Harvard University Press.

Kanter, R. M. (1983). *The change masters: Innovations for productivity in the American corporation*. New York: Simon & Schuster.

Kanter, R. M. (1989). *When elephants learn to dance*. New York: Simon & Schuster.

Kaplan, R. S., & Norton, D. P. (1996). In D. P. Norton (Ed.), *The balanced scorecard: Translating strategy into action*. Boston: Harvard Business School Press.

Kaplan, R. S., & Norton, D. P. (2004). *Strategy maps: Converting intangible assets into tangible outcomes*. Boston: Harvard Business School Press.

Kaplan, R. S., & Norton, D. P. (2006). *Alignment: Using the balanced scorecard to create corporate synergies*. Boston: Harvard Business School Press.

Kassel, D. S. (2010). *Managing public sector projects: A strategic framework for success in an era of downsized government*. Boca Raton, FL: CRC Press.

Kaufman, H. (1976). *Are government organizations immortal?* Washington, DC: Brookings Institution Press.

Kaufman, J. L. (1986). Making planners more effective strategists. In B. Checkoway (Ed.), *Strategic perspectives on planning practice* (pp. 87–104). Lexington, MA: Lexington Books.

Kay, J. (2010). *Obliquity*. London: Profile Books.

Kearns, K. P. (1996). *Managing for accountability: Preserving the public trust in public and nonprofit organizations*. San Francisco: Jossey-Bass.

Kellogg, K. C., Orlikowski, W. J., & Yates, J. (2006). Life in the trading zone: Structuring coordination across boundaries in postbureaucratic organizations. *Organization Science, 17*(1), 22–44.

Kelly, G. A. (1963). *A theory of personality: The psychology of personal constructs*. New York: Norton.

Kelly, K. (1994). *Out of control*. Cambridge, MA: Perseus Books.

Kelman, S. (2005). *Unleashing change: A study of organizational renewal in government*. Washington, DC: Brookings Institution Press.

Kelman, S., & Myers, J. (2009). *Successfully executing ambitious strategies in government: An empirical analysis*. HKS Faculty Research Working Papers RWP09–009. Cambridge, MA: John F. Kennedy School of Government, Harvard University.

Kendall, S., Nino, M., & Staley, S. (2008). Collaborative strategic planning: A wiki application. *Journal of Web Librarianship, 2*(1).

Kettl, D. F. (2002). *The transformation of governance: Public administration for twenty-first century America*. Baltimore, MD: Johns Hopkins University Press.

Kettl, D. F. (2008). *The next government of the United States: Why our institutions fail us and how to fix them*. New York: Norton.

Kettl, D. F., & Fesler, J. W. (2008). *The politics of the administrative process* (4th ed.). Washington, DC: CQ Press.

Khademian, A. M. (2002). *Working with culture: How the job gets done in public programs*. Washington, DC: CQ Press.

Kim, S. (2002). Participative management and job satisfaction: Lessons for management leadership. *Public Administration Review, 62*(2), 231–242.

King, C. S., Feltey, K. M., & Susel, B. O. (1998). The question of participation: Toward authentic public participation in public administration. *Public Administration Review, 58*(4), 317–326.

Kingdon, J. W. (2002). *Agendas, alternatives, and public policies* (2nd ed.). New York: Longman.

Kissler, G. R., Fore, K. N., Jacobson, W. S., Kittredge, W. P., & Stewart, S. L. (1998). State strategic planning: Suggestions from the Oregon experience. *Public Administration Review, 58*(4), 353–359.

Knowlton, L. W., & Phillips, C. C. (2009). *The logic model guidebook*. Thousand Oaks, CA: Sage.

Koteen, J. (1997). *Strategic management in public and nonprofit organizations* (2nd ed.). New York: Praeger.

Kotler, P., & Lee, N. R. (Eds.). (2007). *Social marketing: Influencing behaviors for good* (3rd ed.). Thousand Oaks, CA: Sage.

Kotter, J. P. (1996). *Leading change*. Boston: Harvard Business School Press.

Kotter, J. P. (2008). *A sense of urgency*. Boston: Harvard Business School Press.

Kouzes, J. M., & Posner, B. Z. (2002). *The leadership challenge: How to get extraordinary things done in organizations*. San Francisco: Jossey-Bass.

Kouzes, J. M., & Posner, B. Z. (2008). *The leadership challenge: How to get extraordinary things done in organizations* (4th ed.). San Francisco: Jossey-Bass.

Kraatz, M. S., & Zajac, E. J. (2001). How organizational resources affect strategic change and performance in turbulent environments: Theory and evidence. *Organization Science, 12*(5), 632–657.

Krasner, S. D. (1983). Structural causes and regime consequences: Regimes as intervening variables. In S. D. Krasner (Ed.), *International regimes* (pp. 185–205). Ithaca, NY: Cornell University Press.

Krause, H., & Milgrom, M. (2002). *Thirty days without: Public participation issues in the Minnesota Department of Transportation ramp meter study*. Unpublished manuscript. Minneapolis: University of Minnesota, Hubert H. Humphrey School of Public Affairs.

Kretzmann, J. P., & McKnight, J. L. (1997). *Building communities from the inside out: A path toward finding and mobilizing a community's assets*. Chicago: ACTA Publications.

Krieger, M. H. (1996). *Entrepreneurial vocations: Learning from the callings of Augustine, Moses, Mothers, Antigone, Oedipus, and Prospero*. Atlanta: Scholars Press.

Krieger, M. H. (2000). Planning and design as the manufacture of transcendence. *Journal of Planning Education and Research, 19*, 257–264.

Kübler-Ross, E. (1969). *On death and dying.* New York: Macmillan.

Kwak, Y. H., & Anbari, F. T. (2010). *Project management in government: An introduction to earned value management (EVM).* Washington, DC: IBM Center for the Business of Government.

Lake, K. E., Reis, T. K., & Spann, J. (2000). From grantmaking to changemaking: How the W. K. Kellogg Foundation's impact services model evolved to enhance the management and social effects of large initiatives. *Nonprofit and Voluntary Sector Quarterly, 29*(Supp.).

Latham, G. P., Borgogni, L., & Petitta, L. (2008). Goal setting and performance management in the public sector. *International Public Management Journal, 11*(4), 385–403.

Lauria, M. (1996). *Reconstructing urban regime theory.* Thousand Oaks, CA: Sage.

Leighninger, M. (2006). *The next form of democracy: How expert rule is giving way to shared governance—and why politics will never be the same.* Nashville, TN: Vanderbilt University Press.

Lenhart, A. (2009). *Social networks grow: Friending mom and dad.* Retrieved June 15, 2010, from http://pewresearch.org/pubs/1079/social-networks-grow.

Lewin, K. (1951). *Field theory in social science.* New York: Harper.

Lewis, C. (1991). *The ethics challenge in public service: A problem-solving guide.* San Francisco: Jossey-Bass.

Lewis, C. W., & Gilman, S. C. (2005). *The ethics challenge in public service: A problem-solving guide* (2nd ed.). San Francisco: Jossey-Bass.

Light, P. C. (1991). *The President's Agenda.* Baltimore, MD: Johns Hopkins University Press.

Light, P. C. (1997). *The tides of reform: Making government work, 1945–1995.* New Haven: Yale University Press.

Light, P. C. (1998). *Sustaining innovation: Creating nonprofit and government organizations that innovate naturally.* San Francisco: Jossey-Bass.

Light, P. C. (2000). *Making nonprofits work: A report on the tides of nonprofit management reform.* Washington, DC: Brookings Institution Press.

Light, P. C. (2002). *Government's greatest achievements.* Washington, DC: Brookings Institution Press.

Light, P. C. (2005). *The four pillars of high performance: How robust organizations achieve extraordinary results.* New York: McGraw-Hill.

Lindblom, C. E. (1959). The science of muddling through. *Public Administration Review, 19*, 79–88.

Lindblom, C. E. (1965). *The intelligence of democracy.* New York: Free Press.

Lindblom, C. E. (1990). *Inquiry and change.* New Haven, CT: Yale University Press.

Linden, R. M. (2002). *Working across boundaries: Making collaboration work in government and nonprofit organizations.* San Francisco: Jossey-Bass.

Lipman-Blumen, J. (1996). *Connective leadership: Managing in a changing world.* New York: Oxford University Press.

Lipsky, M. (1980). *Street-level bureaucracy: Dilemmas of the individual in public services.* New York: Russell Sage Foundation.

The Loft Literary Center. (n.d.). *About the Loft.* Retrieved August 9, 2010, from http://www.loft.org/about.

Lu, Y. (2007). Performance budgeting: The perspective of state agencies. *Public Budgeting & Finance, 27*(4), 1–17.

Ludema, J. D., Wilmot, T. B., & Srivastva, S. (1997). Organizational hope: Reaffirming the constructive task of social and organizational inquiry. *Human Relations, 50*(8), 1015–1052.

Lynn, L. E., Jr. (1987). *Managing public policy.* Boston: Little, Brown.

Lynn, L. E., Jr. (1996). *Public management as art, science, and profession.* Chatham, NJ: Chatham House.

Lynn. L. E., Jr. (2003). Public management. In B. G. Peters & J. Pierre (Eds.), *Handbook of public administration* (pp. 14–24). Thousand Oaks, CA: Sage.

Majone, G. (1989). *Evidence, arguments, and persuasion in the policy process.* New Haven, CT: Yale University Press.

Mandelbaum, S. J. (2000). *Open moral communities.* Cambridge, MA: MIT Press.

Mangham, I. L., & Overington, M. A. (1987). *Organizations as theatre: A social psychology of dramatic appearances.* New York: Wiley.

Manz, C. C. (1986). Self-leadership: Toward an expanded theory of self-influence processes in organizations. *Academy of Management Review, 11*(3), 585–600.

March, J. G. (1991). Exploration and exploitation in organizational learning. *Organization Science, 2,* 71–87.

March, J. G., & Olsen, J. P. (1989). *Rediscovering institutions: The organizational basis of politics.* New York: Free Press.

March, J. G., & Olsen, J. P. (1995). *Democratic governance.* New York: Free Press.

March, J. G., & Simon, H. A. (1958). *Organizations.* New York: John Wiley.

Marcus, A. (2009). *Strategic foresight: A new look at scenarios.* New York: Palgrave Macmillan.

Margerum, R. (2002). Collaborative planning: Building consensus and a distinct model of practice. *Journal of Planning Education and Research, 21,* 237–253.

Marris, P. (1996). *The politics of uncertainty: Attachment in private and public life.* New York: Routledge.

Mathes, A. (2004). Folksonomies: Cooperative classification and communication through shared metadata. Urbana, IL: University of Illinois at Urbana-Champaign, Graduate School of Library and Information Science, Computer-Mediated Communication, LIS590. Retrieved February 11, 2011, from http://scholar.google.com/scholar?cluster = 15543633405219125&hl = en&as_sdt = 0,24&as_vis = 1.

Mattessich, P. W. (2003). *The manager's guide to program evaluation: Planning, contracting, and managing for useful results.* St Paul, MN: Fieldstone Alliance.

May, P. J. (2003). Policy design and implementation. In B. G. Peters & J. Pierre (Eds.), *Handbook of public administration* (pp. 223–233). Thousand Oaks, CA: Sage.

May, R. (1969). *Love and will.* New York: Norton.

McKnight, J., & Block, P. (2010). *The abundant community: Awakening the power of families and neighborhoods.* San Francisco: Berrett-Koehler.

McLaughlin, J. A., & Jordan, G. B. (2010). Using logic models. In J. S. Wholey, H. P. Hatry, & K. E. Newcomer (Eds.), *Handbook of practical program evaluation* (3rd ed., pp. 55–80). San Francisco: Jossey-Bass.

Meier, K. J., & O'Toole, L. J., Jr. (2009). The proverbs of new public management: Lessons from an evidence-based research agenda. *The American Review of Public Administration, 39*(1), 4–22.

Meltsner, A. J. (1972). Political feasibility and policy analysis. *Public Administration Review, 32,* 859–867.

Meltsner, A. J. (1990). *Rules for rulers: The politics of advice.* Philadelphia: Temple University Press.

Merton, R. K. (1940). Bureaucratic structures and personality. *Journal of Social Forces, 17,* 560–568.

MetroGIS. (2007a). Mission. Retrieved February 5, 2011, from http://www .metrogis.org/about/index.shtml#purpose.

MetroGIS. (2007b). Setting the stage for the next generation of collaboration. Retrieved February 5, 2011, from http://www.metrogis.org/about/business_ planning/sdw/workshop_summary_07_0626.pdf.

MetroGIS. (2009). MetroGIS history. Retrieved August 9, 2010, from http://www .metrogis.org/about/history/index.shtml.

MetroGIS. (2010). Major accomplishments. Retrieved August 9, 2010, from http:// www.metrogis.org/about/accomplishments/index.shtml.

Metropolitan Council. (2010). About the Metropolitan Council. Retrieved August 9, 2010, from http://www.metrocouncil.org/about/about.htm.

Miami-Dade County Government. (2004). Miami-Dade County strategic plan. Retrieved February 5, 2011, from http://www.miamidade.gov/stratplan2003/ home.asp.

Miller, D., & Friesen, P. H. (1984). *Organizations: A quantum view.* Upper Saddle River, NJ: Prentice-Hall.

Milward, H. B., & Provan, K. G. (2000). How networks are governed. In C. J. Heinrich & L. E. Lynn (Eds.), *Governance and performance: New perspectives.* (pp. 238–262). Washington, DC: Georgetown University Press.

Milward, H. B., & Provan, K. G. (2003). Managing the hollow state. *Public Administration Review, 5*(1), 1–18.

Minneapolis Park and Recreation Board. About MPRB. Retrieved August 9, 2010, from http://www.minneapolisparks.org/default.asp?PageID = 70&SearchID = 298193.

Minneapolis Park and Recreation Board. (2007). *Minneapolis Park & Recreation Board's 2007–2020 comprehensive plan*. Minneapolis: Minneapolis Park and Recreation Board.

Minneapolis Park and Recreation Board. (2009). *Superintendent's annual report*. Minneapolis: Minneapolis Park and Recreation Board.

Mintzberg, H. (1973). *The nature of managerial work*. New York: HarperCollins.

Mintzberg, H. (1987, July–August). Crafting strategy. *Harvard Business Review*, 66–75.

Mintzberg, H. (1994). *The rise and fall of strategic planning: Reconceiving roles for planning, plans, planners*. New York: Free Press.

Mintzberg, H., Ahlstrand, B., & Lampel, J. (2009). *Strategy safari: A guided tour through the wilds of strategic management* (2nd ed.). London: Financial Times/ Prentice Hall.

Mintzberg, H., & Westley, F. (1992). Cycles of organizational change. *Strategic Management Journal*, *13*, 39–59.

Mitchell, R. K., Agle, B. R., & Wood, D. J. (1997). Toward a theory of stakeholder identification and salience: Defining the principle of who and what really counts. *Academy of Management Review*, *22*(4), 853–886.

Mitroff, I. I., & Anagnos, W. G. (2005). *Managing crises before they happen: What every executive and manager needs to know about crisis management* (2nd ed.). New York: AMACOM.

MixedInk. (2009). MixedInk. Retrieved September 2, 2009, from http://www .mixedink.com/OpenGov.

Monbiot, G. (2003, July 29). America is a religion. *The Guardian*, p. 19.

Moore, M. H. (1995). *Creating public value*. Cambridge, MA: Harvard University Press.

Moore, M. H. (2000). Managing for value: Organizational strategy in for-profit, nonprofit, and governmental organizations. *Nonprofit and Voluntary Sector Quarterly*, *29*(1), 183–204.

Morgan, G. (2006). *Images of organization*. Thousand Oaks, CA: Sage.

Moynihan, D. P. (2005). Goal-based learning and the future of performance management. *Public Administration Review*, *65*(2), 203–216.

Moynihan, D. P. (2008). *The dynamics of performance management: Constructing information and reform*. Washington, DC: Georgetown University Press.

Moynihan, D. P., & Ingraham, P. W. (2003). Look for the silver lining: When performance-based accountability systems work. *Journal of Public Administration Research and Theory*, *13*(4), 469–490.

Moynihan, D. P., & Landuyt, N. (2009). How do public organizations learn? Bridging structural and cultural divides. *Public Administration Review*, *69*(6), 1097–1105.

Moynihan, D. P., & Pandey, S. K. (2010). The big question for performance management: Why do managers use performance information? *Journal of Public Administration Research and Theory*, *20*, 849–866.

Mulgan, G. (2009). *The art of public strategy*. Oxford, UK: Oxford University Press.

Mumford, M. D., Eubanks, D. L., & Murphy, S. T. (2007). Creating the conditions for success: Best practices in leading for innovation. In J. Conger & R. E. Riggio (Eds.), *The practice of leadership*. San Francisco: Jossey-Bass.

Murnane, R. J., & Nelson, R. B. (1984). Production and innovation when techniques are tacit. *Journal of Economic Behavior and Organization, 5*, 353–373.

Myers, D., & Kitsuse, A. (2000). Constructing the future in planning: A survey of tools and theories. *Journal of Planning Education and Research, 19*, 221–231.

Nadler, G., & Hibino, S. (1998). *Breakthrough thinking: The seven principles of creative problem solving*. Roseville, CA: Prima.

Nahapiet, J., & Ghoshal, S. (1998). Social capital, intellectual capital, and the organizational advantage. *Academy of Management Review, 23*(2), 242–266.

Nanus, B. (1992). *Visionary leadership: Creating a compelling sense of direction for your organization*. San Francisco: Jossey-Bass.

National Academy of Public Administration. (2009). *OpenGov—open government brainstorm—by IdeaScale*. Retrieved September 2, 2009, from http://opengov .ideascale.com.

National Center for Vital Statistics. (2007). *FASTSTATS*. Retrieved February 11, 2011, from http://www.cdc.gov/nchs/fastats/homicide.htm and http://www.cdc.gov/ nchs/fastats/suicide.htm.

National Health Service for England. (2010). *The handbook to the NHS constitution for England*. London: National Health Service.

Neely, R. (1981). *How the courts govern America*. New Haven, CT: Yale University Press.

Nelson, A. C., & French, S. P. (2002). Plan quality and mitigating damage from natural disasters. *Journal of the American Planning Association, 68*(2), 194–208.

NetSquared. (2009). NetSquared: an initiative of TechSoupGlobal.org. Retrieved September 7, 2009, from http://www.netsquared.org/about.

Neuman, M. (Spring 1998). Does planning need the plan? *Journal of the American Planning Association*, pp. 208–220.

Neustadt, R. E. (1990). *Presidential power and the modern president*. New York: Free Press.

Neustadt, R. E., & May, E. R. (1986). *Thinking in time: The uses of history for decision makers*. New York: Free Press.

Niven, P. R. (2008). *Balanced scorecard step-by-step for government and nonprofit agencies* (2nd ed.). New York: John Wiley.

Nonaka, I., & Takeuchi, H. (1995). *The knowledge-creating company*. Oxford, UK: Oxford University Press.

Normann, R. (2000). *Service management: Strategy and leadership in service business* (3rd ed.). New York: John Wiley.

Nutt, P. C. (1992). *Managing planned change*. New York: Macmillan.

Nutt, P. C. (2001). Strategic decision making. In M. A. Hitt, R. E. Freeman, & J. S. Harrison (Eds.), *The Blackwell handbook of strategic management* (pp. 35–69). Oxford, England: Blackwell.

Nutt, P. C. (2002). *Why decisions fail: Avoiding the blunders and traps that lead to debacles*. San Francisco: Berrett-Koehler.

Nutt, P. C. (2004). Prompting the transformation of public organizations. *Public Performance and Management Review, 27*(4), 9–33.

Nutt, P. C., & Backoff, R. W. (1992). *Strategic management of public and third-sector organizations: A handbook for leaders*. San Francisco: Jossey-Bass.

Nutt, P. C., & Backoff, R. W. (1993). Strategy for public and third-sector organizations. *Journal of Public Administration Research and Theory, 3*(2), 209–231.

Nutt, P. C., & Backoff, R. W. (1996). Walking the vision and walking the talk: Transforming public organizations with strategic leadership. *Public Productivity and Management Review, 19*(4), 455–486.

Nutt, P. C., Backoff, R. W., & Hogan, M. F. (2000). Managing the paradoxes of strategic change. *Journal of Applied Management Studies, 9*(1), 5–31.

Nutt, P. C., & Hogan, M. F. (2008). Downsizing guidelines found in a success story. *Public Performance & Management Review, 32*(1), 103–131.

Olsen, J. B., & Eadie, D. C. (1982). *The game plan: Governance with foresight*. Washington, DC: Council of State Planning Agencies.

Olson, R. (2003). Minneapolis park job goes to man who didn't apply. *Minneapolis/St. Paul Star Tribune*, p. 1A.

Open Government Initiative. (2009). Idealab. Retrieved February 1, 2009, from http://www.whitehouse.gov/open/innovations/idealab.

Open Government Initiative. (2010). Office of Science and Technology: Open Government Plan. Retrieved February 10, 2011, from http://www.whitehouse.gov/open/around/eop/ostp/plan.

Ormsby, T., Napoleon, E., Burke, R., Groessl, C., & Feaster, L. (2004). *Getting to know ArcGIS* (2nd ed.). Redlands, CA: ESRI Press.

Ortony, A., Clore, G. L., & Collins, A. (1990). *The cognitive structure of emotions*. New York: Cambridge University Press.

Osborne, D., & Gaebler, T. (1992). *Reinventing government: How the entrepreneurial spirit is transforming the public sector*. New York: Plume Books.

Osborne, D., & Hutchinson, P. (2004). *The price of government: Getting the results we need in an age of permanent fiscal crisis*. New York: Basic Books.

Osborne, D., & Plastrik, P. (1997). *Banishing bureaucracy: The five strategies for reinventing government*. Reading, MA: Addison-Wesley.

Osborne, D., & Plastrik, P. (2000). *The reinventor's fieldbook: Tools for transforming your government*. San Francisco: Jossey-Bass.

Osborne, S. P. (2010). *The new public governance*. New York: Routledge.

Ostrom, E. (1990). *Governing the commons*. New York: Cambridge University Press.

O'Toole, L. J., & Meier, K. J. (2003). Plus ça change: Public management, personal stability, and organizational performance. *Journal of Public Administration Research and Theory, 13*(1), 43–64.

Packer, G. (2006). *The assassins' gate: America in Iraq.* New York: Farrar, Straus and Giroux.

Page, K., Eden, C., & Ackermann, F. (2010, August 6–10). Procedural justice and cooperative behavior: Passion and compassion in innovation. Paper presented at the annual conference of the Academy of Management, Montreal, Canada.

Palmer, P. J. (2000). *Let your life speak: Listening for the voice of vocation.* San Francisco: Jossey-Bass.

Parkinson, C. N. (1957). *Parkinson's law and other studies in administration.* Boston: Houghton Mifflin.

Patton, M. Q. (2001). *Qualitative research and evaluation methods* (3rd ed.). Thousand Oaks, CA: Sage.

Patton, M. Q. (2008). *Utilization-focused evaluation* (4th ed.). Thousand Oaks, CA: Sage.

Perrow, C. (1986). *Complex organizations: A critical essay.* New York: Random House.

Perry, J. L., Mesch, D., & Paarlberg, L. E. (2006). Motivating employees in a new governance era: The performance paradigm revisited. *Public Administration Review, 66*(4), 505–514.

Peter F. Drucker Foundation for Nonprofit Management & Stern, G. J. (1998). *The Drucker Foundation self-assessment tool process guide.* San Francisco: Jossey-Bass.

Peteraf, M. A. (1993). The cornerstones of competitive advantage: A resource-based view. *Strategic Management Journal, 124*, 179–191.

Peters, B. G., & Pierre, J. (2003). *Handbook of public administration.* Thousand Oaks, CA: Sage.

Peters, T. J., & Waterman, R. H. (1982). *In search of excellence: Lessons from America's best-run companies.* New York: HarperCollins.

Pfeffer, J. (2010). *Power: Why some people have it and others don't.* New York: HarperBusiness.

Pfeffer, J., and Salancik, G. (1978). *The external control of organizations: A resource dependence perspective.* New York: Harper & Row.

Pflaum, A., & Delmont, T. (1987). External scanning: A tool for planners. *Journal of the American Planning Association, 53*(1), 56–67.

Piotrowski, S. J., & Rosenbloom, D. H. (2002). Nonmission-based values in results-oriented public management: The case of freedom of information. *Public Administration Review, 62*(6), 643–657.

Poister, T. H. (2003). *Measuring performance in public and nonprofit organizations.* San Francisco: Jossey-Bass.

Poister, T. H., & Streib, G. (1994). Municipal management tools from 1976 to 1993: An overview and update. *Public Productivity and Management Review, 18*(2).

Poister, T. H., & Streib, G. (1999). Performance measurement in municipal government: Assessing the state of the practice. *Public Administration Review, 59*(4), 325–335.

Poister, T. H., & Van Slyke, D. M. (2002). Strategic management innovations in state transportation departments. *Public Performance and Management Review*, *26*(1), 58–74.

Pollitt, C., & Bouckaert, G. (2000). *Public management reform: A comparative analysis*. New York: Oxford University Press.

Porter, M. E. (1985). *Competitive advantage: Creating and sustaining superior performance*. New York: Free Press.

Posner, R. A. (1985). *The federal courts: crisis and reform*. Cambridge, MA: Harvard University Press.

Powers, R. (2001). *Plowing the dark: A novel*. New York: Macmillan/Picador.

Prahalad, C. K., & Hamel, G. (1990, May–June). The core competence of the corporation. *Harvard Business Review*, 79–91.

Pressman, J., & Wildavsky, A. (1973). *Implementation*. Berkeley: University of California Press.

Project Management Institute. (2008). *A guide to the project management body of knowledge* (4th ed.). Newtown Square, PA: Project Management Institute.

Provan, K. G., & Kenis, P. (2005). Modes of network governance: Structure, management, and effectiveness. *Journal of Public Administration Research and Theory*, *18*, 229–252.

Provan, K. G., & Milward, H. B. (1994). Integration of community-based services for the severely mentally ill and the structure of public funding: A comparison of flow systems. *Journal of Health Politics, Policy and Law*, *19*(4901), 865–894.

Provan, K. G., & Milward, H. B. (2001). Do networks really work? A framework for evaluating public-sector organizational networks. *Public Administration Review*, *61*(4), 414–423.

Putnam, R. D. (2000). *Bowling alone: The collapse and revival of American community*. New York: Simon & Schuster.

Putnam, R. D., Feldstein, L., & Cohen, D. J. (2004). *Better together: Restoring the American community*. New York: Simon & Schuster.

Quantcast. (2010). *Docs.google.com: Quantcast audience profile*. Retrieved June 3, 2010, from http://www.quantcast.com/docs.google.com.

Quinn, J. B. (1980). *Strategies for change: Logical incrementalism*. Homewood, IL: Irwin.

Radin, B. A. (2006). *Challenging the performance movement: Accountability, complexity, and democratic values*. Washington, DC: Georgetown University Press.

Raelin, J. A. (2003). *Creating leaderful organizations: How to bring out the leadership in everyone*. San Francisco: Berrett-Koehler.

Rainey, H. (1997). *Understanding and managing public organizations*. San Francisco: Jossey-Bass.

Rainey, H. G. (2009). *Understanding and managing public organizations* (4th ed.). San Francisco: Jossey-Bass.

Rainey, H. G., & Steinbauer, P. (1999). Galloping elephants: Developing elements of a theory of effective government organizations. *Journal of Public Administration Research and Theory, 9*(1), 1–32.

Raisch, S., & Birkenshaw, J. (2008). Organizational ambidexterity: Antecedents, outcomes, and moderators. *Journal of Management, 34*(3), 375–409.

Randolph, W. A., & Posner, B. Z. (2002). *Checkered flag projects: 10 rules for creating and managing projects that win!* Upper Saddle River, NJ: Financial Times/Prentice Hall.

Ray, K. (2002). *The nimble collaboration: Fine-tuning your collaboration for lasting success.* St. Paul, MN: Amherst H. Wilder Foundation.

Rees, M. J. (2003). *Our final century: Will the human race survive the twenty-first century?* New York: Basic Books.

Rheingold, H. (2003). *Smart mobs: The next social revolution.* New York: Basic Books.

Ricks, T. E. (2006). *Fiasco: The American military adventure in Iraq, 2003 to 2005.* New York: Penguin.

Rieff, D. (2003, Nov. 2). Blueprint for a mess. *New York Times Sunday Magazine*, pp. 28–78 passim.

Riggio, R. E., Chaleff, I., & Lipman-Blumen, J. (Eds.). (2008). *The art of followership: How great followers create great leaders and organizations.* San Francisco: Jossey-Bass.

Rifkin, J. (2000). *The age of access.* New York: Tarcher/Putnam.

Riker, W. H. (1962). *The theory of political coalitions.* New Haven, CT: Yale University Press.

Riker, W. H. (1986). *The art of political manipulation.* New Haven, CT: Yale University Press.

Roberts, N. C. (2002). *The transformative power of dialogue.* Amsterdam: JAI.

Roberts, N. C., & King, P. C. (1996). *Transforming public policy: Dynamics of policy entrepreneurship and innovation.* San Francisco: Jossey-Bass.

Roberts, N. C., & Wargo, L. (1994). The dilemma of planning in large-scale public organizations: The case of the United States Navy. *Journal of Public Administration Research and Theory, 4*(4), 469–491.

Robinson, A. H. (1982). *Early thematic mapping in the history of cartography.* Chicago: University of Chicago Press.

Rochefort, D. A., & Cobb, R. W. (1994). *The politics of problem definition: Shaping the policy agenda.* Lawrence: University Press of Kansas.

Rochet, C., Keramidas, O., & Bout, L. (2008). Crisis as change strategy in public organizations. *International Review of Administrative Sciences, 74*(1), 65–77.

Rogers, E. M. (2003). *Diffusion of innovations* (5th ed.). New York: Free Press.

Romme, A.G.L. (2003). Making a difference: Organization as design. *Organization Science, 14*(5), 558–573.

Romzek, B. (1996). Enhancing accountability. In J. L. Perry (Ed.), *Handbook of public administration* (2nd ed.). San Francisco: Jossey-Bass.

Rossi, P. H., Lipsey, M. W., & Freeman, H. E. (2003). *Evaluation: A systematic approach* (7th ed.). Thousand Oaks, CA: Sage.

Rowley, T. J., & Moldoveanu, M. (2003). When will stakeholder groups act? An interest- and identity-based model of stakeholder group mobilization. *Academy of Management Review*, *28*(2), 204–219.

Rubin, H. R., & Rubin, I. S. (2007). *Community organizing and development* (4th ed.). Boston: Allyn & Bacon.

Rubin, I. S. (2009). *The politics of public budgeting: Getting and spending, borrowing and balancing*. Washington, DC: CQ Press.

Rughase, O. (2007). *Identity and strategy*. Northampton, MA: Edward Elgar.

Rushdie, S. (1981). *Midnight's children*. London: Jonathan Cape/Picador.

Ruttan, V. W. (2003). *Technology, growth, and development: An induced innovation perspective*. New York: Oxford University Press.

Sabatier, P. A., & Weible, C. M. (2007). The advocacy coalition framework: Innovations and clarifications. In P. Sabatier (Ed.), *Theories of the policy process* (2nd ed., pp. 189–220). Cambridge, MA: Perseus.

Salamon, L. M. (1995). *Partners in public service: Government-nonprofit relations in the modern welfare state*. Baltimore: Johns Hopkins University Press.

Salamon, L. M. (2002). *The tools of government: A guide to the new governance*. New York: Oxford University Press.

Sandfort, J., & Milward, H. B. (2008). Collaborative service provision in the public sector. In S. Cropper, M. Ebers, C. Huxham, and P. S. Ring (Eds.), *The Oxford handbook of interorganizational relations* (pp. 147–174). New York: Oxford University Press.

Sartre, J. P. (1947). *The flies*. New York: Knopf.

Sawhill, J. C., & Williamson, D. (2001). Mission impossible? Measuring success in nonprofit organizations. *Nonprofit Management and Leadership*, *11*(3), 371–386.

Schachtel, M.R.B. (2001). CitiStat and the Baltimore neighborhood indicators alliance: Using information to improve communication and community. *National Civic Review*, *90*(3), 253–265.

Scharmer, C. O. (2009). *Theory U: Leading from the future as it emerges*. San Francisco: Berrett-Koehler.

Scheffert, D., Horntvedt, J., & Hoelting, J. (2011). *Building leadership programs management guide*. St. Paul, MN: University of Minnesota Extension Service.

Schein, E. H. (1987). *Process consultation volume II: Lessons for managers and consultants*. Reading, MA: Addison-Wesley.

Schein, E. H. (1997). *Organizational culture and leadership* (2nd ed.). San Francisco, CA: Jossey-Bass.

Schein, E. H. (2010). *Organizational culture and leadership*. San Francisco: Jossey-Bass.

Schön, D. A. (1971). *Beyond the stable state*. New York: Norton.

Schön, D. A., & Rein, M. (1994). *Frame reflection: Toward the resolution of intractable policy controversies*. New York: Basic Books.

Schroeder, R. G., Bates, K. A., & Junttila, M. A. (2002). A resource-based view of manufacturing strategy and the relationship to manufacturing performance. *Strategic Management Journal, 23*, 105–117.

Schwartz, P. (1996). *The art of the long view: Planning for the future in an uncertain world*. New York: Doubleday Currency.

Schwartz, P. (2004). *Inevitable surprises*. New York: Gotham.

Schwartz, P., Leyden, P., & Hyatt, J. (1999). *The long boom: A vision for the coming age of prosperity*. Reading, MA: Perseus Books.

Schwarz, R. M. (2002). *The skilled facilitator: A comprehensive resource for consultants, facilitators, managers, trainers, and coaches*. San Francisco: Jossey-Bass.

Scott, J. C. (1998). *Seeing like a state*. New Haven, CT: Yale University Press.

Scott, R. W. (1987). *Organizations: Rational, natural, and open systems* (2nd ed.). Englewood Cliffs, NJ: Prentice Hall.

Scriven, M. S. (1967). The methodology of evaluation. In R. E. Stake (Ed.), *Curriculum evaluation* (pp. 39–83). Skokie, IL: Rand McNally.

Seligman, M.E.P. (1998). *Learned Optimism: How to Change Your Mind and Your Life*. New York: Pocket Books.

Seligman, M.E.P. (2006). *Learned optimism: How to change your mind and your life*. New York: Vintage.

Selznick, P. (1957). *Leadership in administration: A sociological interpretation*. Berkeley: University of California Press.

Senge, P. M. (2006). *The fifth discipline: The art of practice of the learning organization*. New York: Doubleday.

Seuss, Dr. (Geisel, T. S.) (1971). *The lorax*. New York: Random House.

Shamir, B., Arthur, M., & House, R. (1994). The rhetoric of charismatic leadership: A theoretical extension, a case study, and implications for research. *The Leadership Quarterly, 5*(1), 25–42.

Shirky, C. (2008). *Here comes everybody: The power of organizing without organizations*. New York: Penguin.

Siau, K., & Tan, X. (2005). Technical communication in information systems development: The use of cognitive mapping. *IEEE Transactions on Professional Communication, 48*(3), 269–284.

Simon, H. A. (1996). *Sciences of the artificial* (3rd ed.). Cambridge, MA: MIT Press.

Simons, H. W. (2001). *Persuasion in society*. Thousand Oaks, CA: Sage.

Simons, R. (1995). *Levers of control: How managers use innovative control systems to drive strategic renewal*. Boston: Harvard Business Press.

Soss, J., Fording, R. C., & Schram, S. F. (2008). The color of devolution: Race, federalism, and the politics of social control. *American Journal of Political Science, 52*(3), 536–553.

Spencer, L. (1996). *Winning through participation*. Dubuque, IA: Kendall/Hunt.

Spencer, S. A., & Adams, J. D. (1990). *Life changes: Going through personal transitions*. San Luis Obispo, CA: Impact.

Stadtler, L. (2010, May 19–20). Designing collaborative public-private partnerships: Coordination and design challenges. Paper presented at the tenth annual conference of the European Academy of Management, Rome, Italy.

Staw, B. M., Sandelands, L. E., & Dutton, J. E. (1981). Threat-rigidity effects in organizational behavior: A multilevel analysis. *Administrative Science Quarterly, 26*, 501–524.

Sterman, J. (2000). *Business dynamics: Systems thinking and modeling for a complex world*. New York: Irwin/McGraw-Hill.

Stern, G. (1998). *The Drucker Foundation self-assessment tool: Process guide*. San Francisco: Jossey-Bass.

Stevens, W. (1990 [1954]). *Collected poems*. New York: Vintage.

Stiglitz, J. E. (2002). *Globalization and its discontents*. New York: Norton.

Stiglitz, J. E. (2010). *Freefall: America, free markets, and the sinking of the world economy*. New York: Norton.

Stivers, C. (1994). The listening bureaucrat: Responsiveness in public administration. *Public Administration Review, 54*(4), 364–369.

Stone, D. A. (2002). *Policy paradox: The art of political decision making*. New York: Norton.

Stone, M. M. (2000). Exploring the effects of collaborations on member organizations: Washington County's welfare-to-work partnership. *Nonprofit and Voluntary Sector Quarterly, 29*(1), 98–119.

Stone, M. M., Bigelow, B., & Crittenden, W. (1999). Research on strategic management in nonprofit organizations: Synthesis, analysis, and future directions. *Administration and Society, 31*(3), 378–423.

Stone, M. M., & Sandfort, J. R. (2009). Building a policy fields framework to inform research on nonprofit organizations. *Nonprofit and Voluntary Sector Quarterly, 38*(6), 1054–1075.

Suchman, M. C. (1995). Managing legitimacy: Strategic and institutional approaches. *Academy of Management Review, 20*(3), 571–610.

Sullivan, H., Barnes, M., & Matka, E. (2002). Building collaborative capacity through "theories of change." *Evaluation, 8*(2), 205–226.

Sun Tzu. (1910). *The art of war*. (Lionel Giles, Trans.). London: Luzac.

Surowiecki, J. (2005). *The wisdom of crowds*. New York: Anchor Books.

Susskind, L., & Cruikshank, J. L. (1987). *Breaking the impasse: Consensual approaches to resolving public disputes*. New York: Basic Books.

Taleb, N. N. (2007). *The black swan: The impact of the highly improbable*. New York: Random House.

Tan, A. (2001). *The bonesetter's daughter*. New York: Penguin.

Terry, R. W. (1993). *Authentic leadership: Courage in action*. San Francisco: Jossey-Bass.

Terry, R. W. (2001). *Seven zones for leadership: Acting authentically in stability and chaos*. Palo Alto, CA: Davies-Black.

Thomas, J. C. (1993). Public involvement and governmental effectiveness: A decision-making model for public managers. *Administration and Society*, *24*(4), 444–469.

Thomas, J. C. (1995). *Public participation in public decisions*. San Francisco: Jossey-Bass.

Thompson, J. D. (1967). *Organizations in action*. New York: McGraw-Hill.

Thompson, L. (2008). *The mind and heart of the negotiator* (4th ed.). Upper Saddle River, NJ: Prentice Hall.

Throgmorton, J. A. (2003). Planning as persuasive storytelling in a global-scale web of relations. *Planning Theory*, *2*(2), 125–151.

Tilly, C. (2006). *Why? What happens when people give reasons . . . and why*. Princeton, NJ: Princeton University Press.

Toffler, A. (1971). *Future shock*. New York: Bantam.

Tolkien, J.R.R. (1965). *The fellowship of the ring* (2nd ed., rev.). Boston: Houghton Mifflin.

Tolkien, J.R.R. (1982 [1937]). *The hobbit, or, there and back again* (Rev. ed.). Boston: Houghton Mifflin.

Trist, E. (1983). Referent organizations and the development of interorganizational domains. *Human Relations*, *36*(3), 269–284.

Tuchman, B. (1984). *The march of folly: From Troy to Vietnam*. New York: Knopf.

Underhill, P. (1999). *Why we buy: The science of shopping*. New York: Simon & Schuster.

UNICEF. (2007). *Overview: Understanding, measuring and overcoming poverty*. Retrieved August 5, 2010, from http://web.worldbank.org/WBSITE/EXTERNAL/ TOPICS/EXTPOVERTY/0,,contentMDK:20153855~menuPK:373757~pagePK:148956~ piPK:216618~theSitePK:336992,00.html.

U.S. Department of Education. (1994). *The national agenda for achieving better results for children and youth with disabilities*. Washington, DC: Office of Special Education and Rehabilitative Services, U.S. Department of Education.

Ury, W. L., Brett, J. M., & Goldberg, S. B. (1988). *Getting disputes resolved: Designing systems to cut the costs of conflict*. San Francisco: Jossey-Bass.

Van de Ven, A. H., Polley, D. E., Garud, R., & Venkataraman, S. (1999). *The innovation journey*. Oxford, UK: Oxford University Press.

Van de Ven, A. H., & Poole, M. S. (1995). Explaining development and change in organizations. *Academy of Management Review, 20*(3), 510–540.

Van der Heijden, K. (2005). *Scenarios: The art of strategic conversation* (2nd ed.). London: John Wiley.

Veenhoven, R. (2009). *World database of happiness: Trends in nations.* Rotterdam, The Netherlands: Erasmus University. Retrieved February 14, 2010, from http://www.worlddatabaseofhappiness.eur.nl/trendnat/framepage.htm.

Vella, J. A. (2008). *Aristotle: A guide for the perplexed.* London: Continuum.

Vickers, G. (1995). *The art of judgment: A study of policy making.* Thousand Oaks, CA: Sage.

Vila, J., & Carnales, J. I. (2008). Can strategic planning make strategy more relevant and build commitment over time? The case of RACC. *Long-Range Planning, 41*(3), 273–290.

Vinzant, J. C., & Crothers, L. (1998). *Street-level leadership: Discretion and legitimacy in front-line public service.* Washington, DC: Georgetown University Press.

Warkentin, M. E., Sayeed, L., & Hightower, R. (2007). Virtual teams versus face-to-face teams: An exploratory study of a web-based conference system. *Decision Sciences, 28*(4), 975–996.

Watson, R. (2008). *Future files: The five trends that will shape the next fifty years.* Boston: Nicholas Brealey.

Watzlawick, P., Weakland, J., & Fisch, R. (1974). *Change, principles of problem formation and problem resolution.* New York: Norton.

Wechsler, B., & Backoff, R. W. (1987). Dynamics of strategy formulation in public agencies. *Journal of the American Planning Association, 53,* 34–43.

Weick, K. (1995). *Sensemaking in organizations: Small structures with large consequences.* Thousand Oaks, CA: Sage.

Weick, K. E. (1984). Small wins: Redefining the scale of social problems. *American Psychologist, 39*(1), 40–49.

Weick, K. E. (2009). *Making sense of the organization. Volume 2: The impermanent organization.* New York: John Wiley.

Weick, K. E., & Sutcliffe, K. M. (2007). *Managing the unexpected* (2nd ed.). San Francisco: Jossey-Bass.

Weick, K. E., Sutcliffe, K. M., & Obstfeld, D. (2005). Organizing and the process of sensemaking. *Organization Science, 16*(4), 409–421.

Weimer, D., & Vining, A. R. (2010). *Policy analysis: Concepts and practice* (5th ed.). Old Tappan, NJ: Longman.

Weisman, C. (2003). *Secrets of successful retreats: The best from the nonprofit pros.* St. Louis, MO: F. E. Robbins.

Weiss, J. A., & Piderit, S. K. (1999). The value of mission statements in public agencies. *Journal of Public Administration Research and Theory, 9*(2), 193–223.

Wenger, E. (1998). *Communities of practice: Learning, meaning, and identity.* Cambridge, England: Cambridge University Press.

Wernerfelt, B. (1984). A resource-based view of the firm. *Strategic Management Journal*, *5*(2), 171–180.

Wheeland, C. (2004). *Empowering the vision: Community-wide strategic planning in Rock Hill, SC*. Lanham, MD: University Press of America.

White House Open Government Brainstorming. (n.d.). Retrieved February 14, 2010, from http://debategraph.org/Flash/fv.aspx?r = 20843.

Wichowsky, A., & Moynihan, D. P. (2008). Measuring how administration shapes citizenship: A policy feedback perspective on performance management. *Public Administration Review*, *68*(5), 908–920.

Wikipedia. (2010). List of social networking sites. Retrieved October 15, 2010, from http://en.wikipedia.org/wiki/Social-networking_sites.

Wildavsky, A. B. (1979). *Speaking truth to power: The art and craft of policy analysis*. Boston: Little, Brown.

Wildavsky, A. (1984). *The politics of the budgetary process*. (4th ed.). Boston: Little, Brown.

Williams, W., & Lewis, D. (2008). Strategic management tools and public sector management. *Public Management Review*, *10*, 653–671.

Wills, G. (2006). *Lincoln at Gettysburg: The words that remade America*. New York: Simon & Schuster.

Wilson, J. Q. (1989). *Bureaucracy: What government agencies do and why they do it*. New York: Basic Books.

Winer, D. (2003, May 23). Harvard weblogs: What makes a weblog a weblog? Retrieved August 31, 2009, from http://blogs.law.harvard.edu/whatmakesaweblogaweblog.html.

Wood, L. (2005 March). Blogs & wikis: Technologies for enterprise applications? *Gilbane Report*, *12*(10).

World Future Society. (2008). Outlook 2008. http://www.wfs.org/node/568.

Worldwatch Institute. (2010). *State of the World 2010*. Retrieved September 7, 2009, from http://www.worldwatch.org/sow10.

Worldwide Web Consortium. (2011). Web accessibility initiative. Retrieved February 27, 2011, http://www.w3.org/WAI.

Wright, B. E., & Davis, B. S. (2003). Job satisfaction in the public sector: The role of the work environment. *American Review of Public Administration*, *33*(1), 70–90.

Yang, K., & Melitski, J. (2007). Competing and complementary values in information technology strategic planning. *Public Performance & Management Review*, *30*, 426–452.

Zollo, M., & Winter, S. (2002). Deliberate learning and the evolution of dynamic capabilities. *Organization Science*, *13*(3), 339–351.

NAME INDEX

SUBJECT INDEX

Page references followed by *fig* indicate an illustration; followed by *e* indicate an exhibit.